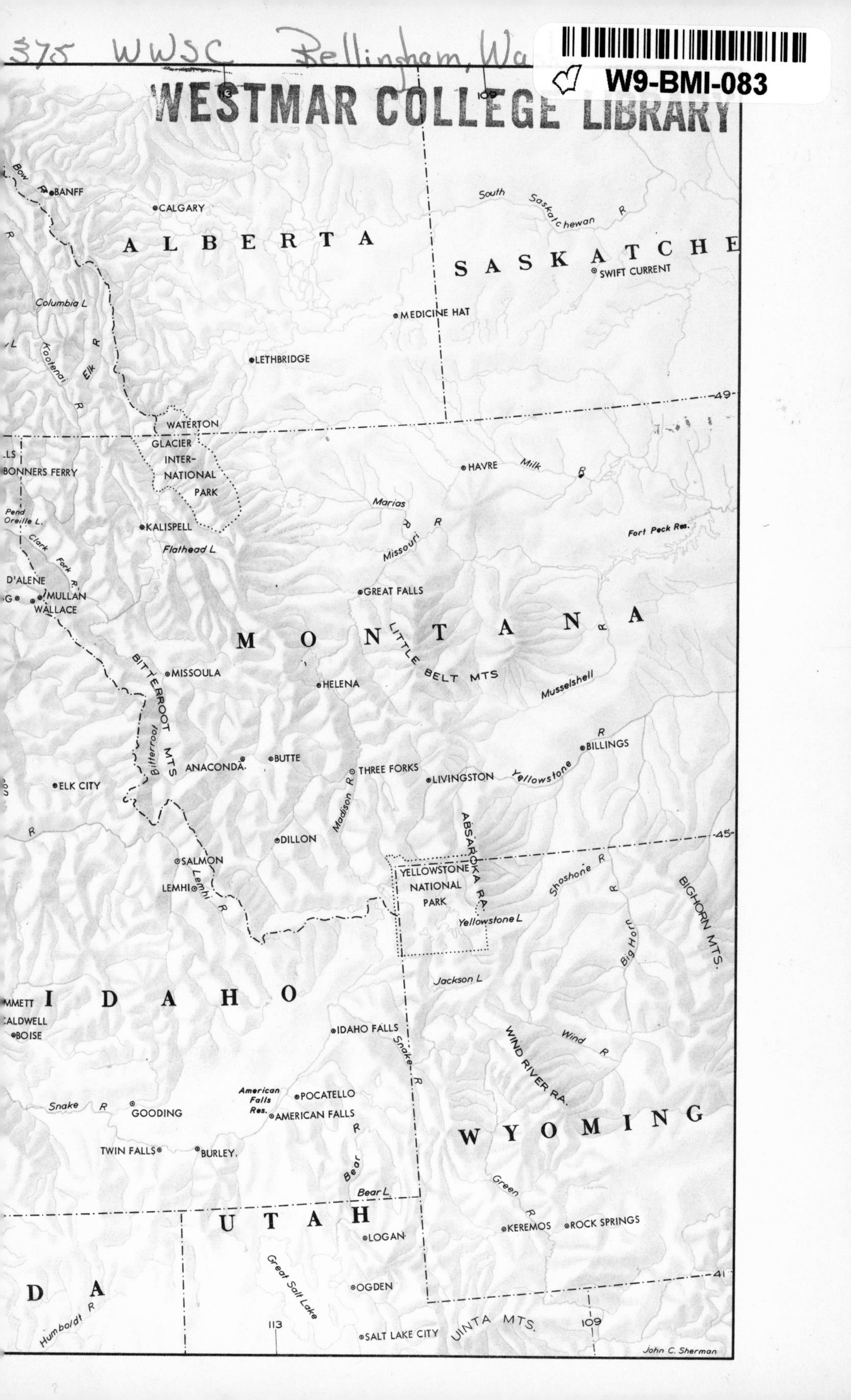
113
109
Bow R
BANFF
CALGARY
South Saskatchewan R
ALBERTA
SASKATCHE
SWIFT CURRENT
Columbia L
MEDICINE HAT
Kootenai
Elk R
LETHBRIDGE
49
WATERTON
GLACIER
INTER-
NATIONAL
PARK
BONNERS FERRY
HAVRE
Milk R
Marias R
Pend Oreille L.
KALISPELL
Missouri R
Fort Peck Res.
Clark Fork R.
Flathead L
D'ALENE
MULLAN
WALLACE
GREAT FALLS
MONTANA
LITTLE BELT MTS
BITTERROOT MTS
MISSOULA
HELENA
Musselshell R
Bitterroot
BILLINGS
ANACONDA
BUTTE
THREE FORKS
LIVINGSTON
Yellowstone
ELK CITY
Madison R
ABSAROKA RA.
DILLON
45
SALMON
YELLOWSTONE
NATIONAL
PARK
Shoshone R
BIGHORN MTS.
LEMHI
Lemhi R
Yellowstone L
Big Horn R
Jackson L
IDAHO
CALDWELL
BOISE
IDAHO FALLS
Snake R
WIND RIVER RA.
Wind R
Snake R
GOODING
American Falls Res.
POCATELLO
AMERICAN FALLS
WYOMING
TWIN FALLS
BURLEY
Bear R
Bear L
Green R
UTAH
LOGAN
KEREMOS
ROCK SPRINGS
Great Salt Lake
41
OGDEN
D A
Humboldt R
113
SALT LAKE CITY
UINTA MTS.
109
John C. Sherman

Empire of the Columbia

A HISTORY OF THE PACIFIC NORTHWEST

EMPIRE OF THE COLUMBIA

A History of the Pacific Northwest

DOROTHY O. JOHANSEN
REED COLLEGE

and

CHARLES M. GATES
UNIVERSITY OF WASHINGTON

HARPER & BROTHERS, PUBLISHERS, NEW YORK

Empire of the Columbia: A History of the Pacific Northwest

Printed in the United States of America

C-L

Library of Congress catalog card number: 56-11074

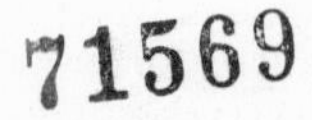

Contents

Preface xi

Part I. The Nations in the Pacific Northwest

1. The Indians of the Northwest 6
2. Spanish and English Explorations 20
3. Maritime Fur Trade: International Rivalries 37
4. Maritime Fur Trade: The Americans in the Northwest 58
5. Continental Fur Trade and Exploration 79
6. Americans and British Cross the Rockies 99
7. Nor'westers and Astorians 120
8. The Hudson's Bay Company in the Pacific Northwest 143
9. The American Rocky Mountain Fur Trade 164
10. Diplomacy of the Nations 184

Part II. The American Colony in the Pacific Northwest

11. Missions and Missionaries 206
12. The Problem of Law and Order: The Provisional Government 225
13. Westward Movement and the Boundary Settlement 246
14. Crisis of the Provisional Government 270
15. Territorial Government and Territorial Problems 289
16. Oregon Statehood and the Division of Washington Territory 315
17. Economic and Social Foundations of Territories and State 334

Part III. A Period of Transition

BEGINNING OF A NEW ERA

18. The Magic of the Steel Rails 368
19. The Boom of the Eighties 383
20. The Statehood Movement in Washington and Idaho 400

POLITICAL ISSUES AND ALIGNMENTS

21. Years of Agrarian Protest 414
22. Politics of the Progressive Era 430

DEVELOPMENT OF SUPPORTING INDUSTRIES TO 1914

23. New Developments in Agriculture 445

24. The Lumber Industry 460
25. Harvests from the Sea 475
26. Metal in the Mountains 488

THE PROGRESS OF URBAN CIVILIZATION

27. Building the Metropolitan Centers 505
28. Patterns of Commerce and Manufacturing 518
29. Cultural Activities in the Northwest Cities 530

Part IV. Frontier No Longer

30. Problems of Industrial Development 543
31. Water for a Thirsty Land 564
32. The Progress of Reclamation 587
33. The Early Conservation Movement 598
34. Advances in Forestry 609
35. The Conservation of North Pacific Fisheries 621
36. Forty Years of Politics, 1916-1956 628
37. Mid-Century Appraisal: A Survey of Cultural Trends 647

Index 669

Plates

following page

Pacific Northwest Indians 96
Tlingit Shaman's Charm in the Shape of a Killer Whale
Spoon Carved from the Horn of a Mountain Goat
Painted Door Posts of a Tlingit House
Articles Used by Northwest Indians
Ceremonial Cape of Cariboo Skin
Dance Mask Worn by the Kwakiutl Indians
Model of a Typical Puget Sound Indian House
Tsimshian Painted Mask from Northern British Columbia
Haida Ornamental Pipe of Carved Slate
Indian Costumes and Basketry from Eastern Washington

Exploration, Missions, Early Settlement 160
Fort Astoria in 1813
Strom Log Cabin, Lane County, Oregon
Catholic Ladder with Illustrations
Joseph Lane
Jason Lee
American Village on the Willamette
Seth Lewelling House in Oregon City
Vancouver's Sloop *Discovery* Temporarily Beached
Sketch of Seattle, the Frontier City

Agriculture and Reclamation 224
Oregon Witch Hazel Farm
Catching Horses for Market
Harvesting in the Palouse Hills
Cultivating an Oregon Wheat Field
Harvesting Machinery at Work near Pullman, Washington
Wheat Sacks Awaiting Shipment
Modern Irrigation Canal Under Construction
Aerial View of Grand Coulee Dam Under Construction

Lumbering 288
Loggers on Their Springboards

Logging Trestle Used to Bridge a Deep Ravine
In the Old Days Logging Was Done With Bulls
Donkey Engine Used Later for Snaking Large Logs
Logs Are Now Towed by Tractors
Trains Carried Logs to the Mills on Railroads
Motor Trucks Are Now Used over Considerable Distances

Fisheries 384
Typical Fish Wheel on the Columbia River
Columbia River Fishing Boats Looked like Butterflies
Launching a Dory from a Halibut Boat
Silhouettes Showing Types of Fishing Boats
Today's Sportsman Takes His Own Salmon
Diagram Showing the Way Halibut Gear Is Set
Mt. Rainier Reflected in a Beautiful Alpine Lake

Cities and Political Figures 480
Flavel House, Astoria
Portland's First Bridge at Morrison Street
Chamber of Commerce, Tacoma
A Fine Oregon Mansion of 60 Years Ago
"They Have Such Lovely Fogs in Seattle"
Lewis and Clark Exposition Buildings, 1905
William S. U'Ren, the Lawgiver
John R. Rogers
Silver-toned Sextette of the Northwest

Industries and Manufacturing 544
May Flower Mine, Bullion, Idaho
Anaconda Hill, a Copper City in the Making, 1894
The Old Tacoma Smelter
Northern Pacific Railroad Shops, Tacoma
Lumber Mills Gave Seattle an Industrial Appearance
Making Pig Iron at Oswego
Interior View of Boeing Airplane Plant, Seattle
Exterior View of Boeing Airplane Plant, Seattle

Travel and Transportation 608
The Wheat Fleet in Portland Harbor
River Steamers Entering Cascade Locks, Columbia River
The Canyon City Stage, Precursor of the Freeway
Fleet of Logging Locomotives, Grays Harbor
Boeing B-52 in Flight Near Mt. Adams
Columbia River Steamers Tied Up to the Bank
Skiing Comes Next to Flying

Preface

This book is an account of the history and development of the Pacific Northwest. It is an essay in regional analysis, an interpretation of a section of the United States which, though diversified and divided within itself because of extremes and contrasts of topography, climate and soil conditions, nevertheless possesses a clear consciousness of its common heritage. History is here a unifying theme which includes the present states of Oregon, Washington and Idaho, and, during its earlier chapters, a vast area to the north as well. We have attempted to recognize the individuality of each of the geographic localities or provinces that make up the Pacific Northwest, and at the same time to emphasize how each one has contributed to the development of the region as a whole.

The writing is the product of collaboration and common endeavor on the part of the two authors. We have exchanged views on many points throughout the narrative in a mutual effort to achieve a genuinely regional perspective. We have tried to maintain a consistent viewpoint on the relation of regional events and trends to the broader history of the nation. We are convinced that regional history should not be provincial, but on the contrary should be a vehicle through which many national problems can be studied at close range, and so be better understood. The purpose in presenting it in this way will be evident in each chapter regardless of its authorship.

With this kind of unifying view we have made a division of the book between us, each of us undertaking to interpret the period which holds the greater interest for us, and the subjects on which our individual research gives us the greater right to speak. Thus Parts I and II have been written by Dorothy Johansen; Parts III and IV, by Charles Gates. Each author has read and criticized the work of the other. In this way we have retained the advantages of our special knowledge and our individual views in particular chapters, while conserving the strength that comes from subjecting the entire book to a double scrutiny. For the sins of omission and commission which, we recognize, unavoidably mar its pages we are jointly responsible.

In matters of acknowledgment each of us would first bow or curtsey to the other. This kind of collaboration is not always easy nor successful, yet for us the experience has been a pleasant one, a prelude, we hope, to other ventures in regional writing. The enrichment of content and the range of understanding which we have been able to achieve are far greater than either of us could have realized alone. For this reason each is under obligation to the other.

Beyond this we are indebted both to colleagues and to the librarians and cartographers who have contributed to make the book what it is. Though many friends have offered us stimulus and encouragement, we owe a special word of appreciation to Professor Herman J. Deutsch of the State College of Washington, and to Professor W. Stull Holt of the University of Washington, whose recognition of the importance of our task has been a constant challenge. To Professor John Sherman and the staff of the Cartographic Laboratory of the University of Washington we express our particular thanks for their interest and technical skill in the preparation of the maps which are an important feature of this volume.

In each of the several libraries we have visited we have received sympathetic and courteous assistance. At the Sutro Branch, California State Library, Mr. Richard Dillon and Mrs. Mary Jane Schmelzle were helpful beyond the call of duty. At the University of Oregon, Martin Schmitt and his staff helped in selecting map data and pictures from the rich Oregon Collection. Mr. Ronald Todd and the good-natured guardians of the Pacific Northwest Collection at the University of Washington have answered a host of hurry-hurry demands through the years, always patiently and generously. The staff of the Reed College Library, especially Miss Jean MacFarland, librarian, and Mrs. Pauline Howard, who has solved all mysteries of government documents, have never been too busy to supply some missing bit of information. Good friends at the Portland Public Library have put us deeply in their debt.

A special word of gratitude goes to Mr. Thomas Vaughan and the staff of the Oregon Historical Society and particularly to Miss Priscilla Knuth, research assistant and associate editor of the Oregon Historical Quarterly, who has taken time, even after hours, to help with problems arising in Parts I and II. She has made herself indispensable to our research and writing in many ways. There are others who have come to our rescue so that the book might become a reality. They must remain unnamed, but the debt is no less because of that. Suffice it to say we are deeply grateful.

DOROTHY O. JOHANSEN
CHARLES M. GATES

February, 1957

Bibliographic Note

In order to simplify footnote citations, the references to supporting documents and source materials are usually given only by author and title, and are indicated at the points in the narrative where they will be found generally useful. In the case of diaries and journals the references are to the more accessible published editions rather than to the originals. Thus there are a number of citations to the *Oregon Historical Quarterly, Pacific Northwest Quarterly* and other periodicals which can be found in most libraries and schools.

Following is a list of abbreviations used:

AHR	*American Historical Review*
BCHQ	*British Columbia Historical Quarterly*
CHR	*Canadian Historical Review*
CHSQ	*California Historical Society Quarterly*
EHR	*English Historical Review*
EWT	*Early Western Travels*
GR	*Geographical Review*
OHQ	*Oregon Historical Quarterly*
OPAT	Oregon Pioneer Association *Transactions*
PHR	*Pacific Historical Review*
PNQ	*Pacific Northwest Quarterly*
WHQ	*Washington Historical Quarterly*
Wis. Hist. Colls.	*Wisconsin Historical Collections*

Part I

The Nations in the Northwest

INTERPRETIVE KEY

The earliest chapters of the Pacific Northwest's history belong to the story of Western Europe's expansion in the sixteenth and seventeenth centuries. The discovery of the Western Hemisphere contributed to the development of new ideas about the nature of the universe, of man and of the world he occupied, and it had its part in inspiring men to adventure in the realms of both imagination and things-as-they-are. Each venture in the latter field replaced speculation with the outlines of reality. The poet gave over to the scientist in delineating the intellectual and physical New World of the eighteenth century.

The conception of an expanding world was represented in the maps of the sixteenth century where the known world was projected against the unknown. Gradually the latter was eradicated as Spanish, French, and English discoveries charted the seas and defined the continents. What was still unknown a century later was a challenge to the nations of Europe in their rivalry to add to science some great new discovery and to their economies rich treasures of land and commerce.

Dreams of finding another treasure of Montezuma and a new Peru, led men to search the Western continent for the fabulous Seven Cities of Cibola and the Kingdom of Quivira, illusory mirages on the horizon of the West. The hope that Europe could reach the Orient by sailing directly westward was equally elusive. It was succeeded by the hope that a sea passage through North America would give the discovering power control of the commerce of the Indies. The search for Quivira, but especially for the Northwest Passage, had a part in sending men toward that unknown land which bordered the Pacific Ocean and which we know today as the Pacific Northwest.

The treasure first found on these shores was neither gold nor pearls nor the western embouchment of the passage to India. It was, rather, the pelt of the sea otter, a commodity that could, temporarily at least, take the place of precious metals in buying the Orient's luxuries. Russia's and England's state-sponsored voyages of discovery, captained by Vitus Bering and James Cook for the purpose of contributing to the glory of the arts and sciences by their explorations, led to the opening of the sea otter trade. Traders, incidentally to their search for furs, discovered some of the principal features of the coastline such as the Juan de Fuca Strait and the entrance to the Columbia River. Within a decade after the inception of the trade, France, Spain, Britain, and Russia had carried out or were engaged in official explorations of the Northwest coast, and England and Spain came close to war in a dispute over the nature of the sovereignty Spain claimed to the region.

Of the powers interested, Spain claimed the most and lost the most of her pretensions. Her efforts to maintain a policy of exclusive sovereignty in the Pacific and elsewhere were futile. In principle and in practice, she was defeated by England, who claimed rights to the commerce and occupation of any land to which title claims were not supported by settlement. As a result of the Nootka incident (1790), the coast between the Russian settlements in Alaska, and Spain's colony in California, was an area of trade, free and open to the nations whose merchants wished to participate in the maritime fur trade.

On the continent the Indian trade, of which the beaver fur trade was an essential part, moved along the waterways of the interior to the West. The Canadian trader Alexander Mackenzie reached the Pacific Coast in 1793 and a decade later, when the acquisition of the Louisiana territory brought the boundary of the United States up to the Rocky Mountains, the Lewis and Clark expedition to the Pacific indicated the course of further American expansion. For forty years thereafter, British and American diplomats at conference tables argued the question of joint or exclusive dominion in the region beyond the Rockies.

For the better part of the period from 1807 to 1846, government negotiations were, in a sense, academic. The British Hudson's Bay Company by 1825 had undisputed commercial control of the region.

The Americans were occupied with opening up the Midwest to settlement. The advance of their fur traders into the Rockies, begun on the heels of the Lewis and Clark expedition, had stopped with the War of 1812. The resumption of their activities in 1823 brought into focus a fundamental difference between British and American practices in the fur trade as it was then developing. The English system was that of a privileged monopoly with long-range policies of development and control; the American system, if such it can be called, was one of individual enterprise, competitive and exploitive, and without a policy. In the long run, British fur trade policy eliminated the British as colonizers. Individual enterprise, agricultural as well as commercial, established an American colony in the Northwest and with it American sovereignty in the region.

The occupation of the Pacific Northwest by white men was first brought about by commerce with the original occupants, the Indians. They were the producers of furs for the maritime sea otter trade, and they were the consumers of a limited range of European manufactured goods. The British system of the fur trade encouraged the protection of the Indian and his way of life. The American did not. Nor did the Indian fit into the American pattern of agricultural development. As elsewhere in the history of the North American continent, the Indian occupied the role of a prime mover in the expansion of the white man's commerce in the Pacific Northwest, but in the processes to which he contributed, he was subordinated and destroyed. The aboriginal culture was background to the history of the region. In itself it was so unique and interesting that it deserves some attention as a prelude to our story.

1

The Indians of the Northwest

We may assume that by 5,000 years ago, the environment for human beings in this region was not unlike that in the primitive areas still to be found in isolated portions of the Far West. There is conclusive evidence that there were people occupying the land at least 5,000 years before that. It is believed that even while the glaciers covered parts of the Pacific Northwest, there was still an open, ice-free passage from Asia into North America and that over this came the first people, followed thereafter through the centuries by further waves of migration. They traveled across present Alaska into the Mackenzie Basin, probably, and thence to the central plains of the continent, and/or through the valleys of British Columbia to the Columbia Plateau from which they spread out.

In the Northwest the most ancient habitants found, along the shores of vast lakes that occupied the interior, conditions suitable to life: a steady supply of water, animal life, and shelter in the caves around the waters' edges. By the radiocarbon method of dating, scientists have shown that 10,000 years ago men lived in these caves, preyed upon and were preyed upon by animals long since extinct.

From archaeological research we now know something about these cave dwellers along the lake shores. They were skilled in weaving bark of sagebrush into foot coverings, baskets and mats from tule, cattail leaves, grass, and bark. They had stone awls, flakers, punches, smoothers, and polishers. They first propelled weapons by means of a throwing stick, and then became skilled in the use of bows and arrows. They decorated their persons with strips of fur and feathers and beads made of bone. They engaged in a food-gathering economy, where they made use of nuts, berries, roots, without developing the techniques necessary to cultivate them. Chipped obsidian arrowheads found with the small bones of birds, and the larger bones of bison and deer reveal they were also hunters.[1]

It is probable that these people differed little from one another whether they occupied the lands of Washington, Oregon, or Nevada. But with the passage of the centuries differences began to emerge among them. New waves of migrations destroyed or pushed out some of the ancient people, or mixing with them, stimulated the development of new techniques and living patterns. Changes in climate, the recession of the lake waters, the disappearance of a food supply or contact with people of different customs, all were factors of differentiation.

The Coastal People

An early center of cultural development was along the lower Fraser River in British Columbia. Here have been found evidences of an elaborate civilization that flourished about 2,000 years ago. Stone carvings of animal and human figures of exceptional artistry and craftsmanship indicate that this culture was far beyond subsistence level and that it had developed a body of ritualistic and symbolic lore. When it began is impossible to discover; it was extinct and forgotten long before the white man came.[2]

It is believed, however, that the culture may have influenced the whole northwest coast. Stone sculptures of similar design have been found along the Columbia River, and Sauvie's Island at the mouth of the Willamette River has been an especially rich source of them. The artistic talent and the skills displayed in the making and delicate finishing of canoes, fishing tackle, and utensils common in the Indian's daily life and noted by the first white men, suggested some strong tradition of arts. It is not improbable that the styles and techniques of the ancient people were background for the development of the civilization that flourished along the North Pacific Coast at the end of the eighteenth century.

This civilization centered among the Tsimshian, Tlingit, Nootkas,

---

[1] Luther H. Cressman, Howel Williams, Alex D. Krieger, *Early Man in Oregon: Archaeological Studies in the Northern Great Basin*, Eugene, Oregon, 1940.

[2] Marian W. Smith, *Archaeology of the Columbia-Fraser Region*, Menasha, Wisconsin, 1950.

Bella Coolas, Kwakiutl, and Haidas who occupied the islands and coast of the mainland from Southern Alaska to the Strait of Juan de Fuca. The Kwakiutl was a peculiarly motivated society. It was individualistic in that there were strong drives toward personal prestige values; it was materialistic and competitive in that such values were determined by an individual's "power" to destroy wealth—canoes, blankets, oil, and coppers. The *potlatch* was a feast and a competition in which a chieftain of one house clan or village challenged another to equal or exceed him in the giving away or destruction of goods. It was a social and an economic weapon. The *potlatch,* stratification of classes, cannibal secret societies, carved totems, elaborate masks, and ritualistic dance dramas were unique expressions of what Ruth Benedict has described as a megalomaniac society.[3]

Many of their customs and peculiarities were shared in some measure by natives on other parts of the Western coasts, notably by those of Northwestern Washington and the Puget Sound country, less strikingly to the south. It might be argued that their influence decreased in direct proportion to the distance from its source. The peoples below the Columbia River had less in common with their Northern neighbors. The people of Southern Oregon shared the cultural patterns of Northern California and the Great Basin.

The Northwest was an area of many mutually unintelligible language groupings. In Western Washington, the predominant language group was Coast Salish, but from the mouth of the Columbia south to Tillamook and east through the Cascades, the Chinookan languages were spoken. So many different languages and dialects were used that adjoining neighbors could not communicate with one another.

The coast peoples were politically atomistic. The governmental unit was an autonomous village, which was sometimes a single large household. There was no tribal concept although one village might be known to another as "of our people." Leadership was inherited in a ruling class but reinforced by possession of wealth. Because of personal prestige the chief man of a village might exert influence over other villages.

Nevertheless each village was independent. It had its own lands for berry gathering, hunting, and fishing, and within a given area would

[3] Ruth Benedict, *Patterns of Culture,* New York, 1949, Chap. VI.

move *en masse* from winter to summer habitations. There seems to have been no competition for possession of these locations. Nor were there alliances or combinations of villages traditionally enemies of one another. Wars were local, of short duration, and the exception rather than the rule. The usual cause seems to have been the demand for slaves. The British Columbia Indians were noted raiders upon Indians of the interior and upon the Makahs and the villages of Northwest Washington. These people consequently were more warlike than their neighbors to the south who had less to fear from attacks. The Chinooks got their slaves by trade rather than by war, and the principal source of their supply was Southern Oregon and Northern California.

Intervillage quarrels and slave raids would produce warlike situations, dances, and the massing of canoes. The Columbia River warriors encased themselves in an armor of thick elkskin that could turn an arrow, and carried shields of skins, hardened in fire. Their weapons were bows and arrows and stout clubs. A battle purposed to save face rather than achieve a victory. Seldom, however, was there much bloodshed—one casualty or two and peace was restored. Alexander Ross in 1811 described them as a commercial rather than a warlike people, and the fact that they were willing to trade their leather war dresses tends to bear this out.

The coastal Indians had the advantage of an unusually rich environment. Ruth Underhill has called them the richest Indians of North America because wealth, as consumable goods, was immediately accessible to them and with a minimum of labor.[4] Wood and water were the sources and the means of their livelihood, and of these there was no limit of abundance. Famine and poverty were unknown among them, except as profligate gambling caused them to throw away their freedom and chance to acquire goods for themselves.

The forests of the Northwest extended solidly from Alaska to Northern California and inland to the "rain shadow" of the plateau. While the pine grows almost exclusively east of the Cascades, the coast forests were stands of mingled spruce, fir, hemlock, and cedar. Wherever the straight-grained, easy-to-split cedar was found easily

---

[4] Ruth Underhill, *Indians of the Pacific Northwest*, Education Division of the United States Office of Indian Affairs, Riverside, California, 1945, 9.

accessible to village sites, housing, utensils, and clothing were made from it. Houses were built of split cedar planks set on end around shallow pits. The gabled roof was supported by posts and was covered by overlapping boards. One or more doorways on the long side of the building gave access to a single room large enough to accommodate a number of families. A house of 100-foot length might house 10 to 12 families; a "long house" or feast house would be five or six times as large and would shelter several hundred persons.

Around the interior walls, platforms covered with mats woven of grass or cedar fiber were the sleeping quarters. Family units were sometimes separated one from the other by hanging mats or by wooden chests in which were kept food supplies and personal properties. Open fires served heating and cooking purposes during the wettest months of the year. There were no windows to lighten the dark interior; the smoke escaped through a hole in the roof.

Cedar also provided them with clothing that would protect them from the weather. From the soft inner fiber found between the bark and the wood were woven large conical, umbrellalike hats and rain capes. According to a sharp-eyed observer in the early days the women wore "a kind of fringed petticoat suspended from the waist down to the knees, made of the inner rind of the cedar bark, and twisted into threads which hang loose like a weaver's thrums and keep flapping and twisting about with every motion of the body, giving them a waddle or duck gait. This garment might deserve praise for its simplicity, or rather for its oddity but it does not screen nature. . . . In a calm the sails lie close to the mast, metaphorically speaking, but when the wind blows the bare poles are seen."[5]

A large part of the year the men went naked and the women wore only such light weight skirts. But in the cold wet days of the winter months, they took from their storage chests bearskins, lynx, otter, or beaver robes for further protection against the weather. The Washington Indians wove blankets from the wool of a special breed of dogs and from the hair of mountain goats for which they traded with the Indians of the mountains.

In the north, wood was skillfully fashioned to make household

[5] Alexander Ross, *Adventures of the First Settlers on the Columbia River,* introduction and notes by M. M. Quaife, Chicago, 1923, 96.

articles and utensils. Thin cedar boards, thoroughly wetted and steamed, were bent around partial cuts to form square-cornered boxes capable of holding liquids. The joining ends were sewed together with fibers or thongs and by the same means the bottoms were attached. Lids were similarly constructed and were decorated with painted designs or with inlaid shells and stones. These boxes were used for storage of goods as well as for cooking. For the latter purpose, the users filled the box with water, put in hot rocks and then added the fish or meat to be cooked. By replacing the rocks from time to time a steady boiling could be kept up. The Oregon and Washington Indians made greater use of grasses and less of wood than their northern neighbors. Baskets for carrying objects, berry gathering, fishing, storing of fish, and root gathering were woven of cedar bark and fiber or from tough sea grasses and weeds. These too would contain water and were used for cooking in much the same manner as the northern Indians used their boxes.

A fine large cedar log of straight grain was material for a canoe, an item so important to the coastal people that they have often been referred to as canoe Indians. The art of fashioning a canoe was highly specialized and varied from place to place. The Makahs and Quinaults of Washington were the great artisans of the sea canoes, the Nootka or Chinook craft. These were flat-bottom dugouts, forty to fifty feet long, which could carry fifty warriors or a crew of five and a ton and a half of dead weight. For its construction a very large log was needed. This was split down its length so that something more than half its thickness was left for shaping. This was accomplished by chipping and burning until the rough form was achieved. Then the final finishing was a job of extreme patience with small chipping strokes and expert use of hot coals. The thin walls were then made pliable with water and hot rocks and stretched out with thwarts. When the canoe dried out, the thwarts were fastened in place without danger of cracking the fragile sides. It was then painted inside and out and adorned with high end pieces carved in animal or human figures. One early observer described the result in these words: "if perfect symmetry, smoothness, and proportion constitute beauty, they surpass anything I ever beheld." William Clark in less elegant language and more elementary spelling spoke of them as "butifull," "neeter made than any I have ever seen and calculated to ride the waves and carry emence burthens."[6]

The facility of men, women, and children in handling these craft made it evident they were equally at home in the water and on the land. They could navigate the roughest seas and should their vessel fill or capsize, the occupants would spring into the water, empty and right their canoe, and climb back in again. The Makahs hunted whale with them. The Chinooks at the mouth of the Columbia traveled north to Vancouver Island and south to California in these low, fragile craft powered by matting sail and paddle.

The waters of the coast, of the sea and the rivers and sound, were the larders of the coastal Indians. A diligent hunter armed with arrows with tiny, sharp heads had his choice of swans, geese, and ducks which twice a year migrated to the region or in mild seasons wintered on the river. Snipe could be caught with nets on the beaches, and wild pigeons and grouse were common in the small meadows and burned-over hillsides. While roots, berries, and game meat were important to them, whale, fish, clams, crabs, and mussels were the staples of their diet. From wood, bone, and shell they made hooks and harpoons; from wood fibers and grasses they wove lines and nets both for fishing and for capturing sea fowl. It was not even necessary on the coast, as it was in the interior, to preserve great quantities of fish for a season of short supply, for there was always fish in the waters, clams on the beaches. From September to January an inferior grade of salmon was plentiful, and with the earliest spring, even in February, giant sturgeon could be caught on deep-set lines, and great quantities of the eulachon or smelt were scooped up in nets and preserved by drying and stringing on cord. The delicate flesh of the chinook salmon caught from May to September was smoked over fires and packed in grass baskets lined with fish skin for later use; and fish oil, a delicacy to flavor berries and a cosmetic for hair and skin, was contained in gut or skin bags for individual use or trade. Their diet, like their way of life, concluded an early observer, "neither secures them perpetual

[6] Robert Stuart's "Narrative of His Overland Trip," in Philip A. Rollins, ed., *Discovery of the Oregon Trail*, New York, 1935, 14; *Original Journals of Lewis and Clark . . .* ed. R. G. Thwaite, 8 vols., New York, 1905, III, 151. For canoe construction see Thomas T. Waterman, *The Whaling Equipment of the Makah Indians*, Seattle, 1920; T. T. Waterman and Geraldine Coffin, *Types of Canoes on Puget Sound*, New York, 1920; Ronald L. Olson, *Adze Canoe and House Types of the Pacific Northwest Coast*, Seattle, 1927.

health, nor exposes them to any particular disease . . . an Indian grows old over his smoked salmon just like a citizen at a turtle feast."[7]

The waters were also the dooryard and principal highways of the coastal Indians. The density of forests prohibited easy land travel and the horse was unknown aboriginally and relatively useless later in their culture. Their villages clustered on cleared spots along navigable rivers and streams and on the harbors and inlets of the seashore. Even as late as 1827 a visitor to Juan de Fuca Strait reported that from Tatoosh Island to Port Discovery he never lost sight of the smoke of villages; and the Columbia River from its mouth to the Gorge was equally occupied. The tidewaters of the Quinault, Chehalis, Yaquina, Siuslaw, Umpqua, and Rogue rivers were population centers, as were Neah Bay, Grays Harbor, Willapa, and Tillamook bays.

However, there were trails that joined sandy stretches of beach or led to berry patches on burned-over hills. Where swift shallow streams had cut their way through the Coast Range, access was had to the Puget Trough and the Willamette Valley. The Chehalis River, the Salmon River, and the Yaquina were among such principal routes. North and south routes led from Puget Sound south across the prairie to the Cowlitz River, and thence to the Columbia; and a similar ancient trail led from the Columbia, at St. Helens on the south bank, into the Tualatin and Willamette valleys where prairie meadows fed great herds of game. Over these trails moved a modest traffic in goods from seashore to valley, from the Sound to the south. The principal artery of commerce was the Columbia and its tributaries.

The coastal pattern of life, modified somewhat in the valleys, prevailed from the coast to the Cascade Mountains. Along the Columbia River, coastal characteristics did not terminate so abruptly. But where the climate changed from wet and equable warm to dry with extremes of hot and cold, and the forests of the mountain slopes gave over to sagebrush, juniper, and grass, the Chinook language, the Chinook canoe, and the wooden houses were abandoned.

The Plateau People

For some years students looked upon the plateau culture as transitional, influenced equally by the coastal and

[7] Rollins, *Discovery of the Oregon Trail*, New York, 1935, 15.

plains cultures which surrounded it. Recent scholarship has shown that from the bend of the Fraser River south to the Great Basin, and from the Cascades to the Rockies, a definite pattern of living with its own individuality existed long before it felt the impact of either of its neighbors. It may well have been that this culture was the oldest of the region, having its roots in that of the lake dwellers of antiquity. Elements of it persisted in spite of overlays of adapted customs. " . . . the Southern Okanogan, Colville, San Poil, Lower Spokane and Columbia, may with reasonable safety be viewed as most representative of older levels and fundamental aspects of Plateau culture," is the conclusion of anthropologist and archaeologist.[8]

The peripheral areas of the Plateau reflected but did not absorb completely neighboring influences. The Nez Perces had certain striking characteristics in common with the Plains culture that they did not have with the Okanogans and San Poil of the upper Columbia. On the other hand the Yakimas and Wenatchees shared both Plains and coastal intrusions. In spite of this, the Plateau people had a uniqueness of their own.

Three linguistic stocks prevailed in the Plateau: the Shoshonean in Southeastern Oregon; the Sahaptin of Northern Oregon, the Southern half of Washington, and Central Idaho; the Interior Salish in Northern Washington, Interior British Columbia, Northern Idaho and Western Montana.

Each language group had its numerous dialects, but probably there were fewer than among the coastal Indians. Villages sharing a common tongue had a bond of union among them cemented by intermarriage and the sharing of certain territory. These were cultural and linguistic bonds of union. They were not political.

In *Cultural Relations in the Plateau of Northwestern America,* Verne Ray distinguishes four types of political organization: the strictly local village autonomy such as found among San Poil, Southern Okanogan, and Teninos; the loose bands of villages of interior British Columbia; the "local autonomy with slight tribal tendency" of the other peoples of the Middle Columbia River area; and the tribal organization of the easternmost, the Kootenais, Flat-

[8] Verne Ray, quoted in Collier, Hudson, and Ford, *Archaeology of the Upper Columbia River,* Seattle, 1942, 113.

heads, Coeur d'Alenes, Nez Perces, Cayuses, and Umatillas. Even within the latter category, however, there were degrees of tight and loose tribal structures, the Umatillas being almost unique in having tribe and village practically synonymous.

Heredity and personal achievement determined leadership in both village and tribe. In sharp contrast to the coastal peoples, those of the Plateau did not place the same emphasis upon the possession of material goods or upon social values derived from such goods. The possession of wealth as a basis for political power was not as significant as it was on the coast. There was an "aristocracy of merit" but the rigid caste system of the coast was absent. Slavery was of little significance except to those who had close trading relations with the coast.

Dwellings varied from coastal to plains types. In some parts of the Western Plateau an ancient style of pit house was modified by the addition of a circular wooden wall roofed with mats or planks. Usually these houses were large enough to shelter two or three families and provide storage space. It would appear, however, that this type of house was no longer consistent with the pattern of life of the majority of the Plateau people after they acquired horses. Different styles of grass mat lodges had taken their place. The eastern Kootenais, Flatheads, and some of the Nez Perces used the hide *tipis* common among the hunting peoples of the Plains. Hides and basketry served them as wood and woven grass served the coastal Indians, for houses, containers, and clothing. During the cold seasons, soft skins and furs were used for garments; in the warm weather men and women wore loincloths, if anything. Bear claws, feathers, bright-colored stones and stone beads, and copper were used for adornment.

These people combined four types of economies appropriate to the varied resources to which they had access. On prairies they gathered roots, such as the camas; wherever the salmon ran they had their fishing sites or traded with those who did have them; on the slopes of the mountains they gathered berries; where the deer grazed they hunted them. In the first half of the eighteenth century, the Shoshones secured horses from the Southwest and distributed them to the peoples of the eastern part of the Plateau. Thereafter they traveled across the Rockies to hunt buffalo.

The horse made these people more mobile. The Nez Perces, for example, traded—and raided—horses with the Plains Indians. They may even have been instrumental in introducing the horse to them. Through this contact, in return, the Nez Perces may have derived their tribal organization, which was a late development in their culture and coincided with the coming of the horse.

Mobility made possible wars farther afield, as well as the development of extended peaceful trading relationships. The Shoshones, Paiutes, and Bannocks roamed over wide areas; the Paiutes so often attacked the villages of the south bank of the Columbia that the enmity was inherited through generations. Yet the San Poil and Okanogans of Northern Washington, who were little dependent upon horses, were extremely pacifistic; and the Indians of British Columbia's Thompson River mountains had no horses and were continually at war.

Where originally salmon festivals were common causes for assembling, horse "fairs" came to attract thousands of natives to annual meeting spots. The grassy valleys of the Yakima and Wenatchee rivers, and the protected valley of Grand Ronde in Oregon were scenes of such gatherings where races were held, treaties were arranged, and other goods as well as horses were exchanged. Intermediary villages carried goods from Northern California, from Western Montana, from the Plains and from the coast to these affairs.

The Indians of the Eastern Plateau had summer and winter villages in widely separated areas. For example, the Nez Perces, who wintered in the Clearwater Valley, traveled to the Beaverhead country in Montana, and followed well-worn trails to the buffalo prairies of Wyoming. Similarly they moved from place to place to gather camas root and berries, for seldom could they satisfy all their food requirements in any one locality.

Although the horse had become important in their economy by the middle of the eighteenth century and the hunt was one of their means of livelihood, the interior Indians, like those of the coast, were also dependent upon fish. Where the latter had access to sea foods at all times of the year, the interior natives were mainly dependent upon the annual salmon run which occurred in the spring and early summer when the fish made their way to the spawning grounds of the head-streams. A failure of the fish run meant disaster to many of these people. Especially was this true of the Indians of Northern Washington and interior British Columbia. The people of the latter region who sang the news of a good harvest expressed a sentiment common to a great part of the region:

I approach the village,
Ya ha he ha, ya ha ha ha;
And hear the voices of many people,
Ya ha, [etc.]
The barking of dogs,
Ya ha, [etc.]
Salmon is plentiful,
Ya ha, [etc.]
The berry season is good,
Ya ha, [etc.].[9]

The salmon were trapped in weirs, harpooned from rocky outthrusts at narrows, or dipped from the pools at the foot of rapids and falls where they milled about trying to make the leap over the obstruction. One of the most famous of these sites was the Dalles of the Columbia. There the Indians constructed fragile scaffoldings extended out over the swift and surging waters, for the choice sites were always where the water was strongest, and where the salmon were forced to pass close to the rocks to avoid the strongest current. At the end of the scaffold, dangerously teetering over the water, the fisherman plied his dip net. Robert Stuart, who observed them in 1812, estimated that an experienced fisherman with industry could catch at least 500 salmon daily at this spot.

Because the Plateau peoples combined fluvial and nomadic ways of life, they were almost as adept in water skills as the Indians on the coast, and may at one time have equaled them. Wherever a river was navigable, the Plateau dwellers made use of it. Their dugout canoes were made from pine logs, and were less skillfully constructed than those on the coast.

Because of the role fishing played in the lives of these people, the Cascades-Dalles section of the river was not only a favored fishing spot

[9] John McLean, *Notes of a Twenty-five Year's Service in the Hudson's Bay Territory*, 2 vols., London, 1849, I, 260.

but the "great emporium" of the Columbia, and according to Alexander Ross, one of its earlier white visitors, "the general theater of . . . roguery" as well.

For a distance of 40 miles between Celilo Falls and the Cascades the Columbia River turned and twisted through narrow channels with many rocky obstructions. A permanent village of Indians lived on the north shore at the Dalles, a site which probably had been occupied for thousands of years. But to both shores of the river within this area thousands of Plateau Indians trekked yearly to fish, to purchase fish if the run had been short in the upper rivers, and to gamble —which to them was another means of exchanging goods.

Slaves and abalone shells from California found their way to the Dalles by way of Indians of Central Oregon and the Willamette Valley; the Eastern Plateau people brought horses, buffalo robes, native tobacco, pipestone, pigments which they had traded or stolen from Plains people. Intermediary tribes traded some of these items to the coast dwellers using the dentalium, *hiqua*, as a medium of exchange since few goods from the seashore had value to the Plateau people. The Spokane villagers traveled to this native fair and became middlemen for the stationary villagers of the upper Columbia or for such people as the Okanogans who traded via the Methow River with the coast. The Yakimas, Klickitat, and Wenatchi used a trail via Chinook Pass to bring goods from the coastal people to the mart.

Similar, if not so large or regular trade gatherings took place at other locations along the Columbia River and its tributaries. Although it is difficult to delineate today the patterns of commerce which existed in prehistoric times, one piece of evidence will suggest their complexity. The abalone is a marine gastropod mollusk found in warm waters of California but nowhere in the Northwest. Yet pendants made from these shells have been found in interior British Columbia, the Yakima Valley, the Dalles area, and in the region of the Nez Perce.[10]

[10] Collier, *et al.*, *Archaeology of the Upper Columbia River*, 97. Other works used in this chapter: Verne Ray, *Cultural Relations in the Plateau of Northwestern America*, Anthropological Records, 8:99-258, Berkeley, California, 1942; Verne Ray, "Native Villages and Tribal Distribution in the Columbia Basin," *PNQ*, XXVII, April, 1936, 99-152; Alexander Ross, *Fur Hunters of the Far West*, introduction and notes by M. M. Quaife, Chicago, 1924; James H. Teit, *The Salishan Tribes of the Western Plateau*, ed. Franz Boas, Bureau of American Ethnology, 45th Annual Report, Washington, 1930.

Geography, resources of land and water, influenced the patterns of life of coastal and Plateau peoples. Within their environments they developed ways to break the hold of brute nature upon them—religions, codes of morals, language, song, commerce, and warfare. The contrast between the Nez Perce, for example, and the Chinooks, or between the Clallams and the Flatheads was illustrated in physical appearance and in social attitudes. Early observers reacted unfavorably to the coastal peoples, noting characteristics of ugliness, grossness, and immorality. Their practice of head flattening was always commented on. They were more favorably impressed with the Plateau people whom they described as tall with well formed bodies and sharply defined features. They noticed, but did not respect the latter's strong feeling for family. In spite of polygamous practices the interior people were chaste before marriage. Basic moral differences between the two native cultures, coastal and Plateau, can be described if not explained in the statement that the former early succumbed to the white men's diseases, of which syphilis was common; the Plateau people took to the warpath and lived longer.

These, then, were the peoples of the Pacific Northwest. They lived well, some even in abundance, upon the resources of the land. When the white man came to share in those resources, he changed the patterns of their lives as he had done elsewhere in his contact with the aborigines. The Indians were the producers of the goods for which ships first came regularly to the Northwest's shores; they became a market for their wares; they were the trailmakers for those who came by land. Both white man and Indian took toll of one another's lives, the Indian less than the other. The white man destroyed the ecology of native life to create his own civilization. He had a larger view of the land's resources.

2

Spanish and English Explorations

The northwest coast was only vaguely outlined and of incidental importance in the affairs of men and nations until late in the eighteenth century. The American colonies had just begun their revolution against Britain when, in July, 1775, the first white man, so far as we know, touched the shores of the far Northwest. But 25 years later the main features of the coastline had been mapped; there was hardly a bay or inlet that had not been entered; and already there had been a quarrel over the rights of nations in this new land.

The search for wealth and power which in the last of the fifteenth and throughout the sixteenth century had brought Europeans to the New World eventually carried them to this northwestern corner of the continent. After four voyages to the "Other World," as he called it, Columbus began to suspect that his discovery was not the much-sought-for Orient and that the Indies still lay to the west. The ill-shapen pearls and the small treasures of gold he carried back to Spain led his successors to their sources and to the conquest of Mexico and Peru. But the plundered riches only stirred their imaginations to dream of further conquests and of "pearls and riches on the coast of the South Sea and all the best and most opulent countries" near there. Quivira and the Seven Cities of Cibola were the names given to fabulous kingdoms whose people "used plates of gold and covered the walls of their temples with it," and which lay, miragelike, always somewhere on the Western horizon. Different map makers at various times placed Quivira on the Missouri River, in the Colorado Rockies, in California, and in the Northwest near a hypothetical inland sea. But more important than the search for Quivira was the anticipation

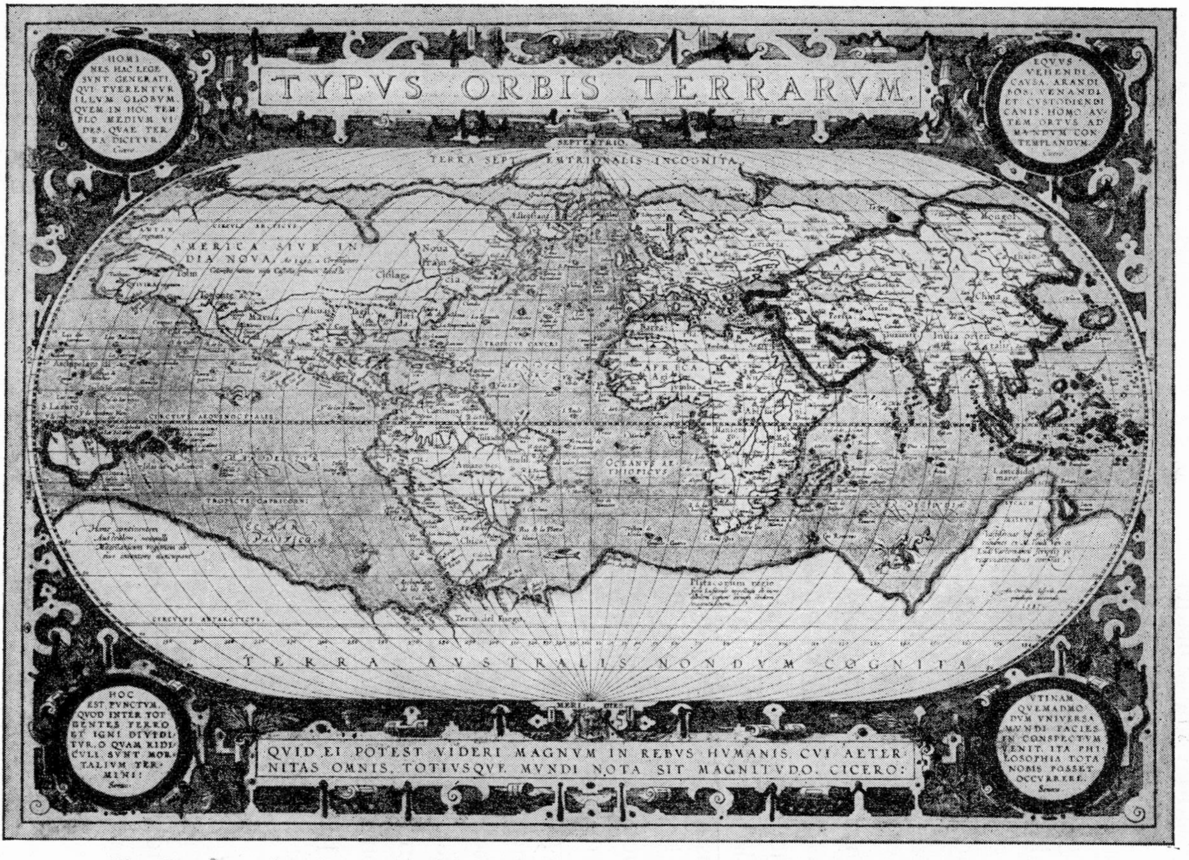

The Known and Unknown Worlds, Sixteenth Century: Typus Orbis Terrarum, Joan Martines of Messina, 1587. (Copy of a photograph of the original in the Charles H. Carey Collection, Oregon Historical Society Library.)

of opening the highway of the Pacific Ocean to the commerce of Europe. For Spain, whose colonies were on both seas, this appeared a relatively simple matter.[1]

On the basis of a papal decree in 1493, Spain claimed the new-found Western Hemisphere and as much of the East as was not occupied by the powers. The following year, by the treaty of Tordesillas, Spain and her maritime rival, Portugal, divided the Atlantic into "spheres of influence" which a subsequent treaty extended to the Pacific. Diplomacy thus provided Spain a shadowy title to the western shores of the Pacific rim, and Portugal, following up the discoveries of Vasco da Gama, secured a foothold in the Orient, over which she sought to retain control. But once established in the Americas Spain looked forward to a trade across the Pacific even though it encroached upon the sphere of her treaty partner. The Philippine Islands, discovered by Magellan and colonized in 1564, were her most eastern outpost.

The voyage of Magellan and Juan del Cano (1519-1522) showed the terrifying extent of the Pacific and the impossibility of navigating it on a two-way voyage with the facilities of that day. The prevailing northeasterly trade winds which carried them to the East made it impossible to return by the same route. In 1565 Andres de Urdaneta discovered that by sailing north in a wide arc from the islands he caught the westerly winds which brought him to the shores of California and thence down the coast to Mexico. This determined the route which made traffic possible on the Pacific Ocean and across it passed the annual trading ships of Spain.

Search for a Northwest Passage

But Spain did not ignore reports of Quivira nor of a passage through the Americas, the Strait of the Indies, which was presumed to debouch somewhere on the western coast north of Mexico. In 1540 Francisco Vasquez de Coronado was sent by land into what is now Arizona and Colorado, and Juan Roderiguez Cabrillo by sea in 1542 to explore the coast of the Cali-

[1] An excellent narration of Spanish explorations is found in John Brebner, *The Explorers of North America, 1492-1806*, London, 1933. The Spanish-Portuguese division of the New World is discussed in Charles E. Nowell, "The Treaty of Tordesillas and the Diplomatic Background of American History" in *Greater America: Essays in Honor of Herbert Eugene Bolton*, Berkeley, 1945; Nellis M. Crouse, *The Search for the Northwest Passage*, New York, 1934, has also been used for this section.

fornias. Coronado failed to find Quivira, and Cabrillo and his pilot, Bartolome Ferrelo, failed to find any strait as far as the latter sailed, which was north to the 42nd or 44th parallels. After the initiation of the Philippine trade, Spain was content to explore the California coast for harbors into which the Philippine ships might take refuge from enemies or storms. She moved farther only to protect her claims when others threatened them.

To Spain's rival, England, a passage through or around the continent was essential if she was to break into the Oriental trade by a western route. The continent lay between her ports and her goal. Under letters patent from Henry VII, the merchant John Cabot in 1497 and 1498 had explored a portion of the coast of Nova Scotia and the shores of Greenland, seeking the entrance of a strait. His son Sebastian became an influential figure in English efforts to expand their foreign trade. As governor of the Merchant Adventurers of London, he was instrumental in sending out two expeditions (1553, 1555-1556) to search for a Northeast Passage to the Orient through the polar regions. Arctic ice thwarted their ambition, but a profitable trade was opened with Archangel. The idea of a Northeast Passage was long favored by the Muscovy traders, but others encouraged and sponsored voyages to seek a Northwest Passage around or across the North American continent. Anian, the Strait of the Indies, appeared on the maps as the imagination of geographers dictated, and its hypothetical location shifted as new discoveries or speculations changed the outlines of the Northern Hemisphere. At one time the Strait was thought to separate the North American continent from Asia; at another time it was the passage through North America and the route joining Europe to the East.

The first and most persistent search was for a western passage opening from some northern inlet on Hudson's or Baffin Bay or through Davis Strait, and debouching on the Pacific coast somewhere above the 60th parallel. This was designated the Northwest Passage. An especially ardent advocate was a London merchant by the name of Michael Lok, or Lock. He had been the chief promoter and financier of the expeditions of Davis and Frobisher to search the North Atlantic seaboard for an entrance. The ice-locked waters of Davis and Frobisher Straits did not encourage further search.

Lock, however, did not give up agitation for continued search, even contributing to a prize of 20,000 pounds for the discovery of a passage. He purported to have a letter from a Greek explorer, Juan de Fuca, in the service of Spain who claimed to have found the western opening of the Northwest Passage. According to this account, Juan de Fuca in 1592 had entered a broad inlet on the Pacific coast located between 47° and 48° north latitude in the vicinity where almost 200 years later the strait leading into Puget Sound was to be discovered.

De Fuca reported he had sailed inland more than 20 days, finding the people there wearing the skins of beasts and the land rich in gold, silver, and pearls. His story was a part of the romance of discovery common to the day, and at best the overenthusiastic propaganda of an ambitious entrepreneur; it was responsible for placing of the inland sea upon the maps, and for the association of that sea with the Kingdom of Quivira.[2]

Francis Drake

England did not enter the Pacific Ocean until 1578, and then her interest was less in exploration than in piracy. In 1567, John Hawkins had raided Vera Cruz, Spain's chief eastern port in Mexico, and in subsequent years others followed suit. Notorious among these freebooters was Francis Drake, who having tasted the fruits of piracy with Hawkins, returned to the Spanish colonies in 1571, 1572, and 1573. In 1577 he was dispatched with the Queen's approval to seek a trade route to the Moluccas, but instead of sailing east around Cape Hope, he crossed the Atlantic, rounded the Horn into the Pacific and raided the undefended Spanish ports. This was immediately profitable although disastrous to Anglo-Spanish relations.

Because Drake sailed northward to some undetermined point on the coast of North America, it has been assumed that he was seeking the western entrance of the Northwest Passage, that because he took possession of the land at a California bay, he was the agent of an early English national interest in the Pacific. One of the best authorities leads us to conclude, however, that, in "all his enterprises, booty seems to have been somewhere in sight."[3] There was no booty on the

---

[2] Charles H. Carey, "Some Early Maps and Myths," *OHQ*, XXX, March, 1929, 19.

[3] Henry R. Wagner, *Sir Francis Drake's Voyage Around the World: Its Aim and Achievement*, San Francisco, 1926, 212. For a British interpretation of Drake's voyage, its purpose and results, see the popular but excellent work by James A. Williamson,

northern coast between the 38th and 48th parallels, the possible range of his voyage. At his highest point he found only a region where ". . . the rain which fell was an unnatural congealed and frozen substance," and where two days later, "there followed most vile, thicke and stinking fogges."

From this unpleasant climate Drake turned south again, and in a bay—Trinidad, Bodega, or Drake's Bay—sought shelter for a month's recuperation of his crew. Before his departure to circumnavigate the globe and return to England, he was reported to have given the name New Albion to the region. This name subsequently appeared on maps of the West, but was shifted north to designate the coast of Oregon and Washington.

The profitable results of Drake's voyage inspired other English sea dogs to like piratical ventures with the result that the Spanish were forced not only to defend their Caribbean colonies but also their ports and trade in the Pacific. After a resounding punishment of English privateers in 1594 Spain set the slow and cumbersome wheels of her colonial administration toward an expedition of discovery in the Pacific. In 1602-1603 Sebastian Viscaino and Martin Aguilar were dispatched, according to one report, to look for the city of Quivira, but more probably to search for harbors as far north as the forty-third parallel. Viscaino carefully explored the California coast; Aguilar may have reached 43° north latitude. Through an error of the historian Torquemada, a "rapid and abundant river" noted by Aguilar in the vicinity of 41° was placed on the map at 43°. His river was probably Tomales Bay; but in subsequent maps it appeared at almost the location where the Columbia River was to be discovered in 1792.

The maps of the day by accident and design took on features which approximated the truth. But the Northwest was still unknown and unexplored north of Mendocino or Cape Blanco, and for more than a century and a half after the voyage of Aguilar no vessel purposely came to explore its coast. Legends of the Oregon Indians tell of

---

Sir Francis Drake, Brief Lives Series, London, 1953. For arguments on whether Drake sailed to 40° or 48° north latitude, see Wagner, Chap. VII, and works of George Davidson, especially *Identification of Sir Francis Drake's Anchorage on the Coast of California*, San Francisco, 1890. For information on the brass plate discovered twenty years ago, see Herbert E. Bolton, "Francis Drake's Plate of Brass," *CHSQ*, XVI, March, 1937, 1-18; also issues of September, 1937, and December, 1938.

white-sailed ships coming ashore, of white men burying treasure on Neahkahnie Mountain, and mysteriously marked wax found in the vicinity lends some substance to the tales.[4]

The Eighteenth Century

Maritime exploration of the Northern Pacific Ocean was at a standstill until the middle of the eighteenth century. From 1603 to 1769 Spain gave her attention to other matters: to voyages in the south seas in search of the Unknown Continent and to the development of her Japanese-Philippine-Mexico trade.

In 1763, as a result of the Seven Years' War (the French and Indian War), Spain acquired French Louisiana, a further burden of administration but a welcome barrier between her and aggressive English colonies to the east and north. Financial difficulties and the complexities of European politics were reducing Spain to a secondary power in spite of her great colonial possessions. She was put on the defensive to protect both her empire, especially the mineral-rich internal provinces, and her peculiar colonial policy. At almost the same time she acquired Louisana, she began the occupation of California as an extension of that continental frontier.[5] Russian expansion into the Pacific was the immediate cause of renewed Spanish interest on the coast.

The eighteenth century was an age of tremendous energy. Ideas of colonial expansion which had dominated the seventeenth century were giving way to policies of commercial colonialism. It was also an age of scientific interests, of enlightenment, in which competition in the arts and sciences was widespread. In some cases it was possible to serve both science and empire.

Russia in the Pacific

Peter the Great of isolated Russia was aware of what was going on in the rest of the world, and he too wished to expand his frontiers and to find an outlet by which Russia also might share in the riches of the East. By 1639 the Russians, enticed

[4] A. F. Stafford, "The Wax of Nehalem Beach," *OHQ*, IX, March, 1908.

[5] Naojiro Murakami, "Japan's Early Attempts to Establish Commercial Relations with Mexico" in *The Pacific Ocean in History*, H. M. Stephens and H. E. Bolton, New York, 1917; A. P. Nasatir, *Before Lewis and Clark: Documents Illustrating the History of the Missouri, 1785-1804*, 2 vols., St. Louis, 1952.

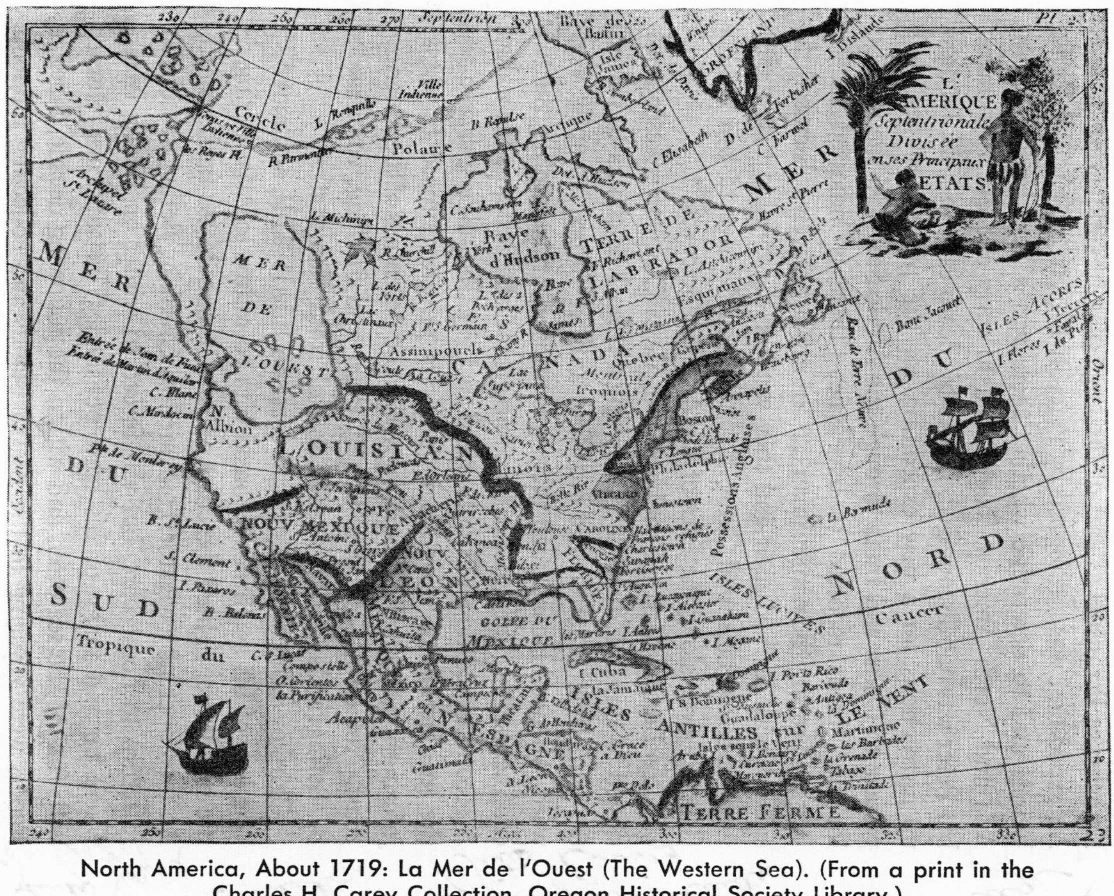

North America, About 1719: La Mer de l'Ouest (The Western Sea). (From a print in the Charles H. Carey Collection, Oregon Historical Society Library.)

by the rich fur resources of the region, had undertaken the conquest of Siberia, had reached the Pacific, and had founded the port of Okhotsk. Trading posts were established across Siberia and on the Kamchatka Peninsula as part of the large plan of conquering Siberia. An expedition was authorized by Peter in 1719 to explore the Kurile Islands and to determine whether there was a land bridge uniting Asia and North America. They failed to carry out the assignment, but Peter was not discouraged. Before his death early in 1725, he drew up instructions for a new expedition for the purpose of finding a passage to China and India through the Arctic Sea. "On the map befor me," he is reported to have said, "there is indicated such a passage bearing the name Anian. . . . In my last travels I discussed the subject with learned men and they were of the opinion that such a passage could be found. Now . . . we should strive to win for her [Russia] glory along the lines of the Arts and Sciences."[6]

Vitus Bering, Martin Spanberg, and Alexei Chirikov were commissioned to this task. In 1728 Bering sailed from Kamchatka to beyond 64° and then followed the coastline until it turned abruptly westward, whence he concluded there was no land bridge uniting the two continents, but that America lay at no great distance across the waters. A second expedition was authorized in 1734. Its public purpose was the satisfaction of scientific inquiry; its private purpose to obtain information about the geography and trade potentials of the American coast. Not until 1740 were the *St. Peter* and *St. Paul*, commanded by Bering and Chirikov, ready to sail from Kamchatka.

Chirikov sighted the American coast on July 15, 1741, at about 57°. The loss of his small boats forced him to return to Asia. Bering, in the meantime, sighted the coast on July 16 one degree farther north. An incompetent navigator, compared to Chirikov, Bering was unable to return to home base, but was forced to winter on Bering Island, where he and many of his crew perished. The survivors returned with furs of the sea otter, and within the following decade, Siberian traders were voyaging to the Alaska islands and collecting immense quantities of fine furs.

---

[6] Quoted in Frank A. Golder, *Russian Expansion in the Pacific*, Cleveland, 1914, 133; J. C. Beaglehole, *Exploration of the Pacific*, London, 1934; Sven Wexel, *American Expedition*, introduction and notes by M. A. Michael, Edinburgh, 1952.

Russia's contributions to the glory of the Arts and Sciences in these voyages were not of immediate concern to the Spanish if they knew about them. But the publication of German and French translations of Russian reports revealed to Western Europeans that they were expanding their interest in the New World beyond the sphere of knowledge alone. The *promishlennik*, or fur traders, were making annual trading voyages among the Aleutian Islands. Three official Russian expeditions commissioned in 1766, 1767, 1768 were interpreted as threats to Spanish claims in the Pacific.

Spanish Ships on the Northwest Coast

Under these circumstances, then, the Spaniards undertook to strengthen their position by the settlement of Upper California and the further exploration of the coast. Between 1769 and 1776 missions and presidios were set up at San Diego, Monterey, San Gabriel, and San Francisco. And in 1774, Juan Perez was dispatched to sail north to 60°, to explore, and to take possession of the whole coast.

Perez reached the 54th parallel where he was forced to turn back because of scurvy which had seriously weakened his crew. He reported he had found no Russian settlements as far as he had gone, had discovered no ports, and had not taken possession of any lands, but he did describe the western coasts of Vancouver and Queen Charlotte Islands, and gave a vague description of the coasts of Oregon and Washington. His was the most thorough report on the Northwestern coast to date, and no doubt it was for this experience that he was chosen pilot of the next and most important expedition sent out in 1775. This consisted of two vessels under Bruno Heceta and with Juan Francisco de Bodega y Quadra (whom we shall call Quadra) second in command. Their commission directed them to explore to the 65th parallel. Misfortune plagued the ships. Heceta turned back at 49° and Quadra at 58° because of scurvy. But their surveys gave shape to the coastline and Spanish claims were based upon their explorations and landings.

On July 14, 1775, the flagship *Santiago* anchored off Point Grenville where Heceta landed and took possession of the region for Spain. At the same time, Quadra in the Schooner *Sonora* had anchored at the mouth of the Hoh River where seven men went ashore to take on fresh water. They were attacked and massacred by the Indians with the result that the rocky island near the spot was named Isla de Dolores, the Isle of Sorrows.

Turning south again, on August 17 Heceta discovered a large bay which he named Assumption Bay in honor of the feast day on which he made his discovery. The northern headland he called Cape San Roque and the southern spit, Cape Frondoso. In the bay, he noted, "currents and eddies . . . caused me to believe that the place is the mouth of some great river, or of some passage to another sea. Had I not been certain of the latitude of this bay . . . I might easily have believed it to be the passage discovered by Juan de Fuca, in 1592, which is placed on the charts between the 47th and 48th degrees; where I am certain that no such strait exists."[7]

Heceta did not explore the bay even with these promising signs. His crew, depleted by death and illness, could not spare men to man the longboat, and if the anchor were lowered "we should not have men enough to get it up." So Heceta put out to sea again, and thus failed to find the Columbia River. The "Rio San Roque," however, appeared on subsequent maps.

The voyages of Perez, Heceta, and Quadra resulted in the greater definition of the northwest coastline. These explorers gave names to many features of the landscape—mountains, harbors, and bays. In most cases these have been abandoned and the names applied by later English explorers and settlers have survived in their stead. But their explorations gave Spain her claim to have been the original discoverer of the northwest coast.

The Spanish as usual did not follow up their discoveries. Their fear of Russian expansion and settlement was allayed because it did not appear that Russia at this time was intent upon any permanent occupation of the land. It was the British who were next to challenge the Spanish, and in so doing to involve the Pacific Northwest in an international incident.

---

[7] Complete quotation given in Robert Greenhow, *The History of Oregon and California*, Boston, 1845, Appendix, 432-433. See also Hubert H. Bancroft, *History of the Northwest Coast*, 2 vols., San Francisco, 1886, I, 152-157.

Cook in the North Pacific

As we have seen, the English first came into the Pacific Ocean to prey upon Spanish treasure ships. In the intervening two centuries they had sent many expeditions of discovery into the South Pacific looking for the Unknown Continent and vying with the Spanish in taking possession of south sea islands. They had secured a foothold for commerce in the Orient and in India, and pursued a rich trade through the East India Company. Their route hence was via known Atlantic waters, and the Northwest Passage had only intermittently occupied their attention.

After the European and American war with France, 1754-1763, England embarked upon a new imperial policy of expansion. Her determination to control her colonies and to fit them to the contemporary theory of imperial needs resulted in the American Revolution. But while England was pursuing measures that led to the breakup of her first empire, she was engaged in creating a new one in the Orient and the Pacific. And, as in the case of Russia's interest in the Pacific, so could England's be justified on the grounds that she served both commerce and science.

In 1768 the English government was encouraged to support an expedition for the purpose of observing the transit of the planet Venus in the south Pacific Ocean. Captain James Cook of the Royal Navy, who had spent the major portion of his life as geographer and surveyor on the north Atlantic coast, was given command of the *Endeavor* for this purpose. He was also instructed to look for the Unknown Continent that was supposed to be in those waters. As a result of his voyage, doubt was thrown upon the possible existence of the continent; astronomical research was, unfortunately, no better off than before, but England had a claim to New Zealand, Tasmania, and Australia, whose coasts were explored and mapped. A second voyage, 1772-1775, conclusively proved that there was no southern continent inviting occupation and his suspicions of the existence of Antarctic lands were left to a later century to prove.

His two expeditions in the Antipodes and the reports of the world they opened stirred the imaginations of all who heard of them. Boswell, biographer of Dr. Samuel Johnson and London's literary set, even "catched the enthusiasm of curiosity and adventure, and felt a strong inclination to go with him on his next voyage." He was not alone in being "carried away with the general grand and indistinct notion of *A Voyage Round the World*."[8]

It was Cook's third voyage, 1776-1780, that had historical significance for the Pacific Northwest. Having abandoned, now, the pursuit of the Unknown Continent, Britain turned to other practicalities of statesmanship. The objective of this voyage of the *Resolution* and the *Discovery* was a final determination of the question of the Northwest Passage. A public and private subscription offered 20,000 pounds as prize for the discoverer. The Northwest Passage had new meaning in 1776. Britain's interests were turning more and more toward India and the Orient and the Pacific, while in the very spring of Cook's sailing, the Atlantic American colonies were debating their declaration of independence.

Previous English searches for a Northwest Passage—by Davis, Baffin, Foxe, Middleton, and Phipps—had approached the North American continent from the Atlantic. Cook was directed to proceed via the Cape of Good Hope into the Pacific, to cross from the Society Islands to the coast of North America, and to lose no time in exploration until he reached 65° north latitude. His search was to concentrate about this parallel upon a channel that might offer a route to Hudson's or Baffin Bay. If he failed to find such a passage, he was to continue to the Arctic through Bering Strait and look for a northeast or northwest polar passage. So much confidence was placed in Cook's talents as a discoverer and navigator that the Admiralty dispatched naval vessels to meet him in Baffin Bay.

Cook blazed the trail, so to speak, for those who were to come after him. *En route* from the Society Islands he discovered islands which he honored with the name of his nation and first lord of the Admiralty, the Earl of Sandwich. The Sandwich Islands (now the Hawaiian) became a regular stopping place and food supply depot for ships destined for the coast.

On March 7, 1778, Cook sighted the Oregon coast off Yaquina Bay. His instructions did not permit any close examination of that

[8] G. B. Hill, ed., *Boswell's Life of Johnson*, revised by S. F. Powell, 6 vols., Oxford, 1934, III, 7.

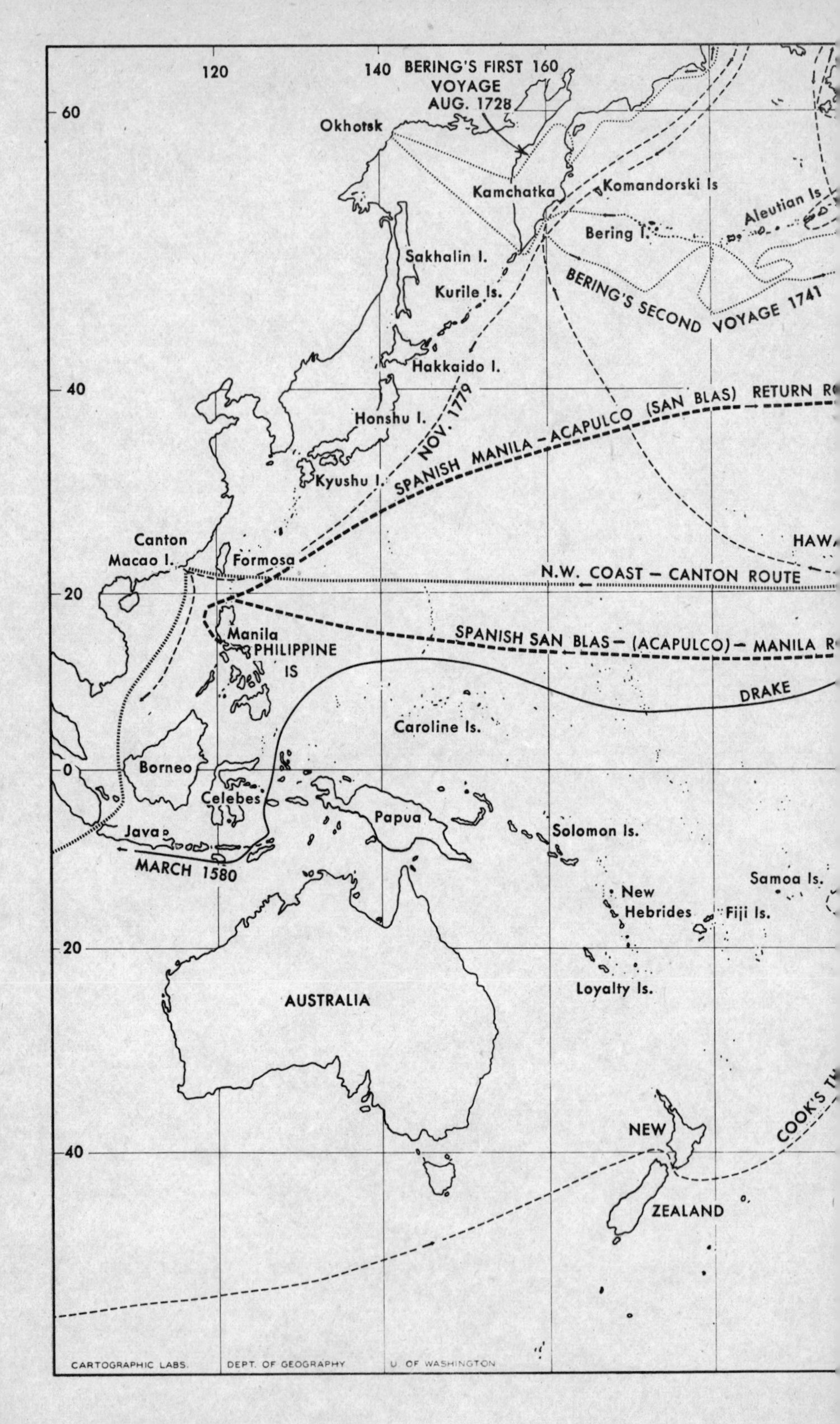

120
140
160
60
40
20
0
20
40
BERING'S FIRST VOYAGE AUG. 1728
Okhotsk
Kamchatka
Komandorski Is
Aleutian Is
Bering I.
BERING'S SECOND VOYAGE 1741
Sakhalin I.
Kurile Is.
Hakkaido I.
Honshu I.
Kyushu I.
NOV. 1779
SPANISH MANILA – ACAPULCO (SAN BLAS) RETURN
Canton
Macao I.
Formosa
N.W. COAST – CANTON ROUTE
Manila
PHILIPPINE IS
SPANISH SAN BLAS – (ACAPULCO) – MANILA
DRAKE
Caroline Is.
Borneo
Celebes
Papua
Java
MARCH 1580
Solomon Is.
Samoa Is.
New Hebrides
Fiji Is.
Loyalty Is.
AUSTRALIA
NEW ZEALAND
CARTOGRAPHIC LABS. DEPT. OF GEOGRAPHY U. OF WASHINGTON

ROUTES OF PA

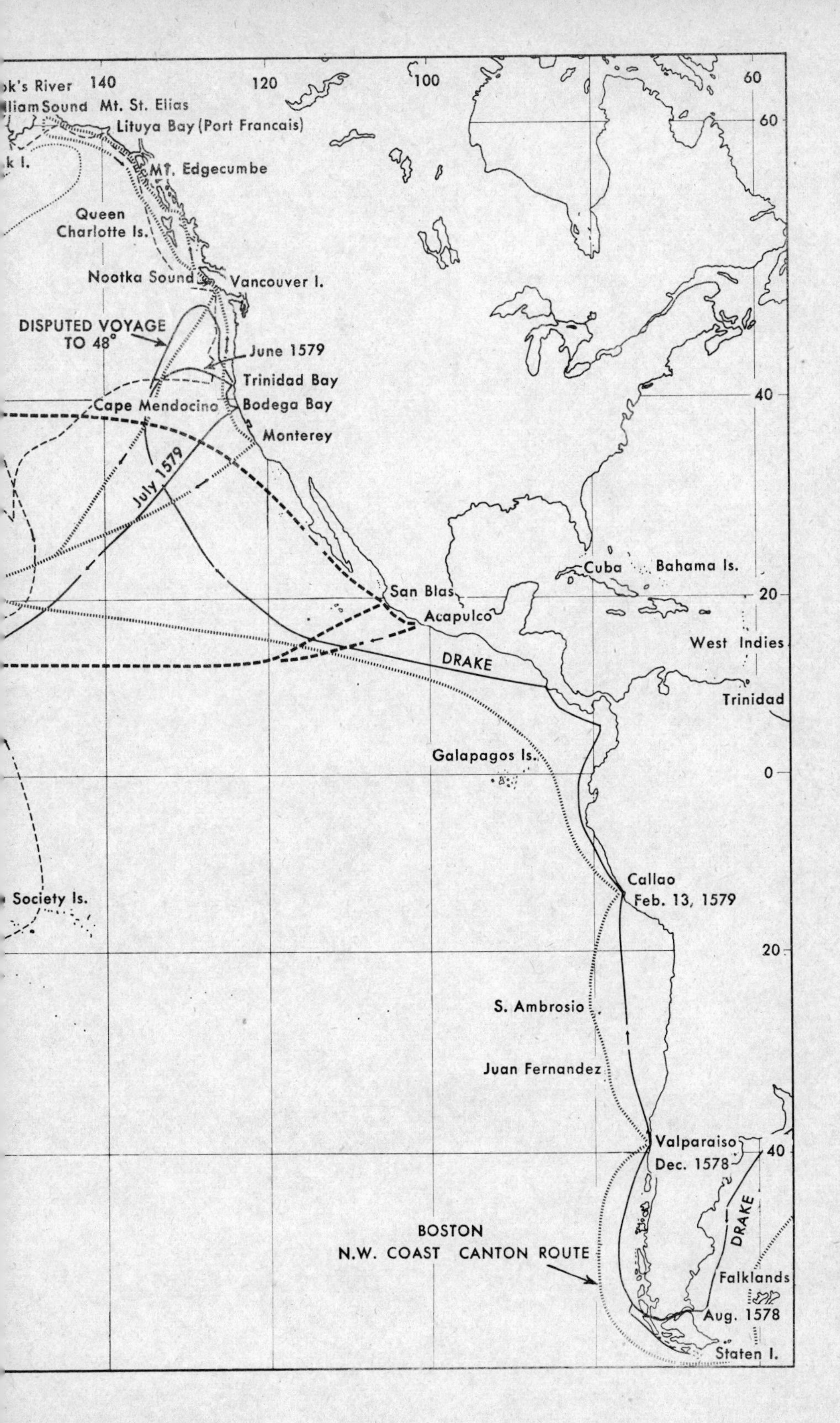

EXPLORATION

part of the coast, but he named Capes Gregory (now Arago), Foulweather, and Perpetua, which, he said, he found at almost the exact location previous geographers had given to Cape Blanco. His haste and bad weather conspired to make him miss the mouth of the Columbia River. On March 22 he sighted a cape at the opening of the strait between Vancouver Island and the continent, which he named Cape Flattery with nice attention to the meaning of the word. As he approached, he said, "there appeared to be a small opening, which flattered us with the hopes of finding an harbour. . . . It is in this very latitude where we now were, that geographers have placed the pretended Strait of Juan de Fuca. But," he concluded, "we saw nothing like it; nor is there the least probability that ever any such thing existed."[9]

Cook failed to recognize that his first landing was on an island, later to be known as Vancouver Island. He spent almost the whole month of April in Nootka Sound repairing and rerigging his ships. Here, as elsewhere in landings made along the northern coast, his crew carried on a lively trade with the natives for furs which they used for bedding or to repair their worn-out clothes. He found the Indians had some fishhooks and other implements of brass and iron, and he noted two silver spoons of Spanish make as evidence of Spanish visits to the coast. The natives' eagerness for metal led to dexterous thieving which practically stripped the ships of iron work in spite of watchful guards.

We also found, that many of the principal natives, who lived near us, carried on a trade with more distant tribes, in the articles they had procured from us. For we observed, that they would frequently disappear for four or five days at a time, and then return with fresh cargoes of skins and curiosities, which our people were so passionately fond of, that they always came to a good market. But we received most benefit from such of the natives who visited us daily. These, after disposing of all their little trifles, turned their attention to fishing; and we never failed to partake of what they caught. We also got from these people a considerable quantity of very good animal oil, which they had reserved in bladders. In this traffic some would attempt to cheat us, by mixing water with the oil; and, once or

[9] James Cook and James King, A *Voyage to the Pacific Ocean . . . in 1776, 1777, 1778, 1779, and 1780*, 3 vols., London, 1784, II, 263. Other quotations and references from Vols. II and III, *passim;* see also, Crouse, *Search for the Northwest Passage* and James A. Williamson, *Cook and the Opening of the Pacific*, London, 1948.

twice, they had the address to carry their imposition so far, as to fill their bladders with mere water, without a single drop of oil. It was always better to bear with these tricks, than to make them the foundation of a quarrel; for our articles of traffic consisted, for the most part, of mere trifles; and yet we were put to our shifts to find a constant supply even of these. Beads, and such other toys, of which I had still some left, were in little estimation. Nothing would go down with our visitors but metal; and brass had, by this time, supplanted iron; being so eagerly sought after, that before we left this place, hardly a bit of it was left in the ships, except what belonged to our necessary instruments. Whole suits of clothes were stripped of every button; bureaus of their furniture; and copper kettles, so that our American friends here got a greater medley and variety of things from us, than any other nation whom we had visited in the course of the voyage.

The remainder of the season Cook examined the coastline northward and westward through the Aleutian Islands. On August 9 he passed through Bering Strait, where, he said, he reached the "hitherto unknown" western extremity of North America. To his left he saw Asia, ahead of him the frozen Arctic Sea, and at his right, the frozen wastes of Northern America. There was no passage here for English ships to sail from China to their island home either by an eastern or western route through the Arctic.

Cook's Pacific voyages are proof that he was a great seaman and a great discoverer. He initiated a new era in maritime exploration when he applied sanitation and health requirements to life at sea. In the four years of the voyage, only five men were lost by sickness, three of whom were ill when they left England. Antiscorbutics, malt and hops, were taken along, but fortunately there was no sign of scurvy, the dread disease of long voyages. Cook used "sour krout and portable soup" as preventives and every effort was made to limit the use of salt foods, the common diet of sailors. Some of the substitutes tried, native foods, for example, were so nauseous that to try them required "the joint aid of persuasion, authority and example, to conquer their prejudices and disgusts."

The third voyage was a training experience for ambitious young explorers. Six names enrolled on Cook's personnel lists appear again in the history of the Pacific Northwest: Lieutenant George Vancouver was to be Cook's great successor in the exploration of the coast; Nathaniel Portlock and George Dixon were to return in 1785 as explorers and pioneers of trade as did James Colnett in 1787; Corporal John Ledyard of the Marines was to be a publicist of the area; and the experiences of Joseph Billings, seaman, were to lead to his career as an explorer of Siberia and the Pacific, and as a commodore of the Russian navy.

As a discoverer Cook opened up the waters of the South Pacific and found a continent and scores of islands. The Sandwich or Hawaiian Islands were to become the principal depot of the mid-Pacific, and a link between the Northwest and the rest of the world. His third voyage proved to all except the most prejudiced that the Northwest Passage, as visualized by armchair explorers, did not open off the coast he had explored. Not until the summer of 1954 did specially-built and powered vessels manage to break through the icy waters of the Arctic passage between the Atlantic and Pacific Oceans. Cook's widely read *Voyages*, published in 1784, inspired European nations to new efforts on behalf of the "arts and sciences," but subsequent search for the Northwest Passage was more in the way of justifying his conclusions than challenging them. After this date, as we shall see, explorers turned their attention to the interior of the continent and the possible linkage of its river systems for transcontinental travel.

It can hardly be held against Cook that he failed to find two notable features of the Pacific Northwest's coastline: the entrances to the Columbia River and Strait of Juan de Fuca. His instructions had directed his search elsewhere. The careful mapping of this particular coastline was to be the work of his successors, but that, in turn, was set in motion by unexpected results of his last voyage.

In the history of this region Cook's name is usually associated with the beginning of the fur trade. Actually the trade had already been initiated by the Russians in the north, and in small measure by Spanish garrisons in California. But both the extent and the effect of these instances were limited. Cook himself had no part in the matter, except to go on record as to the possibilities of the trade. "There is not the least doubt," he said, "that a very beneficial fur trade might be carried on with the inhabitants of this vast coast." He recognized, too, that the most valuable fur of the many available was that of the sea otter. But he had concluded that this trade would not be profitable for Great Britain "unless a Northern passage should be found practicable," in his opinion a very remote possibility.

After Cook's death in the Hawaiian Islands, in the spring of 1779, the *Resolution* and *Discovery* under command of Captain Clerke and then of Captain Gore returned once more to the north Pacific, and in the winter sailed for China. There his men were surprised to find that the sea otter skins for which they had paid trifles were objects of brisk trade. One seaman sold his stock for 800 dollars; a few prime skins, clean and well-preserved, brought their owners 120 silver dollars each. This unexpected windfall almost led the crews to mutiny in their eagerness to return to its source. Even the officers were inspired to plan projects for the development of the trade, and one proposed to the Canton merchants of the East India Company the outfitting of two small vessels to set out immediately. Within five years, two of them, Portlock and Dixon, were pioneers of a "fur rush" to the Pacific Northwest.

Thus Cook's last voyage may be said to have ended one phase of maritime exploration and discovery and instituted a second. The first was principally concerned with the efforts of the Spanish and English to find a route to the Indies, the elusive Northwest Passage, and the equally elusive Kingdom of Quivira, and only incidentally to extend their claims to the land. The second period opened when it was discovered that the lands of the Pacific Northwest had a resource of value in the world's trade. A principal result of Cook's voyage was the beginning of the maritime trade of the region.

The men who followed this pursuit in their sailing ships came primarily to reap profits from the Indian trade or to protect their interests in it. With few exceptions subsequent discoveries and explorations of the area were only incidental to trade. It was a trader who discovered the entrance to the Strait of Juan de Fuca and made a reality of a legend. It was a trader who discovered the Columbia River and eradicated from the maps the River of the West. And it was the fur trade which led not only to the determination of the ownership of the region, but also to the settlement of it.

3

Maritime Fur Trade: International Rivalries

The official report of Cook's third voyage was published in 1784, and commanded equal attention, if not more, than the narratives of his earlier voyages. "The extraordinary discoveries of . . . Cook," wrote a contemporary, "inspired all Europe with an enthusiastic desire of being acquainted with the parts of the globe still remaining unknown."[1] It would appear that such enthusiastic desires were intensified when unknown parts of the globe were reported to be rich in fur resources and especially the sea otter so much in demand in the Chinese market.

Voyage of Lapérouse

Within two years after the publication of Cook's third voyage, the governments of France, Russia, and Spain turned their attention to the Pacific Northwest and to the fur trade. In 1785, Louis XVI took a personal interest in planning and instructing an expedition of discovery into Pacific and Asiatic waters. Two ships, the *Boussole* and the *Astrolabe,* under Jean Galaup, Count Lapérouse, were staffed with scientists and observers to rival the much admired Cook expedition. The interests of science were to be served by examining lands not seen by Cook or Russian and Spanish explorers of the western coast of North America, and Lapérouse was instructed to look especially for "some river, some narrow gulf," which might open up a communication with Hudson's Bay.[2]

---

[1] Martin Sauer, *An Account of a Geographical and Astronomical Expedition to the Northern Parts of Russia* by *Commodore Joseph Billings in the years 1785 &c to 1794,* London, 1802, Preface, 13.

[2] *Le Voyage de Lapérouse sur les Côtes de L'Alaska et de la California* (1786), Historical Documents, Institut Français de Washington, Cahier X, Baltimore, 1937, xvii. Interpretation of Lapérouse's voyage is based upon materials from this and M. L. A.

Thomas Jefferson, United States minister to Paris, asked John Paul Jones to determine, if he could, what lay behind France's sudden interest in the Pacific. Jones reported that the Crown intended to extend French commerce by "Establishing Factories at a future Day, for the Fur Trade on the North West Coast of America." Lapérouse's instructions indicated that scientific knowledge and commercial or colonial opportunities were both of interest to France.

He was to examine the "possibility of establishing a colony or at least a factory in a region not yet occupied." This involved not only the location of a favorable site but an opinion on the nature of any opposition that might develop and on the market opportunities in the Orient. After rounding the Horn, he sighted the coast on June 23, 1786, near Mt. St. Elias at 60° north latitude. One month was spent examining the vicinity.

Lapérouse reported some discoveries which had escaped his predecessors, and took possession of Port des Français (present Lituya Bay south of Mt. St. Elias). This he believed a fitting site for a factory which a hundred men could defend against considerably larger forces. From here he sailed south to observe the strength and character of the Spanish settlements in California, and thence across the Pacific where at Macao he tested the market by disposing of 1,000 furs. At Kamchatka, at the end of September, 1787, he put ashore his Russian interpreter, de Lesseps, to make his way overland to Paris with reports and maps of his voyage to date.

The expedition was shadowed by tragedy. Twenty-one marines were lost in a heavy storm while surveying Port des Français, and sometime in 1788 the gallant Frenchman, his faculty of scholars and crews were lost with their two vessels on an island in the Hebrides. Not only the lives but the observations of the scientific corps were lost. And the voyage did not encourage French colonial enterprise. France could not draw sufficient benefit from the fur trade to justify the risk of offending Spain who would regard any occupation of the

Milet-Mureau, trans., *Voyage de la Pérouse*, 4 vols., Paris, 1797. See also A. P. Nasatir, *French Activities in California, an Archival Calendar-Guide*, Stanford University, California, 1945, Introductory Sketch, pp. 1-3. References to Thomas Jefferson and John Paul Jones and quotations, from *Jefferson Papers*, Julian P. Boyd, ed., Princeton, 1950-1954, Vol. VIII; *Writings of Thomas Jefferson*, Monticello ed., Washington, D. C., 1904-1905, Vol. 5.

region as an usurpation of her rights. The strength of Spanish-French dynastic ties were sufficiently great to excuse France from partaking in a colonial venture she was in no way fitted for at the time.

The preparations for and sailing of Lapérouse's expedition on the first of August, 1785, had been noted by others than Jefferson. There were repercussions in Russia, where up to this time there had been little interest shown in the Alaskan islands which Siberian traders annually visited. In 1783, without any encouragement from the government, the first colony of a permanent nature was established on Kodiak Island. The reports of Cook's voyage brought this colonial outpost into new perspective, the Shelikoff family that supported it into prominence, and Catherine II toyed with the notion of a Russian expedition of discovery into Northeastern Asia and the Pacific. In July, 1785, informed of the outfitting of Lapérouse's expedition at Brest, she gave the orders to proceed.[3] By October, Captain Joseph Billings and a large force were off on a venture that was to last nine years.

Spanish Fears Aroused

Spain too was showing unusual attention to the commerce of her colonies. In 1784 the Viceroy of New Spain submitted a plan for exporting California sea otter pelts to Manila for that island's trade with China. The next year a Spanish version of an East India trading company, the Royal Philippine Company, was charged with the duty of carrying from Europe or America goods suited to the China trade. The sea otter trade of California was made a state monopoly and the first cargo exported in 1786. Such speedy action was unusual in Spanish colonial history and indicates the importance the Pacific Coast was suddenly acquiring in European eyes. At Monterery, Lapérouse noted Spain's new attention to the fur trade and reported his surprise that Spain had not undertaken it earlier, considering the abundant supply on her coast.

Spain did not neglect the region north of her California settlements. Since the Perez-Heceta-Quadra expeditions of 1774-1775, the northwest coast had been considered its legitimate possession on the grounds of discovery and exploration. A further exploration of the

[3] Sauer, *Billings Expedition,* ix.

coast north of 55° in 1779 by Ignacio Arteaga and Quadra completed what was considered the necessary basis for her claims to the whole coast, and the next year the king ordered the termination of all voyages to the north for further exploration. In 1787 this order was rescinded and New Spain's viceroy was informed "that the western coasts of Spanish America and islands and seas adjacent should be more frequently navigated and explored."[4]

The next year a Spanish expedition under Don Esteban Jose Martinez and Lopez de Haro was dispatched to find out what the Russians were doing in the north. Martinez was less excited by what he saw of the Russians than by what he learned of English activities in the vicinity of Nootka Sound, which he himself claimed to have discovered and named San Lorenzo four years before Cook had been there.[5]

English Traders

The English were relatively slow in getting to the northwest coast in view of the fact that their merchants congregated at Canton where Cook's men had sold their furs so profitably in the winter of 1779. Initiation of the trade was handicapped by the Crown chartered monopolies, the South Sea and East India companies. The former had sole rights to British trade on the western shores of the Pacific; the latter had similar exclusive privileges east of the Cape of Good Hope, and consequently controlled British dealings in the Canton market. Only merchants licensed through the East India Company and under bond that might range from five to twenty-five thousand pounds sterling, could trade with the Hong merchants. The alternative was to deal with the Company at its own prices. Trading without license led to seizure of ships and cargoes and British subjects who ran the risk adopted the subterfuge of sailing under other countries' flags. But even so, between 1785 and 1789

[4] "Declaration of His Catholic Majesty," June 4, 1790, in *Annual Register* for 1790, London, 1793, XXXII, 292-294. For report that Spain was active with regard to colonial commerce, see *Annual Register* for 1786, p. 35. For Spanish explorations of 1774-1787, see Bancroft, *History of the Northwest Coast*, Vol. I; Henry R. Wagner, *The Cartography of the Northwest Coast of America to the year 1800*, 2 vols., Berkeley, 1937.

[5] Diary of Esteban Jose Martinez, July 2 to July 14, 1789, in the *Journal of Captain James Colnett Aboard the Argonaut*, Champlain Society Publications XXVI, Toronto, 1940, 309.

there were at least sixteen British vessels on the northwest coast.

The pioneer trader was Captain James Hanna, who made two trips to the coast, the first in 1785 and the second the next year. Almost in his wake came James Strange, representing his own commercial interests and those of David Scott, a prominent Bombay merchant and a member of the East India Company. He also acted as an informal observer of the trading field for the British government.[6] His two vessels, the *Captain Cook* and the *Experiment* under captains Laurie and Guize arrived at Nootka in June, 1786, and remained a month while the crews recuperated from scurvy and trade was made with the friendly natives. The ship's surgeon, John Mackay, volunteered to stay as a commercial agent to encourage the Indians to collect furs and to hold them for Strange on his return voyage. Before leaving the coast, Strange "explored that part . . . not seen by Captain Cook," discovered an extensive sound to which he gave the name Queen Charlotte's Sound, and an island he named for his partner Scott's Island.

In 1785 the British India-merchant Richard Cadman Etches and associates of the King George's Sound Company, an organization of continually changing partnerships, dispatched two licensed vessels from London for a large adventure of exploration and trade on the northwest coast. Captains Nathaniel Portlock and George Dixon, who

[6] John Norris, "The Policy of the British Cabinet in the Nootka Crisis," in *EHR*, LXX, October, 1955, 566-567. Account of the British activities in the Pacific waters and of the controversy with Spain based upon such sources as F. W. Howey, ed., *The Dixon-Meares Controversy*, Canadian Historical Studies, Toronto, 1929; James Strange's *Journal and Narrative of the Commercial Expedition from Bombay to the North West Coast of America*, introduction by A. V. Venkatarama Ayyar, curator Madras Record Office, Madras, 1928; (William Beresford) George Dixon, *A Voyage Around the World*, London, 1789; F. A. Howay, "Early Navigation of the Straits of Fuca," *OHQ*, XII, March, 1911; W. Kaye Lamb, "The Mystery of Mrs. Barkley's Diary," *BCHQ*, VI, January, 1942; John Meares, *Voyages Made in the Years 1788 and 1789 . . .*, London, 1790; S. F. Bemis, *John Quincy Adams and the Foundation of American Foreign Diplomacy*, New York, 1949; George V. Blue, "Anglo-French Diplomacy, 1790," *OHQ*, XXXIX, June, 1938; William R. Manning, "The Nootka Sound Controversy" in American Historical Association *Annual Report*, 1904; Cecil Jane, trans., *A Spanish Voyage to Vancouver and the Northwest Coast of America*, London, 1930; Henry R. Wagner, *Spanish Exploration in the Strait of Juan de Fuca*, Santa Ana, California, 1933. Of special importance are memoranda, letters, notes from the Sir Joseph Banks Collection, Sutro Library, San Francisco. Among these are four letters of R. Cadman Etches to Sir Joseph written between 1788-1792 and published by F. W. Howay under the title "Four Letters from Richard Cadman Etches to Sir Joseph Banks, 1788-1792" in the *BCHQ*, VI, April, 1942. Another item of significance is a clipping from *The World* for October 6 and 13, 1788, containing an account of recent voyages to the Pacific coast.

had been with Cook in 1776, were put in command of the *King George* and *Queen Charlotte*, and elaborately equipped for trade with the natives, as well as with "implements of husbandry," officers, and settlers for several factories.

In July, 1786, their vessels approached the coast in the vicinity of Cook's River and until November their masters carefully explored any inlet that might lead to the interior. After wintering in the Sandwich Islands, they returned the following March to trade and pursue their exploration of the coastline.[7]

In the course of the season they met other traders in the northern waters. John Meares in the *Nootka* and William Tipping in the *Sea Otter* were independents. They also met Captain Charles Barkley in the *Imperial Eagle*, and Captains James Colnett and Charles Duncan in the *Prince of Wales* and the *Princess Royal*, fellow employees of the Etches company. They heard there were Spanish ships in northern waters and that the Spaniards were making settlements "Somewhere a little south of King George's Sound [Nootka]." This rumor may have deterred them from founding the settlement for which they had been provided. Upon their return to England in the summer of 1788, having disposed of their 2,500 sea otter pelts at Macao, they explained that they had used their discretionary powers to decide against settlement.[8]

Cadman Etches and his fellow merchants were disappointed with the results of the Portlock-Dixon voyage, but they were encouraged to believe that if and when they could establish permanent posts they could develop a profitable trade between Great Britain, the Northwest, and the Orient, in which English goods bartered for natives' furs would purchase Chinese produce. Toward this end they sought the assistance of the government, first to break the monopoly of the East India and South Sea companies, second to protect the projected colony by making it a state, or government enterprise, and third, to people it with convicts from English prisons, as was being done in New Holland. The government turned a deaf ear to their solicitations, and the Etches company had to carry on either legally, with licenses

[7] Undated memorandum from "Captain Dickson" in Banks Collection, Sutro Library, San Francisco.

[8] R. Cadman Etches to Sir Joseph Banks, July 17, 1788.

from the monopolies, or under the subterfuge of foreign flags and ownership. The idea of commercial colonization was only temporarily abandoned.

The Discovery of Juan de Fuca Strait

Another of their traders, Captain Charles Barkley, returned a handsome profit and a new discovery. His ship, the *Loudoun* sailed under a fictional Austrian East India Company's flag to escape the heavy hand of the British monopolies, and was renamed the *Imperial Eagle* to fit the circumstances. Accompanied by his young wife, the first white woman of record to visit the Northwest, he left Ostende in November, 1786, and was at Nootka Sound early in June, 1787. He had an excellent trade with the Indians through the help of Mackay, left behind the previous year by Captain Strange. Mackay was reported to have adjusted himself so thoroughly to the Indian way of life that he was hardly different from them, unpleasant in appearance and odor, but he chose to leave his friends and sail with the Barkleys.

Leaving Nootka, Barkley sailed south among the islands that dotted the bays and inlets, anchoring in Clayoquot Sound and in the Sound to which his name has been given. The Indians he found to be a "very Hospitable and well-governed People." It was on a July day that Barkley made the discovery which gives him a special place in the history of the Pacific Northwest. According to his wife's diary: "to our great astonishment, we arrived off a large opening extending to the eastward, the entrance to which appeared to be about four leagues wide and remained about that width as far as the eye could see, with a clear westerly horizon, which my husband immediately recognized as the long lost strait of Juan de Fuca, and to which he gave the name of the original discoverer, my husband placing it on his chart."[9]

Barkley did not venture far into the waters he had discovered. As far as he went, it appeared the strait was of uniform width, with a very strong tide and its north shore was "all Islands." Anchored near a small one on the north side, Barkley's men found the natives, like those they had met earlier, friendly and well disposed. But to the

[9] Quoted in W. Kaye Lamb, "The Mystery of Mrs. Barkley's Diary," *BCHQ*, VI, January, 1942, 41.

south of the strait, where the shore was "like the Main [land]," the people were "more of the Bandity Kind." According to Etches' informant, Barkley crossed to the south shore, anchored near an island, and "at a Town at the entrance (this side) . . . they lost four Men (which went on shore with too much confidence, and unarm'd)."[10] A party of twenty sent in search of them found their clothes and evidence that they had been murdered. The party burned the village in retaliation. A brief report of Barkley's voyage published in 1788 says that he sailed as far south as 47° 30′ which would have brought him to the vicinity of the Queets River mouth; and that the murder of his men occurred at 47° 46′ in the vicinity of the Hoh River. Quadra's Isla de Dolores (present Destruction Island) was thus a monument to two Indian massacres.

Returning north to more friendly people, Barkley continued his trade. Having acquired about 4,000 pelts, one of the richest cargoes of the time, he sailed from Nootka for Macao where he arrived in January, 1788. In 1792 he returned to the Alaskan coast, but never again, so far as is known, to the scene of his major discovery. The next ship sent out by the Etches company probably carried Barkley's maps and charts, and the man who used them was already acquainted with the coast.

Captain John Meares

Captain John Meares was a controversial figure in his own day and his voyages to the Northwest have led to controversy among historians. He was neither modest nor reliable, and in the testimony of those who knew him, as associate or rival in the trade, there was little truth in him. Yet he played an important role in the history of the Northwest.

Meares was an independent trader when he came first to the coast in the late fall of 1786, arriving so late he was forced to winter at Prince William Sound. Twenty-three of the crew of the *Nootka* suffered from scurvy, or as it was charged, from overuse of rum, when in the spring of 1787, Captains Portlock and Dixon gave him much-needed assistance. As licensed operators under the South Sea and East India companies they forced him to leave the coast under bond not to return.

---

[10] Etches to Banks, July 30, 1788.

The next year he was back on the coast with two ships, the *Felice* and *Iphigenia*, Captain William Douglas, under Portuguese flags and with nominal ownership registered to a Portuguese merchant. Actually he was sailing for the Etches company, and he was equipped on this voyage for a large-scale attack upon the coastal trade. At Nootka, a fort was built and carpenters were sent ashore to put together the framework of a small schooner brought over in the *Iphigenia.* The *North West America* was launched in September, 1788.

In the meantime Meares in the *Felice* made a trading expedition and, as he later claimed, a voyage of exploration. Little that he reported can be credited. He saw and named Mount Olympus. He sent his longboat into the Strait of Juan de Fuca as far as Port San Juan, and claimed that he was the strait's original discoverer, whereas he very probably had in his possession, or had seen at Canton or Macao Barkley's charts and heard from his lips the story of his discovery. At the approximate location where Heceta had found evidence of a large river, Meares found nothing. He denied that such a river existed, and to emphasize his exposure of Spanish inefficiency, ascribed to the promontory north of the river the name Cape Disappointment, and to the large bay into which he said he steered "with every encouraging expectation," he gave the name of Deception Bay, and concluded, "We can now with safety assert that . . . no such river as that of Saint Roc exists, as laid down in the Spanish charts."[11] Surprisingly, he accurately described the cape he named Lookout, now Cape Meares. Three Arch Rocks were probably his Three Brothers, and Quicksand Bay may have been a reasonably accurate description of the entrance to Tillamook Bay when he saw it.

In the fall of 1788 Meares returned to China with a cargo of furs and mast timbers. He had noted, as did others before him, that the region possessed other resources than furs; "the woods of this part of America," he reported, "are capable of supplying, with these valuable materials [topmasts and spars], all the navies of Europe." Meares now joined the Etches circle in a new company, the Associated Merchants trading to the North West Coast of America. Properly, although reluctantly, they secured licenses from the East India and South Sea companies, and the *Princess Royal*, Captain Thomas Hudson, and the *Argonaut*, Captain James Colnett, were on their way back to the coast

[11] John Meares, *Voyages Made in the Years 1788 and 1789*, 168.

in the spring of 1789. In the hold of the *Argonaut* were supplies and equipment for a settlement, and for the building of another schooner for the coastal trade. A number of Chinese and Hawaiian laborers were brought along, and it was anticipated that further importations of these, men and women, would people a colony.

But when the *Princess Royal* and the *Argonaut* arrived at Nootka in the summer of 1789, their captains were surprised to find Spain's Don Esteban Jose Martinez, Spanish ships, and a primitive Spanish settlement.

Trouble at Nootka Sound

It will be recalled that in 1788, Martinez had been sent north to investigate Russian activities, and had learned of the English voyages. He was ordered to return immediately to guard Spanish claimed lands against foreign settlements. His subsequent acts were in keeping with the spirit if not the letter of his instructions.

On his arrival at Nootka he found and confiscated Meares's *Iphigenia* and the schooner, *North West America*. When Colnett and later, Hudson, arrived, he seized them and their ships also, having good and sufficient proof in Colnett's papers and cargo that he planned to erect a fortified establishment at Nootka. On the fourteenth of July the *Argonaut* and the *Princess Royal*, their officers and crews were dispatched to Mexico, where the surprised viceroy eventually found reasons to release them in the hope of avoiding an international incident.

On July 9, 1790, "at Ten P.M., the day and hour of release of a Twelve Month and four days' Cruelty, Robbery, and Oppressive treatment of the Spaniards," an indignant Colnett with an exaggerated sense of the wrongs he had suffered, sailed from San Blas harbor in the *Argonaut* for Nootka Sound again.[12] En route he mapped several California bays, and at Port Sir Francis Drake, identified today as Bodega Bay, he dispatched his large longboat, in command of Robert Gibson, to trade along the coast and to meet him at Barkley's Sound. Gibson, however, made only light trades north of Port Trinidad. Between that place, 41° 45′, and 46°, he noted several

[12] *Colnett's Journal*, 169.

"Barr'd Rivers and much smoke on the Land," but no natives came off. At 46° he saw a good harbor "laid down by the Spaniards," which may have been the entrance to the Columbia, and in the vicinity of Destruction Island (47° 30′ is his given latitude, but Gibson was off on other reckonings) he purchased 59 skins before the Indians commenced hostilities.

International Crisis

On March 3, 1791, Colnett left Nootka for the Hawaiian Islands and on May 30, he arrived at Macao. The Nootka incident might have ended here, but Meares, having heard of the seizure of the vessels in the fall of 1789, had immediately gone to London where he and the Etches made loud demands for government intervention to secure indemnities for his losses. He asked over a half million dollars damages. Through wide publicity given his charges, jingoistic pressures, and its own desire to humiliate Spain, the cabinet made an issue of the affair, although restitution was already being made in Mexico.[13]

The government was not very anxious to unravel the thread of events at Nootka, nor to weigh the pros and cons of the incident. It posed two general questions upon which to hinge war or peace: Did the Spanish claim the Pacific to be a closed sea over which Spain exercised all rights and jurisdiction, or was it an open sea with reciprocal freedom for subjects of both powers to fish and trade in its unsettled parts? Could claims to sovereignty be established simply on the grounds of discovery and the act of taking possession, or were occupation and settlement fundamental requirements?

The Spanish court's first reaction to British demands was a stubborn insistence upon sticking to the case at issue. It was quickly made clear that much more was involved: Spain's colonial empire and its exclusive system of intra empire trade. His Catholic Majesty called for aid from his ally, France. The British cabinet prepared for a continental war by alerting its allies, Holland and Prussia. The Canadian colonies were advised to cultivate friendly relations with the young United States, and that government was cautiously approached

[13] Norris, "The British Cabinet in the Nootka Incident," *EHR*, LXX, October, 1955, 580.

to see if it would collaborate with Great Britain in case of war. A war budget was voted by Parliament. Finally the Spaniards, alternating between warlike gestures and apologies, and finding their French ally at first dubious of Spain's legal position and then immobilized by a revolution at home, decided in favor of peaceful settlement.

A convention signed at the Escurial late in October, 1790, terminated the dispute with all practical advantages going to the British. The latter agreed to curb British subjects' "illicit trade with the Spanish settlements" and to forbid navigating or "fishery" (e.g., hunting of the sea otter) within "ten maritime leagues from any part of the coast already occupied by Spain." Spain's large concession was her agreement that the British might fish, trade, and make settlements "in the Pacific Ocean or in the South Seas . . . in places not already occupied." By this article, the British government formalized a principle upon which it acted when it served its purpose: Occupation was a weightier argument for sovereignty than merely exploration or discovery.[14]

Discovery and Diplomacy

To carry out the terms of restoration each government appointed commissioners to a meeting at Nootka. Spain was represented by the commandant of San Blas, Bodega y Quadra, who had explored portions of the coast in 1775 and again in 1779, England by Captain George Vancouver, a former member of Cook's third expedition, and already prepared to sail on a voyage of exploration to the northwest coast.

Before the commissioners arrived, however, the Spanish were busily at work remedying some of their past errors of omission. In February, 1790, three vessels sailed from San Blas under Lieutenant Francisco Eliza, appointed Commandant for Nootka, in the *Concepcion*, with Lieutenants Salvador Fidalgo and Manuel Quimper commanding the *San Carlos* and *Princesa Real* (which was no other than the confiscated *Princess Royal* to be restored to Colnett). The vessels were equipped for explorations along the coast, and carried provisions, including livestock for settlements, and soldiers and artillery for forti-

[14] The text of the treaty is found in William R. Manning, "The Nootka Sound Controversy" in the American Historical Association *Annual Report* for 1904, 454-456.

fied posts or presidios. The result was a settlement of some pretensions at Nootka Sound. According to one report there were 50 houses in 1792—but more accurately, probably 25. The fort was described as "no great thing," but it had mounted cannon to protect an estimated 200 population of Spanish and Peruvian Indians, all males.[15] There were six missionary priests in 1789, there were probably no less in 1792. In 1792 a fortified village, Nuñez Gaona, of some ten houses with gardens was founded at Neah Bay on the south side of the Strait of Juan De Fuca.

Fidalgo made a detailed exploration of the coast. Quimper concentrated on the Strait of Juan de Fuca. He followed its northern shore as far as the present site of Victoria, named the northern channel Canal de López de Haro, explored the entrance to Rosario Strait, and returned along the south shore from present Sequim to Neah Bay. He failed, however, to note the inlet leading to the southern waters later known as Puget Sound. In 1791 Eliza charted the islands and channels from Caamano Bight into the Gulf of Georgia. The names of these navigators identify Fidalgo and Eliza islands.

In the spring of 1792 Lieutenant Jacinto Caamano in the *Aranzazu* and Galiano and Valdes in the *Sutil* and *Mexicana* joined in the task of surveying the waters, mainland, and islands between Juan de Fuca Strait and Queen Charlotte Islands. To this work Vancouver and Quadra contributed when they arrived, so that in a general way, it can be said that the thorough job of exploring done in the summer of 1792 was the joint work of the Spaniards and British.

According to Galiano's and Valdes' reports, the four months of exploration around Vancouver Island in 1792 were wasted. Curiosity had been satisfied, but the explorers had discovered no passage to the Atlantic—not even any sea otter. Actually, the fur traders on the coast had already made the discoveries. "There was hardly a single point on the coast between 37° north and 60° north which had not been visited by these ships, and so, if we have no detailed and accurate map based on the results of these voyages, it is because those who discovered a harbour or entry which had not been known before, and where they . . . were able to secure skins at a profit . . . concealed the news of their discovery, in the expectation that they would be

[15] John Boit, "Log of the Columbia," *OHQ*, XXII, December, 1921, 324.

able for a long while to carry on an exclusive trade. . . ."[16]

Nootka Sound was a busy port in the early spring and summer of 1792. In its waters were, according to Galiano and Valdes, beside five Spanish ships, 22 other vessels, 11 English, two Portuguese, one French, and eight American.

In the month of August Quadra and Vancouver met in Spanish quarters in Friendly Cove, compared maps and charts of their countrymen's explorations, argued their interpretations of the treaty terms, and glossed over irreconcilable differences with glittering social events. At one momentous affair, the courtly Quadra entertained all officers of the vessels in port. "Fifty four persons sat down to Dinner," wrote one amazed and youthful guest, "and the plates, which was *solid silver* was shifted five times, which made 270 Plates. . . ."

In spite of such amicable relations the commissioners could come to no agreement. Vancouver read his instructions to mean that the Spanish should surrender their settlement; Quadra that only the plot of ground where Meares's house had stood was to be restored—at most he offered a division of their interests. They agreed to notify their governments of the impasse in their negotiations; but to prove there were no hard feelings between them they named the island, finally defined and charted, on whose western shore Nootka Sound was located, Quadra's and Vancouver's Island. Quadra returned to California, and Vancouver to an exploration of the coasts of Washington, Oregon, and Northern California. Still without orders concerning the negotiation, Vancouver left the Pacific in 1794, and returned to England in October of the following year.

In the meantime, tedious arbitration in Madrid and London wrestled with the other terms of the convention. In February, 1793, the Nootka Claims Convention was signed. Meares and his associates were awarded indemnities of $210,000, half of what they had claimed. A year later diplomats agreed to solve Vancouver's and Quadra's dilemma of interpreting Article V of the treaty by mutually abandoning the site.

. . . the subjects of both nations shall have the liberty of frequenting the . . . port whenever they wish and of constructing there temporary buildings

[16] Cecil Jane, trans., *A Spanish Voyage to Vancouver and the Northwest Coast of America*, 89-90.

to accommodate them during their residence. . . . But neither of the said parties shall form any permanent establishment in the said port or claim any right of sovereignty or territorial dominion there to the exclusion of the other.[17]

It was not until 1795 that other commissioners arrived to go through the forms demanded by the convention and to bring to an end the long-drawn-out dispute. By then the Spaniards had abandoned Neah Bay and Nootka. English and American traders occasionally stopped at the port, but it was never again occupied.

Captain George Vancouver

Spain's last years in the region were her most successful in the sense of adding to the geographical knowledge of it. Unfortunately the reports of her distinguished explorers were not published until the nineteen thirties. On the other hand, those of Captain George Vancouver were published within a short time after his return to England and added to the prestige of the British as explorers of the Northwest. They also provided grounds for later British claims to certain areas by virtue of prior discovery and act of possession.

Vancouver's expedition was planned to supplement the work of James Cook by exploring the coast from the Spanish to the Russian settlements. How and where he conducted his explorations were determined by details of his instructions. He was to search for a river or entrance to an inland sea which might yet provide a substitute for the discredited Arctic Northwest Passage. While he was to determine the direction and extent of all considerable inlets, and mouths of rivers, he was "not to pursue any inlet or river further than it shall appear to be navigable by vessels of such burthen as might safely navigate the Pacific Ocean." He was to give special attention to Juan de Fuca Strait. He carried out his instructions to the letter. The obvious purpose of his voyage was such exploration as would facilitate Great Britain's commerce in the Pacific, and his careful descriptions of natives, their habits and habitats, and his surveys of anchorages and ports are evidence of British interests in the region.

Vancouver belonged to the best tradition of British seamanship.

[17] Manning, "The Nootka Sound Controversy," 470-471.

He was a cautious and skilled navigator, a leader who carefully guarded the lives and health of his men. His official narrative reveals his intent to be accurate in matters of description and observation whether astronomical or geographical, and the reader almost comes to share his worry over two chronometers which would not stay synchronized. His concern for sanitation and food paid off. He experimented with a diet including sauerkraut, portable soup, wheat, malt and spruce beer, dried yeast, and seed mustard. Oranges and lemons were used medicinally. His crew suffered no ill effects from their long journey through the south Atlantic and Pacific oceans. He was devoted in all ways to the "noble science of discovery," as he called it.

He arrived on the coast, south of Cape Mendocino, on April 17, 1792. His flagship was the sloop of war *Discovery,* and it was accompanied by the *Chatham,* an armed tender. In the summer, the supply ship *Daedalus* joined them. As he progressed north he identified the capes and headlands mapped by his predecessors, changed old names for new, and added features previously missed. Aguilar's Cape Blanco was renamed Cape Orford; Cook's Cape Gregory (modern Arago) was identified, and the difference in his and Cook's latitudes was noted.

Discovery of Columbia River

At noon on the 27th of April he came to an opening which he identified as Meares's Deception Bay. "The sea had now changed from its natural, to river coloured water, the probable consequence of some streams falling into the bay, or into the ocean to the north of it, through the low land," he wrote in his journal. "Not considering this opening worthy of more attention, I continued our pursuit to the N. W. being desirous to embrace the advantages of the prevailing breeze. . . ."[18] With this remark Captain Vancouver dismissed the entrance to the Columbia River. He was to return to the location in

[18] *A Voyage of Discovery to the North Pacific Ocean . . . under the Command of Captain George Vancouver,* 6 vols., London, 1801, is the source of all quotations for this presentation, unless otherwise noted. For Vancouver in Puget Sound see Robert B. Whitebrook, "Vancouver's Anchorages on Puget Sound" *PNQ,* XLIV, July, 1953, 115-128; for the Columbia River exploration, J. Neilson Barry, ed., "Columbia River Exploration, 1792" *OHQ,* XXXIII, March, 1932, for the journal, presumably written by Edward Bell; J. Neilson Barry, "Broughton on the Columbia in 1792," *OHQ,* XXVII, December, 1926, and "Who Discovered the Columbia River," *OHQ,* XXXIX, June, 1938.

a few months with a changed mind, but he honestly refrained from changing the original entry in his journal.

He continued north, keeping a sharp lookout for Barkley's Juan de Fuca Strait. On Sunday the 29th a sail was seen, a "great novelty," as Vancouver put it, since no other ship than the *Chatham* had been sighted for eight months. This proved to be the *Columbia*, an American vessel commanded by Captain Robert Gray. Vancouver sent off several of his officers to talk with Gray, and among other things, learned that nine days before, the American had been "off the mouth of a river in the latitude of 46° 10′, where the outlet, or reflux, was so strong as to prevent his entering. . . ." "This," wrote Vancouver, "was, probably, the opening passed by us on the forenoon of the 27th."

Vancouver on Puget Sound

It is clear that Vancouver's principal interest was the Strait. On the 29th he anchored within its entrance, and the next day at New Dungeness. From a height of land Vancouver looked with immense satisfaction upon a landscape, "almost as enchantingly beautiful as the most elegantly finished pleasure grounds in Europe."

The official narrative reveals the writer's excitement as wonder on wonder was unfolded. "I could not possibly believe," he wrote, "that any uncultivated country had ever been discovered exhibiting so rich a picture."

The delightful serenity of the weather greatly aided the beautiful scenery that was now presented; the surface of the seas was perfectly smooth, and the country before us exhibited every thing that bounteous nature could be expected to draw into one point of view. . . . The land which interrupted the horizon between the N.W. and the northern quarters, seemed . . . to be much broken; from whence its eastern extent round to the S.E. was bounded by a ridge of snowy mountains, appearing to lie nearly in a north and south direction, on which mount Baker rose conspicuously; remarkable for its height, and the snowy mountains that stretch from its base to the north and south. Between us and this snowy range, the land, which on the sea shore terminated . . . in low perpendicular cliffs, or on beaches of sand or stone, rose here in a very gentle ascent, and was covered with a variety of stately forest trees. These, however, did not conceal the whole face of the country in one uninterrupted wilderness, but pleasingly clothed its eminences, and chequered the vallies; presenting, in many directions, extensive spaces that wore the appearance of having been cleared by art. . . . As we passed along the shore near one of these charming spots, the tracks of deer, or of some such animal, were very numerous, and flattered us with the hope of not wanting refreshments of that nature, whilst we remained in this quarter.

The weather was mild, the sky clear, and the snow peaks stood out sharply in the sunshine. They saw Meares's Olympus, which Vancouver described as "a very elegant double fork" and Mounts Baker and Rainier to which Vancouver gave their names. The contrast between snow-covered mountains and the blue sky was emphasized by the green forests crowding from the foothills to the green-blue water's edge. Occasional bare cliffs broke into sandy beaches, or scarred slopes, ravaged by some old forest fire, picked up the theme of mountain snows in the white blossoms of the dogwood.

Following the shoreline in their longboats, they found continuous surprises in store for them: innumerable bays, harbors, inlets, and islands, large and small. An apparent headland was an island, and an island turned out to be a peninsula narrowly joined to the mainland. A long inlet of even width so much resembled a monumental man-made canal it was named Hood's Canal.

Two months were spent exploring the inland waters. In all 18 anchorages were made and have been identified and located on modern maps. At the southern tip of Bainbridge Island longboats and cutter were dispatched to survey the extensive inlet to which Vancouver gave the name Puget's Sound in honor of its chief explorer, Lt. Peter Puget. To the principal bays, inlets, and waterways, he gave the names which in many instances still distinguish them, among these Admiralty Inlet, Cape Dungeness, Port Orchard, Port Discovery, Possession Sound, Restoration Point, Whidbey and Vashon Islands, Deception Pass and Bellingham Bay, and the Georgian Gulf. His exploration of the eastern shore of Puget Sound and Georgia Gulf, and a long trip in a yawl to Jervis Inlet beyond present Vancouver, B.C., showed there was no inlet leading deep into the heart of the continent. But it was a land well worth claiming for Great Britain. "The serenity of the climate, the innumerable pleasing landscapes, and the abundant fertility that unassisted nature puts forth, require only to be enriched by the industry of man with villages, mansions, cottages, and other buildings, to render it the most lovely country that can be imagined; whilst the labour of the inhabitants would be amply rewarded, in the bounties which nature seems ready to bestow on cultivation."

On the fourth day of June, 1792, at the site of the present city of Everett, Vancouver took possession of the whole region, and called it New Georgia, in honor of George III, whose birthday it was. Vancouver then proceeded through the inland passage east of Vancouver Island, around the island's northern tip and down to Nootka and his meeting with Quadra. While negotiations were under way, his lieutenants, Johnstone and Broughton, carried on explorations of the island and along the mainland shore. Leaving Nootka at the end of August, Vancouver took both vessels north as far as Bentinck's Arm and then turned out into the Pacific and south to where muddy waters of a river had colored the sea the previous spring, and where Vancouver had denied the existence of anything but a confluence of small streams. As his vessels hove to on October 19, he was better informed. He had learned from Quadra that the American trader, Robert Gray, had entered the river the previous May and had named it the Columbia.

Broughton on the Columbia

Quadra had given Vancouver Gray's sketch of the river's entrance, but even with this he approached the river convinced it was unnavigable for a vessel of any size. When the previous April his officers had spoken with Gray and learned that he had tried to enter but had been unable to do so because of the strong current, Vancouver had decided, "If any river or inlet should be found, it must be a very intricate one, and inaccessible to vessels of our burthen. . . ." The geography of the coastline alone was a reasonable argument against "any safe navigable opening, harbour, or place of security for shipping on this coast."

Vancouver could hardly risk the 340-ton *Discovery* on the initial entry, so the 135-ton *Chatham*, under Lieutenant Broughton, was sent in, while Vancouver continued on to California.

The *Chatham* had had a rough entry and Broughton's overcaution was almost disastrous. Fearful of crossing the bar he anchored for the night in four fathoms of water and almost on the bar. "I never felt more alarmed & frightened in my life," a clerk confided to his journal. "The Channel was narrow, the water very Shoal, and the Tide running against the Wind . . . raised a Surf that broke entirely around us, and I am confident that in going in, we were not twice the Ship's length from Breakers, that had we struck on, we must inevitably have gone to pieces." The next day the *Chatham* cleared with only a shallow strike and entered the safe anchorage of a bay on the north bank. Here Broughton was surprised to find a fellow countryman, Captain James Baker, in the small schooner *Jenny* of Bristol. He was after trade with the Indians and reported he had been in the river earlier in the year.

It was Broughton's task to explore the river and to take possession of its tributary lands if it appeared a claim to discovery and exploration could be supported. Broughton spent three weeks on this mission. Having carefully examined the shores and principal streams of the wide tidal waters near the mouth, he proceeded upstream in the longboat. He placed on his maps Baker's Bay, Young's River, Tongue Point, Coffin Mountain, Oak Point, Puget's Island, and Mounts St. Helens (named by Vancouver) and Hood. Opposite a sandy point to which he gave his commander's name, and probably near the present town of Corbett, Oregon, he performed the ceremony of taking possession in the moonlight of the night of October 30, 1792. Later, on behalf of British claims and against the United States's claim of prior discovery, the fine point was argued that Gray had discovered the saline bay of the Columbia, but Broughton the river, and upon it he had placed the symbol of sovereignty.

Vancouver's exploration of the Northwest Coast was the last significant effort of a European power to establish its sovereignty on the Pacific Coast. At the close of the eighteenth century, as far as national interests were concerned, the British had eliminated contenders to title over the region between Russian Alaska and Spanish California. Their extensive surveys had mapped the coastline and had answered the century-old question of a Northwest Passage. To Cook's conclusions Vancouver added, "the complete certainty, that, within the limits of his researches . . . no internal sea, or other navigable communication whatever exists. . . ."

At strategic locations the formal rite of taking possession had been performed—a hollow ritual if what the British maintained in the Nootka incident prevailed—that titles to unoccupied lands were hard to defend. But there was as yet no challenger.

European interest in the Northwest had been stimulated by the discovery of new markets "for the productive labors of the civilized world" in the fur trade with the Indians.[19] For ten years the British traders harvested the larger share of the shore's produce. But within three years after Vancouver's arrival on its shores the trade of the Northwest Coast had fallen into other hands.

[19] *Vancouver's Voyages*, 3 vols., London, 1798, Dedication, Vol. I; Introduction, p. *a*.

4

Maritime Fur Trade: The Americans in the Northwest

Between 1785 and 1794 about 35 British vessels traded on the northwest coast; in the next decade there were nine, and between 1805 and 1814, three. This decline can be explained in part by three factors: (1) the East India Company's control of British trade in the Orient; (2) the prolonged European wars growing out of the French Revolution which affected both British manpower and investment; and (3) the entry into the trade of American interests.

The first two factors also contributed to the phenomenal growth of American activity on the coast. Two vessels pioneered the New England-Northwest Coast-Oriental trade in 1788; at least 15 ships followed in the next seven years, and close to 70 between 1794 and 1805.[1] Americans were "free traders" in the sense that there were no privileged corporations with monopoly powers in the United States. A proposal to create one comparable to the East India Company was rejected in 1786 when the Continental Congress expressed the prevailing opinion that "commercial intercourse between the United States and the Indians would be more prosperous if left unfettered in the hands of private adventurers, than if regulated by any system of national complexion."[2]

The Napoleonic Wars, which led to a decline in British shipping, gave the Americans a profitable and almost world-wide opportunity for trade, in spite of efforts of the warring powers to curtail this

[1] F. W. Howay, "A List of Trading Vessels in the Maritime Fur Trade, 1785-1814," in *Proceedings and Transactions of the Royal Society of Canada*, 3d Series, Sec. 2, 1930, 1931, 1932. Vol. XXIV, 111-134; XXVI, 43-86; XXV, 117-149.

[2] Rufus King to John Adams, February 3, 1786, in King's *Life and Correspondence*, ed. Charles R. King, 6 vols., New York, 1894, I, 155.

neutral enterprise. During the era, American trade with the Orient ranked second to that of Great Britain, and continued in that place until the middle of the nineteenth century. The maritime trade of the northwest coast becomes meaningful when it is understood in relation to the larger pattern of early American commerce, and for this reason we must examine with some care the nature of that commerce in the late years of the eighteenth century.

At the conclusion of the American Revolution, the independent Americans found their brief period of postwar prosperity blighted by England's refusal to admit American traders to their former position in the West Indies trade. By August, 1784, business houses were failing in Philadelphia, "trade stagnated" and merchants complained of the "languor of our direct trade with Europe." The result was an almost desperate search for new commercial openings. But six years later President Washington wrote to Lafayette of a flourishing trade to the East Indies and of vessels profitably trading to the northwest coast and Canton. This was the commerce which was to help set the young republic on its feet, and to it, the Pacific Northwest made an important contribution.[3]

John Ledyard's "Great Adventure"

The initial project to bring American ships into western waters never got out of the planning stage, yet it gave a direction to the search for commerce. Its originator was a precocious young New Englander whose restless and imaginative nature was attracted to adventure, and whose quest for it and wealthy family connections had taken him to London. John Ledyard was 25 years old and "hungering for fame" when in 1776, he sailed as a corporal of marines on Cook's momentous third voyage. In 1782 he deserted from the British navy, returned to his home, and the following year published his *Journal of Captain Cook's Last Voyage to the Pacific Ocean.* In this Ledyard revealed the western shores of the still unexplored continent as a field for adventurous and profitable enterprise. He wrote enthusiastically of the richness and variety

[3] Samuel House to Thomas Jefferson, August 10, 1784, in *Jefferson Papers*, Boyd ed. VII, 393; James Madison to Jefferson, August 20, 1784, *ibid.*, 402; George Washington to Lafayette, June 3, 1790, in Washington *Writings*, 39 vols., Washington, D.C., 1931-1944, XXXI, 45.

of animal pelts Cook's men had bought, and of the beautiful sea otter skins which "did not cost the purchaser six pence sterling," but sold in China "for one hundred dollars."

He tried to interest prominent merchants in a trading voyage to the coast under his command and received some encouragement and a retaining fee from Robert Morris, one of the most influential of them all. Ledyard submitted a plan for the voyage and estimates on outfits, and wrote about the "dawn of bright prospects" and a great adventure in which he was about to engage. But Morris' support was withdrawn in favor of another scheme, and the disappointed Ledyard went to Europe where, in the capitals of Spain, France, and England, he sought financial backing for his scheme.

In Paris he told his story to Thomas Jefferson and John Paul Jones, the popular American naval hero of the Revolutionary War and, to the French, the authority on all things maritime. While Jefferson was struck with the exploratory aspect of the project, having already had a notion of an expedition into the West for reasons of state, Jones, it appeared, was interested solely in its commercial possibilities. Ledyard and Jones worked out a plan in which they hoped French merchants would invest. Their plan was practical and became the common pattern for large-scale enterprise in the Pacific Northwest. It called for

> two vessels . . . to proceed in company to the Northwest Coast, and commence a factory there under the American flag. The first six months were to be spent in collecting furs, and looking out for a suitable spot to establish a post, either on the main land, or on an island. A small stockade was then to be built, in which Ledyard was to be left with a surgeon, an assistant, and twenty soldiers; one of the vessels was to be despatched, with its cargo of furs, under the command of Paul Jones, to China, while the other was to remain in order to facilitate the collecting of another cargo during his absence. Jones was to return with both the vessels to China, sell their cargoes of furs, load them with silks and teas, and continue his voyage around the Cape of Good Hope to Europe, or the United States. He was then to replenish his vessels with suitable articles for traffic with the Indians, and proceed as expeditiously as possible . . . to the point of his departure in the Northern Pacific.[4]

[4] Jared Sparks, *Life of John Ledyard*, Cambridge, 1828, 155. Other references for the Ledyard story: Clarence L. Ver Steeg, "Financing and Outfitting the First United States Ship to China," *PHR*, XXII, February, 1953; J. S. C. Abbott, *John Paul Jones*,

They had advanced so far as to consider the outfitting of vessels when they had two pieces of discouraging news. The *King George* and the *Queen Charlotte* under Captains Portlock and Dixon had sailed from England for the northwest coast. "[They] have actually sailed on an expedition which was thought of by Mr. Ledyard. . . ," complained Jones, "which I should suppose must interfere with, and very much lessen the profits of any similar undertaking by others." The other discouragement came from Spanish sources. Jones was informed that the government of Spain would look with resentment upon any enterprise which would encroach upon its rights on the northwest coast. He thereupon withdrew from the project.

Ledyard was still an enthusiast about the northwest venture, but he shifted the spotlight from the business enterprise to himself—to Ledyard, genius, hero, and explorer. He achieved special fame as the would-be solitary explorer of North America's unknown interior. He proposed to go to the northwest coast and cross the continent to the Atlantic seaboard.

Three possible routes were opened to him. He might get passage directly to the coast and strike out toward the Missouri River which was believed to have its source in the coastal mountains; he might return to the United States, and from Kentucky's Mississippi shore "penetrate Westwardly to the South sea." Or, following Jefferson's suggestion, he could traverse Russia and Siberia, and from Kamchatka cross to the Russian colonies where some trader might be found to take him to Nootka. His journey into Western America would then begin. He applied through friends for the patronage of Catherine of Russia, but the Empress was not interested. She thought his project "chimaerical." Eventually he found a patron in Sir Joseph Banks, president of London's Royal Society, who headed a subscription to send him on his way. In the fall of 1786 Ledyard wrote Jefferson, "I am now going across Siberia as I had once before intended from

---

New York, 1904; A. F. DeKoven, *Life and Letters of John Paul Jones,* 2 vols; New York, 1913; *Jefferson Papers,* Boyd ed., Vols. IX, X, and XII; Jefferson's "Autobiography" in *Writings of Thomas Jefferson,* 20 vols. in 10, Monticello ed., Washington, D. C., 1905, Vol. I; Helen Augur, *Passage to Glory,* New York, 1946; *Dictionary of American Biography;* Martin Sauer, *Billings Expedition,* also French ed., J. Castera, trans., 2 vols. Paris, 1802; "Account of the Late Mr. Ledyard; from Proceedings of the Society for Promoting the Discovery of the Interior Parts of Africa," in *Annual Register* for 1790, pp. 16-18; several items from the Banks Collection.

Paris this time twelve month. . . ."

With Sir Joseph's letters of introduction to influential people, Ledyard started his Great Adventure. His subsequent story is only remotely related to the history of the Pacific Northwest, but it serves to illustrate the complex interactions in which that history originated. He made his way to Hamburg, then to Sweden with the idea of crossing the Gulf of Bothnia on the ice. Reaching the middle of the gulf he found open water before him. He returned to Stockholm and made a new start. This time he went northward into the Arctic Circle and around the head of the gulf, descending its eastern shore to St. Petersburg.

In St. Petersburg at the end of March (1787) Ledyard was put in touch with a detachment carrying supplies to Captain Billings in Siberia. Billings, it will be recalled, was carrying out the Empress Catherine's command to explore Northeastern Asia and the Pacific coast. In 1778-1779, Ledyard and Joseph Billings had been shipmates on Cook's flagship, the *Resolution:* Ledyard, a corporal of marines, Billings an even humbler seaman. Now on November 13, 1787, Captain Billings, soon to be a commodore of the Russian navy, was much astonished to meet "Colonel" Ledyard, 6,000 miles east of St. Petersburg, at Yakutsk in Siberia, and to be informed that Ledyard wished to cross over to the American continent with his expedition, "for the purpose of exploring it on foot. . . ."

With Billings, Ledyard traveled to Irkutsk where they were to wait for the ice to break up before continuing their journey. On the evening of February 24, 1788, two hussars appeared at his dwelling with orders to take him into custody and return him to Moscow for an inquiry. It was believed his presence in the country was prejudicial to the best interests of the Russian fur trade.

In the early summer of 1788 Ledyard was back in London at the door of his benefactor Sir Joseph. He was now referred to the Society for Promoting the Discovery of the Interior Parts of Africa, an organization of which Banks was a founder. The gentlemen who interviewed Ledyard later testified that he was impressed with his visitor's "manliness . . . the breadth of his chest, the openness of his countenance and the inquietude of his eye," and offered him a commission to explore Africa. When asked when he could start out, Ledyard replied, "tomorrow morning." On August 19 Ledyard was in Cairo. He wrote Jefferson that if he survived Africa he would yet go "to America and penetrate from Kentuske [Kentucky] to the Western side of the continent." The following January (1789) "mad, dreaming, romantic" John Ledyard was dead.

In September, 1787, when John Ledyard was at Yakutsk on his way to Kamchatka, in hope of reaching the western continent the next year, Ferdinand de Lesseps, having been on that continent's northwest shores, was making his way from Kamchatka toward Yakutsk, carrying the dispatches, journals, and maps that described Lapérouse's voyage to date. By this mission de Lesseps became the sole survivor of the expedition.

Not John Ledyard but others were to make the continental crossing of North America. Others were to reap fortunes from the northwest coast's sea otter. In the year of Ledyard's death, his former shipmates Dixon and Portlock published their stories of their two-year voyage to the northwest coast. His patron, Sir Joseph Banks, received news of more successful explorers: of Charles Barkley, who in the summer of 1787 discovered the Strait of Juan de Fuca; of Ledyard's cool friend Billings, who reached the Asian coast of the Pacific the year of Ledyard's death, and from 1789 to 1791 explored the northern waters; of Alexander Mackenzie, in 1789 traversing the northern river which bears his name, and four years later the first across the continent.

Opening the China Market

As Ledyard lay dying in Cairo, the first American vessels to the northwest coast of America were wintering near Nootka, and the next summer their captains were to witness Spanish resentment to invaders of her lands. Ledyard had a part in sending these American ships to the northwest coast. He had pointed out to American merchants the resources it had to offer. But he was premature. His countrymen had not yet explored the other angle of the trade—the China market.

In 1783, Robert Morris had been interested in Ledyard's descriptions of the fur trade possibilities and momentarily considered sending out two vessels, but he was dissuaded by his partners, who preferred adventuring in more customary channels. They put their capital in a vessel sent directly to China to find out how an American ship with American products might be received there. When the *Empress of China* sailed from New York, February, 1784, she carried a cargo of ginseng, wine and brandy, tar and turpentine, and 20,000 dollars in specie, representing a total investment of 120,000 dollars. The liquors, tar and turpentine, and specie were traded en route for items in demand in China, such as lead, raw cotton, cotton cloth, and pepper. At Canton the Americans were well received, and the supercargo, Samuel Shaw, invested the proceeds from his sales in Chinese goods for the American market: tea, nankeens, chinaware, woven silk, and cassia, an inferior grade of cinnamon. In December the *Empress of China* left Canton and on May 10, 1785, arrived in New York with a salute of thirteen guns.[5]

The voyage brought a profit of 30 percent on the investment, only about one-tenth of what was reported on some later ventures, but sufficient to start a rage for East India voyages and speculations in East India goods. It was a long time before a direct trade between the United States and China developed. In the early years, Americans found their profits in buying Chinese goods, especially nankeens, and in selling them in the ports of Europe, in the West Indies, and in the markets of luxury-hungry Americans. But the problem was to find commodities with which to make the original purchase. Their only product in demand in Canton was ginseng, but the American preparation was so faulty it brought a low price.[6] Wines and brandies could be traded in India for raw cotton which was always in good trade at Canton; but the larger part of the China investment had to

[5] On the China Trade: C. Ver Steeg, "First United States Ship to China" *PHR*, XXII, February, 1953; Robert Morris to John Jay, November 27, 1783, in *John Jay, Correspondence and Public Papers*, 4 vols., New York, 1890, III; R. H. Lee to James Madison, May 30, 1785, in George Bancroft, *History of the Formation of the Constitution*, 2 vols., New York, 1882, I, Appendix; John Adams to John Jay, November 11, 1785, in Adams' *Works*, 10 vols., Boston, 1850-1856, VIII; "Letters of Phineas Bond to the Foreign Office of Great Britain 1787, 1788, 1789" in American Historical Association *Annual Report*, 1896; Foster Rhea Dulles, *The Old China Trade*, Cambridge, 1930; Samuel E. Morison, *The Maritime History of Massachusetts, 1783-1860*, Boston, 1941; H. B. Morse, *Chronicles of the East India Company Trading to China, 1635-1834*, 5 vols., Oxford, 1926-1929.

[6] For a description of American ginseng and its preparation for the China market see François André Michaux, "Travels to the West of the Alleghany Mountains in 1802," in *Early Western Travels*, ed., R. G. Thwaites. Vol. III, Cleveland, 1904, 231-233.

be bought with hard cash and of this the Americans had little to spare and it was hard to come by. In 1788, for example, four American ships carried to Canton ginseng and India cotton and 62 chests of treasure probably amounting to 248,000 dollars.

Captains John Kendrick and Robert Gray

Lack of specie and other high-value merchantable stock prompted five Massachusetts merchants and one from New York to adopt Ledyard's idea of using the northwest coast's furs to buy Chinese goods. They subscribed about 50,000 dollars for outfitting two vessels. Command of the 220-ton *Columbia Rediviva* was turned over to Captain John Kendrick, who had spent most of his 47 years at sea.[7] He was an impressive man in size and courage, and his ideas were bold and unconventional. He looked upon the Northwest as a theater for great deeds. "Empires & fortunes broke on his sight," wrote his clerk John Howell, "the paltry two-penny objects of his expedition were swallowed up in the magnitude of his Gulliverian Views. North East America was on the Lilliputian, but he designed N. W. America to be on the Brobdignagian scale." He unfortunately lacked the stubborn persistence and stability to execute his plans; it would appear he was intemperate in habit and disposition, a poor trader, and a man not to be trusted with other people's property.

The consort to the *Columbia* was a 90-ton sloop, the *Lady Washington.* Her captain, 32-year-old Robert Gray, like Kendrick, had served in the navy of the Revolution. He had neither the colorful personality nor the special weaknesses of his superior. He was ruthless

[7] Sources for the account of Kendrick and Gray: F. W. Howay, ed., *Voyages of the Columbia to the North West Coast, 1789-1790 and 1790-1793,* Massachusetts Historical Society, 1941; F. W. Howay, "John Kendrick" in *Dictionary of American Biography;* Robert Greenhow, *The History of Oregon and California,* London, 1844; Diary of Esteban Martinez in *Colnett's Journal; Niles National Register,* Vol. 53, p. 196; "William Sturgis: The Northwest Fur Trade," ed. F. W. Howay in *BCHQ,* VIII, January, 1944; E. W. Wright, Lewis, and Dryden's *Marine History of the Pacific Northwest,* Portland, 1895, for Kendrick's deed to Indian lands; H. H. Bancroft, *History of the Northwest Coast,* Vol. I; Nellie B. Pipes, "Later Affairs of Kendrick: Barrell Letters," *OHQ,* XXX, June, 1929; John Quincy Adams to Abigail Adams, August 14, 1790, in Adams's *Writings,* Vol. 1; John Boit, "Log of the Columbia" *OHQ,* XXII, December, 1921; Henry Wagner, ed., *Spanish Explorations in the Strait of Juan de Fuca;* C. F. Newcombe, ed., *Menzies' Journals of Vancouver's Voyages,* Archives of British Columbia, Memoir No. V, Victoria, 1923; "Official Log of the Columbia" *OHQ,* XXII, December, 1921.

in his practices and strictly attentive to the "two-penny objects" of his business, which was to get sea otter skins and invest them in China goods.

The two vessels left Boston on September 30, 1787. They were heavily armed, carried special papers issued by the Continental Congress, and a cargo of goods ill fitted for the Northwest trade. In the first week of August, 1788, Gray approached Oregon's southern coast. On the 14th he sailed the *Lady Washington* across the shallow bar of a bay most probably the one we know as Tillamook, and anchored in the quiet inside waters. The Indians brought presents of berries and boiled crabs and gave every sign that these were the first white men they had seen. Some otter skins were traded while the crew took on wood and water. Two days later, the apparently friendly situation changed in an instant. An Indian stole a tool and was pursued by Marcus, Gray's personal servant. The Indians seized Marcus and as his friends rushed to his rescue, killed him. The rest, several of them wounded, made their way to their ship and with the changing tide sailed out of Murderers' Harbour. This was but the first of Gray's troubles with Indians. On September 15 the *Lady Washington* was in Nootka Sound where the *Columbia* joined her. Since it was too late in the season for any extended trade, the Americans spent the winter in Clayoquot Sound.

The next summer they were at Nootka when Martinez seized Colnett and Hudson and the English ships. Their role in the incident is ambiguous, but if they were partisan it was for the Spaniards. The day after the seizure and imprisonment of the *Argonaut's* officers and crew, the *Columbia* fired several salvos of thirteen guns to celebrate the Fourth of July and 13 years of American independence. At noon, Kendrick entertained the Spanish missionary priests, Martinez and his officers, and the English prisoners at a splendid banquet. "For his pretended intercession for my Vessel's release," Colnett reported, he gave Kendrick a gold watch, a gesture the giver regretted when he found his intercessor also receiving favors from Martinez. The latter's attitude toward the American is hard to explain. Kendrick had assured him he and Gray were at Nootka only to make repairs to their vessels, an age-old excuse of mariners who entered Spanish closed ports for illegal trade. Martinez was not taken in by this subterfuge.

He reported to his superiors that their principal object was the collection of furs, and he admitted. "I might have taken them prisoners, but I had no orders to do so, and my situation did not permit it. I treated this enemy as friend. . . ." But Martinez had had no orders to seize the British, and he was not a friend to other Americans who had appeared at Nootka. Thomas Metcalfe in the *Fair American* was seized and briefly held. His father, Simon, in the *Eleanora*, was pursued, but escaped. On the other hand Martinez provisioned Gray and Kendrick from Colnett's stock and gave them permission to trade on the coast, on condition they would make no settlement. Kendrick reciprocated by agreeing to carry the English crew of the sloop *North West America* to China, to sell on Martinez' account some otter skins, and to make some personal purchases for him. The relations between Kendrick and the Spaniards were further cemented when his son, John, Junior, accepted the Catholic faith and entered the Spanish naval service under Martinez.

It would appear that a rupture between Kendrick and Gray took place at the same time. After the Spaniards had departed with their prizes, Gray assumed command of the *Columbia* and Kendrick of the *Lady Washington*. Thereafter he used it for his own personal concerns. His "Brobdignagian scale of ambition" did not contemplate its return to its owners. Gray left for China on July 30, 1789. Kendrick followed several months later, and there he used the proceeds from his sales to rerig his ship. The two captains met once more in the Pacific two years later, but as rival traders. At Macao, Gray sold his furs for something more than 21,000 dollars; at Canton, he took on a cargo of tea. In February, he sailed for Boston where he arrived on August 10, 1790, having made a complete encirclement of the globe in the course of his three-year voyage.

Boston received the *Columbia* with a salute of 13 guns. A vast crowd of people swarmed to the wharf to welcome her, and to thrill at the sight of a native from the Hawaiian Islands whom Gray had brought as servant to replace Marcus. But while patriots and the curious were pleased with the *Columbia's* voyage, owners were disappointed to find their investment hardly refunded. According to the report that was circulated, the financial failure was charged to Captain Kendrick whose reputation was now "suspended between the qualifications of egregious knavery and incredible stupidity."

Captain Gray, on the other hand, was taken into the partnership. Outfitted this time with a suitable cargo of blue cloth, copper, and iron, and a knockdown keel and frame for a small sloop for coastal waters, the *Columbia* sailed from Boston on September 28, 1790, and a quick voyage brought her to the northwest coast in June of the following year.

Gray Enters the Columbia River

Gray spent the winter of 1791-1792 at Adventure Cove in Clayoquot Sound, an ideal spot both for protecting the *Columbia* and for assembling the sloop. A clearing was made on the shore and a fortified log shelter protected the men who worked on it. There was a blacksmith shop and a boatbuilder's shed, and two saw pits constantly in use to cut planks from logs towed to the spot. Adventure Cove, indeed, had the appearance of a young shipyard, as one of the *Columbia's* crew reported.

On March 22, 1792, the *Adventure* was hauled down the ways and supplied for a four months' cruise among the Queen Charlotte Islands under Captain Haswell, formerly Gray's second mate. The *Columbia* was rigged, stowed, and made ready for sea again. But before the *Columbia* and the little *Adventure* left on April 2, Captain Gray made his contribution to the steadily deteriorating relations between white men and natives. While the Indians in the Queen Charlotte Islands had already begun to take their toll of white men—Gray lost three men to them—those about Nootka and Clayoquot remained friendly, until Gray's long stay wore out their hospitality. During the winter there were signs of hostility and toward the end of February a critical threat of attack. For these displays of enmity Gray chastised them severely. Young John Boit, fifth mate of the *Columbia*, was ordered to carry out the punishment a few days before they abandoned their winter quarters. His log carries his comment: "It was a command I was no ways tenacious of, and am grieved to think Capt. Gray shou'd let his passions go so far. *This* village was about half a mile in diameter, and contained upwards of 200 Houses, generally well built for *Indians;* every door that you enter'd was in resemblance to an human and Beasts head, the passage being through the mouth, besides which there was much more rude carved work about the dwellings some of which was by no means *inelegant*. This fine village, the work of Ages, was in a short time totally destroy'd."

On April 3, Gray stood the *Columbia* to the south, and when he came to the California coast hauled to the north again. He examined the shoreline for river mouths and bays into which he might enter for trade, but squally weather and strong southerly currents kept the *Columbia* beating about for safe anchorages that were few and far between. In the vicinity of 46° 10′ Gray noticed evidence of a large river, but the outflowing current was too strong to enter.

On April 27, a calm day, he was able to anchor the *Columbia* abreast a village Boit called Kenekomitt which may have been in the vicinity of present Teakwhit Head. Here a fine lot of skins was traded for copper and more were to be had, but a storm coming up, the *Columbia* was weighed offshore for the night. From this position next morning, two sails were sighted and when they neared were found to be Captain Vancouver's *Discovery* and *Chatham*. Vancouver sent Lieutenant Peter Puget and Dr. Archibald Menzies to get information from Gray, particularly about Juan de Fuca Strait which, it will be recalled, was one of the prime objects of his exploration. Vancouver was skeptical of Gray's report of the mouth of a large river to the south. So after amenities were exchanged, Vancouver sailed on to his exploration of the Strait and Puget Sound, and to his negotiations with Quadra at Nootka. Having satisfied himself that the British were not traders, Gray turned south once more, on the chance the good weather would permit him to examine the coast more carefully. On May 7, he saw an inlet "which had a very good appearance of a harbor." With a boat ahead signaling the depth, the *Columbia* stood for the bar. A quick run between the breakers, and she was in a spacious harbor, to which the *Columbia's* officers gave the name of their captain.

A large number of Indians put out in their canoes, and Boit noted that their language was different from that of other peoples they had met, and that "without doubt we are the first Civilized people that ever visited this port, and these poor fellows view'd us and the Ship with the greatest astonishment." They had a good trade on the eighth, but in the evening the natives began hostile movements. In the moonlight the white men saw their war canoes approaching, and after several warning shots, fired a broadside on the nearest one, containing about twenty men, and "dash'd her all to peices [sic], and no doubt kill'd every soul in her." This introduction to the power of artillery seemed to have no damaging effect upon the trade the next day, for numbers of Indians came from the Chehalis River to trade salmon, beaver skins, and otter for the white men's blankets, iron, and copper.

Toward sunset on the tenth of May (1792) the *Columbia* was clear of the bar of Grays Harbor and her course set to the southward, and the location where, several weeks before, Gray had seen evidences of a large river's mouth.

The next morning, according to his official log: "At four, A.M., saw the entrance of our desired port bearing east-south-east, distance six leagues; in steering sails, and hauled our wind in shore. At eight A.M., being a little to windward of the entrance of the Harbor, bore away, and run in east-north-east between the breakers, having from five to seven fathoms of water."

Thus Captain Robert Gray described the *Columbia's* entrance into the waters of the river which, up to that moment, had been like the inland sea Vancouver was exploring, a matter of legend and speculation.

It was a fresh clear morning with the wind from the north, and if Gray had not been so intent upon the progress of the pinnace that preceded his ship over the bar he might have noted the river lay before him like a widening stream of silver in the morning sun; that the hills were flushed with clear tints of the sunrise; that wisps of fog were caught in the trees that crowded close to the water's edge. If Gray had been an eager discoverer he would have felt the thrill of his life as he ran into the broad estuary of the river men had speculated about so long.

But Gray, so far as we know, had no eye for a spring morning's beauty. There is nothing to suggest he was moved by the explorer's urge to make known the unknown. He was a fur trader and whatever exploration he made, it was with the purpose of finding harbors and inlets, where natives, eager to exchange furs for beads and bright bits of cloth, would increase the profits of his voyage. His hope of a brisk trade in this spot was fulfilled. The natives "appear'd to view the

Ship with the greatest astonishment," reported John Boit. They were eager to sell two salmon for a nail, four otter skins for a sheet of copper, a beaver skin for two spikes, and less valuable furs for one. During his stay in the river he traded 150 sea otter, 300 beaver skins, and numerous other less valuable ones.

With the exception of a short run up the river to Gray's Bay on the Washington shore, the *Columbia's* captain made no attempt at exploration. There is no evidence he had a patriotic or national interest in the river he had discovered. There were too few of the otter, and Indians coming down the river to see the white men and trade with them added nothing to his stock. John Boit's log contains these words: "I landed abrest the Ship with Capt. Gray to view the Country and take possession," but modern scholarship has shown the last three words were inserted later and in a different ink from that used in the rest of the sentence. The official log of the *Columbia* says nothing about taking possession.

On May 20 the *Columbia* again stood out to sea, and turned north to Nootka, where Gray gave Quadra a sketch of the river's entrance. This, as we have seen, Quadra then gave to Vancouver when he made his visit to the river in the following October. From Nootka, Gray sailed to Canton where he disposed of his furs, and thence around the world to Boston, where he dropped anchor July 29, 1793.

Gray's voyage served a dual purpose: it added further clarification to the maps of the northwest coastline and entered on them Grays Harbor and the Columbia River; and it established the American phase of the Northwest-Canton trade, a trade built around the fur of the sea otter.

The Sea Otter

This was an especially beautiful fur and highly prized by those who could afford it. A thick, fine underfur of silver white, tipped to brownish black and sprinkled with silver hairs, gave a shimmering rippling effect when moved by so little as a breath of air. The common size of an adult pelt was between five and six feet in length and twenty-five to thirty inches in width. A number of these carefully pieced together made royal robes for wealthy mandarins; tail pieces and oddments were used for caps or for borders on elaborate gowns. The natives of the Northwest, too, valued the otter skin above all others; two skins would purchase a slave, and only chieftains could afford to wear robes made of them.

These aquatic mammals (*Lutra enhydris marina*) were found only on the Pacific shores where there were reefs, rocks, kelp beds, and some protection from storms and heavy surf. They fed on crustaceans found on rocks and in the kelp; they bore their pups and raised them in these floating beds and came ashore to sheltered reefs only during the winter storms. Conditions suitable for their habitat were limited to rocky or islanded areas of the coast. Alaska and the British Columbia coast were heavily productive and the first exploited. Washington's northern coast, south to and including Grays Harbor, was also a favorable habitat, but the Harbor and the vicinity of Teakwhit Head were the only safe anchorages for vessels. The Oregon coast was on the whole unfavorable.[8] Gray traded a few skins at Cape Orford and Tillamook Bay, and he got 150 skins in the Columbia River.

From its initiation in 1787 to 1796 the sea otter trade was focused on the northwest coast between the Columbia River and the Russian settlements. Subsequently it shifted to the California coast where, between the Farallone Islands and Lower California, the otter found an almost ideal habitat. For several years traders dallied along the California shore seeking to trade for them with the natives wherever they could avoid Spanish officials or find those who, for a price, would coöperate.

It appears to be impossible to arrive at an accurate estimate of the numbers of otter pelts taken on the Pacific coast and marketed by Americans in China, for any interval of time.[9] The trade was highly competitive, hence highly secretive. Collections, if reported, were understated and their sources undisclosed. A figure of 2,500,000 fine

[8] Adele Ogden, *California Sea Otter Trade, 1784-1848*, University of California Publications in History, Vol. 26, Berkeley, 1941; Robert Stuart's description of the killing of sea otter in Rollins, ed., *Discovery of the Oregon Trail;* Victor B. Scheffer, "The Sea Otter on the Washington Coast," *PNQ*, XXI, October, 1940; Karl Kenyon, *The Seals, Sea-Lion, and Sea Otter of the Pacific Coast*, United States Department of the Interior, Washington, 1955; Alan May, "The North Sea Otter," in *Natural History*, June, 1943.

[9] In addition to entries under Note 5, are such sources of information for the maritime fur trade as T. C. Elliott, ed., "Journal of Captain Charles Bishop of the 'Ruby' in 1795" *OHQ*, XXIX, December, 1928; Richard W. Van Alstyne, "International Rivalries in the Pacific Northwest," *OHQ*, XLVI, September, 1945; John D'Wolf, *Voyage to the North Pacific and a Journey Through Siberia More Than Half a Century Ago*, Cambridge, 1861.

furs sold between 1794 and 1810 does not seem an unreasonable estimate. But fine furs included beaver, marten, seal, and sea otter. Dulles, in *The Old China Trade,* states that between 1790 and 1812, "the average importation of sea-otter skins into Canton by the American traders was about twelve thousand each year. . . ." This is perhaps a high figure. William Sturgis, who participated in the trade says, in *The Northwest Fur Trade,* that in 1801-1802, when 15 vessels were on the coast, 15,000 skins were carried to Canton. This seems to have been a peak year both in the number of ships and size of cargoes. A trader who reported 2,500 or 3,000 skins was indeed fortunate; and it is probable that few had so large a take. Nor is it possible to discover what part of the sea otter sold in the China trade came from the Pacific Northwest. In the traders' vocabulary the Northwest Coast of America meant the shore from the Spanish settlements to Bering Strait. The furs they reported might have come from California or Alaska.

The sea otter pelt consistently brought higher prices than any other fur in the China market. The top price of 100 dollars for a complete skin reportedly paid Cook's men in 1779, was bettered by Captain Hanna in 1785, who was reported as receiving 140 dollars a pelt. The market was sometimes glutted and the Hong merchants prohibited further importations. The range of prices ran from 70 to 20 dollars and it seems that with the exception of 1804, when furs brought 50 dollars, the prevailing price was about 22 dollars. While otter were selling at the latter figure, a beaver skin brought six dollars and seal, 80 cents.

The returns were attractive enough to keep the traders coming, and fortunes of at least a dozen Boston merchant families were made from the China trade made possible by sea otter pelts. Sturgis reported instances of a 40,000-dollar investment in ship and Indian goods bringing in 150,000 dollars. In 1810 the *Pearl,* outfit and trade goods costing a like amount, brought home a China cargo sold at auction for 261,000 dollars.

The Schedule of Voyages

The great period of the Pacific Northwest maritime trade was from 1787 to the outbreak of the war with Great

Britain, when it practically ceased. During these years the trade had so largely fallen in the hands of men from Boston that the Indians called Americans Boston men, as distinguished from the British King George's men.

The small vessels engaged in this city's trade usually set out in the early fall, stopped at the Falkland Islands, San Juan Fernandez, or some South American Pacific port, and with good luck reached the Hawaiian Islands the following spring. Having refitted and replenished ship, the master then directed it toward the Pacific coast. A favored port was Newettee, a small inlet on the northwestern promontory of Vancouver Island. There were many Indian villages in the vicinity, and hundreds of natives appeared to trade shortly after a ship arrived. Because this was a principal mart it was one of the first stops on the northern coast. Another was Kygarney, or Kargahnee, north of Newettee and centrally located for trading along the coast. According to one trader, in 1804-1805 this was "the best place of resort for ships on their first arrival, to obtain information for establishing a rate of trade." Most traders spent the summer in the northern waters and when winter came returned to the Hawaiian Islands' more congenial climate. Some, on the other hand, and particularly in the early days of the trade, wintered on the coast, wherever there might be a protected port, friendly Indians, and food resources. Nootka had once been the favored winter quarters, and we have seen how Gray and Kendrick spent two winters in Clayoquot Sound.

A second summer was spent on the coast to the north, or cruising along the California shores, and with the autumn the ship was directed back to the islands and thence to the China ports. Here the furs were sold and their returns invested in Chinese goods. The voyage home was by way of the Cape of Good Hope, sometimes with leisurely port-to-port calls through the Mediterranean before continuing to the West Indies and then to Boston.

The Columbia as a Port of Call

Although there were relatively few otter to be traded in the Columbia River, it became a port of call for some and a few traders wintered in the river. Gray had no sooner reported its discovery at Nootka than Captain James Baker of the little 78-ton

Jenny hove his ship into the bay on the north bank, where he was found by Lieutenant Broughton in October, 1792. Her sister ship, the *Ruby*, wintered there in 1795-1796. Her captain, Charles Bishop, first came in the spring, and in preparation for his return, had his crew clear and plant a small island in the bay with peas, beans, potatoes, radishes, mustard, cress, and celery seeds. When he returned in October for the winter, he found the potatoes plentiful and good, but the "red-dishes" had gone to seed, and with the exception of several beans, the rest of the garden stuff had disappeared.

In 1805 Lewis and Clark obtained from the Indians a list of fourteen names purporting to be of traders who visited the Columbia River, but the explorers' interpretation of the native rendering of these names makes most of them difficult if not impossible to identify. One is inclined to believe more traders than this had traded or wintered in the river. Between 1792 and 1805 the Indians had achieved considerable facility in the English language. Lewis and Clark reported they used "many blackguard phrases" and common profanities with ease and had learned a trading vocabulary of such words as musket, powder, shot, knife, and file. A commercial people themselves, the Chinookan peoples of the lower river had quickly adapted themselves to the white man's commerce.

So long as the white man wanted what the Indian had in abundance and which he did not value, and so long as there was no rival to bid up prices, trading was a simple matter. In the early days, a nail, a piece of iron, a castoff jacket, a piece of copper, or a mirror, or a string of thimbles would buy prime otter skins. But those times passed very quickly. In 1795 Captain Bishop found the Indians of the Columbia River considerably wiser than they had been three years before when Gray and Baker first opened trade. His journal tells:

> we expected of course from the Information we hitherto had of these People that with the choice goods that compose our cargo, we should have been able to procure them [furs] in way of Barter readily and with ease, but our disappointment might be better conceived than expressed when after bartering and shewing them a great variety of articles for the whole day we did not purchase a single Fur. Tea Kettles, sheet Copper, a variety of fine cloths and in short the most valuable articles of our Cargo

were shewn without producing the desired Effect, and in the Evening the whole of them took to their canoes, and paddled to the shore, leaving us not more disappointed than surprised.[10]

The next day the natives came out in even greater numbers, and "began to set their own Price on the Skins which as may be seen from their behaviour yesterday was not moderate." On the third day, Bishop "broke trade," but not at prices as cheap as he wished.

In one interesting respect the Columbia River trade apparently differed from that of other coastal localities. A local product of Chinookan handicraft was found to be a valuable item in trade for furs with other natives of the northern coast. After describing his purchases of furs, Bishop says:

> the best trade is the Leather War Dresses, articles to be disposed of, on other parts of the Coast, to great advantage, we procured such a Quantity, that at the least estimation is expected will procure us near 700 Prime Sea otter Skins. These dresses are made from the Hide of the Moose Deer which are very large and thick, this is dressed into a kind of White leather, and doubled, & is when properly made up, a complete defence against a Spear or an Arrow, and sufficient almost to resist a Pistol Ball.

By 1805 demands of both whites and natives had expanded. The traders brought guns, outmoded British and American muskets, powder, balls, and shot, brass kettles and pots, blankets, scarlet and blue cloth, sheets of copper, wire, knives, buttons, beads, tobaccos, sailor clothing, and rum. They took in exchange skins of all animals, dressed or undressed elk hides, packed dried salmon, and a baked breadstuff made from pounded *wapato* root—commodities that the Chinook Indians secured by trading with other peoples up the Columbia and north and south along the coast. When guns were put into the hands of the Indians, the manufacture of leather war dresses—the *clamons*—was abandoned.

Elsewhere the character of the trade, and the early patterns of traders' movements began to change. Wherever competition was strong increasing amounts of liquor and firearms were bartered. At Kygarney, ermine skins were a highly prized commodity. Sturgis imported 5,000 ermine from Leipzig, worth less than 30 cents in the Boston market, and traded them to northwest Indians at the rate

[10] T. C. Elliott, " Journal of the Ruby" *OHQ*, XXVIII, 262.

of five skins for one sea otter. He reported having got in one afternoon 560 prime otter, at that time (1804) worth 50 dollars each in the China trade. On the northern coast the depletion of the sea otter made trading less profitable and more hazardous. California's shores were rich in supply, but the Spanish were enforcing their prohibitions of trade with greater vigor. New methods had to be devised to break or circumvent this barrier. In 1805, Captain John D'Wolf, master of the *Juno* and a guest of Governor Baranof at the Russian settlement on Norfolk Sound, suggested his host share in an expedition to California. "My idea" he explained, "was to take on board forty or fifty Kodiak Indians, with their canoes, for the purpose of catching sea otter."[11] The plan was acceptable to the Russians but its execution was delayed, first to await the Indians, who were on a hunting trip, and second to accommodate the Russians, who had need of D'Wolf's vessel and which they eventually purchased from him. It was used to bring supplies from California.

The Winship family, with enterprising leadership and large capital resources, also looked to the development of a less haphazard trade by integrating a supply system for the Russian colonies and the hunting of the sea otter. As D'Wolf had offered to do, they contracted with the Russians to use Aleut hunters on the California coast and to supply the Russian posts with goods. They carried the coast's products to the Hawaiian Islands, where they supplemented their cargo with sandalwood for the China ports.

To carry on such an involved trade they needed a depot at some well-located site midway between the Russian posts and the California hunting grounds. The Columbia River was beyond both the Spanish and Russian active spheres, it was navigable, and its shores could provide food to support a settlement. Furthermore it was no longer an unknown river, and there were already bases for claiming it was an American river, since Lewis and Clark had wintered at its mouth in 1805-1806. In late May, 1810, the *Albatross*, carrying supplies and live stock for a settlement arrived in the Columbia. Captain Nathan Winship chose a site some 30 miles up the river and about opposite present Oak Point, Washington. On the fourth of June, some of the crew started to hew logs for a fort, while others cleared a garden spot. Four

[11] D'Wolf, *Voyage to the Pacific*, 29-30.

days later they were flooded out and moved their location a quarter mile farther downstream. Work had hardly started again when a massing of Indians signified trouble; the repeated warnings of the natives that the white men should return down the river were finally heeded, and the project was abandoned.[12]

The significance of the Winships' attempt at settlement is not simply that it was the first effort to build an American post in the Pacific Northwest. It is important evidence that enterprising mercantile interests saw the Columbia River as a vital link in an enlarged commerce involving Russian Alaska, Spanish California, the Hawaiian Islands, the Orient, and the ports of Southern Europe and South America. The Winships were pioneers of the idea only by a matter of months. Born of American maritime trade, it was to develop when it was associated with a plan for a simultaneous development of the land fur trade. It was in the air, so to speak, that the Columbia River should become the western depot of a trade that spanned the continent.

[12] Bancroft, *Northwest Coast*, II, 131-135.

5

Continental Fur Trade and Exploration

By 1793 maritime exploration of the western shores of the Pacific had completed the general outline of the North American continent except for the Arctic area. Vancouver's years of survey had revealed no inlet or bay that broke the mountain barriers with waters navigable by seagoing vessels. Only in the most stubborn minds lingered a hope that somewhere between 50° and the Arctic, Vancouver had missed the entrance of a waterway connecting with Baffin or Hudson's Bay. An alternative to such a passage was an interior river system, a portage of the Rocky Mountain barrier, and connection with a passable river flowing to the sea. The search for a transcontinental route was intimately related to the fur trade, or more accurately, the Indian trade in which furs were a principal item.

The Indian trade had an important part in the colonial history of North America. Furs as well as proselytizing zeal had led the French to colonize the New World. In their search for pelts and souls, *coureurs des bois* and the long-robed fathers had penetrated into the heart of the continent by the end of the seventeenth century. The Dutch at New Amsterdam were agents of Netherlands merchants engaged in the Indian trade. The Pilgrims' first export from their wilderness homes was a cargo of furs, and the Massachusetts Bay Colony had hardly been settled when its traders began the expansion of New England along the forested shores of Maine. The colonists of Virginia, Pennsylvania, and the Carolinas had outposts and routes of trade across the Appalachians long before their settlements left tidewater. The Indian trade was one of the British colonies' principal enterprises, and the mother country's effort to regulate it was a major cause of colonial discontent. Even dissensions among and within the colonies were sometimes caused by competition for the Indian markets.

French Fur Trade

The trade attracted a sturdy breed of men and its demands made them adventurers and explorers. In the English colonies, settlers followed upon the heels of the Indian trader and since settlement was incompatible with the fur trade, the latter was forced inexorably toward the unmapped, unexplored regions of the West. In Canada, settlement was retarded by French and British trade monopolies; but competition and the exploitation of fur resources led to a race of rival interests to open up new and untapped regions. French *coureurs des bois* pushed up the St. Lawrence, into the Great Lakes country, the Canadian plains, and the Mississippi Valley by the end of the seventeenth century. By the beginning of the nineteenth century, their English and American successors were intent upon establishing a Pacific terminal for a trade that spanned the continent.

In the course of the eighteenth century attention focused upon two areas in which river systems or rivers, lakes, and portages made at least canoe transportation into the West a possibility. These were the Mississippi-Missouri system and the Hudson's Bay, Nelson River, Lake Winnipeg, and Saskatchewan route.

Since Marquette's discovery of it in 1673, the Missouri River had been considered a promising route to the western sea. Reports of La Salle's explorations of the Mississippi strengthened the belief that its tributary, the "grand rivière des Esmourites," was navigable for at least 1,000 miles. Fact and fiction combined to create a Missouri legend or legends. The Baron Lahontan's fictitious travels contributed the notion that the river's source lay in a tremendous mountain range; that in its upper reaches was a series of violent cataracts by which the waters leaped from their mountain origin into the level plains; that a short portage over the mountains would take the adventurer to a westward-flowing river and thence to the sea.[1] The mountains (variously called Shining, White, Stony, and Rocky Mountains), the

---

[1] Baron Lahontan, *Nouveaux Voyages . . . dans L'Amérique Septentrionale*, Paris, 1703, Lettre XVI; Lawrence J. Burpee, *Search for the Western Sea*, Toronto, 1908.

Missouri's source in them, a great salt lake, and a westward-flowing river were fixed ideas of geography before white men had ventured very far up the river itself. Not until the last quarter of the eighteenth century did explorers push up the muddy waters to the upper river.

La Verendrye

French colonials, primarily fur traders, were active explorers in the north. As a crown monopoly the fur trade was administered through military outposts, but unlicensed traders, the *coureurs des bois*, opened up the routes the Crown's agents followed. While English traders were content with timid expansion along the west shore of Hudson's Bay, the French pushed steadily into the heart of the continent. By the middle of the eighteenth century they had posts on the Great Lakes, in the Illinois country, and had advanced into the Canadian prairies. At Fort Nipigon, on the lake of that name, Pierre Gaultier, Sieur de La Verendrye, was in charge of the trade from 1726 to 1731. From the Indians who came to his post, he heard of a westward-flowing river which they had never seen but had learned about from people with whom they traded. From 1731 to 1753 La Verendrye and his sons persisted with almost fanatical devotion to discover it. In the first ten years they built no less than six forts from the western end of Lake Superior to Lake Winnipeg, and as far as the forks of the Saskatchewan. In their expedition of 1738 they explored to the south and discovered the Mandan Indians on the Missouri which they thought might lead them eventually to the sea. A second expedition led by his sons in 1742-1743 traveled through the Dakotas until they came within sight of mountains—perhaps the Wyoming Big Horns, more likely the Black Hills—which they were "vexed not to be able to ascend because of the hostility of the Indians."[2]

The report of their journeys in the region of the Upper Missouri was probably used in 1765 by Major Robert Rogers, a Massachusetts colonial who had served in British campaigns against the French in the St. Lawrence, in support of a petition to the British Crown to

[2] Grace Flandrau, ed., "Verendrye Expeditions in Quest of the Pacific," *OHQ*, XXVI, June, 1925; M. Q. Innis, *An Economic History of Canada*, Toronto, 1935; L. J. Burpee, ed., *Letters of La Verendrye and His Sons*, Toronto, 1927; J. B. Brebner, *The Explorers of North America*.

lead an expedition to the same region. He proposed to go "from the Great Lakes towards the Head of the Mississippi and from thence to the River called by the Indians Ouragon."

Nothing came of Rogers' project but encouragement of the idea that the headwaters of east- and west-flowing rivers were in some common locale. An associate of Rogers by the name of Jonathan Carver furthered the notion by claiming, on the basis of his so-called travels, certainty of "the River Oregon, or the River of the West, that falls into the Pacific Ocean at the Strait of Anian." Today both Rogers and Carver are remembered chiefly because they were the first to use the name Oregon, later to be applied to the whole Pacific Northwest.[3]

English Traders and Canadian Pedlars

With the conclusion of the French and Indian Wars in 1763, France lost her colonial empire in the New World. The English inherited the St. Lawrence and Great Lakes region and the Spanish acquired France's Louisiana, with the Mississippi as a common boundary between her lands and those of Great Britain.

The principal agent of English policies north of the St. Lawrence had been, since 1670, the Hudson's Bay Company. A chartered joint-stock company, properly described in its full title as the "Governor and Company of Adventurers of England trading into Hudson's Bay," it was granted a trade monopoly over all the area drained by waters flowing into Hudson's Bay which, in time, was claimed to be the greater part of Canada north of the St. Lawrence drainage and to extend to the Rocky Mountains. In exchange for his royal domain, the Company was obligated to deliver up to the King on occasions of his visits to the region, a feudal token of "two elks and two black beaver," and to carry out a search for the Northwest Passage presumed to open off the bay.[4]

In 1774 the Company's rivals were no longer French colonials but their successors, Montreal merchants of Scottish blood, many of whom had come to the New World since the conquest of New France.

[3] T. C. Elliott, "The Origin of the Name Oregon," *OHQ*, XXII, June, 1921; Jonathan Carver, *Travels through the Interior Parts of North America*, London, 1781.

[4] The Hudson's Bay Company charter can be found in Appendix of Beckles Willson, *The Great Company*, Toronto, 1899, and in numerous other references.

The Montreal merchants were Canadian and colonial as distinct from the Hudson's Bay Company, which had its roots in London and was English. In order to reduce competition among themselves, the Canadian "pedlars" from time to time formed combinations to meet the larger competition of the Hudson's Bay Company. In 1783-1784 such a combination was formed under the name of the North West Company, and indicative of the fragile nature of such combinations, re-formed again in 1787 and 1804.

The North West Company, according to one of its founders, was "no more than an association of commercial men, agreeing among themselves to carry on the fur trade."[5] The merchant partners purchased trading goods and marketed the furs; their partners-in-the-field, stationed at the posts in the interior, conducted the trade and secured the furs. At annual meetings held at some principal depot such as Michilimachinac or Fort William, the partners settled their accounts, divided their profits, and determined their policies for the next year. Where the British Company imported officials from the home country as need for them arose, and used Orkney men and Iroquois Indians in the field, the North West Company employed the skilled French Canadians as its *voyageurs*, and as the older partners retired, promoted to partnerships able and energetic young clerks whose talents had been tested with responsibilities. "This regular and equitable mode of providing for the clerks of the company excited a spirit of emulation in the discharge of their various duties, and in fact, made every agent a principal, who perceived his own prosperity to be immediately connected with that of his employers." The secret of the North West Company's success in extending its posts and opening up new areas to the trade was largely due to its enterprising personnel.

Alexander Mackenzie

A pioneer, both in exploration and in plans for an enterprise of continental scope, was Alexander Mackenzie, one of the founders of the company of 1787. He was born in Scotland, brought to New York as a child, and at the outbreak of the Revolution

[5] Alexander Mackenzie, *Voyages from Montreal on the River St. Lawrence, Through the Continent of North America . . . with a Preliminary Account of the Rise, Progress, and Present State of the Fur trade of that Country*, London, 1801.

sent to Montreal to school. He entered the fur trade when he was 16 as an employee of merchants who later joined forces to form the North West Company. As a partner in the latter organization he planned and carried out two amazing explorations. His first trip in 1789 took him to the Arctic by way of the river which bears his name, and which proved that from the headwaters of the Mackenzie River to the Arctic there was no east-west water passage.

His second expedition was started from the North West Company's Fort Chipewyan in 1792. On October 19, the day Captain Vancouver was attempting to enter the Columbia River, Mackenzie was going into winter quarters on the Peace River. The following May 9 he set out to follow the Peace, hoping it would lead him through the mountains to a westward-flowing river and the sea. A 25-foot bark canoe, "exclusive of the curves of stem and stern," and "so light, that two men could carry her on a good road three or four miles without resting," was loaded with 3,000 pounds of baggage and ten people: Mackenzie, Alexander Mackay, six *voyageurs* and two Indian hunters and interpreters. On the seventeenth of May they saw the snow-covered summits of the Rocky Mountains. Their journey up the river against violent currents confined in narrow rock-walled chasms was hazardous and exhausting. At times they had to carry canoe and goods over crude portage paths they first had to break and hew out of the forest; other times they cordelled, or lined, their fragile craft over cascades, where the linesmen had to hug the face of the cliff and measure their margin of safety in inches.

Mackenzie literally pushed his way up the Parsnip River branch of the Peace to its headwaters. Here he portaged a short distance to a "great river" which the Indians called the Tacoutche Tesse, but which we know today as the Frazer. "At length," he wrote, "we enjoyed after all our toil and anxiety, the inexpressible satisfaction of finding ourselves on the bank of a navigable river, on the west side of the first great range of mountains" and he concluded the Tacoutche Tesse was the River of the West.

Since his canoe was badly damaged, supplies short, his men both exhausted and discouraged, and the course of the river to the sea presumed to be long and arduous, Mackenzie decided to abandon it and head overland for the coast. They retraced their route up the

125
121
CANOE ENCAMPMENT
Queen Charlotte Strait
Chilko L
Fraser R
Canim L
North Thompson R
Columbia R
Adams L
Shuswap L
Thompson
FORT THOMPSON
Lillooet R
Fraser R
Nootka Sound
Okanogan L
Strait of Georgia
49
Similkameen R
Lower Arrow L
FORT LANGLEY
Barkley Sound
Cape Flattery
Strait of Juan de Fuca
FORT VICTORIA
Skagit R
Methow R
Okanogan
FORT COLVILLE
Lake Chelan
FORT OKANOGAN
FORT NISQUALLY
Chehalis R
Snake R
COWLITZ FARMS
Yakima R
FORT CLATSOP
ASTORIA
FORT NEZ PERCE
WAIILATPU
Columbia R
Umatilla R
FORT VANCOUVER
THE DALLES (MISSION)
Grande Ronde
45
R
Willamette
John Day R
Deschutes R
Umpqua R
Malheur L
Harney L
Malheur R
Owyhee R
Rogue R
Klamath L
Klamath R
41
125
Scale
0 30 60 90
121
Cartographic Laboratories, Dept. of Geography, U of Wash.

THE PACIFIC NORTHWEST
FUR TRADE and MISSIONS
113
109
49
45
41
Bow R
Columbia L
Kootenai R
Elk R
KULLYSPELL HOUSE
Clark Fork R
SALEESH HOUSE
Flathead L
Frenchman R
Milk R
Marias R
Missouri R
Musselshell
ST. MARYS (MISSION)
Bitterroot R
Big Hole R
Jefferson R
THREE FORKS
Madison R
Gallatin R
Red Rock R
Yellowstone R
Clark Fork R
Shoshone R
Big Horn R
Salmon R
Yellowstone L
Henry's Fork
FORT HENRY
Jackson L
PIERRE'S HOLE
JACKSON HOLE
Teton Pass
Union Pass
Wind R
Snake R
Payette R
FORT HALL
South Pass
Sweetwater R
Bear R
Bear L
Green R
Great Salt Lake
Humboldt R
John C. Sherman

river until on July 4 they came to a well-defined Indian trail leading west. Thirteen days later they arrived at a substantial village on the Bella Coola River near Point Menzies. Borrowing a canoe from the friendly chieftain, Mackenzie then went out North Bentinck Arm into Dean Channel, where he learned of the visit only a month before of Lieutenant Johnstone of Vancouver's surveying party. To mark the western terminus of his overland voyage Mackenzie used a mixture of grease and vermillion to paint on a rocky ledge the words: "Alexander Mackenzie, from Canada, by land, the twenty-second of July, one thousand seven hundred and ninety three."

The return trip was remarkably short. Thirty-three days after leaving the coast the party was safely back at Fort Chipewyan. "Here," he later recorded, "my voyages of discovery terminate. Their toils and their dangers, their solicitudes and sufferings, have not been exaggerated in my description. On the contrary, in many instances, language has failed me in the attempt to describe them. I received, however, the reward of my labours, for they were crowned with success."

His *Voyages*, published in 1801, is a classic narrative of adventure and exploration. His two explorations offered final and convincing proof that there was no Northwest Passage within the continent north of 50°. The "immense ridge, or succession of stony mountains" through which he had passed in 1793 divided the "waters of the Atlantic from those which run into the Pacific. In those snow-clad mountains rises the Mississippi, if we admit the Missisouri to be its source, which flows into the Gulph of Mexico; the River Nelson, which is lost in Hudson's Bay; Mackenzie's River, that discharges itself into the North Sea; and the Columbia emptying itself into the Pacific Ocean."

While his fundamental conclusion was correct, its details were still in error. When he was composing his book he knew of Gray's discovery and Broughton's exploration of the lower Columbia River. He assumed therefore that his Tacoutche Tesse was the upper part of the Columbia. On the strength of this assumption he projected a plan for a fur trade of continental scope, with the Nelson, Saskatchewan, and Columbia rivers as east-west highways and the latter's mouth as the western terminus.

. . . Whatever course may be taken from the Atlantic, the Columbia is the line of communication from the Pacific Ocean, pointed out by nature, as it is the only navigable river in the whole extent of Vancouver's minute survey of that coast; its banks . . . [are] the most northern situation fit for colonization, and suitable to the residence of a civilized people. By opening this intercourse between the Atlantic and Pacific Oceans, and forming regular establishments through the interior, and at both extremes, as well as along the coasts and islands, the entire command of the fur trade of North America might be obtained, from latitude 48 North to the pole. . . . To this may be added the fishing in both seas, and the markets of the four quarters of the globe.

In 1802 he followed up this broad statement with a proposal for a "Fishery and Fur Company" which would combine whale fisheries and the land and sea fur trade of the north. He urged the British government to provide protection for establishments at Nootka Sound, Sea Otter Harbor (at Dixon Entrance), and on the Columbia River, and to force the East India and Hudson's Bay companies either to abandon their exclusive monopolies or to license the new company and coöperate with it in the Orient and in Canada.[6]

While geography provided the framework of Mackenzie's plan, the competitive situation forced him to make the merger of rival interests a primary condition of its execution. His large view of the industry and the disastrous effects of competition upon it and the Indians was not shared by either the British government or the Hudson's Bay Company, nor for that matter by his associates in the North West Company. He withdrew from the Company in 1799, re-entered the partnership in the reorganized new North West Company upon the death of his principal opponent in 1804, but was "excluded from interference" in the fur trade. His ideas eventually became a reality. Their implementation was brought about in part by a challenge to the Nor'westers from citizens of the United States in the old Northwest.

Spanish Defenses

While the Canadians were making their advances into the interior of the continent, the Spanish in Louisiana were trying to build up their defenses against their powerful neighbors.

[6] Gordon C. Davidson, *The North West Company*, Berkeley, 1918, 75-76. This is the principal study of the North West Company. See also W. Stewart Wallace, *The Pedlars from Quebec, and Other Papers on the Nor'Westers*, Toronto, 1954.

In acquiring Louisiana (Treaty of Utrecht, 1763) and the Floridas (Treaty of Paris, 1783), Spain secured what she hoped was a broad protective belt for her provinces of New Spain. Louisiana, with its northern boundary presumed to be a great arc extending from the headwaters of the Mississippi to the Pacific, was a cushion of defense for the precious metal-producing *provincias internas* of old and new Mexico against British, American, or other aggression.[7] The establishment of *presidios* in California after 1769 was a rounding out of this defense against Russia and England in the Pacific. "Supposing that Louisiana extended no farther [north] than the Missouri," wrote a colonial governor in 1794, "it would be sufficient to glance at the map in order to recognize its importance with respect to the preservation of the internal provinces of New Spain and the kingdom of Mexico, which the Mississippi and Missouri Rivers encircle from the gulf [of Mexico] almost to the South Sea . . . [Pacific]."

What was actually known about this frontier was extremely limited. The headwaters of the Mississippi had not been discovered, and those of the Missouri were still unknown. Until the turn of the century the Missouri was described in terms of the persistent French legend, as "navigable in all parts," as having its rise "a short distance from a very lofty chain of mountains not more than forty leagues" from the sea and within portage distance of another "large navigable river" flowing to the Pacific. The Spaniards did little to further exploration until, in 1792, it was reported that the natives of the Mandan villages on the Upper Missouri were trading with the Canadian nor'westers who were "established and fortified about fifteen day's march" from them.

The advance of the British was a double threat to Spain. Since the Mandan Indians were reported to have communication with New Mexico, directly or indirectly, the same channels might serve the British to the detriment of Spanish trade and security. Considered in relation to the recent Nootka Sound incident, their westward movement suggested a possible union of internal and coastal trade and an

[7] Sources and studies used in this connection are: Annie H. Abel, *Tabeau's Narrative of Loisel's Expedition to the Upper Missouri*, Norman, Oklahoma, 1939; A. P. Nasatir, *Before Lewis and Clark;* Lawrence Kinnaird, ed., *Spain in the Mississippi Valley, 1765-1794*, Part III: *Problems of Frontier Defense, 1792-1794*, American Historical Association *Annual Report* for 1945.

inevitable attack upon the commerce of the Californias as well as the interior provinces. Furthermore, the Nootka Controversy had made Spain's colonial officials extremely aware of the need of supporting their claims to lands by evidences of occupation.

Colonial policy and commercial interests were combined therefore in 1793 when St. Louis merchants were encouraged to form a syndicate for the purpose of exploring and garrisoning the Upper Missouri, which in the geography of the early fur trade, was the river above the mouth of the Platte marked by the beginning of the open plains. During the next five years the employees of the "Company of Explorers of the Upper Missouri," or hardy independents associated with them, pushed beyond the Mandan villages of North Dakota to the waters of the Rivière Roches Jaunes, the Yellow Stones. But the interests of the syndicate were directed more to trade, only incidentally to exploration for its own sake, and they were reluctant to support defensive garrisons. Desperate colonial governors pleaded for some speedy help "to restrain the usurpations of the English," but Spanish officials were only partially aware of their true plight. The Nootka incident had served notice to the world that Spain's empire in North America had lived its term, and was ready for the taking. The question was merely one of when and by whom, and between 1790 and 1800 there emerged three potential takers: Great Britain, France, and the United States.

Thomas Jefferson and the Mississippi Frontier

The principal architect of the United States' policy with regard to the West was Thomas Jefferson.[8] As private citizen and as public officer, his interest in the West, and by that he referred to all the region that lay beyond his Virginia homeland, was both intellectual and political. In 1782 he asked an acquaintance going beyond the mountains to send him descriptions of "animals, vegetables, minerals, or other curious things, notes as to

[8] The writings of Jefferson in the Monticello, Federal, and Boyd ed. have been used; Samuel F. Bemis, *John Quincy Adams and the Foundations of American Foreign Policy*, New York, 1949; Theodore C. Pease, "The Mississippi Boundary of 1793: a Reappraisal of Responsibility," *AHR*, XL, January, 1935; *Canadian Archives*, 1889 and 1890; R. G. Thwaites, ed., *Original Journals of Lewis and Clark*, 8 vols., New York, 1904-1905.

Indians, information of the country between the Mississippi and waters of the South Sea," and we have already pointed out his interest in Ledyard's abortive efforts to explore the continent. During his whole life Jefferson purchased and studied books of western travels and maps, and was considered both at home and abroad as something of an authority on the subject.

He was sensitive to the potentialities of the West as the home of the republic's children and as a resource of the nation's prosperity, and he was concerned with the protection of the region from foreign powers whose politics were antithetical to those of the United States. Two years before he had met Ledyard he had raised the question of an American exploration when rumor reported British interest in an overland expedition to the Far West.

Essential to an understanding of Jefferson are several persistent themes in his public career. He envisioned the development of commerce and the nation within a continental framework as free as possible from the monarchical politics and aggressive commercial imperialism of Europe. He therefore sought "peace, commerce, and honest friendship with all nations, entangling alliances with none." He had a deep-rooted distrust of British imperialism, territorial and commercial. He had a passion for peace, which, if necessary, he might fight to keep. These themes are evident in the instances in which his deeds contributed to the history of the nation—and to the history of the Far West.

From his own experience in Western Virginia and from experiences as a delegate to the Continental and Confederation Congresses, Jefferson knew of the close relation between the Indian trade and the opening up of new lands to settlement. Jefferson was fully aware of the means and the motives that had led Americans across the Alleghenies to the Mississippi boundary. He was intimately aware of frontiersmen's feelings about that boundary and their right of deposit at New Orleans, for on the basis of them, in part, he had created a political following.

There were frontier plots and counterplots on the part of frontiersmen to infiltrate and conquer Louisiana, of Spain to subvert the trans-Allegheny West and incorporate it in her empire. Americans trespassed into the Floridas and surged up to the Mississippi. While some moved into Spanish lands and became Spanish subjects, the majority of westerners waited impatiently on the eastern bank of the river for an incident to invite them to cross. How long the frontier of a weak, overextended, poorly administered colonial power could hold against them was a question that concerned not only Spain but the government of the United States.

The problem was complicated by domestic politics. The frontiersmen felt the Atlantic seaboard interests were opposed to theirs; that the Federalist party was little inclined to champion their cause and force Spain to accede to their demands to have a guaranteed right to transship their goods from river craft to ocean vessels at New Orleans. Kentuckians were ripe for revolt against the new republic, and it became a matter of speculation how long their strained loyalties would hold fast. British observers in Canada considered them potential allies when the Nootka incident took place.[9]

Jefferson was Secretary of State when the questions raised by the Nootka affair came to a head. The first question concerned the role that the United States should play in a threatening world war, when a principal battlefield would be at its boundary if not across its territory. This was decided in favor of neutrality. But Jefferson took the opportunity to point out that, if Spain and Great Britain went to war, the odds were all in favor of the latter. If Britain should occupy the Spanish territory, she would then reduce the American territory east of the Mississippi "by her language, laws, religion, manners, government, commerce, capital," and with her fleet on the Atlantic and her possessions in the interior encircle the United States completely. "Instead of two neighbors balancing each other, we shall have one, with more than the strength of both."[10]

There is little evidence to suggest Jefferson changed his mind in the following ten years. And these were not unrealistic suppositions. Strongly prejudiced as he was against England, Jefferson represented a good part of western opinion. For while settlers on the Spanish border might from time to time be amenable to British influences, American traders and settlers in Wisconsin were bitterly opposed

[9] *Canadian Archives*, 1890, Toronto, 1891, 97-174, "Note E—Relations with the United States after the Peace of 1783."

[10] Jefferson to Washington, July 12, 1790, "Opinions on war between Great Britain and Spain," Jefferson *Works*, Federal Ed., VI, 91-93.

to them. The northern boundary in the vicinity of the headwaters of the Mississippi had not been defined at the conclusion of the Revolution, and the Canadian fur traders occupied the region, and held the Indians completely in their control. Hides and furs from American territory were drawn off to Montreal and, it was charged, American scalps decorated the lodge poles of British-inspired Indian allies.

The Nootka Convention relieved the prospects of a war between Spain and Britain, but the question of whether Britain or the United States would inherit Spain's power in the Mississippi was raised. The year of 1793 witnessed a new crisis, largely manifested in domestic politics in the United States. The course of its Revolution had led France to war with Great Britain, with the result that American sentiment divided sharply into pro-British and pro-French camps, with Jefferson the leader of the Francophiles. Through the erratic and ill-inspired Citizen Genêt, Jefferson's party was led to believe that the French republic could and would help in relieving the United States of both its bothersome monarchical neighbors, Britain and Spain, and would substitute a strong and friendly republican one. The plan was that

> . . . the Naval Forces of the Republic [French] should seize the Mouth of the Mississippi, declare that the Country belonged to them by right of Conquest and invite the Americans of the Western Country to take advantage of the freedom of Navigation. Then, if the Spaniards situated higher up the river molested the Vessels carrying the provisions conveyed by the Americans, the latter would have the right to repel Constraint and force by force. Thus the Spanish Government would have no reason to complain of the United States having broken through inasmuch as the country would be reputed in the possession of the French Republic.[11]

Implicit in the French plot was the idea that from its Mississippi base, the French would attack the British West Indies, while the Americans would rout the British from their northern outposts if not from Canada as well. This was the circumstance which lay behind a project for "exploring the west" and which also led to its failure.

In January, 1793, Jefferson, vice-president of the American Philo-

[11] André Michaux, *Journal of Travels into Kentucky, 1793-1796*, in Thwaites, *Early Western Travels, III*, 44-45.

sophical Society at Philadelphia, laid before the members a suggestion that the society underwrite the expenses of a single individual who would explore the country along the Missouri and thence westward to the Pacific Ocean. Two candidates were considered. One was a 19-year-old army lieutenant and close friend of Jefferson, Meriwether Lewis. The successful candidate was André Michaux, a man of mature years and famous as a world traveler and botanist. He was also an agent of Citizen Genêt and a proponent of the plan of French participation in Mississippi Valley politics. Unfortunately, the scientific objectives of the expedition were smothered in frontier politics and plots and his exploration took him no farther than they required.

The questions in 1793 were how firm the Spanish boundaries might hold and what were the intentions of the British with regard to the Spanish possessions. These questions continued to perplex western politics for the following six years. Mackenzie had made his journey to the Pacific; Gray's discovery of the Columbia River had been reported, and American ships were on the northwest coast, but one of the principal worries of the nation's diplomatic corps was the expanding activities of the British in the Northwest and another, the future of Spain in Louisiana.

Considering Spain's declining fortunes, the obvious policy for the Americans was to let nature take its course. As long as there was no strong and militant power interested in replacing Spain as a western neighbor, there was no immediate threat to the nation's expansion or security.

The Louisiana Crisis

But Jefferson had hardly assumed office as president in 1801, when he learned that by the Treaty of Ildefonso, December, 1800, Spain had ceded Louisiana to France. He at once recognized this was a matter of momentous importance to the United States. With Napoleon directing policies, Louisiana could become the opening wedge for a French conquest of the New World. The tender issues of joint navigation of the Mississippi and of American rights of deposit at New Orleans could easily be the cause of war between the United States and her old ally. Jefferson argued that France and the United States could not continue friends "when they meet in so irritable a position," that France in North America would force the United States to "marry" the British fleet and become a maritime power, and that this change of friendships would necessarily embark the United States as a belligerent power in the next war in Europe.

Since that war was imminent, the Peace of Amiens providing merely a truce between France and England, it was necessary to try to relieve at least one element of the "irritable position" in which the United States now found itself. Jefferson suggested, through his minister in Paris, that Napoleon sell to the United States the island of New Orleans and a part if not both of the Floridas.[12]

That the anti-British Jefferson should have gone so far as to threaten an alliance with Britain and participation in European wars in order to protect American interests in the Mississippi Valley is evidence of the serious light in which he considered the Spanish cession and the consequences for his country. From the moment he had definite news of it (April, 1802) his administration was "making preparations to seize Louisiana as soon as the French and English started war. . . ." Reviewing the situation a year later he explained the temper of his close advisors and the Congress in these words:

> The exchange of a peaceable for a warring neighbor at New Orleans, was, undoubtedly, ground of just and great disquietude on our part; and the necessity of acquiring the country could not be unperceived by any. The question which divided the Legislature . . . was, whether we should take it at once, and enter singlehanded into war with the most powerful nation on the earth, or place things on the best footing practicable for the present, and avail ourselves of the first war in Europe, which it was clear was at no great distance, to obtain the country as the price of our neutrality, or as a reprisal for wrongs which we were sure enough to receive.[13]

His cabinet agreed that as soon as it was found no arrangement could be made with Napoleon, the government should enter into conference with the British government "to fix principles of alliance."

---

[12] Jefferson to Livingston, April 12, 1802, *State Papers and Correspondence Bearing Upon the Purchase of the Territory of Louisiana,* Washington, D. C., 1903, 16, 17; Jefferson's Writings; *Diplomatic Correspondence of the United States: Canadian Relations,* 1784-1860, W. R. Manning, ed., Washington, 1940; John Quincy Adams, *Parties in the United States,* New York, 1941; Mary P. Adams, "Jefferson's Reaction to the Treaty of San Ildefonso," *JSH,* XXI, May, 1955.

[13] Jefferson to William Dunbar, July 17, 1803, *Works,* Federal Ed., X, 20n.

A British alliance, however, was not a palatable idea for Jeffersonian Republicans, nor was Britain considered a disinterested party with respect to Louisiana. In September, 1801, when the Peace of Amiens was being made James Madison had cause to warn France that it was not in the interest of the United States "to favor any voluntary or compulsive transfer" of the region from Spain to Great Britain. In April, 1803, when war was once more renewed between England and France, the threat of British ambitions on the Mississippi loomed as large as Napoleon's. "The anxiety which Great Britain has shewn to extend her domain to the Mississippi, the uncertain extent of her claims, from North to South, beyond the Western limits of the United States, and the attention she has paid to the North West coast of America," warned Madison, "make it probable that she will connect with a war . . . a pretension to the acquisition of the country on the West side of the Mississippi. . . ."

It appears that Jefferson was more sanguine in his hopes of answering the French threat than he was of escaping a dangerous alliance with Great Britain. He had great hopes for the negotiation with Napoleon for the purchase of the island of New Orleans when war in Europe once again ended an uneasy peace. He and his advisors concluded the war gave them an interval of preparation for emergency. If negotiations failed, they must go it alone so long as they could. They debated whether they should take New Orleans directly, or "encourage a decl[aratio]n of independence and then enter into an Alliance" with the Louisianans.[14]

In the meantime, Jefferson had other plans afoot by which he might forestall British activities in the disturbed West, the equally significant long-range threat to American security. He set up a land and Indian policy designed for occupation and defense of the interior, garrisoned western posts and planned a military reconnaissance of the unknown Missouri region which was a part of the problem at issue.

In April, 1802, Jefferson had taken into his official family a private secretary whom he at the same time promoted to a captaincy in the army. It will be recalled that Meriwether Lewis had been an applicant for the 1793 project of the American Philosophical Society. Jefferson's acquaintance with him went back to Lewis' childhood days. Young

[14] *Anas*, May 7, 1803, *Works*, Federal Ed., I, 372.

Lewis shared with his friend a common party affiliation, an enduring interest in the West, and a mutual distrust of the British. It seems beyond coincidence that Jefferson should have chosen him his secretary at this particular moment if he were not contemplating a special purpose for which Lewis was eminently fitted. That special purpose was the western expedition.

Under the circumstances that prevailed between April, 1802, and June, 1803, and in the light of Jefferson's fear of British as well as French ambitions, this expedition can justifiably be considered a military reconnaissance among potential enemies. Long experience in frontier wars had taught Americans properly to appreciate Indians as allies—and Indians as allies of the enemy. Their friendship depended upon their trading relations, trading posts able to supply goods regularly, tactful flattery of influential chieftains, and the observance of certain elementary ideas of justice. The British had been very successful in their Indian relations and their influence was spreading into the Upper Missouri. It was to counteract this influence, to win over the Indians, and to conduct a military reconnaissance against a possible war that Jefferson originally projected the Lewis and Clark expedition.

Domestic politics, international diplomacy, and national interests forced Jefferson to devious means to explain his projected expedition. He had to make sure he would offend neither France, with whom delicate negotiations were pending, nor Spain, whose officials were still in control of Louisiana, resentful of the cession to France, and suspicious of everyone. In November, 1802, he asked the Spanish minister at Washington whether he thought his government "would take it badly" if Congress would send a group of travelers to explore the Missouri River. Jefferson explained that the expedition "would nominally have the objective of investigating everything which might contribute to the progress of commerce; but that in reality it would have no other view than the advancement of geography." This subterfuge was made necessary, he pointed out, because Congress had no power of voting appropriations for "a purely literary expedition." The Spanish minister, Yrujo, replied that such an expedition "could not fail to give umbrage" to his government.

Jefferson argued that he could see no reason for offense when the object would be "no other than to observe the territories . . . from the mouth of the Missouri to the Pacific Ocean," complete the discoveries made by Mackenzie in 1793, and "be sure if it were possible . . . to establish a continual communication, or little interrupted, by water as far as the South Sea." Yrujo's review of the fruitlessness of such attempts, appeared, he thought, to calm the President's spirit. And he characterized Jefferson in an interesting passage: "The President has been all his life a man of letters, very speculative and a lover of glory, and it would be possible he might attempt to perpetuate the fame of his administration not only by the measures of frugality and economy which characterize him, but also by discovering or attempting at least to discover the way by which the Americans may some day extend their population and their influence up to the coast of the South Sea." This discerning analysis of Jefferson caught the full implications of his interest in the West. It did not plumb his capacity for diplomatic double talk.[15]

On January 18, 1803, Jefferson presented "to the special Confidence" of the two houses of Congress a message asking an appropriation for an expedition. He explained that for reasons of state, the expedition must be known as a literary pursuit, and he surprisingly testified that in this light Spain would not be disposed to view it with jealousy, even if the "expiring state of its interests there would not render it a matter of indifference." He asked for an appropriation of 2,500 dollars under the innocuous heading, "for the purpose of extending the external commerce of the United States," which, he said, "while understood and considered by the executive as giving legislative sanction, would cover the undertaking from notice. . . ." Meanwhile, ". . . an intelligent officer, with ten or twelve chosen men . . . might explore the whole line, even to the western ocean; have conferences with the natives on the subject of commercial intercourse; get admission among them for our traders, as others are admitted; agree on convenient deposits for an interchange of articles; and return with the information acquired, in the course of two summers." Thus is explained an expedition secretly organized, military in personnel and supply, including no trained scientific observer, nor any experienced Indian trader, but equipped for winning friends and reconnoitering a strategic area.

[15] Yrujo to Cevallos, December 2, 1802, Nasatir, *Before Lewis and Clark*, II, 713.

Tlingit Shaman's Charm in the Shape of a Killer Whale. (Courtesy, Portland Art Museum.) Right top

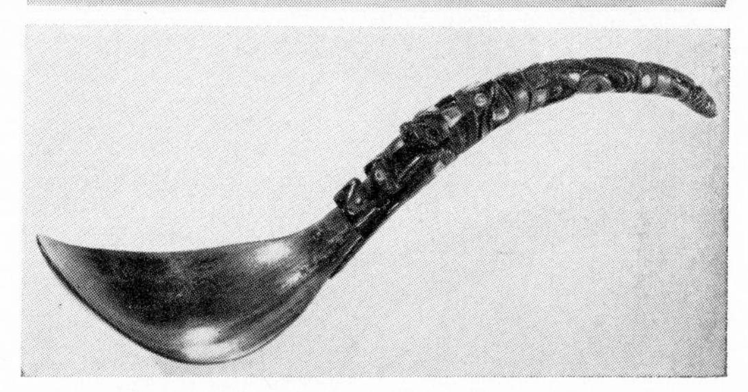

Spoon carved from the Horn of a Mountain Goat. (Courtesy, Portland Art Museum.) Right center

Painted Door Posts of a Tlingit House. (Courtesy, Portland Art Museum.) Below

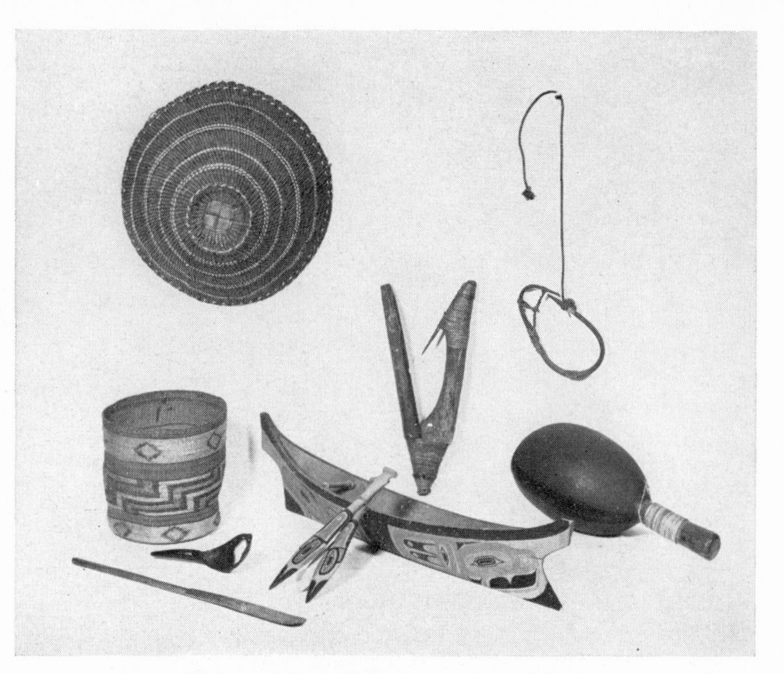

Articles Used by Northwest Indians: Rain Hat of Cedar Bark, Tlingit Basket, Spoons, Model Canoe and Paddles, Halibut Hooks, Rattle. (Courtesy, Washington State Museum.)

Ceremonial Cape of Cariboo Skin, Wolf and Eagle Design. (Courtesy, Washington State Museum.)

Dance Mask Worn by the Kwakiutl Indians. (Courtesy, Portland Art Museum.)

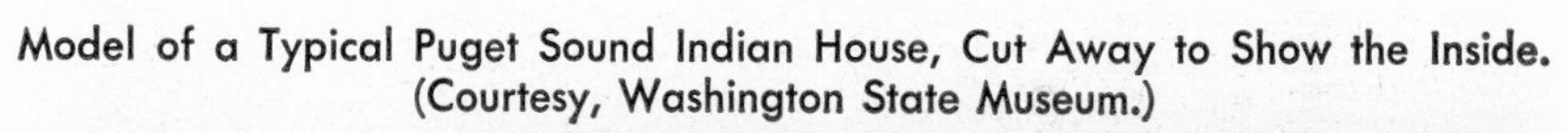

Model of a Typical Puget Sound Indian House, Cut Away to Show the Inside. (Courtesy, Washington State Museum.)

Tsimshian Painted Mask from Northern British Columbia. (Courtesy, Portland Art Museum.)

Haida Ornamental Pipe of Carved Slate. (Courtesy, Portland Art Museum.)

Indian Costumes and Basketry from Eastern Washington. (Courtesy, Washington State Museum.)

However, Jefferson was not one to miss an opportunity to accomplish, with economy, more than one objective at a time. He sent Meriwether Lewis to Philadelphia for coaching in various technical matters that would lead to its successful execution and contribute to the satisfaction of scientific interests. Dr. Benjamin Rush gave him a list of questions to guide him in studying the Indians, and advised him on rules of health for his expedition: to wear flannel next to the skin in wet weather, to wear shoes without heels and to wash the feet in the morning with cold water, and to rely upon "opening pills" for digestive troubles. Dr. Benjamin Barton helped him with botany and zoology; Robert Patterson and Andrew Ellicott with mathematics, astronomy, surveying, and map making.[16]

In the meantime encouraging dispatches were received from France: first, that Napoleon's minister had listened to an offer to buy the island of New Orleans, and second, the totally unexpected news that he had offered to sell the whole of Louisiana.

Jefferson was highly pleased—and relieved. For the sum of fifteen million dollars the United States had acquired a territory which included "all the waters of the Missouri and Mississippi . . . more than double the area of the United States," and a region "not inferior to the old in soil, climate, productions and communications." This was a goodly inheritance and, to be fully appreciated by the skeptics, should be explored and reported. Furthermore, one threat to national security and peace had been removed; but a potential one remained. The British traders, with their Union Jacks and King George medals, moved westward along the Missouri. The expedition, ready to leave, was not canceled.

Jefferson's instructions for the expedition were drawn up on June 20, when news of the purchase had been received but not yet "authentically known." They were changed only slightly later—to the effect that as sovereign of the territory, the government through its agents could propose direct terms under which commerce with the Indians could be instituted. The leaders were directed to inform themselves about the character of the country, its plants and animals, about its Indian population, their customs and trade, and about "the circum-

[16] Jefferson's Writings; *Letters of Benjamin Rush*, ed. by L. H. Butterfield, Princeton, 1951; Benjamin Rush, *Autobiography*, Princeton, 1948; Thwaites, ed., *Original Journals of Lewis and Clark*, VII.

stances which may decide whether the furs of those parts may not be collected as advantageously at the head of the Missouri (convenient, as is supposed to the waters of the Colorado & Oregon or Columbia) as at Nootka sound or any other point of that coast; & that trade be consequently conducted through the Missouri & the U.S. more beneficially than by the circumnavigation now practiced."

It is to be noted here that Jefferson envisioned a trade system that would avoid dependence upon British connections either at Nootka or within the continent; it would flow via the Missouri to the United States east and west by land. It did not, however, exclude a maritime trade, as the last six words of quotation would suggest on a superficial reading. The assumed convenience of the waters of the Columbia to the headwaters of the Missouri was an important factor in his consideration. Jefferson's ideas did not differ from those of Alexander Mackenzie with regard to the geography of a continental trade.

In the first part of July, Meriwether Lewis left for the Ohio where he met his coleader and old friend, Lieutenant William Clark. By early December they were at St. Louis where Captain Lewis presented his credentials to the Spanish officials.

On December 20, 1803, the ceremony of transfer was carried out and the fifteen-starred flag of the United States flew over Louisiana and "the heart of the continent." When the expedition got under way in May, 1804, it traveled from the mouth of the Missouri to the Rockies on American soil.

6

Americans and British Cross the Rockies

The success of the Lewis and Clark expedition, as of any such adventure, depended upon its leadership, and for this Jefferson had made wise choices. Twenty-nine-year-old Meriwether Lewis was a man of some education, he was intelligent, aware of and appreciative of the purposes of the expedition. "Whatever he should report would be as certain as if seen, by ourselves," Jefferson believed, and Lewis' journals supported the President's confidence. He rapidly mastered the arts essential to survival in the western plains and mountains. He shared all hazards with his men. His quick temper and demands for military conduct on the part of every member of the group led to the desertion of two boatmen at the Platte, but it had been his purpose to use the months from December, 1803, until May, 1804, and the early part of the journey, to train the men and to weed out the unfit. There seems to be no evidence to disprove Jefferson's conclusion that he was "careful as a father of those committed to his charge, yet steady in the maintenance of order and discipline."[1]

The coleader of the expedition, William Clark, 33 years old, was the son of a frontier family, and younger brother of George Rogers Clark, of Ohio Valley exploits. He was awkward with the pen, but expert with a gun, experienced in Indian warfare and the handling of *peroques* and canoes. Even-tempered and patient, Clark was unusually successful in negotiations with the Indians, who called him the "red-haired chief, our brother."

[1] The principal source for the Lewis and Clark expedition is of course the *Original Journals*, ed. R. G. Thwaites. Helpful to this part are the following: Annie H. Abel, "A New Lewis and Clark Map," *GR*, May, 1916; Aubrey Diller, "Maps of the Missouri River," in *Studies and Essays . . . in Homage to George Sarton*, ed. M. F. Ashley Montagu, New York, 1946; A. H. Abel, *Tabeau's Narrative*.

A common background helped these men to work well together and in harmony with Jefferson's instructions. Both were born and had lived a part of their lives as neighbors to Jefferson at Shadwell. Both were army men and had fought in the Ohio Valley Indian wars. Lewis had been a young officer under Clark for several years. Through a mix-up and army red tape, Clark did not get his captain's commission before the expedition left St. Louis, but this made no difference in the relation of the two men. He was Captain Clark to the party. Their leadership of the expedition was a joint enterprise and a careful reading of their journals reveals how in personalities and training they complemented one another.

It was a well-equipped expedition, carrying arms for defense and gifts for the Indians, tested means of winning friendships. The leaders were supplied with instruments for determining longitudes and latitudes and materials for preserving specimens of plant life. Efforts were made to give them helpful direction drawn from reliable sources. Before setting out they talked with St. Louis men who had traveled the river: Louis Labeaume, Hugh Haney, and Regis Loisel, who "gave us a good Deel of information." They carried Mackenzie's *Voyages*, and printed and rough maps embodying the latest reports of the region.

It was also a well-reported adventure, there being no less than seven journals kept, of which two have not yet been found. Lewis and Clark were meticulous in entering every detail, and their accounts, read together as they can be in the R. G. Thwaites edition, give a dimensional picture of the whole venture, and are a treasure house of information about the country and the Indians.

The expedition as it finally set out for the West consisted of 33 persons, including one Indian woman and her two-months-old child. Sacajawea was the Shoshone "wife" of the interpreter Toussaint Charbonneau who had purchased her from her captors, the Minnetarees. She was not a guide for the expedition, for the route it traveled was new to her also. But when the expedition reached her homeland and people on the Beaverhead River of Western Montana, her assurance of the peaceful purposes of the party won over her people to supply essential horses. Occasional references to her in the leaders' journals reveal a woman of adaptability and personality.

Brackenridge, writing in 1811, described her then as ". . . a good creature, of a mild and gentle disposition, greatly attached to the whites, whose manners and dress she tries to imitate."[2] Her child, Pompey, affectionately called Little Pomp in Clark's journal, is commemorated in the name Pompey's Pillar, a rocky outthrust on the upper Yellowstone River.

Charbonneau was enrolled as interpreter of the expedition, but turned out to be an almost useless person, unacquainted with the Indian languages after leaving his haunts among the Mandans and Crees and undependable as well. Captain Clark's personal servant, York, on the contrary, was useful as an object of marvel among the natives, who had never before seen a negro and who were amazed at his black skin, tremendous strength, and gay dances.

With the exception of these persons, the expedition was a detachment of the United States Army on special service. Eight volunteers from Kentucky and 16 soldiers were enrolled as privates, from whom the leaders chose three sergeants. A skilled game hunter, George Drouillard, and two "watermen," or *voyageurs*, also enrolled as privates, completed the party.

Special skills or talents distinguished various members' parts in the adventure. One liked to fish and his pleasure provided a supplement to the game diet. One was skilled in making clothes for the men. Two were gunsmiths and blacksmiths, and one of them a boatbuilder; several were cooks, two played the violin. All were experienced woodmen, and most had had experience in Indian wars.

Although Kentucky was the origin of the larger number, Pennsylvania was represented by almost as many. Several came from Virginia, New Hampshire, and Massachusetts, and one each from Indiana, Vermont, and Maryland. After their discharge upon completion of the journey, some returned to their homes, others settled in Missouri. George Shannon studied law and ran for the office of United States senator from that state, but was defeated. Sergeant Ordway acquired

[2] Henry M. Brackenridge, *Journal*, in *Early Western Travels*, VI, 32-33; for members of the expedition, etc., see Charles G. Clarke, "The Roster of the Expedition of Lewis and Clark," *OHQ*, XLV, December, 1944; Stella Drumm, "More About Astorians," *OHQ*, XXIV, December, 1923; John R. McBride, "Oregon in 1946," a chapter of reminiscences in typed copy at the Oregon Historical Society, which has a small item on Robert Frazier; Burton Harris, *John Colter: His Years in the Rockies*, New York, 1952.

property there; Robert Frazier, who had once been a dancing master, left no record of his later years, except in the memory of an Oregon pioneer who remembered Frazier as "a man advanced in years" who often visited his father's house in Missouri and related his adventures with the explorers' party forty years before.

Six of the men later joined fur trading expeditions to the mountains. John Colter was a guide for several parties that reached the headwaters of the Missouri, was the discoverer of Yellowstone Lake, and traversed the wonderland of geysers, springs, and the Teton Mountains. John Potts was back at the Three Forks in 1807 and was killed by the Blackfeet near there in 1810, as was the famous hunter, George Drouillard. Alexander Carson was on the Columbia again with the Astorians in 1811, and became a free trapper. He was killed by Indians near Lafayette, Oregon, in 1836, and Alec's Butte marks his place of death and burial.

From St. Charles, a village about 24 miles upriver from St. Louis, the expedition set out on May 21, 1804. A corporal with six soldiers for added protection against hostile Indians, and nine *voyageurs* to man a 55-foot-long keelboat and two *peroques* accompanied the party to the Mandan Villages, where they arrived late in October. *En route* they had held councils with the Indians at which they distributed gifts—flags and medals to chieftains—and announced a new Great Father to them. Sometimes the men of the expedition were paraded and the white men's "curiosities," their boats, air gun and whisky, for example, were displayed and sampled. Several times the situation was charged with hostility and warfare threatened. The Sioux put on a show for the explorers. As Clark described it: "We Smoked for an hour till Dark & all was Cleared away a large fire made in the Center, about 10 Musitions playing on tambereens . . . , long Sticks with Deer & Goats Hoofs tied so as to make a gingling noise, and many others . . . those Men began to Sing, & Beet on the Tamboren, the Women Came forward highly Deckerated in their Way, with Scalps and Tropies of War of their fathers Husbands Brother . . . & proceeded to Dance the War Dance . . . which they done with great Chearfullness until about 12 oClock. . . ."

Among the Mandans they set up winter quarters not only because it was late in the season, but because this was also a center of British traders' activities. The Indians were advised to accept no more British flags or medals, their principal chieftain was promised a trip to Washington when the party returned, and the prospects of new trading establishments and regular supplies were attractively presented. An interesting and revealing comment was written by one of several Nor'westers who visited the camp in the early winter: ". . . we became intimate with the Gentlemen of the American expedition; who on all occasions . . . treated us with civility and Kindness. It is true Captain Lewis could not make himself agreeable to us—he could speak fluently and learnedly on all subjects, but this inveterate disposition against the British stained, at least in our eyes, all his eloquence."[3]

In April, 1805, they again set out, using their boats as far as they could go on the Missouri's waters. Their route led them to the Three Forks of the Missouri, then up the Jefferson River branch to the Continental Divide. Lewis, traveling ahead of the main party, was following an Indian trail when he discovered that the valley through which he was passing turned "abruptly to the West through a narrow bottom between the mountains," and, says his journal entry for August 12, he "did not dispair of shortly finding a passage over the mountains and of taisting the waters of the great Columbia this evening."

Four miles further on

. . . the road took us to the most distant fountain of the waters of the Mighty Missouri in surch of which we have spent so many toilsome days and wristless nights. thus far I had accomplished one of those great objects on which my mind has been unalterably fixed for many years, judge then of the pleasure I felt in all[a]ying my thirst with this pure and ice-cold water which issues from the base of a low mountain or hill . . . the mountains are high on either hand leave this gap at the head of this rivulet through which the road passes. here I halted a few minutes and rested myself. two miles below McNeal had exultingly stood with a foot on each side of this little rivulet and thanked his god that he had lived to bestride the mighty & heretofore deemed endless missouri. after refreshing ourselves we proceeded on to the top of the dividing ridge from which I discovered immence ranges of high mountains still to the West of us with their tops partially covered with snow. I now descended the mountain about ¾ of a mile . . . to a handsome bold running Creek of cold Clear water. here I first tasted the water of the great Columbia river.

---

[3] Quoted in A. H. Abel, *Tabeau's Narrative*, 88 n.

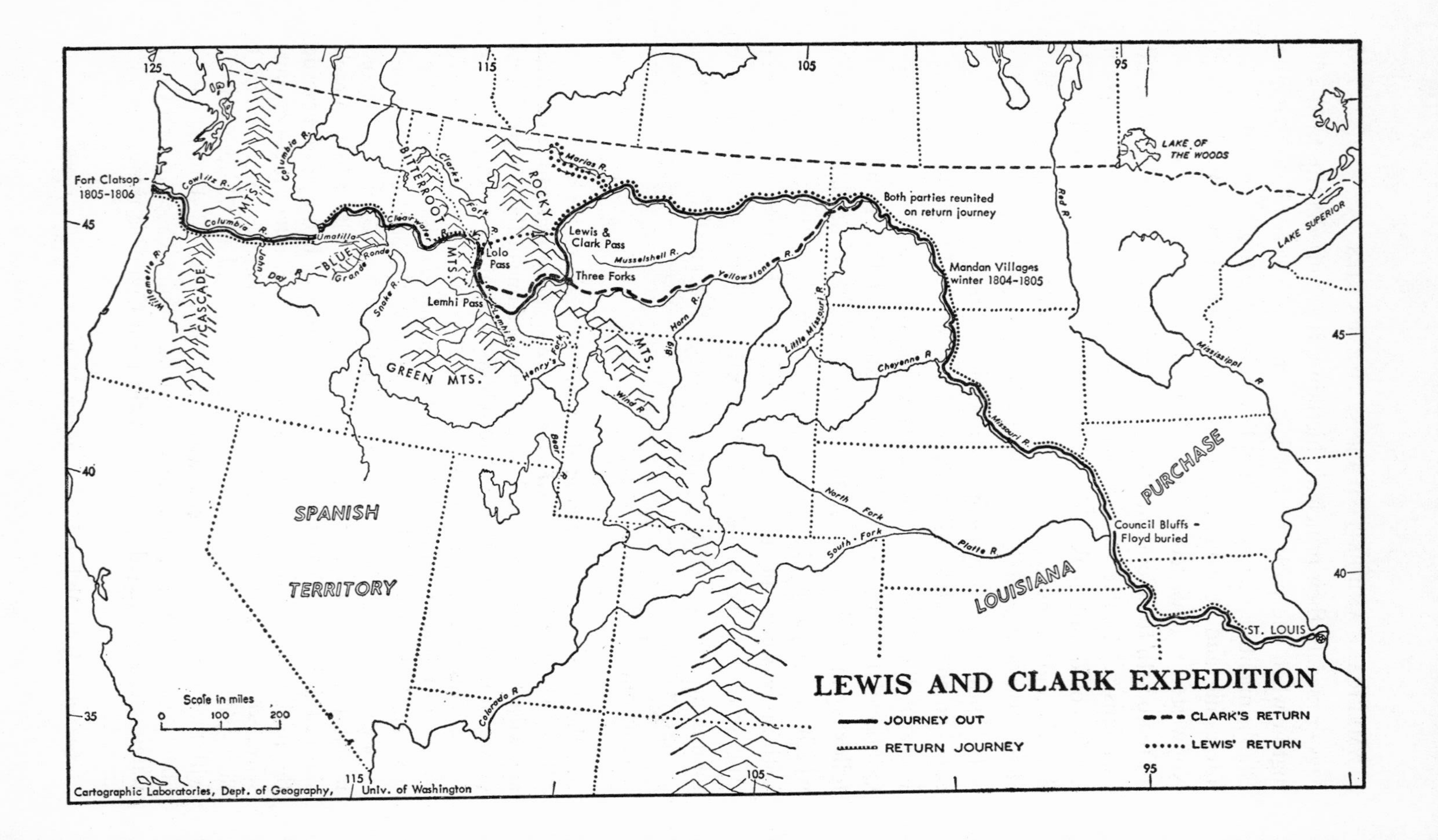
LEWIS AND CLARK EXPEDITION
JOURNEY OUT
RETURN JOURNEY
CLARK'S RETURN
LEWIS' RETURN
Fort Clatsop
1805-1806
Both parties reunited
on return journey
Mandan Villages
winter 1804-1805
Council Bluffs -
Floyd buried
ST. LOUIS
Lewis &
Clark Pass
Three Forks
Lolo
Pass
Lemhi Pass
LAKE OF
THE WOODS
LAKE SUPERIOR
PURCHASE
LOUISIANA
SPANISH
TERRITORY
ROCKY
MTS.
BITTERROOT
MTS.
GREEN MTS.
BLUE
CASCADE
MTS.
Cowlitz R.
Columbia R.
Willamette R.
John Day R.
Umatilla
Grande Ronde
Clearwater R.
Clarks Fork R.
Snake R.
Lemhi R.
Henry's Fork
Marias R.
Musselshell R.
Yellowstone R.
Big Horn R.
Wind R.
Little Missouri R.
Cheyenne R.
Missouri R.
North Fork
South Fork
Platte R.
Bear R.
Colorado R.
Red R.
Mississippi R.
Scale in miles
0 100 200
125
115
105
95
45
40
35
Cartographic Laboratories, Dept. of Geography, Univ. of Washington

Lewis had crossed the Divide by Lemhi Pass and the rivulet from which he drank was one of the streams that formed the Little Lemhi River but the Columbia lay beyond the snow-covered mountains he saw in the distance.

They proceeded north by horse through the Bitterroot Valley, following a Nez Perce Indian trail to Clark's Fork, and thence through Lolo Pass to the Clearwater. The trail was either stony and steep or crossed by fallen timber. Game was scarce and it began to snow. "I have been wet and as cold in every part as I ever was in my life," Clark wrote in his journal: "indeed I was at one time fearfull my feet would freeze in the thin Mockirsons which I wore."

When they reached the Nez Perce villages on the Clearwater they were given dried salmon and roots to eat. The men were already weakened by hunger and exhaustion and a violent dysentery followed the new diet, cured, however, with the help of Dr. Rush's "opening pills." With the help of the friendly natives they made dugout canoes and continued to the Columbia. On October 16 they entered the waters of that river, and two days later caught sight of a snow-covered conical peak which was Mount Hood. The next day they saw Mount Adams. A month later, after a pounding rainstorm lasting several days, they camped on the shore of the inner bay and from the high land north of it took their first view of the Pacific Ocean. According to Clark this western sea had been badly named; it "roars like a repeeted roling thunder and have rored in that way ever since our arrival . . . I can't say Pasific as since I have seen it, it has been the reverse."

Here, Lewis, Clark, and several of the men inscribed their names on a tree. Clark's legend read: "William Clark December 3rd 1805. By Land from U. States in 1804 & 1805." They then moved camp to the south side of the Columbia on the Lewis and Clark River, calling their primitive shelter of logs Fort Clatsop after the Indians of the vicinity.

Lewis and Clark at Fort Clatsop

Christmas was celebrated in the yet incomplete stockade; gifts were exchanged, salutes were fired, and the men shouted and sang. "We would have Spent this day . . . in feasting, had we any thing either to raise our Sperits or even gratify our appetites, our Diner concisted of pore Elk, so much Spoiled that we eate it thro' mear necessity, Some Spoiled pounded fish and a fiew roots," lamented Clark.

To make their monotonous diet palatable and to preserve food for their return journey, salt was needed. A detachment of men was sent to the coast (at the present site of Seaside), where they erected a camp and a rock cairn, and managed to evaporate some three quarts to a gallon of salt a day. A whale cast up on the shore south of Tillamook Head was worth reporting to Fort Clatsop, with the result a number of men were permitted to go with Clark to see it. Sacajawea, who had not yet even seen the ocean's waves, was in the party, although it would appear she had to argue for the privilege. "She observed that she had traveled a long way with us to see the great waters," wrote Lewis, "and that now that monstrous fish was also to be seen, she thought it very hard she could not be permitted to see either."

The excellent hunter, George Drouillard ("Drewyer" in Clark's spelling), was kept busy hunting elk, the only game animal they found in the vicinity of a day's travel. The hungry men consumed the fresh meat so fast the leaders were forced to have it jerked to conserve it. The hides were worked up into clothing and the fat into candles. Lewis and Clark worked over their notes and maps, talked with the Indians about the topography of the country and their lives and customs, and laid their plans for the return journey. There were the usual illnesses, winter colds, food poisonings, and petty accidents, and some infections avoidable only if the men stayed away from the native women.

The stormy weather continued through the winter. Clark, thoroughly disliking the wet coastal climate, counted only six days with sunshine from January until March 23, when they left Fort Clatsop. They had no regrets when they turned their quarters over to the friendly Chinook chieftain and started up the Columbia for the long trip home.

While at Fort Clatsop Clark had entered the note: "There is a large river which falls into the Columbia on its south side at what point we could not lern; which passes thro those extencive Columbian Plains from the South East. . . ." On April 1st they were camped on an island east of the mouth of that river, where the Indians gave them a sketch, drawn with a piece of charcoal on a woven mat, of the river they called the Multnomah. Clark and seven men, guided by a native who accepted a burning glass as pay, returned to the islands which hid the many-channeled entrance of the river. In the foggy dawn of the next morning he had got as far as the bend below Swan Island and "being perfectly satisfied of the size and magnitude of this great river which must water that vast tract of Country between the western range of mountains [Cascades] and those on the sea coast and as farr as the Waters of Callifornia," he returned to the Columbia and Captain Lewis. When the journals of the expedition were published in 1814, they carried a map showing the Multnomah's sources in the Rockies at about 37° north latitude. This error was not corrected until after 1830, when maps showed the Willamette River to be much more limited in length than early speculations had assumed.[4]

The Return Journey

By the end of June an uneventful trip had brought the explorers to Lolo Pass, the last divide through the Bitterroot Mountains. Here, according to plan, they separated. Lewis and nine men followed up the Lolo Canyon by a well-worn Indian road over the mountain pass which bears the explorers' joint names. From Lewis and Clark Pass, via the Sun River, they came to the Great Falls of the Missouri, where the year before they had left a cache of goods. Lewis and five men then cut across to the Marias River, which proved not to extend as far north as he "wished and expected." Although he believed that the watershed of the Marias was only a short distance from that of the Saskatchewan, he "lost all hope" of its extending to 50° north latitude. This is a significant reminder that the original purpose of the expedition had been influenced by English interests in the vicinity of that parallel and by Mackenzie's great plan for a transcontinental trade having the "entire command of the fur trade . . . from 48° North to the Pole."

---

[4] Clarence R. Allen, "The Myth of the Multnomah: The History of a Geographical Misconception," Frances Greenburg Armitage Essay, *Reed College Bulletin*, Vol. 27, June, 1949.

The only Indian trouble on the whole journey occurred in this vicinity, and evidently Lewis handled it badly. A small party of Piegans of the Blackfeet tribe attempted to steal their guns and horses. One Indian was stabbed and a second shot by Lewis who left an expedition medal around the neck of the dead man to inform the natives "who we were." The Piegans were already in trade with the North West Company's western posts and the incident was no doubt played up by the British to turn the Blackfeet Indians against the Americans. However, it would appear the Blackfeet were subsequently enemies of all white men and of any Indians who traded with them.

On July 28, Lewis met the rest of his party at the mouth of the Marias and in the white *peroque* in which they had traveled up the Missouri the previous year, made a rapid trip downstream to the mouth of the Yellowstone where they were to meet Clark.

Captain Clark and his party, in the meantime, had retraced their route from Lolo Pass up the Bitterroot Valley, crossed the Continental Divide at Gibbon's Pass, and on July 8 found their cache and dugouts on the Jefferson River. Within three days they were at the Three Forks. Here Clark divided his party. Ordway and some of the men now took the boats on to the Great Falls to join Lewis' party. Clark, Sacajawea, Little Pomp, Charbonneau and the rest traveled by horse across the Gallatin Valley to the Yellowstone River, which they reached on July 15. The trip down the Yellowstone, by dugout and bullboat in its lower stretches, was a pleasant one. There was plenty of game, the river was full and not obstructed, and the weather pleasant. In fact, there were so few hazards Clark assumed this was the route by which large *bateaux* could reach the mountains.

On August 12 they were reunited with Lewis and in a few days were at the Mandan Villages once again. It is fair to assume they let it be known among the friends of the British, Indians or traders, that their mission had been accomplished and that the Americans had reached the Pacific. As we shall see, the implications were that the northern and western boundaries of Louisiana had been defined by their exploration.

Before arriving at the Mandans John Colter was discharged and equipped to return to the mountains with two trappers who offered to share their traps with him. They spent the winter of 1806-1807 on the tributaries of the Upper Missouri, ranging the valleys of the Yellowstone and Big Horn. Thus Colter became the first guide into the Yellowstone country and a pioneer of the American fur industry in the Rockies. At the villages, Charbonneau was dismissed from the expedition's service and Little Pomp was promised a home with Captain Clark when he might be sent to them.

On September 23, 1806, accompanied by the principal chieftains of the Mandans, whom Lewis had promised a visit with President Jefferson, the expedition arrived at St. Louis. "We Suffered the party to fire off their pieces as a Salute to the Town," wrote Lewis. "We were met by all the village and received a harty welcom from it's inhabitants. . . . I sleped but little last night."

Reporting their return to Congress, Jefferson pointed out that the explorers deserved well of their country for their arduous service. Lewis was appointed governor and Clark superintendent of Indian affairs of Missouri Territory, rewards which carried more burdens than pleasures. Their names are indelibly fixed in American history and the highways that today follow portions of their trail are continual reminders of their exploit. It must be borne in mind, however, that they had predecessors in exploring the Missouri to the Yellowstone; that their field of original discovery lay farther west.[5] They did not trace a commercial route, for the Upper Missouri was not a practicable waterway, nor was the Columbia conveniently near its source. The Missouri legend died as a result of the explorers' struggles to navigate violent mountain streams and rivers that could not wait to flow gently to the sea. Their explorations confined to a limited area revealed no easy mountain passes.

There may have been white men in the upper Yellowstone before Clark, but from the Three Forks of the Missouri they traversed the mountains by routes strange even to their Indian guides. From this unknown West they reported plant, animal, and human life. They brought or sent back animal skins and Indian objects, some of which Jefferson displayed in his Indian Room at Monticello, and others were exhibited in Peale's American Museum in Philadelphia. Seeds and plants were consigned to a Philadelphia gardener for cultivation.

[5] Diller, "Maps of the Missouri River," 519.

Years later a flourishing snowberry, so common to the Northwest, moved Jefferson proudly to describe it as "singular as it is beautiful."

The completion of the journey without serious accident glossed over the genuine hardships it had entailed. The explorers had crossed the continent and that was enough. Popular versions of their trip stimulated an already high interest in the newly acquired Trans-Mississippi West, an interest which did not stop with Louisiana's boundary at the Rockies, but leaped them to contemplate the land where "roll'd the Oregon." The Lewis and Clark expedition was an instrument in the opening of the Pacific Northwest as well as a foundation for a future claim of the United States to the region.

American Traders Enter the Upper Missouri

The acquisition of Louisiana had opened a vast region formerly closed to American traders. The expedition of Lewis and Clark, the extended explorations of Zebulon Pike (1805-1807), and the minor one of Thomas Freeman on the Red River in 1806 not only laid open the geography of a large part of the West but began the converting of the natives from old alliances to new ones. This was to be a long and costly process, and ultimately a failure. The entering wedge made by Lewis and Clark was not followed up by skilled representatives of American official policy. It was many years before the Upper Missouri country was safe for their travel, and as late as 1831, General William Clark—then superintendent of Indian affairs at St. Louis—had to report the Indians still showed a preference for the English.

In spite of Indian hostilities, traders and trappers were not slow to enter the new country. Within the year after the return of the expedition, it was estimated that at St. Louis no less, and probably many more, than 100 traders were licensed to trade with the Indians of the Missouri country, and the number who did not bother with the legal requirements of the government of the new territory may have far exceeded those who did. Several large parties were reported to have left St. Louis early in the spring of 1807 for the Rockies.[6]

[6] William Clark to Secretary of War Dearborn, February 9, 1807, *Territorial Papers of the United States*, ed. C. E. Carter, Washington, D. C., 1949, XIV, 122.

The movement in this direction was stimulated by the report current in early 1807 that "a party of British Traders have passed over by land from the North" moving toward the same objective—the headwaters of the Missouri.

Nor'westers Move to the Rockies

The British traders were a party of Nor'westers. It was characteristic of the Montreal merchants who were partners in this enterprise that they kept abreast of all events in the world of commerce and diplomacy which might affect their interests. The partners in the field, the so-called wintering partners, were equally alert to what was happening in the vicinity of their trade. At annual rendezvous, either at Michilimackinac or later at Fort William on the western shore of Lake Superior, the field partners and Montreal partners met to settle their accounts, distribute outfits, make promotions, and determine policies. Here was shared information from the market place and Indian country, and on both fronts defense and attacks could be planned.

The company was well aware that the purchase of Louisiana would strengthen the American position in the Mississippi Valley and would lead to some vital readjustments of their policies in the Wisconsin country. These, in turn, affected their plans for the Far West and will be taken up in a subsequent chapter. It was realized that the Lewis and Clark expedition was a prelude to American expansion up the Missouri River and into the Far West, where already their trading ships were monopolizing the maritime commerce of the Pacific. Furthermore, the North West Company's rival, the Hudson's Bay Company, was strengthening its establishments on the Saskatchewan River, the alternative to the Missouri as a highway to the sea. From 1804 to 1812, the policies of the North West Company were directed toward holding the Canadian plains against the English company and in securing footholds in the Far West against any competitor's advance. In 1804, a bold move was made to establish the company in the Canadian Rockies.

Simon Fraser

Twenty-nine-year-old Simon Fraser was given the job of continuing Mackenzie's exploration and of establishing posts in Northern British Columbia to which, at that time, he gave the name of New Caledonia. Like a number of his associates, he was a native of the New World, of Scottish descent. His Tory family had fled from the American colonies at the time of the Revolution. He was not a man of learning; his journal, aptly described in his own words, was "ill-wrote, worse worded, and not well-spelt." He was apprenticed to the North West Company in 1792, and became a partner in 1801, evidence that he was a successful trader in spite of his youth. His fame as an explorer rests on his accomplishment in the Rockies.

In 1805 he was assigned the Far West mission. Following Mackenzie's route, he built Rocky Mountain Fort on the upper Peace River. Fort McLeod on McLeod Lake, Fort St. James on Stuart Lake, and Fort Fraser on Fraser Lake were established during the next two years. In 1808, with John Stuart, Jules Quesnell, 19 *voyageurs* and two Indian guides, he undertook the exploration of the length of the "mighty river"—the Tacoutche Tesse which Mackenzie had presumed to be the Columbia.

South of the confluence of the Quesnell River where Mackenzie had found passage impossible and had turned back, Fraser too was forced to abandon canoes. A grueling journey, most of it on foot and only occasionally by canoe, brought the party to the river's estuary, near the present site of New Westminster. Observations of their latitude disclosed the disappointing fact that the river they had explored was not the Columbia. Mackenzie's Tacoutche Tesse was then named the Fraser after the leader who had explored its perils.

While Fraser was traveling down his river, over the eastern ridges of mountains one of his fellow Nor'westers was wintering at the headwaters of the Columbia River. But he too was temporarily a victim of the mountain topography which confused men's understanding as it did the courses of the rivers, and he did not know that he had found the river of Fraser's hopes.

David Thompson

It was the requirements of the trade that brought David Thompson into the Northwest, but he is remembered today for his exploration of the Columbia River and for his skill as a geographer and map maker.

At the age of 14, with an elementary but thorough mathematical education behind him, the young Welshman entered the service of the Hudson's Bay Company in 1784 as an apprentice.[7] After 13 years in the employ of the company, mostly in the Athabaska and Saskatchewan countries, he went over to the more aggressive North West Company, also more appreciative of his technical training. His various assignments during the next ten years acquainted him with the plains country from the Missouri River to the Lesser Slave Lake region, and from Hudson's Bay to the Rockies. In 1804 he was made a partner, and in 1806 assigned the task of developing the trade west of the Rockies and south of the Peace River.

From his headquarters at Rocky Mountain House on the North Saskatchewan River on May 10, 1807, Thompson, accompanied by his wife and three small children, three men, and ten pack horses, set out for the mountains where he was to spend most of the next 12 years. On June 10 Thompson and his party were in the "stupendous a[nd] solitary Wilds covered with eternal Snow, a Mountain connected to Mountain by immense Glaciers, the collection of Ages a[nd] on which the Beams of the Sun makes hardly any Impression." Here he waited 14 days for the snows on the heights to melt. "The Weather was often very severe, cloathing all the Trees with Snow as in the Depth of Winter, a[nd] the Wind seldom less than a Storm we had no Thunder, very little Lightning, a[nd] that very mild; but in return the rushing of the Snows down the Sides of the Mountains equalled the Thunder in Sound, overturning everything less than solid Rock in its Course, sweeping Mountain Forests, whole acres at a Time from the very Roots, leaving not a Vestige behind; scarcely an Hour passed, without hearing one or more of these threatening Noises. . . ."[8]

On the 24th of June they crossed the heights and came to the welcome sight of a ravine "where the Springs send their Rills to the Pacific Ocean," and followed down the Blaeberry River, "a Torrent that seemingly nothing can resist," until on June 30 they came to a

[7] M. Catherine White, ed., *David Thompson's Journals Relating to Montana and Adjacent Regions, 1806-1812*, Missoula, 1950; *David Thompson's Narrative of His Explorations in Western America, 1784-1812*, ed. J. B. Tyrell, Toronto, 1916; Selections of David Thompson's journals, ed. T. C. Elliott, are found in *WHQ*, VII, VIII, IX, X, XI and XXIII; in *OHQ*, XV and XXVI.

[8] T. C. Elliott, ed., "The Discovery of the Source of the Columbia River," *OHQ*, XXVI, March, 1925, 29.

river where, "thank God, we camped all safe."

This was the Columbia River, though Thompson did not know it. Nor is this surprising when one examines a map of the region. It will be noted that the Columbia has its source in two lakes, the lovely large Windemere, and to the south of it, shallow reedy Columbia Lake. From these lakes, the Columbia flows north some 700 miles before it turns around the Selkirk Range to take up its long southwesterly course. Thompson was looking for a river which flowed to the south and west, not to the north. Hence he turned his attention as soon as possible to another river which he called both the Flat Bow and McGillivray's River. This river, which we know as the Kootenai, had its source in a canyon east and north of the Columbia's upper waters and not very far from the mouth of Blaeberry Creek. It flowed parallel to but in the opposite direction from the Columbia, coming within a few miles of the latter's source at Columbia Lake. It continued south and east into Northwestern Montana, then reversed its direction and flowed north to Kootenai Lake, joining the Columbia above the 49th parallel. Before the winter closed in, Thompson had explored the Columbia River to Columbia Lake, and the two-mile portage to the Kootenai River, and had he not been concerned with building quarters, trading with the Indians, and getting food supplies, he would have taken time to "explore at least the Flat Bow Country, a[nd] by the Course of the large River, determine whether it is the Columbia or not."

The winter was spent at Kootenai House, at the northern end of Lake Windemere and at the junction of Tobey Creek with the Columbia. Indians from far and near came to trade and to seek an alliance with the white men against their traditional enemies. From them Thompson had encouraging news about the river he wished to explore. ". . . After drawing a Chart of their Country . . . from thence to the Sea, a[nd] describing the Nations along the River, they assured me that from this House to the sea a[nd] back again was only the Voyage of a Summer Moon. . . ."

It was not, however, until early in 1811 that Thompson could embark on this Voyage of a Summer Moon. In the meantime, his work as a trader took precedence over his desire to carry out his explorations. Trade with the Indians took him through the vast wilderness of Northwestern Montana, Northern Idaho, and Northeastern Washington. At his direction, Finan McDonald built a temporary depot near Kootenai Falls in 1808. In September of the next year Thompson selected the site for Kullyspel House on the eastern shore of Lake Pend Oreille. Saleesh House, near Thompson Falls on the Clark Fork River, was built the same fall. In 1810 or 1811, Spokane House was built by McDonald and Jacques Finlay near the present city of Spokane.

In the course of these years of driving labor, Thompson also made three trips out of the country with packs of furs and back again with trading supplies. In 1808 he left Kootenai House early in June, arrived at Rainy Lake on August 2 and was back on the Columbia in October. The next year he descended the Saskatchewan to Fort Augustus, and returning, crossed by Howse Pass to the Columbia in 35 days. At the annual meeting of the partners in 1810 he was directed to return to the mountains and continue the exploration of the Columbia River.

It is unfortunate that we must leave David Thompson at the moment he was undertaking the trip that resulted in his traversing the Columbia from the sea to the river's source. But the circumstances under which the voyage was finally made are related to other contemporary events, and are part of another story. At this time, however, we can consider why in 1807 Thompson delayed his exploration of the Columbia. The reason was the advance of American competitors.

Competitors and Patriots

In August of his first winter on the Columbia River (1807), Thompson was informed by the Indians that "about 3 weeks ago the Americans to the number of 42 arrived to settle a military Post, at the confluence of the two most southern a[nd] considerable Branches of the Columbia a[nd] that they were preparing to make a small advance Post lower down on the River." Two of the men in this party, the Indians reported, had been with Lewis and Clark. "This establishment of the Americans will give a new Turn to our so long delayed settling of this Country, on which we have entered it seems too late," Thompson reported, "but, in my opinion the most valuable part of the Country still remains to us. . . ."

He learned that Flathead Indians who had been coming to trade with him "had pitched away" to the American camp. To meet his competitors it was necessary to win over the Indians and hold them with a regular supply of the kinds of goods they wanted, so they could not be coaxed away by occasional opposition. It is in this light that we understand Thompson's distress over the "difficulty of getting Goods from Fort des Prairies, a[nd] the still more formidable poverty of the Country in Animals"—that is, horses which could be used on the well-defined Indian trails to distribute trade supplies from post to post. The threat of competition explains Thompson's concentration upon the establishment of posts in the region and his delay in exploring the Columbia.

The identity of the Americans has been a puzzling matter. It is very probable that they were a party which had set out from St. Louis the previous spring when it was reported that British traders were *en route* to the headwaters of the Missouri. Only one of the several parties that set out at that time met the specific identifying features mentioned by Thompson: 42 men of whom two were of the Lewis and Clark expedition. Manuel Lisa of the Missouri Fur Company led such a group in which there were two and probably three former Lewis and Clark men. Colter had been discharged by the explorers at the Mandan villages to return to the mountains. As Lisa ascended the Missouri, he met Colter and prevailed upon him to make another trip. With the expert guidance of this man who was now making his third trip to the Yellowstone country, at least some of Lisa's party could have arrived at the mouth of that river early in July. From there, an open letter was addressed to "the Foreigners who may at present be carrying on a Traffic with the Indians within our Territories." The news of the American party and their communication was brought to Thompson by two Kootenais who had received it from a "more southerly Tribe."

Some of the contents of this paper were probably familar to him. Eight of its ten paragraphs were similar to instructions issued for foreign traders in the Upper Mississippi River country and dealt with the sale of liquor, use and distribution of foreign flags and medals, price codes, misdemeanors, and customs duties. The tenth paragraph, however, was specifically concerned with the Far West, and revealed a writer familiar with the politics of boundaries and possessed of a zealous expansionist attitude not yet shared by the American government.

> The new ceded Territories to the American States northward and westward of the Illinois, comprehend the Mississourie Red River and all the Lands westward to the Coast of California and the Columbia River with all its Branches; of which we have now taken Possession and on which we are now settled down to the Pacific ocean; extending northward to about 50 Degrees north Latitude, according to the Boundaries settled at the Treaty of Peace, between the united States and the Court of Great Britian, [sic] although it is by no means allowed here nor does any of our Expressions bear the Sense that, Great Britain has any special right to any of the Lands on the Pacific Ocean or to the Commerce of any of the Rivers that flow into the said Ocean, all of which we shall comprehend as within our said Territories until some further Explanation takes place on this head between the united States of America and the Court of St. James.[9]

This was dated July 10, 1807, from "Fort Lewis, Yellow River, Columbia," and was signed "James Roseman Lieutenant" and "Zachary Perch Captain & Commanding Officer." Thompson neither mentioned the missive in his journal, nor replied to it. He simply forwarded it with the narrative of his travels to date to Rocky Mountain House on September 23.

It was probably on December 24 that he received another letter addressed this time specifically to "the British Mercht. Trafficking with the Cabanaws [Kootenais]." It referred to the previous communication which the writer was informed had been delivered, but since no answer had been received, silence was construed as "a tacit disrespect," and, it was concluded, Thompson did not properly "acknowledge the authority of Congress over these Countries, which are certainly the property of the United States both by discovery and Cession." Thompson was then threatened with force and demanded to submit "with a good grace" before military posts were fortified and patrols sent out. This was dated September 29 from Poltito Palton Lake and was signed "Jeremy Pinch Lieut."

To this man whom he characterized as "one of these petty officers . . . [with] as much arrogance as Buonaparte at the head of his Invincibles," Thompson replied on December 26. Politely he confessed

---

[9] J. B. Tyrell, "Letter of Roseman and Perch, July 10th, 1807," *OHQ*, XXXVIII, December, 1937, 393-394.

himself "neither authorized nor competent" to discuss boundary issues and advised that customs matters would be considered by all the partners of the North West Company.[10]

The Mysterious Jeremy Pinch

Thompson's identification of his correspondents as of the military was only natural under the circumstances. However, research has failed to find any persons of these names in army records, nor was there any army post authorized on the Upper Missouri. It must be inferred then that the names Roseman, Perch, and Pinch disguised the authors of a hoax which depended upon military disguise for its authority. While we have no hope of contributing a final solution to the mystery of who was Jeremy Pinch, we do believe there are grounds sufficiently firm to support the identification of Thompson's correspondents as members of Lisa's party.

Several other perplexing questions arise from this incident: Where were the Americans when they addressed their messages to Thompson? What did they mean by "Yellow River, Columbia"? We have assumed the Yellow River to be the Yellowstone where in the fall of 1807 Lisa set up Fort Manuel. Where was Poltito Palton Lake? Flathead Lake has been suggested as a possible identification of the latter, but it seems less probable than Yellowstone, or Jackson Lake in the Tetons which Colter and Lisa's men explored. These questions become important only if one is concerned with "firsts"—such, for example, as when did American trappers first cross the Divide?

So far, it appears the answer to this question must lie in Lisa's activities between 1807-1810. His attempts to establish permanent

[10] T. C. Elliott, "The Strange Case of David Thompson and Jeremy Pinch," *OHQ*, XL, June, 1939, 191. The literature on this episode is as follows: Robert C. Clark, *History of the Willamette Valley*, Chicago, 1927, I:122-123, 839-840. Professor Clark was the discoverer of the Pinch letter in the Hudson's Bay Company archives. The Roseman-Perch letter of July 10, 1807, was found by J. B. Tyrrell, *OHQ*, XXXVIII, December, 1937, 391-397. Arguments on identities are found in T. C. Elliott, "The Strange Case of Thompson and Pinch," *OHQ*, XL:188-199, where the Pinch and Thompson letters are given; Jesse S. Douglas, "Jeremy Pinch and the War Department," *OHQ*, XXXIX, December, 1938, 425-431; W. J. Ghent, "Jeremy Pinch Again," *OHQ*, XL, December, 1939, 309-314; Frank E. Ross, "Early Fur Trade of the Great Northwest," *OHQ*, XXXIX, December, 1938, 396-401; J. Neilson Barry, "Lieutenant Jeremy Pinch," *OHQ*, XXXVIII, September, 1937, 323-337. A brief paragraph is also found in George W. Fuller, *History of the Pacific Northwest*, New York, 1931, 75-76; Charles H. Carey, *A General History of Oregon*, 2 vols., Portland, 1935, I:146-147.

trading posts at the mouths of the Yellowstone and Big Horn, and at the Three Forks of the Missouri had to be abandoned under vicious Blackfeet attacks. One of Manuel Lisa's partners, Andrew Henry, and a small party crossed over the Continental Divide from Three Forks, and in 1810 established a winter camp on the north fork of the Snake, in the vicinity of Elgin, Idaho. Although safe from hostile Indians, they were short of game, and in the spring the party broke up. Some returned to the Missouri but others remained in the mountains and became the first of that "reckless breed of men" whose short lives were spent and expended in trapping in the Rocky Mountain beaver grounds. Henry's Fort, like "Fort Lewis" and the camp at Poltito Palton, was only a winter encampment and its temporary nature foreshadowed the trend the American Rocky Mountain trade was eventually to follow.

The Thompson-Jeremy Pinch episode, following so close on the heels of the Lewis and Clark expedition, fulfilled Canadian anticipations of an American entry into the West. Uninformed of the incident, Sir Alexander Mackenzie in London in the spring of 1808 was seeking government support of a Columbia River settlement on the ground that the Lewis and Clark expedition would provide the Americans with arguments for exclusive claims to the country between Spanish settlements and 50° north latitude. The Pacific Northwest had now become part of the main stream of western fur trade politics and commercial rivalry which plagued American-British relations.

7

Nor'westers and Astorians

The nature of the fur trade, the exploitation of fur-bearing animals usually without regard for conservation and strenuous competition, demanded the continuous opening of new fields. This led inevitably to the West where the geography of of the central plains, both Canadian and American, made the principal river systems, the Missouri, Saskatchewan, and after 1811, the Athabaska, and the waters with which they connected by portages, highways of the trade's expansion. The Rockies were an obstacle but not a barrier to enterprises of continental dimensions, and by the end of the first decade of the nineteenth century, they were looking for outlets on the Pacific for their interior trade.

The North West Company initiated the beaver trade in the Pacific Northwest. Between 1807, the year of David Thompson's first coming, and 1821, its activities and its opposition comprise the principal chapter of the region's history. In its progress to the West it was challenged in the Saskatchewan and Athabaskan plains by the Hudson's Bay Company; but the latter made only one brief attempt to invade the Rockies. In the spring of 1810 Joseph Howse with a party of 17 crossed over the pass used by David Thompson, and following his trail to Flathead Lake, built a trading house in the vicinity of present Kalispell, Montana. Trade was good, but after leaving the country the following spring, he recommended no further expeditions into the region because of Indian troubles. Nevertheless, the Nor'westers interpreted Howse's venture as evidence of the Company's intention to expand into the Rockies. For this and other reasons they petitioned the Board of Trade and Privy Council to restrict the Hudson's Bay Company to its chartered lands and to grant them the exclusive trade of the British on the coast between the 42d and 50th parallels.[1]

[1] Davidson, *North West Company*, Chap. VI and Appendices K and L containing the petition of 1811 and the memorial of 1812.

The Canadian company had also had a threat of competition from "Jeremy Pinch," as we have seen, but its more serious threat lay in the plans of a trade rival with whom it had had a long experience in Wisconsin.

John Jacob Astor

John Jacob Astor was a man of outstanding entrepreneurial talent. In 1784 he had come to New York from London, an emigrant originally from Germany. Twenty years later he was the foremost fur dealer and one of the most successful merchants in New York. His career illustrates his capacity for large planning and patient execution, and his great dexterity in manipulating situations to serve his own interests. The "Old Man," "Old Cock," and "Old Tyger," as he was called by young and disrespectful employees, would never lose sight of them, as one who knew his techniques reported, "until some kind friend will put his . . . fingers over his eyelids."[2] The Louisiana territory whetted Astor's appetite for enlarging those interests.

The blueprint of his ambitions detailed a monopoly of the American fur industry from the Appalachians to the Pacific coast, a coastal trade, the supplying of Russian posts in Alaska, and a tie-in with his Canton-New York commerce. It called for the creation of regional companies which could eventually be welded into one. It required the elimination of competitors or coöperation with them, which ever would best serve his purpose.

[2] Robert Stuart to Ramsay Crooks, March 21, 1815, *Wisc. Hist. Coll.*, XIX, Madison, 1910, 369-371. The outstanding work on John Jacob Astor and the Astorians is Kenneth W. Porter's *John Jacob Astor*, Harvard Studies in Business History, 2 vols., Cambridge, 1931. In developing the interpretation presented here the following have been used: John Perry Pritchett, *The Red River Valley, 1811-1849: a Regional Study*, New Haven, 1942; Grace P. Morris, "Some Letters from 1792-1800 on the China Trade," *OHQ*, XLII, March, 1941; *Territorial Papers of the United States*, ed. Clarence E. Carter, Washington, D.C., 1942, Vol. XIV; Julius W. Pratt, "Fur Trade Strategy and the American Left Flank in the War of 1812," *AHR*, XL, January, 1936; *Wisc. Hist. Coll.*, XIX; Arthur S. Morton, "The North West Company's Columbian Enterprise and David Thompson," *CHR*, XVII, September, 1936; W. Stewart Wallace, ed., *Documents Relating to the North West Company*, Toronto, 1934; Washington Irving, *Astoria*, 2 vols., Philadelphia, 1836; *House Doc.* 45, 17th Cong., 2 Sess., 1823; Gabriel Franchère, "Narrative" in *Early Western Travels*, ed. R. G. Thwaites, Vol. VI; *The Discovery of the Oregon Trail*, ed. Philip A. Rollins, which contains Robert Stuart's Narrative and Wilson Price Hunt's Diary; Hiram H. Chittenden, *The American Fur Trade of the Far West*, 2 vols., New Work, 1935; T. C. Elliott, "Sale of Astoria, 1813," *OHQ*, XXXIII, March, 1932; Stella M. Drumm, "More About Some Astorians," *OHQ*, XXIV, December, 1923; Kenneth W. Porter, "Cruise of Astor's Brig Pedler," *OHQ*, XXXI, September, 1930; Alexander Ross, *Adventures*.

The American Fur Company was incorporated by Astor in 1808, but remained dormant until he had established himself openly or covertly through regional companies. To entrench himself in the Wisconsin area he had affiliated with independent American and some North West Company traders in 1807. In January, 1811, the South West Company emerged from this connection. In 1808 he announced his intention to enter the trade of the upper Missouri and west of the Rockies; two years later the Pacific Fur Company was formed for this purpose.

Astor had long since found it expedient to have friendly associations among the merchants of Montreal, especially those who were prominently a part of the North West Company. These amiable relations continued even when his traders and theirs were in vigorous competition in the field. Similar to the North West Company in name and organization, the South West Company was a combination of merchants, Canadian on the one hand, and John Jacob Astor on the other, who undertook to supply the trade and market the furs of their "partners in the field." Although Astor had a 50 percent interest in the South West Company, its management remained in the hands of the Canadian partners and was directed by them during the War of 1812 to win the war for England in the Old Northwest. Between the North West and South West companies there was also a firm agreement that the latter would not intrude in the trade of the upper Missouri or west of the Rockies. This did not prohibit Astor from forming a new company for this special purpose, nor did it prevent Northwesters, as individuals, merchants, or field men, from joining him.

In 1808 he had invited the North West Company to take a one-third interest in his Pacific Fur Company, but the partners in the field had rejected the offer. When this new company was taking shape in the spring of 1810, it was understood by one North West merchant that Astor was "to be conected with the N W Company to make settlements on the North West Coast of America, to communicate with the inland N W Trade."[3]

[3] Alexander Henry, Sr., to John Askin, February 26, 1810, *Wisc. Hist. Coll.*, XIX, 336-337.

Partners and Rivals

There were definite advantages in such a connection. Astor was financially able to risk a half million dollars, if needed, in western establishments; he had no threatening opposition in other areas of his trade; he had a fleet of vessels which could supply them and supplement the Indian trade with the provisioning of Russian posts and the exporting of their furs for them; he had free access to the China market. The North West Company, on the other hand, was engaged in a struggle for survival with the Hudson's Bay Company in the Canadian plains; it had no ships in western waters; and it was excluded from the China trade. However, it chose not to join Astor in 1810—at least in any formal agreement. It had one very practical advantage over Astor since it already had a foothold in the Rocky Mountain trade. It also had a persistent, although so far a relatively dim hope, that the British government would intervene on its behalf by erecting a military post on the Pacific coast. The United States, at this time under diverse pressures of a mounting war tension, was indifferent to the Northwest as a possible territorial acquisition. The Rockies were considered its natural western boundary, and if the transmontane area should be occupied by Americans, it was assumed, it would be the germ of a friendly but independent republic. The governments of Great Britain, however, had become in recent years more responsive to the demands of their mercantile constituencies, and in so far as the Northwest had commercial potentialities they could not afford to ignore Britain's claims to it. The Nor'westers used all evidence of American interest, slight as it was, to argue for state intervention. In November, 1810, Simon McGillivray, the company's London agent, learned of the departure the month before of Astor's sea expedition, and wrote Lord Liverpool, the Prime Minister:

> I have now to inform your Lordship that the American expedition to the Columbia River has actually sailed from New York, and consequently I fear it may almost be too late to accomplish the object which the North west Company had in view, if they could have obtained the Sanction of His Majesty's Government in sufficient time. That object was to establish Settlements on the Columbia River, and so to secure the right of Possession to Great Britain before the arrival of the Americans.

Still however this object might probably be accomplished and His Majesty's right to the Territorial possession of the Northwest Coast of America preserved, if one of His Majesty's Ships could immediately be dispatched to take formal possession of and establish a Fort or Settlement in the Country. The Ship [Astor's vessel] is to make a trading Voyage on her way along the Coast of South America, and His Majesty's Ship would probably get to the Columbia River before her. . . .

If the Plan which I have presumed to suggest should be adopted . . . the Northwest Compy would send an Expedition across the Continent to meet her, and to form trading Establishments under the protection of His Majesty's Fort; But unless they can obtain such protection, they cannot embark in their intended undertaking, and that Country and its Trade will be left to the possession of the Americans.[4]

Thus, the North West Company was gambling on the chance it would not have to carry on a long and expensive trade war with Astor in the Pacific Northwest. Yet it did not want to jeopardize its opportunities of a possible coöperation with Astor if, by chance, he should succeed and they should fail to get government help. Since Astor too was taking a large risk in going it alone, it was in keeping with the circumstances that both he and the North West Company should have arrived at a tacit agreement to keep their competition on a friendly basis—perhaps they even had agreed upon a division of spheres in the new Northwest as they had in the old. In the absence of any other explanation of the situation this hypothesis seems feasible. Two things must be remembered in attempting to interpret Astor: he hated to lose money, and he was not naïve even though he sometimes pretended to be.

The Pacific Fur Company

A tentative agreement was drawn up between Astor and three former Nor'westers, Alexander McKay, Donald McKenzie, and Duncan McDougall, to form the Pacific Fur Company in March, 1810. It is interesting that this agreement should have been made when the representatives of the two leading merchant firms of the North West Company were also in New York and were completing arrangements with Astor for organizing the South West

[4] Arthur S. Morton, "The North West Company's Columbia Enterprise and David Thompson," *CHR*, XVII, September, 1936, 310-311; see also W. Stewart Wallace, ed., *Documents Relating to the Northwest Company*, 239-245, 266-268.

Company. A firm agreement of June 23 brought in others and provided for a distribution of 100 shares of stock on the following basis: Astor retained 50 shares; 35 were assigned to his partners. Alexander McKay, Donald McKenzie, Duncan McDougall, David Stuart, Wilson Price Hunt, and Ramsay Crooks each received five shares. Robert McClellan and Joseph Miller each got two and a half shares, and David Stuart released to his nephew Robert two of his five shares. Fifteen shares were left undistributed at the time. But provision was made that when they were assigned, Astor was to have the power of nominating four of the five three-share partnerships. Astor assumed all risks for five years, and profits, if there were any, were to be prorated among the shareholders. He was also to have the management of the concern for the first five years and to be represented by an agent he would appoint. Annual meetings of the partners were to be held at the Columbia River establishment and absent members were to vote by proxy. If the business proved to be unprofitable the company could be dissolved by vote of the partners at any annual meeting.

The Astorians

Five of Astor's nine partners had only recently severed their connections with the North West Company. Alexander McKay, who had been a clerk with Alexander McKenzie on his expedition to the Pacific in 1793, had retired as a partner after a long service with the company. Donald McKenzie, a chronically discontented young clerk related to Sir Alexander, and with two brothers and several other relatives in the North West Company, resigned from its service in 1808. David Stuart was a cousin of John Stuart, partner in charge of the company's posts in Northern New Caledonia. His nephew Robert was relatively a newcomer to the trade. Of Duncan McDougall strangely little is known before his attachment to Astor's enterprise, and it is a matter of question what part he had played, if any, in the North West Company.

A sixth partner, Ramsay Crooks, was a Scottish-born Canadian and had been affiliated with Astor in the Wisconsin trade, as had been Robert McClellan and Joseph Miller, Americans and tough veterans of the Indian wars of Wisconsin. In 1807 these three men were trading out of St. Louis. Wilson Price Hunt of New Jersey was also a newcomer to St. Louis, where he had set up as a merchant.

There was an interesting balance of assignments among the partners. Hunt was appointed Astor's agent. Originally it was intended he would share command of the overland party with Donald McKenzie, but before the expedition left winter quarters on the Missouri River he receiver an order placing him in full command with McKenzie as second officer. For whatever reason the change was made, it was unfortunate, for McKenzie was both able and experienced. Duncan McDougall was in command of the sea expedition and was to be principal when Hunt was absent from the Columbia River post. Alexander McKay was in charge of trading along the coast.

There was nothing petty about Astor's plans for the company nor in its first outfitting. While one party was crossing by land to the sea and locating sites for future posts, a second party was dispatched by ship to carry supplies, establish a factory, trade along the coast, and send expeditions into the interior. The success of his plan depended in large measure upon observing a set time schedule and upon a harmony of talents and personalities.

The Sea Party

The *Tonquin* sailed from New York September 8, 1810, and almost immediately there was trouble between the Canadians and the ship's captain. While justified in insisting that he was master of the ship, Jonathan Thorn could hardly be excused for his attempts to discipline his pasengers, and for his ruthless disregard of his sailors' lives. Several times guns were drawn and mutiny was threatened. After a two-week stop at the Hawaiian Islands for fresh food supplies, the *Tonquin* arrived at the mouth of the Columbia on March 22, 1811. Thorn insisted upon entering the river in a heavy sea instead of lying offshore until the breakers calmed. He ordered his chief mate and four men, three of whom were *voyageurs* but not sailors, to sound the channel. The whale boat and its crew disappeared in the waves. Three other attempts were made, and three more men lost—a sacrifice of eight lives, owing as much to Thorn's unreasoning stubborness as to the hazards of the Columbia's mouth.

Thorn considered his responsibility ended when he deposited his cargo and passengers on the shore of Baker's Bay. McDougall, however, decided otherwise, and after a survey of the north and south shores, chose Point George on the south for the site of Fort Astoria, to which they moved on the 12th of April. Buildings were started, and in the first week of June, Thorn, accompanied by Alexander McKay and James Lewis, a clerk, left the river for summer trading along the northern coast. Because there was no place to store trading goods on land, the *Tonquin* carried in its hold the greater part of the year's supply. In August the Astorians heard from Indians rumors shortly after confirmed of the massacre of the men and the destruction of the ship. The actual details of what happened will never be known, but it would appear that at Nootka Sound Thorn antagonized the natives, who had a widespread reputation for treachery, and then did not take proper precautions to guard against them.

An appalling loss of life had been chalked up against the Astoria venture in its first six months, eight men in entering the Columbia, 27 at least with the *Tonquin*. The land party had no such serious loss, but they had other misfortunes. From the time they left St. Louis 18 months passed before Hunt arrived at Fort Astoria. Sixty-two men, one woman (the wife of Pierre Dorion), and two children left the Aricara villages on the Missouri July 18, 1811; there were desertions, replacements, and not all who started arrived at Astoria, but only two lives were lost in the course of the journey. Considering the conduct of the expedition and the sufferings its people endured, this was indeed remarkable.

Wilson P. Hunt and the Land Party

Hunt and McKenzie were in St. Louis early in September, 1810, "preparing to proceed up the Missouri and prosue my trail to the Columbia," reported General William Clark.[5] It was not until June 12, the following spring, that they reached the Aricara villages near Council Bluffs. Reports of Indian hostilities on the upper river led Hunt to abandon boats, purchase horses, and strike off across the plains. They left the villages on July 18.

Their route lay generally to the southwest, and for some days they traveled across prairies of knee-deep grass; they followed the Big

[5] To Secretary of War Eustice, September 12, 1810, *Territorial Papers*, XIV, 414.

Horn to the Wind River; traversed its beautiful valley where game was plentiful; and, by an Indian road, reached the Grand Teton Range. Somewhere in this vicinity they were joined by three trappers who had been with Andrew Henry the previous winter. With these men as guides they had no trouble crossing over Union Pass to the Green River where they "were surrounded by mountains in which were disclosed beautiful green valleys where numerous herds of bison graze. . . ."[6] Four trappers were left here to hunt and follow later with their catch to the Columbia.

Two weeks later, in a flurry of snow, they came to Andrew Henry's Fort on the north fork of the Snake, or as Hunt described it, "a tributary of the Columbia." This misinformation led them to hope they could take to canoes again. While the men cut willows and shaped them into canoes, Hunt sent out another party of trappers.

When the saddles were cached, the 77 horses entrusted to two Snake Indians, and the new-made canoes ready for the water, Joseph Miller decided to surrender his partnership and stay with the trappers. Washington Irving in his *Astoria* suggests Miller was dissatisfied with the enterprise. There is no hint of what the trouble might have been. So far there had been no extraordinary hardships for which Hunt could be blamed. That Miller chose to cast his lot with experienced mountain men indicates he did not have confidence in Hunt's leadership on the threshold of a strange and forbidding country.

In ten grueling days of portages, cordelling, and hazardous traveling, they made an amazing distance of some 360 miles. They had, however, lost several canoes and considerable goods. On the 28th a man was lost. The character of the river was intimated but not fully revealed to Hunt, when on the 29th of October he scouted the north bank. From the precipitous cliffs he noted the riverbed as "full of rapids and intersected by falls from ten to forty feet high." But Hunt, from his vantage, saw only the crests of these falls: Shoshone, 212 feet, and Twin Falls, 182 feet. At Caldron Linn they abandoned the river.

The season was advancing and they were still far from their destination. Their supplies were giving out, game was now scarce, and the few Indians they met were also short of food. The course they were forced to follow promised little relief. Donald McKenzie and five

[6] Hunt's diary in *The Discovery of the Oregon Trail,* Appendix A, 287.

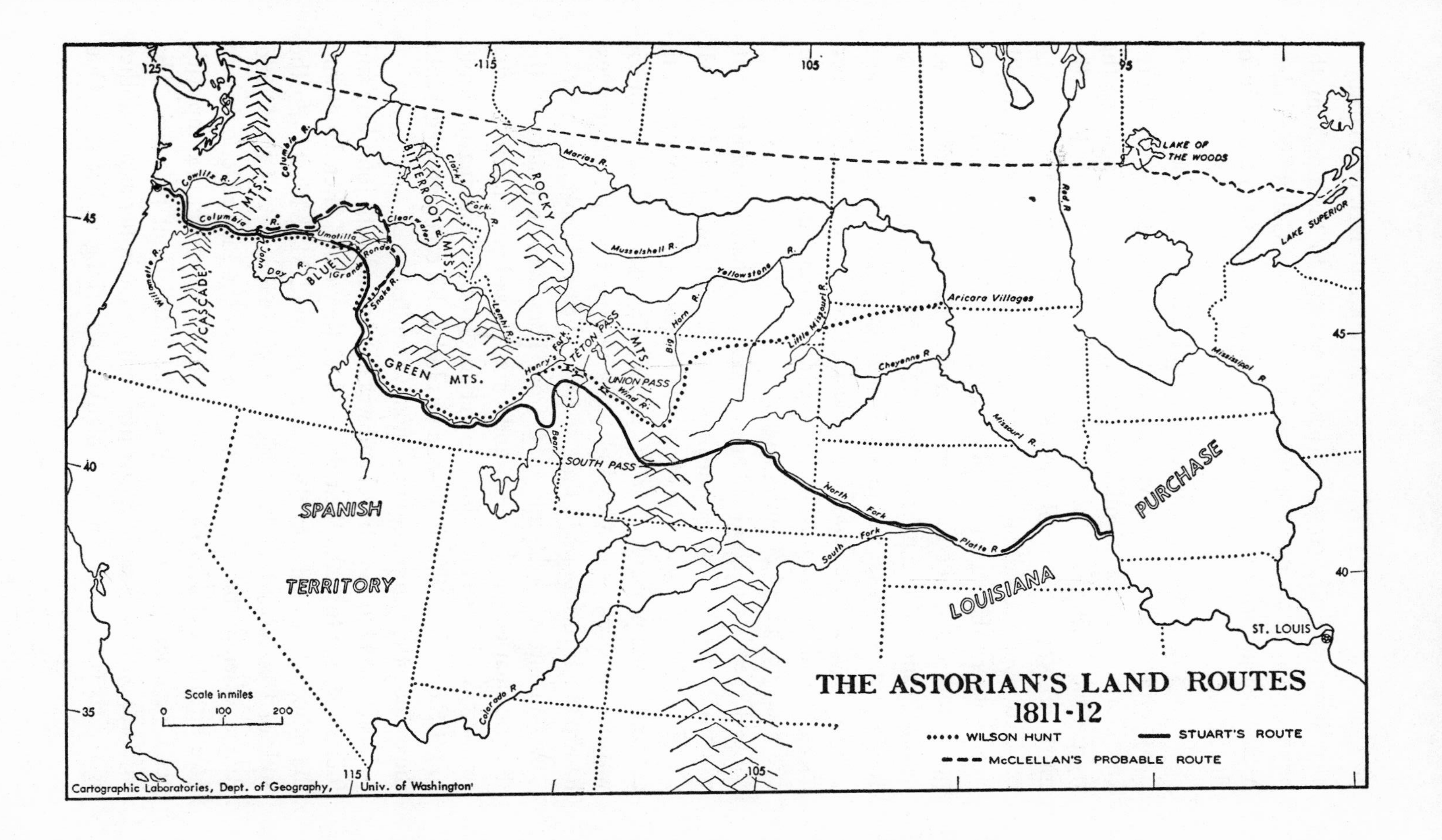
THE ASTORIAN'S LAND ROUTES
1811-12
WILSON HUNT
STUART'S ROUTE
McCLELLAN'S PROBABLE ROUTE
Scale in miles
0
100
200
LAKE OF THE WOODS
LAKE SUPERIOR
Red R.
Mississippi R.
Aricara Villages
Missouri R.
Cheyenne R.
Little Missouri R.
Yellowstone R.
Musselshell R.
Marias R.
Big Horn R.
ROCKY
MTS.
TETON PASS
UNION PASS
Wind R.
Henry's Fork
SOUTH PASS
Bear
North Fork
South Fork
Platte R.
PURCHASE
LOUISIANA
ST. LOUIS
Colorado R.
SPANISH
TERRITORY
GREEN
MTS.
Lemhi R.
Clark's Fork R.
BITTERROOT MTS.
Clearwater R.
Snake R.
Grande Ronde
BLUE
Umatilla
John Day R.
Columbia R.
Cowlitz R.
Willamette R.
CASCADE
MTS.
125
115
105
95
45
40
35
Cartographic Laboratories, Dept. of Geography, Univ. of Washington

men were sent off across the barren country to the north in the hope they might strike the main stream of the Columbia. Robert McClellan and three men were to push ahead along the canyon of the Snake.

Having cached their goods and distributed their paltry food supplies, the main party then was divided into two groups. Hunt with 19 men and Dorion's wife and children were to travel the left bank of the river; Crooks with the other 18 were to try the right bank. From the ninth of November until the sixth of December the two parties traveled along the sides of the canyon, parallel but out of touch with one another. Although their principal courses lay along the river, the precipitous cliffs shut them off from drinking water, except for occasional rain water caught in hollows of rocks. Hunt's party found Indian camps and he was able to trade for a few fish, a horse, and several dogs, but he had 20 people to feed. They pushed on persistently, making remarkable traveling time on foot in snow and rain, and averaging about 28 miles a day.

On December 6 Hunt's diary records: "we had just started out, when—What was my astonishment and distress!—I beheld Mr Crooks and his party on the other side of the river." The place of this encounter was probably near the present Homestead, Oregon. But it was not a happy one. Crooks's party was near starvation, and exhausted by futile efforts to traverse rocky cliffs and broken country.

A skin raft carried some food from Hunt's meager store to the starving men across the river, and Crooks was brought across. After two weeks of desperate effort to get food for the starving men and to get them across the river—one was lost in his eagerness to get into the canoe—the two parties were finally reunited.

Crooks was too ill to travel and was left behind with John Day and four *voyageurs* to make their way as best they could later. Hunt and the others struck off west from the "accursed Mad River." By the 30th of December they had reached the lovely valley of the Grand Ronde, where in the cold hours of the morning, Pierre Dorion's wife gave birth to a child. "Dorion, her husband, remained in camp with her for a day; then rejoined us on the 31st," Hunt recorded. "His wife was on horseback with her newborn infant in her arms; another aged two years, wrapped in a blanket, was slung at her side. One would have said, from her air, that nothing had happened to her." New Year's Day, 1812, was celebrated in the valley.

The following six days took them through the Blue Mountain range. Here the Dorion baby died. On the eighth of January they reached the Umatilla River and friendly prosperous natives. Almost a month later they arrived at Astoria, where Hunt found McKenzie, McClellan, and John Reed from whom he had separated at Caldron Linn and who had arrived at Astoria a month earlier. Crooks and John Day, destitute even of clothing, having suffered terrible experiences of want and abuse from the Indians, arrived May 11.

While the overland party was undergoing these miseries, those who had come by sea were having troubles of another kind. McDougall turned out to be a poor leader in a situation which required energy and firmness. Elementary provisions for health were ignored and little was done to guard the men against diseases carried by the Indian women. Attempts at discipline brought threats of mutiny. The loss of the *Tonquin* was more than a loss of human life. Thorn had carried away in its hold the greater part of their trading goods, and they had no means of seeking supplies elsewhere. Without trading goods their schedule for the interior trade was upset. Furthermore, they were afraid the attack upon the *Tonquin* was part of a general Indian uprising, and their fears were fed by repeated rumors of plots against them on the part of the Columbia River natives. Not until the early part of July (1811) was it considered safe to allow David Stuart and a small party to start up the river on a trading expedition. He had not yet started when the Astorians were surprised by a visit from their old associate, David Thompson.

David Thompson's Journey of a Summer Moon

Thompson was at last making his long anticipated Voyage of a Summer Moon. The partners, meeting at Fort William the summer before, without doubt knew all the details of Astor's project. This made an examination of the Columbia River and its mouth imperative in view of the company's gradually unfolding plan.

Returning to the mountains, Thompson was forced by the Indian situation to seek a new route through the Rockies. He crossed over them by the pass he discovered and named Athabaska. He reached the Columbia River at the mouth of Canoe River, ascended to the Columbia's headwaters, and following a route via the Kootenai, Clark Fork, and Pend Oreille, eventually arrived at Spokane House. From there he proceeded to the falls of the Columbia (Kettle Falls). Having constructed a large canoe, he set out with seven men, July 3, "by the Grace of God . . . on a voyage down the Columbia River to explore this river in order to open out a passage for the interior trade with the Pacific Ocean."[7]

The trip was made without trouble. On the ninth, at the junction of the Snake with the Columbia, Thompson erected a pole and attached to it a notice which read: "Know hereby that this country is claimed by Great Britain as part of its territories, and that the N. W. Company of Merchants from Canada, finding the factory for this people inconvenient for them, do hereby intend to erect a factory in this place for the commerce of the country around." The next day he learned of the arrival of the *Tonquin* four months before. This was, of course, no surprise to Thompson, but his appearance at Fort Astoria five days later was a surprise to the Astorians, who evidently did not expect so sudden a proof that their rivals were in the vicinity. However, he was received "in the most polite manner" by McDougall and the Stuarts.

After a week of rest during which he examined the river's entrance in company with his hosts, Thompson left the post for the voyage up the river. At the same time, David Stuart with eight men set out to establish a trading post "somewhere below the Falls of the Columbia." They erected a house at the confluence of the Okanogan and Colum-

---

[7] T. C. Elliott, ed., "Journal of David Thompson," *OHQ*, XV, March, 1914, 42-43. For the Nor'westers' part in the Astoria incident and for the story of Fort George the following provided materials: Wallace, *Documents Relating to the North West Company;* Kenneth W. Porter, "Jane Barnes, First White Woman in Oregon," *OHQ*, XXI, June, 1930; Mary W. Avery, "An Additional Chapter on Jane Barnes," *PNQ*, XLII, October, 1951; Peter Corney, *Early Voyages in the Northern Pacific* reprinted from the *London Literary Gazette* of 1821, Honolulu, 1896; Simpson's 1828 *Journey to the Columbia*, Hudson's Bay Series 10, Toronto, 1947; Katharine B. Judson, "Restoration of Astoria," *OHQ*, XX, December, 1919; W. T. Atkin, "Snake River Fur Trade, 1816-24," *OHQ*, XXXV, December, 1934; George Simpson's Journal, 1824-1825, in Frederick Merk, *Fur Trade and Empire*, Cambridge, 1931; Alexander Ross, *Adventures on the Columbia.*

bia. It is interesting to conjecture how the Astorians decided on this locality, since none of their party had been there. In fact, David Thompson alone knew the course and features of the upper river. They traveled together past the Cascades and Celilo Falls where the Indians were especially treacherous. Thompson pushed on ahead, arriving at Spokane House on August 11. He then returned to Kettle Falls and thence by canoe traversed the Arrow Lakes, and the upper river to Canoe River and Athabaska Pass, where he met the supply brigade. After wintering at Flathead House he returned to Fort William the following spring and a much deserved rotation rest year.

Outpost of a War Front

On his last trip on the Columbia's waters, Thompson had traveled its full course from its mouth to the source he had discovered four years before. He is primarily remembered as its explorer. But contrary to the long accepted notion, Thompson had not made his voyage as a race against the anticipated arrival of the Astorians. He was examining its course and entrance to determine its feasibility as a highway and outlet for the company's interior trade. Whether this was to be in coöperation with Astor or in opposition was decided finally in the spring of 1812. War was declared in June of that year. Thompson was at Fort William for the July meeting of the North West Company partners. His report on the situation of the Astorians no doubt encouraged them to believe they would have no serious opposition. Donald McTavish was ordered to England to arrange a ship and convoy and thence to proceed to the Columbia River as soon as possible. John Stuart was appointed to take charge of New Caledonia, and ordered to "combine his Plans & operations with the Gentlemen on the Columbia, [and] . . . to proceed next Spring as early as possible down to the Sea, there to form a junction with Mr J[ohn] G McTavish and meet the Ship intended to come to the Columbia."[8]

Since Thompson had seen them, the Astorians had experienced new hope and new despair. Their spirits were raised when Hunt and members of his party finally straggled in during the early spring of 1812. Several months later, the *Beaver* arrived with trading goods and

[8] Wallace, *Documents*, 271-272.

additional personnel. Among these were several relatives of Astor's, one of whom, John Clarke, until 1810 a Nor'wester, was a new partner. They were encouraged too by returns from Stuart's expedition. He had left Alexander Ross in charge of the post at Okanogan and had gone north to the Thompson River where he set up a post then called after the river, but later known as Kamloops. When he returned to Astoria in the spring of 1812, he brought evidence of the northern interior's rich possibilities.

The partners decided that Hunt should go about the Company's business with the Russian posts; that Donald McKenzie and newly-arrived John Clarke would move into the interior, Clarke to establish a trading post near the North West's Spokane House and McKenzie to winter on the Snake River. Robert Stuart was to carry reports to Astor overland.

In spite of this burst of energetic planning it would appear that at least two of the partners decided it was a hopeless situation. Ramsay Crooks and Robert McClellan gave up their partnerships and returned with Stuart to St. Louis, even though it involved a journey they had barely survived a few months before. They left Astoria June 29, 1812.

Stuart and his party chose to avoid the upper Snake. They moved up the Green River and thence through the South Pass to the North Platte River, the route subsequently followed by mountain men and immigrant settlers. Stuart's party was the first of record to use the Pass, although it is very possible it had been discovered and perhaps used by Andrew Henry or his trappers a year or two earlier. They reached St. Louis the end of April (1813).

Astor probably was not satisfied with news from Astoria, ten months old. He had cause to worry, for he had sent no supply ship since the *Beaver*, albeit he had tried cautiously, both in New York and London. He had news that the *Beaver* had arrived at Canton. It would be several years before it left again. In the meantime, Astoria would be unsupplied. A cryptic note from Astor to Crooks (November 1, 1813) suggests much but reveals little: "I request you again give no information whatsoever to any person as to our Columbia River buisness [sic]."[9]

[9] *Wisc. Hist. Coll.*, XIX, 348.

Hunt had left Astoria in the *Beaver* in August, 1812, and delivered an assignment of 56,500 dollars' worth of goods for which the Russians had contracted with Astor, and for which he was paid in furs to be sold in China. Instead of returning to the Columbia to pick up the fur packs there as Astor had directed, he proceeded directly to the Hawaiian Islands for needed repairs to the ship and then sent it on to Canton to take advantage of a favorable season in the market. This was a serious mistake. Hunt waited at the Islands for the anticipated arrival of the 1813 supply ship, and finally had to purchase a vessel to return to Astoria.

News of the war reached the Astorians through Nor'wester John G. McTavish, who also told the Astorians at Spokane House that he was *en route* to the mouth of the Columbia to meet Donald McTavish, who was shortly to arrive in the *Isaac Todd* from England. Thus well supplied, the Nor'westers would then show the Astorians what competition could be. McKenzie carried this unhappy news to Astoria in January, 1813.

McDougall and McKenzie agreed their situation was hopeless and that they would have to abandon the enterprise unless their supply ship arrived before the beginning of the next summer. McKenzie returned to the interior to inform Clarke and David Stuart and to collect horses and supplies for transportation out of the country. While he was gone, John McTavish and his party of Nor'westers appeared at Astoria to meet their expected ship. They remained until July and were present when McKenzie, Clarke, David Stuart, and the clerks who had been at a temporary post on the Willamette came down with their furs, but without provisions or horses to carry them away.

The Sale of Fort Astoria

With considerable unanimity, evidently, the partners agreed to make a deal with McTavish, who, embarrassed by the failure of his ship to arrive, was in a position to do nothing else. They agreed to divide their winter's trade, and the Astorians would postpone their departure until the following spring. They also did what their partnership agreement with Astor gave them power to do —dissolved the company. They explained:

The Ship Beaver was to have returned at the end of two months. Eleven months are now elapsed since she set sail. We have had no tidings of her since, and we have every reason to conclude that she must have either perished or taken her final departure from the coast. Another vessel was to have sailed about the usual time for our support, but after every due allowance, we need no longer expect her. We are now destitute of the necessary supplies to carry on the Trade, and we have no hopes of receiving more. We are yet entirely ignorant of the coast, on which we always had great dependence. The interior parts of the country turn out far short of our expectations. Its yearly produce in furs is very far from being equal to the expences the trade incurs, much less will it be able to recover the losses already sustained, or stand against a powerful opposition and support itself. In fine, circumstances are against us on every hand, and nothing operates to lead us into a conclusion that we can succeed.[10]

The company having been dissolved, their task was to salvage as much as possible of the investment.

When Wilson Hunt arrived at Astoria on August 20, he was surprised to learn of the partners' decision but agreed to it. He then left by the ship which had brought him to return to the Islands and charter another vessel to carry off the Astorians and their stock the following spring.

Early in October McTavish and the Nor'westers were back at Astoria again. They brought word that the *Isaac Todd* had sailed from England in March, and they advised the Astorians that she was "accompanied by a Frigate to take and destroy every thing that is American on the N. W. Coast."[11]

This put the Astorians in a new predicament. Their company had been dissolved; what remained of it was a stock of furs and a limited stock of trading goods. There would not be even this if the post were captured. So on the 16th of October, 1813, Duncan McDougall, on behalf of himself and his associates Donald McKenzie, David Stuart, and John Clarke, agreed to sell to the Nor'westers "the whole of their Establishments Furs and present Stock on hands [sic] on the Columbia and Thompson Rivers."[12] No prices had been agreed upon when, at the end of November, a British ship finally arrived at the Columbia. This was not the long-expected North West supply ship,

[10] T. C. Elliott, "Sale of Astoria, 1813," *OHQ*, XXXIII, March, 1932, 45.
[11] Porter, *Astor*, I, 217.
[12] Elliott, "Sale of Astoria, 1813," *OHQ*, XXXIII. 48.

the *Isaac Todd,* but the naval sloop *Racoon,* carrying partner John McDonald, and fulfilling, according to McDonald's testimony, "a duty to the North West Company." This duty was performed when Captain Black took possession of the country and the fort, which he renamed Fort George, and which he left in "possession and charge" of the North West Company, who already possessed its stock and furs. Taking possession was, under the circumstances, an act of war, which later brought Fort Astoria into the peace negotiations that concluded the war.

Hunt arrived in February in the *Pedler* which he had purchased in the Islands. The month of March was spent in settling details of the sale. Disputes over inventories and prices were so bitter as to bring the participants close to fighting. But terms were finally agreed upon and arrangements made for the personnel. On April 3, the North West brigade set out for Montreal, according to agreement taking with them those former members of the Astoria enterprise who asked to return. Alexander Ross, Ross Cox, and Duncan McDougall, several of the *voyageurs,* and two clerks chose to stay in Oregon as employees of the North West Company.

Hunt and three of the clerks, one of whom was Russell Farnham, proceeded to Sitka, Alaska. There Farnham was transferred to Astor's vessel, the *Forester,* which had not dared to enter the Columbia when its captain learned of the fort's "seizure" by the *Racoon.* He was taken to the coast of Kamchatka, and from there made his way across Siberia to St. Petersburg and Copenhagen, and eventually, in 1816 or 1817, he arrived back in New York. Farnham's long journey was for the purpose, it is presumed, of carrying to Europe two bills of exchange, representing some 40,000 dollars of the purchase price the Nor'westers had paid for Astor's furs, which presented in Europe or England had the advantage of a more favorable exchange.

Hunt made at least one voyage between Alaska, California, and China, and in 1816 arrived in New York with a cargo of China goods. The profits of this voyage and the proceeds of Farnham's bills of exchange over and above other settlements for wages and goods were Astor's returns from his investment. But what that was is difficult to say. Astor figured his loss as close to 200,000 dollars. He based this figure on the "true" worth of the furs which was two and a half times as much as he received for them from the North West Company; he figured he received for the goods sold them only one-third of their value. The North West Company made "no material objection" to the terms on which Astor had been bought out, the competition removed, and their posts supplied, but the partners in their annual meeting did note that by the manner in which the bills of credit had been drawn, the company had lost at least 3,000 pounds "owing to the rate of exchange between Canada & England."[13]

Astor blamed the war for his loss of Astoria, and in time encouraged the idea that he had been sold out by disloyal partners. The latter was not true. His post was improperly supplied and mismanaged. The sale made the best of a bad situation. He had taken a large risk in choosing to compete with the Nor'westers when war was imminent. Had the *Isaac Todd* arrived when expected with supplies for the North West Company's post, they probably could have forced him out of the field with even less salvage; its failure to arrive actually strengthened the bargaining power of the Astorians.

It may be consoling to those who believe Astor's venture was a patriotic one sacrificed in the war, to know that he, personally, suffered very little. The Treaty of Ghent reversed the decisions of the battlefield in the old Northwest and in the upper Missouri. Astor's American Fur Company took over the fur trade not only of this region, but of the Mississippi Valley, and eventually the Rockies as well. The war years also had other compensations for Astor. Through his loyal support of the United States in the purchase of government securities he made close to 2,000,000 dollars, and in his speculations in English pounds sterling, he managed to do very well for himself.

That Astor was disappointed, even angered, by the failure of his company was natural. It would appear, however, that his anger was directed at the North West Company for the low prices paid for his stock. ". . . while I breath[e] & so long as I have a dollar to spend I'll pursue a course to have our injuries repair'd & when I am no more I hope you'll act in my place; we have been sold, but I do not dispair [sic]," he wrote Donald McKenzie in 1814.[14] There seems to be no

[13] Stella M. Drumm, "More about Some of Astorians," *OHQ*, XXIV, December, 1923, 340; Wallace, *Documents*, 282; Kenneth W. Porter, "Cruise of Astor's Brig Pedler," *OHQ*, XXXI, September, 1930.

[14] Porter, *Astor*, I, 239.

evidence that he blamed any of his associates for what had happened, although he rapidly cooled off in his relations with McKenzie.

Hunt, Robert Stuart, Crooks, and several of the clerks were employed in highly responsible positions in Astor's American Fur Company. Astor abandoned any further effort to enter the trade on the coast, but by 1836 he had achieved the monopoly of the American mountains and plains which he had wanted. He continued his friendly relations with the Canadians, whom, through his large influence, he helped to circumvent the laws of the United States.[15]

Fort Astoria Becomes Fort George

After the summer of 1813, the North West Company had no further competition in the Pacific Northwest. Indian hostilities and the war kept Americans out of the upper Missouri and Rocky Mountains which the Americans did not again cross until 1823. The Nor'westers had unwittingly accomplished Alexander MacKenzie's plan for the fur trade, in so far as they had a chain of posts from Montreal to the Columbia's mouth, and a post on the Pacific. For the next ten years Fort Astoria, now Fort George, was the principal depot of their westernmost department. It was connected with Fort William by an annual overland express, and its supplies were brought in and its furs exported via the Pacific.

The annual supply ships reached the Columbia in the spring of the year. The first to arrive was the long-anticipated *Isaac Todd* whose delay had been a great factor in the sale of the Astoria enterprise. With it came Donald McTavish, chief officer or governor of the company's posts west of the Rockies, as well as trade supplies and luxuries for the governor, including a lively barmaid from Portsmouth. The presence of Jane Barnes added no romantic touch to Fort George's social life, rather it complicated the internal affairs of the colony and created troubles with the Indians. Shortly after their arrival, McTavish was drowned and Jane was shipped back to England via Canton.

The supply of Fort George was but one angle of the triangular trade of England, the Northwest coast and the Orient which the North West Company had wished to develop. But British trade in the

[15] See *Wisc. Hist. Coll.*, XIX, 423-424; *American State Papers*, Class II, Vol. 2, 359.

Orient was still monopolized by the East India Company, which refused to allow the North West Company's ships to carry Chinese goods to England. Without this it was unprofitable to supply the Northwest coast from England. In 1815 the company contracted with Boston merchants to supply them and to sell their products in China.

Economy was not a watchword in the administration of the district. The posts were overstaffed for the kind of trade that was carried on. One estimate placed the number of men in the trade on the Pacific slope, which included the New Caledonia posts, at 300. At least 66 men were stationed at Fort George where, according to one observer, they were employed in cutting down the forest and improving the fort. A critic of the Company's practices described the fort in 1824 as "a large pile of buildings covering about an acre of ground . . . [with] an appearance of grandeur & consequence which does not become and is not at all suitable to an Indian Trading post." It was located on a rise of ground overlooking the crescent-shaped shoreline of a small bay where ships could land. According to Alexander Ross, one could see to the west ". . . the breakers on the bar, rolling in wild confusion . . . on the east the country . . . had a wild and varied aspect, while towards the south the impervious and magnificent forest darkened the landscape as far as the eye could reach."

The fort differed only in its size from hundreds of others to be built in the West. It was a square of 200 yards surrounded by a 15-foot palisade of timbers driven into the ground. At the southwest and northeast corners were bastions, or towers, mounted with four- and six-pounders, and a sentry platform topped the large double gate facing the river. Since the natives were peaceful, no close guard was kept, but the Indians were always expelled at night and the gates closed.

Within was a two-story building, the governor's house, and in front of it, two long 18-pound cannon directed toward the gate. Around the inner walls were shops and living quarters, granary, and other buildings that housed the businesses of the post. Outside the wall there was a garden that men struggled to keep from reverting to underbrush, and some neglected livestock.

Below the fort was a sturdy wharf with a loading crane. From this wharf set out the dugouts and canoes that carried men and trading goods to the interior posts—to Fort Okanogan, to Spokane House, Kamloops, or Fort Thompson, Kootenay House, Fort Alexander, and Fort Nez Perce (Walla Walla), and from here also departed the trading and trapping expeditions into the Snake River country.

Donald McKenzie

James Keith, senior partner, was in charge of the fort in 1816 when Donald McKenzie returned to the Columbia to take charge of the interior trade. McKenzie's talents had not been fully used or appreciated when he was an Astorian; Keith distrusted him. It took orders from Fort William to make it possible for him to carry out the Snake country expeditions. He proved to be one of the company's most successful traders and explorers, making three expeditions in four years. A man of huge stature, weighing over 300 pounds, but tireless and fearless and a skilled rifleman able to "drive a dozen balls consecutively at one hundred paces through a Spanish dollar," he was feared and respected by the natives, whom he treated fairly.

In 1818 he built Fort Nez Perce (later Fort Walla Walla) as a trade center for the Nez Perce Indians and a supply depot for the vast country he explored and trapped. In 1819 he ascended the Snake River from the mouth of the Clearwater to the mouth of the Burnt River in a *bateau,* a feat not duplicated until modern times and modern engine-powered craft. Incessantly on the move, he was reported to have met and traded with as many as 10,000 Indians that year. One hundred and fifty-four pack horses were needed to bring out the furs. It is a matter of interest that in this region McKenzie combined Indian trading and trapping, with special emphasis on the latter. On his first expedition he took 55 men, 195 horses, 300 beaver traps, and a stock of merchandise, but no provisions, since he planned to live off the country. In 1820-1821 he had 75 trappers, and after a year's hunt returned without the loss of a man.

The Consequences of the Peace

McKenzie left the Columbia district in 1822. By that time two events of significance in the history of the Pacific Northwest had occurred. The war had raised the issue of national interests in the area. The Treaty of Ghent provided that places and territories captured should be returned to their original holders. The United States government asked for the restoration of Fort Astoria, which had been "captured" by the *Racoon*. Although the Nor'westers argued that Astoria had been a private venture and was located on soil to which the United States had no recognized claim of sovereignty, and that it had been transferred to the Canadian company by sale and purchase, the fact remained that only goods had changed hands, and the fort occupied by an American firm had been taken by navy action and the British flag run up. It took diplomacy three years after the peace to arrive at a convention by which the site of the fort was officially restored to the United States and the American flag once more raised there. This was a mere formality since Astor made no move to reoccupy the fort and it remained in the possession of the North West Company, but it kept alive a United States claim to the Northwest. The convention specified that for a term of ten years, the region west of the Rockies was to be open to both English and American nationals without prejudice to their claims of sovereignty. The terms of the agreement were subject to renegotiation at the end of the period.

The second matter of significance was the conclusion in 1821 of the North West Company's long struggle with the Hudson's Bay Company. While the Nor'westers had acquired a firm foothold in the Far West, they had not achieved a secure monopoly on the continental scale, nor had they created within their own ranks the harmony necessary to hold what they had. The dynamic enterprise which had once characterized the Lords of the Lakes and the Forests was dissipated in quarrels between the merchant proprietors and the wintering partners, and by increasingly violent competition with the Hudson's Bay Company over the Athabasca trade. The scandal of open warfare among its colonials brought the government into action. The result was the merger of the two companies.

8

The Hudson's Bay Company in the Pacific Northwest

The Union of the North West and Hudson's Bay companies was based on the terms of an agreement signed by the principal representatives of each in London in March, 1821. The result was an organization strengthened, in most cases, by the more efficient features of each. The legal title of the older joint-stock company, the Governor and Company of Adventurers of England trading in Hudson's Bay, and its charter of 1670 were continued. A royal license granted exclusive privileges of trade in all territories not already included in that charter. All policy decision rested, as formerly, with the Governor and Committee in London, the representatives of the investors. Administration was placed in the hands of the wintering people: a governor and an annual council composed of 25 Chief Factors and 28 Chief Traders.[1]

[1] Among the sources used for this chapter are: Alexander H. Begg, *The History of the North-West*, 2 vols., Toronto, 1894; *Colin Robertson's Correspondence Book, September 1817 to September 1822*, E. E. Rich, ed., Hudson's Bay Series II, London, 1939; John McLean, *Notes of A Twenty-five Years' Service in the Hudson's Bay Territory*, 2 vols., London, 1849; Frederick H. Merk, ed., *Fur Trade and Empire: George Simpson's Journal, 1824-1825*, Cambridge, 1931; *Simpson's 1828 Journey to the Columbia: Part of Dispatch of 1829*, Hudson's Bay Series X, London, 1947; Walter N. Sage, "Peter Skene Ogden's Notes on Western Caledonia," *BCHQ*, I, January, 1937; John Dunn, *Oregon Territory and the British North American Fur Trade*, Philadelphia, 1845; Joseph Schafer, ed., "Letters of Sir George Simpson, 1841-43," *AHR*, XIV, October, 1908; *Minutes of Council, Northern Department of Rupert Land, 1821-1831*, Hudson's Bay Series, IX, London, 1940; A. G. Morice, *History of the Northern Interior of British Columbia*, 3d ed., Toronto, 1905; David Douglas, "Sketch of a Journey,"*OHQ*, V, September, 1904; *McLoughlin's Fort Vancouver Letters, First Series, 1825-1838*, Hudson's Bay Series IV, London, 1941, *Second Series, 1839-1844*, Hudson's Bay Series VI, London, 1943, *Third Series, 1844-1846*, Hudson's Bay Series VII, London, 1944; Louis Caywood, "Final Report: Fort Vancouver Excavations," U.S. Department of the Interior, National Park Service, San Francisco, July, 1955; *The Hargrave Correspondence*, ed. G. P. deT. Glazebrook, Toronto, 1938; "Edward Ermatingers' York Factory Express Journal," *Transactions of the Royal Society of Canada*, 3d Series, 1912, Vol. VI, Sect. II; A. G. Harvey, "Meredith Gairdner: Doctor of Medicine," *BCHQ*,

George Simpson, Governor

In George Simpson as wintering governor, the Company found so efficient—and some thought so Machiavellian—an administrator, that within several years he was the sole head of the Company in Canada, the architect of its policies, and the dictator of its practices. Under his direction there was better communication between the London Committee and its "servants" in the field, and the independence of wintering and Montreal merchants which had characterized the North West Company was surrendered to management. Centralization of purchasing agencies, standardization of outfits at least within departments, adjustments of tariffs to trading situations, the elimination of competition in all but a few localities and regularity in shipment of supplies made the fur trade of Canada by 1830 considerably different from that of earlier days. Men "of the Country" took the place of Orkney men, and the French Canadians served the Hudson's Bay Company as faithfully as they once had the Nor'westers. Efficiency, whether in man power or provision, was Simpson's objective in management. The word he used for it was economy.

Although he was accused of many pettinesses by his subordinates, Simpson was a man of imperial ideas. His conception of the role the Hudson's Bay Company might play in developing the resources of the Pacific Northwest led to an expansion of the Company's enterprises far beyond the ordinary requirements of the fur trade. His policies evolved from a first-hand acquaintance with the region to which he made two tours of inspection, in 1824 and in 1828, from recommenda-

IX, April 1945; S. F. Tolmie, "My Father William Fraser Tolmie, 1812-1886," *BCHQ*, I, October, 1937; D. O. Johansen, "William Fraser Tolmie of the Hudson's Bay Company," *The Beaver*, September, 1937; E. P. Creech, "Brigade Trails of British Columbia," *The Beaver*, March, 1953; W. Kaye Lamb, "The Advent of the 'Beaver,'" *BCHQ*, II, July, 1938; *Letters of Dr. John McLoughlin*, ed. B. B. Barker, Portland, 1948; *The Journal of John Work, January to October, 1835*, ed. H. D. Dee, Archives of British Columbia, Memoir No. X, Victoria, 1945; Edmund S. Meany, "The History of the Lumber Industry in the Pacific Northwest to 1917," unpublished doctoral dissertation, Harvard University, 1937, microfilm copy; Willard E. Ireland, ed., "James Douglas and the Russian American Company, 1840," *BCHQ*, V, January, 1941; Donald C. Davidson, "Relation of the Hudson's Bay Company with the Russian American Company on the Northwest Coast, 1829-1837," *BCHQ*, V, January, 1941; F. Henry Johnson, "Fur Trading Days at Kamloops," *BCHQ*, I, July, 1937; R. L. Reid, "Early Days at Fort Langley," *BCHQ*, I, April, 1937; "Letters of Sir George Simpson," *AHR*, XIV, October, 1908.

tions of the men in charge of the district, and from the necessities of the diplomatic situation. The Convention of 1818 provided for a joint occupation of the region for ten years. It was renewed in 1827, but thereafter the agreement was for an indefinite period, and could be terminated by either party on a year's notice. Policy had to be formed with due regard for the company's long-range interests and for the possibility that at any time the region it occupied could be subject to negotiation.

The Columbia Department

The Columbia Department comprised the whole Pacific Northwest from the Russian settlements in the north to the Spanish in the south and from the Rockies to the ocean. Simpson was convinced that when a permanent boundary settlement was made with the United States, the area south and east of the Columbia River below the 49th parallel would ultimately go to the Americans. He therefore recommended a policy of trapping out that broad region. This would serve two purposes. In removing the principal attraction of the region for American hunters there would be no temptation to settlers to follow them. The Snake River route, stripped of its fur resources, would become a barrier rather than an inducement to invasion. With the Lewis and Clark route shut off by hostile Indians, the Pacific Northwest might yet remain British for lack of rival occupation. The second purpose was to secure an anticipated rich returns of furs to carry the cost of developing the rest of the department and making it self-supporting. The Snake River expeditions of large parties of trappers, instituted by Donald McKenzie of the North West Company, were placed in charge of another former Nor'wester, Peter Skene Ogden, who took out his first party in 1824. The annual Snake River outfit was an important part of the trade for the next 16 years.

For the rest of the department, Simpson's plans were directed toward permanent occupation. This meant a policy of Indian trading rather than fur trapping, of conservation rather than extermination of the beaver, and of forts and trading posts rather than roving bands of trappers. The richest district in the department was New Caledonia, and it was preserved as such through a careful cultivation of the native trade. Here can be illustrated the features which distinguished the post system.

The Post System of Trade

The principle underlying the trade was the same that justified commerce generally: to satisfy the wants of a people who had some valuable goods, either labor or commodity, which they would exchange for the satisfaction of their wants. To increase the range of wants among a primitive people was profitable and was believed to be a civilizing agency. The Hudson's Bay Company improved upon this principle, as have others before and since, by limiting the opportunities of their market to find satisfactions elsewhere, that is, by eliminating competition. With its license for exclusive trade in the Indian country, e.g., west of the Rockies, the Company had a monopoly on the trade at least so far as other British traders were concerned. By establishing posts where population and the supply of furs were in happy conjunction, the Company was able to control the lives of the natives.

The post system enabled the Company to take advantage of the dual role of the Indian as profitable consumer of goods and producer of profitable goods. They consumed British goods and they produced furs which supplied the London market, and hence, a large part of the world's demand for fine furs. In both instances, the Company made a tidy profit. A district's trade was profitable when its returns in furs exceeded the cost of its outfit. In 1826 the formula for figuring costs of trading goods in the Columbia Department was prime cost plus a 70 percent markup, whereas a 33 1/3 per cent markup would have covered all charges.[2] In bartering with the Indians, the district traders had to set prices to show a profit over the marked-up cost. Using the prime beaver pelt as the unit of trade, a trap, an essential to producing furs, cost the Indians in New Caledonia six skins. The result was that the Indians refused to buy traps, and consequently failed to produce skins. In order to keep up the returns of furs in the district, traders adopted a lending and credit system which tended to keep the Indians forever in debt to the Company, since they seldom returned their loans and often failed to settle their debts. Not until

[2] *Simpson's 1828 Journey to the Columbia: Part of Dispatch of 1829*, 70, 97-99.

1839 were these trading practices discontinued in New Caledonia. Under monopoly conditions, the natives became increasingly dependent upon the Company's posts for food as well as for the goods that had become essential to their living. In the course of time, their trade leveled off to a subsistence standard, and they became, in a sense, wards of the Company.

In 1833-1834, the costs of the outfit for New Caledonia were 3,000 pounds. The estimated return, at the prevailing London prices for furs, was 11,000 pounds.[3] So profitable was this district that others, such as Thompson's River, owed their existence to the fact that they were necessary to the support of New Caledonia.

For diplomatic and commercial reasons, then, the Company concentrated its trading posts north of the Columbia. Factors which determined the location of these were: potentialities of the fur production; facilities for supply and communication; advantages in meeting or forestalling competition and/or opening new avenues of trade; and, so important to George Simpson's economy program, environments which would make the posts and their districts self-supporting in food.

The Fur Trading Posts

In 1824 the Company had four posts in territory which might eventually go to the United States: Flathead House, Spokane House, Fort Nez Perce (Walla Walla), and Fort George. Flathead House was continued as a temporary post, a supply point for trapping expeditions into the Blackfoot and Snake River countries, and as an outpost against Americans. Spokane House was a special object of Simpson's indignation when, on his first visit to it in 1824-1825, he found its people guilty of "an extraordinary predilection for European Provisions," whose cost made their diet like "eating Gold." This post, so gay and cheerful when it was the chief outfitting point for the Snake River expeditions in North West Company days, had an intimation of a different future when Simpson warned that its people had better hoard the luxuries they had as their future supply of them would be scanty. It was removed to Kettle Falls in the spring of

[3] John McLean, *Notes of a Twenty-five Years' Service in the Hudson's Bay Territory*, I. 250.

1825, when Fort Colvile was founded. This post made few returns in furs but it became an important depot on the Columbia overland express route, and by 1840 it functioned as a granary for the northern interior posts.

Fort Nez Perce then became the outfitting post for the Snake River country. It was an especially important post because it was located among Nez Perces who held the "Key of the River" from Okanogan to the Dalles of the Columbia, the Company's chief highway. The success of the Snake River expeditions depended upon horses from their great herds, and upon the peace they kept with their traditional enemies to the south. In case this site fell to the Americans, the fort could easily be moved across the river and its advantages retained. In Simpson's eyes the location had a further advantage, as he pointed out, in that "the River with a Potatoe Garden will abundantly maintain the Post."[4]

Fort George, old Fort Astoria, did not measure up to requirements as a producer of furs or of foods, and its location on the south side of the river was definitely a factor against its continuation as the principal depot of the department. A new site was chosen about 100 miles inland, on the north side of the river, and in a setting favorable for farming.

When Simpson was finally convinced that the Columbia was the only navigable route by which the interior posts could communicate with the sea—and it took a hair-raising voyage down the Fraser in 1828 to convince him that river was not—then Fort Vancouver became the capital and headquarters of the whole department.

Fort Vancouver

This palisaded outpost of empire had a beautiful setting on a bluff overlooking the river. David Douglas, the botanist visitor in 1825, called it "sublimely grand" with its "lofty, well wooded hills, mountains covered with perpetual snow, extensive natural meadows, and plains of deep, fertile, alluvial deposit covered with a rich sward of grass, and a profusion of flowering plants."[5] But eight-foot-tall stalks of wild lupine on the prairie, the blue scilla on the river banks, or blooming salal with shining leaves at the edge of

[4] Merk, *Fur Trade and Empire*, 128-129.
[5] David Douglas, "Sketch of a Journey," *OHQ*, V, September, 1904, 243.

the woods were not as gratifying to Simpson's eyes as prairie lands under cultivation and pastured herds of cattle. Within five years the Vancouver herd and farm supplied not only that post, but added to the stores of less fortunately located posts elsewhere. The prairie produced abundantly grains, vegetables, and fruits under skilled Scottish gardeners. The apples grew so thick upon the limbs of the dwarfed trees that they looked like "onions fastened in rows on a string." Cattle and hogs were imported from California and the Hawaiian Islands and sheep from England, and when their number grew too great to pasture on the plains near the fort, they were swum across the Columbia to Wapato (Sauvies) Island thence across the slough and over the hills to the Tualatin Plains. A farm yield in 1829 of 1,500 bushels of wheat, 306 bushels of white pease, 191 of gray pease, 200 of barley, 205 of Indian corn, and 20 tierces of pork was reported. To live at Fort Vancouver was to live well, and fish and wild game, fowl and venison, were less the regular fare than additions to it.

Removed from the bluff to the plain and nearer the river in the winter of 1828-1829, the rebuilt fort was still located in an idyllic setting from which it commanded a sweeping view of the river to the west, whence came the annual supply ships from England, and to the east, where it was the highway of the overland express brigade and the outfits returning from the interior. Many changes and additions were made to the original structure. By 1846 it was an enclosure roughly 750 x 450 feet surrounded by a high palisade of hewed logs fitted closely together and firmly buttressed on the inside. At its northwest and southwest corners were two-story bastions each mounting two 12-pound cannons which, never used, were tributes to peace rather than symbols of war. Within the walls were two courts around which were ranged one-story buildings housing officers and clerks, and warehouses and workshops. In the first, and opposite the great gates, stood the two-story residence of the Chief Factor, and to the right, the common eating hall and quarters for the commissioned gentlemen and clerks.

While Simpson's part in establishing the Hudson's Bay Company in the Pacific Northwest was paramount, the name synonymous with the Company in the region was that of his subordinate, Chief Factor Dr. John McLoughlin.

Dr. John McLoughlin, Chief Factor

Born at Rivière du Loup, Canada, in 1784, McLoughlin was 39 years old and had already had about 18 years' experience in the fur trade when he was appointed to the department. He had studied medicine in Quebec in the fashion of the time and had entered the service of the North West Company in which he became a partner in 1814. He was involved in the warfare with the Hudson's Bay people in the Red River country, and was one of the representatives of his company when the union was arranged in London in 1821. He was not easily reconciled to the new order and was thought by some of his associates to have been exiled to the Columbia for his partisanship. His exile, if such it was, made him the chief figure of Northwest history for the next 22 years.

From the beginning, Simpson appears to have disliked McLoughlin, who was in so many ways a contrast to himself, and yet in others quite like him. *En route* to the Columbia in 1824, Simpson caught up with McLoughlin, who had a 20-day start. "He was such a figure as I should not like to meet in a dark night in one of the byelanes in the neighbourhood of London," Simpson wrote to a member of the London Committee: "He was dressed in Clothes that had once been fashionable, but now covered with a thousand patches of different Colors, his beard would do honor to the chin of a Grizzly Bear, his face and hands evidently Shewing that he had not lost much time at his Toilette, loaded with Arms and his own herculean dimensions forming a tout ensemble, that would convey a good idea of the highway men of former Days."[6]

McLoughlin never became a dandy, but as Chief Factor of the Columbia River Department he was never again compared in appearance with a highwayman. He was, for his time, herculean in dimension, almost six feet tall, and inclined to weight. He was often described as dignified and of a bland courteous manner. His hair was prematurely gray, but thick and bushy, framing a mobile face. His blue eyes could be kindly, but they could also grow icy, or snap with the temper he displayed on more than one occasion.

Bearing in mind the fact that Simpson was called "the Emperor"

[6] Merk, *Fur Trade and Empire*, 242-245.

by his subordinates in their more confidential utterances, one can discover in his evaluation of McLoughlin after ten years' acquaintance, Simpson's prejudice toward an equally dynamic character. Simpson was also a shrewd and sharp judge of others' characters. In his secret "Book of Servants' Characters" he wrote of McLoughlin in 1832:

> A very bustling active man who can go through a great deal of business but is wanting in system and regularity and has not the talent of managing the few associates and clerks under his authority; has a good deal of influence with Indians and speaks the Soulteaux tolerably well. Very zealous in the discharge of his public duties, and a man of strict honor and integrity but a great stickler for rights & privileges and sets himself up for a righter of wrongs. Very anxious to obtain a lead among his colleagues with whom he had not much influence owing to his ungovernable violent temper and turbulent disposition, and would be a troublesome man to the Comp'y if he had sufficient influence to form and tact to manage a party, in short, would be a Radical in any Country under any Government and under any circumstances; and if he had not pacific people to deal with, would be eternally embroiled in "affairs of honor" on the merest trifles arising I conceive from the irritability of his temper more than a quarrelsome disposition. Altogether a disagreeable man to do business with as it is impossible to go with him in all things and a difference of opinion almost amounts to a declaration of hostilities, yet a good hearted man and a pleasant companion.

To the Indians of the Northwest whom he ruled with a firm but just hand, McLoughlin was *hyas tyee,* a good chief. He was the "good doctor" to those missionaries and settlers who experienced and appreciated his generosity. But he was also a tyrant to many of his subordinates. An able administrator where the trade followed the patterns of his earlier experience, and successful in carrying out Simpson's plans for agricultural development and diversified trade, he nevertheless suffered from the many demands made upon him. He was confident when dealing with Indians, whom he understood; but, faced with decisions on large policy issues not fully comprehended, or with crises in his own personal life, he panicked, suffered from a nervous stomach, and exploded in violent tempers. His all too evident humanity does not detract, but rather enhances, the character often portrayed in Olympian composure and granite serenity.

As Chief Factor he was expected to exercise the powers vested in him alone. These were discretionary powers in matters of appointments, outfits, distribution of personnel, and in all matters in which time and distance made it impossible for him to ask direction from the Governor or Committee. It was his responsibility to see that policies, broadly outlined by the London committee and more minutely by Governor Simpson, were carried out. In application this meant the economical administration of the department and a profitable harvest of furs; the establishment of new posts, the supervision of personnel, of numerous agricultural enterprises, of the Indian trade, of trapping expeditions, and of a marine department; the development of some of the region's resources other than furs, such as timber and fish, and the opening of new markets for them; and the conduct of "foreign" relations with Russians in Alaska, with Californians, and with Americans.

Life at Fort Vancouver

For the conduct of all these affairs, Fort Vancouver was the headquarters, and the metropolis of the Northwest. It was the nerve center of the Company's business. From here runners were dispatched with communications of news and orders to outlying posts: to Colvile that there was a shortage of horses at Fort Nez Perce to outfit the Snake brigade, and 50 were needed; to Chief Trader Black at Fort Nez Perce that since an American trader had slipped up to the Dalles of the Columbia, he was to reduce Company prices temporarily; to John Work, *en route* to Northern California via the Willamette Valley, that he was to meet Michel Laframboise and his men at the Umpqua; to William Connolly at Bear's Lake in Northern Caledonia that leather was needed at Fort Colvile. And to the fort came runners, bringing word of disasters: the *bateaux* had swamped at the Dalles and nine men were lost; the Clallams had attacked a party and killed two Company men; the *Isabel* was wrecked at the mouth of the Columbia and her crew lost; and, bitter news for the man McLoughlin, his son John was murdered at Stikine.

From early summer until late fall the fort was a busy place. The annual ship arrived and goods had to be checked, unloaded, and assigned to outfits. The outfits came in from New Caledonia, from the trapping parties, from the isolated posts of the whole Northwest.

Furs, cleaned and packed, had to be ready to load when the fall came and the sails stood fair for England again. Clerks worked from morning to midnight on bills of lading, the annual accounts, the checking and rechecking of figures to show that the department had not done too badly in the year. The expeditions had to be got off, the returning ones welcomed with salutes and cheers. The overland express must be organized and sent off on schedule to carry special messages, mail, passengers back to Red River, to York, or to Montreal and civilization. Stiff hands worked late to complete a message to family or to friends. ". . . send the old Heron, a few late news papers, to show what is going on in the old countries; with a letter of at least two sheets, closely written to make him knowing in what is going on in this," wrote Chief Trader Francis Heron. Inquiries about the progress of children at school, orders for yardage and clothing, comments on fellows, and on the Company's affairs fill in the human side of the business which McLoughlin officially and impersonally reported to Simpson and the directors. The 70 pounds of paper in a dispatch box, carried painfully over portages and the Athabaska Pass, held written evidences of the hopes, fears, loneliness of the exiled Columbians.

Yet life at the fort was not dismal. It was a welcome relief from the isolated posts where men struggled against an icy wilderness. It was heaven in retrospect for those in roofless camps of the expeditions keeping nightlong watches against Indians. After the formalities of dinner with Dr. McLoughlin in the common eating hall, the gentlemen went into the Bachelors' Hall to smoke their long clay pipes, tell their stories of adventures, or browse among the books William F. Tolmie brought to start the circulating collection known as the Columbia Library. This was different from the field where hunger sometimes pinched so hard the squaws scraped skins and boiled them for food and the only talk could be of the chances of surviving another day.

Occasionally the Fort had distinguished visitors whose special interests made them welcome. David Douglas was an attractive person as well as a distinguished botanist. As a result of his two trips to the Northwest (1825-1827, 1830-1832) he introduced hundreds of northwestern botanical items to the scientific world. His name is familiarly attached to the native pine, mistakenly called in his honor the Douglas fir. Another botanist, John Scouler, came as surgeon-naturalist on board the *William and Ann,* the same vessel that brought Douglas, but he stayed only so long as the ship was in port. Thomas Nuttall accompanied the Wyeth expedition and spent almost a year botanizing the region. Such guests brought the outside world to the Columbia, as did official but sometimes less welcome visitors, such as Edward Belcher in 1839 and Warre and Vavasour in 1845-1846.

When the Company's own employees assembled at the departmental capital they contributed an air of distinction too. The gentlemen who made up the officer class of the Company were required to have something more than trading skill and lore of the forests and plains, as necessary as these were. Lack of an education was a handicap to advancement; its possession a guarantee of caste. The medical men were university graduates: John Kennedy and Meredith Gairdner of Edinburgh, William Tolmie of Glasgow. Gairdner was a specialist on mineral and thermal springs and at 22 the author of a comprehensive work on the subject. Tolmie's interests ranged from *belles lettres* to botany and scientific farming. Charles Ross was a classical scholar. Peter Skene Ogden, a Canadian of American descent, was educated in the law. James Douglas, later to succeed Simpson as Governor, Dugald Mactavish, Alexander Anderson, Roderick Finlayson, George Barnston, among others, revealed in their letters, journals, and histories those characteristics of literacy and understanding that would fit Simpson's criteria of men at least "tolerably educated."

Life at Outlying Posts

Their regular assignments were not to circumstances as pleasant as the Fort. All permanent posts were depots and, if possible, supply centers for their immediate districts; but they were remote, usually dreary, and sometimes so desperate that men were paid an extra wage to compensate for being there. In New Caledonia, Fort St. James on Stuart's Lake was the residence of a Chief Factor equal in rank to McLoughlin, but because of the dependence of the district on Vancouver after 1827, was put under the latter's direction. Poor soil, easily exhausted, made gardening impossible. Fish were so plentiful that quantities were dried and packed for other posts and the Indian trade. Fish, however, was not a popular food with Caledonians. "Where there are no gardens, the men have only dried salmon, as poor fare as civilized man subsists on in any part of the world," wrote one victim of too many years of it. Thirty miles distant, Fort Fraser on Fraser's Lake stood in a valley open to the southwest and protected from the cold northeast winds, and a rich sandy soil and a relatively long growing season produced potatoes and turnips and other vegetables. At New Caledonia's Fort George efforts were made to obey Simpson's orders to become self-supporting. Four acres of land were cleared and planted to wheat. "Pancakes and hot rolls were thenceforward to be the order of the day; Babine salmon and dog's flesh were to be sent 'to Coventry,'" rejoiced Trader McLean. But there was a late spring, a cold summer, early autumn frosts, and no pancakes. Fort McLeod, on the lake of the same name, was, even in Simpson's views, "the most wretched place in the Indian Country," where even the Indian suffered for want of food. Connolly or Bear Lake post and Babine were hardly better, yet these six posts yielded a gross profit of 1,200 pounds and 9,000 pounds in 1828.[7]

It took four months for the "voyage out" and return from Northern Caledonia. The route led by boat from Fort Vancouver to Okanogan, and by horse brigade—250 to 300 in the train—from Okanogan to Kamloops, and many animals died from the rigors of this trip through the winding mountain trails. At Alexandria the brigade was met by the men from the north in their lightweight, but sturdy, swift-water canoes, who carried the supplies back to Stuart's Lake, where they were distributed to the other posts by "large and small canoes, Horses, Dog sleds and Men's backs."

Fort Alexandria, located on the Fraser near present Quesnel, was the northern terminus of the horse brigade and a transshipping point. It enjoyed a setting almost like that of Fort Vancouver. There was a pleasant diversity of hill, plain, and wooded groves—and of food. Excellent crops were raised, although early frosts nipped garden truck. No one exiled to the north complained of Fort Alexandria.

The erection of Forts Langley (1827), Simpson (1831-1834),

---

[7] *Simpson's 1828 Journey*, 25.

McLoughlin (1833), Stikine (1839-1840), Taku (1840), and Victoria (1843) along the coast of British Columbia was part of a plan to stabilize the Indian trade of the interior and to meet competition from the sea. The great days of the sea otter trade were over, but Yankee ships now took off cargoes of beaver, marten, and other skins brought from the mountains to the coast, draining the interior of stock and forcing traders to lower their tariffs. Furthermore, there was still a great untapped and rich fur region in the north that had no other outlet but occasional Yankee ships and the Russian posts. Fort Simpson was intended to answer this purpose.

Fort Langley, on the lower Fraser, was a defense against the American ships, and became a productive farm and provisioner of dried and salted fish. Eight hundred barrels of the latter were put up in 1846, of which more than half was exported to the Hawaiian Islands where it sold for nine dollars a barrel. This was the genesis of the foreign trade of British Columbia.[8] Coastal posts too were required so far as possible to live on country provisions, fish, and game. In one case, much to Simpson's delight, consumption actually returned a profit. At Taku, located between Sitka and the Taku River, the personnel of 24 officers and men were maintained on venison got at "so cheap a rate from the natives, that we absolutely make a profit in our consumption of provisions, the skin of the animal selling for much more than is paid for the whole carcass."[9]

The Marine Department

These posts required vessels to outfit them and to carry off their returns, and ships were also needed to head off opposition wherever it might appear. The *Cadboro* arrived from England in 1827 to take men and supplies to construct Fort Langley. Subsequently she spent most summers in the northern waters, and winters in trading voyages to California or the Hawaiian Islands. The *Vancouver*, a 60-ton schooner built under great handicaps at Fort Vancouver and launched in 1826 was hardly seaworthy for more extended voyages than on the lower Columbia River. A better job was done on the 30-ton sloop *Broughton* launched the same year, but lack of skilled labor and iron works and properly seasoned

[8] R. L. Reid, "Early Days at Fort Langley," *BCHQ*, I, April, 1937, 80.
[9] "Letters of Sir George Simpson," *AHR*, XIV, October, 1908, 76.

timber were reasons for abandoning shipbuilding.

In 1835, the pioneer paddle-wheel steamer *Beaver* was dispatched under sail from England to the Northwest. From the time of its arrival on the coast in the spring of 1836 to its final catastrophe near the entrance to Vancouver (British Columbia) harbor in 1888, it had a memorable career in northern waters. Its two engines of 35 horsepower each and its low draft but protective high sides, would, it was hoped, make it possible to enter coves and inlets where sailing vessels could not go. But its voracious appetite for fuel defeated Simpson's hopes. The Pacific Northwest's first steamer used sails in its early years on the coast.[10]

Although there was only light competition from American traders, their effect on the trade was important. Between 1827 and 1829 two irritatingly persistent American traders, Captain John Dominis in the brig *Owhyhee* and Captain D. W. Thompson in the *Convoy* not only scanned the coast but had the temerity to enter the Columbia River. Since the Americans were carelessly extravagant in their trade, transient and without a long-range prospect of permanent trade, they bid up prices and "excited quite a sensation amongst the natives." Prices went up to five times the normal schedule. Reluctant to use guns and liquor in the Indian trade, competition forced McLoughlin to match or better the Americans' bids, and this was difficult, since the loss of the two supply vessels seriously reduced his stock. When the Americans left the river the tariff returned to its old rates and the Company's hold upon the natives was strengthened by a fortuitous coincidence. A virulent outbreak of influenza struck the Columbia area. In the minds of the few surviving Indians, there was a strong suspicion that the river had been poisoned by the Americans. This was a persistent story told about Americans which may have had its origin in some dramatic threat on the part of Dominis or others. In later times the story was used with disastrous results against the Whitmans, who were suspected of a similar plot.

American Competition by Sea

There were at least six American vessels on the coast for beaver in 1829-1830 before McLoughlin was able to get the coastal trade of the Company on a firm footing. The natives

[10] W. Kaye Lamb, "The Advent of the 'Beaver's' " *BCHQ*, II, July, 1938, 161 ff.

made the most of the presence of opposition and raised their demands. The effect spread into the interior where the Indians threatened to carry their furs to tribes on the coast. In 1832 Duncan Finlayson reported to a friend that rum was sold by the Americans "by the Puncheon, a p[int] of white Salumpon for a Beaver & other articles equally exorbitant." The next year, 1833-1834, there was little or no opposition; but the Indians were loath to trade and preferred to hold their skins against the Americans' return and a rise in price.

What happened when the Hudson's Bay traders met head on with their Yankee rivals was described by John Work, Chief Trader in charge of the *Beaver* and the coastal trade in 1835. At Nass, on a May morning of that year, he recorded:

We have the Mortification to find the *Europa* here, she arrived this morning, and has already been busy trading with the Indians. . . . Early in the [next] morning the Indians began to assemble and were about both vessels and going from one to another all day. We traded 51 Beaver, 5 Land Otters, 9 Bears & and a few Martens. The Americans have 3½ point Blankets, far superior to ours both in size and quality, of which the Indians are well aware. In order that we might have a chance for a share of the trade we were induced to rise our Tariff to a Blanket 3 gall. Ind[ian]. Rum, 6 head Tobacco, per Beaver large. It is high but without we do so we will have no chance to get our share of the trade. We also give 7 gall. Mixed liquor for a beaver which is a gallon more than our opponents give. The Indians glory in having . . . opposition and know well how to take advantage of it.

The Indians assembled again in the morning [third day] as usual, and kept going between us and our opponents as usual. During the day we traded 94 Beaver, 5 Otters, 28 Bears, 21 Martens. We had more customers than our opponents owing to the superior quality of our Rum and Tobacco. Capt. Allan [of the *Europa*] who must have been perfectly aware of our scale of trade, came aboard and enquired what we were giving, and on being told, got in a violent passion and declared that he would do his utmost to rise the price and make us pay as high as possible for all the furs we would trade on the coast this season, that he had plenty of goods to do so (& as our deck was full of Natives busy trading) without waiting to be spoke to went over the side and proclaimed to the Indians that he would give 4 gall. Rum & 8 heads of tobacco with one of his large blankets for a beaver. The Indians received this intimation with several loud hurrahs, and immediately ceased trading, and began to clear off to his vessel. It remained with us now either to lose the beaver or rise our price, the latter was preferred and we accordingly offered 5 gal. Mixed rum & 10 heads tobacco with a blanket per beaver, the result of which was that we secured, as we think, the best share of the day's trade. At this rate the furs cost high, but as our expenses are going on the same, let us get beaver or not, and as we have a good stock of goods, it is deemed best rather than let the furs fall all into the hands of our Opponents, to secure them even at a light profit. The Indians seem perfectly aware that this is not to last, for they are enquiring how long these prices are likely to continue and were promptly told by us only so long as our Opponents remained.[11]

McLoughlin viewed the expansion of the marine department with a jaundiced eye. He believed its purpose was eventually to eliminate the coastal posts which he was convinced were less costly in the long run and made for better trade relations with the natives. When Simpson instituted the department in 1829 and appointed a cousin, Captain Aemilius Simpson, to head it, McLoughlin's obedience was severely tested. At the sudden death of Captain Simpson in 1831, McLoughlin abolished the office and took charge of the vessels. He managed to make them strictly auxiliary to the posts and to the expanded trade in produce other than furs.

McLoughlin had more than his share of troubles with this department. He found sea captains insubordinate, too often drunk, and their crews unruly. He preferred to deal with men of his own experience and way of life. When he usurped the management of the vessels, he placed his own traders, Peter Skene Ogden and John Work, for example, in charge as supervisory officers. He managed to hold his position against that of his superior, Simpson, but the controversy did not improve their relations.

By 1836 there were, besides the *Beaver*, six sailing vessels ranging from 100 to 300 tons burden in the service, including the annual supply ships which arrived in the Columbia, usually in March. On the safe arrival of these vessels and their cargoes depended the following season's trade, the outfitting of expeditions and posts, and in some measure the morale of the personnel. A disaster, such as the wreck of the *William and Ann* in 1829, and of the *Isabella* in 1830, seriously affected the trade by reducing the outfits, and threw out of joint the tight schedule for collections from the coast establishments.

[11] *The Journal of John Work, January to October, 1835*, 41-42.

During the interval of their stay in the Pacific, the vessels distributed supplies and took up cargoes—not only of furs—but of lumber and salmon which they would dispose of in California, the Hawaiian Islands, or in South American ports on their return to England.

Expanded Activities of the Company: The Lumber Trade

McLoughlin anticipated and supported Simpson in the latter's zeal to open up and to protect the avenues of Company business by trading its resources other than furs. "We must avail ourselves of all the resources of this Country if we have to Compete for the trade of it with the Americans as we may depend they will turn everything they possibly can to account," he reported to the Governor and Committee in 1829.[12] In 1827, for example, McLoughlin advocated the development of the lumber trade. He had already built a small water-powered sawmill on a creek six miles east of Fort Vancouver. In 1838, six to ten saws and 25 men were employed. McLoughlin and Simpson together in 1828 selected a site at the Falls of the Willamette where, according to Simpson's enthusiastic report, "whole Forests of Timber can be floated into a very fine Mill Seat . . . [and] Saws enough could be employed to load the British Navy."[13] Timbers for a mill were cut at the spot in 1831, preparatory to building a mill, but the project was abandoned, since the abundant supply of timber was one thing, but markets for lumber were another.

The Fort Vancouver mill was able to supply all that was needed for Company use and for export as well. The first shipment to the Islands in 1828-1829 sold for 100 dollars a thousand feet but the demand was spotty and unpredictable, and American competition and influence were discouraging.[14] Neither were efforts to sell lumber in the South American market or California successful. Nor did export of salmon, dried or salted, fulfill Simpson's and McLoughlin's anticipations. It spoiled on the voyage to England, and was in light

[12] *McLoughlin's Fort Vancouver Letters, First Series,* 77.
[13] *Simpson's 1828 Journey,* 84.
[14] *Ibid.,* 110; Edmund S. Meany, "The History of the Lumber Industry in the Pacific Northwest to 1917," unpublished doctoral dissertation, Harvard University, 1937, microfilm copy, 65, 67.

Fort Astoria in 1813. (From Gabriel Franchère, Narrative of a Voyage to the Northwest Coast of America.)

Strom Log Cabin, Lane County, Oregon. (Courtesy, University of Oregon Library.)

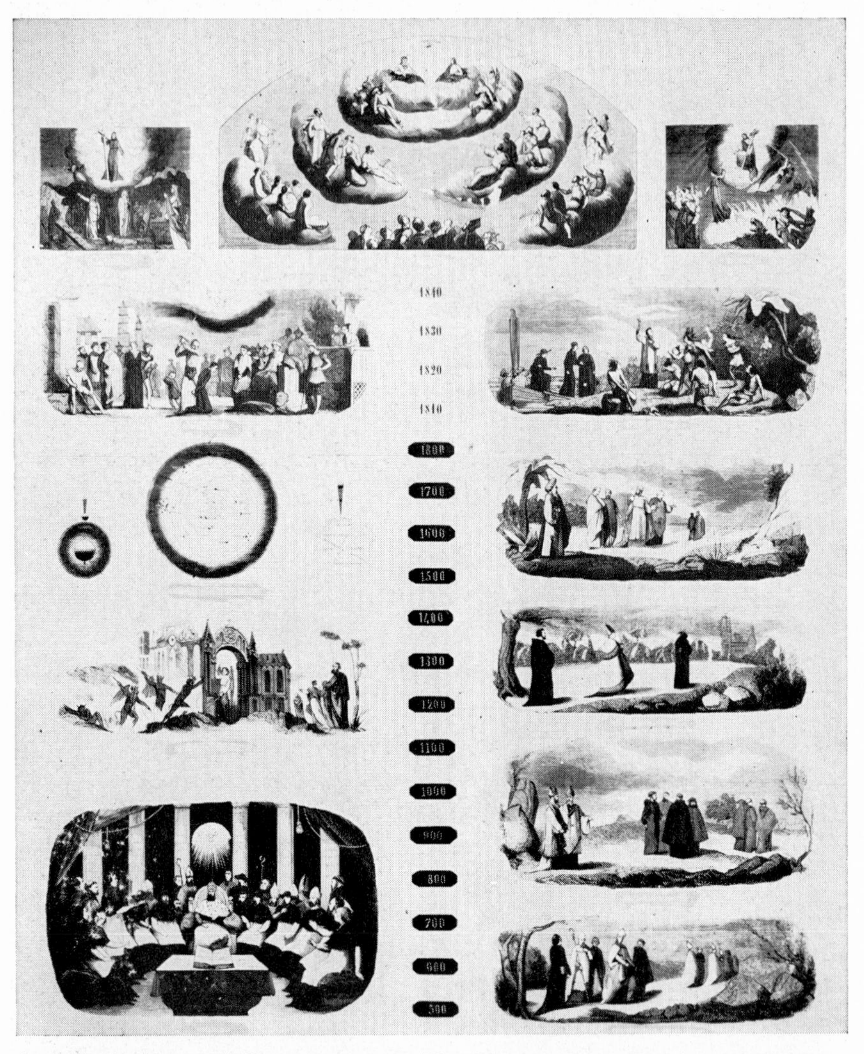

Catholic Ladder with Illustrations, Used by Missionaries in Teaching the History of the Church. (From a French engraving, probably made about 1860. Courtesy, Oregon Historical Society.) Top row: (left) Resurrection; (center) Paradise; (right) Last Judgment. Second row: (left) Martyrs of the Faith; (right) Preaching the Gospel. Third row: (right) Mahomet; Iconoclasts; Luther; Calvin. Lower left: (second from bottom) Triumph of Religion; (bottom) Councils of the Church.

Joseph Lane. (Courtesy, University of Oregon Library.)

Jason Lee. (Courtesy, University of Oregon Library.)

American Village on the Willamette. (From Henry Warre, Sketches in North America and the Oregon Territory.)

Seth Lewelling House in Oregon City. (Courtesy, Oregon Historical Society.)

Sloop of War Discovery Temporarily Beached. (From Vancouver, Voyage of Discovery to the North Pacific Ocean.)

Sketch of Seattle, the Frontier City. (Courtesy, University of Washington Library.)

demand elsewhere. It was no easy matter to make the Pacific Northwest a commercial depot for the Pacific.

Agricultural Developments

Simpson, as had Astor in his time, looked with great interest upon the possibilities the Russian Alaska posts offered for profitable trade. By acquiring this business the Company could achieve a number of goals. It could cut out a principal attraction that drew American traders to the coast; it could furnish British manufactures with reasonable profit to the Company, and it could find an outlet for surplus produce from its local farms. Here at least, the Americans could not underbid them.

In 1829 Simpson made overtures to the Russians to substitute cooperation for rivalry in the interior of Russia's territory. Although the Russian governor was attracted to any reasonable offer that would free his colony of dependence on irresponsible American traders who persisted in selling liquor and ammunition in unlawful trade with the natives, he could not accept the Company's terms.

When the Company established posts in the Far North it came into direct competition and a territorial dispute with the Russians. This was settled in 1839 by a commercial agreement by which the Russian company leased to the Company a strip of the mainland coast, the *lisière,* from Mount Fairweather to Portland Canal, and upon which Forts Stickine (1840) and Taku (1840) were built. In effect, the Russians kept the islands' trade, and left that of the interior to the Hudson's Bay Company.[15] In rental for this lease the Hudson's Bay Company agreed, among other things, to sell the Russians agricultural products at stipulated prices. This led to a new emphasis upon farming enterprises and to a special organization for their management.

The Puget Sound Agricultural Company

The Puget Sound Agricultural Company was a separate organization of the Hudson's Bay Company, but with a board composed of Hudson's Bay Company directors and adminis-

[15] Willard E. Ireland, ed., "James Douglas and the Russian American Company, 1840," *BCHQ,* V, January, 1941, 65 n.

tered locally by Dr. McLoughlin. Its purpose was distinct from that of the fur trade, in that it was organized to establish "an agricultural Settlement with a view to the production of wool, hides, tallow, and other farm produce for the English and other markets, in the Country situated between the head waters of the Cowlitz Portage and Pugets Sound . . .";[16] but it was also a means of "proving up" the Company's claims on behalf of Great Britain, to the disputed region north of the Columbia which after 1828 had narrowed down to the western half of Washington. It was reasoned, with cause, that an agricultural settlement provided a firmer argument for "occupation" than a fur trading post.

Nisqually and the Cowlitz Valley Farms

Fort Nisqually, located at the southern tip of Puget Sound, had been intended as a farm and shipping point since its establishment in 1833. Its returns in furs declined rapidly; but as a part of the Puget Sound Agricultural Company its chief function was agricultural. Early hopes that it would produce bumper wheat crops were disappointed when it was found the soil responded only if heavily fertilized. It grass-fattened beef cattle, but dairy cows gave as little as a pint of milk a day until skilled husbandmen took over their feeding. After 1841 sheep and cattle became the establishment's chief produce. Ploughs broke the heavy sod at Cowlitz Farms in 1839. The turf resisted harrow and drag and the poorly prepared fields dried out in an unusually hot and dry summer that year. But two years later 1,000 acres produced 8,000 bushels of wheat and 4,000 bushels of oats, barley, pease, and quantities of potatoes.

Agricultural development was handicapped by a lack of labor. The Indians were seldom reliable workers, and employees of the Company were hardly accustomed to farming. To meet this problem the Company settled six of its retired employees there, and in 1841 sent out 21 families—116 men, women, and children—from the Red River. Of these, 77 persons, principally English half-breeds, were located at Nisqually where they farmed on halves for the Puget Sound Agricultural Company. Seven families composed of thirty-eight persons, Canadians and half-breeds, were reluctant to accept these terms and were

[16] *McLoughlin's Fort Vancouver Letters, Second Series,* 15 n.

settled at Cowlitz Farms in a semi-independent status.[17] They were advanced seed, implements, and other supplies, and were outside the jurisdiction of the Puget Sound Agricultural Company except for their debts.

Western Washington thus early was becoming a farming community. A similar change was taking place in the Tualatin and Willamette valleys. Early in the 'thirties Company cattle grazed the Tualatin prairies. Retired employees and free men moved into the Willamette and began to farm. At least eight families in 1833 formed the nucleus of a growing Canadian population, and gave the name French Prairie to their locality. They were joined by Americans, missionaries, mountain men, and settlers, and a new chapter of Northwest history was in the making.

The Hudson's Bay Company was at the same time a deterrent and an aid to the occupation of the Oregon Country by Americans. To maintain its monopoly it fought competitors who might get a foothold in the region and it had resources of men and capital to carry the burden. Its policies were aimed at destroying the attractiveness of the Snake country to American trappers, and of preserving the northern region where British claims were strongest. On the other hand, by enlarging the field of its enterprise in agriculture, by disciplining the natives, by maintaining posts at strategic locations, and by establishing routes of travel by water and land throughout the Northwest, it took off the sharpest edge of danger for venturesome Americans who did break through. While the Company frowned upon any practices which made it easy for their rivals, it did not demand a ruthless treatment of the stranger within its gates. John McLoughlin's humanity made Fort Vancouver an outpost of civilization as well as empire.

[17] "Simpson's Letters," *AHR*, XIV, October 1908, 78-79.

9

The American Rocky Mountain Fur Trade

For more than 20 years, from 1824 to 1846, the Pacific Northwest was a department of the Hudson's Bay Company, but American fur interests, as well as expansionists, missionaries, settlers, and diplomats, continually reminded the Company that the land was not yet Britain's. As we have seen, the affairs of the Department of the Columbia were therefore conducted with a view to discourage, if not to prevent, Americans from getting a foothold in the region.

After Astor's unsuccessful attempt, no organized fur enterprise of American origin crossed the Rockies for almost a decade. In 1822, a St. Louis firm composed of General William H. Ashley and Andrew Henry, who had wintered on the north fork of the Snake in 1810-1811, advertised for "one hundred young men to ascend the Missouri River to its source, there to be employed for one, two, or three years."[1] The next year a fort was built at the mouth of the Yellowstone and no less than 200 men were hunting in the vicinity. By the following year the distinctive features of Ashley's enterprise emerged, were adopted by his rivals and successors, and prevailed throughout the moun-

[1] Quoted in Robert G. Cleland, *This Reckless Breed of Men*, New York, 1950, 56. Among the basic sources for this chapter are: Frances F. Victor, *River of the West*, San Francisco, 1870; Dale L. Morgan, *Jedediah Smith and the Opening of the West*, New York, 1953; H. M. Chittenden, *The History of the Fur Trade of the Far West*, 3 vols., New York, 1902; *McLoughlin's Fort Vancouver Letters*, First, Second, and Third Series, Hudson's Bay Series, IV, VI, VII, London, 1941-1944; *Ogden's Snake Country Journals, 1824-26*, Hudson's Bay Series IV, London, 1941; Maurice S. Sullivan, *The Travels of Jedediah Smith*, Santa Ana, California, 1934; *Senate Ex. Doc.*, No. 39, 21 Cong., 2 Sess. Washington, 1931; "Report on the Fur Trade, 1830," *OHQ*, XLVIII, March, 1947; Fred Wilbur Powell, "Hall Jackson Kelley: Prophet of Oregon," *OHQ*, XVIII, March 1917; *Correspondence and Journals of Captain Nathaniel J. Wyeth, 1831-6*, ed. F. G. Young, Eugene, Oregon, 1899; John Ball, "Across the Continent Seventy Years Ago," *OHQ*, III, March, 1902; Philip Overmeyer, "Members of the First Wyeth Expedition," *OHQ*, XXXVI, March, 1935.

tainous region of the West until the trade declined in 1840.

Ashley's contribution to the trade was not original, but it gave a new direction to it. He abandoned the practice of building forts or trading houses, which had been characteristic of the American trade as it moved across the Mississippi and into Indian country. Instead, he employed trappers, who in large and small groups hunted the rivers and streams, and brought in their accumulated catch to some previously agreed place of meeting. This yearly rendezvous, usually held in July, very soon became a gathering not only of employees, but also of free trappers and Indians from the Rocky Mountain region. At the height of the trade in the early 'thirties, several thousand Indians and hundreds of white men would assemble and settle accounts. Rival outfits sometimes had their rendezvous within a few miles of one another. Sometimes as much as two weeks was given over to lusty carousal, during which great quantities of high-priced rum and alcohol were consumed. After the men recovered from their spree, they separated again for the year's assignment in the dangerous, lonely mountain country.

The Mountain Men

To qualify as a mountain man one had to be able to survive both rendezvous and mountain life. Those who proudly carried the title were expert hunters and trappers, bear fighters, and Indian killers. The hazards of the occupation were many. No less than 94 men were killed by Indians between 1823 and 1829.[2] The figures were probably higher in the next six years. The rewards, in most cases, were the freedom of the wilds, adventure, and the rendezvous. Few lived to retire to civilization, and those who did had little more than scars to show for their years of hazardous toil.

Ashley and his successors, Smith, Jackson, and Sublette, and the Rocky Mountain Fur Company, supplied their indentured employees, free trappers, and Indian allies with goods priced to assure them a generous margin of profit. In 1826, gunpowder was sold at $1.50 a pound, scarlet cloth at $6.00 a yard, beaver traps were $9.00, sugar $1.00, coffee $1.25, flour $1.50 per pound, and alcohol, oiling the wheels of the industry, was $13.50 a gallon. The same year free trap-

[2] Morgan, *Jedediah Smith,* 344-345.

pers received $3.00 a pound for beaver pelts. The wages paid hired trappers ranged from $120 to $600 a year depending upon the competition for their services. When accounts were settled, the trapper usually was in debt for the goods he had purchased.

Chittenden, the historian of the trade, estimated that Ashley's returns from 1823-1827 were something like 500 packs of skins worth more than 250,000 dollars in the St. Louis market. Estimating the partners' annual investments in goods, including costs of transportation at a generous 20,000 dollars, the profits were in the neighborhood of 50,000 to 60,000 dollars a year. By 1832, however, the prime costs mounted, and there was increasing competition. Astor's American Fur Company had eliminated its rivals by 1835, and achieved a monopoly of the trade. Within the next four years the trade declined: the beaver were practically destroyed, the market had changed, and the rendezvous was abandoned. The great period of the trade was its first ten years, from 1823 to 1833. And this was the period of its famous leaders and exploits.

The partners who developed and extended the Rocky Mountain fur trade combined the talents of entrepreneurs, frontiersmen, and explorers. The names of Ashley, Henry, Jedediah Smith, the Sublette brothers, David E. Jackson, Tom Fitzpatrick, and Jim Bridger are associated with places and routes of travel as well as with sagas of adventure and commerce. They filled in the geographical outlines of the West and in the process linked the Pacific coast to the Mississippi Valley by narrow but well-traveled trails.

The Clash of British and American Trappers

In 1824 the mountain men had crossed the continental divide at South Pass. The next year Ashley explored the Green River, principal northern tributary of the Colorado. The valley of the Green, Bear Lake in Cache Valley, Jackson's Hole, and Pierre's Hole became the chosen rendezvous sites. In 1827, Ashley sent a howitzer along the North Platte route, through the pass, and proved that wheels could travel to the mountains. In 1829 Smith, Sublette, and Jackson used a wagon caravan to transport their goods to the Pass. The road to Oregon was taking shape.

The American trappers' approach coincided with the Hudson's

Bay Company's decision to trap out the Snake River country and destroy its attractiveness for them. Before Peter Skene Ogden took over this task, Alexander Ross was in charge of the Snake River expedition. In 1824 he met Jedediah Smith and six trappers and permitted the Americans to travel with him from the Bear River north to the Flathead post. Ogden later referred to "that damn'd all cursed day" as the one which brought the Americans into the region for which the Hudson's Bay Company had not yet undertaken a thorough defense.[3] When Ogden took his first expedition back to the Snake River that December, Smith journeyed with him part way. The following May, Ogden met more of Smith's fellows on the Bear River, and almost came into direct conflict with them. The Americans claimed Ogden was trespassing on American soil, but Ogden refused any such admission until notified by his government. It was a slight matter of concern, had either party known it, that they both probably were within the boundaries of Spanish claims.

Immediately infuriating to the quick-tempered Ogden was the fact that the Americans induced 23 of his free trappers to desert, taking with them some 700 beaver skins and leaving behind them the debts they owed the Company. But more disturbing in the long run was the news that no less than 150 American trappers were working west of the divide. Their presence kept Ogden in the field and so successfully did he hunt that some streams he worked were destitute of beaver thereafter. But while Ogden was on the Snake River front, the Company's nemesis, Jedediah Smith, suddenly appeared, as it were, behind the lines.

Jedediah Smith

Smith was one of the most unusual men in the Rocky mountain trade. Even his rivals admitted he was "a very intelligent man."[4] What was more surprising in a mountain man, he was deeply religious. He was one of the young men (he was only 23 years old) who entered Ashley's employment in 1822; three years later his abilities earned him a partnership. His biographer, Dale Morgan, convincingly argues that he was the outstanding field operator of the fur trade until his death in 1831.

[3] *McLoughlin's Fort Vancouver Letters*, First Series, 296-297.
[4] Morgan, *Jedediah Smith*, 129.

In August, 1826, Smith led a party of 18 men from the rendezvous at Bear Lake south through the Uintah mountains to the Virgin and Colorado rivers, and from there across the Mojave Desert to the mission settlement at San Gabriel. After some difficulties with the dismayed governor of California, Smith was permitted to leave California by the same route by which he had come. However, he chose to ignore this restriction and trapped as far north as the American River. Unable to take his full party over the mountains, he left them to hunt in the San Joaquin Valley, while he and two companions crossed the snow-covered Sierras, the desert Nevada plain, and survived to reach the rendezvous in Bear Valley.

His 45-day exploit was followed by nine days of rest and Smith was again on the California trail he had pioneered. His purpose was to join the party he had left behind and then to "proceed further in examination of the country beyond . . . and along the sea coast." He was himself aware that he had been captivated by the fever of discovery: "I of course expected to find Beaver, which with us hunters is a primary object, but I was also led on by the love of novelty common to all, which is much increased by the pursuit of its gratification."

His first venture had been a grueling one; the second was disastrous. Nine men were killed by the Mojaves before he reached California. He again had trouble with officials who were fearful that he was getting into the habit of dropping in on their guarded settlements. After having tasted even a bit of Mexican prison fare, Smith was permitted to outfit and depart, providing he got out as quickly as possible and stayed out. With a party of 20, nine survivors of his recent trip, nine remaining from his previous one, and two added from the settlements, Smith left on December 30, 1827, and headed north. Though well supplied with horses and mules, he was short of traps, but beaver were plentiful on the lower San Joaquin River, and he was carrying about 800 pelts when catastrophe overwhelmed him.

Smith approached the northern California seacoast over the almost impassable terrain of the South Fork of the Trinity River and lower Klamath. Dale Morgan, his biographer, tells that to drive his animals one mile through tangled underbrush and dense forest, down canyons that ended in vertical cliffs, or along the sides of hazardous chasms, sometimes took a whole day. It took the exhausted man and beasts six months to reach the coast. On June 23 they crossed the 42d parallel and were in the Oregon country. Four days later they reached the mouth of the Rogue, and on July 12, the Umpqua. Here they had trouble with the Indians. An ax was stolen and to force the thief to give it up, Smith put a rope around his neck while his men held their guns on some 50 others watching the humiliation. Two days later, while Smith and two of his men were scouting the country ahead, the angered natives caught up with his party and massacred all but one. Arthur Black escaped and made his way to Fort Vancouver. Smith, John Turner, and Richard Leland, who had returned to the shocking scene and thought themselves the sole survivors, arrived two days later on August 10.

John McLoughlin, who had resented "to the utmost" Ogden's contretemps with Smith in 1825, now received his enemy with kindness, even generosity. He had been preparing an expedition to the Umpqua to trap, and he now ordered it to proceed, with Smith, to rescue his goods and to punish the Indians. Sir George Simpson, arriving on a tour of inspection, consented to buy the recovered furs, "the worst he had even seen," for $2369.06. The following March, Smith and Black left Vancouver, traveled up the Columbia and across the route which later became part of the Oregon Trail, to Pierre's Hole where he met his partners.

Sir George did not have a very high regard for participants in the American fur trade: ". . . the Trappers themselves are generally speaking, people of the worst character, run-aways from Jails, and outcasts from Society . . . [they] acknowledge no master, will conform to no rules or regulations. . . ." He underestimated the capacities of their leaders, such men as Jedediah Smith, and the role they were playing in opening up the West. ". . . The heads of the concern or Outfitters, are merely adventurers who have nothing to lose," he reported to London. "The conductors or Leaders of parties, are men who have been common Trappers, and therefore possess no influence."

He anticipated no serious consequences of Smith's invasion, for he assumed, or was led to believe, that Smith's experiences had convinced him there were geographic deterrents to American migration to Oregon.

We learn from our American visitant Smith, that the flattering reports which reached St. Louis of the Wilhamot Country, as a field for Agricultural speculation, had induced many people in the States to direct their attention to that quarter; but he has on his present journey, discovered difficulties which never occurred to their minds, and which are likely to deter his Countrymen from attempting that enterprise. In the American Charts this River, (the Wilhamot or Moltnomah) is laid down, as taking its rise in the Rocky Mountains . . . and the opinion was, that it would merely be necessary for Settlers with their Horses, Cattle, Agricultural implements &c.&c. to get (by the main communication from St. Louis to S[an]ta Fee) to the height of Land in about Lat. 38, there to embark on large Rafts & Batteaux and glide down current about 800 or 1000 Miles at their ease to this "Land of Promise." But it now turns out, that the Sources of the Wilhamot are not 150 Miles distant from Fort Vancouver, in Mountains which even Hunters cannot attempt to pass, beyond which, is a Sandy desert of about 200 miles, likewise impassable. . . . And the other route by Louis's River [Snake], Settlers could never think of attempting. So that I am of opinion, we have little to apprehend from Settlers in this quarter, and from Indian Traders nothing. . . .[5]

The Outline of a Road to Oregon

But Simpson would have been less sanguine had he read Smith's communication to the Secretary of War in 1830. Speaking of the trade commenced by Ashley in 1822 and continued since 1826 by himself, William Sublette, and David Jackson, Smith pointed out that where pack horses and mules had previously been used, in the Spring of 1830 a caravan including two light-weight wagons, ten five-mule team heavy wagons carrying about 1,800 pounds each, 12 head of oxen, and a milk cow had left St. Louis April 10 and arrived at the Wind River-Popo Agie junction on July 16 without mishap. Buffalo provided more food than they could use, and although the mountains were white with snow, the passes and valleys were green and the stock was easily fed. A few pioneers moved ahead of the caravan to cut down the banks of creeks and ravines over which the wagons had to pass, but otherwise the route along the Great Platte to the Wind River was open level prairie with no obstructions.

"This is the first time that wagons ever went to the Rocky mountains," he reported, "and the ease and safety with which it was done prove the facility of communicating over land with the Pacific ocean.

[5] *Simpson's 1828 Journey: Part of Dispatch of 1829*, Hudson's Bay Series, X, London, 1947, 64, 66-67.

The route from the *Southern Pass*, where the wagons stopped, to the Great Falls of the Columbia, being easier and better than on this side of the mountains, with grass enough for horses and mules, but a scarcity of game for the support of men."

Several other points were made in the letter tied in with a rising issue of American politics: the conflict of British and American commercial interests and the unsolved boundary issue. Smith reported that Fort Vancouver was protected only by 12-pounders; that its gardens, herds, mills, and artisans, were evidence of its being a permanent establishment; that the annual value of furs shipped from the fort would be worth more than a quarter of a million dollars on the New York market; and that in 1824-1825 the Hudson's Bay Company's trappers first crossed the Rockies, and were confining their destructive practices "to the territory of the United States." He concluded that the Convention of 1818 had given privileges to the British and enabled them "to take possession of the Columbia River, and spread over the country south of it; while no Americans have ever gone, or can venture to go on the British side."[6]

So it was that reports of profits enjoyed by an ancient enemy and of the potentials of a practically unknown land—reports that probably lost nothing as they were repeated by word of mouth—invited new adventurers into the fur trade and a new interest in the Oregon country. In 1833 Chief Trader Francis Heron of the Hudson's Bay Company summarized the situation as of that date:

> The Americans . . . seem determined on making a bold push for the trade of the country— Upwards of 400 Men well equipped with all sorts of goods, have forced their way across land from St. Louis, and passed the Winter on this side of the Mountains, at Salmon River, with the intention of scattering over the country this summer. . . . They also propose bringing out future supplies by sea, and to form establishments on the Coast; but these are principally intended for carrying on Salmon fisheries— By all these movements you will well perceive that Jonathan is determined to have, at least, his share of what the country produces—[7]

Heron's estimate of the number of Americans in the mountains in the winter of 1832 was probably close to correct. The American Fur Company was in the field. It had accomplished what had for-

[6] *Sen. Ex. Doc.*, No. 39, 21st Cong., 2d Sess., 22-23; see also Morgan, *Jedediah Smith*, 346-348.

[7] *The Hargrave Correspondence, 1821-1843*, Toronto, 1938, 112.

merly seemed an impossibility—the establishment of forts on the Upper Missouri among the Blackfeet: Fort Union on the Yellowstone, Fort McKenzie on the Missouri near the mouth of the Marias, Fort Cass at the junction of the Big Horn and Yellowstone. From these posts its trappers spread out through the country to compete with the Hudson's Bay Company expeditions and with the Rocky Mountain Fur Company, successor in 1830 to Smith, Sublette, and Jackson. The American Fur Company used the Blackfeet as powerful weapons against its opponents' trapping parties. It set up rendezvous in the neighborhood of its rivals, and with the backing of almost unlimited capital, paid higher wages and higher tariffs, if necessary to defeat its enemies. Besides the American Fur Company there were the forces of the Rocky Mountain Fur Company, probably 200 men at least, and the men of two newcomers to the trade, Nathaniel J. Wyeth and Captain Bonneville.

Captain Bonneville

Benjamin Louis Eulalie de Bonneville, a West Point graduate, became interested in the fur trade while stationed on the frontier. He secured a two years' leave, ostensibly for the purpose of exploration, but there is no evidence to support the claim he was on a secret mission for any department of government. His outfit was provided by Alfred Seton, a New York merchant and former Astorian, and it appears conclusive that Bonneville's principal purpose was to break into the fur trade. Instead, he was broken by his experienced competitors and withdrew bankrupt in 1836.

Chittenden calls Bonneville a "history-made" man, and it was Washington Irving's facile pen that made the adventures of Captain Bonneville famous. His travels were limited to the region crossed and recrossed by his competitors, the American and Rocky Mountain companies, between the Green and the headwaters of the Salmon River, with the exception of two sorties he made to the Snake and Columbia in 1833 and 1834.

Bonneville did make two contributions to an otherwise futile role in the history of the Far West. Jedediah Smith and his partners used wagons in 1830 to transport goods to the mountains, but they did not go farther than to the South Pass and they did not continue the practice. Bonneville, with his company of 110 to 120 men, took 20 light wagons carrying two years' supplies through the pass to the Green River. He thus added another stretch to the developing western highway. At the junction of Horse Creek with the Green River near present Daniel, Wyoming, he built Fort Bonneville. This was strategically located to command the principal route of travel to the Snake and was in the heart of the rendezvous country, but it was not well situated for a profitable trade, nor was it a good location for year-round occupation. However, the establishment, temporary as it was, indicated a new emphasis upon this gateway to the West. Before Bonneville left the country, two other forts, Hall and Boise, were located in the Snake region.

The efforts of Nathaniel J. Wyeth to get a foothold in the Far West were likewise a failure, but his activities have a peculiar interest in themselves, as well as an important bearing upon American-British commercial rivalry in the Pacific Northwest.

Wyeth was a young man 29 years of age and a successful Cambridge ice dealer when he became interested in the plan of Hall Jackson Kelley to colonize in Oregon.

Hall Jackson Kelley, "Prophet of Oregon"

Kelley was a Boston schoolteacher in 1817, when according to his own testimony, the Biddle edition of Lewis and Clark's journals and conferences with seamen and hunters convinced him that the Pacific Northwest "must, at no remote period, become of vast importance to our Government. . . . I foresaw that Oregon must, eventually, become a favorite field of modern enterprise, and the abode of civilization." A strong religious overtone invaded Kelley's thinking, but the principal task to which he devoted himself was the colonization of the Oregon country.

In 1829 he organized the American Society for Encouraging the Settlement of the Oregon Territory and by means of circulars and personal appeals sought to form a company to colonize at the mouth of the Willamette River. There was no doubt in Kelley's burning mind that the Oregon country was legitimately a territory of the United States though occupied by a foreign power whose grasp could be broken only by no less than "three thousand active sons of American freedom" as colonists. The colony "planned by Providence, made easy by Nature," would improve the moral condition of the Indians, open the continent to the trade of the Orient through the Columbia River, provide a refuge under a paternal government for the virtuous but unfortunate elements of American villages and seaports, and break the hold of the "bold and lawless spirit of enterprise" by which England held the land.

Kelley did not neglect the economic arguments that might invite colonists. Because of the wide circulation given his plans and writings, his assurances of the Oregon Country's prospects became part of the common thinking about the region.

> Much of the country within two hundred miles of the Ocean, is favorable to cultivation. The valley of the Multnomah is particularly so, being extremely fertile. The advantages, generally, for acquiring property are paramount to those on the prairies of the West, or in any other part of the world. . . . The Oregon is covered with heavy forests of timber. . . . The production of vegetables, grain, and cattle will require comparatively but little labor; these articles, together with the spontaneous growth of the soil, and the fruits of laborious industry, in general, will find a market, *at home,* and thereby comfort and enrich the settlers. Surplus staple articles may be shipped from their doors to distant ports, and return a vast profit in trade. Lumber, ship timber, &c. may be sent to the western coast of South America, the islands in the Pacific; bread stuffs, furs, salmon, and many other articles of domestic manufactures, to the East Indies.[8]

Nathaniel Wyeth, Colonizer

The origin of Wyeth's interest in Oregon lay in words like these. But when he was convinced of Kelley's inability to lead an organization, and of Kelley's apparent indifference to the actual purpose for which Wyeth was considering joining the company, that of making money, he decided to form his own company. He was ready to go in the spring of 1832.

His idea was to organize a joint-stock company, as he put it, like the Hudson's Bay and North West companies, under the name Pacific Trading Company, whose shareholders would actually participate in an expedition to the Columbia where they would ulti-

[8] Fred W. Powell, "Hall Jackson Kelley," *OHQ*, XVIII, March, 1917, 35.

mately develop a commerce based on the region's diverse resources. Until he had thorough information as to these potentialities, he planned to engage in the fur trade on so large a scale that he would force the Hudson's Bay Company to come to terms with him. He believed the joint occupation agreement with Great Britain would be terminated in 1838 with Oregon falling to the Americans, and he assumed the British company would withdraw, leaving his association as successor to its monopoly position.[9] To accomplish this ambitious hope, he planned to supplement his fur trade in the interior with a coastal salmon canning enterprise, the latter to carry the cost of supplying his interior trade by sea and from the coast.

Between Boston and St. Louis, Wyeth gathered up the party of 24 who paid him 40 dollars apiece to help defray expenses of transportation, and who hoped, by this small investment, to become partners in a profitable enterprise. They were uniformed in coarse woolen jackets, pantaloons, striped cotton shirts, and cowhide boots. They carried muskets or rifles, but that they marched to the tune of the bugle, as Wyeth had hoped they might, is highly improbable.

Desertions *en route* to the mountains, and at Pierre's Hole where the party had a sample of what competition meant in the trade, sadly reduced his party. An additional factor may have been Wyeth's personality. He was a brilliant planner, but according to one of his companions, he "was not a man easily diverted by the advice of others."[10] Among those who gave up the enterprise were his eldest brother, Dr. Jacob Wyeth, and his 18-year-old unruly nephew, John B. Wyeth. Eleven men chose to continue to the mouth of the Columbia.

At the end of October, Wyeth arrived at Fort Vancouver practically destitute, having had to cache some of his goods in the mountains when he could not procure horses. He was kindly received by McLoughlin, although he was given clearly to understand that hospitality did not cover his business affairs.

Wyeth was not discouraged, but on the contrary convinced that there were opportunities in the Oregon country and the fur trade for his exploitation. His experience thus far had shown a small enterprise

[9] *Correspondence and Journals of Captain Nathaniel J. Wyeth,* 32.
[10] Ball, "Across the Continent," *OHQ,* III, March, 1902, 88.

could not break into a trade backed with generous capital, as in the case of the Hudson's Bay Company, or years of experience as in the case of the American companies. The latter, however, were in a process of disintegration or reorganization, and he saw an opportunity to step in as a supplier for independent trappers. He believed that they could be supplied more profitably from the coast than from St. Louis, and that a coastal depot, supported by fishing and farming in the Willamette Valley, would eventually pay off. In anticipation of returning to Oregon he journeyed to the mouth of the Columbia "with a view to the Salmon buisness [*sic*]" and spent a few days examining the Willamette Valley for a farm site. "I have never seen country of equal beauty except the Kanzas country," he wrote in his journal, "and I doubt not will one day sustain a large population." Here he found eight or nine retired Hudson's Bay Company employees settled with their families, and their prosperous gardens confirmed his opinion that if the country was ever to be colonized, this was the place to begin.

Having released the 11 men who had stayed with him, Wyeth rehired two of them to accompany him on his return trip. Others found temporary employment with the Hudson's Bay Company. John Ball, a New Yorker trained in law and a successful businessman who had joined Wyeth to fulfill an old dream of western adventure, taught school at Fort Vancouver during the winter of 1832-1833. In the spring after Wyeth left, he decided to farm in the Willamette Valley in partnership with John Sinclair, another Wyeth man. Choosing their lands on the prairies near present Salem, they built a house "the walls of which are the cylindrical fir, and the roof thereof cypress and yew," made horse harness of deerskins, and with tools and seeds lent by Dr. McLoughlin, plowed and sowed. It was a beautiful and fruitful country to which Ball responded appreciatively: ". . . Strawberries and other plants are in flower, and trees in leaf in April. By April 15 the camas are in bloom, and plants of many kinds full grown. By May 15 strawberries are ripe and roses are in bloom. . . . Deer and elk are plentiful, and one can always get salmon at the falls to eat. Hogs, horses, and cattle are easily raised."[11]

But for all the richness of the valley and the grandeur of the moun-

[11] *Ibid.*, 104.

tain peaks, there were persistent strains of evil in the garden: its inhabitants made the country one of "falsehood and low cunning" and the white men lived too close to the ways of the natives. And the "fever and the ague" burned out the enthusiasm already weakened by loneliness. Ball and Sinclair sold their first crops to the Hudson's Bay Company and left the country the following September.

Two other members of Wyeth's first expedition, Solomon H. Smith and Calvin E. Tibbetts, a Maine stonecutter, became permanent settlers. Smith, a New Englander with some training in medicine and a varied experience in business and fishing, succeeded Ball as teacher at Vancouver for almost two years. He married an Indian woman, and moved to the valley, joining the settlement of former Hudson's Bay Company employees known as French Prairie. Here he farmed and in 1834 started a school for his neighbors' children.

In the meantime, Wyeth had left Fort Vancouver in February, 1833, in company with Francis Ermatinger of the Hudson's Bay Company, who was in charge of the Snake River expedition that year. Wyeth was full of new schemes of a commercial venture, which while still incorporating farming and salmon canning, had shifted emphasis with regard to the fur trade. He proposed now not to concern himself with the trapping part of the industry but to become a supplier of goods to those already in the field. From Fort Colvile, he sent a proposal to Governor Simpson to coöperate with the Company in such a capacity outside the field of its immediate interests, that is, south of the Columbia and away from its established posts. This proposal was not accepted by the governor, but the principle behind it was adopted by Dr. McLoughlin, who the next year sent Thomas McKay to the Snake country with an outfit to trade with the American trappers, "so as to Introduce Our Goods Among them. . . ."[12]

Unaware of this turn of events, Wyeth based his future plans upon the probable acceptance of his proposal. Before reaching the rendezvous of the mountain men he made arrangements to hunt in partnership with Captain Bonneville south of the Columbia River, even to the Spanish settlements. Wyeth planned to lead a party to California himself, but for this purpose Bonneville sent his lieutenant, Joseph

[12] *McLoughlin's Fort Vancouver Letters*, First Series, 168.

Walker, on an expedition of extreme hardship across Nevada to San Francisco Bay. Walker's experiences did not encourage further efforts in this direction. Besides entering into partnership with Bonneville, Wyeth also contracted with Milton Sublette and Thomas Fitzpatrick, of the recently collapsed Rocky Mountain Fur Company, to deliver goods from the United States to them at the next rendezvous. He intended to transport the furs taken in exchange to the Hudson's Bay Company at Fort Walla Walla or Vancouver in line with his proposition made to the Company.

In early November (1833) Wyeth was back in Cambridge trying to find backers for his second expedition to the Oregon country. The firm of Tucker and Williams of Boston advanced him funds for his inventory of goods under the name of the Columbia River Company, and some financial assistance probably came from Bonneville's backer, Alfred Seton of New York.

Wyeth's Second Expedition

In March, 1834, Wyeth was in St. Louis once more. Jealous competitors, well entrenched there, forced him to pay high for horses, and to get men he had to make heavy advances on wages. When he started from Independence at the end of April, he was racing against time to get to the rendezvous July 1, before his chief rival, William Sublette, Milton's brother. He failed to do so. Milton Sublette and Fitzpatrick alleged they were unable to continue in business and refused to buy his stock. What Wyeth learned of Bonneville's dawdling winter activities did not encourage him or his men, 30 of whom were hired away from him. With 130 horses and mules, 40 remaining employees, and a large stock of goods, Wyeth had but one alternative: to set up a post in the hope that a successful trading house might yet save his venture.

Fort Hall

On the Snake River above the Falls he built Fort Hall, and to celebrate its erection "manufactured a magnificent flag from some unbleached sheeting a little red flannel and a few blue patches, saluted it with damaged powder and wet it in vilanous [sic] alcohol . . . after all it makes . . . a very respectable appearance amid the dry and desolate regions of central America."[13] Always hopeful in spite of reverses, he now saw new possibilities in having several such permanent forts in the interior. Their establishment, however, would depend upon the success of his efforts at the mouth of the Columbia. He then hurried on to the Columbia where he expected to find his ship the *May Dacre* and a salmon preserving industry under way. But the ship was delayed at Valparaiso three months and did not arrive until the 11th of September, too late to do anything with salmon that fall.

Although his prospects were as dismal as those of two years before, Wyeth still tried to secure a foothold in the country. He put men to work on a farm at French Prairie. Another crew worked on Fort William, located on Sauvies' Island, then called Wapato Island, near the mouth of the Willamette, and which he planned as the center of his fishing enterprise. He reported he had a few buildings for storehouses, some dwellings, and a blacksmith's and cooper's shop erected by October 6.

Misfortune dogged his efforts. The Sandwich Islanders he had imported as laborers deserted, and accidents and, in the interior, Indian scalpings took the lives of 14 of his employees. "Our people are sick and dying off like rotten sheep of bilious disorders," he wrote in September, 1835. The Indians did not bring their salmon to his plant, no doubt discouraged from doing so by the Hudson's Bay Company, which otherwise did nothing overt to interfere with his affairs. Before the ship sailed only a half cargo was obtained and that was not properly cured. During the winter of 1834-1835, Wyeth explored the Deschutes River a considerable distance into the interior, but spent most of his time at Fort William. He wintered at Fort Hall in 1835-1836. In the spring he returned once more to Vancouver where he arranged for Courtney M. Walker to take charge of Fort William and left a tenant on the farm he had started in the valley. In June of 1836 Wyeth started back to the United States by way of Taos (New Mexico) and the Arkansas. The next year he sold Fort Hall and its outfit to the Hudson's Bay Company. Fort William was abandoned, but for some years Wyeth continued to believe he was still possessed of lands in the Willamette Valley.

---

[13] Wyeth, *Correspondence*, 72.

Nathaniel Wyeth's attempts to establish a commercial colony in the Oregon country were unsuccessful, but even their failure was significant. The enterprise was based initially upon the fur trade of the Rocky Mountains. He attempted to enter it against heavy opposition and at the very time a decline in its fortunes had set in. He had neither the capital nor experience to compete on the one hand with the well-entrenched Hudson's Bay Company, and on the other with the hardened leaders of the mountain men whom he described as scoundrels. His hope of developing a Columbia River salmon industry for export trade was premature. He had to depend upon the Indians' primitive methods of catching the fish and of transporting it to his processing plant. It was essential that the fish be fresh but this was a requirement the Indians could not appreciate. Nor could he, in his brief experience, break through the customary trade practices the Hudson's Bay Company had built up and through which the Indians had become dependent. These factors alone were sufficient to defeat him. All the Company had to do was to wait patiently for his expectations to fail.

Unknowingly, Wyeth contributed to the settlement of Oregon by inducing the Hudson's Bay Company to shift its policies with regard to the Snake River country. McLoughlin saw the point of Wyeth's idea of supplying the American trappers and turned it to the Company's account. When Wyeth built Fort Hall, McLoughlin had Fort Boise built and when Wyeth offered his fort for sale, McLoughlin purchased it and maintained it to supply Americans and interior Indians with British goods. When emigration began to flow along the Oregon Trail, Fort Hall and Fort Boise became important supply stations on this long and barren stretch.

Wyeth's failure also contributed to American settlement when men from his two expeditions chose to remain in the West. Smith and Tibbets of the first company were the original citizen-settlers. No roster of the second expedition has survived, but it has been estimated that no less than seven of his men began farming in the valley. With his party in 1834 were several "dignitaries," as he called them, among them the naturalist John K. Townsend, and botanist Thomas Nuttall, the Methodist missionaries Jason and Daniel Lee, and the laymen Cyrus Shepard and Philip Edwards who were to accomplish what Wyeth aspired to and failed to complete. Their role and the part of other missionaries in the settlement of Oregon are the subject for another chapter.

When Wyeth left the mountains in 1836, the era of the fur trade was drawing rapidly to a close. The American trade was in the hands of the American Fur Company. The mountain men had to work harder and roam farther to find the increasingly scarce beaver; the price they received from the unopposed American Fur Company was less rewarding than it had ever been. By 1840 many had deserted the Rockies. Some drifted to California and entered the horse and cattle trade of the Southwest; some came to the Willamette Valley and reluctantly but of necessity turned to farming.

The Mountain Men Turn to Oregon

The first of these appeared in 1834, the year McLoughlin politely welcomed Wyeth back to the fort and received the Lees as guests. No such welcome was given Ewing Young and the party of eight or 12 who accompanied him. Young was a hardened product of the southwest frontier whose career had included mountain trapping, the Santa Fe trade, and driving horses from California to Taos. His companions with one exception comprised a cross section of the reckless breed of mountain men, from well-educated, energetic, and versatile Joseph Gale and steady Webley Hauxhurst down the scale to roistering irresponsibles. The one exception was Hall Jackson Kelley, who after the failure of his colonizing companies to get started in 1832, undertook to come to Oregon alone.

Kelley's Unhappy Journey to Oregon

Kelley's story is an unhappy one of a brilliant, erratic man driven by compulsions to a leadership he was temperamentally unfitted to exert. These led him to become a promoter of schemes of which the more enduring was Oregon. In 1817 he had a vision in which " 'the word came expressly to me' to go and labor in the fields of philanthropic enterprise and promote the propagation of Christianity in the dark and cruel places about the shores of the Pacific. . . ." This, in 1829, had become a vision of an Oregon colony of which he became the principal promoter. Determined to go to Oregon to civilize it, alone if need be, in 1833 he started from New Orleans and sailed to Vera Cruz. In Mexico he distributed religious tracts and almost was deflected from his Oregon destination by a new consuming passion to confer benefit on Mexico by planning a railroad between Vera Cruz and Mexico City. After numerous hardships he crossed to Acapulco, and finally reached California where near San Diego he fell in with Ewing Young. According to his story, he converted Young and his companions to a desire to live in Oregon. By the time the caravan got started for the Columbia it was joined by others who were driving horses they had not bothered to purchase. Young and other Americans of his kind were barely tolerated by the Mexican officials when they were on legitimate business and more often than not were subject to suspicion of being horse thieves rather than traders. What may have been an unfortunate misunderstanding led the governor of California to notify McLoughlin by means of a Company ship then at Monterey, that the Young Party was driving stolen horses.

When they arrived at Fort Vancouver, they were coolly received. Kelley was obviously a mentally sick man suffering from a persecution mania. He was given housing outside the fort until March 15, 1835, when he was sent off at Company expense to the Islands and the following October sailed for Boston on a whaling ship. He never forgot that his treatment, while within more than the modicum bounds of humanity, was still disinterested and impersonal. He overlooked completely the fact that he was notoriously anti-British and anti-Hudson's Bay Company even before his visit to its western fort, and that McLoughlin was informed in this regard. Kelley subsequently became even more than before a principal propagandist for American occupation of Oregon, and a bitter antagonist of the British Company.

The affairs of Ewing Young and his companions were only slightly better, in that they were in health and used to hardship, but that was all. They moved into the Chehalem Valley and erected cabins, but were unable to get supplies from the Hudson's Bay Company. Young and Lawrence Carmichael retaliated against the "tyranizing oppression" of McLoughlin by starting a whisky distillery in the winter of 1836. This sure means of acquiring a livelihood was frowned upon by other members of the community, both French Canadians and missionaries, and upon their solicitation, Young abandoned his still. In 1837 he led an expedition to California and returned with cattle for himself and the other settlers.

As a rancher and storekeeper he formed the core of a growing community of ex-mountain men. In 1840 Robert Newell, his brother-in-law, Joseph L. Meek and George W. Ebberts, came down from the mountains and took up land on Tualatin Plains. The fur trade era was at an end. The future of Oregon lay in the plowed earth and in the fields of grain ripening in the August sun.

10

Diplomacy of the Nations

The preceding chapters have considered the era of the fur trade, maritime and continental, in terms of the enterprise of British subjects and American citizens. We have indicated that the governments of Spain, Russia, England, and the United States, and in a slight degree, France, had interests in the region, and that the development of the trade affected, and was affected by, these interests. Allowing for the restless stirrings of expansive ambitions on the part of European nations in the eighteenth century and for the promptings of scientific curiosity which attracted them to the region, it still can be said with reasonable justification that, in the cases of Russia and France, their national interests in the Pacific Northwest evolved from the fur trade. In the cases of Spain, England, and the United States, this form of commercial enterprise was only incidental to large and more comprehensive ideas of national interest. Common boundaries and different conceptions of government and policies of trade contributed to bringing these interests into conflict.

As we have seen, Spain's interest in the Northwest grew out of her concern for the defense of her cherished internal provinces. To protect them she claimed a widely extended continental frontier and fortified her vulnerable California coast colonies. Her structure of government—dynastic, autocratic—and her colonial system, structured in the old mercantilism, which closed her empire to the rest of the world politically and economically, were almost anachronisms in an age when dynasties were toppling and the idea of free trade—the new mercantilism—was gaining ground. In contrast to Spain, the English state was no longer a "monolithic structure" which society existed to serve, but rather it was the aggregate of interests that composed the society and government served to protect and prosper that society.

British Policy

By the mid-eighteenth century, England was experiencing the impact of the Industrial Revolution. Commerce, which included the whole range of economic activity from the development of resources to the processing and distribution of goods, and was considered a means of expanding the wealth of the nation, was becoming a primary interest of the state. The nation's power was inextricably interwoven with the prosperity and expansion of the mercantile classes. Some members of this important element in British society influenced statecraft toward a revision of old ideas about the balance of power, the balance of trade, and colonialism. Merchants were becoming increasingly interested in achieving a free trade of goods throughout the world and the capture of the world's markets for British manufactures. They were less interested in the state's acquiring territorial possessions which would burden it with expenses of administration and defense, and political dilemmas of theory and practice such as had developed with relation to the American colonies on the Atlantic. They were concerned with colonies not as producers of raw materials but as markets. Their emphasis was upon trade rather than territorial possessions. The Nootka incident gave Britain's commercial interests an opportunity to direct their developing ideas of a new imperial sovereignty and of free trade toward the overthrow of traditional exclusiveness of the old mercantilism which especially characterized the Spanish empire.

Redefining Sovereignty at Nootka

Issues of domestic politics in part explain the British position in this controversy in 1790: the opposing viewpoints of "Big" and "Little" Englanders, the jingoistic pressures in an election year, and the efforts of merchants, who wanted free trade to mean also freedom to trade, to use the northwest coast trade as a lever against the East India Company's monopoly in China. But it may also be explained as a manifestation of the government's "desire to establish a new principle of imperial sovereignty" and as a major step toward the institution of free trade practices among the nations.[1]

[1] John M. Morris, "The Policy of the British Cabinet in the Nootka Crisis" in *EHR*, LXX, October, 1955; Lennox Mills, "The Real Significance of the Nootka Sound Incident," *CHR*, VI, June, 1925.

The New Interpretation of Sovereignty

In the Nootka incident, Spain interpreted sovereignty as a consequence of title, and title was based upon prior discovery, exploration, and formal acts of possession. The power to exclude was inherent in a declaration of sovereignty. England, on the other hand, admittedly with weak claims to title on the customary grounds, in effect chose to interpret sovereignty as effective only as a consequence of occupation, and this meant, to all practical purposes, on-the-spot power to exclude. She did not claim that Meares's establishment at Nootka was evidence of English occupation. It was, rather, evidence that the Spanish were not there, in occupation, to prevent it. Since they were not in a position to exclude, it followed they had no exclusive sovereignty. Therefore, the Northwest coast was open to England's commerce. And this was the Spanish interpretation of the British position.[2]

A significant item of fact supports the thesis that the British argument was mainly directed toward development of an expedient theory of sovereignty which would permit the exploitation of colonial domains by mercantile enterprise. Having displayed an aggressive belligerence to break down Spain's claims to exclusive sovereignty, the British government did not proceed to establish its own. In spite of the pleas of Cadman Etches and his associates for state support in founding commercial outposts, the government gave them no direct encouragement and took no steps to build up a case for British territorial dominion. *Laissez-faire; laissez aller*. It was alert, however, to any circumstances which might jeopardize the principle it had threatened war to establish: The region was open to the commerce of nations without prejudice to claims of title. Although changes of government brought fluctuations of emphasis with regard to both the emerging concept of free trade and British interests generally, this remained essentially the policy of England in the Pacific Northwest.

---

[2] Luis de Las Casas to Alcudia, February 1, 1793, in *Spain in the Mississippi Valley, 1765-1794*. Ed. Lawrence Kinnaird. American Historical Association *Annual Report 1945*, Part III. *Problems of Frontier Defense 1792-1794*, Washington, 1945, 136.

American Policy

Happening almost simultaneously with the initiation of American commerce on the coast, the Nootka incident precipitated a small-scale crisis for the new government of the United States. It contributed to the formulation of the nation's foreign and continental policy. The prospect of a war between England and Spain, whose possessions bordered the nation's restless frontiers, brought about the first statement of a neutrality policy and reinforced the idea already prevalent among its statesmen that European neighbors, whether at war or in peace, were hazards to the Republic's security.

The new nation inherited from its colonial experience a continental viewpoint. British imperialism of the mid-eighteenth century had required the expulsion of the French Empire (1754-1763) from North America. The United States's imperialism now required, at most the elimination of the British Empire or at least its containment. During the Revolution and the making of the peace, it was hoped that Britain might surrender Canada. Such hopes remained in some breasts until late in the nineteenth century, but realistic politics were satisfied in 1783 with a boundary that would exclude the British from south of the 49th parallel.

The idea of exclusive sovereignty was inherent in American continentalism. It was early associated with the notion that republican ideology and institutions must be protected from European monarchical hostility. And both ideas were basic to the expansionist ambitions of the American people. During the 50 years in which the United States and Great Britain found cause for dispute over the Pacific Northwest, policies of state and the deeds of the American people were directed toward the realization of the nation's sovereignty from sea to sea. Jefferson's role in bringing the nation's western boundaries up to the Rockies has been described. It is sufficient to recall that he did not look upon the mountains as a barrier to further American expansion, even though he did not believe the transmontane region would ever become a part of the republic. The Columbia River, "pointed out by nature," according to Alexander Mackenzie, as "the only navigable river" on the northern Pacific coast, was clearly intended to lie within the sphere of American and republican interests. But there was no formal agreement between the United States and England as to what the legal boundaries of those interests were.

Following the purchase of Louisiana and the Lewis and Clark expedition, negotiations between the United States and Great Britain in 1807 led to the acceptance of the 49th parallel as the international boundary "as far as the respective Territories of the parties" extended to the west. This ambiguous phraseology was temporarily satisfactory for diplomatic purposes even though this particular agreement failed of ratification. Officially the United States had surrendered nothing. In the popular mind there was no doubt, and there never was, that the western boundary of the United States was the Pacific Ocean. It will be recalled that this was the gist of the message the mysterious Jeremy Pinch sent to David Thompson. The matter rested between the governments or was, more properly perhaps, lost in the welter of other issues that plagued them, until peace commissioners began the treaty negotiations that concluded the War of 1812.

In his directions to the commissioners, Secretary of State James Monroe admitted he was not sure whether John Jacob Astor's fur trading post at the mouth of the Columbia had been wrested from the United States during the war, and whether its restoration should become a part of the peace stipulation. He was firm, however, in his warning to the negotiators that they should admit no British claims to territory south of 49°. "It is not believed that they have any claim whatever to Territory on the Pacific Ocean," he instructed them, "You will . . . be careful . . . not to countenance in any manner or in any quarter a pretension in the British Government to Territory South of that line."[3] This was the position consistently maintained in American diplomatic proceedings with Great Britain.

Restoration of Fort Astoria

The Treaty of Ghent which concluded the war (1815) provided for the restoration of all locations, except certain islands in Passamaquoddy Bay, taken in military action by either party during the war. In July, 1815, Monroe called to the attention of the British *chargé d'affaires* that the Columbia River post

[3] *Canadian Relations,* I, 218.

came under this stipulation and would be reoccupied without delay. Two years passed, however, before any measures were taken toward this end. John Quincy Adams, succeeding Monroe as Secretary of State when the latter became president, instituted a vigorous policy with regard to the United States's claims wherever the nation was still at variance with the British. John Bartow Prevost was ordered as special agent to proceed to the Columbia River on the United States sloop *Ontario*, and in collaboration with Captain James Biddle, "to assert there the claim of sovereignty in the name and on behalf of the United States by some symbolical or other appropriate mode of setting up a claim to national authority and dominion."[4]

The British immediately protested this sudden assertion of American rights. Adams's ironical instructions to Richard Rush, minister to London, revealed his pleasure in pushing the British on this issue. He could not see how they could be offended since they had no "authorized" establishment on the Columbia; they had "intimated no question whatever of the title of the United States" to Astor's settlement before the war, and it had not occurred, therefore, to the state department that any question had arisen which would make the United States's title now "an object of interest to Great Britain." He suggested Rush point out to Lord Castlereagh "the minuteness of the present interest" to both nations, but that "should it ever *become* an object of serious importance to the United States," it could scarcely be supposed that Great Britain would find it either "useful or advisable" to resist. Deprecation of the issue as unimportant at the time was nullified by the unveiled threat as to the future. It is probable that Rush did not submit to Castlereagh verbatim the bald statement summarizing Adams' instructions: "If the United States leave her [Great Britain] in undisputed possession of all of her holds upon Europe, Asia, and Africa, with all her actual possessions in this hemisphere, we may very fairly expect that she will not think it consistent either with a wise or a friendly policy, to watch with eyes of jealousy and alarm, every possibility of extension to our natural dominion in North America, which she can have no solid interest to prevent, until all possibility of her preventing it shall have vanished. . . .[5]

British arguments that Astor's fort had been sold to the North

[4] *Canadian Relations*, I, 262-263.
[5] *Canadian Relations*, I, 268-269.

West Company previous to its capture did not prevail. Castlereagh admitted that, on the same principle on which Britain had demanded restoration in the Nootka controversy, the Americans were justified in claiming the restoration of Fort Astoria. But he would not admit that agreement to restore settled the matter of sovereignty, and he requested a further examination of that subject.

In the meantime, Astoria was, in effect, doubly restored. In August, Captain Biddle arrived on the *Ontario* and on the 19th took possession of both shores of the Columbia. Two months later Prevost arrived on board the British naval vessel *Blossom*, whose captain lowered the British flag. Prevost hoisted the Stars and Stripes in token of possession and sovereignty. These formalities did not change the actual situation with regard to the occupancy of the fort. Prevost notified James Keith, factor in charge of the post, that the Company might continue to occupy and protect the fort, under the American flag, until the United States should order its withdrawal. Such a time depended upon a settlement of the question of title to the region, and the British did not admit this as concluded.

The Boundary Issue—1818

This was made very clear during the eight conferences held by American and British commissioners during the fall of 1818 on three categories of problems connected with the peace treaty. The Pacific Northwest question was linked with the one concerning the boundary line in the old Northwest.

Albert Gallatin and Richard Rush, the American commissioners, suggested an extension of the 49th parallel to the Pacific. They admitted that the United States did not have an unassailable right to the whole territory south of that line westward of the mountains, but asserted that their claims were at least as good as those of the British. So far as the country drained by the Columbia was concerned, however, they argued indisputable rights on the basis of discovery, exploration, and settlement, and Fort Astoria was offered as evidence of the latter. The British commissioners, Frederick Robinson and Henry Goulburn, presented counterarguments, and intimated they would accept as a boundary the 49th parallel to where it crossed the Columbia River, and the course of the River thereafter, providing the two powers held a common ownership of its mouth.[6]

The Americans could not accept these provisions since they were instructed not to consider any British claims south of the 49th parallel. Since the commissioners had before them other matters of greater immediate concern, they agreed to postpone final settlement of the Columbia River issue, but at the same time to provide against its becoming a source of continuing discussion between the two states.

Joint Occupation Agreement

To this end it was agreed that the boundary between the United States and Canada should follow the 49th parallel to the Rocky Mountains, as formerly, and that

> . . . any such country as may be claimed by either party on the North West Coast of America, or on the continent of America Westward of the Stony Mountains shall together with its harbours, bays and creeks and the navigation of all rivers within the same, be free and open, for the term of ten years . . . to the vessels, citizens and subjects of the two powers; it being well understood that this agreement is not to be construed to the prejudice of any claim, which either of the two high contracting parties may have to any part of the . . . country; nor shall it be taken to affect the claims of any other power or State to any part of the said country. . . .[7]

This article of the Convention of 1818 has, through customary usage become known as the "joint occupation" agreement. It simply meant that the citizens and subjects of the two powers could enter the region without prejudice to either nation's claims to title.

It should also be noted that with regard to the latter, the agreement recognized that other powers might also have claims to the area and that the temporary solution of the British-American dispute did not eliminate these contenders to title in this area. In the next six years, American diplomacy accomplished the formal abrogation of Spanish and Russian claims.

The Enlarging Idea of National Dominion

The circumstances of American politics which at that time brought experienced diplomats into the state department and then to the presidency gave national continental

[6] *Canadian Relations*, I, 879.
[7] Hunter Miller, *Treaties*, II, 574-578.

policy and diplomacy a basic consistency over a long period of years. James Madison was Jefferson's secretary of state, and James Monroe, an experienced if not a brilliant diplomat, succeeded to the state office when Madison became president. Similarly, John Quincy Adams, one of the commissioners at the peace conference in 1814, became Secretary of State under Monroe, and succeeded him as chief executive. Throughout the period from Jefferson through Adams' administrations, there was no relinquishment of the nation's claim to the Pacific Northwest, even when it was held to be extremely unlikely that it would ever become a part of the United States. By Adams' time it was not inconceivable that the expanding nation would march to the Pacific. The government therefore was not indifferent to the protection of the most remote frontiers of what Adams called the "natural dominion"; neither was the government indifferent to the means by which destiny could be encouraged through diplomatic channels.

Elimination of Spanish Claims to Title: Florida Treaty

To Adams must be given credit, not only for standing firm on the 49th parallel line, but also for narrowing the field of title contenders, actual or potential, to the Pacific Northwest. In concluding a treaty with Spain by which the United States secured the Floridas in 1819, he also secured Spain's surrender of claims to all lands west of the source of the Arkansas River and north of the 42nd parallel to the Pacific.[8] It was thereafter argued that the United States through this treaty succeeded to the original Spanish claims in the Pacific Northwest. The argument was academic, but it indicated Adams' determination to leave no loophole through which the American case for sovereignty to its "natural dominion" might be lost.

The Russian Threat

Adams was also alert to the possible claims Russia might extend southward from Alaska. The Russians had not been especially concerned with extending their territorial claims in the New World until, in 1806, an imperial inspector, Baron Rezanov, who was also the son-in-law of the influential head of the

[8] Hunter Miller, *Treaties*, III, 3-18.

Russian American Company, urged the founding of a colony at the mouth of the Columbia River. Here, he pointed out, the Russians "could attract population . . . and become strong enough to make use of any turn in European politics to include the coast of California in the Russian possessions."[9]

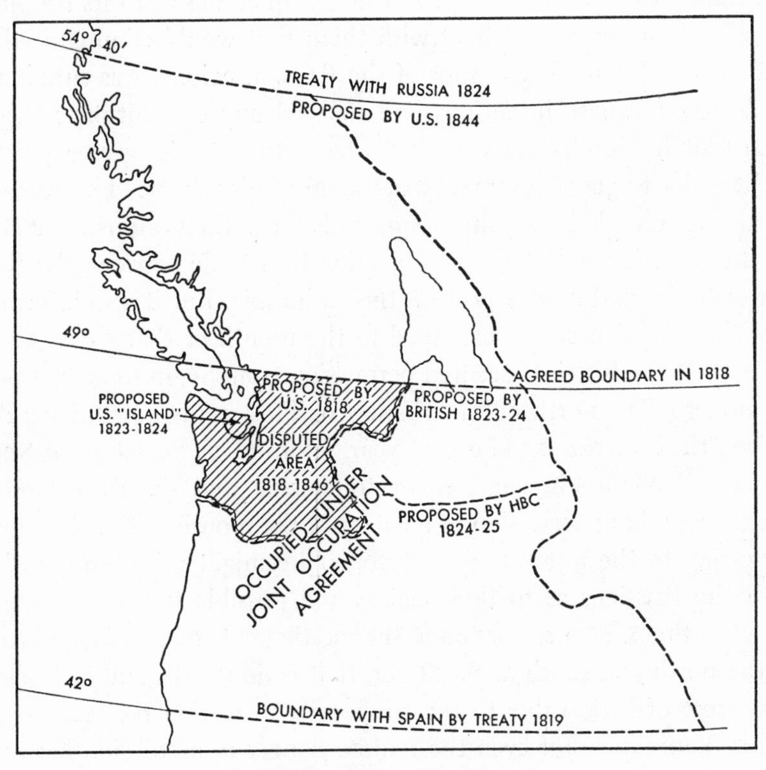

Oregon Boundary Negotiations

Rezanov's encouragement of Russian expansion reflected his concern with serious problems related to the Alaskan trading posts. They were endangered immediately by the establishment of the North West Company's posts in Northern New Caledonia, more remotely by the probable consequences of the Lewis and Clark expedition in which it was presumed the United States would extend its claims to the river's mouth. Furthermore, the Russian posts' dependence upon irresponsible American traders for food supplies and trading goods

[9] Bancroft, *The North West Coast*, I, 321.

exposed them, they claimed, to dangers from the natives supplied also with American firearms and firewater. The acquisition of the coast, including the Columbia River's entrance and California, would solve these problems by providing the produce they needed and excluding the Americans from access to Russian waters.

When Astor had heard of the Russian dilemma as to its supplies, he offered to make a contract with them that would eliminate other traders, but Baranoff, governor of the Russian colony, was suspicious of Astor's ultimate intentions and delayed any commitment. Astor even sent his son-in-law, Count Bentzon, to Petersburg as a private ambassador to get governmental approval of his scheme. The Russian Chancery revealed to John Quincy Adams, then minister at the capital, that it would have no objection to a trade between the Russian colonies and Astor's post on the Columbia. But it also informed him that Russian claims extended to the mouth of that river.[10]

In 1815, the Russians secured permission from Spain to erect a post on Bodega Bay, north of San Francisco. This seems not to have disturbed the Americans. The next year, Monroe, as Secretary of State advised William Pinckney, envoy to Russia, that since the United States was taking possession of territory at the mouth of the Columbia (referring to the restoration of Astoria) he might raise the question with the Russians as to their claims and possible future differences between them. Monroe assumed that settlements of Russian subjects to the north and south of the River, that is, in Alaska and at Bodega Bay, were of little value to the Emperor considering the vast extent of his dominions; but even the remote danger of a collision between them ought to be guarded against. He therefore suggested that, in adjusting their mutual claims, the United States would be satisfied to adopt the 49th parallel as the northern boundary between their interests. Noteworthy is the fact that in this suggestion, Monroe ignored British claims north of 49°.

When Adams succeeded Monroe as Secretary of State, he added nothing to these instructions, but suggested that the United States's minister "observe attentively the movements of Russia with regard to their settlements on the North-Western Coast." He believed that Russian policy in 1818 did not make it appear Russia was much to be feared: Emperor Alexander displayed no "symptoms of the Passion

[10] Adams, *Writings*, III, 487-488.

which so vehemently prompted his ancestor Peter to make Russia a naval Power." Hence it might be concluded that Alexander would not attempt on the coast of America what he had accomplished in the way of conquest on the shores of the Baltic. But, ever cautious, Adams could not neglect the fact that the "whole System of Russian Policy, as it bears on her Relations with Great-Britain, with the European Alliance, with Spain and the South American affairs, may require the most steady and attentive observation, as it may link itself with objects of importance to the interests and welfare of the United States."[11]

These references to European politics of the post-Napoleonic period are outside the immediate problem of the Northwest boundary, but Adams did not wholly separate them in his long-range view of American welfare and the nation's natural dominion.

The alliance to which he referred, the Holy Alliance, was aimed at restoring the old regime and the old balance of power in Europe. A step in this direction was the restoration to Spain of her South American colonies which had revolted during the world upheaval; another was the curtailment of British power. While no friend of Britain, Adams was even less friendly to Russian-led reactionaryism. The need for attentive observation to Russian movements on the northwest coast had been pointed up by John Prevost's report, following his journey to the Columbia to accept the restoration of Fort Astoria. He had visited the Spanish settlements in California, found them weak and defenseless; he also found what he considered evidence of Russian ambition to acquire an empire in the Pacific. He referred to the newly formed establishment of the Russians in the Hawaiian Islands, and to the post at Bodega Bay. The location of the latter, near San Francisco Bay, one of the "most convenient capacious and safe in the world, wholly without defence and in the neighborhood of a feeble diffused and disaffected population," made feasible the inference that Russians had in mind aspiration to "early possession of this Harbor and ultimately to the sovereignty of entire California." He warned his superior: "Surely the growth of a race on these shores, scarcely emerged from the savage state, guided by a Chief who seeks not to emancipate but to inthrall, is an event by all to be deprecated! An event the mere apprehension of which I should

[11] *Canadian Relations*, I, 275-276.

think ought to excite the jealousies of the United States. . . ."[12]

In September, 1821, Alexander issued a *ukase* in which "the pursuits of commerce, whaling, and fishery, and of all other industry" on the northwest coast from Bering Strait down to the 51st parallel were "exclusively granted to Russian subjects," and all foreign vessels were prohibited from approaching within 100 Italian miles of the shore, and of carrying on trade with the natives.[13] While the *ukase* could have an impact upon American commercial interests in the northern Pacific, Adams was principally concerned with the fact that Russian assumption of jurisdiction over seas and shore to the northern tip of Vancouver Island, taken in conjunction with their activity in California and the Hawaiian Islands, might mean the initiation of an active program of territorial colonization. He instructed Henry Middleton, ambassador to the Emperor's Court, that the United States could admit no part of Russian territorial claims, that is, of colonies other than trading outposts such as those of the Russian American Company.

He went further in his warning to the Russian minister at Washington. The United States, he affirmed, "would contest the right of Russia to *any* territorial establishment on this continent, and that we should assume distinctly the principle that the American continents are no longer subject for *any* new colonial establishments."[14] The same principle was reiterated in instructions to Richard Rush in London to inform him of the trend of American policy.

> . . . The American continents, henceforth, will no longer be subject to *colonization.* Occupied by civilized, independent nations, they will be accessible to Europeans, and to each other, on that footing alone; and the Pacific Ocean, in every part of it, will remain open to the navigation of all nations in like manner with the Atlantic.
>
> Incidental to the condition of national independence and sovereignty, the rights of interior navigation of their rivers will belong to each of the American nations within its own territories. The application of colonial principles of exclusion, therefore, cannot be admitted by the United States as lawful, upon any part of the Northwest Coast of America, or as belonging to any European nation. Their own settlements there, when organized as territorial Governments, will be adapted to the freedom of their own

[12] *Canadian Relations,* I, 891.

[13] *Sen. Ex. Doc. No. 162,* 58 Cong., 2 Sess., 25-26.

[14] *Memoirs of John Quincy Adams,* ed. C. F. Adams, 12 vols., Philadelphia, 1874-1877, VI, 163.

institutions, and as constituent parts of the Union, be subject to the principles and provisions of the Constitution.[15]

The principle of noncolonization set forth here was the main thesis of President Monroe's annual message to Congress in December of the same year (1823). The Monroe Doctrine was the crystallization of a long-developing policy of American continentalism. Its extension to the South American continent was, in a sense, as unrealistic as the emperor's *ukase* of exclusion in the North Pacific, but it served the purpose of publishing to the world the fact that American policy was independent from European politics. While it is true that Adams and Monroe had in mind this large diplomatic purpose, it must be borne in mind that Adams seized the incident of the Russian *ukase* to drive it home, and he followed up the incident to further narrow the problem of title contenders to the Northwest Coast. In doing so he sharpened the issue between the United States and Great Britain.

The *ukase* was, of course, ineffectual unless implemented, and evidently the emperor had no intention of doing so. England and the United States both protested it, and Adams, in 1823, took the occasion to reopen negotiations between the two governments over the Oregon boundary.

The American minister, Rush, proposed the extension of the joint occupation agreement for another ten years, but on the stipulation that British subjects should make no settlements south of 51° nor north of 55°, and Americans none north of 51°. The British objected to these restrictions and offered a counterproposal that the boundary line should be the 49th parallel to the point where that line struck the "northeasternmost branch of the Columbia," thence down the Columbia to the ocean; that the river be forever free to citizens and subjects of both powers; and that thereafter no settlements would be permitted by either power within the limits thus assigned, except where there were already settlements made (such, for example, as Spokane House, Forts Okanogan, and Nez Perce), where the proprietors would have ten years of grace before removal.[16]

The negotiations were futile except to establish what would henceforth be the British position: a partition of the Oregon country. The

[15] *American State Papers, Foreign Relations,* V, 793.
[16] *Canadian Relations,* 468-469. Rush's summary of negotiations up to August 12, 1824.

Americans remained adamant: nothing less than the 49th parallel to the coast. It was inevitable under the circumstances that the negotiations should fail. Prime Minister Canning was enraged by the Adams' doctrine of noncolonization, and further so when he learned of the treaty the United States had negotiated with Russia and which had been signed late in April, 1824. This accepted Russia's exclusive jurisdiction down to 54° 40′, and between this latitude and 49°, it was agreed the two powers should enjoy free and equal access to navigation and commerce. This cavalier dismissal of British interests in the area was hardly tactful at the moment.

Further to complicate matters, Senator John Floyd of Virginia in January, 1822, had introduced a bill to organize the Oregon Territory. Another bill passed the House in December, 1824, authorizing the President to occupy Oregon with a military establishment and to organize a government. The latter failed in the Senate, but it led Richard Rush to warn his government in March, 1825, that if it commenced, "under an act of legislation or otherwise, the exercise of exclusive jurisdiction over both sides of the Columbia river, though keeping within the limit of 49 north, serious difficulties" would result. The British were in an unyielding mood.[17]

A little more than a year later and two years before the expiration of the joint occupation agreement, Canning himself reopened the Oregon issue. Frederick Merk in *Albert Gallatin and the Oregon Question* has argued that it was because the Hudson's Bay Company required a clarification of government's position before it undertook further development of its establishment in the region. It already was acting on the assumption that the Lower Columbia, that is, from the junction of the Snake west, would be the boundary line. It now suggested to Canning that this line be extended east along the Snake in the vicinity of 46° 20′ to the Continental Divide and thence north to where the Divide and the 49th parallel intersected. This would assure the Company the trade of the Northern Idaho region as well as the posts that would, in the proposal of 1823-1824, have fallen outside the British line. Why the Hudson's Bay Company or Canning thought this proposal would be more acceptable to the United States than the former which had been rejected is difficult to explain. The other explanation is the continuing white heat at which Canning

[17] *Canadian Relations*, I, 488.

seethed in resentment to Adams' noncolonization doctrine and to the Congress' repeated measures to occupy Oregon. We are led to conclude then that Canning's reopening of the issue was principally caused by a passion of resentment generated in 1823 and 1824 and brought to a head in 1826 by the Hudson's Bay Company's demands. Even though British opinion was solidly behind Canning, he was facing a stubborn Adams in the presidency—not only a stubborn man but one capable of as much wrath as his British antagonist. An unpopular president, especially with the West, his position on the Oregon question would nevertheless be supported in a crisis.

The circumstances did not promise a peaceful solution of the problem. It required all the tact and diplomacy of Albert Gallatin, special minister to London, to arrive at an anticlimactic renewal of the joint occupation agreement of 1818, with the one difference, that it could be terminated by either power with one year's notice.

Several futile concessions were made by each side in the course of the negotiations. The principal one Gallatin offered was the perpetual free navigation of the Columbia south of 49°. The British retreated to their 1823-1824 proposal of the Columbia as the boundary, and offered a small strip of shoreline on Puget Sound as compensation for the loss of that inland sea. What emerged clearly was that the area of dispute lay between the Columbia and the sea, roughly the western half of Washington. The rest of the Oregon country was conceded as American territory.

Two points were made repeatedly during the conferences: The British emphasized that they had no intention of colonizing the Oregon Country and that they wished only to protect their right to trade there; and the other was the equally repetitive claim on the part of the United States that it expected eventually to achieve exclusive dominion over the area south of 49°.

The Oregon question did not reach the diplomatic level of negotiation again until 1842, but it was by no means an unarticulated question. American fur trade interests, western Congressmen riding a subject popular with their constituents, enthusiasts like Hall Jackson Kelley, expansionists, even railroad promoters, and missionaries kept the subject alive.

Nor did the administrations, Democratic or Whig, ignore the issue. Adams' principal contribution was made before he became president.

Jackson's second term was almost expired when, in 1836, suspecting a British plot to subvert the newly created Republic of Texas and to combine with it a strengthening of its position on the Pacific coast, he sent special agent William A. Slacum to gather "useful information" about the British and the inhabitants in the Northwest. His report, among other things, emphasized the strategic military importance of Puget Sound to protect the Willamette Valley from northern Indians who might be inspired, by "some foreign power" to attack it.

A second investigation was set in motion almost simultaneously. In 1837 Lieutenant Charles Wilkes was given command of a Pacific and Antarctic exploration, which was scheduled to take him also to the Columbia River. At the same time an overland exploration under Lieutenant John C. Fremont was to head toward the same destination. The latter reached the Rockies in 1839, and a second expedition in 1842-1843 brought him to the coast. Like the Lewis and Clark expedition, Fremont's was a scientific exploration and a reconnaissance. Wilkes arrived in the Columbia in 1841 and in the months he was on the west coast he surveyed its rivers and harbors. Having lost one of his ships on the Columbia bar, he was not very enthusiastic about the potentials of the River, but he reported Puget Sound provided ideal harbors and recommended that it should never be surrendered in any boundary negotiations.

The heightening of interest in the military aspects of the Oregon country between 1836 and 1843 was the result of a situation foreseen decades before—the march of the American people into the West and into Oregon. Slacum found a handful of American missionaries and mountain men in 1836-1837; Wilkes, something more than 150; Fremont, close to 300. The linking of the Pacific Northwest with the international politics back of the Texas question, almost as enduring a one as the Oregon, suggests the scope of problems a continental policy and a continental-minded people involved. So long as the British—or the Spanish or Mexicans after 1822—continued to have any national interests whatever within what the United States considered to be its natural dominion, their interests were in conflict. The rivalries of the fur trade era were but preludes to the rivalries of a new era.

The American Colony in the Pacific Northwest

INTERPRETIVE KEY

Part II is concerned with the founding and development of an American colony in the Pacific Northwest. The first settlers were a few mountain men who arrived almost simultaneously with Wyeth's party in 1834. From his group a half-dozen remained, some only temporarily, and others became permanent settlers. The active founders of the colony were the missionaries, the Methodists under Jason Lee, and the Congregationalist-Presbyterian group led by Dr. Marcus Whitman and Henry H. Spalding. The missionaries had every intention of permanent settlement, for their work of converting and civilizing the Indians was not to be accomplished in a brief visit. They brought families into the West, farmed, and engaged in mercantile enterprises. For reasons beyond their control they were more successful as colonizers than missionaries to the Indians. They advertised the country and worked assiduously to attract to it the sober, industrious type of settler who would insure the Oregon Country to the United States politically and to the Protestant faith religiously. They helped to lay the foundations of a temporary government which served the colony until the settlement of the boundary issue with Great Britain brought the region into the orbit of national government as a territory, and they exerted an influence over the region that did not cease when their missions were closed.

The immigrants who followed the mountain men and missionaries, beginning in 1842 and in increasing numbers thereafter, belonged in the tradition of a westward moving people. Their pasts and their futures were linked with the development of the United States as a continental power. Many, if not most, of Oregon's early inhabitants had pioneered some part of the Middle West before they started to

Oregon. Whether they came originally from north or south of the Mason-Dixon line, they were predominantly a frontier farming people. As farmers they were seekers for the "Garden of the World." But this idyllic concept of an agricultural paradise had been corrupted by a counterbalancing trend toward urbanization which was beginning to prevail as the Middle West became settled and industrialization took hold in the East. The people who moved to Oregon, like those who moved into Iowa and Kansas, were town builders as well as farmers. Oregon promised what Kansas and Iowa did not—a gateway to the Pacific and the commerce of the Orient.

Politically oriented to the ideology of continental expansion and self-determination, the emigrants to Oregon like Westerners generally were intolerant of the slow processes of diplomacy which might or might not achieve for them the rounding out of the nation's natural dominions as they ambitiously conceived them. Their spirit of enterprise and aggrandizement ignored boundaries; yet, sticklers for legal forms, they abided the decisions of state their actions made inevitable. The same token respect for law impelled them to build a temporary government in the pattern they had known before they moved to Oregon, and to welcome the settlement of the boundary issue which assured them political unification with the nation. Yet their independence and their assertiveness made them resent the restrictions of territorial status and yearn for the sovereignty of statehood.

As territorials, the inhabitants of the Oregon country faced the problems of reconciling their anticipations of economic opportunity with the facts of the case. The commerce of the Orient did not flow in their direction. Their most encouraging development came from the happy accident of gold discoveries which gave the farmers markets first in California and then in the gold fields of the Pacific Northwest. But contemporary with the exploitation of the region's first natural resources, the Oregonians had to fight their most serious Indian wars, combat the elements of lawlessness which followed the mining frontier, and reach out by ship and rail for closer contacts with the commerce of the nation and the world.

In 1840, a few Americans in the Willamette Valley petitioned the United States to consider their plight as a colony isolated from its parent and faced with dangers their isolation magnified. Forty years later, the state of Oregon and the territories of Washington and Idaho were on the eve of their victory over isolation. A transcontinental railroad was approaching, their ships were carrying wheat and lumber to South America and Europe, and the town builders anticipated cities where villages existed. Optimism, that great quality of the American folk, which could burn down forests and till the deserts, and build wagon roads and railroads into virgin country, prevailed in the Pacific Northwest.

It was optimism too which brought the missionaries into Oregon in the 1830's to found the American colony in the Far West. We turn now to the early years of that colony and to the trials which forged its character and outlined its future.

11

Missions and Missionaries

Religious piety was not an outstanding characteristic of men engaged in the fur trade, although there were some exceptions. Among the mountain men, the Bible had a place along with Sir Walter Scott's works, Byron's poems, and Jane Porter's *Scottish Chiefs* as popular reading matter in winter camps, but a praying man, like Jedediah Smith, was unusual. Religious teaching had been a part of the education of most of the gentlemen officers of the Hudson's Bay Company, but so had the skeptical philosophies of the eighteenth century. When conflicts of orthodoxy and the new science were argued in Bachellor's Hall at Fort Vancouver, or in a lonely trading post of the north, as argued they must have been, the chances were the deistical or agnostic views were advanced equally with those of the Church of England, of Scottish Presbyterianism or Catholicism. The noncommissioned classes, largely French Canadian, by virtue of their ancestry and training were predominantly Catholic. Their church followed them to the Red River settlements, but not until 1838 did it cross the Rockies.

The Company was obligated by its 1821 royal license to provide for the moral improvement and religious instruction of the Indians. This was ignored, although Governor Simpson ordered divine services to be read on Sundays at Company posts. At Fort Vancouver, the Sabbath was observed. A bell summoned its inhabitants to the Hall to hear the reading in French of the Scriptures and a "Penser y Bien" and to unite in prayer.

In 1833, Dr. William Fraser Tolmie, a devout young Scotchman assigned as trader to Fort Nisqually, was shocked to find the trading post opened on Sundays. He stopped the practice and summoning the Indians to meet with him began to instruct them in religious history. Says the post clerk's journal of occurrences, in one lesson Dr.

Tolmie "explained the creation of the World, the reason why Christians and Jews abstained from work on Sundays; and had got as far as the Deluge in sacred history" when he was requested to stop as the Indians "could not comprehend things clearly."

Pressed by critics at home who seized on the fact that the Company was not fulfilling its charter obligations, the Governor and Committee in London decided in 1834 to attach a chaplain to the Vancouver post. Two years later, the Church of England's Herbert Beaver and wife Jane arrived at the Columbia. The peculiar affinity of his name with the trade was not borne out either in his personality or in his preparation for his task. Strongly anti-Catholic, he found to his "utter grief and astonishment" that he was "in the very stronghold of Popery. . . ." This he promptly attacked. Interpreting his appointment to mean he was to form "without forcing the consciences of Men . . . a Christian, a Protestant, and a Church of England Congregation," he began his work in the fort school he was assigned to teach. Since the majority of its pupils were from French Canadian families of the Catholic faith, McLoughlin feared the consequences of instruction based upon the Church of England catechism, and after one week, withdrew Beaver from the schoolroom.

The chaplain and his wife seemed to miss no opportunity to annoy or offend McLoughlin, and when Beaver accused him and others of living in sin because their marriages had no religious sanction, he was caned by the enraged Chief Factor. The Beavers returned to England after twenty-six months of bitter controversy. Reporting on the Beaver affair, James Douglas, McLoughlin's colleague, summarized for the Governor and Committee the qualifications of a clergyman for the heterogeneous community of the Company's western district: "A Clergyman in this Country must quit the closet & live a life of beneficent activity, devoted to the support of principles, rather than of forms; he must shun discord, avoid uncharitable feelings, temper zeal with discretion, illustrate precept by example, and the obdurate rock upon which we have been so long hammering in vain will soon be broken into fragments."[1]

[1] W. Kaye Lamb, ed., "The James Douglas Report on the 'Beaver Affair,'" *OHQ*, XLVII, March, 1946, 28. See also *McLoughlin Letters, First Series*; R. C. Clark, ed., "Experiences of a Chaplain at Fort Vancouver, 1836-38, by Herbert Beaver," *OHQ*, XXXIX, March, 1938.

The "obdurate rock" of religious controversy was not sealed off from the Oregon country with the departure of the Beavers. It was already firmly fixed there when Douglas described his ideal cleric.

The Methodist Mission Society: Jason Lee

Between 1820 and 1840, a great upsurge of religious awakening coincided with the accelerated movement of American people to the West, and missionary societies were formed, or their attention redirected toward pioneer communities. In 1832 the *Christian Advocate and Journal* (New York) carried an emotionally charged story of four Indians, Nez Perce or Flatheads, who had come to St. Louis, according to the report, seeking the "whiteman's Book of Heaven." This was interpreted as a Macedonian Cry of heathens seeking Christ and inspired societies and individuals to answer the call. One of the first to respond was the Reverend Jason Lee, who volunteered to take on the work for the Mission Society of the Methodist Episcopal Church. At its New England Conference in June, 1833, he was dedicated to the task of setting up a mission among the Flatheads. His nephew, Daniel Lee, also an ordained minister, was appointed his colleague. With lay-helpers Philip L. Edwards and Cyrus Shepard, and Courtney M. Walker, a nonprofessor, the Lees joined the Wyeth expedition to the West in 1834.

Jason Lee, of New England parentage, born in 1803 in the northern part of Vermont which later became a part of Quebec Province, was a powerfully built, slow-moving man of tremendous endurance. He was devout, practical-minded, friendly, and lacking in the firmness his responsibilities required. He was hospitably received by Dr. McLoughlin, who advised him to establish his mission in the Willamette Valley. That the mission intended for the Flatheads should have located in the Valley, where there were few Indians and those with no special yearning for Christian teachings, has suggested that either McLoughlin purposely diverted Lee from his original purpose for reasons peculiar to the Hudson's Bay Company, or Lee early became more enamored with the secular matters of farming lands and American colonization than with the task of saving souls.

Willamette Mission

There was no reason for McLoughlin to advise against the Flathead country on the grounds of the Company's best interests. The long history of hostilities between Flatheads and Blackfeet which made the region dangerous to traders, and the isolation of the region were arguments sufficient in themselves. Lee was either misinformed about these people or allowed his Board to get the impression that he did not locate among them because "the real Flathead Indians were few in number, and had no settled habitations." Lee did not arrive at his decision to locate in the Valley quickly or easily. ". . . My mind is greatly exercised with regard to the place of location," he noted in his journal, and he yearned to know "the identicle [sic] place that the Lord designs."[2] Probably the more influential factors in his decision were the advantages of the Valley for the farming necessary to the missionaries' survival and independence, and the prospects of its colonization by Americans. Lee had traveled to Oregon with Wyeth whose hopes of starting such a movement himself were strong. That Lee came also to this conclusion is indicated in the information he sent to the Board, that the Mission in the Willamette was "so situated as to form a central position from whence missionary labors may be extended in almost every direction among the natives and those emigrants who may hereafter settle in that vast and fertile territory." Lee's choice was a beautiful prairie site, on the southern edge of the French Canadian settlement, ten miles north of the present site of Salem, and near a village of thirty Indians, a "filthy, miserable company," he noted, but contentedly subsisting on camas roots.

His first preachings were to a surprisingly heterogeneous congregation at Fort Vancouver: English, French, Scotch Irish, American, Indian, Hawaiians, half-breeds, and three Japanese, survivors of a wrecked junk found on the coast in 1833. After he and associates moved up the valley, he walked two miles each Sunday to preach to his Canadian neighbors.

[2] Jason Lee, "Diary," *OHQ*, XVII, December, 1916, 398. Among sources for the Methodist Mission experiences are: "Oregon Mission Record Book," *OHQ*, XXIII, September, 1922; C. H. Carey, ed., "Methodist Annual Reports," *OHQ*, XXIII, December, 1922; Robert M. Gatke, "A Document of Mission History," *OHQ*, XXVI, March, 1935.

Weekdays were spent in building a mission house and in planting crops, and before the shelter was properly roofed, the first of his Indian pupils arrived. In the next four years, he reported a total of 52 such admissions to the mission family. Of these eight died, some stayed only a short time, either running away or being removed by their parents. Epidemic influenza and other diseases which had almost obliterated the native population continued to ravage their numbers, weakened the missionaries themselves, and forced heavy burdens upon them.

In 1836, as a response to the encouraging news of the first year's experience, the Mission Society sent 13 men and women as helpers, among them Dr. Elijah White, a medical missionary who was to become a controversial figure in the valley community. As superintendent of this growing mission, Lee was forced to spend more and more time in providing for its physical needs. In his journal, at the end of the third year, he noted that the "main object I have kept in view has been the Glory of God in the salvation of souls," but the spring of his spiritual strength was drained: ". . . the *filling up*, the *Filling Up*, there is the difficulty," he cried.

The Great Reinforcement

The reinforcement permitted the establishment of a mission at the Dalles of the Columbia. W. H. Willson and Daniel Lee chose a suitable site on the south bank of the River, where the Indians had permanent villages and annually gathered in great numbers for the fishing season. The prospects of a successful mission here encouraged the missionaries to believe that with more help their work among the Indians could be extended. This hope, and incidents of the times and situation which will be suggested later, moved Lee to plans of great magnitude for the Oregon mission. In 1838 he went East to lay them before the Mission Board, and so successfully did he arouse its enthusiasm and that of the congregations he spoke to, that $100,000 was subscribed to send out with him the Great Reinforcement of 50 persons, 32 adults and 18 children. With them on the *Lausanne* came supplies, tools, and goods for the equipment of the enlarged mission family and for new stations.

No sooner had the passengers disembarked in the spring of 1840 than they were dispersed to the stations. J. H. Frost and Daniel Lee and their families were sent to the Clatsops at the mouth of the Columbia, where they built a mission one mile from Point Adams. Dr. John P. Richmond and his wife were sent to Fort Nisqually, the first breach into the area tacitly assumed to be British. Alvin F. Waller was sent with W. H. Willson to the Falls of the Willamette, where a permanent village and a spring gathering of Indians from the Valley to fish temporarily promised a larger field of work than either Clatsop or Nisqually.

The headquarters of the mission family was at the original station, to which David Leslie and Gustavus Hines were assigned to help Lee. Here no less than 25 adults, ministers and laymen, farmed several hundred acres with herds of horses and cows, taught the 18 or 19 children of their own families and a continually changing number of Indian children. There was a sharp contrast between the living of the missionaries assigned to new stations and those so fortunate as to be located at the Willamette Mission where, in the opinion of one disgruntled newcomer "the Mission family live better than they would at home."[3]

Christianizing the Western Indians

While the Willamette Mission was important as a farm and as a nucleus of civilization, the Dalles station ranked second in its appurtenances and probably first with regard to the size of the Indian population it sought to serve. In the fall of 1841 Jason Lee preached at a camp meeting from which he reported 130 baptisms and 500 partaking in the sacrament. But in spite of the work of the labors of Perkins, Leslie, and others at this station the Indians showed few evidences of any permanent effect of either teachings or conversions. Instead, the Indians let it be known they expected to be paid for attending worship. Since the Indians did not let religious duties interfere with their seasonal occupations, the missionaries even followed them to the berrying grounds on the slopes of Mt. Adams. Their principal reward was a climb almost to the summit and a dazzling view of the Cascade Mountains.

[3] Z. A. Mudge, *Sketches of Mission Life Among the Indians of Oregon*, New York, 1854, 87.

From the north shore of the Columbia River one November day in 1843, the missionaries watched an eruption of Mt. St. Helens, and were inspired to sing a hymn whose first line read: "How awful is our God." The Indians failed to comprehend the lessons their teachers read in such a phenomenon. It has been suggested that Christianity did not take hold among the Clackamas Indians of the Willamette Valley because they were unable "to conceive any universal principle of power, force, or deity."[4] This may explain the failure of Christian missions generally west of the Cascades and the resulting discouragement of those who had come with such high hopes. At Clatsop Plains, John Frost found the Indians had "no correct knowledge of the relation they sustain to God, as rational and accountable human beings, nor of the future state as a place of retribution." A paltry number occasionally attended services, and on many Sundays the missionaries preached to congregations composed only of themselves and their wives.

Disheartened by the indifference of the natives, their gross habits and materialism, a number of the newly arrived missionaries were further discouraged by what they believed to have been misrepresentations of the task to which they had been called. "Instead of thousands [of Indians] I have found but a few hundreds," wrote John Richmond from Nisqually, "and these are fast sinking into the grave. Extinction seems to be their inevitable doom, and their habits are such that I am fearful that they will never be reached by the gospel." W. W. Kone, probably temperamentally unfitted for his work, nevertheless justifiably complained that there were already too many missionaries in the field and noted some were leaving the country, while others were becoming farmers in the valley. Jason Lee's own nephew, and his fellow pioneer of Oregon Methodism, concluded: ". . . the Church has been led to an improper estimate upon the prospects of Christianizing and civilizing the natives . . . and must now realize . . . disappointment. . . ."[5]

---

[4] Melville Jacobs, "A Few Observations on the World View of the Clackamas Chinook Indians," *Journal of American Folklore* LXVIII, September, 1955, 289. See also Daniel Lee and J. H. Frost, *Ten Years in Oregon*, New York, 1844, 233.

[5] Lee and Frost, *Ten Years in Oregon*, 234. See also Gatke, ed., "A Document of Mission History," *OHQ*, XXXVI, 82.

The American Board of Commissioners for Foreign Missions: The Whitmans and Spaldings

Such, in effect, was the conclusion of other Protestants who independently or in organized efforts tried to work with the natives. But most reluctant to concede the fact were the Whitmans and Spaldings sent out by the American Board of Commissioners for Foreign Missions (ABCFM) in 1836.[6] The Board, representing the coöperative effort of Congregationalist, Presbyterian, and Dutch Reformed membership, authorized Samuel Parker and Dr. Marcus Whitman to survey the Oregon field in 1835. At the fur traders' rendezvous, they talked with Flatheads and Nez Perce whose eagerness to be taught deeply stirred them. Whitman from here returned to the East with two Indian boys to raise money and secure helpers. The following year he, his recent bride Narcissa Prentiss Whitman, Henry Harmon Spalding and his wife Eliza, and layman William H. Gray, with the help of several Indian boys and hired men, joined the fur traders' caravan to the West. Taking a cue from the early experiences of the traders, the party traveled with wagons as well as horses and mules, and drove along a small herd of cattle. The heavy wagon was abandoned at Fort Laramie when its slow progress threatened to put the missionaries too far behind; Spalding's light wagon, reduced to a two-wheel cart, was taken through to Fort Boise, the first vehicle to go so far on the western trail.

On September 12, McLoughlin welcomed the tired travelers to Fort Vancouver, where Mrs. Whitman and Mrs. Spalding, the first white women to make the continental crossing, were delighted to meet Mrs. Beaver and Mrs. William Capendale, the post farmer's wife, who had recently made the long sea voyage from England, and

[6] The Pacific Northwest was a "foreign" field in 1836. After the boundary settlement and after the region had become a part of the United States, the Congregationalists and Presbyterians supported the work through the American Home Missionary Society. For the work of this organization see Colin B. Goodykoontz, *Home Missions of the American Frontier*, Caldwell, Idaho, 1939. For the Whitman-Spalding mission story see T. C. Elliott, ed., "The Coming of the White Women, 1836," *OHQ*, XXXVII, September, 1936, and "Spalding and Whitman Letters, 1837," *OHQ*, XXXVII, June, 1936; Clifford M. Drury, *Marcus Whitman*, Caldwell, Idaho, 1937, and *Henry Harmon Spalding*, Caldwell, Idaho, 1939; *Oregon Pioneer Association Transactions*, 1891, 1893.

to find friendliness, the luxury of variety at table, and an offer of hospitality while their husbands located mission sites. In her first letters home, Narcissa Whitman described the congenial life of the fort and pointed up her reactions to her adventures thus far by inviting others to follow: "If anyone wishes to come by land (& by the by it is the best for health & the cheapest) let them send all their outfit to Oahu [Hawaiian Islands] by ship & take only the suit they wish to wear & a few changes of undergarments, packing their provisions only & they will make an easy pleasant trip & less expensive than we made. . . . *We see now* that it was not necessary to bring anything *because we find it all here.*"

Waiilatpu and Lapwai

At Waiilatpu, "the place of the rye grass," at the junction of Mill Creek and the Walla Walla River and about 25 miles east of Fort Walla Walla, the first shelter at the Whitman Station was built and occupied by November, 1836. "We shall not have access to as many Indians at first as Brother Spalding," Whitman reported, "but in the end I think as many will be benefited by this station as that. We have far more good land for cultivation here than there probably more than at any place in the upper Columbia."

The Spaldings located on a small prairie where Lapwai Creek flowed into the Clearwater. They were among the Nez Perces who had given most promising evidence of adaptability to Christian discipline, and under the Spaldings' influence showed a reluctant interest in adopting an agricultural way of life. This was a strong contrast to the Whitman's experience with the Cayuses in their vicinity. Although they spoke the Nez Perce tongue and were closely bound to them through intermarriage, the Cayuses early revealed themselves as proud, arrogant, and troublesome.

Problems and Personalities

In the fall of 1838 a small reinforcement guided out by William H. Gray, who had returned East on personal matters, made possible several other stations. Unlike the Methodist mission under the superintendency of Jason Lee, the American Board's missionaries decided policies and made assignments as a group, presided over by an elected moderator, but they too had trouble in satisfying some of their fellows. Elkanah Walker and Cushing Eells and their wives were sent to Tshimakain, "the place of the springs," on the trail between forts Colville and Walla Walla, and about 25 miles northwest of the present city of Spokane. Their work among the Indians there was not spectacular, but they labored without complaint. Possessed of quiet but not colorless personalities, they were, fortunately for their own peace of mind, remote from Waiilatpu and Lapwai and the conflicts of the partisans. Timid Asa Bowen Smith, a scholar and able linguist, and his wife were at Kamiah until intimidated by the Indians. Before he left the Oregon country in 1841, Smith devised a practicable alphabet which Spalding used in printing a Nez Perce text of the Book of Matthew. This pioneer publication was made possible by the gift of an old press from the Hawaiian mission. William H. Gray, who had been sent out as an artisan to serve mission needs, continually agitated for a mission of his own, and acted as a catalytic agent of disharmony.

There were personal reasons for conflict between the Spaldings and Whitmans. Their sympathetic biographer, Clifford Drury, has found a basic, if not wholly clear cause in a mutual antipathy between Henry Spalding and Narcissa Whitman. A rejected suitor for Narcissa's hand, Spalding had questioned her fitness for a mission, and before her marriage to Whitman had said that he would not go on one with her. This old wound was opened up from time to time and had to be cleansed with Spalding's repeated confessions of guilt and temporarily healed with promises to forgive and forget.

Spalding was a talented man with great physical energy, and he gave himself unremittingly to his heavy task. He was a skilled teacher as was his unusually well-educated wife. He early became convinced that the spiritual salvation of the Nez Perces, as well as their physical survival, depended upon their abandoning their traditional hunting economy and becoming settled farmers. His emphasis upon the secular side of mission work was not always approved by his co-workers. Disagreement over this or any other matter of policy was intensified by clashes of personalities. Spalding was exceptionally thin-skinned, defensively critical of others, and, one is inclined to believe, jealous of the more aggressive, positive Whitman. The latter was also a man of great energy, who drove himself under compulsions too complex to unravel here. He was decisive, but impatient; he believed in disciplining his charges and was determined that others should accept his point of view. He not only developed a highly productive farm, with grist and pit-saw mills, and attempted to supply the other stations, but he worked assiduously as a physician among ungrateful natives, and often rode hundreds of miles to care for his fellow missionaries. He was not an ordained minister, but he preached and taught, and in the mission family assumed a leadership, needed perhaps, but not specifically constituted in its organization.

Narcissa's letters reveal a devout, observant woman with a gift for describing the life around her, the thoughts and things that composed a well-ordered Christian home. In spite of earnest efforts and tireless work, she lacked understanding of the Indians and of mentalities different from her own. In the ten years at Waiilatpu, the burden of running a large household, taking care of sick and hungry Indians and immigrants, teaching school, and raising orphaned children makes her occasional sharp tongue understandable today. It was not always understood by her fellows. The pathos of the drowning of her two-year-old daughter, her lonely forebodings, and the tragic conclusion to years of an increasing fear of the Indians, have endowed her character with a saintliness neither she nor her immediate contemporaries would have recognized.

The troubles between the Spaldings and Whitmans reached a climax in the winter of 1839-1840. Complaints from Smith and Gray and from Whitman led the American Board to order Spalding's dismissal, Gray's and the Smiths' return to the States, the closure of Lapwai and Waiilatpu, and the removal of the Whitmans to Tshimakain. By the time these orders were received in the fall of 1842, a reconciliation had again taken place, and the unhappy news strengthened a newly-forged bond of harmony. To get the Board to rescind its orders and to report the latest developments in mission affairs and its prospects for the future, Whitman decided to return east even though the season was late and such a journey hazardous.

Whitman Saves His Mission

The cause he had to plead had taken on new meaning in the fall of 1842. The number of immigrants coming into the region each year had been steadily mounting. That year more than 100 had passed the door of Waiilatpu mission. A greater migration was promised for the next. To abandon the station, particularly at this time, was to abandon the settlers and the Indians who more than ever would need the missionaries' help to meet the changes inherent in the situation. The importance of Waiilatpu was pointed out in Elkanah Walker's statement that if the Board felt a mission should be abandoned, it had better be Tshimakain "with far less disastrous consequences both as respects white settlers and the natives."[7]

The arrival of white settlers was the fulfillment of all the American missionaries' hopes. Only under the pressure of a strong civilized community could the Indian be forced into the pattern of life he now chose to ignore. To plead the mission's cause was to plead the cause of settlement, of occupation by Americans. Whitman's ride in the winter of 1842-1843 was successful in both respects. In the East, he talked with government officials about Oregon, and he convinced the American Board it should continue its missions. He preached Oregon to audiences already smitten with the Oregon fever, and he helped guide the wagons of the Great Migration of 1843 across the trail he had first traveled seven years before. Upon his return to Oregon he turned Waiilatpu into a provision center, a rest station, and a hospital for the immigrants of 1844 to 1847. In that latter year, the wagons had hardly rolled down the river road when the Cayuses turned on the Whitmans and their crowded household in a fury of butchery, and crowned Narcissa and Marcus Whitman's missionary labors with martyrdom.

Independent Missionaries

From time to time, independent missionaries appeared in the Oregon country. In 1839 "arrived a new order of missionaries styled 'Self Supporters,' " McLoughlin reported, "to bewilder our poor Indians already perplexed beyond measure by the number and variety of their instructors." Some of these became permanent settlers, resorting to farming as a necessity. Some passed through the country, as did several in 1839, looking for a proper setting for a utopian community. Some were transients, like 64-year-old Joseph

[7] Quoted in Drury, *Marcus Whitman*, 277.

Williams who traveled to Oregon and returned to Indiana in 1841-1842, part of the time journeying alone, because he wanted "to preach to the people . . . and . . . to the Indians, as well as to see the country." He was shocked by the profanity and "deistical" thinking of the nonreligious people he met, and he disapproved of the Oregon missionaries' secular activities, although by means of these he was clothed and fed. In the light of his interpretation of the command "to go and preach," he was grieved "to see some of them so high-minded, and doing so little in the cause of God," and he feared they had "lost the spirit of their station, and have turned their attention too much to speculation."[8]

The Catholics and the French Canadians: Father Blanchet

Such criticisms were borne with more or less Christian fortitude, but a new element for religious controversy appeared with the arrival in the Northwest of the first Catholic priests. Within two years after Jason Lee had set up his mission on the edge of French Prairie, the French Canadians there had expressed a desire for priests to instruct them in their old religion, and Dr. McLoughlin had sent a petition from them to the Bishop of Quebec asking for the establishment of a church. In anticipation of a favorable answer, the inhabitants of the small but growing community started construction of a church building. When the Bishop asked permission that priests be allowed to travel with the Company's express, the London Committee expressed strong doubts about the wisdom of allowing priests to enter the Willamette settlement on the grounds that it was not "a sufficiently extended field for further missionary labor" and that the presence in the same locality of Protestants and Catholics with widely differing viewpoints about religion might lead to Indian troubles. McLoughlin, however, argued that the presence of the priests "would prevent the American missionaries acquiring influence over the Canadians" there. Permission was finally given the priests to travel to Oregon at their own expense with the Company's express brigade, but on condition that they would not set up a mission south of the Columbia River. Within a year after their arrival this condition

[8] Joseph Williams, *Narrative of a Tour . . . to the Oregon Country in the Years 1841-42*, New York, 1921, 24, 63-64.

was withdrawn, and Governor Simpson ordered McLoughlin to "facilitate" the priests' mission.[9]

Father François Norbert Blanchet was a member of a family distinguished in its services to the church, and had already proved his abilities when he was appointed Vicar General of the Oregon country. His assistant, Modeste Demers, had spent a few months of missionary work in the Red River country. Their instructions directed them to "withdraw from barbarity . . . the Indians . . . and to tender services to the wicked Christians who have adopted there the vices of the Indians and live in licentiousness and the forgetfulness of their duties." They preached to the Indians *en route,* but after their arrival at Vancouver their work was primarily among the French Canadians. Mission St. Francis was founded in the Cowlitz Valley where Demers was in residence when he was not on missions to Walla Walla, Colville, and Okanogan. Father Blanchet was stationed at French Prairie where on January 6, 1840, St. Paul's mission was dedicated in a moving ceremony. This was the largest congregation of Catholics and in 1842 St. Joseph's school for boys was founded; two years later six sisters of Notre Dame de Namur founded a convent and school for girls. In December, 1843, the Oregon mission was created a vicariate apostolic with Father Blanchet as Bishop. At the conclusion of a tour of Europe to raise funds and secure workers for his vineyard, he was elevated to Archbishop and Oregon was made an ecclesiastical province. The seat of the province was located at the Falls of the Willamette, where the church of St. John the Apostle was erected in 1846. Father Demers was consecrated Bishop of Vancouver Island, and the Archbishop's brother, A. M. A. Blanchet, Bishop of Walla Walla.

The Jesuit Missions

In the meantime, missionary work among the Indians of the interior became the principal task of the Jesuit fathers. The Flathead and Nez Perce delegation to St. Louis in 1831, which had started the movement to establish Protestant missions, was followed by no less than three other delegations asking for "black robes" to teach them. These people had had living among them for some time a number of Catholic Iroquois from whom they had

[9] William N. Bischoff, *The Jesuits in Old Oregon,* Caldwell, Idaho, 1945, 4. See *McLoughlin Letters, Second Series,* 202, 202 n, 227.

learned about prayer and about the black-robed men who taught how to pray. Two Iroquois, among the last of these native lay missionaries to the Rocky Mountains, came to St. Louis in 1839, and in response to their entreaties the Bishop of St. Louis promised a mission the next spring.

The man chosen "to sound out the disposition of the Indians," and to survey the chances for success of a mission among them, was Father Peter John DeSmet, a 39-year-old Belgian whose classical studies had been made in pioneer Missouri.[10] He had worked among the Indians at Council Bluffs for nearly two years with success, but his great work was to be as the Missionary of the Rockies.

Traveling to the mountains with the fur caravan in 1840, Father DeSmet was received at the rendezvous by a deputation of Flatheads and taken into their country at the headwaters of the Missouri. Everywhere he found encouraging evidence of the Indians' desire for teaching. After reporting back to St. Louis, he returned again to the mountains in 1841 with Fathers Point and Mengarini and three lay brothers to begin the arduous labor of converting and holding the Indians. Their work was directed toward combatting "the avarice and cupidity of civilized man," the "abominable influences of frontier vices," and the "Apostles of Protestantism." Within the first year the Mission of the Sacred Heart was founded among the Coeur d'Alenes, and the next year, St. Mary in the Bitterroot Valley. Reinforcements of priests and lay brothers recruited from the order in Europe and North America extended the work of the mother missions. St. Ignatius was founded in 1844, removed to its present site at Spokane in 1854, and has had the longest continuous history in the interior. The same year St. Francis Xavier was erected in the Willamette Valley near St. Paul's and was intended to serve as headquarters for the order, but its distance from the interior posts led to it abandonment three years later.

Successes and Failures

In 1847 there were 14 Jesuits in the Northwest. The rush to the California gold fields opened a new missionary

---

[10] William L. Davis, "Peter John DeSmet: The Journey of 1840," *PNQ*, XXXV, January, 1941, 33; see also XXXII, April, 1941, XXXIII, April, 1942, and XXXIV, January, April, 1944.

field and some of the Fathers were withdrawn but the work of the Jesuits among the Northwest Indians was never wholly abandoned. Their persistence and endurance among a recalcitrant people were due in part to their organization and their concentration on one goal. They had the satisfaction of working with relatively unspoiled Indians of the interior and the measure of their expectations was related to the capacities of their students. They did not require the examination of doctrinal problems; rather they sought from their converts the simplest expressions of faith. These expectations were so different from those of the Protestants that where the latter often labored hard and long to convert their tens, the Fathers' labors were to keep to their Christian duties a few of the thousands they converted.

Where the work of the Protestant and Catholic missionaries overlapped, as among the Spokanes and Nez Perces, the confusion of sectarian differences undermined whatever progress the natives might have been making toward universal concepts of deity. A case in point was the Catholic Ladder, a visual teaching aid devised by Father Blanchet and systematically used by the Jesuits, but adopted and adapted by the Spaldings to tell a different and Protestant story. Each version graphically illustrated the torments of damnation awaiting the other.

If continuous missionary service were the final test of the two religions' success among the Indians, the laurels would go to the Catholics. After the Whitman massacre the Protestants withdrew from the interior. But while their work temporarily declined among the natives, their churches in the Willamette Valley multiplied and flourished, and the Catholics' declined.

When Father Blanchet first arrived in the Oregon country he ministered to 26 families of French Canadians in the Willamette Valley. When he returned from Europe in 1847 as Archbishop of the ecclesiastical province of Oregon, he and his recruited priests served the needs of an estimated 1,200 local parishioners.[11] By 1850, however, the Catholic community in the valley began to disperse. In the

[11] Robert C. Clark, *History of the Willamette Valley, Oregon*, 3 vols., Chicago, 1927, I, 231. Professor Clark estimated there were 50 families in 1840, 61 in 1841, 83 in 1842. By 1845, 600 or 700 persons, which with an addition of 200 in that year, brought the possible Catholic population, French-Canadian, half-breed, and "imported" Indians to 1,200 in 1847.

course of the decade many French Canadians sold their lands to the Americans and moved away.

The Closing of the Methodist Mission

While the Catholic fortunes rose and fell, the Methodists likewise saw the end of their great hopes for their missions. As with the Congregationalists at Lapwai and Waiilatpu, Lee's followers were beset with conflicts over such issues as secular versus spiritual needs. Some felt too much effort went into such private interests as farms and trade. A crisis was precipitated in 1840 when the mission set up a store at the Falls of the Willamette and the next year led the organization of a joint stock company to manufacture flour for the Hawaiian Island trade. Others rebelled against Lee's concentration of authority and supplies at the Willamette mission. What William H. Gray was to the Whitmans and Spaldings, Dr. Elijah White was to Lee. In 1841, he brought his complaints and others' before the Mission Society which, already disturbed by Lee's failure to return financial statements regarding the large funds at his disposal, suspended him as superintendent and appointed George Gary in his place. Lee received the news of his removal from Whitman upon the latter's return in the fall of 1843, and just when he was prepared to move the mission to its new site at Chemeketa (present Salem). The next spring he left for the East and never returned.

Gary arrived in 1844 authorized "to ascertain . . . whether the mercantile, agricultural and mechanical operations, as they are now carried on in connection with that mission are necessary to its successful operation . . ." and to dispose of mission property, dismiss personnel, and to give to the "mission as far as practicable, a strictly spiritual character."[12] His findings led him to close the mission and to sell its properties.

This decision has been variously interpreted. It suggests that the Board was reversing its policy of 1838, which through generous financing had enlarged the opportunities for secular activity, and that it was only now understanding the full implications of its activities. It

[12] Gatke, ed., "A Document of Mission History, *OHQ*, XXXVI, 170-171.

also unfortunately suggests that there was something unethical in the secular activities of the mission.

The Secular Work of the Methodists

The latter interpretation has been the basis of a common criticism of the Methodists. It overlooks the fact that it was the original intention of the Board and its agents in the field to Christianize and civilize. These objectives could not be separated; the secular basis of the civilizing process could not be ignored. The missionaries did not come as had Joseph Williams to preach and to see the country. They came to establish themselves on the land and to mold the inhabitants to fit their conception of civilization. It is worthy of notice that the Mission Society considered this a long-range process; it would pay the return transportation of the missionaries only after ten years of service in the field. Cultivating the land, raising herds of cattle, building grist and saw mills, the buying and selling of goods were necessary activities of a people who intended not merely to survive a short time, but to root themselves in the country. McLoughlin was being realistic when he reported "the formation of a Colony of the United States Citizens on the banks of the Columbia . . . [was] the main or fundamental part" of the missionaries' plans. If such had not been their intention, they would not have placed so much emphasis upon recruiting married couples or upon encouraging the addition to their bachelor ranks of marriageable women teachers. Nor would they have been so active in efforts to bring to Oregon and to encourage the settlement there of what they considered the right kind of people and to discourage elements incompatible with their social concepts. The rapid decline of the Indian population of the Valley proved conclusively that Oregon's future belonged to white men, and it was their intention that these white men should be predominantly American. Nor was it surprising that they also expected them to be and remain Protestant in their faith.

Protestants Versus Catholics

It must be borne in mind that the first half of the nineteenth century witnessed the emergence of a strong

American nationalism; its frontier people were expansive and aggressive, proud and sensitive, inexperienced with and hence suspicious of foreigners. They were traditionally anti-British, and also traditionally anti-Catholic. The era that formulated "Manifest Destiny" waged as well a Protestant Crusade. The religious fervor of those years was evident in both Catholic and Protestant circles but in the latter it was intensified by a militant reaction against increasing numbers of Catholic foreigners in the United States and against their church's enlarged activities. The elements necessary for a Protestant Crusade were present in Oregon in the strong prejudices of the missionaries even before the Catholic priests arrived there in 1838.

It is impossible to believe that when Jason Lee went east in 1838 to lay his plans for an expanded mission endeavor, he was unaware that the Catholics were *en route* to Oregon and that he did not use this as one of his strong arguments for increasing the mission's resources. The men and women who came in the Great Reinforcement were as much bound to save souls from Catholicism as they were to save them with a Protestant doctrine. The circulation of anti-Catholic tracts, of hard words between professors over the binding character of the marriage rites that their ministers and priests performed, aroused controversies even among men who otherwise did not take religion seriously.

The organization of anti-Catholic sentiment and the countermovement of the Catholics, while gentlemanly and moderate compared to the situation in the East, was sanctioned by the political and economic circumstances of the Willamette community. Inextricably woven into the fiber of that community were national as well as religious antipathies. It is interesting to observe that the strongest overt expression of anti-Catholicism occurred after the treaty settlement of 1846 released from Great Britain's protection a large number of Catholics of foreign extraction, the French Canadians. The occasion was the Whitman massacre, erroneously but firmly held by some to be the result of a Catholic plot. The missionary era of Pacific Northwest history, from 1834 to 1843, was not one of simple spiritual activities. It was a period of colony building, but of a colony in which, quantitatively and qualitatively, religious elements dominated. The influence from these formative years persisted in the history of that part of the Northwest later organized as the state of Oregon.

Oregon Witch Hazel Farm. (From West Shore Magazine.)

Catching Horses for Market on the Ranges of Eastern Washington. (From West Shore Magazine.)

Harvesting in the Palouse Hills. (Courtesy, Washington State Historical Society.)

Cultivating an Oregon Wheat Field. (Courtesy, Oregon Historical Society.)

Harvesting Machinery at Work near Pullman, Washington. (Courtesy, Washington State Historical Society.)

Wheat Sacks Awaiting Shipment. (From West Coast Trade, 1910.)

Modern Irrigation Canal Under Construction. (Courtesy, U.S. Reclamation Bureau.)

Aerial View of Grand Coulee Dam Under Construction. (Courtesy, U.S. Reclamation Bureau.)

12

The Problem of Law and Order: The Provisional Government

As colonists and religious workers the missionaries were concerned with law and order—with the moral life of the community that between 1834 and 1840 was developing in the Willamette Valley. In their efforts to maintain civil order and to enhance the moral conduct of the inhabitants they had a strong ally in Dr. John McLoughlin. Together he and Jason Lee "wielded the entire influence over this small population," according to Dr. Elijah White who was not sympathetic with this dyarchy.[1] The Hudson's Bay Company, by virtue of its royal license and an act of Parliament, could administer local jurisdiction over British subjects involved in minor civil and criminal offenses. This gave control not only over their own employees but over their retired servants, the French Canadian families who had settled in the valley. The Company also had a tremendous moral and civil influence over non-British persons through its economic position and its man power resources. Everyone was in some measure dependent upon the Company.

The Mission's Moral and Economic Influence

The missions too had an increasing economic power as they became "the life and soul of the [American] Settlement, dispensing," according to McLoughlin's deputy, James Douglas, "bounties with a liberal hand."[2] Outside the missionaries

[1] Elijah White, *Ten Years in Oregon*, Ithaca, N. Y., 1848, 197.

[2] James Douglas to Governor and Committee, October 18, 1838, *McLoughlin Letters*, 1st Series (H.B.S., IV) 241: "Last winter its Members laid out upwards of £500 in various improvements, purchases of Land & Farm stock, which gave an extraordinary impulse to industry and greatly inhanced [*sic*] the price of labour. A good working horse valued formerly at £2 now sells for £5 or 6. . . ."

themselves, the settlement consisted of those few American mountain men who had come with Ewing Young and Hall Jackson Kelley in 1834 and those who had chosen to remain from Wyeth's party of the same year. To those whom the missionaries chose to help, they gave credit or issued, in exchange for labor, drafts on the mission's stores or negotiable at Fort Vancouver.

Lee and McLoughlin made a great mistake when they chose not to help Ewing Young. In retaliation for what Young called the tyrannizing oppression of McLoughlin, he and Lawrence Carmichael set up a distillery, using the equipment from Wyeth's abandoned Fort William. This was, indeed, a certain way to get ahead in a community where the Indians, French-Canadians, and other mountain men suffered continuous thirsts, but it was as certain a way to corrupt the infant society as could be devised. Lee countered with the organization of a temperance society to which he induced even reluctant members of the community to join, and to which Dr. McLoughlin contributed a substantial gift in cash. The society addressed a letter to Young and Carmichael asking them to desist from their manufacture, and offering to make a monetary payment to them to cover their losses. But Lee also had another means of persuasion. The settlers were in need of livestock. What they had was borrowed from the Hudson's Bay Company's farms, but all the calves had to be returned to the Company. Hence the settlers could not build up herds. With McLoughlin's financial assistance, Lee promoted a cattle-drive company to bring stock in from California, and was able to offer Young the leadership of the drive. This was more in keeping with Young's temper and pride. He and his partner gave up their distillery, led the drive to the Spanish settlement, and returned with some 600 head. Distributed among the subscribers to the company, these cattle were the foundation of independent herds, and gave Young a position in the community which he formerly had not had.

Jason Lee also exercised leadership and influence in civil matters. In 1834-1835 he had arbitrated a quarrel between Wyeth and his men. In 1837 or 1838 when two mountain men had a shooting fray over an Indian woman each claimed as wife, Lee acted as judge.

These incidents combined to make the missionaries concerned over the continuing peacefulness of the community. The question was, how long could moral suasion alone act upon men who were unused to or rebellious against law and order?

Lee's 1838 Journey East

As they mulled over their experiences in the winter of 1837-1838, and contemplated the future—a future suddenly made darker by the arrival of the Catholic priests—they concluded that their prospects would be greatly enhanced if settlement of the "right kind" of people could be encouraged and laws could be obtained to curb the wrong kind. It was then that Lee decided to return East to ask the Mission Board to expand its work among the Indians and to equip the missionaries to serve the American colony's physical as well as spiritual needs. He was evidently encouraged in his decision by Lieutenant William Slacum who arrived in the Columbia in the summer of 1837 on a tour of inspection on behalf of the United States. His presence was evidence that the government was not indifferent to what was happening on the Pacific Coast, and Slacum led the missionaries to believe that Congress might respond to an appeal for help. The missionaries believed that the government had a fund which it sometimes used to subsidize missionary work; and Congress had the power, if it cared to provoke the British, of building a military post, or of settling the boundary issue and asserting the United States' sovereignty over the region. Civil government, in a territorial organization, would follow the latter. To get financial help and an authorized government were the purposes of Lee's journey east in 1838.[3]

The 1838 Petition

He carried with him a petition to Congress, composed by Philip Edwards and signed by 36 out of a possible 51 settlers south of the Columbia River. Nine of these were Canadians,

[3] Clifford M. Drury, *Marcus Whitman*, Caldwell, Idaho, 1937, 192-193, makes the point that Lee's enthusiastic plans swept Whitman off his feet to the point of making unreasonable demands for reinforcements for their ABCFM missions. It is very possible too that Whitman's troubles with Spalding were complicated by this. It would be natural for Spalding, feeling as he did that the Indians should become settled before they could become practicing Christians, should wish this to become accomplished before white immigration occurred. Whitman, on the other hand, despairing of the Indians' ever reforming their lives, might have placed all his hopes equally strongly on immigration.

the remainder was almost equally divided between the members of the mission and the Americans who followed its leadership—in short, a mission party.[4]

The petition reviewed the history and agricultural and commercial possibilities of the region as "strong inducements for the Government of the United States to take formal and speedy possession." But the main plea was for some agency of law and order. It pointed out that thus far the colony had carried on without courts or law, dependent upon the Hudson's Bay Company "and their moral influence." This could not continue when the resources of the country attracted more immigrants and dependence on the Company diminished. "We are anxious when we imagine what will be—what must be—the condition of so mixed a community, free from all legal restraint, and superior to that moral influence which has hitherto been the pledge of our safety." A "good community" would not emigrate to a country which has no law. "We can boast of no civil code. We can promise no protection but the ulterior resort of self-defense. By whom, then, shall the country be populated? By the reckless and unprincipled adventurer . . . by the Botany Bay refugee; by the renegade of civilization from the Rocky Mountains; by the profligate deserted seamen from Polynesia; and the unprincipled sharpers from Spanish America."[5]

Although it made direct but brief reference to the need for regulating intercourse with the Indians, it only obliquely referred to the British neighbors in the Pacific Northwest. Speaking of the renegade inhabitants, it warned that the petitioners could not "suppose that so vicious a population could be relied on in case of a rupture between the United States and any other power."

The Congress was hearing a considerable number of reports about the Far West from ardent champions of American expansion, but it was in no mood to act. The petition was accepted; it inspired sev-

[4] Of these nine Canadians, eight were among the earliest settlers in the valley and were probably those who had questioned Wyeth about their status should the United States take over; seven of the same names appear on the letter to Ewing Young in the distillery episode.

[5] Cornelius J. Brosnan, ed., "The Oregon Memorial of 1838," *OHQ*, XXXIV, March, 1933, 74-77. According to James Douglas, the petition in asking for a "form of government" from the United States, revealed the "natural bias of our neighbours," but he did not believe it would attract much attention unless "in accord with the tide of public feeling." Douglas to Governor and Committee, October 18, 1838, *McLoughlin Letters*, 1st Series, H.B.S., IV:241.

eral bills to provide a military post and to authorize the "occupation" of the Oregon country. But Lee was refused permission to address the Congress, and the bills were laid on the table.[6] He was more successful in presenting his case to the Mission Society. As we have related, he secured the Great Reinforcement, the provision of a mercantile establishment for the mission, and, as a consequence, the lessening of the American settlers' dependence upon the Hudson's Bay Company.

Troubles in the Community

The petition of 1838 was a product of weakness in the community, of fear, and perhaps of disappointment that there should be evil and disorder where the missionaries wanted to build a Zion. While Lee was absent, the missionary party elected two magistrates to serve where they could in disputes. There were some folk, however, who saw no reason they should coöperate with a self-constituted tribunal. McLoughlin and James Douglas shared the missionaries' fears for what the future might bring, as they anticipated 1840 and the influx of men from the mountains, or the Missouri frontier. Douglas reported that he looked "with much anxiety" to the immigration that was expected, "attracted to this country by the overcharged pictures of its fertility and commercial importance transmitted through a variety of channels, but chiefly emanating from the Missionary stations."[7] In 1840 the population of mountain men and their families was increased to perhaps 30 or 35. They settled down and conducted themselves as law-abiding people. True, they made and consumed "blue ruin," they gambled and ran the *correr el gallo*—a cruel race in which a greased goose or chicken might be torn to shreds. Many of them, but not all, carried over from their mountain days a strong antagonism to the Hudson's Bay Company which represented in their eyes an aristocracy as well as a monopoly. Some, but not many, got religion and moved at least temporarily in the missionary circle. All were patriotically American; some called themselves Jacksonian Democrats, others Clay Whigs.

The mission party no longer had its old solidarity, but was plagued

[6] C. J. Pike, "Petitions of Oregon Settlers," *OHQ*, XXXIV, September, 1933, 220-221.

[7] James Douglas to Governor and Committee, October 14, 1839, *McLoughlin Letters*, 2d Series, H.B.S., VI:226.

with internal quarrels. Dr. Elijah White publicly broke with Lee, and left the country. His complaints and those of others, principally those who had come with the Great Reinforcement, led the Board of Missions eventually to recall Lee, but his power was already declining both within and without the mission. There was opposition to his having assumed the role of a judge and of having magistrates from among his followers acting on the community's civil affairs. There was a decided movement away from the former position of moral solidarity with McLoughlin, a position that had fortified Lee in his earlier magistracy. There was opposition to the growing secularity of the mission and the missionaries. Yet, on the other hand, even those who objected to commercial enterprises of store and mill benefited as did the rest of the community by the increasing economic independence these gave to the Americans.

The Missions as Mercantile Posts

In 1838, James Douglas, McLoughlin's deputy while he was on leave, suspected the Methodists were nourishing plans at variance with the Company's interests. "It is my opinion," he reported to London, "they will engage directly or indirectly in trade," and he continued, "I really wish such an event could be averted, by means of a settlement with them; but if that cannot be done, we must . . . take the field, heart and hand, against them. It is a contest . . . from which we can derive nether [*sic*] honour nor advantage. . . . If the eager spirit of rivalry should unfortunately beget a mutual hostility, their cause will attract general sympathy, and by raising the cry of persecution against us, they may perhaps rouse the attention of government to the subject. . . ."[8] The Company, under McLoughlin's management of the Department, did not take the field against the mission. On the contrary it supplied goods and cooperated in keeping up prices. But as the American community grew stronger and it was less directly dependent on the Company, there was a rising resentment and greater antagonism toward it and the nation of which it was part.

[8] Douglas to Governor and Committee, October 1, 1838, in *McLoughlin Letters*, 1st Series, H.B.S., IV:242-43.

The Catholic Community

The Catholic priests were one cause of this. Immediately upon their arrival they exerted a strong influence over the lives of most of the French Canadians, who as neighbors of the Methodists had once been to some extent parishioners as well. For example, marriages by Protestant rites were not recognized and Catholic ceremonies were required. As the Canadian population increased by nature and by immigration, this largest group in the valley became isolated from the rest of the population. In the eyes of the Americans this was the result of the priests' persuasion. The priests also appeared to be especially favored by the Hudson's Bay Company, a not unnatural circumstance perhaps when one considers that the French Canadians they ministered to were a Company responsibility, morally and legally. The docility of the French Canadians to the paternalism of both church and Company further separated them from the American community. Resentment against them continued even after their number had declined and they were but a small minority in the valley's population. Writing in the late 1850's, Major A. N. Armstrong, government surveyor, reported that "the French are not liked at all by the other citizens of Oregon. They speak their own language, and have no more manners than the Indians—care nothing for schools—and are kept in ignorance by their Romish priesthood."[9]

Suspicions of the British

The Company had undertaken a colonization of its own in the Cowlitz Valley, north of the Columbia, and had organized the Puget Sound Agricultural Company to manage its farm enterprises there. A start had been made to build a company mill at the Falls of the Willamette, but though the project had been abandoned, it was evidence of a continuing claim upon a valuable water-power site. A quarrel between McLoughlin and Alvin F. Waller, the Methodist missionary at the Falls, over land rights at this place, raised a furore that eventually divided the community into hostile

[9] A. N. Armstrong, *Oregon: Comprising a Brief History and Full Description*, Chicago, 1857, 15.

camps and embittered McLoughlin's relations with the Americans for the remainder of his life. To top it all off, in 1839 a British naval squadron under Captain Edward Belcher arrived in the Columbia. Belcher's purpose was primarily to investigate Hudson's Bay Company-Russian relations on the Stikine River, and the politics of that situation had given a sudden importance to the Columbia River bar, channels, and inner anchorages.[10] But the American settlers interpreted his surveys as a prelude to seizure of the country.

The Petition of 1840

This complex of antagonisms led to a new petition to Congress. Its author was David Leslie of the mission. There were 67 signers, citizens of the United States or persons who expected to become so.[11] It described the settlers as exposed to the attacks of the savages around them, and "others that would do them harm," and it elaborated on British efforts to hold the country north of the Columbia River as their own, and to exploit its resources. It stated briefly that theft, murder, infanticide, etc., were increasing at an alarming rate, and that the people's only means of protecting themselves, other than force of arms, were "self-constituted tribunals, originated and sustained by the power of an ill-instructed public opinion," a reference to Jason Lee's magistracy. It asked "for the civil institutions of the American Republic"; prayed "for the high privileges of American citizenship; the peaceful enjoyment of life; the right of acquiring, possessing, and using property; and the unrestrained pursuit of rational happiness."[12]

In response to this petition and for other reasons as well, Senator Lewis F. Linn on January 8, 1841, introduced a joint resolution to occupy, settle, grant lands, and extend certain laws of the United States to the Oregon country. Again no action was taken on the bill

[10] H. H. Bancroft, *History of Oregon*, 2 vols., San Francisco, 1886, I:232-233.

[11] Known as the Farnham petition of 1840 after the man who presented it to Congress in June of that year. Thomas J. Farnham was captain of a party of 14 individualists who left Peoria, Illinois, in 1839, of which half eventually arrived in Oregon. Asked by "several American citizens, unconnected with the mission," why the Oregon colony was neglected, why foreigners "were permitted to domineer" over them, drive traders from the country, and reduce them to dependence, Farnham suggested a petition to Congress. He carried such a petition to Washington on his return. Farnham, *Travels in the Great Prairie Wilderness*, R. G. Thwaites, ed., *EWT*, XXIX:23.

[12] W. H. Gray, *History of Oregon*, Portland, 1870, 194-196.

but it focused attention on what was coming to be known as the Oregon Question, and created an interest in the area of mounting intensity.

A Happy People?

While one finds, on the one hand, the missionaries' concern over the character and future of the American colony, one also finds an interesting expression of contentment with the situation on the other hand. The itinerant missionary, Joseph Williams, who was a severe critic of his fellow religious workers, found at least one American settler who saw nothing wrong with Oregon. From James O'Neill, one of the Wyeth settlers, he learned that "the white people live without any forms of law; but in general are very honorable in paying their debts, and give notes and bonds. They have no sheriffs, constables, fees, nor taxes to pay. They profess to be very hospitable to strangers, and kind to one another. No breaking each other up for debts. Here are no distilleries, no drunkenness, nor much swearing. They seem, indeed, to be a very happy people."[13] There is other evidence that in the spring of 1841 there was lacking unanimity with the missionary viewpoint and with those who sought the strong hand of government in the colony.

Need for a Probate Judge

The test of the law and order movement came when Ewing Young died, possessed of worldly goods but apparently without an heir. His illness in the winter of 1840 had given Jason Lee and his fellow missionaries time to prepare for this contingency. After the funeral on February 17, Lee discussed the problem of the disposal of the estate, making it clear to the mourners, no doubt, that such a situation might arise again, and that it was advisable to prepare for it. The settlers were urged to take steps toward this end and toward "the better preservation of peace and good order." From the discussion came group consent to a committee of seven to draft a code of laws for the government of the settlements south of the Columbia River.

---

[13] Joseph Williams, *Narrative of a Tour . . . to Oregon Territory, 1841-2*, New York, 1921, 57.

It would appear that so far there was considerable harmony in the meeting. But when a list of offices and of the candidates to fill them was proposed, there was less agreement. The motion called for a governor, a supreme judge with probate powers, three constables, three road commissioners, an attorney general, a clerk of court and public recorder, a treasurer, and, somewhat ironically it seems, two overseers of the poor. It would appear there was not a complete consensus on this matter, and there was reason to wonder whether the meeting was being rushed into an organization for which the community was not prepared. While a majority appears to have approved the list of recommended officers, it was moved to adjourn until the following day, when a larger attendance could consider further the proposition of government.

There must have been a great deal of coming and going, of talking and listening, during the evening and night of the 17th of February, 1841. On the next day, "at a full meeting of the inhabitants of the Willamette Valley," there was, in effect, a referendum on the actions of the day before. The inhabitants now approved only such offices and candidates as would be necessary to handle probate cases and matters affecting the public peace. They elected a judge with probate powers, a clerk, a sheriff, and three constables, but they drew the line sharply at setting up authority in the person of a governor. They approved the appointment of a committee headed by Father Blanchet to draft a code of laws, and the meeting adjourned until June 1, when the committee was to report. When that day came, Father Blanchet reported that his committee had not met.

Discouragements for Organization

The real drive behind the effort to create a government had come from Jason Lee and the mission. Its failure to go further than the handling of the Young estate probably came from a suspicion that the missionaries would control that government. The Canadians could not genuinely support it and their priests opposed it. McLoughlin did not subscribe to it, and without his assistance, or at least his tacit consent, many believed no such movement could succeed.

Lt. Charles Wilkes of the United States Navy, currently observing affairs in the Oregon country, discouraged it. He found no cause for alarm as to the security of lives and property. The 150 Americans, as far as he could tell, were "orderly, and some industrious," although they were "with the exception of the missionaries, men who have for the most part led dissolute lives." The greater part of the white population, including Canadians and half-breeds, some 700 or 800 persons, were kept in order by the Hudson's Bay Company, and since Catholics formed "A large majority of the inhabitants," their priest was supposed to act "in unison with the others [that is, the Protestant missionaries and the Company] in the proper punishment of all bad order." He felt, therefore, "fully satisfied" that the colonists needed no further laws.[14]

New Reasons for Organization

In spite of Wilkes's opinion that an organization of government was not needed, the idea of government and of at least a minimum of officialdom was slowly taking hold in the community. The proceeds from the sales of Young's estate, largely promissory notes, eventually provided a fund amounting to more than 3,000 dollars which was the property of the community. It is an interesting commentary on the character of the community, and incidentally raises questions about its idyllic state, that this money was invested in a jail house. But the existence of this treasury was evidence that a corporate community existed in fact if not in law.

Between 1841-1843 there was reason to reconsider the matter of government in the light of new circumstances. That was the beginning of the mass migration to the Oregon country. In 1841 the Hudson's Bay Company sent out 21 families from the Red River in Canada to settle in the Cowlitz Valley and work the Company lands on shares. Enticed by more fertile pastures and the prospect of lands of their own, these gradually moved down to the Tualatin Plains and the Willamette Valley. In 1842 a party of 114 persons led by Dr. Elijah White arrived from the United States. This important immigration was the first consequence of the Oregon fever and the spirit of Manifest Destiny, generated on lyceum platforms and "Oregon meetings" in Iowa and Illinois villages, and encouraged by the

[14] "Charles Wilkes' Report on Oregon Territory," *OHQ*, XII, September, 1911, 292-293. As to the Willamette missionary settlement, he was "on the whole, disappointed from the reports that had been made, not to find it in a greater state of forwardness . . . ," 285.

number of bills introduced in Congress by Senator Linn and others to occupy Oregon and reward its settlers with free lands. Tilghman Howard's remarks addressed to citizens of Bloomington in 1841 were typical. In urging emigration to Oregon he "had in view the establishment of an American society, under American laws, and influenced by American feelings, manners, habits, principles and institutions. The idea that the great country west of the Rocky Mountains, is to remain under foreign influence . . . is altogether inadmissible. The glory of our country and its future safety, as well as the progress of our free institutions, all require its occupation and settlement by the United States."[15] He stressed the fact that the present lack of United States laws in Oregon "should not deter one emigrant from going. A colony could protect and govern itself until the general government should be driven by a sense of duty, and from a regard to the interests of the United States, to protect the people."

Land Titles

The immigrants of the fall of 1842 had some evidence, slight and premature to be sure, that the general government was interested in Oregon. They brought with them the news that Senator Linn had once again, in January of that year, introduced in the Senate his bill that would extend the laws of the United States to the region south of the 49th parallel, and grant emigrants a section of free land. The prospects of its passage were so favorable that people were gathering in Missouri preparatory to coming out the next year to take up those free lands. The question was now: What would protect the lands of those already in Oregon?

The importance of this question cannot be exaggerated. In 1833 when Wyeth first arrived in the valley, he found some of the French Canadians already concerned with this matter. Assuming that the United States would ultimately exercise its sovereignty over the Willamette Valley, the French-Canadians wanted to know under what conditions they, as noncitizens, could get title to their lands.[16] Even

[15] Tilghman A. Howard, *Remarks on the Settlement of Oregon Delivered Before the Monroe County Lyceum, May 24, 1841*, Bloomington, Iowa, 1841, 16-17.

[16] Wyeth undertook to find out for the Canadians just what would be the conditions under which as noncitizens they could get title to their lands. Wyeth to Lewis Cass, December 9, 1833, *Correspondence and Journals*, 92-93.

citizens could be similarly concerned, for once sovereignty was exercised, the land became a part of the public domain to be sold as was customary, at the average price of $1.25 per acre. The Linn bill had contained a provision granting immigrants to Oregon a section of land free. Should this pass, as was expected in the fall of 1842, future arrivals might easily overlook the claims of earlier settlers in their eagerness to make their selections. And furthermore, the occupants of lands at the time had no registry of claims, no system of records, no enforcement officers, but custom which had proved satisfactory so far in every case but that of McLoughlin's disputed claims at Oregon City. This was, in itself, a warning of the dangers that beset them.

Dr. Elijah White

A second question of importance arose from the news that Dr. Elijah White, the leader of the 1842 immigration, had a presidential appointment as sub-Indian agent for the Oregon country. This was construed to mean the United States was not indifferent to the welfare of its citizens, and indicated that the leadership of the American colony was now to pass out of the hands of Jason Lee and the mission. But to whom?

White, it will be recalled, had left Oregon in 1840 after a quarrel with Lee. His appointment as Indian agent anticipated a provision of the Linn Bill, which authorized the president to appoint agents for the territory west of Iowa. The failure of the Linn Bill to pass the House early in 1843 was not known in Oregon until late the next fall. In the meantime, White acted in an official capacity to keep the peace between natives and settlers and thereby serve the American interest somewhat in the same capacity as McLoughlin served the British. His coming in this capacity was a cause for happiness among those who, with his encouragement, interpreted it as a first step in a firm national policy toward the colony.[17] But Elijah White was not one to neglect his duties or minimize the extent of his powers, real or implied. He allowed it to be known that in the absence of any other authority, he was government itself. He was, on the whole, an energetic and reasonable administrator in a most difficult position,

[17] For resolutions of citizens in this connection, see W. H. Gray, *History of Oregon*, 215.

yet every opportunity was taken to discredit him. His dealings with the Indians were decried as arbitrary, costly, and futile. They were, it is true, futile.

Problems of the Indian Agent

At the Whitman mission the Indians had been growing increasingly impudent. While her husband was east in the winter of 1842-1843, Mrs. Whitman had been so frightened by a ruffian that she went to the Dalles to stay with the Methodist missionaries there. During her absence the Waiilatpu mill mysteriously burned. The news reached the valley and aroused there a wave of suspicion and fear.

White made blind but interesting efforts to keep the interior Indians peaceable. In a series of conferences with the principal chieftains of the Nez Perces, but unfortunately failing to reach all the Cayuse chiefs, he prevailed upon them to accept 11 fundamental laws regulating their conduct toward the white men. (These were printed by Spalding on the mission press.) White's strength and weakness as an Indian administrator were revealed in the manner in which he handled the situation. He urged the Indians to choose a head chieftain who would be responsible for enforcing the laws, but he failed to realize that the atomistic structure of the Indian society prevented this kind of united action and that responsible power was equally foreign to their thinking. The Nez Perces attempted the impossible and failed.

White was also severely critized for his methods of handling Indian problems in the valley, where rumors of Indian restlessness created needless fear and suspicion. An incident of a drunken Indian ended in a pitched battle in which two white men were killed. White was held indirectly accountable.

White was an ambitious man, a fact he did not hide, and this was used against him by equally ambitious men. Any idea he advocated, either seriously or in humor, was immediately challenged. It was suspected that he intended to use his experience as Indian agent to build himself a political career in the territory, when and if it was erected.

The Pioneer Lyceum and Literary Club, a debating society formed at

Oregon City in 1842, provided a forum for public discussion of some of the Oregonians' problems. On one occasion debate was held on the resolution that "it is expedient for the settlers on this coast to establish an independent government," and the decision was in favor of the affirmative. Shortly after, a similar decision was reached on the resolution that it was inexpedient to form an independent government "if the United States extends its jurisdiction over this country within the next four years."

White was ardently in favor of the extension of United States jurisdiction, but in connection with the first debate he had been overheard to say that he was in favor of independence providing he was elected governor of the new country. Whether this was said in jest, and in its repetition a serious intent was added, is impossible to determine now, but it is clear that thereafter Elijah White was suspect in many minds. It was felt that if there was to be a government, independent or provisional until Oregon was absorbed into the Union as a territory, it should be devised and administered by others than Elijah White.

Further Efforts Toward Organization

Patriotism, land problems, and ambitions, then, were impelling motives toward organization. Discussion was resolved into action in the early spring of 1843 when a nonpolitical but common problem was the pretext used by the patriots for a general meeting of the inhabitants of the valley. One of the principal sources of livelihood of the community was its livestock. Horses and cattle were harassed by wolves which attacked the animals in the unfenced pastures and grazing areas. A meeting called for the second of February for the purpose of discussing ways and means of controlling depredations on their flocks brought a large turnout of settlers.

At a second meeting the next month, it was agreed that everyone should kill wolves, and to stimulate extermination of the pests, the meeting voted to pay a bounty for every skin. This entailed the setting up of a system of voluntary taxation to pay the bounties, and to this also there was agreement.

The temper of the so-called "second wolf meeting" was so agreeable that just at its conclusion it was moved, probably by William H. Gray, notably unfriendly to White but a strong advocate of government, that "a committee be appointed to take into consideration the propriety of taking measures for the civil and military protection of this colony." The resolution was passed and a committee of 12 was appointed for this purpose, a committee which attempted to represent all the interests of the community except those of the Hudson's Bay Company.

Some of the settlers felt at the time that there were greater dangers than wild animals and ambitious men. Indians were one; the Hudson's Bay Company was the other. New elements had entered into the anti-Hudson's Bay Company sentiment. The Company was the sole purchaser of the wheat crop of the valley and was believed to be making immense profits in the trade of this commodity to the Russians in Alaska and to the Hawaiian Islands. The idea was circulated that the settlers were being exploited by this grasping monopoly. That the Company was British and the agent of British power in a region of disputed title was an additional source of trouble. McLoughlin symbolized that nation's imperialism, and to Protestants, his recent conversion to the Catholic faith was a call to battle with Anti-Christ. These emotional issues became involved with personal differences, private interests and ambitions, and inevitably crystallized into action.

The Vote to Organize

The committee appointed at the Second Wolf Meeting prepared a report on organization which was presented to a gathering of settlers on May 2, 1843. The report bore considerable resemblance to that of February 17, 1841, which Jason Lee had outlined to the mourners at Young's funeral. It too called for a large number of offices but it also provided for executive, legislative, and judicial committees, popularly elected.

To the French Canadians who attended, and there were probably fewer than the popular tradition has claimed, it appeared they were being invited into an American framework of government which would jeopardize their positions as British subjects and their relations with the paternally watchful Hudson's Bay Company. Whereas none appeared averse to the American form of government, they were hesitant about advocating it. If the boundary decision should be in favor of the British and the Willamette Valley became British soil, they would be in the embarrassing position of having been disloyal to the British cause. On the other hand, if the boundary settlement gave the Oregon country to the United States, they feared they would be in an equally anomalous position. They were not citizens of the United States, and they did not know what protection might be given their land claims under a new jurisdiction.

It is not clear that opposition arose only from the French Canadians. There was confusion as to what acceptance of the report actually meant. Did it mean a step toward eventual absorption into the expanding United States? Did it, on the other hand, mean the foundation of an independent republic? Or did it mean the setting up of prohibitions and regulations that would subject men resentful of law to its restraints? And did it mean that numerous and unnecessary public officers would have to be supported by taxes from an impoverished people?

A motion was made to accept the report of the committee recommending a "provisional" government—that is, to last only until some other authority was imposed. It was voted down. The skeletal minutes of the meeting say that after the rejection of the motion, "considerable confusion existed in consequence." There is no way of knowing how long the confusion lasted, but when order was restored, so say the minutes, "It was moved by Mr. [George] LeBreton and seconded by Mr. [W. H.] Gray, that the meeting divide, preparatory to being counted; those in favour of the objects of this meeting taking the right, and those of a contrary mind taking the left. . . ."

According to Gray's later version of the affair, which mountain man Joe Meek corroborated, it was Meek who took the center of the stage and broke the deadlock. He is reported to have stepped out into the yard, drawn a line across the dirt with a stick, and cried in his clearest and loudest voice, "Who's for a divide? All for the report of the committee and an organization follow me."

That there was a close vote of 50 French Canadians and a few Hudson's Bay men on one side of the line and 50 Americans and two French Canadians on the other side is justifiably disputed. But the results were clear. A considerable number, mostly French Canadians, had withdrawn from the meeting. Those remaining were Americans —how many is not known—and they voted to adopt the report of the committee. They elected a legislative committee of nine members to formulate a code of laws and to report to a meeting of the inhabitants to be held on July 5, at Champoeg.

A Government Adopted

There was a rollicking celebration on the Fourth of July, the favorite holiday of mountain men and isolated frontiersmen. The next day the Willamette Valley's solemn conclave of democracy took place as scheduled. Again it is not known how many were present but it is safe to assume that most, if not all were Americans. Some were merely curious about the affair, some hesitant about accepting its conclusions, some openly antagonistic, and others ardently supporting the idea of government.

The code adopted by the assemblage was drawn from the laws of Iowa enacted in its first territorial session in 1839, and from the Ordinance of 1787, which was contained in the Iowa "Little Blue Book." It was not, as has been said, only because some one "happened" to have a copy of this code that it became Oregon's model. The Linn Bill introduced in the Senate, January 1842, provided that "the civil and criminal jurisdiction of the supreme court and district courts of the territory of Iowa be . . . extended" over the whole West including the Oregon country. It also authorized the president to appoint two additional Indian agents "to superintend the interests of the United States . . . west of any agency now established by law." Elijah White was appointed one of these agents, on the assumption the law would pass. It is very reasonable to assume he brought with him a copy of the laws he would have to administer.[18] There were, however, unique provisions in the Oregon code devised to fit the special needs and desires of its framers. An article on lands generously provided the mission with a township (36 square miles) and every adult male settler with a section (640 acres). There were no requirements of proof for claims other than a description of the boundaries. Also palatable to the voters was the omission of a taxing authority. Volun-

[18] Pertinent sections of the Linn Bill are easily accessible in Thomas Benton, *Thirty Years' View*, 2 vols., New York, 1856, II:469-470.

tary subscriptions and fees were to support the government. Machinery was provided to create counties and county officers, and the three traditional branches of the state, legislative, judicial, and executive, with the innovation, however, of having an executive committee in place of a governor. After the code was adopted, election of officers followed. The diminishing power of the missionary party was evident when only one of the Committee was chosen from among them.[19] The others were Independents, that is, they belonged to those settlers who were associated with neither the Hudson's Bay Company nor with the missionary party.

The Provisional Government

The government instituted that May applied only to the American community; it was agreed to be a provisional government and was to function only until a permanent one would be set up. Although Americans generally assumed this unquestionably would be under the United States, the still moot boundary issue left room for doubt among others. There was little unanimity about the functions or the propriety of the state they had just organized. In spite of the apparent willingness with which the report of the Committee had been accepted and the peaceable election of officers, the 1843 government hardly survived its first year, and the arrival of 900 new settlers. Almost at once the newcomers were at variance with the old settlers and the old influences. They began to agitate for a revision of the land laws, particularly to reduce the Mission's 36 square miles to one, and for a strengthening of the governmental structure.

Parties

There emerged two factions, an Independence and an American party. The Independence party supported the idea that the settlers were occupying the country on a permanent basis; that the Hudson's Bay Company was merely a temporary resi-

[19] In the election of 1844, after an influx of new settlers, lessening of the early religious influence was even more clearly discernible. The executive committee was composed of Osborne Russell, a mountain man, but one of unusual education and ability who had come to the valley in 1842 and who received 244 of the 454 votes; P. G. Stewart of the 1843 migration received 140 votes, and Dr. W. J. Bailey, an old-timer and associated only casually with the mission party, received 70 votes.

dent; and that the settlers formed a sovereign body over which neither the United States nor Great Britain could exercise control without their consent.[20] Their purpose was, therefore, to strengthen the government of 1843 and remove from it the idea that it was simply a provisional structure.

The American party, on the other hand, was composed of two elements. They were in agreement in wishing to be attached to the United States, but they disagreed upon the methods by which this was to be accomplished. One, the moderates, recognized that a boundary settlement had to precede any such act, unless war was made the arbiter. Until there was such a settlement, under the joint occupation convention the Hudson's Bay Company had rights in the country, and the community could be better ordered if it worked in harmony with it than against it. Because of their attitude, such men as Robert Newell, Jesse Applegate, were called sycophants of the British. The other group, the ultras, were opposed to the Independents but did not go along with the moderates as to the kind or measure of coöperation with the Hudson's Bay Company.

The Independents controlled the legislature in the early summer of 1844. Despite a petition of the French Canadians against reorganization of the government, taxes, and changes in land laws, certain changes were accomplished. Emphasis upon the "provisional" character of the laws was dropped, the mission claims were reduced, and a tax schedule was erected. The latter called for a poll tax and taxes on "all merchandize brought into the country for sale, improvements on farm lots, mills, pleasure carriages, clocks, watches, mules, cattle, and hogs."[21]

This was directed against the entrenched "old-timers" and especially the Hudson's Bay Company, for any person refusing to pay these taxes was excluded from the benefits "of the laws of Oregon." The ace card the Independents held was to withhold protection to the Company from themselves unless it allied itself with them.

The immigration of the fall of 1844 added perhaps 1,200 people to the community now grown to as many as 2,500, at least. With them

[20] *Accompaniment to Mitchell's New Map of Texas, Oregon, and California,* Philadelphia, 1846, 18.

[21] Tax law printed in F. G. Young, "Financial History of Oregon," *OHQ,* VII, December, 1906, 390-391.

came lawyers and men of considerable experience in government, who, joining the moderate elements of the American party, demanded a more conservative and efficient government. Their attitudes were reflected in the spring session of the 1845 legislature which returned to the "provisional" emphasis. The executive committee was replaced with a governor, and George Abernethy, former mission steward and now a storekeeper at the Falls of the Willamette, was elected to the office. The personalty and poll taxes were retained but the new legislature's willingness to work constructively toward law and order won McLoughlin's participation in the reorganized compact of government. With his claims at the Falls continually under attack and with attempts on the part of some Americans to occupy lands at the very gates of Fort Vancouver, and for other reasons he explained to his superiors, "we saw no means so well calculated to preserve the rights and property of the Company, to prevent outrage and ruin, [and] to promote British influence, . . . as to take part in the Association."[22]

The government of the American colony thus emerged through trial and error, and with changing emphasis to a consensus of opinion sufficiently large and influential as to make its articles of compact the nucleus of an ordered community. It was at first so weak that a real government could not be said to have existed in practice until 1845. It drifted with the winds for two years, but the provisional government, founded in May, 1843, lasted until March, 1849, and it maintained law and order with increasing effectiveness.

[22] Katherine B. Judson, ed., "John McLoughlin's Last Letter," *AHR*, XXI, October, 1915, 113.

13

Westward Movement and the Boundary Settlement

In tracing the emergence of a governmental structure in the American colony from its origin in the simple magistracy of the missionaries to the code adopted in 1845, we have touched but not focused upon the critical meaning this had to the solution of the problem of national sovereignty in the Pacific Northwest. In considering the character and motivations of immigration to this region it may become clear why joint occupation became an anomaly the moment the American settlers agreed to adopt a civil government, even though that government's jurisdiction was limited to their own community. The determining factor was not so much the numerical strength of the organized community as the strength of the political inheritance back of the organization.

Territorial Expansion

The settlement of Oregon was part of the phenomenon of territorial expansion which, in one decade, realized the continental vision of early statesmen and extended the nation's natural dominion from the Atlantic and Pacific oceans, roughly, between the 49th and 30th parallels. The western movement had been a characteristic of America since the first colonies were founded on the Atlantic seaboard. Benjamin Franklin early pointed out that the ease with which colonials could acquire lands permitted them to marry young and raise large families. Thus the population was bound to grow so rapidly that the American people would shortly become numerically the most powerful people in the world. The inference was that as they multiplied, nothing would stop their occupation of the continent. Franklin recognized the significance of the continental hinterland and the force it would exert upon the formulation of the American character and future.[1] By 1800 the Americans were well on their way to occupying the continent, and it, in turn, had already made its mark upon their character.

In the first decade of the nineteenth century a French traveler had noted that, as a consequence of the Louisiana purchase, the Americans were seized with "a general spirit of enterprise and aggrandizement . . . that sets boundaries at naught."[2] The spirit did not diminish with the passing of years, and it fortunately came up against no strongly defended boundaries that would exclude them except that along the 49th parallel to the Rockies which, since 1818, divided them from British Canada. Even this, however, was not completely secured against pressures from the expanding Americans as was evident in 1837 when a short-lived insurrection of French Canadians was supported by Americans on the border and led to several critical "incidents" which almost brought England and the United States to war. The unfortified boundary of which both Canadians and Americans are so justifiably proud today was only possible after the spirit of enterprise and aggrandizement had changed its direction in post-Civil War days. On the other hand, the Mexicans in Texas and California put up ineffectual defenses against the invading Americans who came against them originally in the innocent guise of settlers. And such they were. But settlement was prelude to their assertion of sovereignty.

The Middle West received the greatest accretions of population during the mid-century wave of western migration. Between 1800 and 1850 the north central states alone grew from 51,000 to 5,400,000. More than four-fifths of this number settled there during the 1830's and 1840's when agitation over the Oregon question was at its height. Yet from 1840 to 1850, while Wisconsin added 275,000 new inhabitants and Iowa 175,000, Oregon grew from approximately 150 persons to 13,000. The occupation of this farthest western area was the work of relatively few people. The decision against British interests was

[1] Gerald Stourzh, *Benjamin Franklin and American Foreign Policy*, Chicago, 1954. See also Franklin's *Observations*.

[2] Félix de Beaujois, *Sketch of the United States of North America at the Commencement of the Nineteenth Century, from 1800-1810*, translated from the French by William Walton, London, 1814, xxvii.

made by a paltry several hundred, reinforced in 1843 by a migration of less than 1,000. In 1846 there were probably between 5,000 and 6,000 in the whole region.

Manifest Destiny

But they were the vanguard, and only the vanguard, of the greater movement which the mid-century called the fulfillment of the nation's "Manifest Destiny." "Who shall undertake to define the limits of the expansibility of the population of the United States?" asked Caleb Cushing in his Report on the Territory of Oregon in 1839.

> Does it not flow westward with the never-ceasing advance of a rising tide of the sea? Along a line of more than a thousand miles from the lakes to the Gulf of Mexico, perpetually moves forward the western frontier. . . . Here, stretched along the whole length of this line, is the vanguard, as it were, of the onward march of the Anglo American race, advancing, it has been calculated, at the average rate of about a half a degree of longitude each succeeding year. Occasionally, an obstacle presents itself, in some unproductive region of the country; or some Indian tribe; the column is checked; its wings incline toward each other; it breaks; but it speedily reunites again beyond the obstacle, and resumes its forward program, ever facing and approaching nearer and nearer to the remotest regions of the west.

And he gave to the fact the impress of providential sanction: "This movement goes on with predestined certainty, and the unerring precision of the great works of eternal Providence, rather than as an act of feeble man. Another generation may see the settlement of our people diffused over the Pacific slopes of the Rocky Mountains."[3]

Expansion, as the national destiny, was the constant theme of orations, in Congress and out, and the greater the conception of destiny the greater was the patriotism it represented. The patriotic deed was to expand and to remove whatever stood in the way of destiny. "The idea that the great country West of the Rocky mountains, is to remain under foreign influence . . . is altogether inadmissible," declared an Iowa lyceum orator. "The glory of our country and its future safety,

[3] Caleb Cushing's Report on the Territory of Oregon in *Niles National Register*, Vol. XXXIX, June 8, 1839, pp. 234-238.

as well as the progress of our free institutions, all require its occupation and settlement by the United States."[4]

The constant reiteration of this theme in the thirties and forties had its impact particularly upon those who were already attracted to the idea of a new move—perhaps to the farthest West. There was a type of American who could not resist the call of the frontier. The patriotism which manifested itself in expansion and in the removal of barriers to expansion was a product of the West, of the continental-orientation of that segment of the American people who turned their backs to the Atlantic and looked toward the interior of the country. The West, the frontier, was as much psychological as it was geographical. The Westerner, the frontiersman, was a product of an interacting personality and environment. He emerged with the founding of the colonies when the unbroken forest invited him to enter either alone or with his family. Whether it was a state of mind produced by the proximity of the unexplored, the unknown, or an escape from the restrictions and responsibilities of a settled society, or ambitions that could be satisfied by the "free" lands that lay beyond the thin line of settlement, or ideals that could be realized only in some new start in some new place, the result was the same: A type of American was created.

The Frontiersman

Within the type there was a range of great variety. Crevecoeur, in his *Letters of an American Farmer* (1787), gives an early and classical description of this spread, from the rough individualist who fled to the deeper wilderness when he could see the smoke of his neighbor's chimney, and the lawless who sought the refuge of Indian life to escape the law and find freedom for the exercise of baser instincts, to the farmer pioneer, building his roads as a life line to his old home and carrying his church and school and law and order to his new one.

In William Byrd's *History of the Dividing Line* is found one of the ancestors of the southern frontiersman, in the first quarter of the eighteenth century, the landlubber, who when he moved to the

[4] Tilghman A. Howard, *Remarks on the Settlement of Oregon Delivered before the Monroe County Lyceum, May 24, 1841*, Bloomington, 1841, 5.

Mississippi Valley, acquired more energy and became the half-man half-alligator folk hero, Mike Fink or Davy Crockett; or, lacking the energy except to move to some new corn patch among some girdled trees, became Thomas Lincoln and the father of Abraham.

At one extreme was the frontiersman who lived closer to the elements; he was the Mississippi River boatman, the mountain man of the fur trade in the Rockies, the driver on the Santa Fe trail. In the opinion of some folk he was better fit for Botany Bay's penal colony than the society of civilized men. Yet something of his brutality, his crudity, his ingenuity and individualism, his cockiness, courage, and humor rubbed off on those with whom he came into contact, and he left his mark on each frontier he opened. He was in Kentucky, Ohio, Iowa, Missouri, Texas, California. And he was early in Oregon.

The other extreme of the frontier type has been romanticized almost as much as the eye-gouging, cockadoodledooing, bear-killing Davy Crockett who could ride a flash of lightning. But if the frontier farmer was not always the noble individual carrying his rifle in one hand and the Bible in the other, or the pious Aeneas carrying his father on his shoulders and leading his son by the hand, he was nevertheless a rich character in his own right. He too was an individualist but he could tolerate other individuals without having to gouge out their eyes. He carried government with him, wherever he went; he was interested in political organization and surprisingly well informed about it. He was litigious, but he had no respect for lawyers. He liked to have his law specific, clear, and understandable, but he did not feel bound to obey it if it interfered with what he believed to be his customary rights and privileges or his interests. He could be generous in large matters, petty in small; he could be religious or impious at a quick turn. He had the curiosity and directness of the child, and at times the deviousness of a childish old man. As a rule he was sharp-witted with facility for poetic concreteness, but he lacked the broad, slowly-built-up anecdotal humor of the southwestern frontiersman. He was undramatic but not colorless; he was confident, practical, cautious and stubborn. Outside his respect for his customary privileges—and duties—he had no feeling for history and the past, but he had an exaggerated confidence and optimism with regard to the future. And above all, he was restless. He could not unharness his team as long as he heard the sound of wagon wheels grinding out a road to a new land. He identified himself with an expanding, westward moving America. He was a patriot, according to the orators.

The Garden of the World

It was, of course, a pleasant coincidence that in doing one's patriotic duty of opening up the continent, one also satisfied a restless drive and at the same time enhanced one's circumstances. The presence of unoccupied land and of opportunities beyond the settlements, of a great domain inhabited only by Indians or a few scattered traders, or indolent Mexicans was a factor of great significance in the settlement of the West. These lands were invariably reported as possessed of ". . . Rivers, a very fine wholesome Air, and Soil, capable of producing Food and Physic, and all Things necessary for the convenience and Delight in Life"; in fine, each was in its turn, "the Garden of the World."[5] The search for the Garden played a part in bringing settlers into Kentucky, into Iowa—and to Oregon.

The optimism of expansionists, as well as the publicity of speculators in western lands, emphasized the remarkable advantages of each new country as it was opened. Oregon was described in Congressional debates by congressmen who had read Robert Greenhow's, Charles Wilkes's and William Slacum's reports and improved upon them, as a paradise of natural beauty, rich well-watered valleys, mild climate, and excellent facilities for trade with the Orient. Anti-expansionists, and there were some, might point out that there was a great part of the region west of the Rockies that was arid and uncultivable, mountainous, and forested, but even they could not underwrite the lush beauty of the region west of the Cascades. An anonymous British writer, writing to minimize the value of the country, nevertheless painted an enviable picture of "the most fertile region of the whole of this fertile district" west of the Cascades, the Willamette Valley:

> . . . it is a region of great beauty and luxuriance, with lakes and pools, and green meadows shaded by noble rivers. The country bordering this river [the Willamette] is finely diversified with prairies and hills, and forests of oak, ash, maple, and cedar. It abounds with elk and deer, and the

[5] Quoted from *Nathaniel Ames Almanac for 1758* in Percy H. Boynton, *The Rediscovery of the Frontier*, Chicago, 1931, 2.

stream itself is well stocked with beaver. In the vicinity of the mountains it is interspersed with glens and ravines well wooded; its copses abound in game, and the land, in its natural state, is usually ready for the plough, and exceedingly productive. The climate is mild, and the air is loaded with the perfume of the odoriferous shrubs which nature has profusely scattered over the domain.[6]

The Oregon country "holds out more inducements to the emigrant than any other point in the limits of the United States," was the opinion of the orator who thought the idea of British control there inadmissible. Immigrants already in Oregon who found the country good sent home a steady stream of letters urging their families and friends to join them. While there were among these professionals who "puffed" the town site or land they wished to promote, there were also sincere men and women who gave information for the sake of information. They spoke well of Oregon as a rule, and their words, published in midwest weekly newspapers and quoted far and wide, spread the Oregon fever. "I was much opposed to coming as anyone could be," wrote one young woman after her arrival in 1846, "if I were back there and knew what I know now I should be perfectly willing to come. . . . It is an easy place to make a living."

Town Builders

Land was an attraction but even farmers looking for the Garden of the World were not unresponsive to other potentials of a new country. The population which moved to Oregon in the forties was composed of two almost equally divided groups, geographically derived. A study of the 1850 census shows that 46 percent of the adult population was born south of the Mason-Dixon line, 53 percent north. But 80 percent of the child population was born in the newer states of the Middle West. This indicates that the adults had lived for some time in that region, which could therefore be considered the "crucible in which the population of the Pacific Northwest was molded."[7] In one respect at least the experiences of the midwest in the thirties may well have affected those who decided to go on

[6] *The Oregon Territory, consisting of a brief Description of the Country and its Productions*, London, 1846, 23.

[7] Jesse S. Douglas, "Origins of the Population of Oregon in 1850," *PNQ*, XLI, April, 1950, 106-108.

to Oregon. It illustrated that in an expanding economy and in a rapidly growing country, there were advantages to be had from owning townsites, millsites, and land where railroads might locate.

The town-builder was very much in evidence in the midwest in the thirties and forties. He was in the vanguard of the pioneers to Oregon. Oftentimes he was the other self of the farmer. It was more than likely, however, that he was not of southern origin. In Oregon the immigrants who came from the south were more likely to settle up the Willamette Valley. Those who came originally from the midwest, or had lived there long enough to have witnessed the phenomenal growth of towns and the profits made in rapidly rising land values, and to have caught the fever of railroad building, or those who came from New England, New York, and Pennsylvania and had the blood of village-farmer-merchants in their veins, settled down-river, at the Falls of the Willamette, at the head of navigation, or if they crossed to the north of the Columbia, settled along the shores of the deep-watered well-wooded Puget Sound. The town-builder was a product of the later frontier of the midwest, but he was a frontiersman just the same. His optimism was undampened by the panic of 1837 and the instances of foreclosures on lands mortgaged to bring in a railroad. He was ready to try again. His vision of the Garden of the World had an image, faint perhaps, of a city skyline in the background, and he hoped that somewhere he would find it.

A persistent illusion of Oregon advocates was the potential greatness of the country as the gateway of trade with the Orient. Senator Thomas Benton predicted an "emporium of Asiatic commerce" at the Columbia River's mouth, and "a stream of Asiatic trade pouring into the valley of the Mississippi through the channel of Oregon."[8] George Wilkes, promoter of a national railroad designed to span the continent, argued that, as an agricultural country Oregon was of no great importance since its products were the same as those of other and nearer parts of the country; "but as a commercial avenue to the wealth of the Indies and the riches of the Pacific, its value is incalculable. . . . *Our* destiny now offers it to us."[9]

[8] Thomas Benton, "Letter to the People of Oregon," March, 1847, in *Oregon Spectator*, September 16, 1847.

[9] George Wilkes, *The History of Oregon, Geographical and Political* . . . , New York, 1845, 47-48.

Politics and Frontier

The frontier society which created the Middle West and then fed its people into the streams of the movement to Oregon developed a politics as distinguished from that of the Atlantic coast as was its orientation. It was derived from Jefferson and Jackson and was democratic, states' rightist, and antimonopoly. Almost everyone who lived for any time in this crucible of the frontier, had some experience with the territorial system of government. If anything, this created in them a more self-conscious attitude toward their own individual roles in governing a republic. It sharpened their views on the role of government itself. They wanted it on the local level and they wanted it responsible to them. It may well have been that it was not frontier conditions *per se* that bred in them a paramount urge for self-determination. It was, rather, the reaction against territorial status that fostered the rebirth of democracy on each succeeding frontier. Only men who had lived west of the Appalachians knew what this was. Then too, Westerners were inclined to think that in the national government their special agricultural interests were too often sacrificed to the interests of the seaboard commerce. And they carried in their bosoms, long after they had cause to do so, a strong anti-British sentiment and accused the East of being pro-British for reasons of its commercial ties with that country. These were in part some of the distinguishing features of the Westerner, of the frontiersman, and of the general motivations that contributed to the westward movement, and to the movement to Oregon. There were others, however, which may be considered as special reasons why people chose to go to Oregon rather than to some less distant paradise. The trail to Oregon was more forbidding, it took longer to travel, and required more of an investment to start on than did the road to Iowa, for example.

Special Motivations for the Move to Oregon

There were, of course, private reasons that impelled men then as they do now. The attraction of a new location might be great, but for many the pull of the old had to be weaker. Every man and woman who moved to Oregon had to answer the question "Shall we go or stay?" The factor that might weigh the answer in favor of Oregon might be no more than the sound of a wagon train passing the door, so tenuous was the balance of argument. A special circumstance helped decide some families who lived in the south or in the border states. They wanted to escape the social disruption and the destructive competition of the slave economy. A few slave owners chose to do likewise on the theory that in so remote a place as the Pacific Northwest their slave property would be secured and themselves safe from slave revolts. But these were so few they hardly counted. On the other hand, it is told that Lindsay Applegate came to Oregon because a proslavery mob drove him from a voting-place in Missouri. His brother Jesse believed slavery more degrading to the master than to the Negro and he could not live in such an environment. Captain Robert W. Morrison is reported as having said his motives for migrating were, first, that he believed Oregon by right belonged to the United States and he was going "to help make that right good"; second, he "supposed there were many of the native race . . . who needed instruction to a better condition of life," and although he was no missionary, he "had no objection to help in that work"; and third, "he was unsatisfied to live longer so far from the markets, that there were few products he could raise whose value in the world's markets would pay the cost of production and shipment—especially when the producer, who could neither own nor be a slave, had to compete with breeders and owners of slaves."[10]

Tilghman Howard testified before a Bloomington, Iowa, lyceum in 1841 that he desired to live in a milder climate; he wanted to leave his children in a milder climate; he was unwilling to live in a slave country, and he was unwilling to leave his children in one; therefore, he was inclined to the coast of the Pacific. For those who wished "to unite a *mild climate* with a *free country*, as their home," he pointed to "the valley of the Oregon as that country."[11]

---

[10] See George B. Currey, "Address before the Oregon Pioneer Association," *Oregon Pioneer Association Transactions*, 1887, p. 35; Charlotte Odgers, "Jesse Applegate," Armitage Essay in *Reed College Bulletin*, January, 1945; John Minto, "Antecedents of the Oregon Pioneers and the Light These Throw on Their Motives," *OHQ*, V, March, 1904, 40.

[11] Tilghman A. Howard, *Remarks on the Settlement of Oregon*, 5.

The fact that Oregon was reported as a land of mild and healthful climate seemed to have an especial appeal for those who had suffered the fever-ridden valley of the Mississippi. Almost every pioneer's letter home reported the absence of the miasma, the plague, the ague, the shaking fits. Peter Burnett gave as one of his reasons for migrating the desire to restore the health of his wife, and two years after their arrival he reported this object had been achieved. Robert V. Short, troubled with the chills and fever in Illinois, "one day while lying under a tree, unable to work" made up his mind to go to Oregon. With tongue in cheek wrote Tallmadge B. Wood from Clatsop Plains in 1846:

I believe it to be one of the most healthy places on the globe. It is now four years since the first whites settled here, and yet there has not been a case of sickness nor a death as yet, and but ten or fifteen births, for there is not a woman who has a husband but what well fulfills the Commandment by about every year giving birth to a fine chub, and very often two at a time, and some instances of women, without husbands, lending a hand in populating our valuable country, and all owing to the climate and the shellfish (?) which we have in abundance.[12]

"It is now the 1st of April," wrote Maria King to her mother, "and not a particle of snow has fallen . . . it rains nearly all winter but this does not hinder them from plowing and sowing. We have the most frost in the spring. They don't make garden until the last of April or the 1st of May, but it comes good when it does come."

Then there were those who came to Oregon because there were no fences there—the young men, adventure bound with nothing but their lives to risk—who joined the wagon trains as drivers or chore boys. Had they been born twenty years earlier they would have joined Joe Meek and Robert Newell and gone up the Missouri to trap beaver. These youth became a problem in the Oregon country. According to one old settler, "They are not content," he complained, "with any country where corn and pork are not the staple products. Besides, they are not as industrious or moral as our New Englanders.

---

[12] "Two Letters of Tallmadge B. Wood, written from Oregon, 1846 and 1847," *OHQ*, IV, March, 1903, 82; Peter H. Burnett, "Recollections of an Old Pioneer," *OHQ*, V, June, 1904, 183; Robert V. Short, "Autobiography," *OHQ*, VII, March, 1906, 53; and Maria King, April 1, 1846, a copy of this letter was given the authors by Margaret Ann Swart.

Some of them complain that they cannot get the necessaries of life, such as *whiskey*. . . ."[13]

The Oregon fever attacked not only these young malcontents, but the sober men of property whose migrating tradition was sometimes a generation or more behind them. They picked up the trail again because it was reported Oregon was a "good country to grow up with," or because "there was room for the boys to grow in." There was a future in the West. And whether idealism or practicality, determination or shiftlessness composed their secret reason, no one who started for Oregon between 1843 and 1849 was indifferent to the prospect that, should Senator Lewis F. Linn's Oregon bill, or one like it, pass Congress, every one who journeyed to Oregon would be rewarded with free land.

The Linn measure promised 640 acres of Oregon to every adult male and 160 acres to every child. When it had passed the Senate in February, 1843, the pioneers, certain that it would also pass the House of Representatives, gathered in trains to set out for the new Utopia, where the land was flowing with milk and honey, where there would be land, and milk, and honey for everyone, where old debts could be paid—or forgotten—and new fortunes made. There were not a few among these who were familiar with the ways of the frontier, who understood the advantages of being among the first to pick up lands and to hold them for sale to the late-comers. On the distant Oregon frontier there were opportunities for those with courage to risk the journey, with foresight to seize what it offered.

The Long Road to Oregon

Because Oregon was so distant, the road so long, and the investment so considerable, not everyone who wanted to go could do so. To travel 2,000 miles by wagon was not lightly undertaken. It has been estimated that proper equipment required an investment of $800 to $1,200. There was the prospect of a total loss of this capital, not easily acquired when wages were less than $1.50 a day, and lands in Illinois were selling for $3 to $6 per acre. To

[13] "Extracts from a letter (published in the *Newburyport Herald*) dated October 20, 1843, from Wallammette Falls," in *Niles National Register*, March 2, August 31, 1844, p. 101; Editorial, *Oregonian*, July 4, 1883.

purchase supplies at Forts Laramie, Bridger, and Hall required cash, and prices were shockingly high: a dollar a pound for flour, coffee, sugar.

The would-be pioneers pored over maps that showed a "Great American Desert," the plains that were not a desert until men made them so, stretching from the mouth of the Platte to the Rockies. The earliest wagon trains to cross found its hazards overestimated: grass and game were plentiful, the traveler could live off the country. The trail had been outlined by Indians and fur hunters; and the passing of heavy wagon wheels stamped out a road. But with traffic, the game was driven from the vicinity, grass was consumed by the first passers, and hunger, dust and monotony cursed the late. Indians were a continuous annoyance, a threat to security and a strain on taut nerves, but there were relatively few attacks during the forties. Hostilities and the cholera were serious handicaps to travel in the fifties.

The South Pass was an easy crossing of the mountains, but the Snake River country was truly barren, hot, dusty, and rough to travel. Thus far, and one was still a long way from the Willamette Valley.

They consulted the guidebooks that appeared on the market and plotted their journey. Those who found J. M. Shively's *Route and Distances to Oregon and California with a Description of Watering-Places, Crossings, Dangerous Indians, &c &c* had a breezy, cheerful guide.

When the emigrants start to the sun-down diggings of Oregon, they should not fancy that they are doing some great thing; and that they need military array, officers, non-commissioned officers, &c: all this is folly. They will quarrel, and try to enforce non-essential duties, till the company will divide and subdivide, the whole way to Oregon. When you start over these wide plains, let no one leave dependent on his best friend for anything; if you do, you will certainly have a blow-out before you get far.

The Elijah White party in 1842 took its cue of organization from the fur trade caravans. Captains were elected, pilots appointed, and a rudimentary military discipline enforced. The 1843 migration started with somewhat the same notion, but abandoned it for more democratic procedures. They learned too that the wagon train could not be expected to wait for the cow column and so it split into two sections—Jesse Applegate's *Day With the Cow Column* is a classic description of a typical day. Pioneers' letters and journals tell essentially the same story but less gracefully:

From six to seven o'clock is a busy time; breakfast is to be eaten, the tents struck, the wagons loaded, and the teams yoked and brought up in readiness to be attached to their respective wagons. All know when, at seven o'clock, the signal to march sounds, that those not ready to take their proper places in the lines of march must fall into the dusty rear for the day.

There are sixty wagons. They have been divided into fifteen divisions or platoons of four wagons each, and each platoon is entitled to lead in its turn. The leading platoon of today will be the rear one of tomorrow, and will bring up the rear unless some teamster, through indolence or negligence, has lost his place in the line, and is condemned to that uncomfortable post. It is within ten minutes of seven; the corral but now a strong barricade is everywhere broken, the teams being attached to the wagons. The women and children have taken their places in them. The pilot (a borderer who has passed his life on the verge of civilization, and has been chosen to the post of leader from his knowledge of the savages and his experience in travel through roadless wastes) stands ready in the midst of his pioneers, and aids to mount and lead the way. Ten or fifteen young men, not today on duty, form another cluster. They are ready to start on a buffalo hunt, are well mounted and well armed as they need be, for the unfriendly Sioux have driven the buffalo out of the Platte, and the hunters must ride fifteen or twenty miles to reach them. The cowdrivers are hastening, as they get ready, to the rear of their charge, to collect and prepare them for the day's march.

It is on the stroke of seven; the rushing to and fro, the cracking of whips, the loud command to oxen, and what seemed to be the inextricable confusion of the last ten minutes has ceased. Fortunately everyone has been found and every teamster is at his post. The clear notes of a trumpet sound in the front; the pilot and his guards mount their horses; the leading division of wagons move out of the encampment, and take up the line of march; the rest fall into their places with the precision of clockwork, until the spot so lately full of life sinks back into that solitude that seems to reign over the broad plain and rushing river as the caravan draws its lazy length towards the distant El Dorado. . . .

The pilot, by measuring the ground and timing the speed of the wagons and the walk of his horses, has determined the rate of each, so as to enable him to select the nooning place, as nearly as the requisite grass and water can be had at the end of five hours' travel of the wagons. Today, the ground being favorable, little time has been lost in preparing the road, so that he and his pioneers are at the nooning place an hour in advance of the wagons, which time is spent in preparing convenient watering places for the animals, and digging little wells near the bank of the Platte. As the teams are not unyoked, but simply turned loose from the wagons, a corral is not formed at noon, but the wagons are drawn up in columns, four abreast, the leading wagon of each platoon on the left—the platoons being formed with that view. This brings friends together at noon as well as night . . . the sun is now getting low in the west, and at length the pains-taking pilot is standing ready to conduct the train in the circle which he has previously measured and marked out, which is to form the invariable fortification for the night. The leading wagons follow him so nearly round the circle, that but a wagon length separates them. Each wagon follows in its track, the rear closing on the front, until its tongue and ox-chains will perfectly reach from one to the other, and so accurate the measurement and perfect the practice, that the hindmost wagon of the train always precisely closes the gateway, as each wagon is brought into position. It is dropped from its team (the teams being inside the circle) the team unyoked, and the yokes and chains are used to connect the wagon strongly with that in its front. Within ten minutes from the time the leading wagon halted, the barricade is formed, the teams unyoked and driven out to pasture. Everyone is busy preparing fires of buffalo chips to cook the evening meal, pitching tents and otherwise preparing for the night. . . .

All able to bear arms in the party have been formed into three companies, and each of these into four watches; every third night it is the duty of one of these companies to keep watch and ward over the camp, and it is so arranged that each watch takes its turn of guard duty through the different watches of the night. Those forming the first watch tonight will be second on duty, then third and fourth, which brings them through all the watches of the night. They begin at eight o'clock, P.M., and end at four o'clock A.M. . . .

But time passes; the watch is set for the night, the council of old men has broken up, and each has returned to his own quarter. The flute has whispered its last lament to the deeping night. The violin is silent, and the dancers have dispersed. . . . All is hushed and repose from the fatigues of the day, save the vigilant guard, and the wakeful leader who still has cares upon his mind that forbid sleep.

Multiplied by 150 to 180 days, this routine took the emigrants to the Columbia River. From the point where the trail reached the river, the pioneers were more or less on their own, and some of the hardest traveling lay before them. The Columbia was not hospitable to wagon travel. There was no bench for any distance on the north bank, and rugged cliffs were insurmountable, but wagons could trail the high bank on the south around Celilo Falls and the Dalles to the Mission House. Here they had to hire Indians to transport them or make rafts to float them down the 40 miles to the Upper Cascades, where they portaged about three miles. If they were fortunate they might be met by Hudson's Bay Company bateaux or by earlier arrivals who came to help them. Wagons were knocked down and loaded on the boats or floated down the river, and the cattle were swum across to the north side and down an Indian trail through dense forest to Fort Vancouver, where they had to be swum once again back across the Columbia. The 1844 immigrants lost over half their stock in this grueling experience.

The arrivals of 1845 found the number of boats inadequate for their needs. With provisions dangerously low and famine and disease prevalent, they were faced with imminent disaster unless some radical steps were taken. Because of the inadequacy of facilities on the river the pioneers tried a land route. Samuel K. Barlow determined to take his party over the Indian trail around the south slope of Mount Hood which had been used for cattle but over which no wagons had been driven. This trail ran from the Tygh Valley to the Sandy River, to the Falls of the Willamette and the Willamette Valley. Through dense forests, swamps, and over the broken slopes of the western side of the Cascade Mountains, the Barlow party cut its way, to come eventually to the welcome hospitality of Philip Foster's house at the foot of the mountains. The next year the provisional legislature authorized Barlow and Foster, who between them had the engineering ability, teams, and funds, to build a wagon toll road along that route.[14]

Barlow Road

For several years the Barlow Trail was the principal highway into the Willamette Valley, but it brought little joy to those who chose to travel it. Theodore Wygant in 1850 found it one of the most depressing stretches of his long journey.

[14] Mary Barlow, "History of the Barlow Road," *OHQ*, III, March, 1902; *Oregon Spectator*, August 6, 1846; July 9, 1846.

> For over eight days we struggled through snow, rain, mud and cold and witnessed suffering and despair among the poor emigrants, beyond anything we had before encountered—deserted wagons, hundreds of dead cattle mired in the mud, with only their backs sticking out,—cattle lying dead around wagons, with the immigrant families and their camp fires near, the people waiting for help to come to them from the Wallamette Valley; such were the scenes that we passed through the Cascade Mountains, ourselves nearly all the time on foot, picking our way as best we could and driving our poor animals.[15]

On Laurel Hill wagons had to be chained to trees to keep them from going too fast and running over the oxen. The worst part behind them, the immigrants arrived at Toll Gate, where they paid five dollars per wagon and ten cents per head of stock in cash, note, or kind. Even in 1848 when the settlers were better off financially than those who preceded them, 56 out of 118 could not then pay, and one ran "like a turkey."[16]

In spite of the inhospitable approach to the Oregon country via the Columbia River, it was the route most commonly used. In 1845 and again in 1853, parties attempted to reach the Willamette Valley by way of the Malheur River in central Oregon, and met with sufferings and disasters before they gave up the attempt to find a pass through the Cascades and turned north to the Columbia River. Jesse Applegate in 1846 undertook to lead a party across northern Nevada and California into Southern Oregon. After a journey of three months and intense hardships, the settlers reached the Willamette Valley. A feud between members of the party and its leaders led to unfavorable publicity for the route and it was seldom used.

Not many pilgrims to the western shores of this new world approached by sea until after 1850. The first settlers were used to land migrations and the covered wagon.

The People, Their Government, and the Land

This, then, was the people and the long road they traveled to Oregon. They brought with them their preju-

[15] Theodore Wygant, Notes. Typed manuscript of reminiscences dictated in 1896 from the diary he kept on the overland journey, Reed College Library.

[16] Toll receipts for September, 1848, are in the Foster Papers, photostatic copies bound and at Oregon Historical Society Library, Portland Public Library, and Reed College Library.

dices and their principles and sometimes they did not sharply separate them, but they brought especially the tradition of a local government based upon an exclusive jurisdiction over the land. Government to them was not authority, a rule, that could be separated, except for a temporary situation, from the possession of land. Government existed for the purpose of mutual protection of private person and private property, but the nature and extent of the exercise of that protection was decided by the people of the community acting through their laws. They incorporated, as it were, for this purpose, or their government, already incorporated, extended its laws to them. This dependence of the American people upon their peculiar institutions of government was pointed out to the British in 1827, even before there was an American colony in Oregon. Speaking of the need of Americans for government, Albert Gallatin contrasted the British and American systems: "A powerful incorporated Company [like the Hudson's Bay Company], to the exclusion of private British traders, was in itself a territorial government . . . when there was but one exclusive Company, its agents were the Governors, all the other British subjects in the territory were the servants of that Company; they might be and were kept under perfect subordination; restrained from committing any outrages on the Indians and forming a force sufficient for protection against them. Peace and order had through these means been effectually preserved." He also pointed out that the Company, by Act of Parliament in 1821, had civil jurisdiction over its subjects in the region.[17] But the United States could not obtain the same objects by the same means since exclusive corporations were incompatible with American habits and institutions. Hence, it was to be expected that there would be several independent companies and individuals moving into the Oregon Country. "We had always been in the habit," he pointed out, "in our most remote settlements of carrying laws, courts, justices of the peace with us. There was an absolute necessity on our part to have some species of Government."[18]

The point to be emphasized, and the one which Britain failed to appreciate and Gallatin did not make wholly clear to them in 1827, was that the Americans were not dependent upon the national government to provide them with one. But having one would lead either

[17] *Diplomatic Correspondence of the United States, Canadian Relations,* II, 609.
[18] *Canadian Relations,* II, 569.

to independence or annexation by the United States. The British objected to the extension of the national government's power in 1827 on the ground that it would lead to exclusive jurisdiction. In 1844, it was made clear that the self-created government of the Oregon colony, whether a part of the United States or "independent," was occupying the region in exactly the terms of the principle Britain had set up at Nootka: organized, they had the power to exclude, and they would use it the moment the joint occupation agreement was terminated. Whether their power would be sufficient was another matter; but to debate the matter by force of arms would be a major war undertaking in any case. In January, 1843, John C. Calhoun, debating the bill for the creation of an Oregon Territory, warned the Senate against a measure that might precipitate a war situation. He advised "wise and masterly inactivity" on the grounds that "Our population is rolling toward the shores of the Pacific . . . and [will] be ready to pour into Oregon . . . when it will come into our possession without resistance or struggle. . . ." Two years later, Daniel Webster, writing to the secretary of the British Board of Trade, wished ". . . both Governments would consider how soon it must be, that Oregon will have a Government of its own. The character of the settlers, the temper of the times, the great distance of the place, as well from the United States as England, all concur, I think, to prove that Oregon, a poor country at best, will be its own master by the time 50 or 100 thousand Englishmen & Americans are found there."[19] Webster's reference to the character of the settlers and the temper of the times and the consequences of their conjunction in Oregon were discerning, but his time schedule was off. When he wrote his letter, the Americans had a government by compact, and the Hudson's Bay Company, through John McLoughlin, had become a part of it.

"54—40 or Fight"

In the campaign for the election of James Knox Polk in 1844, the slogan of "54—40 or fight" emerged as an effort to win votes from expansionists who might for other reasons be

[19] "Two Letters on the Oregon Treaty found in Bingley Public Library (York) addressed to John MacGregor, joint secretary of the Board of Trade, 1840-1847," submitted by E. E. Dodd, in *History Today,* June, 1955, 417.

lukewarm to the Democratic candidate. It created a veritable flurry of excitement and passionate addictions to this unrealistic expansion of American claims to the Russian boundary. It also embarrassed Polk who as president could little justify the demand or the alternative. Simultaneously bills were introduced in Congress to organize the Oregon territory and to advise the president to notify Great Britain of its desire to terminate the joint occupation agreement within the year.

The British Reaction

The British were alarmed at this coincidence, since the 54° 40′ demand went far beyond the previous position of the United States and over which government had not been overly excited since their principal concern had been to protect the Hudson's Bay Company. With the new demand, popularly supported, the situation was altogether different. Between 49° and 54° 40′ was a territory to which British claims had never been questioned. In anticipation of the worst, Warre and Vavasour were dispatched to the Pacific to make a reconnaissance of defenses. It must be borne in mind that the British had consistently maintained they were not interested in establishing a colony in the Pacific Northwest; that they wished only for joint privileges in the region, and they held firmly to their opposition to any claims to exclusive jurisdiction. Their objective was to protect the interests of the Hudson's Bay Company in its trade route via the Columbia River and its access to seaports. This aspect of the national interest was considerably changed when in 1842, the Hudson's Bay Company built Fort Victoria on the southern tip of Vancouver Island, and shortly thereafter had informed the Foreign Office that it was gradually removing its principal depot from Fort Vancouver to the new location. The lower Columbia and the long-disputed area west of the Cascades, between the river and Puget Sound, no longer had the same significance in British policy. This did not mitigate its interest in the area above 49°, however.

In the early part of 1846 the Oregon question had reached a crisis. It was not a simple crisis but one complicated by the internal politics of the United States and by strained relations with Mexico over Texas which threatened a war. The last word from the Oregon country was to the effect that in the preceding year there was a strong movement toward independence in the colony on the Columbia River. In California, Polk had his hands deep in a plot to overthrow the Mexican government by 1848; events were moving in that direction more rapidly than had been anticipated. The slogan of "54—40 or fight" was an onerous burden hard to shake.

The Termination of Joint Occupation

At the end of April, 1846, the Congress passed its resolution recommending to the president that he terminate the joint occupation agreement. This made two alternatives possible within the following year: (1) a new treaty with satisfaction of the boundary question, or (2) a war with Great Britain. Facing up to the alternatives calmed down many, if not all, of the 54-40 advocates. Indubitably British repeal of its Corn Laws, establishing free trade with the British Isles and opening them to American wheat and cotton staples at just the right moment made western farmers hesitate to fight this market. Antiwar sentiment was stronger than the resentment of American Whigs who believed a projected reduction of tariff protection on British manufactures was too high a price to pay for Oregon.

In England there was almost, if not complete, unanimity in Lord Aberdeen's cabinet that the Oregon question be settled without war. Even influential figures outside the cabinet pressed toward the same end although, as in the United States, domestic politics sometimes put public and private opinions in opposition. Lord John Russell in the fall of 1845, indirectly advised Lord Aberdeen to accept the 49° line with the British, "reserving to themselves to refuse, modify or ask for compensation for Vancouver's Island." Along this line of negotiation, "The quarrel . . . ought never to come to a war." And he added as a postscript, "All boundary questions once arranged, we might live on brotherly terms with Jonathan."[20] A masterly campaign of propaganda issuing from the Foreign Office prepared the way for peace with Brother Jonathan, while negotiations were undertaken to write a treaty. With remarkable speed—perhaps not so

[20] "Two Letters," *History Today*, 414.

remarkable considering how many years the issue had been discussed —a document was agreed upon. It was signed at Washington, June 15, 1846.

The Oregon Treaty

The essential features of the treaty were: (1) the boundary was extended along the 49th parallel "to the middle of the channel which separates the continent from Vancouver's Island, and thence southerly from the middle of the said channel, and of Juan De Fuca Straits, to the Pacific Ocean"; (2) the navigation of the channel and straits south of 49° was to remain free and open to both parties; (3) the Hudson's Bay Company was to have free navigation of the Columbia River from the 49th parallel to the ocean; (4) the possessory rights of the Hudson's Bay Company and all British subjects occupying land lawfully acquired in the Oregon Country were to be respected; (5) the properties of the Puget Sound Agricultural Company were confirmed to it, but if the United States wished to acquire them, for public and political reasons, the properties were to be transferred to the United States at a proper agreed valuation.

The treaty was accepted by the Senate without any significant debate. The "54—40" spirit had vanished and the expansionists' attention was occupied with the Mexican War and the revolution in California.

Further Boundary Troubles

It would seem that Lord Russell's hope for amity with Brother Jonathan—at least with regard to the Oregon boundary—was realized. Unfortunately, two provisions of the Treaty further plagued their relations.

Almost immediately after its signing, the Hudson's Bay Company decided it had better dispose of its properties in the Oregon Country before it had trouble with settlers who might encroach upon its lands. In 1855 a bill authorizing an appropriation of 300,000 dollars, an amount acceptable to the Company, for this purpose passed the House but failed in the Senate. During the Indian Wars north of the Columbia the officers and employees of the Puget Sound Agricultural Company were accused of being friendly to the Indians, and settlers staked out claims on Company lands and raided their cattle herds. During the same period, the Federal army was using Fort Vancouver as its own military establishment. In 1858, the Company agreed to take 650,000 dollars for its claims; two years later it offered to settle for 600,000 dollars, but no appropriations were made by Congress. In 1863, the matter still dragging, the governments of Great Britain and the United States, decidedly cool toward one another as a result of incidents connected with the Civil War, agreed to submit the matter to an arbitration commission. The agents of the two powers, without a third party, arrived at a decision which awarded the Hudson's Bay Company 450,000 dollars, and the Puget Sound Agricultural Company 200,000 dollars for their properties.

The second issue aggravated by the first arose almost immediately over the interpretation of that portion of the boundary line described as the "middle of the channel," separating Vancouver's Island from the mainland. There were two channels, Haro, which lay nearest Vancouver Island, and Rosario, or Vancouver's channel, nearer the mainland. Between the two were the San Juan Islands. The Hudson's Bay Company set up a sheep ranch on the largest of these after which the group was named, and by 1852 they were having trouble with a few Americans who settled there also. While the boundary line was being studied by commissioners, the island was presumed to be in a neutral situation. But the killing of a Hudson's Bay Company pig by an American, an incident that grew disproportionately as its details were passed along to various authorities, caused a near-crisis. As a result, British warships hovered off the island and American troops occupied the southern part of it. The Pig War was bloodless, but the tensions it created between England and the United States, and in the Northwest between civil and military authorities gave it a seriousness its cause did not justify. In 1860, the island was jointly occupied by troops of the two powers and remained in an uneasy state of suspension for 12 long years. In 1871 the United States and Britain agreed to arbitrate their difference and the German Emperor was chosen arbiter. The decision of his experts was in favor of the American arguments and the Canal de Haro became the boundary line. The San Juan Islands, in the jurisdiction of the United States, were evacuated and peace finally reigned along the whole length of the 49th parallel.[21]

The problem basic in this boundary dispute and essential in the adjustment of the Hudson's Bay Company claims was the determination of the American settlers to have the fullest measure of what they believed to be their natural dominion. Their method of achieving it was to occupy and then argue the principle. The spirit of enterprise and aggression moved them mightily. Having acquired the Northwest, the spirit was directed to new objectives: to develop the land they had won and to govern it wisely.

---

[21] *Northwest American water boundary case of government of Her Brittanic Majesty*, London, 1873; Hunter Miller, *San Juan Archipelago: Study of the Joint Occupation of San Juan Island*, Bellows Falls, Vermont, 1943; *Northwest Water Boundary: Report of the Experts*, ed., with trans. by Hunter Miller, University of Washington Publications in Social Sciences, January, 1942. For the settlement of the Hudson's Bay Company's possessory rights claims see British and American Joint Commission for the Final Settlement of the Hudson's Bay and Puget Sound Companies, *Papers*, Washington and Montreal, 1865-1867.

14

Crisis of the Provisional Government

The news of the signing of the Treaty of 1846 by which Britain relinquished her claims to the Oregon country south of the 49th parallel was welcome news to Oregonians. They believed it would be but a matter of months before they would be organized as a territory. National politics, the Mexican War, the mounting struggle of free states versus slave states delayed such action.

The "Aristocracy of the Land"

The provisional government continued to function although there was practically unanimous hope that its duration would be short. Bitter factional quarrels of which the causes of some are difficult to discover divided the community. The issues were strictly local, but were sometimes confused by the attachment to them of national party labels. The editor of the *Oregon Spectator*, William G. T'Vault, was dismissed, not because of his bad spelling as was charged, but because his views were at variance with those of his paper's owner. "The political sentiments here avowed," he explained in his valedictory editorial, "were at war with some of the present aristocracy of the land." His "Jeffersonian democracy" was not the issue even though Governor George T. Abernethy, owner of the *Spectator* and leading merchant at Willamette Falls, may have been at heart a Whig. The trouble was that Abernethy's party was composed of the old mission group and the older settlers who, to the newcomers, did represent an entrenched aristocracy. An old settler was one who had arrived no later than 1843. Those who came as late as 1846 found town sites laid out, the water-power sites at the Falls claimed, choice lands with river frontages occupied. There were among the later arrivals some whose antagonisms went so far as to lead them to threaten to jump claims in order to possess themselves of land. Anticlaim-jumping associations were formed for mutual protection, joining old settlers on at least one issue, while they might be at variance on others. All were sensitive and worried about land titles, for no one knew, as yet, what provisions the federal government would make for them, if and when it set up a territorial government. Suspicions of trickery and chicanery, even where none existed, were fed by recollections of stories heard in Missouri of how speculators usurped the claims of early settlers in Louisana territory.

Many of the farmers who came to Oregon had been "well-to-do farmers or, rather, graziers, in the valley of the Mississippi," according to one of them.[1] Their resources were limited when they got to Oregon and many of them bore the scars of the 1837 depression and such antipathies toward monopoly and privilege as characterized the Jacksonian era. These they transferred to the first settlers and the occupants of town sites.

The Town Builders

Town building had not progressed far by 1846 but sites were laid out and campaigns were waged to attract settlers.

Philip Foster, a "wild speculator" according to a sharp-tongued contemporary, arrived in Oregon from Calais, Maine, in April, 1843, and settled at the Falls, whence he wrote: "I am situate in a business part of the Town oposit [*sic*] the ferry which will become valuable land property has risen three hundred per cent in this town within eight months and I have taken care to Share Some in the Speculation."[2]

This was the center of population until 1846 when other towns began to add to their numbers sufficiently to challenge its supremacy. Its location was important. Although handicapped by the rapids just

---

[1] "Letter of Jesse Applegate," *OHQ*, XX, December, 1919, 399.

[2] Foster to Grimes, December 1, 1843, in the Foster Papers, photostatic reproductions of papers in the possession of Mrs. Meyers, Eagle Creek, Oregon. An anonymous but enthusiastic writer exaggerated considerably in a report to a Middle Western paper, reprinted in *OHQ*, II, June, 1901, 202: "Lots that I was offered for $5.00 can not now be bought for $1.000."

below the city, a circumstance which made it necessary to reship goods to the foot of the falls, it was nevertheless the point at which portage was made around Willamette Falls for the trip to the upper valley. With an abundance of water power and the early construction of grist and saw mills, its future seemed assured. Portland and Linnton were other towns laid out at this period, each in the hope of becoming the great metropolis of the West.

The future depended upon population. Peter Burnett, who with General Morton M. McCarver[3] located and surveyed Linnton, carried on a regular campaign by letter to stimulate immigration. He discussed the costs of the journey, the route to be taken, and provisions to be made. "The trip to Oregon is not a costly or expensive one. An individual can move here as cheap, if not cheaper, than he can from Tennessee or Kentucky to Missouri. All the property you start with you can bring through, and it is worth thribble as much as when you started. There is no country in the world where the wants of man can be so easily supplied, upon such easy terms as this. . . ." He described the navigation of the Columbia and Willamette rivers, the water power, timber, fishing, climate, commercial advantages, and location of towns.

> . . . of late towns have become quite common. As all the towns yet laid out in the country are upon the water, I shall begin at the mouth of the Columbia, and come upwards. First, there is old Astoria revived. Captain Applegate and others are now laying off a town at old Astoria. . . . They have not yet sold any lots. Next is Linnton, laid off by Burnett and McCown [McCarver]. This place is on the west bank of the Wallamette River, four miles above its mouth, and is the nearest point on the river to the Fallatry [Tualatin] Plains, and the nearest eligible point to the head of ship navigation for large vessels on the Wallamette. Next in order is Oregon City, laid out by Dr. McLoughlin, at the falls. At this place there are four stores, two sawmills, one gristmill, and there will soon be another built by the Doctor. . . . There is quite a village here. The last town I shall mention is Champoe [*sic*], on the Wallamette, at the head of navigation. I do not know that any lots have as yet been sold at that place.[4]

---

[3] Morton Matthew McCarver was a professional promoter. He was also instrumental in founding the towns of The Dalles, Oregon, and Tacoma, Washington. See Thomas W. Prosch, *McCarver and Tacoma*, Seattle, 1906.

[4] "Letters of Peter H. Burnett," in *OHQ*, III, December, 1902, 405-426, 420-421, 425-426.

Philip Foster reported that at the Willamette Falls "We have something like seventy-five buildings in this place; and the people are still going ahead . . .";[5] and he wagered with Overton Johnson, a co-founder of Portland, that he would pay 500 dollars if any town below the Willamette River's mouth would excel the Falls settlement in "amount of value and population in ten year's time."[6]

Lot Whitcomb platted a town at the foot of the Clackamas rapids in 1846 and ran an advertisement in the *Oregon Spectator* pointing out its virtues: "As the eligibility of this site for a town, has been attested by nearly all nautical men who have visited the river, and particularly by those navigating it during the summer season, it will be unnecessary to say anything farther in its favour. The situation of the ground is dry, level, and at least ten feet above the highest water mark; and from it to the crossing of the Clackamas, where a bridge will be built the coming season, an almost level road can be opened."[7]

Four years later Milwaukee had a population of 500. The go-ahead spirit permeated the pages of the *Spectator* which in the same issue that carried Whitcomb's notice carried an editorial extolling the health, fertility, soil, industry, water power of the country, inviting "the attention and investment of capitalists in the establishment of machinery . . . with bays and rivers traversing our rich and fertile plains, affording the greatest facilities to commerce" and prophesied that, in a short time, it would become "one of the greatest commercial countries on the Pacific." The decade of the fifties was to witness a greater passion for town building and more strenuous rivalry to become the commercial depot of the region, but healthy ambition was not lacking in the earliest settlements.

The enterprise of town builders gave the immigrants arriving penniless an opportunity to get a stock of supplies to start their farms or to get established in a growing village. They engaged in the carpentering trade, in cutting lumber for building, or in working as common laborers. "Any man," wrote a correspondent in 1843, "with a *reason-*

[5] Foster to Grimes, December 1, 1843, in Foster Papers.

[6] Note of Overton Johnson to Philip Foster, March 12, 1844, in Foster Papers. Johnson left Oregon in 1846, and the unpaid note remains in the possession of Foster's descendants.

[7] Advertisement, *Oregon Spectator*, Oregon City, February 5, 1846.

able degree of industry, can in two years make himself perfectly independent. . . ." There is ". . . plenty of employment at $1.00 to $2.50 per day for mechanics."[8] A year later Peter Burnett reported, "Carpenters and other mechanics obtain $3.00 per day and found, and ordinary hands $1.00 per day and found." This was somewhat higher than the cash wages being paid in other parts of the country, but in Oregon cash was a scarce commodity, and they were paid in kind, or with scrip on the mission or Hudson's Bay Company stores.

The Merchant Class

The Hudson's Bay Company, represented in Dr. John McLoughlin, was the first and continued to be the most important mercantile establishment in the Oregon country. It had provisioned the French-Canadians, the stray Americans and the missions until 1840, when the Methodist Mission itself established a store. The same year Captain John H. Couch, the first of the merchant sea captains to arrive, brought a cargo for the Cushings of Newburyport, Massachusetts, and sold the goods directly from his ship. In 1842, Couch set up a store of his own at the Falls and later removed to the new town of Portland. Couch and a Captain Chapman offered strong opposition to the Hudson's Bay Company.[9]

In the spring of 1843, Francis W. Pettygrove and his brother-in-law, Philip Foster, came to Oregon via the Hawaiian Islands, bringing with them a shipment of goods valued at $1,146.05, which they were to sell for John H. Colcord of Oahu. In December, Foster wrote E. & H. Grimes, commission merchants at Oahu:

Some considerable cash is now coming into the country and if I could have a good stock of goods I could do a good business . . . hides are gitting to be plentyer here than usual some beaver & other can be traded for . . . it wants Indian trade for that, which consists of blankets beads knives powder led cot hdkfs cheap calicos cottons jewshars &'c Some mustard seed beeds of different couler are fine for working moccasins I hope you will send me all I have sent to you for and in large the amount to about double that I have written to you for previous to this. Such as

---

[8] "Extracts from a letter [published in the Newburyport *Herald*] dated October 20, 1843," in *Niles National Register*, April 13, 1844, Vol. 16, n.s., 101.

[9] Katharine B. Judson, ed., "John McLoughlin's Last Letter," in *AHR*, XXI, October, 1915, 124.

axes of good quality and various kinds of other tools. I should like a large quantity of sugar and molasses say three tons Sugar and twentyfive Bbls molasses . . . if you please you may send me a general asortment of goods to the amount of three or four thousand dollars as I am perswaded that I can sell that amount in one year and git my pay and make remittenances twice in the time to you.[10]

"Clothing is cheaper here than in Iowa," William Perry wrote to friends in the spring of the same year, "There is nothing to be found in your stores, but what we have an abundance of, and that at a cheap rate, as they are brought here free of duty."

Conflicting reports of the condition of the country may have been due to the interests of those reporting. In 1843, Captain Avery Sylvester "found the trade very dull, not because they did not want my goods, for they were in want of everything but provisions, but because they had nothing to give me in return. . . ." Yet the same year Burnett, the promoter, wrote: "Business of all kinds . . . is very active, and times are flourishing. . . . When an individual here has any idle time he can make shingles which are worth $4 for fir and $5 per thousand for cedar."

Credit

The problem of local trade was complicated by the lack of money. An order on a merchant could be paid only in the goods available at that particular merchant's store. If the latter's credit with the importing captain was low, or a ship delayed, he could not satisfy his customers. Peter Burnett tells that he had 49 dollars credit upon the books of an Oregon City merchant for legal services and that for this sum he was able to get only brown sugar at the usual price of 12½ cents a pound. The other available goods, few of which he wanted, were of excessive price and more than would have been charged at the Vancouver store of the Hudson's Bay Company. On the other hand, the merchant could sell only by accepting produce in exchange for his goods, by accepting orders on other merchants, or by giving credit. In the spring of 1844, according to Dr. McLoughlin, the Methodist Mission store offered to sell him 27,000 dollars worth of debts owed by the settlers and John Couch

[10] Foster to Messrs. E. and H. Grimes, Oahu, December 1, 1843, Foster Papers.

offered his which he said amounted to 30,000 dollars.[11]

Two years later, Pettygrove advertised a large shipment of goods, which had arrived on the *Toulon* and were for sale at his "Red House" at the Falls and at Portland:

> 20 cases of wooden clocks; 20 barrels dried apples; 3 small mills; 1 doz. cross cut saws; mill saws and saw sets; mill cranks, plough shares, pitch-forks; 1 winnowing machine; 100 casks cut nails; 50 boxes saddlers' tacks; 6 boxes carpenters tools; 12 doz. hand axes; 20 boxes manufactured tobacco, 5000 cigars [in subsequent issues, 50,000]; 50 kegs white lead, 100 kegs paints; ½ doz. medicine chests; fifty bags Rio Coffee; 25 bags of pepper; 200 boxes soap; 50 cases boots and shoes; 6 doz. slippers; 50 cane seat chairs; 40 doz. wooden seat do., 50 dozen sarsaparilla; 10 bales sheetings; 4 cases assorted prints; 1 bale damask tartan shawls; 5 pieces striped jeans; 6 doz. satinett jackets; 10 doz. cotton do. do.; 12 dozen linen duck pants; 12 doz. red flannel shirts; 200 doz. cottn hdk'fs; 6 cases white cot. flannels; 6 bales extra heavy indigo blue cotton; 2 cases negro prints; 1 case black velveteen; 4 cases Mackanaw blankets; 150 casks and bbls. molasses; 450 bags sugar . . . for sale at reduced prices for cash.

Considering the fact that there were three other stores at the Falls at this time, such a stock of goods suggests a heavy demand for more than minimum essentials in 1846 and a market more able than formerly to pay for the goods in some profitable medium of exchange, or such large orders would not have been placed. The economy, however, was almost exclusively based on credit. The fall session of the 1845 legislature attempted to make "available orders, wheat, hides, tallow, beef, pork, butter, lard, peas, lumber . . . at their current value . . . lawful tender," but the governor vetoed this provision, explaining to the December session that although precious metals were scarce and by most persons not to be had, the provision to make all produce legal tender would be inconvenient. He pointed out that if all articles produced in the country were made legal tender, "no person will sell anything he has to dispose of unless there is a special contract drawn up designating how and in what manner the seller is to receive his pay. . . ."[12]

The stringencies of 1844-1845 were somewhat abated in 1846 when,

[11] Katharine B. Judson, ed., "John McLoughlin's Last Letter," *AHR*, XXI, October, 1915, 124.

[12] F. G. Young, "Finances of the Provisional Government," in *OHQ*, VII, December, 1906, 371-372.

as Foster noted, more cash began to come in with the settlers. Some defaced Spanish-American coins were circulated at varying rates of exchange. Crops had been good and there was a limited market with the Hudson's Bay Company for the surplus wheat. But the accumulation of debt quickly drained off the cash into a few hands.

The legislature sought to relieve this situation by a measure that made "approved orders on solvent merchants, and good merchantable wheat" legal tender for the payment of taxes and judgments rendered in the courts.[13] One result was that when Sheriff Joe Meek collected taxes, he testified, he had more need for a warehouse than he had for a wallet. The legislation was actually discriminatory against the merchants and immigrants. For example, in making wheat legal tender, it sought to save those already producing that commodity and already in debt to the merchants from having to use the small amounts of currency coming in to pay off their debts. It applied only to judgments at law and not to original trade transactions. Illustrative of the manner in which the legislation worked out is a notice in the *Spectator*, on December 24, 1846: "I hereby give notice that my note, in favor either of John McLoughlin, or the Hudson's Bay Company,—I do not now distinctly remember which party—dated in October, 1845, will not be paid unless the payment is compelled by law, as the payment of said note in 'good merchantable wheat' has been refused at the granary at Linton. Signed Jacob Hoover." The immediate result was to slow up all credit transactions. Merchants were affected since they were reluctant to engage in litigation in the existing courts, but the legislation also worked a hardship on recent immigrants who were dependent in large measure upon credit the merchants were now loath to extend.

There were plenty of reasons why the settlers looked upon the two years from 1846 through 1848 as years of hard times. The production of wheat on a large scale reduced the market price but the costs of goods wheat purchased was not correspondingly reduced. Commodities were 300 to 400 percent higher in Oregon than in the middle Western

---

[13] *Oregon Laws, 1843-49*, Salem, 1853, 33. ". . . in addition to gold and silver, treasury drafts, approved orders on solvent merchants, and good merchantable wheat, at the market price . . . shall be a lawful tender for the payment of taxes and judgments rendered in the courts of Oregon Territory, and for the payment of all debts contracted Oregon Territory, where no special contract has been made to the contrary."

states.[14] Two prices were quoted: a nominal price of exchange on wheat orders, and a real price on the basis of coin. In 1846, some goods were one-third lower for cash, and in 1847, 50 percent lower. The difference between the barter or nominal price and the real price tended to shrink as the times grew harder and the price of merchantable grain fell.[15]

The credit system of the frontier made the merchant a vital figure in building a community. Lewis Atherton's description of his role in the Middle West also applies to the Far West: "If the merchant had been satisfied to stop with this service [that is, the retailing of goods] the West would have taken a much longer period to reach economic maturity than proved to be the case. Money was scarce, and the most bountiful supply of goods was worthless unless some medium of exchange was available. Banks and market for western crops would solve the problem, but neither existed. Faced with this situation the merchant had no choice but to assume the double burden of banker and dealer in agricultural crops."[16]

But the settlers in Oregon did not consider the merchant in this light. Whether Hudson's Bay Company, George Abernethy, Philip Foster, or Francis Pettygrove, the merchant was a monopolist, who profited two ways on every transaction—in buying and in selling. The Hudson's Bay Company, because it was the largest buyer of the farmers' wheat, because it acted with the American merchants in controlling credit, and because it was British, received the greatest share of public disapproval, especially when it reached the limit of its buying capacity.

The Wheat Market

It was fortunate for the settlers that the Hudson's Bay Company in 1844-1846 needed their produce to help

[14] J. Quinn Thornton, Memorial to Congress, *Senate Misc. Doc. No. 143*, 30th Cong., 1st Sess., 12-13. Prices current for 1848 listed on p. 15. For prices in 1838-1841, see F. G. Young, "Ewing Young and His Estate," in *OHQ*, XXI, September, 1920, 210-303. For 1843-1846, accounts in the Foster Papers have been used.

[15] James H. Gilbert, *Trade and Currency in Early Oregon*, New York, 1907, 55. See also Neil M. Howison, Report to the Commander of the Pacific Squadron (1848), *House Misc. Doc. No.* 29, 30th Cong., 1st Sess., reprinted in *OHQ*, XIV, March, 1913, 1-60.

[16] Lewis Atherton, "The Pioneer Merchant in Mid-America," in *University of Missouri Studies*, 14, April, 1939, 10-11.

meet its contract for supplying the Russian American Company in Alaska with grain. Besides sending large quantities of grain north, the Company engaged in trade with the Hawaiian Islands and California. In 1846 the pioneers were producing more grain than the Company could use. It was estimated that the surplus in that year was 50,000 bushels of wheat or 10,000 barrels of flour.[17]

Numerous letters to the *Oregon Spectator* reflected the growing antagonism to the concern. The Company was charged with having made exorbitant profits to the detriment of the farmers. On the basis of suppositious figures, one writer claimed there was a "clear profit" of 74,800 dollars from an investment of 24,000 dollars in merchandise. "If justice were done to this infant community, fifty thousand dollars at least of this profit, would be in the hands of our farmers. . . ."

Earlier several attempts had been made by the settlers to solve their market problems. In 1841, a group of farmers headed by ex-mountain-man Joseph Gale built the small schooner, *Star of Oregon,* which they sailed to California and sold. The purchase money was invested in cattle which were driven back to Oregon to break the monoply in that industry in the hands of the Hudson's Bay Company, the Methodist Mission, and the independent settler, Ewing Young. In 1843, the merchant, Philip Foster, received word from sources in the Hawaiian Islands that the market there was picking up and that Captain Avery Sylvester was planning to establish a regular run from the Northwest Coast to the Islands. In the spring of the next year, Foster exported a cargo of goods with Sylvester, whose ship, the *Chenamus,* was the only American vessel to enter the river that summer. Foster's cargo consisted of 29,000 shingles, seven barrels of salmon, and two barrels of peas, for which he received, net, $200.75.

On his outward trip in April, 1845, Captain Sylvester also loaded for the Islands 50,000 feet of lumber at H. H. Hunt's mill, 30 miles above Astoria. Earlier he had carried salmon which he bargained for and cured on the Clackamas River.[18] But this industrious

[17] *Oregon Spectator,* January 7, 1847.
[18] Sylvester, "Voyages," *OHQ,* XXXIV, September, 1933, 360, 363.

Yankee trader left the river in 1845, and for the next two years only the *Toulon* and the *Henry* came to trade. The *Henry* in 1847 carried a cargo of lumber, flour, salmon, beef, potatoes, butter, cheese, cranberries, turnips, cabbage, and onions from Oregon to California. This cargo was an exception rather than the rule, however, as most often the boats carried mainly lumber, flour, and dried salmon.

Anti-Monopoly Sentiments

On December 10, 1846, the *Oregon Spectator* carried a communication from "A Friend to Fair Trade" addressed to the "Farmers and mechanics of Oregon," which embodied the complaint of a part of the community, not only against the Hudson's Bay Company but American merchants as well.

> You are all fully aware of our situation as it regards the state of our commerce. The most of us have left the interior or western part of the United States, in hope to find a better price for the reward of our labor. The soil yields a rich reward to the cultivator, and the merchant's coffers groan with the profit thereof; whilst we are groaning under the consequences. Men of capital dare not venture to engage in merchandising whilst the monster Hudson's Bay Company reigns over the land. And now, fellow citizens, while the petty merchants and lawyers and would be politicians, are trying to mend the matter by memorializing Congress, let us help ourselves. . . .

In a second letter he suggested the formation of a farmer's coöperative to compete with the Hudson's Bay Company and the merchant clique controlling the local exchange of goods and the export trade. He proposed a joint stock company with a capital of 600,000 or 800,000 bushels of wheat, subscribed by shares of 100 bushels each. Bonds were to be issued on this capital stock and the funds thus raised were to be used to build lumber and flour mills and a schooner to export their produce. He argued that such a company would be "entitled to credit; so much so, that their bills payable in wheat, lumber and goods will furnish an excellent currency, such as will be good wheresoever their trade extends, if that should be to Canton; for flour and lumber is better than gold and silver."

The writer had no question as to their ability to sell the bonds, "For," he wrote, "the money is already in the country, and can be had for such bonds." The belief that there was money in the country evidently prevailed rather generally. Those who possessed capital would, according to his reasoning, buy the bonds issued on the commodity which the farmers possessed in lieu of money. Since other evidence leads one to the conclusion that the capital extant in the community was largely in the hands of members of the Hudson's Bay Company and of the American merchants, it is difficult to understand how "A Friend to Fair Trade" expected to sell the bonds of the farmers' coöperative company to its business rivals.

It is impossible to determine how much "wealth" there was in Oregon before 1850. Certain groups recognized the existence of a moneyed class in 1846-1847. Dr. John McLoughlin was, undoubtedly, the wealthiest individual in the territory, but there were others, who, before the gold rush in 1848, were considered in the ranks of the wealthy. In the February 21, 1850, issue of the *Oregon Spectator*, "pro Bono Publico," writing of a program of city improvements, ironically referred to "Wealthy merchants and other capitalists" who "should not spend all that they have for the benefit of the public." "I understand," he went on, "that several of them are each worth, at least, one hundred thousand dollars, and one is supposed to be worth half a million." Partisan exaggeration may account for this statement. It is difficult to believe any individual was able to make such a fortune before 1849, and there is no evidence of anyone returning so early from the California gold fields with a half million dollars and setting himself up as a merchant in Oregon City.

In January, 1847, a writer who signed himself "M," also advanced plans for the marketing of the farmers' crops. He proposed a stock company similar to the one previously described, but he was less optimistic about selling bonds locally, and suggested an agency in New York to dispose of them. But of greater importance was his suggestion that the farmers engage in the shipping business for themselves. According to this writer, the company would be able to sell its produce to the military garrisons in Oregon and to the commissaries of the "Navy in the Pacific." The weakness of the writer's argument is nowhere more evident than in this matter of markets. If in 1847 the Hudson's Bay Company had more than enough grain to fulfill the requirements of the Sandwich Islands, Alaska, and California trade, which it controlled in large part by company contracts, there would be no opening for the new company in these areas. As for the military and naval stations to be supplied, there were as yet none.

In the same issue of the *Spectator* "A Rocky Mountain Boy" called a public meeting of farmers "to take measures to prevent our ruin, by the combined operation of the merchants and shippers, who have united to tie us down and prevent us from getting the just reward of our labor, by refusing to ship produce for us, and combining to force us to take their goods for it, at prices ruinous to us and destructive to the interest of the country."

At such a meeting in April, it was pointed out that the "present oppression upon the producers . . . by mercantile extortion and refusal to do a freighting business, calls upon the producers generally, to engage as a united whole in the business of exchanging products. . . ."[19] The Oregon Producers' Exporting and Importing Company was projected, but nothing further came of this movement, generated during the farmers' quiet winter months. As crops demanded attention, and a California market emerged, the farmers forgot their griefs or laid them aside for the time being. In 1848 settlers on Clatsop Plains, although inexperienced as shipbuilders and navigators, built a two-masted 40-ton schooner, which they loaded with butter, bacon, eggs, and potatoes and sailed to California. Their success in selling both schooner and cargo was an indication of the striking change in the economic situation of the Oregon country the discovery of gold in California was to bring about.

Economic discontent in 1846-1847 offers an explanation at least in part, of the political situation in Oregon at this time. There were social issues that created almost as bitter interactions. Prohibition, for example, was supported by a majority of those who were looked upon as the "entrenched aristocracy." Either prohibitory or regulatory laws were the subject of acrimonious debates at legislative sessions, and it was sure that whatever kind of measure was passed at one session would be repealed at the next.

Indian War

There was little light and sunshine in Oregon's politics in 1846-1847. There was less in 1847-1848, when the

[19] *Oregon Spectator,* April 29, 1847.

provisional government faced its severest test and one for which it was least prepared, an Indian war. The valley Indians had been so depleted in number by the epidemic of 1830-1833 and the remainder so debilitated by disease and starvation in the following decade that they were more an annoyance than a threat. Those in the interior were of a different character and were still numerous. Of these, the Cayuse, a proud, arrogant people, according to the Whitmans, had shown the only serious evidences of hostility. This was directed towards the Whitmans, who early realized they were living on the thin edge of security.

The Whitman Massacre

The deep-rooted cause of their particular trouble lay in their understandable inability to handle a complex situation. They were harsh with the Indians when they broke the white man's moral code or ignored the rights of privacy and possession, concepts which the natives did not understand. They were meek when they were subjected to indignities the Cayuses would not tolerate in their own code. When Whitman was slapped by a native, he turned the other cheek. Marcus Whitman fought a heroic but losing battle when he persisted in trying to cure their illnesses, even when he knew the tribal medicine man often had to pay with his life when his patient died. The long lines of immigrant wagons that were stopping at Waiilatpu in 1845, 1846, and 1847 brought white men sick with diseases from which they often recovered, but from which the Indians died in epidemic numbers. They believed they were being poisoned, and as lodge after lodge sent up the death chant, even those who had been friendly to the Whitmans wavered in their loyalty. Panic fed on rumor, agitated by half-educated Indians who realized that their ancient way of life, their hunting lands, and their freedom were menaced by the immigrants the Whitmans welcomed and helped. On November 29, 1847, the mission, crowded with such immigrants and children, was attacked. The first victims were Marcus and Narcissa Whitman. In all, 14 were massacred, two died of exposure, and 47, of whom 34 were children, were captured.

When the news was brought to Fort Vancouver, James Douglas immediately sent a relief party under Peter Skene Ogden with goods to ransom the captives, and to use his influence to prevent a general rising of the Indians. The Spaldings with the help of the Nez Perces escaped from Lapwai to the Willamette Valley. The Walkers and Eellses remained with their faithful Spokanes until the spring.

The Cayuses, all fury spent, were willing to give up their captives in the hope that a peace could be negotiated to prevent a war which, Ogden assured them, would lead to their extermination. A tense situation prevailed among the interior Indians who, had they had any tradition of united action or a common understanding of the crisis they faced, could at this time have opened up a disastrous war against the whites and perhaps exterminated them.

The Cayuse War

A tense situation likewise prevailed in the Valley where the news of the massacre had arrived on December 8. The first reaction was a fear of a general uprising, a fear which did not lessen as a month later reports were heard that the Walla Wallas, Nez Perces, and Yakimas were in alliance with the Cayuses.[20] The legislature had just assembled at Oregon City and took immediate steps to prepare for war and protect the community. By the end of December a company of local militia arrived at the Dalles to protect the missionaries there. With less alacrity a regiment of 500 men was enlisted. Reluctance to leave their homes which might need protection, the lack of finances to provision the force, and the ever-present politics of commands delayed their setting out. Supplies from the Hudson's Bay Company were secured on personal pledges of Governor Abernethy, Jesse Applegate, and A. L. Lovejoy. By the middle of January Colonel Cornelius Gilliam was *en route* to the upper river with 130 men. More troops followed, and a desultory campaign against the Cayuses, fortunately of few casualties, continued until April, 1850, when the natives surrendered to the new territorial governor five men as the murderers of the Whitman party.

To call the military activities of the provisional government a war is to distort the meaning of the word. There was no war in the sense of attacks and counterattacks. The Cayuse Indians were trying to avoid the consequences of the Whitman massacre, whether those were a retributive war or the surrender of the murderers for legal

[20] *Oregon Spectator*, January 20, 1848.

action. The Americans had no taste for aggressive attack which might well coalesce the interior Indians against them. It was not a war of white men against red men, but an armed effort on the part of the American population to enforce its law and order, and to protect its settlements against raids. Negotiations went on with the various Indians; garrisons were set up at The Dalles and on the site of the Whitman mission. Troops were kept in the field. The Hudson's Bay Company remained neutral, but alert to the situation, which was potentially explosive.

To protect the colony and to keep troops in the field placed a heavy strain on the finances of the provisional government. There was no resort to a system of uniform taxation. There was practically no cash in the country. The expenses of the war amounted to more than $175,000, to which $2,885.02 was contributed in cash.[21] Individuals able to do so made contributions from their resources to meet particular emergencies, and signed notes for supplies. A commissary general was appointed, and through his agents bought goods if they had the cash, gave due bills, or commandeered wheat from those best able to spare it. The war was financed on credit. The situation was relieved only by the anticipation that the United States government would assume responsibility for the colony's debts and its further protection.

Petition for Help

The news of the massacre had no sooner been received than the legislature set up a committee to formulate a petition of the citizens to the Congress that the laws of the United States might be extended to them. This interesting document composed by Peter H. Burnett, later to become California's first governor, and George L. Curry, to be Oregon's fourth and last territorial governor, and L. A. Rice, was less concerned with the colony's threatened danger than it was with the need of government.

Embarrassed as we were, and finding by actual experiment that a resident and civilized people could not exist without government of some kind,

[21] F. G. Young, analyst of the provisional government's finances, has pointed out that because of the anomalous status of the government, "its previous rather pusillanimous financial policy on the one hand, and the patriotic public spirit hampered by the primitive economic and monetary facilities on the other hand," the methods used to finance the operation were unique. F. G. Young, "Financial History of Oregon," *OHQ*, VII, December, 1906, 422.

however imperfect, we were forced, as a community, to organize a temporary system of laws for the preservation of peace and order. Whatever civilized people may hereafter be compelled to try the unhappy experiment, will find, as we have done, this truth undeniable, that no civilized race of men can possibly exist, as such, without government. Even a despotism is better than no government at all. In organizing and putting in operation our plans of temporary government, we were met by, and had to overcome, great and serious difficulties. That it is, with even the same means, much more difficult to administer a mere temporary system of laws, where all is new and fluctuating, than a regular and permanent one, is a truth so sensible and apparent as not to need illustration. No people can, or will, be contented and happy under a government where all is painful suspense and uncertainty. . . .

Furthermore, it stated a philosophy of rights inherent in citizenship under the government of the United States. ". . . We have acted under the firm conviction that there exists a mutual duty between our government and all its citizens; and that, while we owe and observe a most willing allegiance towards the United States, we have a right to claim their protection and care. Our forefathers complained that they were oppressed by the mother country, and they had a just right to complain. We do not complain of oppression, but of neglect. Even the tyrant has his moments of relaxation and kindness, but neglect never wears a smile. . . ."[22]

Scurrying for Office

There was unanimity apparently with regard to the petition. But there was none in the legislature or outside over recommendations that might accompany it concerning land laws and appointments to the new government. According to the one cynical observer, Oregon's politics in the winter of 1847-1848 were "filthy party strife," to promote Democratic ends. While there was, no doubt, strife of this nature, the attachment of national party labels to it was an error. The large majority of the Oregon population were Democrats, if for no other reason than inheritance. There were no organized parties as such. The strife was rooted in old antagonisms to the "entrenched aristocracy," to the Hudson's Bay Company, and to George Abernethy and his adherents: prohibitionists, merchants,

[22] "Petition of Citizens of Oregon," in *PNQ*, XL, January, 1949, 6, 7.

possessers of McLoughlin's mill site at the Falls. It has been suggested that the feud was so bitter and that the anti-Abernethy party was so fearful its enemies would secure appointments in the government that the legislature which represented it "practically requested" the president to give the more important positions to persons not resident in the territory.[23]

Oregon Country Becomes Oregon Territory

The legislature chose Joe Meek its emissary, and the governor's party delegated J. Quinn Thornton to act for it. Thornton, proceeding by ship, reached Washington before Meek. The colorful mountain man crossed the Rockies in the early spring of 1848 with nine companions in the record time of two months. In Washington he had the advantage of being the president's cousin, but this did not essentially change the customary practice for territorial appointments. Joe Meek was appointed United States Marshal, and Peter H. Burnett Associate Justice. Both were anti-Abernethy. The rest of the appointments were made outside the territory. But, on the other hand, Thornton worked diligently with the Congress on the organic law and toward a land law which met the rival groups' desires.

President Polk signed the bill creating Oregon Territory on August 14, 1848.

One period of colonial experience was concluded the following March when the Territorial Government was declared in operation. The provisional period is one of great interest for the student of American institutions and character. Under circumstances complicated by social, national, racial, religious issues—because the Roman Catholic French Canadians were a factor in the complex—social, and personal issues, a politically mature people worked out their problems as they arose in spite of differences, antagonisms, and distrust. The methods they used were those that had served them and their forefathers on earlier frontiers—the public forum, the newspaper, and the legislative hall. Their confidence in their ability and their ardor for governing

[23] Lester B. Shippee, "The Federal Relations of Oregon—Part VII," *OHQ*, XX, December, 1919, 349.

themselves, their resentment of injustice and of coercion, real or fancied, and their proud independence were exhibited in a memorial addressed to Congress by the legislature of the newly organized territory in 1849. They acknowledged "that providential care which had guided them to their present enviable and prosperous condition" and presented to the Congress, not the supplicating hand of a people asking favors, but "the hand of kinsman and friend," seeking their rights.[24] In this frame of mind, the American colony in the far Northwest began its territorial experience.

[24] Copy of Memorial in Papers of the Territorial Government, 102-109, Mss. File 353, Oregon Historical Society Library; *Journal of the House of Representatives*, 1849; *Journal of the Council*, 1849, 13, 14.

Loggers on Their Springboards. (Courtesy, University of Washington Library.)

Logging Trestle Used to Bridge a Deep Ravine. (Courtesy, Oregon Historical Society.)

In the Old Days Logging Was Done with Bulls. (Courtesy, University of Washington Library.)

Donkey Engine Used Later for Snaking Large Logs. (Courtesy, University of Washington Library.)

Logs Are Now Towed by Tractors. (Courtesy, University of Washington Library.)

Trains Carried Logs to the Mills on Specially Constructed Railroads. (Courtesy, University of Washington Library.)

Motor Trucks Are Now Used over Considerable Distances. (Courtesy, University of Washington Library.)

15

Territorial Government and Territorial Problems

The territorial form of government was the American answer to the problem of ruling colonies of its citizens settled in areas outside the boundaries of the states.[1] The Ordinance of 1787, first devised for the Territory north of the Ohio River, provided the framework of such government for all of the trans-Mississippi West, with the exception of Texas and California. The feature of the ordinance which distinguished it from previous colonial systems was its provision for a terminal date to colonial status. When the population of a territory was sufficiently large to support a state government, and other conditions were favorable, the territory could apply to Congress for admission. If Congress approved, it passed an enabling act authorizing the residents of the territory to form a constitution. If this was in the tradition of republican government, an admission act enabled the new state to take its place on equal footing with others of the union.

To far-off Oregonians, as to others who had pushed out the frontier of the expanding United States, territorial status was a prelude to statehood and to the sovereignty western pre-Civil War political theory held inherent to statehood. Territorial status was something to be desired; it was also something to be endured.

Advantages of Territorial Status

The advantages were many. The federal government assumed the responsibility of protecting settlers and immigrants. The army moved in with garrisons and mounted riflemen wherever trouble was brewing. Long-standing policies with regard

[1] This chapter owes much to Robert C. Clark's *History of the Willamette Valley*, 3 vols., Chicago, 1937, and especially to Robert Johannsen's *Frontier Politics and Sectional Conflict*, Seattle, 1955.

to internal improvements prevented the government from building roads for civilian needs, but it could be expected to construct some for military purposes. Aids to navigation such as lighthouses and harbor improvements, and the establishment of ports of entry, customhouses, and mail service were anticipated by territorials, not only for the direct services they would perform, but also because they would bring money into the area, starved for a circulating medium. So did the construction of territorial buildings, legislative hall, penitentiary, the inevitable insane asylum; and the location of the capitol and government buildings created new land values for the community so fortunate as to get them. The machinery of government was supported by federal moneys. The salaries of the territorial officers and the *per diem* and mileage of jurors and legislators not only relieved the local tax budget, but put government vouchers to work as credit capital. These were some of the things the settlers of the Oregon country could look forward to as territorials.

Outweighing all these in importance, however, was the assurance of land titles. Official surveys replaced with township and range the old method of designating corners by familiar but changeable features of the landscape. Backed by the authority of the federal law, settlers would no longer need to rely upon voluntary associations to protect their lands from claim jumpers. For Oregonians it was a matter of extreme concern whether the Congress would recognize the land laws of its provisional government and the claims of its early settlers.

The Donation Land Act

The Organic Act which set up Oregon Territory provided generously for the support of public education in the new country. Where the Ordinance of 1787 had set aside section 36 of every township for this purpose, at the behest of Samuel Thurston, sections 16 and 36 were so designated in the Oregon law. On the other hand, it voided the provisional government's land laws. The Oregon Donation Land Law of 1850 restored their essential features. It was charged that, as devised by Samuel Thurston, this law perpetuated the old "junto of aristocracy" and purposely defrauded Dr. McLoughlin of his claims to the Williamette Falls site.[2] It granted

[2] F. V. Holman, *Dr. John McLoughlin, the Father of Oregon*, Cleveland, 1907, 123-130; *Orgeon Spectator*, March 20, 1851, May 1, 1851.

a half section, or 320 acres, to every settler (including American half-breeds) over the age of eighteen, who was a citizen or declared his intention to become one before December 1, 1851, and who had occupied and cultivated his land for four consecutive years. If he married by December 1, 1851, his wife was granted a like amount to be held in her own right. This took care of the claims of those who had settled Oregon before 1850. Those settling between December of that year and December, 1853, had to be white male citizens of 21 years of age, to qualify for half as much land, 160 acres. Wives of such qualified settlers were entitled to a like amount. In February, 1853, an amendment extended the expiration date of the act to 1855, and permitted settlers to patent their claims after two years' occupancy and the payment of $1.25 an acre.[3]

The Oregon Donation Land Law was the only Congressional legislation to make an outright gift of western public land to individuals and was designed to reward and encourage the settlement of the Pacific Northwest. It had several interesting features and significant consequences. It recognized the part women had in the task of pioneering by allowing wives the privilege, uncommon at that time, of holding real property in their own names. A minor consequence of the double allotment for married couples was an increased number of marriages, and since single women were as scarce in Oregon as in other frontier societies, very young girls suddenly became marriageable and were married.

More significant was the long-range effect of the act upon the economy of the territory and especially of the Willamette Valley. The size of many of the grants, one square mile, isolated the settlers, impeded the growth of towns, and the diversification of occupations, industry, and crops. It increased a tendency already characteristic of Oregon's pioneers toward provincialism and localism. The long residence requirement prevented settlers from supplementing a meager farm income with other kinds of labor to bring in cash or its equivalent. Many settlers were reduced to a subsistence level and a diet of boiled wheat, at least during the difficult first two years of residence.

[3] The amendment also allowed widows to receive title even though the full period of occupancy had not been fulfilled. An amendment of July, 1854, granted orphans of settlers who took land under any of these acts 160 acres. M. P. Deady, comp., *General Laws of Oregon,* Portland, 1866, 85-96.

The size of the unit reduced opportunities for speculators to engross large acreages, but it was an uneconomical unit with regard to the supply of labor. Within the boundaries of the state of Oregon, 7,437 patents covering about 2,500,000 acres were eventually granted. North of the Columbia in what became Washington Territory in 1853, 1,018 patents accounted for more than 300,000 acres of the public domain.[4]

Those who were so fortunate as to hold their claims profited in the long run, especially if their lands became the site of a city or a water-power development. But a study of 100 square miles of the richest farm lands in the Willamette Valley illustrates the characteristic fluidity of American frontier settlement, showing that before the end of the century two-thirds of the donation land claim lands had passed out of the hands of the original claimants and their descendants.[5]

But the Donation Land Law was an inducement to emigrate to the Pacific Northwest, for the gift of free lands could not be resisted by a people still traditionally land hungry.[6] It has been said that by 1855 the lands of Western Oregon, considered the only fertile lands in the region according to the practices and information of the day, had been taken up.[7]

Disadvantages of Territorial Status

While Oregonians generally welcomed the advantages of territorial status, many who had experienced it

---

[4] Mrs. Dorothy Peterson at the Bureau of Land Management (Portland) helped in verifying figures on Oregon patents. The Genealogical Forum of Portland has been working on Donation Land Claim data. I am grateful to Mrs. William Irvine, Portland, for information resulting from their work. Robert C. Clark's *History of the Willamette Valley*, I:405-409, so thoroughly analyzed the Donation Land Act and its effects that much of what one might say about it simply echoes him. He gives 7,317 as the number of patented claims. The discrepancy between his and the Forum's figures is not significant. Land totals I give on the Washington Territory claims are derived from data to be found in Charlotte Shackleford, "Donation Land Claims," in *Building a State: Washington 1889-1939*, Washington Historical Society Publications, Vol. III, Tacoma, 1940, 410-446.

[5] Timothy W. Davenport, "An Object Lesson in Paternalism," *OHQ*, IV, March, 1903, 50-51. Davenport was state land agent from 1895-1899. His interpretation of his data does not necessarily disqualify the study he made.

[6] The Donation Land Act has been considered as practically the sole explanation for the increase in population in the census period of 1850-1860. This does not take into consideration other factors, of which a not unimportant one is the fact that there were other causes to curtail immigration after 1854 beside the expiration of the act.

[7] Harvey Scott, editorial, *Oregonian*, October 7, 1906.

elsewhere were aware of the drawbacks of the system, and others quickly learned them. Congress appropriated the funds which determined the kind and extent of improvements and help the territory could get. What the territorials expected and what they got were often at variance. The red tape of bureaucracy and an apparent indifference of the treasury department to the time and space which separated Oregon from the national capitol delayed the payment of territorial vouchers. The War Department was ill prepared through lack of funds, personnel, and plans to provide garrisons or troops for protection of immigrant routes and settlements. Congress legislated in significant matters affecting the territory and it had the power, seldom used, to declare territorial legislation null and void; but citizens of the territory had no voting representative in Congress, nor could they vote in national elections for president and vice-president.

Their only part in national affairs was in the person of their elected delegate, who could speak, although he could not vote, on their behalf in Congress. His election was the most important political affair in territorial politics. The successful candidate had an opportunity to build his political fences at home and abroad in anticipation of the day when his territory became a state and entered the national political scene. The strength of the delegate in Congress lay in his ability to win support for desired territorial legislation, and this was most often less a matter of the logic of the legislation than of party affiliation and influence. Through the delegate national party politics entered territorial politics, but the issues which usually figured in elections were local ones. Samuel Thurston, Oregon's first delegate, won an almost uncontested election because of his part in securing the Donation Land Law. His successor was Joseph Lane, first territorial governor. Lane's popularity in Oregon and his standing in the national Democratic party, which put patronage in his hands, kept him in office for eight of Oregon's ten years as a territory. He was defeated on a national issue.

The territorial officers—governor, secretary, attorney general, treasurer, marshal, and three judges—were appointed by the president, and hence came under the patronage system. Because of this they were exposed to criticism they did not always deserve; but the records of territorial experiences show evidence to support charges that appointees were often incompetent, absent from their duties, and willing to exploit their offices for political as well as financial gain. In any case, officers could be unpopular if for no other reason than that they were "foreigners," that is, they were imported and had not previously been residents of the territory.

The case against territorial governors was summarized, in one instance, in a reference to them as "usually obscure strikers, who do the dirty work of parties, and being sent out as governors, assume proconsular powers, and endeavor to 'mold public sentiment' into sending them to Congress."[8]

Territorial Governors

In the last year of his administration President Polk had the opportunity to reward a faithful democrat of favorite son rating in Indiana with the governorship of Oregon Territory. Joseph Lane's reputation as a general in the Mexican War, his politics, and his personality pleased the Oregonians. His term as governor was short, but his influence in politics was of long duration. He arrived in Oregon City on March 2, 1849. On the third he declared the territorial government in operation, and on the fourth, his appointment expired with Polk's presidential term. He continued to carry on the duties of the office, including the important one of superintendent of Indian affairs, until his successor arrived. He also built up a strong political machine, supported by the vitriolic pen of Asahel Bush, editor of the *Oregon Statesman*, the organ of the democratic party. He was elected delegate to Congress in 1851 and served until 1859, when he resigned to become vice-presidential candidate on the Breckenridge ticket of the southern extremist party in the critical campaign of 1860.

John P. Gaines was President Taylor's second choice for Oregon Territory's governorship. The position was first offered to Abraham Lincoln, who refused it.[9] Gaines's career as governor was short and full of contention. He had everything against him. He was a Whig and Oregonians were Democrats; he was dignified, even pompous

[8] Quoted from The Dalles, Oregon, *Mountaineer*, in Earl Pomeroy, *The Territories and the United States; 1861-1890; Studies in Colonial Administration*, Philadelphia, 1947, 88.

[9] Paul I. Miller, "Lincoln and the Governorship of Oregon," *Mississippi Valley Historical Review*, XXIII, December, 1936, 391-394.

according to his enemies, and a marked contrast to the easy-going frontiersman, Joe Lane. In less than a year Gaines was at swords' points with the greater number of Oregonians. Controversy over the location of the capitol, a common cause for quarrels in territories, led to a situation where the governor recognized as the legal legislature an assembly of four members at the Falls of the Willamette, now Oregon City, while the rest of that body convened and legislated at Salem, under the watchful eye of the democratic machine.

Gaines's successor, John W. Davis, was a Democrat, but he had an equally unfortunate experience. He survived only nine months of attack and invective in the best of Oregon's uninhibited newspaper style. The editor of the Whig *Oregonian* ironically explained that local Democrats would not accept Davis because he was "a foreigner. . . . He had neither driven his team across the plains nor been to the mines."[10] That he was a "foreigner" was an important reason for the opposition to him, but it was not the sole reason, nor the most important one. That was found in the ambitions of the tightly knit Democratic machine which, under the epithet of the "Salem clique," dominated Oregon's politics, and intended to continue to do so. The clique's strong card was Joseph Lane, Oregon's territorial delegate, who was able to prevent local revolts and, after Davis, to secure the appointment of a local Democrat, George L. Curry, to the governorship.

The Judges

Almost as important as the governor in the politics of the frontier were the judges. It was their duty to hold district courts and, sitting with a quorum of two out of three, to compose the supreme court of the territory. Judges were supposed to reside in their assigned districts but some found this inconvenient, and one found it so even to reside in the territory. No charges of corruption or willful misdeeds in office could be charged against Oregon's governors, but the first chief justice and the first associate justice fulfilled the worst expectations of the cynical. William P. Bryant was described euphemistically as "in reduced circumstances" when he arrived in Oregon in April, 1849. When he left the following

[10] Quoted from *Oregonian*, August 5, 1854, by W. C. Woodward, *Political Parties in Oregon*, Portland, 1913, 81.

November he was financially well off. In the six months he was in the territory he held two terms of his district court and one term of two days of the supreme court. He purchased interests in the disputed McLoughlin land claim at Oregon City for which title could be adjudicated only before his own court. His fortunes were restored at McLoughlin's expense. He continued to hold the office of chief justice and drew salary for a year and a half after he had left his duties in the territory.[11]

Peter Burnett, a pioneer of 1843, had been appointed associate justice by Polk, but had left for California before his commission arrived. The position for the third district remained unfilled until 1851. After Bryant left, Orville C. Pratt, appointed to the second district, was the only judge in the whole territory until Judge William Strong arrived in August, 1850. Pratt added nothing to the dignity of the bench, although like Bryant he missed no opportunity to add to his own fortune. His private business and political interests often took him from the territory; and when he was present, he was a center of controversy and political machination. He quarreled with Strong and with Bryant's successor, Chief Justice Thomas Nelson, who arrived in April, 1851, and he brought so much confusion into the processes of justice that the courts suffered in prestige. Both Nelson and Strong were Whig appointees but of high moral character and judicial integrity. In the capitol controversy and in its related quarrel over the statutory code (the battle of the Iowa Big Blue Book versus the Iowa Little Blue Book), Nelson and Strong concurred with the governor's constitutional position, while Pratt moved to Salem with the Democratic partisans and, ruling that he presided over the legal court, used his office to play an injudicial role in politics. On the happier side of the picture, in filling Bryant's unexpired term, Nelson contributed to the territory's legal history "as a preëminent exemplar of judicial dignity and independence in an atmosphere of political animosities."[12] Strong remained a permanent resident in Oregon and enjoyed an unblemished reputation.

---

[11] Sidney Teiser, "The First Chief Justice of Oregon Territory: William P. Bryant," *OHQ*, XLVIII, June, 1947, 48, 49, 53-54.

[12] Teiser, "The Second Chief Justice of Oregon Territory: Thomas Nelson," *OHQ*, XLVIII, September, 1947, 223-224. For Pratt, see Teiser, "First Associate Justice of Oregon Territory: O. C. Pratt," *OHQ*, IL, September, 1948, 177, 180.

Bryant and Pratt were symbolic of the evils to which a territory could be subjected when its highest offices were considered spoils for a party and offered opportunities for speculation and aggrandizement.[13] One year after the territory had been organized, the editor of the *Oregon Spectator,* contemplating the fact that Pratt, the territory's only judge at the moment, was in California and the governor and other officers out of the capital city on Indian business, concluded there was no civil government, and that he could see "no remedy for this state of things but in the erection of a State Government and the elevation of our own officers."[14] The 1850 legislature considered a resolution calling for a convention to form a state constitution, but passed instead one asking its delegate to try to secure a change in territorial law to permit the election of their own governor and secretary.

Reaction to "Colonialism"

Absenteeism and "foreigners" were not the issues which started and eventually enlisted Oregonians in a movement toward statehood. In spite of its disguises in local party conflicts and personal feuds, the fundamental issue was the right of self-determination. This was an idea very much in men's minds in the fifties, the era of sectional strife, when every constitutional or political turn of the slavery question opened up the same issue: the right of men, in state or territory, to determine for themselves the institutions with which and under which they would live. For the inhabitants of Oregon, slavery was still an abstract question, but the measure of their freedom was not. Territorial status was, according to a member of the legislature, "repugnant to the true spirit of our Constitution" which intended that men should govern themselves.[15] In the pages of the weekly newspapers Jesse Applegate, called by his contemporaries the "Sage of Yoncalla" and a man who often raised his voice on behalf of principles, pointed out that the disenfranchisement of American citizens in a territory was comparable to the practices of the British toward their American colonists. He advocated the immediate application to the Pacific Northwest of the principle of self-determina-

[13] Jesse Applegate, "An Old Oregonian" to the editor, in *Oregon Statesman,* December 9, 1851.

[14] *Oregon Spectator,* March 7, 1850.

[15] *Oregon Weekly Times,* December 20, 1851.

tion, not only for the whole Oregon Territory but for a part of it as well. He recommended that Congress "divide the Territory by the Columbia river," set up a new territory in the north, and "restore to the people of said Territories their political rights, by allowing them to adopt their own form of Government—to choose their own officers—as a body politic, to have their voice in the councils of the nation. . . ."[16] This was, in effect, asking for political advantages of statehood without the burden of its support.

In asking for the division of the territory and the organization of the region north of the Columbia, Applegate was recommending a step toward independence for its inhabitants—independence from the domination of the Willamette Valley. And this is what they wanted too.

Territory North of the Columbia: 1845-1853

The first settlers north of the river were Canadians, employees and colonists of the Hudson's Bay Company. Although there were no Americans there, the provisional government in 1843 included it in Clackamas and Twality (Tualatin) districts.[17] Probably in recognition of the fact that this was inconsistent with their contention that the provisional government was intended only to apply to American citizens, and that it could not help but be offensive to McLoughlin, the next year's legislature withdrew the northern boundaries of its districts to the Columbia.

In February of 1845, several Americans attempted to establish claims to lands practically at the gates of Fort Vancouver and within

[16] *Oregon Statesman*, December 16, 1851, also November 25, December 2, 9, 1851, "Letter From an Old Oregonian." See D. O. Johansen, "A Tentative Appraisal of Territorial Government in Oregon," *PHR*, XVIII, November, 1949, 485-499.

[17] There were four districts in all. Twality, the first district, included the region between the Willamette River and the Coast Range, from the Yamhill River to 54° 40′; Yamhill, the second, south to the 42nd parallel; and Clackamas, the third, everything east of the Willamette to the Rockies and from the Pudding River north to the 54th parallel; Champoich (Champoeg), the fourth district, comprised the area south of Clackamas from the Willamette to the Rockies and to the 42nd parallel. For the boundaries of Oregon counties see Frederick V. Holman, "Oregon Counties, Their Creations and the Origins of Their Names," *OHQ*, XI, March, 1910, 1-81; for the boundaries of the northern districts which included Washington in 1843-1850, see Jesse S. Douglas, "The Clackamas-Clark Boundary, 1850," *OHQ*, XXXIX, June, 1938, 147-151.

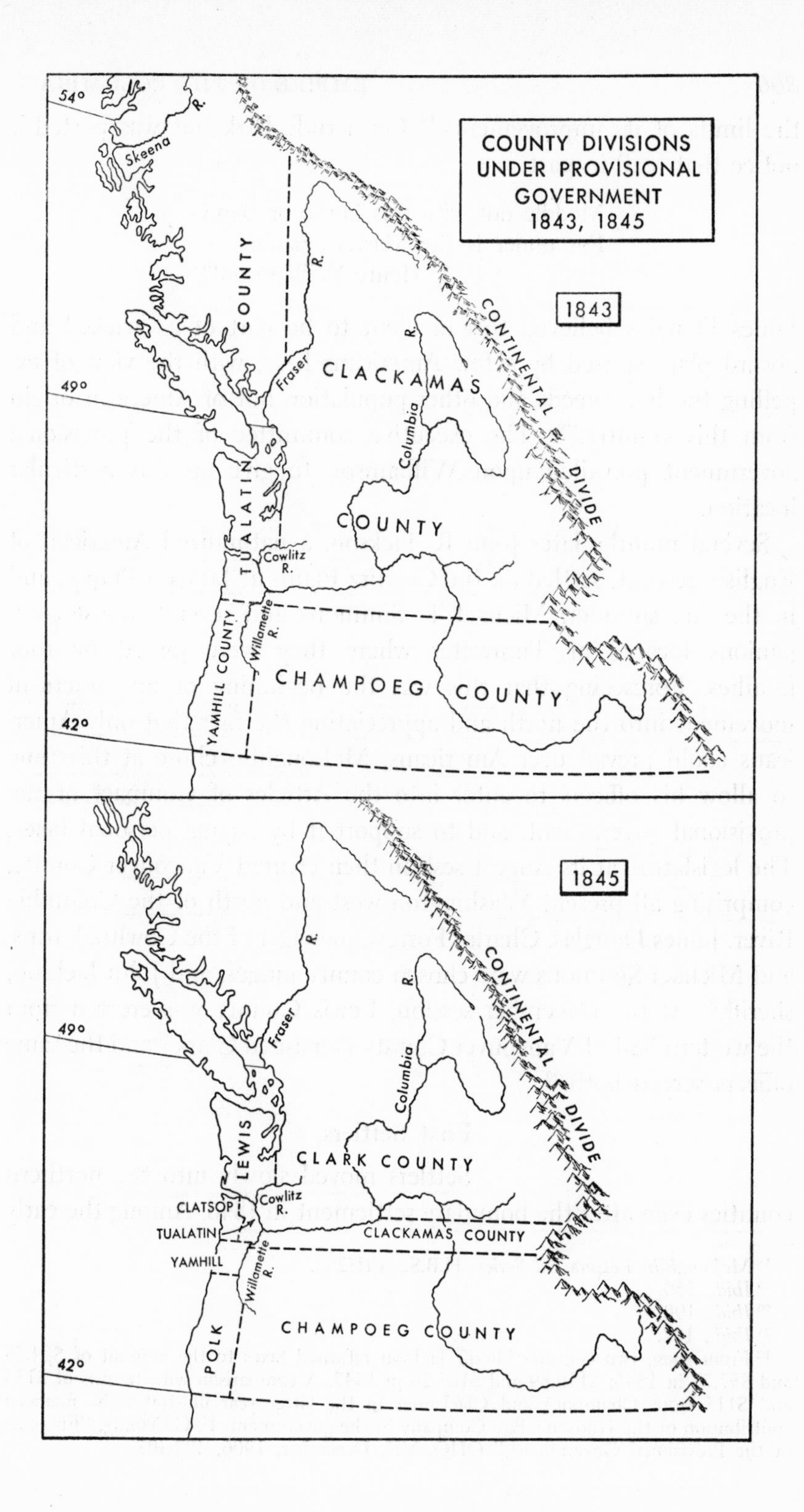
COUNTY DIVISIONS
UNDER PROVISIONAL
GOVERNMENT
1843, 1845
1843
54°
Skeena
R.
COUNTY
Fraser
R.
CLACKAMAS
Columbia
R.
CONTINENTAL
DIVIDE
49°
TUALATIN
COUNTY
Cowlitz
R.
YAMHILL COUNTY
Willamette
R.
CHAMPOEG
COUNTY
42°
1845
Fraser
R.
Columbia
R.
CONTINENTAL
DIVIDE
49°
LEWIS
CLARK COUNTY
CLATSOP
Cowlitz
R.
TUALATIN
CLACKAMAS COUNTY
YAMHILL
Willamette
R.
POLK
CHAMPOEG COUNTY
42°

the limits of its improvements.[18] On a rude bark hut was posted a notice that read in part:

> Meddle not with this house or claim
> For under is the Master's name
> Henry Williamson[19]

James Douglas believed this incident to be part of a "wicked and absurd plan, started by a few Americans here, with the view of expelling the half breeds and other population not of American origin from this country."[20] The executive committee of the provisional government prevailed upon Williamson to give up this particular location.

Several months later John R. Jackson, a naturalized American of English descent, settled on the Cowlitz Plains at Jackson Prairie, and in the late summer, Michael T. Simmons and several robust companions located at Tumwater where they were joined by four families. Foreseeing that this was the beginning of an American movement into the north and appreciating the fact that only Americans could prevail over Americans, McLoughlin chose at this time to allow his officers to enter into the Articles of Compact of the provisional government, and to support it by paying personal taxes. The legislature at its August session then created Vancouver County, comprising all present Washington west and north of the Columbia River. James Douglas, Charles Forrest, manager of the Cowlitz Farms, and Michael Simmons were chosen county judges, and John Jackson, sheriff.[21] At the December session, Lewis County was erected from the western half of Vancouver County (renamed Clark) and the same officers served both.[22]

First Settlers

Settlers moved slowly into the northern counties even after the boundary settlement in 1846. Among the early

---

[18] *McLoughlin Letters, 3d Series,* H.B.S., VII:267.
[19] *Ibid.,* 260.
[20] *Ibid.,* 190.
[21] *Ibid.,* 107.
[22] From these two counties Sheriff Jackson returned taxes to the amount of $24.58 and $57.73 in 1846; $110.89 and $165.26 in 1847. A comparison with returns of $133 and $115 from Champoeg and Clackamas in the latter year illustrates the financial contribution of the Hudson's Bay Company to the government. F. G. Young, "Finances of the Provisional Government," *OHQ,* VII, December, 1906, 402-405.

comers were Sidney Ford and Joseph Borst, who located on Ford Prairie near present Chehalis. Edmund Sylvester joined Simmons and his friends near Tumwater, and Levi Smith built a cabin at Chambers Prairie two miles distant on the site of the present capitol.[23] In 1849 Marshal Joe Meek reported in an unofficial census 304 persons north of the river. Of these probably two-thirds were Canadians. Lewis County was so thinly populated that to fill the panels of grand and petit juries for the trial of Indians accused of murdering Leander Wallace, Meek had to draw jurors from Vancouver County.[24]

Two things militated against the growth of the area. One was the attraction of the Willamette Valley with its settled conditions, growing villages, and greater conveniences. The other was the hostility of the Valley's inhabitants toward its northern neighbors. They encouraged, if they did not actively circulate, reports of poor lands for farming, and of a population representative of the crudest elements of the frontier. What George Gibbs reported of Oregonians generally in 1850 was often applied especially to the inhabitants of Northern Oregon: "There is . . . a general recklessness of character pervading all men—Money is of but little consideration to any but those who look forward to a return to civilized life. They therefore spend it as freely as they make it, gambling and drinking are the every day vices of the country . . . the farmers . . . although indolent, are excellent people. But it is no country for one who has not the power of self-denial, and a strong inducement to labor."[25]

Either Meek's first census of the Oregon Territory in 1849 was a mere approximation of the number of inhabitants north of the river, or a large immigration crossed over in the next 12 months, for the official census of 1850 showed a population of 1,049. Three years later there was an estimated 4,000 scattered in small villages on the eastern and southern shores of Puget Sound and on the prairies of the Cowlitz. Port Townsend was a rough lumbering town, and the Terrys, Hortons, and Yeslers had laid the foundations of Seattle.

---

[23] Levi Lathrop Smith's journal for 1847-1848, is an unusually poignant document revealing the lonely days of a frail and sick pioneer. Ed. James R. Tanis in *PNQ*, XLIII, October, 1952, 277-301.

[24] Panel list in Meek Papers in possession of Mrs. John R. Gates, Hillsboro, Oregon. Photostat copies at Reed College Library.

[25] Vernon Carstensen, ed., "The Pacific Northwest Letters of George Gibbs," *OHQ*, LIV, September, 1953, 200.

Movement to Independence from Oregon

But the dependence of the northern communities upon the Willamette Valley, politically and economically, had not lessened. To free themselves "from the shackles" of "their Willamette masters," they began their agitation for separate territorial status as early as July, 1851. The Cowlitz Convention of that year organized the movement, and on November 25, 1852, "delegates of the citizens of Northern Oregon, in convention assembled" at Monticello drew up a memorial to Congress, requesting the creation of the "Territory of Columbia."

Their case rested on the arguments that the Oregon Territory was too large to form a single state and that division was inevitable; that because of their geographical position, the residents north and south of the Columbia would "always rival each other in commercial advantages . . . [and] as they now are and always have been, be actuated by a spirit of opposition"; that the territorial capital at Salem was 500 miles from the citizens in the north; and that the southern part of the territory "having a majority of voters . . . controlled the Territorial Legislature" and kept from them the benefits of congressional appropriations.[26]

Creation of Washington Territory

Joseph Lane presented the memorial to Congress in February, 1853, and argued its cause. There was no opposition. On March 2, President Millard Fillmore signed the bill creating Washington Territory.[27] The news was received in the new territory with the firing of guns and celebrations. "No longer in the hands of go-betweens, we have become 'a people' within ourselves," exulted the *Columbian*'s editor. " 'Progress' is our watchword. Our destiny is in the keeping of God, the National Government, and our own judgment. . . . So, *nous verrons*."[28]

---

[26] Memorial in Charles M. Gates, *Readings in Pacific Northwest History: Washington, 1790-1895*, Seattle, 1941, 116-117.

[27] The name requested in the memorial was changed to avoid confusing it with the District of Columbia. It is questionable whether this is not a worse confusion.

[28] Olympia *Columbian*, May 7, 1853, in Gates, *Readings*, 128-129.

Washington Territory was then defined as the land lying between the summit of the Rockies and the Pacific Ocean and from the Canadian line at the 49th parallel to the middle of the main channel of the Columbia River until its direction changed at Walla Walla and thence eastwardly to the mountains along the line of the 46th parallel. The Organic Code by which it was to be governed for 36 years differed in no essential matter from that of the Oregon Territory.[29]

The Administration of Washington Territory

The first decade of its political experience followed the general pattern of older territories and in considerable measure paralleled that of Oregon. Its first governor served three years and then became territorial delegate. In rapid succession three governors followed him between 1857 and 1861. Again between 1866 and 1872 three governors sampled the Far West and departed. But between the latter date and 1889, three local men, as local was defined, served the territory long and well. Using the election of the territorial delegate as an indication of the prevailing party preference, it would appear that only three times in 36 years was the governor not of the local majority's party preference.

In times of crisis during the early years of Washington's territorial history there was the usual anguish over rule by "foreigners." A correspondent to the *Puget Sound Herald* in 1860 referred to Henry M. McGill, secretary of the territory and acting governor at the time, as a "stranger, recently exported from the political rubbish floating about Washington [D. C.]."[30] Political life in the Territory was never dull. It had its democratic machine, the Olympia clique, and uninhibited editors of party newspapers such as the *Pioneer and Democrat* (Olympia) and *Puget Sound Courier*, who gave to Washington's politics a

[29] All legislation passed by its assembly had to be submitted to Congress for approval. Federal and territorial laws passed for Oregon Territory before the division were to be in effect in the new territory where applicable. The Washingtonians immediately set up a commission to prepare a statutory code that would eliminate some confusions in Oregon's statutes. See Arthur S. Beardsley, "Compiling the Territorial Codes of Washington," reprinted from *PNQ*, XXVIII, January, 1937, 4.

[30] Quoted in Arthur S. Beardsley, "Early Efforts to Locate the Capital of Washington Territory," *PNQ*, XXXII, July, 1941, 263.

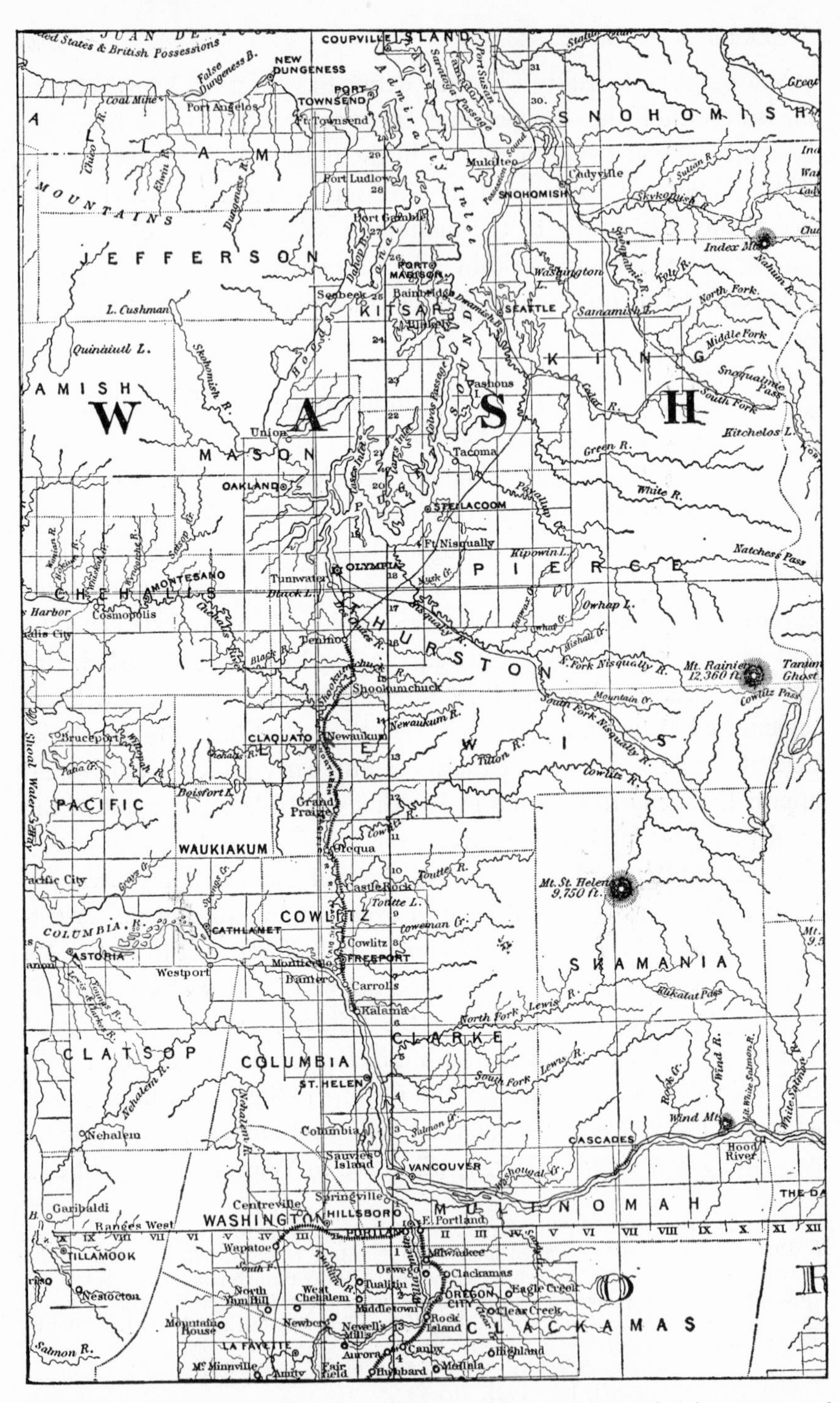

Population Centers in Western Washington. (From Asher and Adams, Map of Washington Territory, 1873.) See companion map facing p. 336.

flavor comparable to that provided Oregonians in the pages of the *Oregon Statesman* and *Oregonian*. When there was nothing else to get excited about there was the capitol controversy which almost monopolized politics throughout the territorial period and in which national party labels were attached to partisans.

The courts suffered no scandals involving the personal integrity of their judges, but they were, from time to time, part and parcel of whatever controversy was in the air. In 1856, the first chief justice, Edward Lander, ordered the arrest of the governor for contempt of court and was himself arrested by the militia on the governor's orders.

Washington Territory's First Governor: Isaac Ingalls Stevens

Governor Isaac I. Stevens had the personality and knew the techniques to build a following among Washington's individualistic citizenry, even though he aroused widespread opposition. A West Point graduate originally from Massachusetts, Stevens compensated for his lack of a frontier background by a successful military career in the Topographic Engineers Corps during the Mexican War from which he emerged a major general. In 1849 he was assigned to the United States Coast Survey headquarters, where as chief assistant to Alexander D. Bache he gained invaluable experience and scientific training. Like many army men, Stevens supported General Franklin Pierce when he ran for the presidency. For his political services and because of his unusual training and manifest abilities, Stevens was rewarded with the concurrent offices of governor of Washington Territory, Superintendent of Indian Affairs, and leader of the northern Pacific Railroad Survey.

The Pacific Railroad Surveys (1854-1861), of which there were five, were intended to ascertain a practicable route for a railroad from the Mississippi River to the Pacific. They were extremely important not only in furthering the development of transcontinental communication and in joining the isolated West to the rest of the nation, but also in acquiring more accurate knowledge about the West. Unfortunately political considerations and the reluctance of men to examine the grounds of their preconceptions led Stevens' superiors and the public to ignore or misinterpret some of his basic conclusions.

Stevens' explorations were confined to the area between the 47th and 49th parallels. His assistant, Lieutenant George B. McClellan, explored the Rocky Mountain and Cascade passes, but both *en route* to Puget Sound and in the course of his duties as governor and superintendent of Indian affairs, Stevens became thoroughly familiar with what he called "the Great Plains of the Columbia." From his observations and from comparisons with other similar regions he concluded that the character of this country had been grossly misunderstood. On the thesis that where there was a good growth of grass there was good cereal land, he argued that the "Plains" would support a farming population and that Washington Territory's resources were not limited to the western wet valleys. His enthusiasm for the territory and his championship of the railroad route that would open it up have been interpreted as merely the promotion of his own political interests. Such a viewpoint ignores his integrity as "a practical geographer of uncommon stature," as he has recently been described.[31]

Stevens, the politician, managed to build a powerful clique at Olympia which supported him as governor and from 1857 to 1861 as delegate to Congress. In the words of his opponents, the Olympians were guilty of "perpetuating a political dynasty which stinks in the nostrils of all honest men";[32] but to the majority of Washingtonians Stevens was a hero. To even the most unbiased observer it is evident that Stevens was engaged in more than political quarrels during those busy years. As well as governor, he was superintendent of Indian affairs and commander of the territorial militia. In these capacities he led the territorials in a critical era of Indian wars.

The Background of Indian Troubles

To understand this episode it is necessary to consider the interrelated land and Indian policies in which the troubles were rooted. Through the Donation Land Law of 1850, the federal government gave settlers a free choice of lands from the public domain in the Pacific Northwest, but by its own customary practice, it did not have title to that domain. It was a basic assumption

[31] Donald W. Meinig, "Isaac Stevens: Practical Geographer of the Early Northwest," *GR*, XLV, October, 1955, 542-558.

[32] Quoted in Beardsley, "Early Efforts to Locate the Capital of Washington Territory," *PNQ*, XXXII, 258 n.

of American law that property rights could be surrendered only through lawful processes. From colonial times, government had recognized the sovereignty of Indians, whether tribes, nations, or villages, over their traditional lands. To acquire title to these, it made treaties with the natives who, in exchange for gifts, annuities, and promises of perpetual peace thereafter, ceded their rights to the soil. Having surrendered the lands which supported the theory of their sovereignty, the Indians then became wards of the state. In the early nineteenth century the policy was adopted of removing the Indians, by force if necessary, to some remote location where it was hoped they would be adjusted to civilization.

Settlers in Oregon expected the same policy to be applied in Oregon. Governor Lane's first message to the legislature showed his awareness of the mutual problem of the settlers and Indians; of the former in getting titles to lands, of the latter in surrendering them. He indicated his sympathy for the Indians "surrounded . . . by the whites, whose arts of civilization, by destroying the resources of the Indians doom them to poverty want and crime," and he urged a memorial to Congress asking for the "extinguishment of their title by purchase, and the locating them in a district removed from settlement."[33] The Donation Act was in full effect, however, before these matters were concluded by Congress, and in many cases titles were not extinguished until after the lands had been occupied.

Authority to negotiate with the Indians was granted under the Indian Treaty Act of 1850. Commissioners were appointed to make treaties with the western Indians and remove them to unsettled areas east of the Cascade Mountains. The commissioners found these Indians willing to cede their lands, but they refused to move from the locality. Considering the distinct patterns of life which had evolved in the two environmental situations—the wet wooded region and the barren dry plateau—it is not hard to see the reasonableness of the western Indians' position or that of the interior peoples who objected to having among them those of such different ways of life. The commissioners thereupon departed from their instructions and agreed that the Indians should retain a portion of their old lands, while

[33] Priscilla Knuth and Charles M. Gates, eds., "Oregon Territory in 1849-1850," *PNQ*, XL, January, 1949, 12.

ceding the remainder. Between 1851 and 1853 treaties were concluded on this basis with some of the Willamette Valley and coastal bands.

The Commissioner of Indian Affairs in Washington, D.C., recognized the fact that these treaties contained "novel provisions the practical operation of which could not be foreseen" and neither recommended nor opposed their ratification.[34] Although these particular treaties were not ratified by the Senate, their "novel provisions" eventually became a basic part of northwest Indian treaties. In essence, what they did was to allow the Indians a continuing fiction of sovereignty over a portion of their original lands, now "reserved" for their exclusive use. The presence of the Indians in a settled area and their occupation of reservations for which white men believed they had a better use led to abuse of the natives and a continuous process of reducing their holdings.

It is a matter of significance that the Indians of the western part of the territory were on the whole willing to make the cessions in exchange for annuities, providing they did not have to remove. The interior Indians, on the other hand, being less commercial in attitude, and having a different attitude toward the land, were loath to part with any of it. The Yakimas, for example, had a sense of exclusive ownership uncommon among northwest Indians. They required outsiders to get permission to cross their lands and even posted guards at their boundaries.[35] The different value scales of whites and Indians and among Indians was illustrated in the words reported as spoken by Chief Peu Peu Mox Mox at the Walla Walla Treaty Council in 1855: "Suppose you show me goods, shall I run up and take them? Goods and earth are not equal. Goods are for using on the earth. I do not know where they have given lands for goods."[36]

This was the general background for the Northwest's Indian problem. The failure of the Senate to ratify the 1851-1853 treaties left the situation and the matter of land titles wide open. The settlers did not

[34] C. F. Coan, "The First Stage of the Federal Indian Policy in the Pacific Northwest, 1849-1852," *OHQ*, XXII, March, 1921, 56.

[35] Verne F. Ray, "Native Villages," *PNQ*, XXVII, April, 1936, 119; *Cultural Relations in the Plateau of North West America*, Anthropological Records VIII, Berkeley, 1942, 17.

[36] As reported in Hazard Stevens, *Life of Isaac I. Stevens*, 2 vols., Boston, 1900, II:45-46.

wait, but hastened to spread out and take up claims. In 1852 gold was discovered in Southern Oregon, and miners from California moved into the Rogue and Umpqua valleys. Rumors of gold discoveries elsewhere in the Northwest sent prospectors far and wide—and into regions where only fur traders had ventured before. A brief but bloody war with the Rogue River Indians in 1853 emphasized the need for some firm settlement. This was settled by the Table Rock Treaty of 1853 and ratified by the Senate the following year.

Indian Outbreaks

One of Governor Stevens' first duties was to conclude treaties with the Indians of Washington Territory, that is, roughly, north of the Columbia and as far east as Nebraska Territory. The same Congressional act which authorized him gave similar powers to Superintendent Joel Palmer for Oregon Territory, the southern part of the Pacific Northwest. It would appear they were instructed to use as models the treaties that had been made, and rejected, in 1851-1853. Beginning in the winter of 1854 and continuing through the following summer, the two men held councils and concluded treaties with the major bands. Each treaty provided a special reservation of land or, as in some cases, a reservation of lands and of rights to customary fishing sites. Palmer had little trouble with the reduced Oregon Indians except with Rogues who went on the warpath again in 1855-1856. Their outbreak coincided with a general uprising that was thought at first to be the result of a concerted plan. This was not the case. The Indians had no precedent of unified action among so many people with widely differing customs and languages to separate them; they had no tradition of leadership or strategy in warfare. They had in common only fear, suspicion, and a compulsion to act before it was too late.

Peu Peu Mox Mox, at the Walla Walla Council, tense with suspicion, had asked for time—"We require time to think quietly, slowly." But there was no time. Treaties were signed, and the lands were ceded. There were questions about the signings: whether Leschi —for example—signed at all; in other cases whether chieftains had the power to sign for their people. There were promises that if the Indians ceded, they would receive gifts and annuities. Before the

Indians had any tokens of good faith and before they had begun to move to their assigned reservations, the white men entered their lands, building their cabins and creeping snake rail fences, or trespassing jealously guarded trails with their pack trains and cattle drives.

Even while the treaties were in the process of negotiation, rumors of gold in the vicinity of Fort Colville had started a movement of local citizens in that direction. They found gold, and in a brief time, increasing numbers traveled north via the Columbia River and the valleys of its western tributaries, which meant they crossed Yakima lands. Several parties of miners were murdered as was the investigating Indian agent. Major G. O. Haller with a company of regulars was repulsed with losses when he attempted to enter the valley. Simultaneously the Indians on the Sound struck at the settlers, massacring a colony on the White River, besieging the citizens of Seattle. The blockhouse winter succeeded the treaty-making summer.

The Indian Wars: 1855-1858

It was reported from the Puget Sound settlements that the Indians committed acts of violence and cruelty "of which they were heretofore judged incapable."[37] Cabins were burned, cattle driven off, trails and roads ambushed, and frightened people took refuge in blockhouses hastily erected or converted from church, barn, or schoolhouse. The crisis of Indian attack brought into being or to a head other conflicts. In Western Washington, the governor's volunteer militia was hard put to catch up with the marauding Indians who seemed to vanish mysteriously after a raid. Furthermore, some settlers continued to live peaceably on their lands, while their neighbors' cabins were burned and the occupants murdered. Suspected of helping the Indians, they claimed in their defense that they had escaped attack because they were "neutral."

Martial Law in Washington Territory

There was no such word as "neutral" in Stevens' vocabulary at the time, and he ordered them into the block-

[37] David E. Blaine's diary, entry made at Portland, March 19, 1856, in "Seattle's First Taste of Battle, 1856," *PNQ*, XLVII, January, 1956, 6.

houses where they could be watched. When five men (it is interesting that they were former employees of the Hudson's Bay Company) refused, Stevens declared martial law and arrested them for trial in a military court. Chief Justice Edward Lander, on service with the volunteers, left his post to open his court to *habeas corpus* proceedings. When two of the prisoners were still held even though Lander had proved the civil court was functioning, the judge ordered Governor Stevens arrested for contempt. The Governor retaliated by having the militia arrest Lander, holding him prisoner on the charge that he had absented himself from his military duties without leave. This dilemma was finally resolved in a unique fashion. When Lander was released he slapped a fine on Stevens who thereupon pardoned himself.[38] Although censured by the legislature, Stevens' popularity survived the incident and he was elected delegate by a vote of 986 to 549.

Militia Versus the Regulars

A less amusing conflict was that between the governor and the settlers on one hand and General John E. Wool and the regular army on the other—a conflict which handicapped the job of pacifying the Indians. General Wool, commandant of the Pacific military district with headquarters at San Francisco, like many regular army men believed that in most instances settlers were responsible for their troubles with the natives; and that the army's duty was also to protect the Indians. In the case of the Northwest, Wool explicitly affirmed that the troubles were fomented by the whites. They hoped, he charged, to relieve a depressed condition of their economy in 1854-1855 with army war expenditures and with the issuance of scrip to pay their volunteer companies. He blamed Stevens' treaties which did not protect the Indians' interests before permitting settlers to enter ceded lands and did not provide for a total removal of the Indians to an "Indian Country," but permitted them reservations in country otherwise open to settlement. He ordered the interior closed to white men to remove further causes of disturbance in that area.

The governor, as spokesman for the settlers, denied the general's charges and countered with his own: that the army refused to protect

[38] Edmond S. Meany, *History of the State of Washington,* New York, 1909, 197.

the settlers, that the general had disbanded companies of volunteers when there were insufficient regular troops to protect the settlements, and had used technicalities to evade arming and equipping the settlers for their own defense. Bitter personal recriminations, extending even to their soldierly experiences in the Mexican War, did nothing to relieve the quarrel. The Oregon and Washington legislatures petitioned for General Wool's removal from the Pacific command, and expressed a common lack of confidence in the army.

There was some reason to share the army's distrust of volunteer militia, its inexperienced command, lack of discipline, and three months and six months terms of enlistment. The volunteers did a great deal of marching but were guided by no plan of attack or defense. On the other hand, the citizen's army had seen no striking evidence of brilliant leadership on the part of the regulars. The subsequent records of George McClellan, Phil Sheridan, and George Wright in the Civil War suggest they were not incompetent in orthodox war situations.

General Wool was relieved of his command and Brigadier-General N. S. Clark adopted a more energetic policy with regard to the Indians of the interior. The Yakima War was prosecuted with vigor after the disastrous defeat of Colonel Steptoe. Ordered to Fort Colville to protect about 40 miners there who feared attack, Steptoe was stopped by a combined force of hundreds—possibly as many as 1,000 to 1,200 eastern tribesmen—who warned him not to cross the boundary of the latter's lands. He agreed to withdraw, but his retreat to Walla Walla was harassed by a series of running battles. Colonel George Wright was then placed in command of a punitive expedition.

The Wright Campaign

While Major Robert Garnett reduced the Yakima Valley natives, Wright advanced with more than 500 troops into the Spokane country. By his skillfull deployments at Four Lakes and Spokane Plains he convinced the enemy they had no chance to win and further fighting meant extinction. This was brought home to them in a hard way when Wright rounded up and slaughtered 800 or 900 of their horses and destroyed their caches of winter food. As they surrendered, summary justice was dealt a quota of ringleaders from each band. Qualchian, a young Yakima warrior accused of murdering the Indian agent, was sent word that his father Owhi would be hanged if he did not come to Wright's camp. "Qualchian came to me at 9 o'clock," Wright reported, "and at 9¼ A.M. he was hung."[39]

The war in the West was over by 1857, in the Columbia Plateau in 1858. In the Snake country it continued sporadically until 1867. Hostilities along this portion of the Oregon Trail had begun in earnest in 1854 when 19 out of 21 persons in the Ward party were massacred just east of Fort Boise. Regulars and volunteers did what they could to patrol the region. With the outbreak of the Civil War, and just when a heavy migration of miners was beginning in Southern Idaho, federal troops were withdrawn. The protection of this area's trade routes with California, and its fast-growing settlements had to be handled by volunteer corps from Washington, Oregon, and California. Fort Boise, abandoned by the Hudson's Bay Company in 1856 was rebuilt near the old location and garrisoned. At the conclusion of the Civil War the army returned and by 1870 the Indians were confined to their reservations.

Effects of the Indian Wars

The Indian wars had a profound effect upon the Pacific Northwest, and especially upon Washington Territory. They deflected its enterprise from some areas of peaceful enterprise. The essential task of road-building to join the interior and the coast had to be abandoned. Farms had to be rebuilt and restocked and the accumulation of capital for other types of venture was delayed. Immigration of a much wanted type of settler—the sturdy farmer with a family—was curtailed, postponed, or deflected to Oregon.

On the other hand, the Northwest as a whole derived benefits from the wars. Special agent John Ross Browne found no evidence to support Wool's charge that the wars had been promoted to relieve their depressed economic condition. There had been hard times in 1854-

[39] Report to W. W. Machall, September 24, 1858, in John Mullan's "Topographical Memoir of Col. Geo. E. Wright's Campaign against the hostile Northern Indians in Oregon and Washington Territories," *Sen. Ex. Doc. No.* 32, 35th Cong., 2d Sess., 69.

1855 but the wars alone did not change that. The depression was caused by the hard winter of 1853-1854 which prevented the miners of Southern Oregon from working. This set up a chain of reactions in San Francisco and Portland that in turn affected credit and commerce in the Willamette Valley and Puget Sound country. The reopening of the mines improved matters the following summer. It is true, nevertheless, that army expenditure and the circulation of scrip with which the volunteers were paid were advantageous to farmers and merchants alike. Stevens in 1857 reported to the legislature the issuance of close to one million dollars in scrip redeemable by federal funds. This was not an insignificant sum in a frontier economy.

The wars—and the mines—drained the chronically short-supply labor market. Farm help in the Willamette Valley in 1857 was receiving 50 dollars a month, board and room, and mechanics and carpenters $3.75 to $5.00 a day. These signs of inflation were multiplied when demands for goods to supply the miners' markets increased.

Two major outcomes of the war were the removal of the Indian threat and, after the withdrawal of Wool's exclusion order, the opening of the interior to settlers and gold seekers. Ten years after the Yakima War was concluded farmers at Walla Walla were beginning to ship out wheat. Within those ten years Oregon became a state, Idaho Territory emerged from Eastern Washington Territory, and a large part of the Pacific Northwest became a mining frontier.

16

Oregon Statehood and the Division of Washington Territory

A movement for statehood originated almost simultaneously with Oregon's organization as a territory. It arose from discontent with a system which Oregonians believed reduced American citizens to a position of colonial subjection. Self-determination was a principle of government which the territorial experience made popular.

From 1850 to 1854 the statehood issue was largely confined to legislative debates on resolutions calling for a constitutional convention. In this period while both Democrats and Whigs subscribed to the idea of self-determination, their enthusiasm waxed or waned according to the dictates of party expediency. The Democrats more consistently favored statehood, especially when, as in 1851-1852, a Whig national administration placed a Whig governor in the territory. The Whigs, on the other hand, were reluctant for statehood when it would mean putting the Democrats in control of a government they, as the minority, could not hope to win. In both cases the assumption was that the Oregon Democracy was a firm cohesive party and that it had no opposition sufficiently strong to break it.

Such was not the case, however. The high-handed methods of the Salem clique which ran the party had created factions within it which were only waiting for an opportunity to throw the rascals out and put themselves in. The emergence of the short-lived but controversial nativist party, the Know-Nothings, represented more of an anti-Salem revolt than the anti-Catholic, antiforeigner movement it was in the East.[1] It was scotched when the clique put through the legislature a *viva voce* voting measure to ferret out its membership.

[1] Priscilla Knuth, "Nativism in Oregon," *Reed College Bulletin,* January, 1946, 24.

One of the strongholds of the democratic party was the mining district in Southern Oregon. But here opposition not only to the clique but to Willamette Valley farmers and Portland merchants as well, encouraged a movement to withdraw from Oregon Territory and, uniting with Northern California, to form a new territory of homogeneous political and economic interests. This local secession movement had its effect upon the statehood issue.

The Slavery Issue and Statehood Movement

The question of calling a constitutional convention was first submitted to the voters in 1854 and rejected by a majority of 869 with solid opposition from the miners. It was also defeated in the next two years' elections, but by so narrow a margin in 1856 that Delegate Lane introduced into Congress the necessary measure to enable Oregonians to proceed toward statehood. It was not even considered by a Congress distraught with "bleeding Kansas." By 1857 local politics were almost obscured by the national crisis over the slavery issue. As Oregonians interpreted the course of events, this involved more than the freedom of Negroes. The right of citizens to determine their own institutions was the critical issue at stake.

Immigrants to Oregon had early expressed their sentiments with regard to slavery. The provisional government had not only reaffirmed the prohibition of slavery in the Ordinance of 1787, but had legislated to exclude free Negroes and mulattos. Although the majority of Oregonians were of southern origin they were not of the slave-holding class, and it would appear that those who came with slaves did not hold them in bondage. This attitude had led the proslavery forces in the Senate to defeat an Oregon territorial bill offered in 1847, and the Organic Act of the next year had been passed without reference to slavery. There were few Negroes in Oregon; the census of 1850 showed a population of 207 free colored, which may have included some Hawaiians. Oregonians wanted no more of free Negroes than they did Negroes in bondage. They were anti-Negro rather than anti-slavery. Yet it was in the temper of the territory's inhabitants to prefer slavery if any outside influence should try to dictate to them on the matter. Asahel Bush, editor of the *Statesman*, pointed out in 1857 that if some abolitionist society should attempt to "abolitionize" Oregon, the latter would become a slave state. "Such is the temper of the Oregonians; they want no outside interference."[2]

The same dilemma that split the national Democracy cracked the Oregon party wide open. Democrats were forced into positions of being proslavery or antislavery in so far as they adhered to the "hard" or "soft" wing of the party. The softs called themselves the National Democrats and subscribed to Stephen A. Douglas' device of popular sovereignty for determining whether or not a territory should have a free or slave constitution. The "hard" faction in the national party held to the theory that Congress had the power and obligation to protect slavery wherever it was or wherever it wished to go. The Oregon "hards" were the Salem clique in so far as they sought at all costs to maintain party regularity and prevent the split apparent within the national organization, but they could not go along with it on this issue. They could be proslavery in theory, but could not straddle the fence on popular sovereignty. This was appealing to too many persons within the clique.

It was difficult for Oregonians, as it was for citizens in the whole country in those troubled days, to find a party refuge for their dilemmas. Some Oregon democrats found they were not at home in either the hard or soft camps. The Republican party was radical, and not yet respectable. The Whig party, always anemic in Oregon, was dead, and some of its members were moving toward republicanism. "The Whigs are all dead out here—they call themselves the *Republican* party—which means negro worshippers," wrote a member of that moribund group. "I can't go the Locofocos [a faction of the Democratic party] and I'll see the Republicans to the Devil before I'll vote with them. I don't know what I am exactly, but any thing but an abolitionist."[3]

The Civil War in Kansas, the position of the incoming Buchanan administration with respect to slavery in the territories, the Dred Scott decision which, in effect denied the right of territories to decide

---

[2] *Statesman*, March 31, 1857.

[3] David Logan to Mary Logan, November 28, 1855, "22 Letters of David Logan," *OHQ*, XLIV, September, 1943, 272. Compare this Whig's dilemma with that of Lincoln the same year in a letter to Joshua F. Speed, August 24, 1855, in Philip Van Doren Stern, *The Life and Writings of Abraham Lincoln*, Random House, 1940, 395.

for themselves whether they would be slave or free, forced Oregonians to a decision irrespective of party affiliations.[4] "If we are to have the institution of slavery fastened upon us here, we desire the people resident in Oregon to do it, and not the will and power of a few politicans in Washington City," wrote Thomas Dryer, editor of the *Oregonian*, former opponent of statehood, and Whig in the process of becoming a republican.[5]

The Constitutional Convention

Under the threat of a limitation to their rights of self-determination Oregonians went to the polls in June, 1857, and by a vote of 5,938 to 1,679 showed they were in favor of a constitutional convention and sovereign statehood. They ignored the fact that Congress had not passed the enabling act which authorized this step. They were asserting their independence of political action.

The convention which met in August of that year wisely avoided complicating its work by arguing whether the constitution should be slave or free. This was left to the voters to decide. They wrote the document without reference to the matter and in submitting it to the voters for ratification added a schedule of three questions: Do you vote for the constitution? Do you vote for slavery in Oregon? Do you vote for free Negroes in Oregon? The results were an interesting illustration of Oregon opinion. The constitution was approved 7,195 to 3,125; slavery rejected, 7,727 to 2,645; and free Negroes excluded, 8,640 to 1,081.

In essence, what the Oregonians had done in writing a constitution without authority from Congress was to act upon the principle of self-determination, or popular sovereignty, the Douglas solution for the problem of slavery in the territories. Consistent with the large principle if not with the slavery issue, they then took the democratic position of states' rights and in June, 1858, elected as their state governor, John Whiteaker, a proslavery, states' rights Democrat, as were their senators, Delazon Smith and Joseph Lane.

This election was an assertion of Oregon's convictions, but it was

[4] For a thorough discussion of this subject see Robert W. Johannsen, *Frontier Politics and the Sectional Conflict: the Pacific Northwest on the Eve of the Civil War*, Seattle, 1955.

[5] *Oregonian*, November 1, 1856.

also an indication of the strength remaining to the Salem clique. A narrow margin of 943 for regularity revealed it was losing ground. Oregon's vote in the presidential election of 1860 showed the effect of the war issue on the sentiments of Oregonians. Self-determination for territory and state and tradition captured 9,000 voters for the Democratic candidates. Douglas, popular sovereignty and soft Democrat, received 4,131 votes; Breckinridge, states' rights, secession, slavery, and party regularity, with Oregon's Joseph Lane as vice-presidential candidate, 5,074. With the Democrats thus split, Lincoln and the new Republican party with a firm position on the one issue of excluding slavery in the territories and an otherwise appealing platform to western interests in the railroad and homestead planks, won with 5,344 votes.

The Constitution Adopted

In adopting a constitution and electing state officers, Oregonians had assumed their statehood as an accomplished fact. Congress was not to be rushed in this manner, however; Oregon had to remain a territory until properly admitted into the Union. The prospect that it would soon be was indeed dark in 1858. The Republicans, gathering strength from every possible source, were opposed to admitting as a state one which had so consistently a Democratic voting record, even though it had, in effect, aligned itself in the slavery issue with the free states. They therefore united with the proslavery Democrats, who did not want to admit another nonslave state, to reject Oregon's statehood. It took a coalition of moderate Democrats and 15 Republicans to pass the Oregon admission act. It was signed by President Buchanan February 14, 1859. Oregon's era of political vassalage thus ended in a victory for the principle of self-determination of a people.

Oregon's Organic Law

What Oregon was to be as a state was foreshadowed in its constitution. This document revealed its framers and its ratifiers to be conservative in the tradition of the agricultural West. During the convention the idea was advanced that "here upon the Pacific Coast . . . we ought to go by the reason of things, and not go so much by precedent." The opinion that prevailed was voiced by a delegate who held that "if he was sent here to form a new Bible he would copy the old one . . . to make a hymn book, he would report an old one—they are better than any he could make."[6] With the exception of one minor article on the judiciary, there was nothing in this one not to be found elsewhere in American state constitutions of the time.[7] The framers drew most heavily upon those of Indiana, Iowa, and Michigan.[8] They chose well from their sources, and if they erred in any major respect it was in an almost penurious thriftiness which burdened a few ill-paid officials with multiple duties. In its economy-mindedness, in limiting state and county indebtedness, in regulating banks and corporations, it expressed the sentiments of a farming people who had memories of the panic of 1837 and the ensuing depression, and who had no understanding or affection for the emerging industrial influences of their day. Judge Matthew P. Deady spoke for them generally when he said: "We have an agricultural community, and the domestic virtues incident to an agricultural people; and there is where you look for the true and solid wealth and happiness of a people. . . . In the manufacturing countries power, political and otherwise, is in the hands of capitalists; there are many people dependent on them, and dependence begets servility. . . . I am not in favor of such a state of things here. . . ."[9] The Constitution of 1857 served Oregon without change until 1902.

Northwest Politics

Politics in the new state were influenced by the Civil War and by the rapid rise of the Republican party. Loyalty to the union was the sentiment that drew war Democrats, Republicans, and old Whigs into the coalition functioning as a Union party. Between 1862 and 1885 Oregonians elected three Democratic governors, six senators, and seven representatives; three Republican governors, three senators, and six representatives. The Salem clique disappeared and the Portland Republican machine took its

[6] Charles H. Carey, ed., *The Oregon Constitution*, Salem, 1926, 75, 109.
[7] Helen Leonard Seagraves, "The Oregon Constitutional Convention of 1857," *Reed College Bulletin*, Vol. 30, June, 1952, 15.
[8] Carey, *The Oregon Constitution*, 482.
[9] Carey, *The Oregon Constitution*, 249.

place as an example of inner core control and direction of politics.

The war years produced a similar metamorphosis in Washington Territory. Democrats tended to act with Republicans in a Union party where support of the federal government was concerned. Its Republican-appointed governors did not add prestige to the territorial system, but they managed to build up a party following sufficiently strong to move the western part of the territory into the Republican camp. There was no dearth of local issues on which it could build its strength. One of the most important of these was the division of the Territory as a result of the Idaho gold rush.

The Northwest's Gold Rushes

In 1860, as Oregon was getting the feel of "flying with her own wings" as her state motto asserted, Washington territory and the whole Pacific Northwest were undergoing changes incident to its recently expanded mining frontier. Reference has already been made to gold rushes in the Northwest in the fifties. Their importance warrants more detailed attention.

As surface mining declined in California, miners moved from Northern California to the Rogue River country of Southern Oregon where, by 1852, a modest gold rush was under way. Jacksonville became the capital of the mining district, Scottsburg its transportation center, and Marshfield a port of entry. In the next several years, as prospectors pushed their explorations across the Cascades, strikes were reported on the Santiam and John Day rivers, and in 1854-1855 substantial discoveries were made on the upper Columbia in the vicinity of Fort Colville. This brought hundreds of miners into the region, whence they spread into Canada, where rich discoveries were made on the Fraser. By 1858 the Fraser was experiencing a rush reminiscent of the early days on the Sacramento. Thousands of Californians came by boat directly to Victoria, a lesser number arrived in Portland and Seattle and thence overland to avoid as much as possible the dangers of the river's trails. During the peak of the rush, there was a temporary cessation of all normal activities in the Northwest as soldiers deserted their posts, sailors their ships, and farmers their plows, to try their luck on the golden river. The miners had to be fed, and every settlement on the waters of Puget Sound suddenly entertained notions of becoming the great supply center for the northern mines. Fleets of sailboats and sternwheelers carried passengers and goods to Victoria, and herds of cattle and strings of pack horses moved north through the Cowlitz, Yakima, Wenatchee, and Okanogan valleys to supply the mushrooming camps. Rich strikes in the Caribou District of the Upper Fraser brought a repeat performance in 1862. Some idea of what this meant to the region's farmers and ranchers can be had from data of 1866 when the first boom days were over. At the Little Dalles, above Colville, the customs office in that year reported 507,479 dollars worth of goods exported over the line. Of this sum close to 350,000 dollars was in livestock, beef cattle, sheep, and pack animals.[10]

Gold Strikes in Washington Territory

On the theory that the sources of gold in gravel bars came from upstream, the pattern of the expanding mining frontier led to the upper Fraser and Columbia rivers and thence fanned out along the numerous tributary waters. In 1860 prospectors began to report almost simultaneously encouraging strikes in Eastern British Columbia and Eastern Washington Territory. The latter, after the creation of the state of Oregon, included all of present Idaho, Western Montana, and a small portion of Western Wyoming. The Snake River country was well traveled by the Oregonians and was a vital part of the communication line for the western settlements, but other than this the whole area had had little part in the events which peopled the Willamette Valley and Puget Sound. Its history had been that of the fur trade and fur traders: of Nor'westers David Thompson, Donald McKenzie, and Alexander Ross; the Hudson's Bay Company's Peter Skene Ogden, John Work, and Francis Ermatinger. The Americans, mysterious Jeremy Pinch, Andrew Henry, John Colter, Captain Bonneville, and Nathaniel Wyeth wrote another chapter, as did the mountain men Jedediah Smith, William Sublette, Tom Fitzpatrick, Robert Newell, Joe Meek, and the nameless others who trapped the Three Forks, Beaver Head, Jackson and Pierre's holes, the Tetons, and the torrential waters of the Salmon,

[10] J. Ross Browne, *Mineral Resources of the States and Territories West of the Rocky Mountains, H.R. Ex. Doc.* 202, 40th Cong., 2d sess., Washington, 1868, 559.

the River of No Return. Its missionary period was the work of Henry and Eliza Spalding at Lapwai, the Smiths and Grays, briefly at Kamiah, and of Fathers De Smet and Point, and other men of the black robes who built the missions of St. Mary's and the Sacred Heart and planted crosses wherever they worked among the Indians. This was the land of the Nez Perces, on the one hand, and the Blackfeet on the other, as contrasting in tempers as the land itself, sharply divided between the barren and the forested, the clear and open plain, and the walled in, rugged valley. Its settlement was one or two old mountain men near Lapwai in the forties and a brief effort of the Mormons in the Lemhi Valley in 1855.

Washington Territory east of the Cascades was hardly occupied in 1860; the region east of Walla Walla was practically in a state of nature when the first reports of gold were heard. It lost its innocence within the year.

Western Montana

The principal gold regions in what is now Western Montana were located in the Jefferson Basin and Gallatin Valley. The former, an old resort of early fur trappers, was known as the Bannack district, where the names of such creeks as Grasshopper, Stinking Water, and Alder Gulch became synonymous with rich placer and quartz diggings. In 1863, the 17-mile length of Alder Gulch's gravel bars were reported to have 10,000 miners and on its steep banks were springing up the four "cities" with names famous in mining history: Virginia, Nevada, Central, and Summit. The Gallatin Valley showed its gold-bearing quartz veins in Last Chance Gulch, and Helena grew up to serve it and other equally famous gulch camps.

Idaho

The mining districts of what is now the state of Idaho were more widely separated. The Oro Fino mines on the Clearwater were discovered in 1860 and within a year Elk City had 1,500 or more men working placers there. The Florence mines in the Salmon River district had a brief, brilliant, and remarkably rich moment of greatness. The diggings were located in a small valley at the head of Meadow Creek, where a granite butte rose to a height of some 1,000 feet. Here on its fair mile-wide summit, marshy crisscrossed ravines filled with bog peat hid coarse gravel which, when exposed, was found to yield about a dollar a pan. When this isolated treasure gave out, Florence declined.

The Boise, or Grimes Basin, is not to be confused with the vicinity of Boise City. It lay to the north where in 1862 placer mines were found at Elk Horn, and Placerville. In spite of Indian troubles, miners left the Clearwater camps and hurried to the new strike. Shortly after the Boise Basin opened, a rush to the Owyhee district brought into existence Ruby City, Booneville, and another famous Oro Fino.

Miners came by wagon train over the Oregon Trail from the east, up the Missouri by boat as far as Fort Benton, by trail from California, Nevada, and Colorado, and up the Columbia by boat to Walla Walla. From the latter point the Mullan Road, built in 1859-1860 as a military road with the purpose of joining the Missouri and Columbia valleys, gave access to the vicinity of present Missoula, Montana. Little more than a pack trail, it was nevertheless an important link between the Columbia and the mining camps. Similarly, the immigrant road between Walla Walla and Southern Idaho came into new prominence as a supply route for the mines. Via the Columbia River 10,500 men were reported to have taken passage for the mines in 1861; 24,500 in 1862; 22,000 in 1863, and 36,000 in 1864.

Mining and Miners

Since these were figures from only one route of travel, it would be natural to assume that the population of the mining region was swelled by comparable additions by other routes, and that the number of men in Eastern Washington must have been in the neighborhood of at least 50,000 or 75,000. However, nothing was more fluid than a mining population. It moved like quicksilver within a given area; it also melted away like the spring snows.

Numbers in this regard have meaning only in the context of the mines' development. The industry had two phases: surface or placer phase and deep or quartz phase. The first occurred where there were streams with gravel bars, or where some ancient water action left gravel deposits close to the surface. The pan was the cheapest and easiest way of washing nuggets, dust, and free gold—free in the sense that the ore was released from its matrix. Rockers made it possible to work heavier rock, and with sluices, fed by ditch and flume, placers could grow into large-scale operations moving tons of free or picked rock. Placer mining attracted the independent, restless, "professional" miner who staked a claim and worked it until some new strike lured him on, and the strike-it-rich-and-go-home amateur. Both types were mobile and often irresponsible.

One class of professionals specialized in prospecting for quartz veins and their discoveries opened up the second phase of the industry. The presence of free gold indicated some source or vein from which the ore had been washed out. Quartz mines were often found at headwaters of streams or in the banks of ravines through which streams had once flowed. The gold was imbedded deep in the rock and revealed by peculiarly colored surface soil, or, in lucky cases, by an outcropping of the quartz itself. The discoverers worked them only to hold their claims and to sink shafts that would show the strike and dip of the vein, and then sold them for development. Quartz mining required large capital investment, not only to sink shafts and run tunnels but also to erect stamp mills to crush the rock so that the metal could be recovered. It also required means of transportation to move the rock from the tunnels to the mills, to bring in machinery, and since quartz mining was more stable than placer, to supply the camps. Miners in these cases worked for wages, and were less fluid in their movements than those who worked one placer field after another.

Under these circumstances, to determine the population of a mining region at any given time was almost impossible until a region had settled down to the second phase of the mining process. During the early phase there was a great rush of thousands of men. Within a few months a gravel bar might have its 10,000 miners and its tent and dug-out cities. In as few months it might be almost deserted, inhabited only by some few Chinese painstakingly working over the same rock skimmed by their impatient predecessors.

If one accepts the usual figures of a population of at least 30,000 in Eastern Washington by 1863, it is not difficult to understand the problem created for the territory. Its population was congregated in the extreme eastern and western portions and separated by practically uninhabited country, with no land communication. Government was located in the west and was representative of a population of about 11,000 whose principal interests were agriculture and lumbering. Administration of law and preservation of order in such a large mobile population so remote from the capital was a problem of overwhelming magnitude.

The Mining Camp

A voluminous literature describes aspects of the life of mining camps. The romantic stories of Bret Harte and the humorous writings of Samuel Clemens and J. Ross Browne are no more distortions than the overdrawn pictures of the penny dreadfuls. Letters and diaries reveal sensitive, hardworking, law-abiding young men trying to make their stake in a hard way. But there are also indisputable records of lawlessness, of highwaymen, of helpless courts and corrupt officials, and vigilante committees; of hangings and shootings; of bawdyhouses and whisky palaces.

Law was not absent on the mining frontier but it was directed toward objectives that were not confused with ideas of sin and social morality. In the Northwest's gold camps, as elswhere, the miners themselves organized their first governments. These were claims associations whose purpose was to define the extent and character of a defensible claim in keeping with the peculiarities of the topography, and to set up the minimum requirements for holding and protecting it. The miners elected judges whose sole qualification was a knowledge of mining and the agreed code of mining law, and whose jurisdiction was limited to disputes in these matters.

The first agency of territorial law was the land office where descriptions of claims were filed. The Washington legislature created counties and voting districts through which the miners then elected officials to administer laws that applied elsewhere in the territory. The execution depended upon the demands of the constituencies as well as upon the integrity of the elected officers. The camps got as much order as they wanted, as much integrity as they supported. In the earliest days judicial proceedings were obstructed when lawyers and judges, unfamiliar with Washington statutes, were unable to secure copies of them. The common law did not always apply to mining situations, and criminal law was not respected and unfortunately little enforced.

Lawlessness

The camps' reputations for lawlessness were no doubt exaggerated, but in contrast to the agricultural communities of the western parts of the territory, their character was not considered socially stable. There were also significant differences to separate the political sentiments of the mining regions from the rest of the territory during the war years. Western Washington was Unionist, tending toward Republicanism. The mining camps had their Unionists, but they also had their southern sympathizers and the Democrats were in large majority. Many miners from both sides of the line that divided the nation in civil war had come to the mines to escape the military drafts, but they patriotically defended their homelands and causes with torchlight parades and fist fights in saloons on Saturday nights. For the politically ambitious in Western Washington it was a matter of concern that when Shoshone, Missoula, and Walla Walla counties were set up, the vote in them was strongly Democratic. It was with considerable relief that Olympia and the Republican party shook off their eastern stepchild when it was organized as a separate territory.

Movement to Create Idaho Territory

The movement for the organization of Idaho Territory originated in Western Washington and was assisted by Oregon. It did not originate among the residents of the area involved. Separation was supported by the Washingtonians for a number of reasons with little agreement on any one, except separation from an uncongenial population which was able, by sheer force of numbers, to take over the legislature and dominate the whole territory if it so wished. What made the creation of the new territory an issue was the western boundary of the proposed organization: whether it should include all the territory west to the Cascades, or divide on an extension of the north-south line of the Snake River to the 49th parallel. The former would reduce Washington to a small coastal section, and rivalry among Olympia, Vancouver, and the booming town of Walla Walla for the capital of Washington Territory, influenced their attitude toward the boundary as they wished to be the seat of a large or small territory.

Oregon entered the controversy by virtue of her economic interest in the mining country. The Columbia River was the principal highway to the mines; Portland was the commercial depot which served them, and Portland transportation interests controlled the traffic on the river. In the light of antagonisms resulting from this situation, it was to Portland's interest that the mining region be set off as a separate territory so that it could not control the Washington territorial legislature and emancipate itself from Portland influence.

In the mining region there was more opposition than support for separation. The charge was made that the vociferous supporters both there and in Olympia hoped for political preferment in a new territory, and that Portland had a heavy hand in the matter. But the principle of self-determination, so recently championed in Oregon, was not to be allowed in this case. Through extensive lobbying on the part of William H. Wallace, Washington's delegate to Congress, and with the help of Oregon's congressman, John R. McBride, both of whom received appointments to the new territory, the Idaho bill was passed and signed by President Lincoln on March 4, 1863.

The way was cleared for the measure by the political situation in the national capital.

> In Congress the Radical Republicans and Lincoln both were receptive to schemes for the admission of new states and the creation of new territories. Additional western states might serve to offset the return of Southern Democrats to Congress in case the North should win the war. The Republicans were aware that without additional Western support, they would be able to retain control of the federal government only with great difficulty. . . . Thus the distraction of the Civil War actually encouraged, rather than disrupted, the Olympia Radical Republican movement for purging the politically hostile Idaho miners from Washington territory.[11]

[11] Merle W. Wells, "The Creation of the Territory of Idaho," *PNQ*, XL, April, 1949, 117.

Idaho Territory's Administration

The conditions under which Idaho, constituting all of Washington Territory east of the extended Snake River line, was organized did not presage a happy history as a territory, and its experiences illustrate many of the worst features of the system. Federal patronage was used to build up the Republican party although, as it has been previously pointed out, the population was primarily Democrat—copperhead, according to the radical Republicans. The party machines in Salem and Olympia had a large part in the distribution of this patronage and they used it to strengthen their own positions. According to Earl Pomeroy's study of this problem, Senator John H. Mitchell from Oregon "endorsed candidates on a baldly political basis, intervened in departmental channels, and, together with certain colleagues from the Pacific Coast, exercised a sort of guardianship" over both Washington and Idaho territories. The latter was a "political dependency of Oregon," a contemporary testified. "In rewarding political and personal services, men unfit and unacceptable in Oregon, were billeted upon Idaho."[12]

Absenteeism, voluntary or otherwise, was common. There were more acting governors than commissioned. Opinions of the integrity, competence, and performance of those who actually did serve as governors were and have been widely discrepant. The struggle between President Johnson and Congress led to controversies over his appointments to territorial offices in which charges of malfeasance were hurled about and led to suspensions and restorations in the cases of two of the earlier governors.

Governors

The first commissioned governor, William H. Wallace, had been a delegate to Congress from Washington Territory and a promoter of the division creating the new territory. Three months after he declared it organized, July, 1863, he ran for the office of delegate and was elected. In this role he acted in conformance to Olympia's and Portland's direction. In August, 1864,

---

[12] Earl Pomeroy, *The Territories and the United States*, 67.

Caleb Lyon succeeded him as governor. Lyon had served in the New York legislature, in Congress, been first consul to China, and participated in the erection of state government in California. His short career in Idaho was not distinguished. Reappointed at the expiration of his first year after a delay caused by controversy as to his fitness for the office, he shortly thereafter left the Territory without a formal farewell. A large sum of territorial money departed either with him or with the territorial secretary who left about the same time. One of his critics described him as "a revolving light on the coast of scampdom."[13]

After an interlude of irresponsible governors, Dr. David W. Ballard of Yamhill, Oregon, was appointed to share the burden of top administrative offices with two other appointees from the same political hotbed of Oregon. During his four year term of office, 1866-1870, Ballard survived one suspension of office and such bitter feuds that he deserved laurels for persistence at least. His administration was a party administration—radical Republican—but the legislatures with which he had to work were democratic and sympathetic toward the defeated south. The third session, for example, had one Unionist in it. Ballard's first message contained a politely couched but unpopular recommendation that its members economize by giving up their raid on the treasury to supplement their *per diem*. "By the God," exploded one legislator, upon hearing it, ". . . I do not believe the house will submit to it, for the governor to say we shall act thus and so. . . . We didn't elect him governor. He is no part or parcel with us."[14]

Supported by forces almost wholly outside the territory, Ballard remained in office for a four-year term, handicapped not only by the internal situation but by continuous interference from factional struggles in Oregon and efforts of each side to control the appointments in Idaho. These struggles, in turn, were due to the national level controversy over the Tenure Act, and the quarrel between Johnson and the Congress. By the end of his term Ballard had worn away a considerable measure of the early antagonism directed toward him in Idaho, and although he was defeated when he ran for delegate in

[13] H. H. Bancroft, *History of Washington, Idaho and Montana*, San Francisco, 1890, 467.
[14] Bancroft, *History of Washington, Idaho, and Montana*, 468.

1870, he was endorsed by Idaho papers for having conducted his office with dignity under extreme provocation.[15]

His successors were not subjected as he had been to involvement in national politics, but President Grant found it difficult to find men to take the governorship. No less than five men were offered commissions, before he found Thomas W. Bennett, who served from 1871 to 1875. D. P. Thompson of Portland held office one year, 1875-1876, and Mason Brayman for the following four years. Between 1880 and 1885, four appointments were made and three of the appointees served fragmentary terms.

Local Complications

Obviously Idaho had small success in attracting and holding dedicated public officials. While this was due in large measure to outside influences, the situation within Idaho did not hold out bright prospects of a smooth political career. The earliest legislatures were irresponsible. The code adopted by the first "in much haste and with much less consideration than its importance demanded," according to Ballard, was not printed until after the second had met because the territorial secretary had absconded with the entire territorial treasury in 1866. Ignorance of the code did not prevent the second legislature from passing some new laws, and the result was some "perplexing discrepancies," to put it mildly.[16]

Legislature and administration were both seriously handicapped by their failure to receive moneys appropriated by Congress for territorial purposes. Indian funds, a crying necessity considering the hostilities that prevailed, had been carried off by Governor Lyons. Local funds were not judiciously used. The legislators found the congressional appropriations insufficient to their *per diem* expenses and increased the sum by raiding the treasury. Test oaths were a continuing problem in Idaho politics. In 1862 Congress passed a measure requiring persons elected or appointed to public offices in areas under Federal administration to swear that they had never countenanced or encouraged the

[15] Merle W. Wells, "David W. Ballard; Governor of Idaho, 1866-1870," *OHQ*, LIV, March, 1953, 25. Mr. Wells's excellent studies of Idaho politics are satisfying a long-felt want.

[16] Ballard's First Message to the Legislature in *Journal of the Fourth Session of the Council of Idaho Territory*, December 3, 1866—January 11, 1867, Boise, 1867, 15.

southern cause. The legislature of Idaho of which the majority were southern sympathizers eliminated the test oath for its local officials and legislators, even though this meant withholding of Territorial funds. When Ballard vetoed the measure on the ground that territorial legislation could not be in contradiction to congressional legislation, the measure was triumphantly passed over his veto. In later years, Idaho Republicans revived test oaths to purge politics of Democrat Mormons.

Added to these troubles was the enduring issue of division within the territory over the capital location and a separation movement. In 1864 the easternmost part of the territory was withdrawn to form Montana Territory and with it went a large part of Idaho's population. The remainder was divided into two parts by the geography of the country. The greater part of the population was in the south, but with the support of Walla Walla, the Lewiston community fought hard, literally and figuratively, but unsuccessfully, to retain the capital Boise captured the state seal, archives, and Republican administration, but Lewiston countered by a separation movement which would unite the northern part of the territory with Washington. This issue which embittered otherwise innocuous legislation persisted throughout the territorial period and rivalry between the two sections has afflicted Idaho throughout its history as a state.

During tempestuous political controversies fundamental problems of law and order were neglected. Little was done to organize defenses against serious Indian attacks in the southern part of the territory. Travelers on the Oregon Trail were harassed and there were several shocking massacres. Volunteers from Oregon, California, and Washington helped to keep essential communication lines open from Utah, California, and along the Oregon Trail, and they were assisted by small groups of miner-settler volunteers from Idaho. During the Lyons administration and the earlier years of Ballard's, highway robberies, murders, and lynchings perpetrated by white men were widespread. Failure to secure convictions of the few lawbreakers brought to trial led to the organization of vigilante committees who took the law in their own hands.

By the end of the 1860's the territory began to settle down to a more placid existence. The placer mines gave over to quartz mining and the human flotsam of the first era drifted off to Colorado or Nevada. Ranchers stocked the small but fertile valleys and in the Clearwater Valley settlers were beginning to raise more wheat than their local market could use.

The census of 1870 revealed 15,000 residents in Idaho, hardly 50 per cent more than the number of men in Alder Gulch alone seven years before. One enduring problem of Idaho's territorial period and one she shared with Washington Territory was the relatively slow growth of population. In the decade of 1870-1880, when Idaho added about 17,000 people, Washington increased by 51,000 and Oregon by 83,000.

Both territories justifiably complained of their lack of transportation facilities to encourage settlement and develop their economies. During the era of 1860 to 1880 they chose to lay the blame for this upon the selfish machinations of the state of Oregon, and especially upon Oregonians who lived in Portland. What this town was to the Pacific Northwest and how it came to be is the subject for a final chapter on the territorial phase of the region's history.

17

Economic and Social Foundations of Territories and State

From the days of the first settlement of the Pacific Northwest settlers had an eye for any location which had possibilities as a townsite. There was no dearth of hopeful speculators in the fifties and sixties. Upon the passage of the Donation Land Act in 1850, Samuel E. Thurston, Oregon's delegate to Congress urged his constituents to organize an emigration bureau and hire an agent to get up companies to move to Oregon. "All of you," he wrote, "would quadruple your money by the operation, because in proportion as our population becomes more dense your property would rise."[1]

Townsite Speculations

Towns were laid out and inducements offered settlers, just as they were in Midwest when that area was opening up. The speculative fever was quickly reflected in the local papers as proprietors touted the special advantages of their respective sites. The proprietors of Milton City near what is now the town of St. Helens advertised that they would give to every head of a family two town lots, to single men, one lot, if they would become settlers in their town and build a house upon the properties within six months. They would also supply building materials on credit. To any one that would build a grist mill, they offered a mill site and land.[2] A month later the proprietors were projecting a railroad to run from St. Helens over the hills through the Tualatin Valley to Lafayette, and they advertised a "Brilliant chance for investment!"[3] In 1855 Milton

[1] Samuel E. Thurston to Philip Foster, June 30, 1850, in the Foster Papers, photocopies in the Reed College Library.
[2] Advertisement, *The Oregon Spectator*, October 10, 1850.
[3] Advertisement, *The Oregon Spectator*, November 28, 1850.

City was county seat of Columbia County but shortly after it was swept away by a flood. In 1890 it was still trying to get a post office. Its projected railway ran only as advertising matter in the *Oregon Spectator*.

Another "city" first named Lancaster and then Pacific City was laid out by Dr. Elijah White on Baker's Bay near the entrance to the Columbia River, and on the shore opposite Astoria. John Adair, one of those interested in rebuilding the latter and not anxious to see a rival across the river, complained to Samuel Thurston: "I have been informed of a speculation started by Dr. White, formerly a sort of Indian agent in Oregon, which promises to assume a rather portentous form. It is no less than the building of a new city in Baker's Bay to which he proposes to transfer the port of Entry and everything else . . . Dr. White has started a new town there with the name of 'Lancaster City' and sundry good folks above her have taken shares therein. . . . As yet there are only one or two Indian grog shops on the ground, but what may not puffing and petitioning do. Baker's Bay may well set itself up as a rival to Portland. . . ."[4] The "puffing and petitioning" had, by November of 1850, reached such proportions that Astoria's proprietors were seriously alarmed. Of it an Astoria booster wrote: "I see in a letter in the Pacific News of Oct. 24, signed by a man named Morse, puffing Pacific City in a most preposterous style. He is a person whom Dr. White brought in . . . to lecture up his town throughout Oregon. The letter was written before the animal had ever seen the country . . . another of his new importations, a 'Professor Jackman' has written something in a similar vein, but attacking Astoria, and a Weekly Cal. Courier . . . had an article . . . stating that Baker's Bay was the only good harbor. . . . Now is it worth while to answer these things over two or three signatures, or say a dozen?"[5] A number of buildings including a knocked-down hotel brought up from San Francisco were erected at Pacific City by White and his associates, Alonzo Skinner and Joseph D. Holman, and it was estimated that nearly 100,000 dollars was invested before Astori-

[4] John Adair to Samuel E. Thurston, February 15, 1850, Adair Letters, Oregon Historical Society Library.

[5] George Gibbs to Lieutenant Commander William P. McArthur, November 23, 1850, quoted in Lewis A. McArthur, "The Pacific Coast Survey of 1849 and 1850," in *OHQ*, XVI, September, 1915, 272.

ans managed to get the townsite taken over by the United States Government as a military reservation.[6]

Other towns had happier histories. Milwaukee, founded in 1847 by Lot Whitcomb, grew to be something of a rival to the settlement at the falls of the Willamette, having about 500 people in 1850. The Falls maintained its priority until the middle of the fifties when, as Oregon City, it was rapidly eclipsed by its neighboring rival, Portland. The latter also eliminated St. Helens, Rainier, and Linnton as prospective commercial centers on the lower Willamette and Columbia rivers. Peter H. Burnett and Morton M. McCarver hoped to tap the Tualatin Valley by means of the old Hudson's Bay Company's cattle trail across the hills, but it was impassable for loaded wagons, and Linnton did not flourish. Rainier for a short period appeared to be the coming town on the Columbia and claimed to be the head of deep water navigation but like Linnton, St. Helens, and Milton City it had no easy access to the hinterland of the Tualatin, and the west side of the Willamette.

The Building of a Metropolis: Portland

That the site of William Overton's claim between Linnton and Willamette Falls would ever outstrip the latter in size and importance was believed only by its owner who in 1844 wagered 500 dollars on its future. Asa L. Lovejoy and Francis Pettygrove took up claims just to the north of Overton's, in a forest whose almost level plain sloped gradually to the Willamette, drained by an alder-lined creek fed by springs and streams from the canyons of the hills behind it. In 1845 they platted their lands and flipped a coin to name the site Portland.

Ocean-going vessels could reach Portland. What it needed was settlers and a hinterland from which to draw cargoes for the ships. In 1850, the inhabitants of the village sent a river boat up to the Cascades with help for stranded immigrants, and thus diverted settlers from the Barlow Road and Oregon City. At the same time they tried to find a practical route over the hills into the Tualatin Valley. A

[6] Frances Fuller Victor, *All Over Oregon and Washington*, San Francisco, 1872, 39. One of the wonders of the day was the expenditure of 28,000 dollars for a hotel, fully equipped, purchased in San Francisco, knocked down and brought to Pacific City on the *Caroline*, and reassembled there.

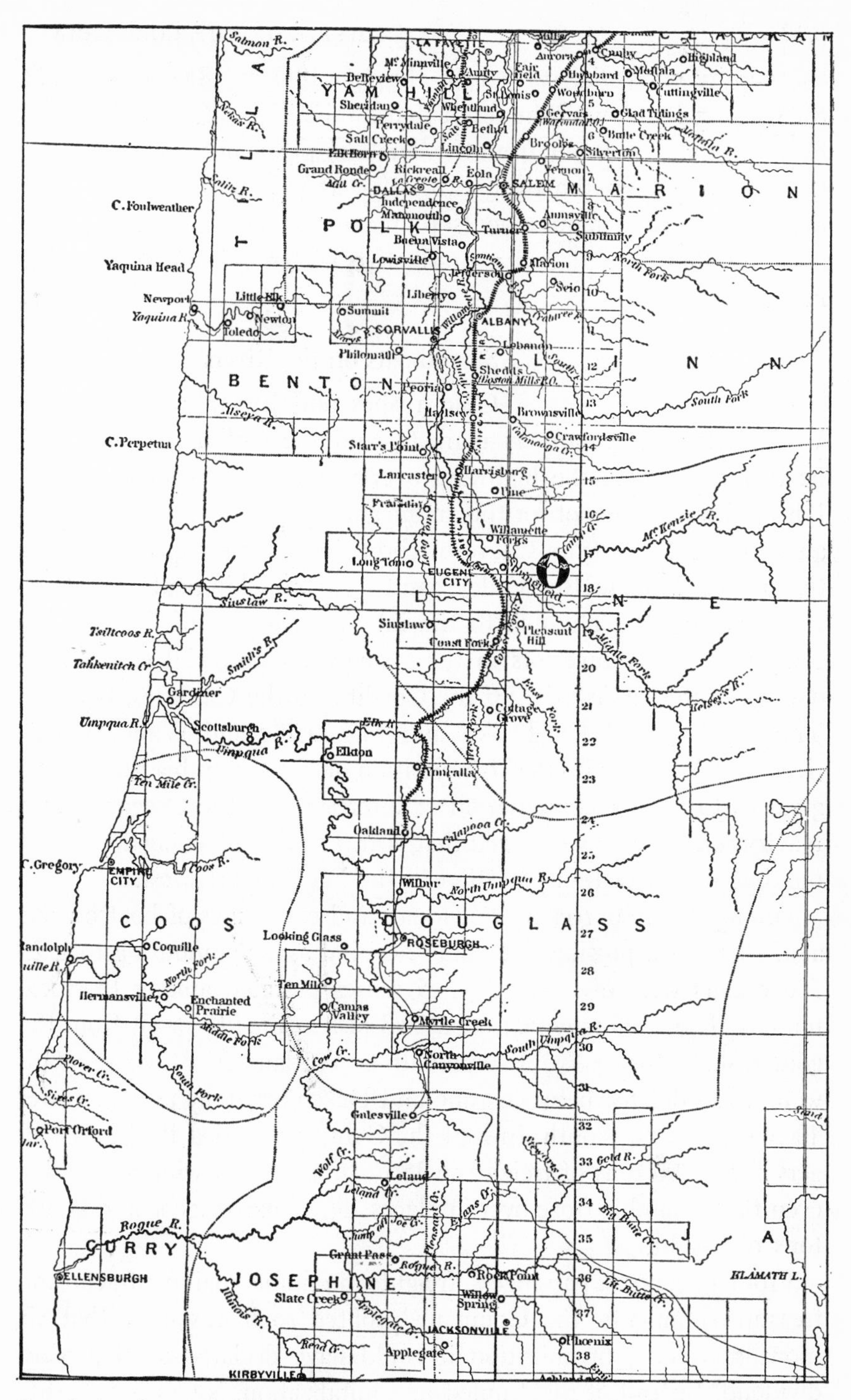

Population Centers in Western Oregon. (From Asher and Adams, Map of Oregon, 1872.) See companion map facing p. 305.

community enterprise carried on through 1851 to 1853 finally built the Canyon Road, with the result that lumbering wheat wagons could reach Portland, not only from the Tualatin plains but from the Yamhill settlements on the river's west side as well. Portland then had the two principal requirements to make it a city in terms of the needs of that day: It had a productive hinterland and deep water navigation.

Steamboats on the Rivers

Gold rushes and Indian wars gave the Willamette Valley farmers markets, and the Columbia River and its tributaries were the highways over which their produce moved. Portland was the depot for this traffic and by 1858 had overshadowed all its rivals. Ships from California brought goods for distribution to the upper Willamette Valley, and for transshipment on sternwheelers up the Columbia to the interior. Citizens of the growing town were heavy investors in these small but powerful vessels that opened routes to Astoria, up the Cowlitz, to the Cascades, between The Cascades and The Dalles, and The Dalles and Walla Walla's river port, Wallula. By 1860 competition on the Columbia runs was so great as to force a combination of interests, and the Oregon Steam Navigation Company emerged that year. For the following 20 years it monopolized river transportation in the Pacific Northwest.

Pooling the resources of individuals and companies of boat owners at their highest possible evaluation, capital assets amounting to 172,500 dollars were divided into 345 shares prorated among 14 stockholders. The Company was organized just in time to profit from the gold rush to Idaho. Gold shipments to Portland in February, 1861, were 4,700 dollars; between June and December, they averaged over 400,000 dollars a month. In 1861 the Company carried 10,500 passengers and 6,290 tons of freight; in 1862, in spite of a winter in which even the Columbia froze over in places, 24,500 passengers, and 14,500 tons of freight.

From all sources, passengers, freights, profitable mail contracts, and treasure shipments, the Company profited so handsomely that six months after its organization it could have declared a 20 percent dividend. Instead, it quadrupled its capitalization, issued four certificates of stock for each original share and paid a 5 percent dividend. A month later it increased capitalization to 1,000,000 dollars and paid a 2 percent dividend. In the first 12 months fortunate investors had a return of 240 dollars on an investment of 500 dollars. Further increases in capitalization of the same kind made it a 5,000,000-dollar corporation in 1868. In the 20 years of its history the company paid a conservatively estimated 4,600,000 dollars in dividends.

The small steamers, sail boats, and barges which had formed its first working capital were quickly replaced with powerful, and in the language of that day, elegant stern-wheelers. The 400-ton *New World* was queen of a fleet of 18 passenger and cargo vessels in 1865. In 1880, there were 26 boats. The *Wide West*, 1,200 tons, built at Portland yards in 1877, lacked nothing in safety or comfort from the sturdily built hull to velvet-draped, floral carpeted salon. The *R. R. Thompson*, 1,158 tons, built at the Dalles the next year, was equally grand. The Company invested more than 3,000,000 dollars in its facilities. There was nothing shabby about its wharves at Portland; at The Dalles it had a 900-foot inclined wharf to load and unload conveniently at any water stage.

The character of the Columbia route made portages necessary at the Cascades and at The Dalles. Mule-powered railroads served the six-mile Cascade portages on each side of the river until 1862 when the Company got possession of both and put on engine-drawn coaches and flatcars. The same year it acquired and similarly improved the 14-mile Dalles Portage. Possessed of these strategic locations, the Oregon Steam Navigation Company firmly established its grasp on river traffic.

The men principally responsible for the founding and management of the Oregon Steam Navigation Company were Captain J. C. Ainsworth and Simeon G. Reed of Portland, and Robert R. Thompson, originally of The Dalles. This triumvirate, with the assistance of William S. Ladd, Portland's principal banker, was the Oregon Steam Navigation Company to all practical purposes until 1867, when they also become the sole owners of its stock. Their planning, management, and resources, kept out San Francisco's Ben Holladay who would have liked to have made the Columbia part of his coastal navigation system and the Wright brothers of Puget Sound who had ambitions along the same lines. They eliminated competitors as fast as they came on the river, with the exception of the People's Transportation Company, composed largely of Salem interests. An almost disastrous rate war in 1862-1863 ended when the Oregon Steam Navigation Company turned over the Willamette run to its rivals on condition they stay off the Columbia. A stern-wheeler on the Cowlitz paid off with mail contracts and in keeping down competitors. On the Astoria-Portland run they reduced rates to a free ride if necessary to eliminate any opposition that might try to put a boat on the river.

Their possession of the portages at the Cascades and The Dalles assured them control of the Columbia as far as their vessels could go. They drew the interior trade to them by combining land and water routes. At Wallula, pack and wagon trains took their cargoes over the Walla Walla-Spokane-Colville trail to the Little Dalles of the Columbia, where their *Forty Nine* ran from that place to the head of Upper Arrow Lake and tapped the trade of the Caribou and Kootenay mines. To compete with the Missouri River-Fort Benton route they organized the Oregon and Montana Transportation Company to carry cargo and passengers from White Bluffs on the Columbia to Lake Pend Oreille where they built and ran the *Mary Moody* from the lower end of the Lake to Cabinet Rapids on Clark's Fork. A portage connected with the steamer *Cabinet* which ran to Thompson Falls, where the *Missoula* continued to the mouth of the Jocko, and thence by road their shipments went to the mining camps of Helena.

From Umatilla Landing four stagecoach lines ran to Old's Ferry on the Snake, where in 1866, the *Shoshone* was built at a cost of 100,000 dollars to run to the mouth of the Bruneau River and intercept the Utah-Boise stagecoach traffic. The cost of building boats and navigating them on these interior waters was greater than any income they brought in, but it was part of a necessary overhead in keeping down competitors who might draw off some of the heavy-paying load that traveled from Portland to Umatilla, Wallula, and Lewiston.

The Company's growth in financial power was unusual in western history. In most instances, frontier enterprises were financed by outside capital, but the Oregon Steam Navigation Company was completely home-owned. The need for investment capital in Oregon was sufficient to keep interest rates at a 12 percent legal charge, with a 5 percent bonus in addition. If a quarter of a million dollars were available, the *Oregonian* reported in 1872, it could readily be invested at 17 percent.[7] Yet the Oregon Steam Navigation Company never put its stock on the market and only once, to buy rails and engines for its portage roads, it went to San Francisco for a six months' loan of 200,000 dollars.

The Oregon Steam Navigation Company never lost sight of its own interests, and those were irretrievably tied to Portland. Whatever detracted from that town's prosperity was to its detriment as well. Compared to San Francisco, Portland in the 1860's was a mere village. The Bay City was the terminus of the first transcontinental railroad completed in 1869 and in size, transportation facilities, capital resources, and enterprise the commercial capital of the West. With it connected overland stages and express lines that tapped the mining districts of Idaho and Montana as well as the Willamette Valley. Wells Fargo Express with headquarters at San Francisco provided banking as well as transportation services. Ben Holladay's Overland Mail fanned out from Salt Lake City to Alder Gulch, the Boise Basin, and The Dalles. His Pacific Mail Steamship Company controlled the coastal trade, and in 1868 he entered the railroad field in Oregon.

Oregon's First Railroads

In all these respects, the Pacific Northwest was made tributary to San Francisco. On the other hand the region needed and wanted railway connections to end its isolation from the East. A California group of investors first proposed a railroad up the east bank of the Willamette Valley to connect with the Central Pacific at San Francisco; a local company in which the Oregon Steam Navigation Company participated was organized to counter with a west bank line to bypass San Francisco and connect with the Union Pacific at Ogden, Utah, via the Winnemucca cutoff. By 1870 Holladay had secured control of both lines, the land grant of 3,800,000 acres of valley lands, and in his Oregon and California Railroad Company combined the Willamette's steamship companies and the portage around the falls of the Willamette.

In the meantime the Oregon Steam Navigation Company threw

[7] *Oregonian*, August 9, 1872.

its support to Jay Cooke who proposed to build the long-delayed Northern Pacific Railroad and give the Pacific Northwest a transcontinental connection at Portland and Tacoma. In 1870 the Company sold 50 percent of its stock to Cooke, but retained management in local hands. Between that date and 1873, Captain J. C. Ainsworth, president of the Oregon Steam Navigation Company, headed a construction company that built a portion of the Northern Pacific line from Portland to Tacoma. Upon the failure of Jay Cooke in 1873, the Oregon Steam Navigation Company proceeded quietly and methodically to buy back its scattered stock which it succeeded in doing at about an average price of 12 cents on the dollar. In 1880 it sold out finally to Henry Villard who completed the Northern Pacific in 1883.

For 20 years, from 1860 to 1880, the Oregon Steam Navigation Company worked to make and to keep Portland the commercial center of the Pacific Northwest, and to break the network that drew its trade to San Francisco. Within the region it had no rival on the navigable waters. But its dominant position in the Northwest's economy made it and Portland the object of envy and bitter hatred.

Years of Moderate Growth

The Pacific Northwest as a whole experienced a relatively slow growth of population during the decade of the sixties. The war years witnessed a phenomenal growth in cities of the eastern part of the nation where industry competed with agriculture as an attraction to a mobile people. Agricultural expansion, encouraged by war prices for wheat, by organized efforts of land and railroad companies to stimulate settlement, and by the Homestead Act of 1862, was notable in the Middle Western states, but dwindled to a small trickle beyond Kansas. The Homestead Act, designed to encourage the continuation if not the increase of the independent yeoman class of American farmers by opening portions of the western public domain as free land, did not attract migration to the Far West in any substantial amount.

The Homestead Act

By the terms of this act, as passed in May, 1862, a citizen or alien who had filed a declaration of intent to become a naturalized citizen, who was 21 years of age or head of a family, or had served at least 14 days in the military of the United States and had not taken up arms against it (thus excluding Confederates) could file on 160 acres of unappropriated land for a fee of ten dollars. Residence or cultivation for five years subsequent to filing was required before a patent would be granted.[8] Among the numerous amendments later added was one which made proof of residence and cultivation necessary, but another permitted commutation of this requirement by the payment of $1.25 per acre, the minimum preëmption price for public lands. The ban against Confederates was lifted in 1866.

The act has been accurately described as an "incongruity" in the pattern of American agricultural development. In the Northwest it was especially so, where the size of the unit was inappropriate for efficient farming in the interior, and its application to the forested regions impossible. Until 1879 it was not possible in many instances to homestead more than 80 acres on the sections of reserved public lands alternating with sections granted to the railroads and held by them at a minimum price of $2.50 an acre. The Homestead Act was not an effective force in encouraging the immigration of farm population to the Pacific Northwest in the sixties; in the seventies, a more important factor was the construction of railroads. Between 1860 and 1870 Oregon's farms increased from 5,806 to 7,587, Washington's from 1,330 to 3,127. In the next decade Oregon's shot up to 16,217 and Washington's to 6,529.

Percentagewise the territories experienced a greater rate of growth between 1860 and 1880 than did Oregon. In actual numbers, the cold hard facts showed that more immigrants located in Oregon than in the territories. Between 1870 and 1880, Oregon's increase was from 90,922 to 174,768; Washington's from 23,955 to 75,116, and Idaho's from 14,999 to 32,610.

Portland's population grew from 821 in 1860 to 9,565 in 1870. In the latter year Washington Territory's largest towns were seats of counties that could boast no greater numbers than 2,488 for Thurston County; 6,801 for Walla Walla County; and 1,709 for King County. According to the census of 1880 Washington Territory had no town

[8] *United States Statutes at Large,* XII, 392 ff.

of 4,000 population, and Multnomah County in Oregon, containing Portland, alone had one-third as many inhabitants as all of Washington, and only 7,000 less than Idaho.

Opposition to Portland

The citizens of Washington blamed this on their lack of transportation and capital which made it impossible for them to compete with their neighbor to the south. It was even charged that the Oregon Steam Navigation Company, in bringing overland immigrants down the Columbia, purposely avoided stopping at Vancouver, a charge the company vigorously denied.

The territory had no means of directing immigration to Puget Sound. Washington had little influence in securing congressional legislation to support wagon roads with land grants. In 1869 Governor Alvan Flanders pointed out that the federal government had granted Oregon 1,256,800 acres of public domain for this purpose. He urged a memorial to Congress asking for two roads from Puget Sound to the Columbia River, one via the Cowlitz, and the other from Seattle to Wallula, and two others from Walla Walla to Colville and from Spokane to Lake Pend Oreille.[9] The inhabitants of the Puget Sound country had tried to make a highway over the Cascades from Steilacoom to Walla Walla in 1853, and private citizens took up pick and axe to create it at their own expense. While they were working on it, they heard that Portlanders had sent out agents to meet the immigrant trains and advise them not to take the route because it was impassable. The first to try it were almost starved before they got help from Steilacoom.[10] The road was unused during the Indian wars and remained no more than a trail.

Attempts to compete with the Oregon Steam Navigation Company on the Columbia were numerous but unsuccessful. Washington's capital was insufficient to meet so powerful an opponent, and locally financed companies were easily bought out after a taste of rate war.

In 1864 the Washington Transportation Company, backed by San Francisco and Victoria (British Columbia) financiers, built a large

---

[9] *Messages of Washington Territorial Governors,* 152.

[10] Blanche B. Mahlberg, "Edward J. Allen, Pioneer and Roadbuilder," *PNQ,* XLIV, October, 1953, 159.

stern-wheeler at Utsalady, Washington, which they brought to the Columbia loaded with machinery for two boats they planned to build above the Cascades. The territorial legislature enthusiastically supported this venture with a charter to the same interests for a railroad on the Washington side at the Cascades, and power to condemn lands and materials, "such as railroads" at that location. Signs of a good practical opposition to "the unscrupulous monopoly" were hailed with joy by the Washingtonians.[11] Although the company had its friends in Washington, the opposition managed to defeat the Oregon Steam Navigation Company in the legislature and in the courts. In the end the company won out, but only by getting Congress to disapprove of the territory's legislation. Simeon Reed, the company's vice-president and manager, gleefully pointed out that it would be "a 'bitter pill' for our friends in W[ashington] T[erritory] and hereafter the Legislature of that Territory will be reminded that there is a 'power above them.' "[12]

Struggles for Economic Independence

The Company was no more popular in the interior than it was in Western Washington. During the mining rushes, it was blamed for the high prices miners had to pay for flour, bacon, beans, and whisky. The slow growth of farming population in Eastern Oregon and Washington and in Idaho was blamed on its exorbitant rates. It often got blame it didn't deserve. It had an expensive transportation system. In the 401 miles from Portland to Lewiston at low-water seasons, cargoes had to be handled 14 times; between Portland and points above the Dalles under any condition at least ten times. Because there was no timber east of the Dalles, fuel for engines consuming 50 cords in the up river trip, had to be transported by barge to fueling stations. The Company followed the rate policy of all transportation companies in the sixties and seventies, and charged all the traffic would bear. It could not bear too much on the Boise Basin route because of the competition of overland stages from Red Bluff, California, and from Salt Lake, Utah. These were the life lines Idaho Territory—and California and Utah—struggled to keep open even under Indian attacks.

[11] *Vancouver (Washington) Register,* November 4, 1865.

[12] Reed to J. C. Ainsworth, May 12, 1866, in Hanley Papers, Reed College Library.

Willamette Valley shippers won out in a competition that left the People's Transportation Company the monopoly on the upper river. It immediately adopted Oregon Steam Navigation rates. The Valley's residents did everything they could to bring in Ben Holladay's Oregon and California Railroad, in the hope that competition would reduce rates. In 1878 the valley had two competitive railway lines and three steamship companies. A cargo of wheat shipped by rail from Eugene to Portland, 124 miles with two handlings of cargo and no transfer, cost 6 dollars per ton, exactly what the Oregon Steam Navigation Company charged from Wallula to Portland using three steamboats, two portage railroads, and requiring ten handlings.

The rise of the Granger movement in the valley along the Columbia and in the Willamette Valley was not due wholly to the Oregon Steam Navigation Company's "grinding monopoly" but to frustrations in not having more facilities for transportation, and especially in the delay of transcontinental railway connections.

In 1872 Corvallis welcomed the charming southern Colonel T. Egenton Hogg and his Corvallis-Yaquina Railroad Company which was to give the Upper Valley an outlet on the coast, and was to become, in time, a link of the Corvallis Eastern line, a rival to Portland's hoped-for Northern Pacific line.[13] The Corvallis road, aptly named the "Frustration Route," almost made a seaport out of shallow tide-bound Yaquina Bay; but the frustrations which perplexed its history made the valley's inhabitants no more resigned to Portland's still dominant position. All parts of the Pacific Northwest had some cause to complain against the Oregon Steam Navigation Company and Portland to which the gravity flow of the rivers brought the inlands' agricultural and mineral products.[14]

Unable to get a transportation foothold in the interior, Western Washington had to be content with its fine harbor on Puget Sound and its lumber export trade. In 1871 its shipyards built nine vessels totaling 1,377 tons; in 1875, 18 with 3,986 tonnage. Its growing lumber industry financed by California capitalists and shipping interests made Seattle and Port Gamble the chief export towns. Of 37 sawmills in the territory producing 130,421,927 board feet of saw lumber, 12 on

[13] Randall V. Mills, *Railroads Down the Valley*, Palo Alto, 1950, 32-72.
[14] Glenn C. Quiett, *They Built the West*, New York, 1934, 339.

the Sound cut more than 117,000,000 feet. Its lumber went principally to South America and Australia; but slightly more than half of the total value of 759,000 dollars in exported goods in 1875 was of other commodities shipped to British Columbia.[15] This indicated the trend of Puget Sound's trade direction in the future.

"The City That Gravity Built"

Neither lumber nor the British Columbia trade built up the Sound cities in population or prosperity comparable to Portland's. In 1867, the latter entered the export trade with a cargo of wheat for Liverpool. By 1875 Portland's wheat fleet rivalled Seattle's lumber draggers in number and outstripped its value of exports by approximately 50 percent. In that year S. J. McCormick's *City Directory* pointed out that on wheat, and wheat "almost alone, can be based the argument in favor of Oregon's stability and Portland's permanency."[16]

By the end of the seventies the grain for the Portland ships was beginning to come from Eastern Oregon and Washington. In 1873-1874 two vessels carried off "the entire crop from eastern Oregon, Washington and Idaho,"[17] the rest came from the Willamette; but by 1885-1886 the interior was sending out three times the amount exported from the Valley. This tied the economy of the interior even more closely to Portland, and as long as ships came to the river from Great Britain, France, Sweden, and Germany for this produce, the railroads could not break the bond.

Portland was an island of wealth and prosperity in a sea of jealousy and discontent. In 1872 it was reputed to be one of the richest towns of its size in the United States, a reputation so firmly fixed that statistics could not shake it. In that year, in a population estimated at less than 13,000, there were, according to Frances Fuller Victor, ten men with incomes ranging from 16,000 dollars to 50,000 dollars,

---

[15] *Messages of Washington Territorial Governors*, 169, 186.

[16] S. J. McCormick, *Directory of Portland and East Portland for 1875*, Portland, 1875, Editorial. For the wheat trade see Dorothy D. Hirsch, "Study of the Foreign Wheat Trade of Oregon, 1869-1887," in *Reed College Bulletin*, August, 1953, 47 ff. For vessels carrying Puget Sound lumber and Oregon wheat see *Lewis and Dryden's Marine History of the Pacific Northwest*, Portland, 1895.

[17] A note in the Merchants Exchange Records, Portland, quoted in Hirsch, "Study of the Foreign Wheat Trade," 82.

and 20 more in the range of 5,000 dollars to 12,000 dollars.[18] Their wealth came from transportation, banking, merchandising, and real estate. There were no large industries in the city or its environs. An iron furnace and several casting plants comprised its heavy industry. Its shipbuilding activities were modest. There were about the same number of ship carpenters, riggers, and calkers employed in Oregon and Washington. In 1874, a shipyard on Coos Bay built the largest sailing vessel yet constructed on the Pacific Coast, the 186-foot, 1,118-ton clipper *Western Shore* which broke all coastal records for speed; Puget Sound yards specialized in small schooners, and at Seabeck, Port Ludlow, Utsalady, and Port Madison first-class ships were being constructed by 1876.[19] In that year the Oregon Shipbuilding Company was incorporated, the first of any magnitude involving Portland capital almost exclusively. Indicative of the provincial character of Portland's enterprise was its rejection in the late sixties of a Maine shipbuilding company's offer to build a yard on the Willamette if encouraged by a gift of a site on the waterfront. There were as yet no tycoons of the lumber industry. Portland's mills produced little more than what the growing city could consume. It lived on its hinterland.

In 1875, the City Directory listed four banks, ten brokerage firms, 20 commission houses, six wholesale grocers, and 11 corporations of which eight were engaged in transportation of one kind or another. Commission merchants, exporters, machinery dealers, and general merchandizers as well as bankers and transportation people often combined their interests with other fields of enterprise. Robert R. Thompson, director of the Oregon Steam Navigation Company, and Henry W. Corbett of the California Stage Company were also hardware merchants. Captain J. C. Ainsworth, president of the OSN, was a leading figure in the construction companies which built the western portion of the Canadian Pacific Railroad and the Northern Pacific line between Tacoma and Portland. S. G. Reed and W. S. Ladd were general merchants before starting in transportation and banking respectively. In partnership they also operated 17 farms in the Willamette Valley. Broadmead in Yamhill County, comprising 7,000 acres, was bought in 1871 and became a showplace among valley farms.

[18] Frances F. Victor, *All Over Oregon and Washington*, 153.
[19] *Lewis and Dryden's Marine History*, 219-220.

They imported purebred stock to upgrade sheep, beef, and milk cattle, brought in managers experienced in the latest scientific methods of farming, and experimented with grain and grass seeds, soil drainage, fertilizing, and the newest inventions in farm machinery.

The Hinterland of Farms

Oregon's agriculture needed the encouragement of gentleman farmers who could afford to and were inclined to experiment and branch out. The Willamette Valley farmers had easily fallen into patterns of farming and husbandry that were neither profitable nor enterprising. They were reluctant to change their ways from the methods that they had learned elsewhere to suit the conditions of the new land. Wisdom that went unheeded was uttered in the pages of the *Oregon Statesman* as early as 1853: "There is no part of the world where agricultural and horticultural societies are more necessary, and would be more useful than in Oregon. The experience and experiments of 'the States' are of little or no service here. Our climate, seasons, and soil differ from those of all of them, and agriculture and horticulture here must be conducted upon different systems. New experiments must be tried, and new modes adopted. In a great measure everything is to be learned anew."[20]

Private subscribers instituted a State Agricultural Society in 1860 and several farmer's publications helped to bring new ideas to the region. Fruit farming began to take hold in the Valley by 1870 but the farmers' staples were wheat and cattle.

The cattle industry moved across the mountains with the mining rushes. What survived the hard winter of 1861-1862 provided a nucleus for herds which, by 1876, had far outgrown the local demands. In that year at least two herds were driven from The Dalles to Cheyenne for shipment to the Chicago market, and sheep were trailed to the ranges of Northern Montana.[21] But these outlets did not take up the surplus in production nor remedy the disastrous decline in prices of the seventies. Surpluses and assets were wiped out in many instances by the disastrous winter of 1880-1881, when, as in 1861-1862, temperatures dropped to record lows, and alternate thaws, freezes,

[20] *Oregon Statesman, October* 5, 1853.
[21] Ernest S. Osgood, *The Day of the Cattleman,* St. Paul, 1929, 50, 189.

and heavy snowfalls found farmers, deluded by a belief that winters were consistently mild in the Northwest, unprepared to feed or water their unsheltered herds.[22]

Agriculture was generally in the doldrums in the seventies, and no less so in Oregon and Washington. In 1871, when Portland was experiencing a real estate boom sending prices up 20 percent to 25 percent in older parts of town and 50 percent to 100 percent in new additions, improved farm lands in the Valley on the route of the West Side railroad were offered, with few takers, at 10 dollars to 20 dollars an acre.[23] Four years later, W. G. Scoggins, who owned between 5,000 and 6,000 acres just over the west hills from Portland, added to his holdings at 11 dollars an acre land selling at 25 dollars an acre a few years before.[24] It did not help the farmers' frame of mind that men of capital with diversified sources of income bought up their lands at depressed prices, and as in the case of one of Reed's farms, erected an enclosed track for training his racing horses.

Many of the more prosperous families in Portland were of New England origin. Their influence in politics, as well as socially and economically, significantly outweighed their strength in numbers, and gave such a tone to Portland that it was often described as a New England village transplanted to the West. Actually, this was less true of Portland than of Walla Walla, Salem, or Forest Grove, where the atmospheres were less commercial and where the village aspect was more real than fancied. Portland combined qualities assumed to be characteristic of New England with those of a more rugged and recent frontier.

A Show of City Elegance

The business district lay parallel to the river and by the late 1870's was composed of brick structures with cast-iron façades of fluted columns and Corinthian capitals or with narrowly arched street floors surmounted by second and third stories

[22] See J. Orin Oliphant, "Winter Losses of Cattle in the Oregon Country 1847-1890," *WHQ*, XXIII, 1932, 3-17; "The Cattle Trade from the Far Northwest to Montana," Agricultural History, VI, 1932, 69-83.

[23] S. G. Reed to Benjamin Stark, April 14, 1871, Reed Letter Book 2, No. 143, Reed College Library.

[24] *Washington Independent*, Hillsboro, June 24, 1875.

carrying out the Palladian pattern of the traditional "orders" of architectural decoration. Side by side with these manifestations of the classical revival were found evidences of the eclectic taste of the West for the sharp arched window of the neo-Gothic style pointing to a late Renaissance mansarded roof. And next to an elegant structure of brick, marked only by a neat brass directory plaque, might crouch a frame building with the familiar flat false front bearing its unmistakable identification in foot-high lettering. At the intersection of Ankeny, Vine, and First streets, the shops and better stores were congregated. When the daytime noises of heavy drays and wagons rumbling over the cobblestones ceased, the night reverberated with the quicker beat of high-stepping horses and whir of carriage wheels approaching the New Market Theater, and the more respectable avenue of Portland's night life. At this location in 1888 Olin Levi Warner placed his lovely masterpiece, the Skidmore fountain, initially endowed by a pioneer businessman for "men, horses and dogs."

A desire for a beautiful city was evident in the first planning, when, as the residential district moved back toward the hills, park blocks were laid out and planted. Substantial but not elaborate homes were set in large fenced yards, unimaginatively landscaped, and monotonously repetitious in style and approach. The prevailing style of the sixties was the "Gothic Cottage" made popular in widely circulated books on carpentry. But toward the end of that decade and in the next, the sophisticated tastes of the well-to-do adopted the Italian villa and French Second Empire styles.[25]

As money accumulated among Portland's citizens, a requisite of social leadership was the tour of European capitals and the purchase of private art collections. Simeon G. Reed made two such tours, and, with little taste or training and certainly no helpful advice, purchased scores of second-rate Munich school oils of tediously sentimental themes and dull brownish tones. The Ladds and Corbetts were more fortunately endowed and brought back to Portland fine pieces of Oriental art and popular but good examples of contemporary European schools.

Reed's "Judith with the Head of Holofernes" and pink Carrara

---

[25] Marion D. Ross, "Architecture in Oregon 1845-1895," *OHQ*, LVII, March, 1956, 4-64.

marble "Cupid and Psyche" were beautifully housed in a mansion designed by Henry W. Cleveland of San Francisco. Among the last of the homes of this period is the Kamm House, moved and "restored" in a new location. The architectural style of mansarded roofs, small high-ceiling rooms, and bays of tall shuttered windows, repeated on a lesser scale, prevailed until the end of the century. The art works have perhaps fortunately disappeared. The occupants of these houses lived well, supported civic enterprises, and established the cultural institutions that gave Portland its distinction.

Chinese Laborers

A perennial shortage of domestic help perplexed Portland housewives as their Irish girls married and deserted them. The Irish comprised the largest foreign-born group in Portland in 1870; but within the decade, "China boys" became the laundrymen, gardeners, and chefs for the well-to-do. Seldom did a ship come in from the Orient but brought 300 to 400 Chinese laborers. Their first destination was the railroad construction camps, or the mines, but when the depression following the panic of 1873 halted railway work, they congregated in Portland and Astoria where they worked in the canneries. Clatsop and Multnomah Counties alone had more than 4,000 Chinese in 1880, almost 1,000 more than in the whole of Washington Territory. Later in the decade when anti-Chinese sentiments reached the proportions of civil disturbance in Puget Sound towns, the influence of families dependent upon the Oriental labor in Oregon counteracted the agitation of those who thought them a threat to their livelihood, and the Chinese episode was passed over with relatively little incident.

Heritage from New England: Churches

The New England accent was probably more noticeable in Oregon in connection with its churches and schools. The people of Portland, according to Samuel Bowles, editor of the *Springfield Republican* and editorial mouthpiece of Jay Cooke's Northern Pacific Railroad, "keep Sunday with as much strictness almost as Puritanic New England does, which can be said of no other population this side of the Rocky Mountains at least."[26] It was also a

[26] Samuel Bowles, *Our New West*, Hartford, Conn., 1870, 457.

matter of note that Portland's churches were located in the middle of the business portion of the city. Whether this was because the founding fathers who donated the lands for them in many instances were short-sighted with regard to the growth of the city, or because they found a moral strength in their proximity to their businesses is hard to say at this late date.

The Methodists, Congregationalists, Presbyterians, and Episcopalians were well established in the city by 1872 when the Directory listed 14 Protestant churches. The Methodists had three edifices of substantial size and congregations. The oldest and largest was the Taylor Street Church founded in 1851 by James H. Wilbur, who cleared land and cut timbers for the first frame structure. Father Wilbur, as he was affectionately titled, served several pastorates with this church and spent 18 years as Indian agent on the Yakima reservation. The Congregationalists had two churches under the leadership of George H. Atkinson and Horace Lyman both of whom had been sent to Oregon by the American Home Missionary Society in 1847, and who contributed to secular and religious education in the state. Mr. Atkinson was the father of the territory's public education bill; and Mr. Lyman was connected as a founder and teacher with La Creole Academy in Marion County, the short-lived Montville Institute in Linn County, and Pacific University at Forest Grove.

The First Presbyterian Church was organized in Portland in 1854, and Mr. J. L. Yantis, its pastor, divided his services between this pastorate and one at Calypooia, 80 miles up the Valley. No church was built in Portland until 1865. Then, under the pastorate of A. L. Lindsley, First Presbyterian grew to be one of the city's largest congregations. During his 20 years in the city (1867-1886) Mr. Lindsley also helped establish missions among the Indians of the Northwest and Alaska, and organized no less than 21 congregations of the faith.

Trinity Episcopal parish was organized in 1851, and three years later the first church of the denomination on the Pacific Coast was dedicated by Thomas Fielding Scott, missionary Bishop of Oregon and Washington. Bishop Scott was successful in firmly establishing in the Northwest a church not usually popular in a frontier community. The Baptists were early in Oregon but not until 1872, and 22 years after the first organization, was a church firmly established in Portland. The 1880's witnessed the largest growth of this sect in the

Northwest and especially in Washington Territory.

Among Portland's leading merchants were a number of Jews who in 1858 organized a congregation and three years later built the first synagogue. Temple Beth Israel, completed in 1888, had a seating capacity of more than 700. A second synagogue, Ohavi Sholem, was organized in 1872.

A rough chapel built in 1852 served the few Catholics in Portland until ten years later when the Irish began to settle in the city. By 1880 they comprised the third largest foreign-born group in the city. In 1862 Archbishop Blanchet removed the seat of the diocese to Portland and two years later dedicated a procathedral. The Archbishop saw the completion of the Cathedral of the Immaculate Conception in 1882. His death three years later brought to a close a continuous association with Oregon's religious history for 47 years, a record equaled only by that of Thomas Lamb Eliot, pastor of the Unitarian Church from 1867 to his retirement in 1893, but who continued his services to the community until his death in 1936.

The Unitarians were first organized in 1866 and the congregation, composed of many whose roots lay in the movement in their native New England under the leadership of Dr. Eliot, exerted a strong influence in the molding of public opinion toward social reforms in the city. A noteworthy advance in help for dependent children was pioneered by Dr. Eliot and his friends in founding and encouraging the Boys and Girls Aid Society and in utilizing foster home instead of institutional care when the latter generally prevailed elsewhere.

Schools

Portland had no college, but it had Bishop Scott's Grammar School where emphasis was placed upon ancient and modern languages. In 1872, 250 students attended the Portland Academy and Female Seminary, whose curriculum included studies to be found in the last two years of high school and the first two years of college work. There was a "free school" as early as 1851 but the city's first public school was opened in 1856 and survived having Mr. John Outhouse, properly pronounced Othus, as teacher. In 1872 there were five elementary schools, two offering ninth and tenth grade work, and a high school with an enrollment of 65. Episcopal Bishop B. Wistar Morris' St. Helen's Hall educated the young ladies who would be mistresses of Portland's finer homes. There were two Hebrew schools, a German school, and three Catholic academies.

Portland, however, had no monopoly of religion or education, nor for that matter of a New England inheritance. The capital city Salem also bore the mantle of culture. Willamette University was the culmination of the long struggle to make the Methodist mission school, the Oregon Institute, something more than an elementary academy. Methodism outweighed Calvinism in this valley town, but in Forest Grove, Mother Tabitha Brown's orphanage grew into Pacific University under the care of the Reverend John S. Griffin, and the masterful teaching of the classicist Sidney H. Marsh, all Congregationalists.

Practically all of Oregon's institutions of learning had their roots in church schools. A number of these had only brief histories, starting as academies to serve a local need for secondary schooling or to implement some doctrinal conviction. The Baptists founded institutes at Corvallis and West Union (1856 and 1858); the Disciples of Christ a school at Bethel (1855), which merged with Christian College to form Monmouth University (1864). The Presbyterian Albany Academy was founded in 1858. The same denomination's Corvallis College, chartered by the territorial legislature in 1858, became Oregon Agricultural College (1885) when the church relinquished its control. It was thereafter partially supported as a land-grant college under the terms of the Morrill Act of 1862.

A state university had been projected with the organization of the territory when lands were granted for purposes of higher education, but the sparse population and the small funds that could be derived from this source did not encourage its founding until early in the seventies, when the sum of 100,000 dollars was appropriated for the purpose. A struggle over its location was resolved when Eugene raised money to start Deady Hall on its site. In 1876 the University opened with an unusually fine faculty. Its financial struggles, however, were not over.

Oregon's resources to support education were limited, its school land funds were stolen or abused, and its efforts were spread too thinly over too many institutions. However, the struggles of these schools to maintain themselves were heroic. Those that survived the extension of public education at elementary and secondary levels had to shift from academy to college or university organization, and they existed on minimum financial support. They provided a modest higher education for ambitious young men and women, and after 1870 many of Oregon's most respectable members of bench and bar, of the medical profession, and school staffs had their academic training at these institutions.

The numerous schools founded in Oregon points up the contrast marking the early development of the state compared with that of Washington Territory, where in 1885 the governor reported 24 institutions "of the higher order," but few that fulfilled the description. Washington's ambitions were always on a different scale from Oregon's. It had a vision of greatness, but visions sometimes are slow to materialize. The legislature provided for a state university in Seattle, which in 1861 offered its students a most elementary curriculum. Its first president, Asa Mercer, was an energetic advocate of Puget Sound's great future and is perhaps best remembered as importer of the "Mercer girls" to add a touch of feminine gentility to the territory's bachelor population.[27] Mercer accomplished more in the field of publicity than in higher education. In 1873, Governor Ferry reported that for lack of financial support it was a university in name only and he recommended appropriations that would permit the establishment and maintenance of a curriculum "equal at least to that provided in first-class seminaries and academies."[28] Two years before the University opened, the legislature incorporated a seminary for Walla Walla. Whitman Seminary (1866) in 1883 was reorganized and incorporated as Whitman College. Its original trustees included names associated with the Pacific Northwest's missionary history and indicated the character of the college, founded as a memorial to the Whitmans. Among these were Elkanah Walker, George H. Atkinson, H. H. Spalding, and Cushing Eells. It also marked the end of an era and the beginning of a new one for the city which supported its growth and guarded its standards. Walla Walla had changed remark-

---

[27] Delphine Henderson, "Asa Shinn Mercer, Northwest Publicity Agent," *Reed College Bulletin*, January, 1945, 21 ff.

[28] *Messages of Washington Territorial Governors*, 181.

ably from a rowdy rendezvous for miners to a prosperous farming town as sedate and proper as a western image of a New England Concord.

The Enjoyment of Literature and Music

For pioneer generations that had not had much time for book learning there was nevertheless a great value placed upon books. Oregon was not overly generous to its schools, but it expected great things of them. It did not have large library facilities, but there were books in almost every pioneer home. The Applegate family stands out as perhaps unusual in its collection of fine works. The spirit that created a circulating library at Oregon City in 1844 did not perish as the years passed. A library group formed in Portland in 1850 had a short life of six years. But the Library Association organized in 1864 under the leadership of Banker W. S. Ladd and a board of directors composed of the city's leading citizens has had a continuous history. Starting with donations of $2,611, and supported by an initation fee of 5 dollars and quarterly dues of 3 dollars, it had a collection of 9,872 volumes by 1880, and the annual report of that year showed that the whole number of volumes loaned amounted to 18,208. In 1902 the Library Association contracted with Multnomah County to serve the community as a free public library.

Music and the theater had a part in the city's cultural life. There was, of course, the background of folk singing, the campfire songs, and church hymns which were common to the frontier. The guitar, banjo, trumpet, and drum provided marching music for pioneers. The piano and the portable organ graced pioneer parlors. The 1860 census which found 17 actors and 14 artists located in Oregon listed nine musicians and five music teachers. Oregon's first musical organization was something out of the ordinary on the frontier. Aurora, half-way point between Salem and Portland, was founded in 1857 by a German communist society who had migrated from their mother colony in Bethel, Missouri, under their patriarch and leader, Dr. William Keil. A concert by these music-loving Germans, directed by Heinrich Carl Finck, was an introduction to the classics by performers first instructed by Professor Ruge, the university-trained schoolmaster, and finished off by the sharp-eared, sharp-tongued Meister Heinrich Carl himself. Finck's son, trained in music by his father, in the classics by Aurora's Professor Wolff from Gottingen, entered Harvard in the sophomore class and became a music critic in New York and Philadelphia.[29]

The music standards and tastes of Aurora were shared by a large part of the Portland German community, numbering 1,600 in 1880. *Leiderfests* at the *Turn Verein* may well have been the foundation for the organization of the Handel and Hayden Society. In its first concert in the spring of 1879, it presented the premiere of Dudley Buck's "Legend of Don Munio" especially orchestrated by the composer for the limited local orchestra. To round out an ambitious first season, the fall concert was presented at a reception for General U. S. Grant at which a full orchestra and chorus performed the *Messiah*.

The Portland Philharmonic Society (1866) gave a vocal and instrumental concert at Oro Fino Hall in 1867 for the benefit of "the poor of the city." Helen Ladd Corbett, who was to be social arbiter of Portland's first families for the next 40 years, sang in two duets songs fitting to the occasion and the popular taste, "All Things Are Beautiful," and "Mother, Can This Glory Be." Another grand benefit concert, combining all the talent of the city, was occasioned by the fire which devastated a large part of the city in the summer of 1873.

Theater was popular in mining camps, frontier towns, and in Portland, but not in the upper valley of the Willamette. Portland had variety troupes and minstrel shows as early as 1856, and a theater building in 1858. More elaborate than these earlier performances was that of Mrs. Charles Correll's Vaudeville which at the Masonic Hall in 1872 presented scenes from "Lydia Thompson's Burlesque" with featured songs such as "Her Bright Smile" and "Sleepy Family." The program concluded with an "opera" entitled "Lucretia Boards Here" with a cast of three characters, and "less than one thousand Cho-rusters." At the old Stewart Theater, the Oro Fino, and Adelphi, Portlanders wept over *East Lynne* and *Camille*. But the theater of which the city boasted was the brick-framed, pilastered front New Market. Its builder, A. P. Ankeny, a merchant and navigation man, now speculator in the arts, was delayed in the opening of his theater until 1875,

[29] John E. Simon, "Wilhelm Keil and Communist Colonies," *OHQ*, XXXVI, June, 1935, 143-144; see also Robert J. Hendricks, *Bethel and Aurora*, New York, 1933.

when James A. Hearne played Rip Van Winkle before the local diamond horseshoe.

The Conservative Side of Oregon

"The Oregonians," remarked Samuel Bowles in 1869, "have builded what they have got more slowly and more wisely than the Californians; they have . . . less to unlearn; and they seem sure, not of organizing the first state on the Pacific Coast, indeed, but of a steadily prosperous, healthy, and moral one—they are in the way to be the New England of the Pacific Coast." As the city grew it did not wholly lose this atmosphere. In many ways, it remained a village. But even as villages have their seamier sides of life, so did Portland. With the development of its maritime commerce the once respectable boardinghouses and residences at the north end of First Street became sailors' rooming houses. Saloons and bawdy-houses gave the North End a reputation and a clientele that flourished with the years. Shipmasters were not hesitant to fill crews, depleted by desertions, with the drugged or drunk, "shanghaied" by professionals. When fancy ladies strolled from their haunts to parts of town frequented by their betters, the latter gently dropped their parasols to exclude them from their vision, and when Ben Holladay drove by in his carriage accompanied by a lady who did not "belong," they peeked with caution to avoid acknowledging his bow.

Spreading out across the Willamette to build East Portland, Lents, Alberta, and St. Johns, the permanent inhabitants did not have to crowd together in unwholesome districts. Modest homes, gardens, orchards, dotted the landscape as the forests receded. Spring still comes to Portland in a burst of bloom from the cherry and apple trees planted 80 years ago. It was from its origin a homey town, not robustiously friendly but amiable, cautious in its enthusiasms, reluctant to peer very far out from under its ruffled parasol. Portland was Oregon, conservative and, under most circumstances, contented with itself as it was.

And this was perhaps natural in the course of its history. As an American colony, the first settlement of Oregon laid out the pattern of the future. Sobriety, thrift, mercantile energy combined with agricultural provincialism, simplicity, loyalties, and traditions to create a conservative community. Oregon's conservatism was not reactionary, it did not fight change. It welcomed separation from the elements which disturbed its pattern, as it did in encouraging the separation with Washington. Oregonians did not reject anything new because it was new—whether an "outside" industry such as a shipbuilding firm asking for a spot of land as an inducement to locate, or Abigail Scott Duniway's suffrage agitation—without a reasonably polite hearing.

Its citizens took their politics, business, and morality seriously but not uncomfortably. Portlanders voted Republican as a rule, but until the end of the century there was no incident to rouse political antagonisms among the nonprofessionals. It was told of a prominent Democrat that he marched with his party in the torchlight parade, but at Third and Morrison he slipped away to join his Republican friends when they marched down Second. Business did not keep them from sharing in the duties of city offices, and on commissions to develop the water system and the street railway. The rich supported the city's cultural life, philanthropies, and churches. Yet Simeon Reed played cards on Sunday after church, and he did not pull the shades to hide the fact.

They did not admire ostentation or conspicuousness or overconfidence. To R. R. Thompson, contemplating the sale of the Oregon Steam Navigation Company at a fine profit, the purchaser, Henry Villard, was a windbag. W. S. Ladd replied to his farm manager's letters by turning the paper upside down and writing between the lines. Simeon Reed didn't own a dress coat and to attend the opera in Paris had his wife pin back the tails of his Prince Albert to simulate the proper garb.

The state's principal citizens and wealthiest men might, on occasion, align themselves in rival camps and carry a battle of railway franchises or land grants through the courts; they might finagle laws to get more than their share of the public domain, or squeeze out a competitor; they might buy juries or legislators; or ignore frauds and corruption. But seldom did an individual emerge to notoriety or prominent infamy, or strain after power without regard to public opinion. On the whole, Portland's citizens were "proper Oregonians." Their morals and their values were suspended in a narrow middle range.

Part III

A Period of Transition

INTERPRETIVE KEY

The 30-year period 1880-1910 was a time of transition in the Pacific Northwest which saw changes take place more important than those of any other period in the history of the region. In 1880, despite the first 30 years of growth, it was still an isolated frontier which attracted relatively small numbers of settlers, found little use for its rich natural resources, and maintained its contact with the rest of the world commercially mainly over the ocean sea lanes. By 1910 the population of Oregon, Washington, and Idaho together totaled more than two million. The economy of the region was closely interlocked with that of the rest of the nation, and the general level of growth compared favorably with that of other sections.

The completion of the northern transcontinental railways marked the beginning of this important era and in some measure made it possible. Accessibility was itself a requisite to progress, and the railroads ushered in a new day of easy travel and rapid transportation. Thousands of immigrants came West "by the cars" who doubtless never would have attempted the voyage by schooner around the Horn, nor ventured to cross a continent, as the earlier pioneers had done, "by long and weary marches." Trains carried agricultural produce, lumber, and minerals to markets which hitherto had been quite out of reach.

Yet much more was involved in the transformation of the region than simply the means of travel. Far-reaching developments were taking place in the country as a whole, which made the conditions of living and the patterns of enterprise very different from what they had been ten or 20 years earlier. Large-scale production, which revolutionized many lines of manufacturing, gave Big Business a new interest in the exploitation of natural resources in the West, and placed a correspondingly higher value upon them. Giant corporations with their tremendous working capital and their closely centralized agencies of management brought any frontier, however remote, into the orbit of their control. The man-made environment of steel and stone that appeared so suddenly in the nation's cities was something new whether one lived in Portland, Oregon, or Portland, Maine.

Thus the railroads were particularly important in the Pacific Northwest because they linked the region with the older states at the very time when those states were themselves undergoing profound economic and social change. The far western frontier was doubly transformed, once by the physical conquest of distances, and again by the new forces which were immediately brought to play upon it. Industrialism and urbanization had special implications for these newer sections of the country that stood so near to the pioneer stage of history. In many ways development was greatly accelerated and progress went farther and faster than could have been possible otherwise. On the other hand, the concentration of population and economic power in the East sometimes worked against the kind of dispersion that was essential to the long-range growth of the Pacific coast.

The years of transition were marked by an exuberant optimism. This generation knew the excitement of the region's first big economic boom, and had the satisfaction of seeing the Pacific Northwest reach out, after the long years of slow development, to realize something of its own destiny. Boosters enjoyed a field day and played the drumbeat of progress in the ears of listening Americans everywhere. Colonel Nicholas Owings, who a few years previously had been Secretary of State and head of the Immigration Bureau in Washington Territory, set the tone in an interview for a popular magazine. Washington, he insisted, had more and better timber than the Baltic. It was a better dairy country than Holland, raised better hops than New York and better grain than any other state in the Union. It had the grandest harbor in the world, and would assuredly be the center of America's trade with the Orient. "Here on Puget Sound," he declared, "is the future seat of the western empire of wealth."

Owings could be called without injustice a professional booster and his language was undeniably extravagant. But the statistics of the eighties were given to extravagance. Oregon, Washington, and Idaho received three times as many new settlers in that decade as they had during the preceding one. In Washington the value of manufactures and the estimates of assessed property stood ten times higher in 1890 than in 1880. Farmers doubled their output. Cities arose as if by magic in a few years time. The boom had been long awaited; now at last it was a reality.

Northwesters denied that growth and expansion were simply speculative, or that they would lead to an inescapable "bust." On the contrary, they protested that they were just growing up with the country. But they were nevertheless lifted high by a wave of national prosperity and when the wave passed, they were somewhat becalmed. During the general panic of 1893 and the depression years that followed, the stream of immigration largely disappeared and the flow of investment slowed to a trickle.

Fortunately prosperity soon returned and the Yukon gold rush brought unprecedented opportunities in the outfitting trade to Portland and the Sound cities. The decade 1900-1910 was one of renewed activity. The fine art of boosting reached a climax in the Lewis and Clark exposition in Portland in 1905 and the Alaska-Yukon-Pacific exposition in Seattle in 1909. Behind this sensational showmanship and advertising, solid advances were made in all the major lines of resource enterprise, in construction, in banking and commerce.

Much of this latter story of economic growth was achieved, not by shouting and display, but by a careful analysis of the economic opportunities that the region afforded under conditions of modern industrialism. Tough problems in production and marketing had to be solved. Conditions of competition, despite the new railroad connections, were often unfavorable. Carrying costs were higher than elsewhere, and established industries, situated in other parts of the country, enjoyed in many instances a distinct advantage. Of necessity the Pacific Northwest matched its wits with other sections and caught up with them only as the economies of production made it possible, and as local trade increased with the growing population.

The period was a time of advancement in the political life of the people. Washington and Idaho, which had languished in territorial status for a quarter-century and more, were admitted as sovereign states in the Union. Conventions drew up state constitutions which were ratified and put in force. Delegations from the Far West appeared in Congress to play a new and more significant role in national affairs. The organization of political parties became more full-bodied and more complex in its representation of agricultural areas and of the urban population concentrated for the most part in a few metropolitan centers. Far western names appeared on the roster of administrative officials in the federal government, as leaders from the new states began to assume a larger importance in the shaping of policy and the management of the executive departments.

Society was also profoundly affected by the extension of the newly developing urban civilization to the Pacific Northwest. To be sure, the number of cities of more than 100,000 population could be counted on the fingers of one hand. But these places were focal centers where a truly urban way of living was developed, and where the rich (and the sordid) features of urban culture were accentuated and disseminated. Here the cultural evolution from frontier to a city civilization took place with unusual abruptness, and experiences which in older places extended over several decades were compressed into the space of a few years. Here the technician and professional expert found a community sufficiently large and diversified to support his craft. The artist found a discriminating patronage and the music lover, concerts according to his taste. Science and learning flourished, finding stimulus and nourishment in the growth of schools and colleges. The isolation and provincialism of the earlier years became a thing of the past. Standards of excellence in every field of intellectual and cultural attainment were judged by the general progress of education and research or were appraised in the light of the achievements of leading figures whose work was known and recognized throughout the world.

It would be a mistake to think that living in Seattle or Portland was like living in Boston or Chicago. Frontier characteristics were still discernible, for time would be required to build institutions that were the equal of those in the older states. But the progress of urban culture enriched the interests and activities of the people in the Northwest, just as it did elsewhere, and civilization in all its varied aspects came to be much the same in its essential qualities, whether one lived in the valley of the Columbia or on the Atlantic coast.

Such is the interpretive setting which gives special meaning to the events and developments of the latter years of the nineteenth century and the first decade and a half of the twentieth. It would be hard to magnify the points of difference which set off in sharp contrast the beginning of the period and the end of it, or to exaggerate the rapidity with which important changes took place. In point of time a single generation spanned the years of transition. In the quality and conditions of living the Pacific Northwest of 1914 was part of a new world. These middle chapters in the history of the region tell how the new Northwest came into being.

18

The Magic of the Steel Rails

Of all the agencies that contributed to the development of the American West, none had more magic than the railroad. The very idea of a transcontinental line that would link Chicago and New York with the Pacific coast worked a tremendous excitement in men's minds. Whether one dreamed of a great commerce with the Orient or visioned the peopling of new frontiers in America, the transcontinentals stirred one's imagination long before they were built, and worked their marvels of economic growth from the day they were finished.

George Wilkes, one of the earliest promoters of such a project, thought of the railroad as a means of putting the United States on the "short route to Asia." The possibilities of such a trade were boundless, he declared. "The riches of the most unlimited market in the world would be thrown open to our enterprise, and, obeying the new impulse imparted to it, our commerce would increase till every ocean billow between us and the China seas would twinkle with a sail. By the superior facilities conferred upon us by our position and control of the route, we should become the common carrier of the world for the India trade."[1]

If Wilkes saw sails on the sea, there were others who pointed out that the Pacific railroad would give value to great stretches of American farmland, and stimulate the movement of population to the frontier communities of the Far West. The Westerners pictured it threading its way through a vast and almost illimitable interior, without rival in beauty and resources. Would it not bring an empire in population to the Pacific coast? Over it would pass a constant wave

[1] Robert R. Russel, *Improvement of Communication with the Pacific Coast as an Issue in American Politics, 1783-1864*, Cedar Rapids, 1948, 15.

of exhaustless wealth flowing from the rich farms of the interior out to the seaboard where ere long cities would spring up to rival Boston and New York. "This," protested the Oregon booster who penned the prophecy, "is no fancy picture, but simply words of truth and soberness."[2]

The story of the surveying, financing, and construction of the transcontinentals is a story of private enterprise and government aid on a national scale. Local groups along the proposed routes, as they realized that they would draw their lifeblood from the railroads, sometimes took an active part in the effort to build them. Territorial and state legislatures themselves incorporated railroad companies or memorialized Congress to aid the lines that held national charters. Local mass meetings were staged and local capitalists promised to use their means to raise money. But the roads were built largely from the outside, and while Jay Cooke might speak of the Oregon group as "our Western Associates," the big eastern bankers shouldered the main responsibility and called the tune. During the latter half of the nineteenth century railroading was no longer an enterprise that western communities could undertake for themselves. It was a job for Big Business. If the frontiers of the Far West were to be linked by rail with the rest of the country, it would be because the captains of finance had their own reasons for doing it.[3]

To the settler of the Far Northwest it seemed that the railroads were tragically slow in the building, for the first surveys had been made before the Civil War. Isaac I. Stevens laid out the route between St. Paul and Puget Sound when he came out to take up his duties as Washington's first territorial governor in 1853. However, the rivalry among the advocates of the northern, central, and southern routes, and the mounting tensions over the slavery issue prevented Congress from taking further action at that time, and nearly ten years passed

[2] William L. Adams, *Oregon As It Is; Its Present and Future,* Portland, 1873, 47.

[3] The early history of the transcontinental railroads, and more especially the Northern Pacific, is covered in Lewis H. Haney, *Congressional History of the Railways in the United States to 1887*, 2 vols., Madison, Wisconsin, 1908-1910, Edwin I. Sabin, *Building the Pacific Railway*, Philadelphia, 1919; Glenn C. Quiett, *They Built the West*, New York, 1934, and Enoch Bryan, *Orient Meets Occident, the Advent of the Railways to the Pacific Northwest*, Pullman, Washington, 1936; also in biographies by Henrietta Larson, *Jay Cooke, Private Banker*, Cambridge, Mass., 1936, and Ellis P. Oberholtzer, *Jay Cooke, Financier of the Civil War*, 2 vols., Philadelphia, 1907.

before any of the transcontinentals were chartered. During the Civil War years legislation was passed which chartered the Union Pacific and the Central Pacific (1862), and the Northern Pacific (1864). Save for the chartering little was done until after the war ended.

Land-Grant Railroads

The basic legislation was itself important since it laid down the terms of building and finance, and stated the government policy of subsidy. All three lines were land-grant roads; that is, they were to be subsidized with lands from the public domain. Each was to receive a strip of land 200 feet wide as a right of way and alternate sections of public lands which were to be sold to help finance construction. The Northern Pacific received ten sections per mile in the states through which it passed and 20 sections per mile in the territories. If sufficient lands were not available within this "primary" grant, the other sections could be selected (lieu lands) from a secondary zone which reached back from the tracks another 20 miles. Additional funds were to be secured through the sale of stock.

Government loans in the form of bonds amounting to 16,000 dollars to 48,000 dollars per mile of track laid were provided for in the charters to the Union Pacific and the Central Pacific railroads. The Northern Pacific did not receive aid in this manner, but in 1870 Congress authorized the sale of bonds by the railroad with the land grant, as well as other property, as security. The latter measure was put through by the initiative of Jay Cooke who was by this time under agreement to handle the financing on a commission basis.

Under the terms of these various laws all three railroads began construction. The Union Pacific put General Grenville Dodge in charge of its field force and pushed the laying of rails with such energy that by May of 1869 the ribbons of steel extended from Omaha to northern Utah following the Platte River route. In the meantime the Central Pacific under the vigorous direction of the Big Four (Leland Stanford, Collis P. Huntington, Mark Hopkins, and Charles Crocker) built eastward from Sacramento through the mountains of California and Nevada. On May 10, 1869, the gold spike was hammered home at Promontory Point and a consignment of tea started eastward from the Pacific coast, a token of the beginning of overland trade with

China and Japan. The next morning the first transcontinental passengers from the East passed over the "last tie."

Owing to the financial difficulties which delayed construction, the Northern Pacific failed to complete its main line before Jay Cooke went bankrupt in 1873. The eastern division of the road was finished from Duluth only to the Missouri River at Bismarck, North Dakota. At the western end Cooke completed only a section of road extending from Kalama on the Columbia River northward to Tacoma on Puget Sound.

The building of the Kalama-Tacoma section resulted from a change in the plan first projected. The original charter provided that the main line of the road should run from the Clark's Fork river by way of Spokane Falls to the Columbia River at Ainsworth, and thence up the Yakima River and across the Cascade Mountains directly to Puget Sound. A branch was to follow the Columbia from Ainsworth to Portland. In 1870 the route was changed so that the main line followed the Columbia while the route over the mountains became the branch. This had the advantage of utilizing the twenty-mile portage road which the Oregon Steam Navigation Company had already built, on which $50,000 per mile in bonds could be issued. The route favored Portland's continued preëminence and increased the land grant to include alternate sections along the Columbia River and northward through the Cowlitz Valley. By building this latter section the railroad earned 2,000,000 acres of land on which stood timber estimated to be worth 100,000,000 dollars.

The choice of Tacoma as the terminal city was made in the face of a spirited effort by the people of Seattle, who offered both land and cash as inducements to bring the railroad to their community. The northern town was larger and somewhat more established than Tacoma, but this very fact worked against it, since the possibilities of land speculation were more promising at or near the infant settlement on Commencement Bay. Having chosen Tacoma, the railroad brought the tracks in at water level and built wharves to serve the ships that plied the Sound or picked up cargoes for the ocean trade. The St. Paul and Tacoma Land Co., composed of investors a number of whom were railroad officers, pushed the sale of its lands with considerable vigor, and speedily brought the government of the town under its control. It was a shrewd game, a bit too shrewd to please Cooke, who protested that if land prices were held too high it would discourage settlement instead of promoting it. For a number of years the road went no farther than Tacoma, leaving the other towns on the Sound to be served by steamer. Despite the atmosphere of expectancy, the Northern Pacific brought comparatively little real economic growth so long as great stretches of it remained nothing more than lines on a map.

The people of Washington, disappointed when the eastern connection was not completed, demanded that the Northern Pacific land grant should be taken back by the United States government. The railroad could not perfect its own title to the land or sell it except as it was earned through the progress of construction. Even government lands could not be taken up in areas reserved for lieu land selections. Yet the alternate odd-numbered sections lying within the limits of the grant, according to the maps filed by the railroad, were withheld from individual settlement. In the case of lands that were earned, the railroad company deliberately delayed taking the final steps to secure title since it was possible to escape taxation that way. These were serious complaints which made the railroad land grant a troublesome political issue for a number of years. The grant was never recaptured, but popular resentment against the Northern Pacific became so strong that the railroad was viewed almost as the archenemy of the public. Even after the road was finished Charles S. Voorhees campaigned successfully for the office of territorial delegate on the basis of his vigorous attack on the Northern Pacific.

Oregon and California Railroad

While Washington's economic progress depended largely upon the completion of the Northern Pacific railroad, Oregon's geographic position was such that it was interested in several routes to the east and south. The projected line of the Northern Pacific down the Columbia River was only one such connection. Equally important were the proposals (1) to build through the Columbia and Snake river valleys to a junction point on the Union Pacific, (2) to join the Willamette Valley by rail with the Central Pacific at some point in Northern Nevada, or (3) to cross over the

Siskiyou Mountains from the Rogue River valley to the Sacramento. All of these schemes appeared to be entirely feasible, but most Oregonians felt compelled to choose between them, not realizing that in the end three of the four lines would be completed within the space of five years (1883-1888).[4]

In Oregon's Willamette Valley, railroad projects had local as well as transcontinental importance, for they opened up a large area of fertile farm lands. Some of these tracts to be sure were served by the river boats, and the prospective competition between boat and train was a calculation of some weight in the minds of promoters and financiers. But back from the river on both sides the railroad would tap more inaccessible lands which could be expected to provide a considerable quantity of paying freight. Furthermore, the upper valleys of the Umpqua and the Rogue, which lay beyond the reach of river boats, were potentially rich agricultural areas, as was the district around Klamath Lake.

The early railway surveys in Northern California and Orgeon were carried out with a purpose to serve these more southern areas by linking them with Portland to the north and with San Francisco to the south. The Elliott and Barry surveys made in 1866-1867 were backed by men in Southern Oregon to whom local accessibility was the first prerequisite to any economic progress. Portland men feared that the effect of a railroad in Southern Oregon would be to draw the commerce of the area to California. They therefore favored a route that would join the Central Pacific at Winnemucca, Nevada, rather than at San Francisco.

For a time the railroad projects in the Willamette Valley were enmeshed in a web of promotional rivalry and financial intrigue. Not one Oregon Central but two were chartered. One of these was sponsored by a group of capitalists in Portland and the area lying west of the river; the other represented the interests of a group of men who wanted a railroad to be built south from Portland but to the east of the river. The struggle between them was rendered the more bitter when Congress passed a bill carrying a land grant of 5,000,000 acres lying in the Willamette, Umpqua, and Rogue valleys, and pro-

[4] John T. Ganoe, "History of the Oregon and California Railroad" in *OHQ*, XXV, 1924, 235-283; 330-352.

vided that the state legislature should designate the railroad to which it should go. The stakes were high, the excitement intense. The west side company was first to organize but withdrew its articles of incorporation in order to secure additional signatures. In the meantime the east side company began construction with a great celebration. At this point Ben Holladay, the western express magnate, became interested in the situation and reached an agreement with the east side company which gave him control of that enterprise. Holladay was not one to hesitate over the niceties of business ethics or legislative statesmanship. His hospitality at the sessions of the Oregon legislature was lavish indeed. In a day when legislators were more than ordinarily open to such persuasion, his methods brought results. When the session was over a bill stood on the statute books which stipulated that the east side rather than the west side company was to receive the land grant. Soon afterward Congress was prevailed upon to change the terms of the grant to Holladay's benefit. The whole affair produced indignation and resentment on the part of the west side group, but there was no help for it and they sold out to Holladay on the best terms they could get. Holladay reorganized his enterprise as the Oregon and California Railroad, and sold several million dollars worth of bonds to finance construction, placing a good part of the amount in Germany. Soon afterward the steel rails began to stretch out south from the Portland terminus up the Willamette Valley. By September, 1870, the tracks reached Salem; a year later trains rolled into Eugene. By the end of the year 1872 service extended to Roseburg. There the project rested for more than a decade. The Panic of 1873 did not affect the Oregon and California as severely as it did the Northern Pacific. Holladay brought the Willamette River steamboats under his control, and his railroad served as a feeder which supplemented the water routes. Lacking an eastern connection, however, the rail line brought only limited returns and Holladay suffered an increasing amount of trouble with the German bondholders.

Oregon drew considerable benefit from the Portland-Roseburg section even without an eastern connection. The European and Oregon Land Company, which acted as the colonizing agency for the Oregon and California railroad, opened offices in San Francisco and New

York and offered land for sale on credit, at moderate prices, asking only 20 percent in cash, the balance over a five-year period of payment. Lands already occupied jumped sharply in value as the railroad came within reach of them. Around Salem farm land rose from seven dollars to 30 dollars an acre; by 1878 the more favorably situated tracts at Salem and Albany brought as much as 50 to 60 dollars per acre. Far to the south in the Umpqua Valley prices went up from five dollars to three or four times that amount. Large increases were reported throughout Western Oregon in wool, wheat, oats, and potatoes while gold and treasure accounted for a smaller part of the total trade than formerly.[5]

These evidences of growth may appear to be all that could be wished but they fell far below the expectations of the railroad financiers. To these men the revenues of the Oregon and California line were disappointingly small. The products of local agriculture were inadequate to sustain the road, and sales from the land grant did little to help. Mines in Southern Oregon, which were expected to be large revenue enterprises, failed to materialize. The bondholders had been oversold on Oregon's immediate prospects and they became increasingly disgruntled.

Meanwhile Oregon's connection with the transcontinentals remained a question mark for nearly ten years. From 1867-1869 while the Union Pacific and the Central Pacific were building rapidly toward each other, each line hoped to achieve control of the Columbia River outlet. The Union Pacific ordered a survey of the Snake River route and found encouragement for it in Portland. Soon afterwards two Oregon railroads were incorporated with charters to connect with the central transcontinental route, one by way of the Snake River, the other via the Willamette, Sprague River, and Goose Lake to the Central Pacific line at Winnemucca in the Humboldt Valley, Nevada. The latter route, which was promoted vigorously by Oregon's B. J. Pengra, interested Collis P. Huntington, and for a while it looked as if it might have strong backing in that quarter. However the Holladay interests in Congress secured an amendment to the land-grant bill which provided that the Humboldt branch should connect

[5] William Reid, *Progress of Oregon and Portland, from 1868 to 1878*, Portland, Oregon, 1879.

with Holladay's east side line rather than Pengra's west side route, so Huntington dropped the matter. For several years 1869-1876 the advocates of the Snake River and Humboldt proposals tried to secure favorable action from Congress which would make possible the building of their particular route. But public opinion turned increasingly against further land grants and neither road was built until after Henry Villard completed the northern connection over the tracks of the Oregon Railway and Navigation Company and the Northern Pacific.

Villard's Activities in Oregon

Henry Villard had only an academic knowledge of the intricacies of railroad finance when he first became interested in Oregon. He had come to the United States from Germany, as a young man. After a short experience with farming and the study of law, he turned to journalism, reported the Lincoln-Douglas debates and the progress of the Colorado gold rush, and during the Civil War represented northern newspapers as a war correspondent. He became interested in railroad financing while secretary of the American Social Science Association. Subsequently during a period of ill health he returned to Germany and while there came to know some of the bankers and investment groups that had interests in America. In February, 1873, a friend at Heidelberg asked him for advice regarding the handling of an investment in the bonds of the Oregon and California Railroad. After some negotiation Villard became a member of a committee representing the German Oregon and California bondholders, a responsibility which carried him to Oregon to see the situation for himself.[6]

Villard became very enthusiastic about the possibilities of economic development in Oregon, but he was convinced that basic changes were necessary in management of the railroad. Holladay was not an easy man to deal with. The first agreement Villard worked out left Holladay in nominal control but included safeguards for the bondholders. When these were ignored Villard negotiated a new arrange-

[6] James B. Hedges, *Henry Villard and the Railways of the Northwest*, New Haven, 1930; also Henry Villard, *Early History of Transportation in Oregon*, ed. Oswald Garrison Villard, Eugene, Oregon, 1944.

ment which eliminated Holladay altogether. Villard then became director for the bondholders, who acquired control first of the Holladay rail and steamboat lines on the Willamette, and soon afterward of the Oregon Steam Navigation Company enterprises on the Columbia as well.

In this way the entire system of principal lines in Oregon was brought under one organization. Yet the transportation routes linking Oregon with the rest of the country were still only water routes. Villard therefore addressed himself to the problem of securing transcontinental connections.

Villard's approach to this task brought him to attempt one of the boldest strokes of finance in the annals of American railroading. After studying the several possibilities he came to the conclusion that the best route was the Columbia River route rather than the southern route via California or Nevada. He acquired the Oregon Steam Navigation Company, as Cooke had before him and for the same reasons. It gave him a profitable business and one that united him with the principal capitalists of Oregon. Construction began between Celilo and Wallula in 1880 and by November, 1882, there was unbroken rail service from Portland inland to the Walla Walla wheat fields. Villard was much troubled, however, by the possibility that the Northern Pacific by building down the north bank of the Columbia might parallel his own road and with its connection via Spokane to St. Paul might draw all the traffic leaving the Oregon Steam Navigation Company to wither on the vine. The answer seemed to be to reach some understanding with the Northern Pacific or, failing that, to acquire control of it, if he could.

No one thought that Villard had the resources to buy up a controlling interest in the Northern Pacific, yet that is what he now aimed to do. In 1881, skillfully concealing his purpose, he approached a group of bankers and investment people in Boston and other eastern cities and by a special appeal raised a fund of 8,000,000 dollars which he was free to use as he wished. This fund, usually referred to as the Blind Pool, he used to buy stock in the Northern Pacific until he had enough to demand representation on the Board of Directors. After a short struggle Villard gained control of the Board and became its president.

Portland thus got its first transcontinental connection over the Northern Pacific tracks. Using various corporate organizations, including such new ones as the Oregon Improvement Company and the Oregon and Transcontinental Company, Villard pushed construction vigorously, persuaded in his own mind that once the rails were laid, they would lead to a rapid economic development that would more than repay the tremendous capital outlay that was involved.

The years 1881-1883 were exciting indeed as the construction crews moved like armies across the plains and through the mountains, pushing the rails into country previously traversed only by pack animals. Engineers pressed forward from both ends at once. From Glendive they carried the line westward up the Yellowstone Valley, through Bozeman Pass to the Missouri, and thence through Mullan Pass to the Little Blackfoot River. From Wallula gangs of Chinese laborers toiled to build a right of way across the barren plateau to Lake Pend Oreille and the Clark's Fork River. Tunnels were bored through mountain barriers in the Rockies. Bridges were built across the rivers, and trestles carried the track over the narrow ravines. Along the Clark's Fork the crews struggled to penetrate dense forests which presented "a solid rampart of trunks" and made of broadest day a "somber twilight." Through the winter thousands of men wrestled with the deep snow to clear the grade and lay the track. At some points in the gorge whole mountainsides were exploded into the canyon below with blasts of powder.[7]

The trains were soon running, all the way from Portland to St. Paul. Villard drove the gold spike at Independence Creek 60 miles west of Helena on September 8, 1883. As his special train moved west its progress was attended by festivities and celebration. At Portland business firms and private citizens rivaled one another in the lavishness of their decorations and put on the biggest pageant and parade the Northwest had ever seen. At New Tacoma, where an immense triple arch spanned Pacific Avenue, there was much speech-making and banqueting. Seattle entertained its guests at an immense barbecue and clambake.

---

[7] Eugene V. Smalley, *History of the Northern Pacific Railroad*, New York, 1883.

Seattle, Lake Shore, and Eastern

Though they were encouraged by the completion of the Northern Pacific's main line, the people of Puget Sound were far from satisfied. The indirect route by way of Portland placed them at the mercy of the Oregon Railway and Navigation Company. The Tacoma group in the Northern Pacific demanded the immediate construction of the Cascade Branch which would give them a direct route from Ainsworth up the Yakima Valley and across the mountains to the Sound. The Oregon and Transcontinental, under the leadership of Elijah Smith, resisted and for several years delayed the building of it. Meanwhile Seattle citizens were indignant that the Northern Pacific should be so reluctant to build northward to their city. When the gold spike ceremonies were being held, Villard's party journeyed by train a short distance up into the Puyallup hop fields, then returned to Tacoma and took a boat to Seattle. This was a situation that no good Seattle booster could tolerate. Arthur Denny wrote a long letter to Villard urging the importance of building the line to Seattle. If the Northern Pacific refused to do so, he said, then Seattle would build its own railroad.

Seattle's struggle to become a railway terminus is an important and illuminating chapter in the history of the city. The people of the town did attempt their own railroad despite Villard's remark that it would be suicide to try it. There is something at once bold and amusing in the way the citizenry organized itself to win by energy and "indomitable spirit" what was not to be had by the gift of Congress or Wall Street. The idea that a railroad could be built by calling out the men of the community to dig and make one is typical of a frontier that was largely helpless in the new age of industrialism and Big Business but refused to give up without trying every means at hand however desperate or futile.

The town did not stop with a pick and shovel brigade, but had its own adventures with large-scale financing. Two railroad companies were organized, the Seattle and Walla Walla, and the Seattle, Lake Shore, and Eastern. The Seattle and Walla Walla represented local enterprise. The Lake Shore and Eastern was organized originally by local people, of whom Thomas Burke, a vigorous and enterprising young lawyer, and Daniel H. Gilman were the leaders, but it was launched with the express intention of finding investment capital in the eastern money centers. These promoters hoped to find men of means who would venture their capital in a western enterprise without demanding to have the control of it. Gilman made several trips back to New York and managed to get enough funds to undertake the construction of the road. The plan of organization and finance followed on a lesser scale the pattern of the transcontinentals. The railroad company would issue stocks and sell bonds. Building would be done by a construction company which would take assets of the road in payment. Both the road and the construction company would dodge the problem of raising cash, so far as possible, by depending upon the credit of the contractors who did the actual work. Just where the railroad would go was not altogether clear. It would lead from Seattle east up into the Cascades where it was believed there were iron deposits. From there it would cross the mountains to some point in Eastern Washington, and perhaps would be projected through the Rockies and across the plains to a terminal point in Iowa.[8]

There was nothing small about the plan, but unfortunately the promotional possibilities of the venture far exceeded the ability of its managers to cope with problems of ways and means. Burke was a man fertile in ideas if not in expedients. He outlined the opportunities of the railroad so persuasively that presently the directors were, like Stephen Leacock's plumed knight, "riding off in all directions" but without arriving anywhere. One section of the track led up into the Cascades and stopped. Another ran west from Spokane toward Okanogan but found nothing there. Still a third, which started bravely north from Seattle toward Bellingham, served no more useful a purpose than the others. The construction was poorly done and the eastern investors became increasingly skeptical of the whole affair. In the end the road was purchased primarily for its nuisance value; the Northern Pacific bought it up in 1890 mainly to prevent its being used against them. Though pretty much a failure it is a good example of the interrelations of western promotion and eastern capital. The

[8] For research into the history of the Seattle, Lake Shore and Eastern Railroad, the authors are indebted to Robert C. Nesbit whose work on this topic is part of a projected biography of Thomas Burke, based upon the Burke Papers at the University of Washington Library.

promoters seem to have lost little or nothing, but they failed to win much either, and certainly as railroad builders their record is not impressive. One of them, Burke, did make himself useful to James J. Hill in later years as a local representative and intermediary.

The years 1883-1893 saw the main network of the transcontinentals completed except for the Milwaukee line. In 1884 the Oregon Short Line, which had been building from its junction with the Union Pacific at Granger, Wyoming, northwest through the Snake River valley, met the tracks of the Oregon Railway and Navigation Company at Huntington, Oregon. In 1887 the Northern Pacific finished its Cascade Division through the Yakima Valley and Stampede Pass. That same year the Oregon and California railroad, now a part of the Southern Pacific system, closed the gap between Roseburg and the California line. Thus Tacoma had one direct route to the east, and Portland had two to the east and one to California. With the completion of the Great Northern Railway in 1893, Seattle became a full-fledged western terminus.

Great Northern Railway

The Great Northern illustrates the way a complex of local lines could be made strong and important by knitting them together into a single system. Unlike the Northern Pacific, this was not a land-grant railroad. James J. Hill started out with several short railroads in Minnesota and North Dakota. None of them had pretensions to the status of a transcontinental line, yet all of them served good agricultural country and under good management they developed a modest but profitable traffic. By 1886 Hill was ready to project more ambitious plans. In that year he gave his guidance and support to the organization of the Montana Central Railroad which was to build between Helena, Great Falls, and Butte. During the next two years Hill pushed the construction of his Manitoba line west from Minot, North Dakota, until it joined the Montana Central, permitting his trains to run all the way to the Rocky Mountain copper mines.[9]

The final step was to complete the section between Helena and Puget Sound. Again he supported local efforts, this time in Seattle,

[9] Joseph G. Pyle, *Life of James J. Hill*, 2 vols., Garden City, N. Y., 1917.

Everett, Fairhaven, and Vancouver, B.C. In 1889-1890 the Seattle and Montana Railroad carried its line from Seattle north to Everett and thence east up the Skykomish River. Tracks were laid by other local companies between Vancouver and Fairhaven, and between Fairhaven and Everett. In 1889 the Minneapolis and St. Cloud, a short line in Minnesota that belonged to the Manitoba, changed its name to the Great Northern Railway, and Hill undertook to forge the various parts of his empire into one piece. Building went forward steadily between Helena and Everett, and on January 6, 1893, the last spike was driven home at the tunnel mouth on the west slope of the Cascades.

One could not always count on small lines growing into big ones. The construction of feeder lines did something to distribute the benefits of the transcontinentals over the greater part of the region, but the success and importance of these local links in the chain depended largely upon the potentialities of the particular situation. Thus Port Townsend was joined with Portland and Tacoma by a feeder, yet failed to realize nearly the development that was expected to result from it. Similarly the transverse feeder lines in Oregon which cut across the Willamette Valley proved to be disappointing in their benefits. The Oregon and Southeastern, affectionately called Old Slow and Easy, was "a homely short line that meanders up the valley of the Row River a matter of twenty miles and finally bogs down in the middle of nowhere." The Corvallis and Yaquina Bay Railroad, "the frustration route," found everything perverse and never achieved the fine dream that its promoter, Colonel T. Egenton Hogg, envisioned for it. Most of the small lines in the Northwest either failed or remained only capillaries in the regional distribution. The completion of the main transcontinental arteries, however, provided a tremendous spur to economic growth. The region had been waiting a long time for a good boom. The railroads now made it a reality.[10]

[10] Randall V. Mills, *Railroads Down the Valley; Some Short Lines of the Oregon Country*, Palo Alto, California, 1950.

19

The Boom of the Eighties

The boom which followed the completion of the Northern Pacific Railroad was a double-barreled movement which, in its essential aspects, somewhat resembled a number of previous ones that contributed to the occupation of the upper Middle West. It was in part a migration of farming population to new agricultural areas in the Puget Sound country and the Inland Empire. It was also an urban movement which brought thousands of people west seeking new opportunities in the rising cities. This movement of people was further stimulated by an accelerated exploitation of the region's chief natural resources.

We do not usually turn to the census reports for exciting reading. Yet we should remember that the generation of pioneers was given to counting—population, dollars of assessed property, number of farms, value of manufactures, bushels of wheat, cans of salmon, tons of coal —for in these things they found the measure of their growth. Only a few years before they had counted their new immigration in covered wagons and in the passenger lists of the steamers from California. The railroad changed all that. Who was so dull that he did not thrill at Governor Miles C. Moore's report that 95,000 people arrived in Washington Territory during the years 1887-1889, a figure greater than the total population of the territory at the previous federal census. During the decade of the 1880's Oregon, Washington, and Idaho together gained nearly a half million (481,000) in new population, an increase more than three times as great as that of the preceding decade. Hardly less impressive was the fact that property values as reported to the Census Bureau increased fourfold to reach a total of one and a third billion dollars. In Washington the figures for assessed property and the value of manufactures stood ten times higher in

1890 than in 1880, indicating a rate of growth that was unequaled in any other state.[1]

The Progress of Agriculture

The Sound country had never been thought a good place for farming, despite the earlier successes of the Hudson's Bay Company in raising grain and breeding stock at Nisqually and the Cowlitz flats. The forests pressed in too closely upon the tilled fields and the task of clearing the land of its giant trees was so formidable that few attempted it simply to plant cereal or vegetables. Immigration bureaus made special appeals to those who had "the courage and endurance to hew themselves a home out of the forests," but there was no great response to them. In 1880 there were less than a thousand farms in the area between the Sound and the Cascade Mountains. Throughout the eighties the townspeople of Western Washingon ate flour and provisions from Portland, and beef from Ellensburg and the eastern ranges.

Yet the bottom lands were fertile in the western river valleys, and the farmers who did establish themselves there took astonishingly good crops from them. Puyallup hop ranches increased in extent between 1880 and 1890 from 500 acres to 5,000, yielded one to four tons of hops per acre, and brought to the growers returns which in good years ranged as high as 60,000 dollars. To the north, as the La Conner tidelands were diked, farmers grew oats and hay with great success and some few raised cabbages and other vegetables which because of their superior size and excellence sold for seed at fancy prices.

These were the exceptional farms but they attracted wide notice and farmers came into Western Washington in some numbers. Eighteen hundred new farms were established between the Sound and the Cascade Mountains in ten years, and crop values increased there by nearly 2,000,000 dollars. Such expansion was modest enough compared with the wheat lands across the mountains, but it set a pattern of intensive agriculture which is continued even now. Thanks

[1] In addition to the reports of the Census Bureau, see John S. Hittell, *Commerce and Industries of the Pacific Coast of North America*, San Francisco, 1882, and an article by the same author, "Boom in Western Washington," in *Overland Monthly*, XVI, n.s. September, 1890, 225-237. An excellent descriptive report for the decade of the 1880's is U.S. Treasury Dept. *Report of Internal Commerce of the United States for the Year 1890*, 51st Cong. 2d Sess., House Executive Document 6, Part II, Washington, D. C., 1891.

Typical Fish Wheel on the Columbia River. (Courtesy, Oregon Historical Society.)

Columbia River Fishing Boats Looked like Butterflies. (Courtesy, Oregon Historical Society.)

Launching a Dory from a Halibut Boat. (From Thompson and Freeman, Pacific Halibut Fishery.)

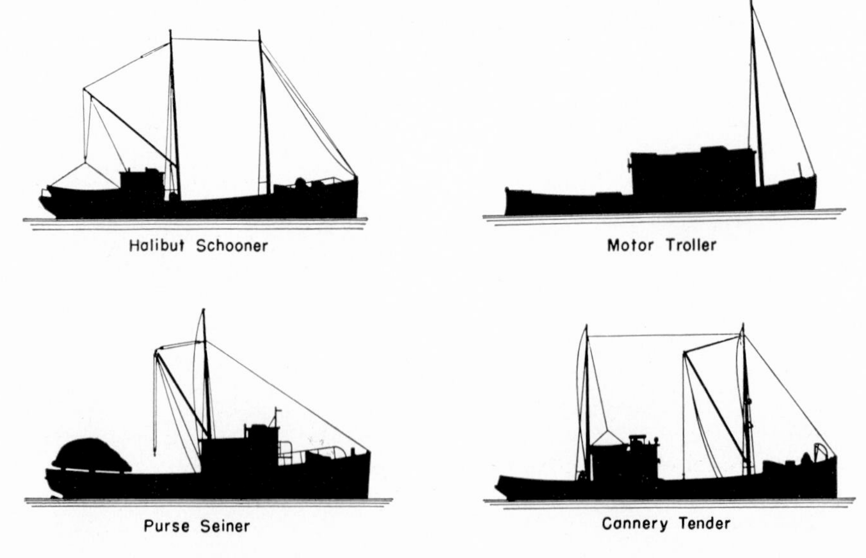

Silhouettes Showing Types of Fishing Boats. (From Pacific Fisherman.)

Today's Sportsman Takes His Own Salmon. (Courtesy, Washington State Department of Fisheries.)

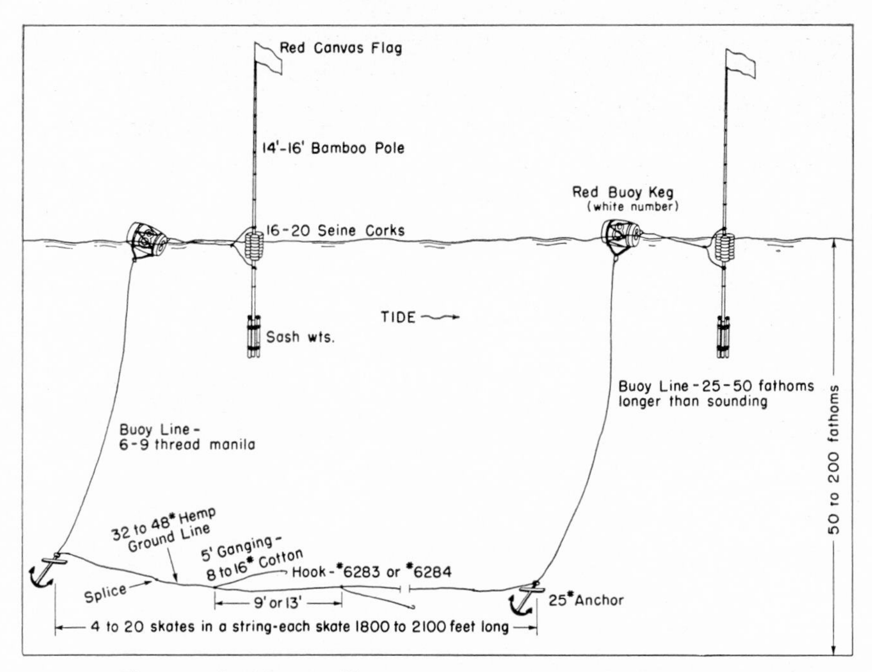

Diagram Showing the Way Halibut Gear Is Set. (From Thompson and Freeman, Pacific Halibut Fishery.)

Mt. Rainier Reflected in a Beautiful Alpine Lake. (Courtesy, University of Washington Library.)

to their specialties and high per-acre yields the Sound counties took on a new importance in agricultural production.

Meanwhile the building of railroads up the Columbia River and through the Walla Walla and Palouse country had the same tonic effect there that the Erie Canal had produced in New York and Ohio half a century earlier. In ten years time some two and a half million acres of new agricultural land was improved in Idaho, the Columbia Basin, and Wallowa districts of Oregon, and the Washington counties lying between Spokane Falls and the Oregon line. Nearly 15,000 new farms were established, and the value of farm products sold jumped from five million to fourteen million dollars representing an advance from 25 per cent to about 40 per cent of the total production of the three states. Here was a development that shifted the balance to a new section altogether. Mother Earth gave generously of her bounty in these areas. Acre for acre wheat harvests ran higher in the Palouse than in Dakota's famed Red River Valley; potato yields were higher than in Maine. Soil samples from Umatilla fields in Oregon, which Senator John Mitchell offered for analysis to the Smithsonian Institution, compared favorably with the best agricultural soils of Europe. Palouse top soils proved to be several feet deep and required nothing more than summer fallow in alternate years to produce repeated crops of grain. Failures were almost unknown and farmers who came early paid but five to ten dollars an acre for land and had no great difficulty in paying off their debts and putting money aside, even though they had only a small capital to start with. Little wonder that the settlers' handbooks warned the old-timers of the Willamette that they had a formidable rival in the Inland Empire.[2]

Under such conditions specialized agriculture took the place of grazing in the places where the rainfall was sufficient to support it. Descriptions of farms in Southeast Washington told of comfortable homes, large barns, well-fenced fields and vegetable gardens, suggesting that general farming was practiced for a time at least. Dairy products found ready markets, too, and some attention was given to them. But for the most part farmers in the grain belt specialized in

---

[2] John F. Carrère, *Spokane Falls, Washington Territory, and Its Tributary Country*, Chicago, 1889; *Settlers' Guide*, Spokane, 1885; William Parsons, *Illustrated History of Umatilla County*, Spokane, 1902; and David S. Halbaken, "History of Wheat Growing in Oregon During the Nineteenth Century," unpublished thesis, University of Oregon, 1948.

wheat, with oats and barley figuring as secondary grains. This was the kind of operation that gave the section its picturesque character. Many a farmer cultivating the steep slopes of the Palouse found the seat on his machine a precarious perch indeed. Twenty mules or horses drew the harvesters and considerable skill was required to manage them. Pictures of steam combines illustrate the way agriculture was mechanized in the Umatilla section where gentler grades permitted it. This was a far cry from the days when Oregon's first farming frontier was occupied by settlers who came over the plains in a wagon, tilled their fields with only the simplest of machinery, and considered themselves lucky to send a little grain to California. In the Inland Empire agriculture was commercial from the beginning, and those who were most successful there were those who equipped themselves with the improved machinery and began at once to use the same large-scale methods that were proving so profitable in California and the Middle West.

Cattle and Sheep

As the plows and harvesters invaded the bunch grass areas of Eastern Oregon and Washington, cattle men from Klickitat and Yakima complained that running large herds was coming to be a thing of the past. The open ranges were fast disappearing and farmers were agitating for herd laws to control the wandering animals. Nevertheless the eighties were good years. There was ample grazing in the more arid and inaccessible parts of the Columbia Basin and in Eastern Oregon where steers might roam at large for the greater part of the year. The larger ranchers secured their own fattening grounds by purchasing extensive tracts of land, and improved their herds by more careful breeding. Many of their smaller competitors gave up and joined the homeseekers. Most important of all, Montana stockmen bought thousands of head of cattle in the Far West to build up the industry on the northern high plains.[3]

[3] James O. Oliphant, "Cattle Trade from the Far Northwest to Montana" in *Agricultural History*, VI, 1932, 69-83; Oliphant, "Eastward Movement of Cattle from the Oregon Country" in *Agricultural History*, XX, 1946, 19-43; also John Minto, "Sheep Husbandry in Oregon" in *OHQ*, III, 1902, 219-247; John Minto, E. A. Carman, and H. A. Heath, *Special Report on the History and Present Condition of the Sheep Industry of the United States*, U.S. Dept. of Agriculture, Washington, D.C., 1892, 976-991.

During the early eighties the herds were moved eastward across the Rockies to the plains in large drives of 600 to 1,000 animals which followed the Mullan road or a more southern route through Boise and the Snake River valley. With the completion of the Northern Pacific, special rates were offered on cattle and large shipments were made by rail. In 1884, 4,000 head went from Idaho to Miles City. The following year heavy shipments were sent from far western territories to the Yellowstone country and to Fort Benton. Cattle were driven to the nearest railroad shipping points from Idaho's Big Bend, from Northeastern Oregon and from the Yakima Valley in Washington. Rail men reported that some 34,000 head of cattle and as many sheep were shipped from stations west of the Rockies just before the disastrous Montana winter of 1886-1887. These heavy purchases put an end to thoughts of overproduction, especially when the growers enjoyed a steadily increasing demand from Portland, San Francisco, and Puget Sound. Even though the Montana trade declined in the latter years of the decade, the rising cities of the Far West promised substantial local markets. Packing houses in Portland increased their production, while Seattle, Tacoma, and Spokane built up their facilities to meet the local demand. Stock men of the Inland Empire took pride in their horses, too. Pendleton sent riding horses and draught animals to farm and city alike, and developed breeds for every purpose from racing to hauling streetcars. The annual round-up at Pendleton and the Ellensburg rodeo recall these early days when the two towns made their reputation from horses and cattle.

Wool-growing likewise expanded eastward across the Cascades and became one of the big industries of the Inland Empire. Sheep men kept bands of from 1,500 to 12,000 head, and in good years made profits of 100 percent on their cost. Herders contested bitterly with the cattle ranchers for the control of the ranges, and more and more of them drove their flocks to the higher feeding grounds well up in the mountains. In Eastern Oregon the Harney Valley became an important sheep area, while Umatilla, Morrow, and Crook counties reported in 1890 572,000 head. Many Washington bands wintered on the Snake River and went for summer pasture to the Idaho mountains. Others from south of the Snake went to the Blue Mountains, while those in Central Washington went to Colville or to summer ranges in the Coeur d'Alenes. In five years in the early eighties Eastern Oregon doubled its wool clip from 3,800,000 pounds to 7,700,000. Fleeces from Southwestern Oregon commanded premium prices because of their even texture, the result of more favorable climate and careful breeding, and the Western Oregon product generally was considered better in quality than that from the interior. But in quantity the eastern counties far outstripped the western. One hundred thousand sheep were sheared near Sprague in 1889. Considerable numbers of animals were driven to Montana, and the railroads took many more, shipping them on cars specially double-decked for the purpose. The sheep industry, like the cattle industry, declined somewhat in importance with the progress of settlement but 10,000,000 pounds of wool were being shipped through Pendleton and the Dalles in the early nineties and by the end of the century Pendleton had become the chief primary market for wool in the United States.

Thus in new areas and in old, agriculture and its allied enterprises held out their promise of greater opportunity during the early railroad period as they had during the years of steamboats and freighting wagons. From his observation post at Port Townsend John B. Alexander, the British vice consul, remarked that the people were "betaking themselves to the country" to engage in farming east of the mountains. Idaho publicists spoke with satisfaction of "our industrious pioneers" who in the space of a few years put 600,000 acres of land under cultivation in the Snake River valley.

Yet the progress of agriculture was less substantial than other forms of enterprise. In 1880 Oregon's farms represented nearly half its total assessed wealth as reported to the federal census bureau; ten years later they stood for only 27 percent. Washington's farms declined similarly from 31 percent to 14 percent of that territory's assessed wealth. In Idaho the figure remained unchanged at 18 percent. The explanation is to be found in the greatly increased exploitation of the region's natural resources and in the tremendously rapid growth of its cities. Illustrative of this new importance of resources is the growth of the lumber industry in Western Washington and of mining in Eastern Washington and Idaho.

Lumbering in the Eighties

Paul Bunyan, hero of the logging camps, hardly showed his strength in Oregon and Washington until the eighties, but then what an amazing young giant he grew to be. Hustling to keep up with the hungry, whining saws, which consumed in 1884 a million board feet a day, he pushed farther and farther along the shores of Puget Sound and back inland up the river courses. In Washington 160,000,000 feet came from his ax in 1880; a decade later his annual cut passed the billion mark. Southwest of Olympia in the Satsop and Chehalis districts great acreages of magnificent forests, averaging 50,000 to 60,000 feet to the acre, fell before him and were brought down to tidewater mills by logging railroads. In Thurston County only half the original stand of timber remained in 1890. Pope and Talbot mills at Port Ludlow and Port Gamble took their logs from a wide area extending up Hood Canal and along the western shore of the Sound as well. Large new mills at Seattle and Tacoma reached out to take in their rafts all along the Sound.

Here was an industry which grew primarily out of a plentiful supply of cheap raw materials and expanded rapidly as new markets opened up. Standing timber cost but a third to a half of the average for the country as a whole, and while the value of the sawed lumber was correspondingly lower, the margin of profit was sufficiently large to stimulate a considerable investment of new capital.[4]

The average mill in Oregon in 1890 was a 25,000-dollar plant instead of the 7,000-dollar mill typical of the earlier years. At Port Blakeley near Seattle a new mill, built after fire had gutted the old one, boasted engines that developed 3,000 horsepower and saws that handled 150-foot logs and counted 300,000 board feet an ordinary day's work. Operating figures for the lumber industry in Washington as a whole ran ten to 15 times larger than they had been a decade before. At the beginning of statehood the logging camps and mills represented a 20,000,000-dollar investment, delivered a 15,000,000-dollar annual product, and supported 10,000 men with their 4,000,000-dollar payroll.

[4] Edmond S. Meany, Jr., "History of the Lumber Industry in the Pacific Northwest to 1917," unpublished thesis, Harvard University, 1935.

Lumbering in the Northwest was a wasteful business which drew sharp criticism upon itself for its spendthrift methods. Paul Bunyan often cut his stumps 20 feet in the air, and while he argued that the lower trunks were shaky and full of pitch, it was nevertheless true that much good wood, if not the best, was left on the ground. At the mills the huge double-bladed rotary saws converted half an inch of log into sawdust at every cut and raised huge piles of slabs and mill ends to be burned. Logs and timbers were cut at random lengths and no one paid much attention to the standard grades and dimensions that were commonly accepted and used in other parts of the country.

Some of these practices were improving, to be sure, as better and more powerful machinery was introduced. The newly developed donkey engine did the work of many oxen in snaking the great logs out of the woods, and band saws were found to be far more efficient than the rotary type for large logs. Yet it was only as stumpage values increased that there was real incentive to develop methods that fully utilized the wood in the entire tree. Such an upward trend was beginning to take place, partly because of wider opportunities in the lumber trade and partly because of the rapid transfer of timber lands from the public domain to private ownership.

The Lumber Trade

Northwest lumber had long been something like Robinson Crusoe's pile of gold; there was lots of it but it was worth very little since there was so little opportunity to use it. The railroads did not altogether change this situation, but they did bring about a striking enlargement of the local market and make possible the shipment of substantial quantities of lumber to the Inland Empire and the western Middle West.

California continued to be the lumberman's best customer, and the ocean trade along the coast rose to nearly 200,000,000 board feet in 1883-1884 and to 323,600,000 in 1889. Exports to foreign countries also increased. Scores of square-riggers found shelter in the protected harbor at Port Townsend while their captains negotiated for cargo at the various mill ports on the Sound. One hundred and forty-eight vessels, registered in a dozen different countries, made up the Sound's lumber fleet. Norwegian barks cleared for Melbourne, and Chilean ships took rough lumber to Valparaiso. American ships weighed anchor at Port Blakeley bound for Buenos Aires, Boston, Honolulu, and for Brisbane and Shanghai. Swedish vessels left for London and Pt. Pirie; British for Adelaide and Sydney. Some of these cargoes amounted to a million feet of lumber, each, and were valued at 10,000 dollars to 12,000 dollars. They were the exceptional ones, however. Ordinary cargoes ranged from 1,000 dollars to 6,000 dollars in value and many were small shipments worth only a few hundred dollars. The export trade was not, therefore, as valuable as the number of ships would suggest. Lumbering was geared mainly to the domestic markets and it was only the surplus that found its way to foreign ports. Even during the latter part of the decade the export trade amounted to little more than 1,000,000 dollars, which compared to the 15,000,000 dollars total is hardly impressive.

The domestic trade was the trade that made the significant gains. Statistics are lacking to measure it accurately, but we have reports that point out in a general way at least the growing importance of local and interior markets. In Washington, where the cargo mills had been cutting only one-tenth of their product for home consumption, firms like Stetson and Post of Seattle began producing entirely for local needs. Building booms that accompanied the influx of large numbers of new immigrants increased the demand tremendously, and the mills were quick to respond to it. New small mills situated east of the Cascades partially met the needs of the Inland Empire and western mills supplied the rest. Treasury officials estimated that this local trade exceeded the California trade in 1885 and grew to be twice as large in the next five years.

The development of the lumber industry in the area tributary to Portland came as a result of the growing trade with the Middle West, carried on via the Union Pacific railway. Experimental shipments to Denver, Salt Lake City, and Omaha led to a trade amounting to some 5,000,000 dollars per month, with a single mill sending as much as 26,000,000 feet to these cities of the Rockies and High Plains. Favorable freight rates gave Oregon an advantage over Puget Sound in commerce with these points and for a number of years she claimed it as her own, save for the cedar shingles which Washington sent to Colorado and Utah as well as to Iowa, Illinois, and Ohio. Rates proved to be a shifting and unpredictable element which worked against the Northwest section as often as for it. Portland's trade with Denver was highly sensitive to any change in the Union Pacific rate level, and Puget Sound found it difficult to supply the Montana market because of rates which favored St. Paul even though that city was much farther away. Rail charges were a factor which might spell the difference between success and failure, and bitter struggles were waged between rival communities and between different sections to secure a revision of rates in favor of one or another. Even with this wider and more complex pattern of competition, the trade of the Northwest with the interior showed an encouraging increase. Lumbermen might have to share their new markets with the producers of southern pine, but their own share grew in encouraging fashion, and was the foundation of a trade that would be expanded rapidly in the future.

Thus the lumber industry experienced a strong stimulus which, both in its brighter and its darker aspects, was typical of frontier experience under the impact of industrialism. Capital was supplied in larger sums than ever before were available. Markets were opened up which hitherto had not existed or could not be reached. Employment rose to levels which had never been attained previously. All these were evidences of greater productivity which did much to support, directly or indirectly, an expanded regional economy.

Rise of Industrial Mining

The development of the mining districts of the Inland Empire revealed in much the same way the importance of industrialized methods for frontiers which were blessed with abundant natural resources. In Idaho, in Western Montana, and in sections of Eastern Washington new machinery and large-scale processes of extraction and reduction revived the mining industry and made it a principal enterprise.[5]

To be sure, placer mining was in the Idaho tradition and the tradition persisted at a number of the places—Elk City, Florence, Oro Fino, Warren's Diggings—which had been famous 25 years before. These lonely villages were still almost completely isolated,

[5] *Spokane Miner*, Columbia World's Fair Edition, 1893; also annual reports, *Mineral Resources of the United States*, published by the U.S. Geological Survey.

linked with the outside world only by 150 miles of primitive trails over which pack animals gingerly picked their way. Only the best mining grounds could be worked profitably under such conditions, but even without roads or railroads Idaho county continued to rank first in the territory for its gold dust and reported recent discoveries of quartz as well. Most of it was gold that a man might have for the digging and washing it out, without going to London for capital or to Denver for machinery. The lure of the placers was still strong in the mountains, and reports of a strike still put fever in the blood. When in 1883 the rumor went around that dust and nuggets had been discovered at Coeur d'Alene, hundreds of prospectors hurried to the new diggings, heedless of the winter's cold and the lack of provisions.

But the day of the placer mine was passing. At many of the old locations the gold was largely gone and the army of miners moved on leaving behind them ghost towns rich only in their memories. Coeur d'Alene was a job for heavy equipment and the placer miners found little there but suffering and disappointment. Placers were for the most part short-lived enterprises which were quite undependable as the base for a stable economy. In 1881 the production of precious metals was only 3,000,000 dollars, a third to a fourth of what it had been during the peak years of 1865-1866. Faced with this prospect of declining returns, Idaho made her comeback through advances in industrialized mining which represented in 1890 a plant value of 44,000,000 dollars and produced ores worth 17,000,000 dollars. Meanwhile prospectors met with some success in the Okanogan and Colville country and over at Butte, Montana, the Anaconda Copper Company, amid operations of some secrecy, began the sinking of shafts which would soon challenge the primacy of Hecla and Calumet, Michigan's famed producers.

Industrial mining lacked some of the picturesqueness and excitement of the placer operations, but there was a good bit of color in it nevertheless. Prospectors were still in evidence and while they might not have the thrill of washing out 50 or 100 dollars in a single pan, they often realized their profits on a much larger scale by selling or bonding their claims to eastern or foreign mining companies. Mining experts examined the ore fields and ledges, developed new hydraulic machinery to exploit the more stubborn placer grounds, and set up elaborate stamp mills and concentrators to handle the complex ores. Steam power was put to the aid of the miner's pick and shovel, and while the big machines might devour two to 20 tons of ore to take out 500 dollars worth of metal, they were of such large capacity that some of them at least brought clear profits to their owners of 25 percent. The Old Dominion boasted a 50-ton concentrator and 80-horsepower compressor which ran four Ingersoll drills to produce three cars of ore per week at 2,300 dollars value for each carload.[6] The Bunker Hill and Sullivan mines at Wardner developed a capacity of 2,000,000 dollars gross production per year, and properties at Canyon Creek produced at a capacity of 5,000,000 dollars per year. In Idaho as a whole the gold and silver mines supported a 3,300,000-dollar payroll and gave direct employment to 4,500 men.

These operations depended upon cheap transportation over great distances, for the chief reduction plants and the markets to which the metals must be sent were hundreds of miles away. Railroads held the secret of successful mining, and those who had an interest in these new enterprises bent their energies to the construction of feeder lines which would make them accessible from the recently completed transcontinentals. Spokane took the lead in this effort. Clearly sensing what the trade with the mining communities would mean to her, she pushed very aggressively the building of lines from Spokane to the Coeur d'Alene mining towns and to the new districts that promised to open up in the Colville and Okanogan country. If she were to become the metropolis of the Inland Empire, the northern mines might mean as much to her as the rich agricultural districts lying to the south.

Urban Expansion

Farming, lumber, and mining thus underlined, each in its own way, the importance of resources for the development of the Pacific Northwest. Hardly less important was the vigorous growth of cities in the region. In some respects this urban growth stood out in sharp contrast to the scattering of population over wide areas of farming country and to the growth of exploitative industries which were not in the main of a type to draw a heavy population at all. In reality, however, the cities, farms, mills, and mines all came

[6] *Ibid.*

together, and each was related to the others. How intimate the relation was it is difficult to say. Certainly the years of rapid growth were marked by speculative expansion which had little real connection with the development of regional resources, but was rather the expression of the boom spirit of the times. On the other hand, the lively growth which these communities enjoyed was part of a strong urban movement which made itself felt in every part of the country. Sociologists expressed their surprise that the urban trend should be as marked in frontier areas as in the older industrial sections, but the figures showed it to be true. The number of cities was indeed small; that was the pattern throughout the trans-Mississippi West. Nevertheless the rise of Seattle and Tacoma on the Sound and of Spokane in the Inland Empire brought about a new balance of metropolitan centers in the Northwest which was considerably more decentralized and complex than that which had existed during the earlier period of Portland's preëminence.

The importance of urban growth during the years of expansion, 1880-1910, is plainly seen in a simple analysis of the census reports. During the decade of the eighties Oregon's city dwellers increased from 14.8 percent of the total population to 26.8 percent. By 1900 the figure had risen to 32.2 percent; in 1910 it was 45.6 percent. In Washington the percentages were even more striking. In 1880 the population in the territory was 90 percent rural. Ten years later when the state was admitted to the Union it was 35.6 percent urban and by 1910, 53 percent urban. This meant that the migration of new population to Oregon and Washington during these years was to a surprising degree an urban movement. One in five of Oregon's new population 1880-1890 could be found (statistically) in Portland and 41 percent settled in the urban counties of Multnomah and Marion. Three urban counties in Washington (King, Pierce, and Spokane) received a full one-half of the new population, and the three cities of Seattle, Tacoma, and Spokane took one of every three new residents who came to the territory. Thus while the rural counties received their thousands of new population, the cities counted their gains in tens of thousands. Portland jumped from 17,500 to 46,385. Seattle, a frontier town of 3,533 population in 1880, became a bustling city nearly as large as Portland in 1890 (42,837). Tacoma enjoyed a similar growth (1,098 to 36,006) and Spokane, which was scarcely more than a village (350), emerged as a lively center of nearly 20,000.

Whether one viewed these rough growing communities sympathetically or wrote of them in a vein of skepticism depended upon the observer's attitude toward them. John Muir who visited Puget Sound in 1888 spoke of Seattle and Tacoma as lively, progressive, and aspiring places, young and loose-jointed but "fast taking on the forms and manners of old cities, putting on airs, some would say, like boys in haste to be men." Rudyard Kipling, passing through the Northwest a year later, commented on the way the men of Portland fought tooth and nail for wharf, rail, and wharfage projects, and worked their lives out for what they conceived to be the city's natural prosperity. "All this is excellent and exactly suitable to the opening of a new country, but when a man tells you it is civilization, you object." At Tacoma the British author found a scene of feverish activity. Apparently he shared the feelings of a friend who protested, "They are all mad here, all mad. A man nearly pulled a gun on me because I didn't agree with him that Tacoma was going to whip San Francisco on the strength of carrots and potatoes." Kipling stopped only briefly at Tacoma then escaped to Victoria "to draw breath." An American city at the height of its boom was too much for him.[7]

The spirited zeal of the northwest city builders produced striking changes and contrasts during these years. One could sit in a bedizened barroom in Portland, complete with telephone and clicker, and in half an hour be out in the depths of the forest. Tacoma's streets were quite likely to end abruptly in a 15-foot drop and nest of brambles. Huge stumps stood at the very doors of her best hotels. Drunken telegraph and light wires clung precariously to tottering posts. In the crowded streets ox drivers mingled with dudes and with agents for everything under the sun. Everywhere was the raw new smell of fresh sawdust.

But there were electric lights and gasworks and five-story business blocks in these cities, and streetcars nosing their way about the hills. There were pretentious residences, built in imitation of the very best on Nob Hill, San Francisco. There were institutions of culture and

[7] John Muir, *Picturesque California and the Region West of the Rocky Mountains, from Alaska to Mexico*, 2 vols., San Francisco, 1888; and Rudyard Kipling, *From Sea to Sea, Letters of Travel*, 2 vols., New York, 1899-1900.

education and public information. Seattle had its university; Tacoma its female seminary at which the natives bade their visitors marvel. Visiting musicians and dramatists drew audiences to the theaters and opera houses. Each city had its churches and social organizations, and long lists of newspapers, dailies and weeklies, including a few Scandinavian and German language papers for the immigrant groups who brought to these places, like those of the East and Middle West, a cosmopolitan atmosphere.

Fire played its part in making changes. Kipling, coming to Seattle only a few weeks after fire had wiped out a good part of the business section of the town, spoke of the "horrible black smudge, as though a Hand had come down and rubbed the place smooth." This city was built up not once but twice in a short space of years, once in the jerry-built wooden structures so characteristic of the frontier town, a second time in permanent buildings of stone and cement.

Commerce and industry utilized the natural resources of the region but they expanded largely in response to the needs of the rapidly growing population. Portland produced not only lumber and wood products but "beer and buggies, and bricks and biscuit." By 1890 the manufacturing plants in the city turned out products valued at 25,400,000 dollars. Flour milling was a million-dollar industry and the flour mills were more important to the city than the sawmills. Four different railroads poured into Portland's lap the varied products of mines and forests and farms. A published list of goods received from the East for distribution included a wide variety of implements and machines, wagons and farm tools, stoves and safes, pianos, organs, and sewing machines. The shipping trade to the Sound by rail amounted to three-quarters of a million dollars. The coastwise trade amounted to nearly 5,000,000 dollars; the foreign export trade to 6,600,000 dollars, 80 percent of which was shipments of wheat and flour.

In Seattle the major lines of manufacturing were those related to construction and to foods and clothing. Lumber mills and slaughterhouses, foundries, carpentry and masonry work, canneries and flour mills—these enterprises gave employment to a full one-half of Seattle's labor force and turned out one-half of its manufactures. The city had a dozen sawmills by 1890 and nearly as many sash and door and furniture plants. Her manufactures produced crackers and canned salmon; soda water, ice, and cigars; pumps, stump-pullers, and donkey engines; heavy castings, brass machine work, and the fancy roof ornaments that gave a touch of elegance to the houses of the day. Tacoma claimed more lumber-working plants than any other city on the coast, and more wholesale drygoods, hardware, and grocery establishments than either Seattle or Spokane. Here were located the big Northern Pacific railroad shops, the smelter, which was the city's bid for importance in the metallurgical industry, and the huge grain elevators capable of storing as much as 2,000,000 bushels of grain. Alert to the importance of linking rail and water transportation, Tacoma made much of the network of steamship lines which offered service twice daily to other Sound communities and twice each week to San Francisco. Wharfage and handling services were provided at one-third the rates charged at Portland, and towing, pilotage and lighterage costs were only a tenth of those on the Columbia. Through these competitive advantages Tacoma sought to challenge Portland's supremacy in the grain trade. Forty-four cargoes, worth nearly 3,000,000 dollars were shipped to England alone during the years 1888-1890.

Spokane's rise was meteoric, but the businessmen there stoutly maintained that theirs was no mushroom growth since it had the strength of the rich surrounding country. The city had natural advantages, to be sure. Its water-power resources, estimated at 150,000 to 215,000 horsepower capacity, were pronounced by a visitor from Lowell, Massachusetts, to be the best on the continent, and Edison Electric quickly installed there what was said to be the largest incandescent light plant west of the Rockies. Its strategic location as a rail center and crossroads of stage and wagon routes permitted it to tap the wealth of the Palouse grain fields and the Coeur d'Alene mines as well, and gave it a commanding position as a marketing and distribution center for the northern intermountain territory. But it was the general development of the country that supported the city. Twenty towns in the wheat belt to the south looked increasingly to Spokane for equipment and supplies. Several thousands of miners in the Idaho mountains had to be fed. This was the reason for the rapid increase of Northern Pacific rail receipts which soon reached 200,000 dollars per month. This was the basis for the 10,000,000-dollar total in business transactions, claimed by the city's 590 business establishments in 1889. With wool and flour near at hand to be processed and ample supplies of lumber at St. Joe and Coeur d'Alene, Spokane had some reason to exclaim exuberantly, "Anything can go here with the surrounding country building up."

The urban boom affected not only the larger centers but some of the smaller ones as well. Centralia in two years time grew from a sleepy village of 600 to a lively trading center of 3,000 population and thought of itself as the future "great inland metropolis of Western Washington." Ellensburg enjoyed a short period of speculative activity based on real estate promotion and schemes involving the supply trade to the Okanogan country and the establishment of an iron and steel industry that would make Ellensburg "the Pittsburgh of the West."[8] Pocatello, Idaho, thrived as the Oregon Short Line went through. Port Townsend developed grandiose ideas from the furnaces at Irondale and dreams of building a navy yard and seaport 70 miles nearer the ocean than the "overgrown towns" up the Sound.

But such townsite booming as this did not always succeed. There was a vast difference between a purely speculative expansion on borrowed money and the growth of a city which was solidly supported by resources and competitive advantages. The pace was a fast one. The leading cities quickly established themselves and the smaller ones soon fell behind and became reconciled to the status of secondary trading centers. The boom as a whole was brought to an abrupt halt during the panic and depression years 1893-1897. Portland had less capital in industry in 1900 than she had ten years before and her manufacturing payroll was smaller by 2,000,000 dollars. Tacoma and Seattle registered gains but they were small ones. For several years trading was dull and a number of aspiring communities never revived the bright dreams of progress which they had cherished so confidently only a few years earlier. Fortune was a fickle goddess and when good times returned again and the Yukon gold rush brought new treasure and new population to the Northwest, the larger centers reaped the profits more than ever while the lesser ones rarely achieved more than a local importance. The boom years of the eighties are still a bright spot in the memory of these communities that expected much of the future only to have History prove them wrong.

[8] Samuel R. Mohler, "Boom Days in Ellensburg, 1888-1891" in *PNQ*, XXXVI, 1945, 289-308.

20

The Statehood Movement in Washington and Idaho

It was no accident of history that brought statehood to six far western territories within the three years 1889-1891. Washington, Montana, and the two Dakotas were admitted to the Union by the Omnibus Bill of 1889. Idaho and Wyoming were admitted under separate enabling acts passed by Benjamin Harrison's Republican Congress the following year. Each of these territories had a history of its own. Washington's was linked with Oregon and dated back to the overland migration to the Pacific coast during the fifties. Territorial government in Idaho and Montana was a natural consequence of the gold rush to the northern Rocky Mountains a decade later. The early settlement of the Dakotas and Wyoming was part of the occupation of the high plains which took place after the Civil War. Yet whatever the circumstances of their first development and organization as territories, the Northern Pacific Railroad was the life line for all of them. Each territory gained rapidly in population, and as it did so the need for a full-fledged state government became greater. At the same time the greater number of inhabitants and the developing industries promised new revenues to pay the costs of government. Thus the several territories not only expanded together economically but advanced together as a group politically as well. Their admission to the Union was in part a matter of national politics which affected them all. But behind this was the fact of common growth and expansion that stemmed from the completion of the northern transcontinental railroad.

To be sure, the territorials did not look upon statehood as something to be deferred until the transcontinentals were finished. The people of Oregon had won statehood for themselves without railroads, as had half a score of other territories in the Mississippi Valley somewhat earlier. Population requirements had not been strictly enforced, and while the general rule was that a territory must have enough people to elect a representative to the lower house of Congress under the federal ratio (125,000 population in 1870), there had been several exceptions to it. The people of Washington and to a lesser extent of Idaho looked ahead to statehood as something to be realized rather quickly and easily. It was a keen disappointment to them that so long a time should elapse before they won it.

Weaknesses of Territorial Government

The settlers of Puget Sound and the Inland Empire were particularly restive under territorial rule. To many of them such a regime was, as Orange Jacobs of Washington asserted in Congress, "in direct conflict with the sentiments of the American people and the genius of our government." Territorial administration was a kind of colonialism little better in their eyes than the British rule from which their colonial forbears had escaped a century before. Jefferson P. Kidder, delegate from Dakota Territory expressed the views of many people in the Far West too when he declared that the territories no less than the states should be guaranteed by the federal constitution a republican, that is, a representative form of government.

In a number of respects territorial government was not representative. Governors, judges, and lesser administrative officials were not chosen by the people but rather were appointed by the president, usually in recognition of services rendered in party politics elsewhere. Some of them identified themselves with the communities to which they were sent, but a number of them looked upon their assignment to the Far West as a kind of exile and found many pretexts and excuses to be absent from their posts. The territorial legislature in Washington found it necessary to memorialize Congress, calling their attention to the fact that "many of the officers, both Executive and Judicial, appointed by the Federal Government for this Territory, have been frequently absent from their posts of duty, and for so long a time as seriously to embarrass the Territory, and interfere, to a very great degree, with the administration of Justice among us." The problem became so serious that penalties had to be enforced so that officers who were absent without sufficient reason suffered deductions in pay. During the later years the situation was somewhat improved. Men were appointed who were residents of the territories they served, and a number of them served faithfully and well. But these happy instances of good appointments did not conceal the weakness of the system, and the territorials complained bitterly about it.

Territorial populations enjoyed somewhat more of the privileges of self-government in the choice of legislators, but here too they had their grievances. Members of the territorial assemblies were locally elected. Their powers in matters of legislation were quite broad and they sometimes contested successfully with the governor for the control of local patronage. On the other hand, they were limited in many matters by restrictions in the organic law. After 1866 they faced the possibility of a governor's veto of legislative bills, and it was always theoretically possible (though it rarely happened in practice) that Congress would disallow some bill that they had passed. While the extent to which Congress could legislate directly for the territories was a somewhat controversial subject, there were a number of instances when it happened and this deepened the feeling in the West that Congress was encroaching in matters that ought to be left to the wishes of the people. The territorial delegate in Congress was popularly elected, but he had only a voice, not a vote. In the election of president and vice-president the territorials had no part whatever.

Certain very practical problems required statehood for their solution. School lands did not become fully available for educational purposes until a territory was admitted to the Union, and other land grants from the public domain and proceeds from the sale of federal lands likewise depended upon admission. Private titles in tidelands were uncertain and the boundaries which set off one territory from another remained subject to change by Congress, making dismemberment a real and present danger. Federal appropriations were niggardly and would doubtless remain so until congressional representatives acquired the political lever of voting power. Population and investment capital could be expected to come to the far Northwest only when the national government expressed its confidence in the area by granting statehood. Territorial government was, then, a kind of administration that was acceptable only so long as a small population, possessed of insufficient means, found advantage in having the federal treasury pay most of the bills.[1]

Proposals of Partition

For some time the problem of stabilizing territorial boundaries was difficult to resolve. Subdividing territories as they became more populous was of course a practice of long standing. Washington had once been part of Oregon Territory and Idaho a part of Washington. Idaho lost territory to Montana in 1864 and to Wyoming four years later. On the whole there was little opposition to dividing large sprawling territories into smaller ones of a size suitable for states. But in the Inland Empire and the Rocky Mountains the future pattern of state boundaries was not yet clear. Who could say whether the Walla Walla country should be part of Washington rather than part of Oregon as the Oregonians proposed in 1858? Was the Idaho panhandle related more naturally to the Boise basin or to Eastern Washington or to the mining districts of Western Montana? These were questions to which one could never be sure he had the final answer so long as the territorial boundaries could be drawn and redrawn at will in Washington, D.C. Statehood would bring a permanent decision, for each state would be protected by the federal constitution against being subdivided except by its own consent.

These questions involved the destinies of several political communities and they were hotly debated whenever the subject of statehood was raised. The transfer of Walla Walla to Oregon was viewed as outright dismemberment in the rest of Washington Territory. The issue caused such an outcry in 1876 that both the major parties declared themselves against it, despite the fact that in Walla Walla itself there was considerable sentiment in favor of it. There it was felt that the area was oriented toward Portland because of the Columbia River waterway, and it was believed that growth would come more quickly if the district were joined to Oregon. The annexation of the Idaho panhandle to Washington encountered less resistance. For a

[1] Earl S. Pomeroy, *Territories and the United States, 1861-90*, Philadelphia, 1947; Robert C. Nesbit, "Territorial Viewpoints: the Popular Election of Officials," *PNQ*, XLV, 1954, 46; Wilfred Airey, "History of the Constitution and Government of Washington Territory," unpublished thesis, University of Washington, 1945; Keith Murray, "Movement Toward Statehood in Washington," unpublished thesis, University of Washington, 1940.

time Southern Idaho acquiesced in the plan and it seemed likely that it would go through. In both cases politics in the end decided against the proposed changes, and the boundaries of 1864 were allowed to stand.[2]

If population was to be the first requirement of statehood then Washington Territory badly needed both Walla Walla and Northern Idaho. In 1878 Washington, Idaho and Wyoming combined could hardly claim a population sufficiently large to entitle them to one representative to the lower house of Congress (125,000). Washington estimated hers at 75,000 including the Idaho panhandle. However, Congress had made several exceptions to the usual 125,000 minimum. Oregon, Nevada, and Nebraska had all joined the Union with less than that.

Washington's First Constitution, 1878

A good case could be made for admitting Washington as well; at least the territorial politicians thought so. A measure was prepared and submitted to a popular vote, which provided for the calling of a convention to draw up a state constitution. It passed by a majority of 4,000; hardly an impressive vote, but a favorable one nonetheless. In December, 1877, Orange Jacobs, the territorial delegate, introduced a bill in Congress which would have admitted Washington as a state as soon as the constitution was ratified by the people. Without waiting for Congress to act, the territorial legislature went ahead with the calling of a convention, which assembled at Walla Walla during the summer of 1878 and drew up a state constitution.

This first draft of Washington's constitution reflected the frontier conditions under which it was written and at the same time expressed the broader current of western agrarian thinking on matters of governmental reform. It was the work of fifteen men, none of whom represented a town of more than 5,000 people. Necessarily it dealt with problems of public administration with which the convention delegates had had little or no experience. When fiscal matters were under consideration, the newspaper reporter, to whom the task of keeping

[2] C. S. Kingston, "Walla Walla Separation Movement," *WHQ*, XXIV, 1933, 91-104; and "North Idaho Annexation," *ibid.*, XXI, 1930, 133-137, 204-217, 281-293; Merle Wells, "Territorial Government in the Inland Empire; the Movement to Create Columbia Territory, 1864-1869," *PNQ*, XLIV, 1953, 80-87.

minutes had been assigned, confessed that he had considerable difficulty in following the discussion and remarked that the speakers seemed to be in deep water. Corruption in government and the exercise of power by private corporations were generally recognized to be serious problems, yet the delegates were unable to devise effective measures to cope with them.

The proposed constitution contained a number of provisions which, though forthright in their purpose, could hardly have been effective. One stipulation considered the possibility that a member of the legislature might have a personal interest in a bill, and required him to declare it and refrain from voting on the measure. Another had to do with the indifference of officials to their public duties, and directed them to devote their personal attention to their office. Since justices were tempted by fees and supplementary considerations, they were forbidden to accept anything but their salaries. Because treasurers might be corrupted by handling the state's money, the constitution limited them to no more than a single term. To prevent corporations from watering and inflating their stock, a clause of the constitution restricted them to the issue of securities for labor, services, money, or property actually received.

In matters of public finance, the convention was so much concerned with the necessity of keeping government inexpensive that they wrote in various requirements of economy that would have been better left to future generations to decide for themselves. Salaries were stipulated at low fixed figures. Public indebtedness was limited to 100,000 dollars which was to be paid off on a ten-year schedule. No debt was to be contracted by the state for work or internal improvements. Cities were limited to a debt not to exceed 3 percent of property valuations, and not greater than could be paid off in 12 years with a 12-mill tax. Such limitations as these may have been appropriate for the existing situation in a poorly developed frontier community. One may, however, question the wisdom of imposing them permanently by including them in the state constitution when the existing circumstances were certain to change.[3]

[3] Edmond S. Meany, *History of the State of Washington*, New York, 1909, Chaps. 24-26; "Washington's First Constitution, 1878," edited by John T. Condon, *WHQ*, X, 1919, 57-68, 110-141; see also the Proceedings of the Constitutional Convention of 1878, *WHQ*, IX, 1918, 129-152, 208-229, 296-307; J. Orin Oliphant, "Additional Notes to the Constitution of 1878," *WHQ*, XVII, 1926, 27-33.

In October, 1878, the constitution as drawn up was referred to the voters and was approved by them 6,462 to 3,231. The territorial legislature then formally memorialized Congress to pass the admission bill.

But Congress never acted upon Jacobs' proposals nor upon the legislature's memorial. The delegate made a good speech in support of admission, but his efforts were unavailing. The bill never got out of committee, never was debated on the floor of the House. One can only conjecture as to the reasons. Economic development on Puget Sound was slow—so slow that a Walla Walla editor spoke of annexation to Oregon as releasing "our beautiful valley from its death embrace with Puget Sound." Save for Walla Walla, Eastern Washington was largely unoccupied. Political gains to be had from admission were problematical for the strength of Republicans and Democrats was very even. Since the Republicans controlled the House by only a slender margin, there was every reason to be cautious when there was no way of knowing with assurance whether the new state would send a Republican or a Democratic delegation to Congress.

Statehood Movement of the 1880's

During most of the decade of the 1880's, the question of statehood continued to involve Washington and Idaho together. The annexation of the Idaho panhandle to Washington appeared regularly in most of the enabling bills that were introduced into Congress and the proposal found favor not only in Washington but in Idaho as well. Separation of the panhandle from Southern Idaho appeared to be in the interests of the local population and the question seemed to be whether the mining communities there should be joined to Washington or to Montana. Statehood for Idaho as a whole seemed unlikely because of its limited population growth and because of the political controversy that raged over polygamy and the political influence of the Mormons in the southern districts. Annexation to Washington was thus partly a matter of geography, and partly of political expediency.

The chief obstacles in the way of statehood were now to be found in the effects that the admission of new states might be expected to have on the balance of Republican and Democratic forces in Congress. The return of prosperity throughout the nation during the latter eighties and the economic invigoration resulting from the completion of the Northern Pacific railroad produced a rapid development of the entire Northwest from Minnesota to Puget Sound. Montana and Dakota territories like Washington aspired to statehood and had the population and the general growth to justify it. Yet the prospect of eight or ten new Senators and even half as many Representatives appearing to take their places in the halls of Congress at once raised questions as to what their party alignments would be. Since it was more than probable that more of the new states would be Republican than Democratic in their politics, and since the Cleveland Democrats controlled both houses of Congress by only slender majorities, practical politics plainly counseled a policy of delay. Congress devoted considerable time to long speeches and debates in which the issues (though not the politics) of admission and annexation were fully discussed, but beyond this no action was taken.

The Democratic dam went out in 1888. Benjamin Harrison defeated Cleveland in the Presidential election and the Republicans established clear majorities in both houses of Congress for the first time in ten years. Realizing now that any further objection was futile, the lame duck Congress passed the Omnibus Bill and Cleveland placed his signature on it on February 22, 1889, a date which was found peculiarly appropriate by the settlers on Puget Sound. After that the territorials in Washington, and in Montana and the Dakotas as well, had statehood within their grasp. The Omnibus Bill was an enabling act which clearly set forth the steps that should be taken, and promised that admission to the Union would follow. Each territory was to elect delegates to a constitutional convention. These conventions were to meet during the summer of 1889 and draw up constitutions. In the fall, elections were to be held for the purpose of ratifying the constitutions and choosing officials to represent the people at their state capitols and in Congress.

Constitutional Conventions, 1889

The constitutional conventions that met in the Omnibus states and the constitutions that they drew up had a good bit in common, so much so that they were reported and analyzed as a group by the observers of the day. The majority of the delegates were fairly young men, well educated and representative of a wide variety of occupations and enterprises. For the most part they were well to do and were emigrants who had arrived fairly recently. Only a few of them in Washington had been members of the Convention of 1878. A number of them were men of larger affairs who had little sympathy with the crusading agrarians and "cranks" who, they claimed, had dominated the earlier convention. Yet despite the presence of this group, who appealed to their fellows to be "liberal and broadminded" in their attitude toward the corporations, the state constitutions of 1889-1890 plainly bore the marks of proposed reform, and included a number of safeguards against the political corruption and the economic centralization which were generally considered to be the greatest threat to genuine self-government.

Their zeal to protect society from these evils led the conventions to write some of the longer constitutions in American history. Skeptical of the honesty of public officials and fearful of the sinister influence of lobbyists, they multiplied stipulations and prohibitions until they quite seriously confused the task of drawing up a constitution with the processes of legislation and administration. The responsibility for the first was theirs; the second inevitably must be left in large measure to the public servants who would be elected later. Nevertheless the constitutions contained general pronouncements regarding corruption and monopoly which were quite meaningless except as they were implemented subsequently. On the other points specific figures and details were included which led to embarrassment and circumvention in matters which could better have been left to the free discretion of later generations.[4]

[4] Hubert H. Bancroft, *History of Washington, Idaho and Montana, 1845-89*, San Francisco, 1890, 264-327; Francis N. Thorpe, "Recent Constitution Making in the United States," *Annals of the American Academy of Political and Social Science*, II, 1891, 145-201; John D. Hicks, "Six Constitutions of the Far Northwest," Mississippi Valley Historical Association, *Proceedings*, IX, 1917-1918, 360-379; Frederic L. Paxson, "Admission of the Omnibus States," Wisconsin Historical Society, *Proceedings*, 1911, 77-96; L. J. Knapp, "Origin of the Constitution of Washington," *WHQ*, IV, 1913, 227-275; Austin Mires, "Remarks on the Constitution of the State of Washington," *WHQ*, XXII, 1931, 276-288, Theodore Stiles, "Constitution of the State and Its Effects Upon Public Interests," *WHQ*, IV, 1913, 281-287.

Proceedings of Washington's Convention

Such observations may be illustrated from the experience of the Washington convention which met in Olympia on July 4, 1889. The delegates to this assembly represented a wide cross section of territorial society. There were elderly farmers from Shelton and Steilacoom, Colfax and Puyallup; stockmen from Pasco and Oakesdale; editors from Davenport and Port Townsend; merchants from Ellensburg, Skokomish, and Mt. Vernon; bankers from Sprague and Vancouver as well as Spokane and Seattle; a mining superintendent from Black Diamond, several physicians, a couple of teachers, even a preacher from North Yakima. But more important than the wide diversity was the considerable number of young lawyers from all parts of the state and the smaller but significant group of leaders who were men of experience in political and economic affairs. J. J. Browne of Spokane and H. G. Blalock of Walla Walla were among the wealthiest men in the territory. J. B. Hoyt was manager of the Dexter Horton bank of Seattle. Hoyt, who was elected chairman of the convention, was likewise a veteran politician, for he had served as the speaker of the lower house of the Michigan state legislature, as governor of Arizona Territory, and as supreme court judge in Washington Territory. George Turner of Spokane had headed the Alabama delegation at three national Republican conventions. C. H. Warner of Colfax was chairman of the Democratic territorial committee. Perhaps one-third of the delegates had lived in Washington more than 15 years; the other two-thirds were men who had emigrated to the territory comparatively recently. Politically they numbered 43 Republicans, 29 Democrats, and three Independents.

The convention favored a number of reform measures which were designed to curtail political corruption and to promote economy in government. Generally speaking, the members advocated a government that was directly responsible to the people. Under the new constitution not only the governor and the legislature were to be elected but the judges and the chief administrative officials as well, including the secretary of state, auditor, treasurer, attorney-general and superintendent of public instruction. On the other hand, the delegates showed considerable distrust of the people's representatives and wrote into the constitution numerous clauses that limited their freedom of action, sought to guarantee their good behavior, and in case of necessity provided a way of removing them from office altogether.

The legislature was particularly the target of constitutional restraint. Much was said about the corruption that had made legislatures an object of scorn in other states. After a heated argument over the issues of civil rights that were involved, the convention approved an article prohibiting corrupt solicitation (Art. II, Sec. 30) and requiring witnesses to give testimony. The legislature's freedom of action was limited in many ways. The length of session could not exceed 60 days. The state was not to incur a public debt exceeding 400,000 dollars and municipalities were not to be allowed to undertake obligations larger than 5 percent of the value of their taxable property, with 5 percent more for water, light, and other utilities (Art. VIII, Sec. 6). The state was not to loan its credit to any individual or company or subscribe to the stock of any corporation. Maximum salaries were set for judges and for the governor and administrative officers. The principal of the common school fund was to remain "permanent and irreducible." No money was to be expended for any religious worship exercise or instruction. Lotteries and individual divorces were not to be authorized by an act of law. No private or special legislation was to be enacted on a list of 18 different subjects which were enumerated in detail. As one of the delegates remarked, "If . . . a stranger from a foreign country were to drop into this convention, he would conclude that we were fighting a great enemy, and that this enemy is the legislature."

The convention shared the nation-wide concern regarding the growing menace of trusts and monopoly. J. R. Kinnear of Seattle introduced a proposition favoring a general antimonopoly clause and a provision phrased in general terms was accepted without debate (Art. XII, Sec. 22). The dangers inherent in the watering and manipulation of corporation stock were pointed out and safeguards were formulated with a view to controlling the practice (Art. XII, Sec. 6). Prohibitions were approved to prevent discriminating charges by the railroads, the issuance of free passes, and the consolidation of competing lines. The legislature was authorized to pass laws establishing reasonable maximum rates for the transportation of both passengers and freight (Sec. 18).

Despite this general disposition toward reform, however, the convention framed a constitution that was essentially a compromise with the demands of the entrepreneur for freedom from governmental interference. Repeatedly the argument was made that if the controls on corporations were too strict, they would discourage the investment of capital in the state and would prevent new businesses from locating there. After much discussion of a proposal to create a railroad commission by constitutional mandate, the convention rejected the committee report on the subject, an action which delayed the establishment of the commission by 15 years. The antitrust section of the constitution proved to be largely a dead-letter provision and the attempt to regulate the management of corporation stock has had little effect. The implementing of constitutional provisions was after all something that they could not control, something which the people themselves and their representatives would determine during the ensuing years.[5]

Idaho and Wyoming

Idaho and Wyoming were not included in the Omnibus Bill, but these territories too held constitutional conventions during the summer and early fall of 1889. The Republican victory presaged a new Congressional attitude toward admission and the territorials were quick to take advantage of it. The Committee on Territories both in the Senate and in the House reported favorably on admission bills early in 1889 and while they were not passed by the outgoing Congress, the territorial governors took action in accordance with their provisions. Governor R. A. Stevenson of Idaho on his own initiative set the machinery in motion for the election of delegates and called the convention to meet on July 4th at Boise. In Wyoming the governor acted upon application of a majority of the county com-

[5] James L. Fitts, "Washington Constitutional Convention of 1889," unpublished thesis, University of Washington, 1951. The full debates of the convention were never transcribed, but the official journal is preserved in the office of the Secretary of State. An analytical index to these proceedings has been prepared by Quentin Smith, unpublished thesis; University of Washington, 1947.

missioners who proposed that the governer, the secretary and the chief justice apportion delegates to a convention (SB 2445). The procedure was somewhat irregular but the election was held and the convention met at Cheyenne during September.

These conventions drafted constitutions which resembled very closely in their essential provisions the ones drawn up in Washington and Montana. Idaho delegates took pains to point out that the business and taxpaying portion of the population was especially prominent and watchful at the convention and they described the constitution as a "conservatively progressive one." To reduce the burden of government they not only placed ceilings on the salaries of officials, but put county officers on a fee basis, a move that enabled them to claim that state government would actually cost less in appropriations for the civil offices, state and county, than the preceding territorial regime. The most controversial feature of the constitution was the section (VI, 3) which disenfranchised the Mormon population on the grounds of polygamy. Perhaps the most significant provisions of both the Wyoming and Idaho fundamental law were those which established state control over water rights and irrigation reservoirs and ditches, explicitly declaring the principle of public and beneficial use. Idaho also included an article for the laboring man which established the eight-hour day on all public works, prohibited child labor in the mines, and authorized the legislature to create boards of arbitration for the settlement of labor disputes.[6]

During the fall of 1889 the electors of each territory voted favorably on the constitutions that were referred to them and chose their state officers. Early in November one territory after another certified to President Harrison that the new governments were ready to assume authority. The president thereupon issued formal proclamations for those included in the Omnibus Bill, declaring them to be states in the Union—for North and South Dakota on the 2d of November, for Montana on the 8th, and for Washingon on the 11th.

The inauguration of the new state governments was celebrated with pomp and ceremony. On November 18 the streets of Olympia were lined with exulting citizens who gathered to watch the parade

---

[6] *Proceedings and Debates of the Constitutional Convention of Idaho, 1889,* ed. I. W. Hart, 2 vols., Caldwell, Idaho, 1912.

of pioneers and notables as they passed in procession to the Capitol grounds, escorted by bands and drum corps, foot soldiers and cavalry. Polished orations called attention to the significance of the occasion. Miles Moore, the last territorial governor, gave his valedictory and Elisha P. Ferry, newly elected governor of the state, saluted the legislature and the people in his inaugural address. Statehood, he said, "is the consummation of hopes long deferred yet ever renewed. It is the accomplishment of the result for which they (the pioneers) had waited with anxious solicitude, and which they now welcome with joy and satisfaction." The boom of cannon closed the ceremony, marking the end of the old regime, the beginning of the new.[7]

Congress took up the question of admitting Idaho and Wyoming at its next session. Statehood bills introduced (HR 4562) early in January, 1890, met with little more than a token opposition. George G. Vest, Democratic Senator from Missouri, saw statehood in Wyoming as the scheme of Republican politicians who gerrymandered the apportionment of electoral districts for party advantage and secured a comfortable local control by ill-concealed manipulation. But the day of Democratic procrastination was over and Vest's objections were in vain. Congress was in a generous mood and admitted new states, as he said, not singly but in bunches. On the eve of Independence Day, 1890, President Harrison signed the bill which formally admitted Idaho and Wyoming to the Union. The last vestiges of territorial vassalage in the Pacific Northwest (save for Alaska) were gone. Political history would henceforth be the history of sovereign states.

[7] *Readings in Pacific Northwest History: Washington, 1790-1895,* ed. Charles M. Gates, Seattle, 1941, Chap. 17.

Political Issues and Alignments

21

Years of Agrarian Protest

Background of Discontent

The reform movement of the 1890's had its roots in agrarian discontent. Northwest farmers, like those of the Middle West, suffered from high transportation costs and declining returns from their crops. Export prices of wheat dropped sharply and freight charges consumed the value of the grain until the railroads were taking nearly as much to carry a bushel 300 miles as the farmer received for raising it. One in every four farms in Washington was mortgaged (1890), many of them at interest rates ranging up to 20 percent. Taxes as well as indebtedness constituted a heavy burden, so much so that in the mid-decade years of depression the published lists of delinquencies filled many columns in the local newspapers. Protective tariffs and commercial profits likewise took their fractions of the consumer's dollar.[1]

Quite apart from these acute economic problems, the people of the region were aroused by more specific abuses which in most cases stemmed from political corruption. Logging companies had been guilty of trespass on the public lands, yet they had been let off with no more than a token gesture of court action. Millions of acres had been set aside in railroad land grants, a good part of which could be neither taxed nor colonized. These giant corporations built their

[1] For accounts of the Grange and Populist movements and the conditions which led to their extension into the Pacific Northwest, see Edna Scott, *Grange Movement in Oregon*, Thesis Series, University of Oregon, 1939; Marion Harrington, *Populist Movement in Oregon, 1889-96*, Thesis Series, University of Oregon, 1940; Homer L. Owen, "Oregon Politics and the Initiative and Referendum," unpublished thesis, Reed College, 1950; Fred Yoder, "Farmers' Alliances in Washington—Prelude to Populism," in State College of Washington, *Research Studies*, XVI, 1948, 123-178; Gordon B. Ridgeway, "Populism in Washington," *PNQ*, XXXIX, 1948, 284-311. Most of the details in the present summary are drawn from these sources.

political fences with great shrewdness and by a careful distribution of campaign funds succeeded in putting their spokesmen into high office.

John H. Mitchell, United States Senator from Oregon for twenty years, was legal counselor for both the Oregon and California Railroad and for the Northern Pacific. He was reported to have remarked, "Ben Holladay's politics are my politics and what Ben Holladay wants I want." Joseph N. Dolph, another prominent Oregon senator, became in 1882 vice-president of the Oregon and Transcontinental Company, a corporation which was closely linked with every important railroad in Oregon. Judge Henry McGinn later recalled that the Northern Pacific did not hesitate to spend 30,000 dollars to elect a senator.

Railroad sympathizers were vigilant in every matter touching the interests of their constituents. By one means or another they warded off every public scrutiny of freight rates, and defeated every effort to establish a genuine regulatory commission. Undoubtedly the standards of that day were different from our own. Nevertheless there was a growing apprehension among the people lest the safeguards of public interest fail, and government come wholly under the domination of the acquisitive and the unscrupulous.

Oregon particularly suffered a succession of unhappy experiences with venal officials and land-hungry speculators. This all but destroyed popular confidence in the state government. Governor George L. Woods certified to the completed construction of the Dalles Military Road when actually it was quite worthless, an oxcart trail wholly unimproved. In this instance the road company secured through a barefaced swindle half a million acres situated in the best part of the John Day Valley. Lands in Southern and Eastern Oregon were surveyed and sold as swamp when the nearest water was 30 feet below the surface. Later it was revealed that the governor, treasurer, and secretary of state were in league with the speculators, practicing gross deception and mismanagement of funds. Clerks issued receipts for moneys never received. Governor William Thayer, himself an applicant for 100,000 acres of swamp land, ignored or nullified provisions of law and allowed Henry C. Owens to acquire large acreages for which he had paid little or nothing. Owens contracted to sell more than a million acres to which he had no claim beyond the act of filing.

Meanwhile the farmers in Baker County were forced to organize a Protective Association to prevent speculators from dispossessing them entirely through manipulation and intrigue.

The school lands in Oregon were likewise the source of much complaint. State officials had shown an amazing lethargy and negligence in making surveys and locating sections 16 and 36 to which the schools were entitled. As a result, much of this land, distributed in individual townships, was taken by private purchasers or claimants. In later years the state took a greater interest, not so much to have the land as to sell it cheaply to any purchaser who might demand it. In 1887 the legislature placed upon the statute books a law that opened every door to speculation and authorized the sale of even the best timber land at a price of $1.25 per acre. In cases where school lands in a particular section had already been taken up, a purchaser might buy other land instead (lieu land) which he might choose from the best in the national domain, provided he could identify the original section (base) for which it was substituted. Since the identification (i.e., "naming the base") could only be made by persons who had access to the land office records, the law of 1887 produced a situation where a few favored persons were able to form a land ring and levy tribute systematically from all who would buy. The resulting land scandals reached a climax after 1900, but the activities of such men as E. P. McCormack and Napoleon Davis, clerks of the Land Board, led to much complaint and eventually to Davis' removal from office. Even the creation of national forest reserves in the Cascade Mountains (1891) was tainted by the zeal of speculators to use the additional base to buy fine forest lands for a pittance.

Reform Organizations

Under such conditions the Northwest was a fertile field for agrarian organizers. The Patrons of Husbandry had organized their Granges in Oregon earlier, and 86 of them were active in 1891 with 3,140 members. Despite the fact that the national organization had begun to decline, these locals and the state Granges newly organized in Washington and Idaho were lively centers of agitation and political activity. The Farmers Alliances came into the region as well and gained membership rapidly, especially in the Inland

Empire. By July, 1891, the Northwestern Alliance had 183 local units in Washington alone. Their picnics attracted several thousand people. The Southern Alliance likewise sent lecturers and organizers into the region and pressed their activities there so aggressively that by 1892 there were in Washington as many members in the one organization as in the other. No love was lost between them, and all attempts to merge the two failed. Jurisdictional disputes led to much bitterness and to charges of misrepresentation and false pretense, as the Southern Alliance invaded even counties that were strongholds of the Northwestern Alliance. In Oregon the Southern Alliance met with even greater success, making that state the 37th to join the national organization of the Farmers' Alliance and Industrial Union. Meanwhile in Idaho, too, farmers' organizations were laying the groundwork for a political effort that would soon offer a vigorous challenge to the conservative Republican control.

These reformers spoke their minds with no little vigor. As they saw it, they were battling not against impersonal conditions of geography and economic competition but against business organizations and people who in a very sinister way controlled the government and used it to their own special advantage. As the Oregon agrarians put it, "the power of trusts and corporations has become an intolerable tyranny, the encroachments of the landgrabbers have almost exhausted the public domain, and the corruption of the ballot has rendered our elections little less than a disgraceful farce." Railroad rates were high, in their view, not because of distance but because of monopoly. Taxes on farm lands were heavy because other forms of property through political connivance either failed to carry their share of the load or perhaps escaped taxation altogether. Money was scarce because the banks of issue, "the pawnshops of American liberty," had arrogated to themselves a control which rightfully belonged to and should be exercised by the government itself. Land was scarce because so much of it had been allowed by designing politicians to come into the hands of the railroads or speculators who cunningly appropriated the public domain of the state or federal government at scandalously low prices.

In drawing up statements of their purposes and objectives, they put forward proposals touching all these complaints. A convention held at Salem in September, 1889, representing Grangers, Knights of Labor, and Prohibitionists, declared for the following:

1. prohibition of the manufacture and sale of intoxicating liquors;
2. a national monetary system "by which a circulating medium in necessary quantity shall issue direct to the people without the intervention of banks";
3. transportation corporations should be regulated "to prevent unjust exactions and discriminations against persons, places or products";
4. a governmental land system that will restore to the public domain all unearned land grants, restrict settlers to the possession of 160 acres and corporations to no more land than necessary for the conduct of their business;
5. impose residence requirements and a test of knowledge of American institutions as conditions of naturalization and suffrage for foreigners;
6. trusts and combinations for maintaining artificial prices to be held a conspiracy against the common welfare, and punished accordingly;
7. a prohibition on the issuance of nontaxable bonds.[2]

These demands were added to from time to time. In 1891 the farmers' organizations spoke out for the abolition of national banks and the free coinage of silver, an income tax, the nationalization of railroads, telephone and telegraph lines "and natural monopolies," and the direct election of all officers. The emphasis might vary as between these different measures. All were, however, considered desirable, and together they comprised a broad program of reform calculated to make government responsible to the people, control monopoly, and limit speculative activity whether by banks or land sharks.

Formation of the People's Party

The Grangers and the Farmers' Alliances did not come at once to the organization of their own political party. For some years they preferred a campaign of education and debate and sought to win the major parties through persuasion to an acceptance of the proposals they advocated. Tracts and pamphlets were written and distributed in some number. Lecturers traveled from place to place and study clubs were organized, like the one at the home of Seth Lewelling in Milwaukee which gave William U'Ren his start in Oregon. At election time Grangers cast their votes for

[2] Harrington, *Populist Movement in Oregon*, 9, 29-36; Owen, "Oregon Politics," 59.

Republicans or Democrats depending upon their position on the issues that the Grange considered important.

At the Salem Convention (1889), however, a new third party called the Union Party was formed in Oregon. Both the major parties took note of it, and Sylvester Pennoyer, Democratic candidate for governor, showed some sympathy for reform principles. He declared his opposition to tax-free bonds, his support of the Australian ballot, and his purpose to look into administration of the Land Board. The Union Party endorsed him and gave him perhaps 5,000 votes. They ran their own candidates for Congress and for the office of Secretary of State, but put up only a partial slate.

During 1891 Alliance leaders in Washington disputed among themselves as to the wisdom of forming a party. G. D. Sutton, president of the Washington Northwestern Alliance, strongly opposed the idea believing that the Alliance would dissolve in political discord and fanaticism if forced to contend with "all the antagonistic elements which are continually crowding to the front of the third party movement." For the Alliance to become a political party would be "as disastrous as leaping from a strong and well made ship into the ocean when the white capped waves begin to roll."

E. B. Williams, vice-president, voiced exactly opposite views. He saw no hope of getting reforms adopted through the old parties, both of which for 20 years "have legislated against us and in favor of our enemies." There must be no more bending the knee and begging the politicians to hear their prayers. "Let us," he urged, "act for ourselves, and be our own leaders. We know that we have the power. Why not use it."

While the local leaders were thus divided in their opinion, a strong trend set in nationally toward independent political action. Delegates from the Northern and Southern Alliances held a national convention at Cincinnati in May, 1891, and decided upon the steps to be taken to draw up a platform and nominate candidates for the 1892 election. Local Alliance organizations in the Northwest fell in line. Sutton stood his ground, but found few to support him and was finally forced out of office with a vote of censure. The new state leaders felt misgivings too, and continued to stress the nonpartisan character of the Alliance organization, the purposes of which were "to ameliorate the condition of the farmers and not to boom the political aspirations of any set of men." But the third-party proposals simmered and boiled in the local Alliances through the winter and spring of 1892, and by campaign time most of the rank and file of the membership favored an independent ticket.[3]

The People's Party, organized early in 1892, therefore found a ready constituency in the Pacific Northwest. Local clubs were formed and state conventions drew up platforms and slates of candidates. General James B. Weaver, Populist candidate for president, made a stumping tour to the Northwest, addressing at Baker, Oregon, a crowd of 1,500 people. Mary Ellen Lease of Kansas, famous for her exhortation to farmers to "raise less corn and more hell," spoke to a large audience in Portland, receiving a friendly introduction by Abigail Scott Duniway, the leading feminist in the region. Though the dominant voice of the press continued to be Republican, a score or more of Populist newspapers were established, to become vigorous agents of electioneering.

Populists made a surprisingly good showing in their first campaigns. Weaver won 56,650 votes in the three Northwest states in 1892, or about 30 percent of the total vote cast. Benjamin Harrison carried Oregon and Washington by a margin of hardly more than 8,000 votes in each state, and in Idaho, where the Democrats joined in supporting Weaver, the Populist electors won by easy majorities.

Strategy of Fusion

Yet the Populist vote by itself was only a minority vote. Populists in the Oregon legislature numbered only four in 1893 and ten in 1895, most of them coming from rural counties of the southwest corner of the state. The party drew from the Republicans in Multnomah and other counties that were normally Republican, and from the Democrats in Democratic counties like Jackson and Linn, but they failed to gain control in any of the more populous districts. In Washington, Populists captured eight seats in the 1893 legislature and 23 seats in 1895, but they fell short

[3] Yoder, "Farmers' Alliances in Washington," 169-173. Results of elections are taken from Appleton's *Annual Encyclopedia*, 1892-1900, and Edgar E. Robinson, *Presidential Vote*, 1896-1932, Stanford University, 1934.

of the votes necessary to put through any of the reforms proposed in their platforms. Here they ran in third place behind the Democrats. In Idaho they equaled or slightly exceeded the Democratic strength and in Oregon they ran well ahead of it, but in no three-cornered contest were they able to challenge the Republican control. Republican governors ruled in the state capitols and congressional delegations were solidly Republican as well. Idaho's Populist candidate A. J. Crook made a good showing in the race for a seat in the Senate, but failed to unseat the veteran Republican George Shoup. In the congressional election of 1894 Populist James Gunn beat his Democratic rival, but trailed 3,000 votes behind Republican Edgar Wilson. If the Republicans were to be turned out of office, the Populists must either register substantial gains in their own right, or they must settle for some kind of alliance or "fusion" with the Democrats, and agree upon a single joint ticket.

The political strategy of fusion produced as much difference of opinion among the Populists as the question of founding a third party had produced in the Farmers' Alliance earlier. One group in the party insisted that the only wise course was to maintain the independence and integrity of the Populist organization by holding aloof from political bargains and following "the middle of the road." Others, however, welcomed the opportunities of fusion, believing that once a change of control was achieved, it would be possible to secure at least some of the reforms they desired.

A decision as between these alternative considerations sometimes depended upon the balance of party strength in one state or another, and the degree to which the Republicans or Democrats accepted the Populist objectives. In Washington fusion was perhaps the easier because the Populists gained in numbers between 1892 and 1896 while the Democrats weakened. In Oregon, on the other hand, the Democratic party was more influenced by reform thinking and was considerably torn in 1894 by the difficulty of supporting Cleveland and Pennoyer at the same time. The Democratic platform included declarations in favor of free silver, direct government, an income tax, and banking reform, which were Populist planks. The saying became current: "Scratch a Western Democrat and you find a Populist." From such a situation it was only a short step to develop the "Popocrat" who figured so conspicuously in the campaign of 1896.

Beyond this, one's views as to tactics were likely to be shaped by one's main purpose. Those who thought of the Populist goal as a comprehensive program, a philosophy, almost a way of life, preferred an independent course and a distinct party, the integrity of which should never be sacrificed. Those who were intent upon specific reforms were willing to achieve them by measures of expediency using any combination of elements from different parties that might come to hand. William U'Ren advocated fusion almost from the start in order to secure the adoption of the initiative and referendum. Free silver men from all three parties joined hands in a common endeavor. Some Populists were skeptical of such an alliance. "Politicians," they said shrewdly, "do not want the Omaha (Populist) platform. They would rather rattle around on Silver, which is a very small reform and a convenient hobby for politicians to ride on." Still the free silver combination promised votes and the Populists, who of necessity must appeal to malcontents of many colors, were in no position to be aloof. There was a touch of irony in the fact that while a restless demand on the part of the rank and file of Alliance men to accomplish something politically brought about the founding of the Populist party, their characteristic nonpartisan attitude led them naturally into the entanglements of fusion which soon destroyed the organization they had made.

Election of 1896

The election of 1896 brought the issue of fusion to a climax. Oregon politics became a tangled skein, the county conventions presenting many diverse views and contradictions on questions of coinage and party alignment. The farmers who converged upon Ellensburg, traveling for days by wagon, bicycle, and even afoot to attend the Populist state convention in Washington were generally considered to be the strongest "middle-of-the-roaders." Yet the convention quickly took to negotiations with the Democrats and Silver Republicans (who met at the same place at the same time) and determined upon fusion with them. The resulting ticket found Populists like John R. Rogers, C. W. Young, Neal Cheatham, and Robert Bridges teamed up with Democrat James Hamilton Lewis and W. C.

Jones, a Silver Republican from Spokane. Populists claimed the chief state offices, while Lewis and Jones were put up for Congress. Each party announced its own platform in language "as noncommital as good politics could make it."

In Idaho fusion was stronger than ever, since politics revolved mainly around free silver. William E. Borah, who was just making a name for himself as a silver-tongued orator and capable politician, expressed the attitude of the majority of Republicans when he insisted that the true Republicans were the Silver Republicans. These men walked out of the hall when the Republican national convention declared itself for the gold standard and only a minority of organization men remained regular and worked for McKinley. Even they did so reluctantly. As one of them put it, "I am for silver but I don't know exactly where I am at."

Borah and his fellows accepted fusion with Democrats and Populists fairly easily. Their Republicanism had a good streak of liberalism in it; in fact, Republican conventions had earlier declared for women suffrage, a federal department of mines, postal savings, and the right of labor to organize. Silver Republicans, Democrats, and Populists had no difficulty in working out a slate which united them for Bryan and for Democrat Frank Steunenberg as candidate for governor. The silver votes were split in the contest for congressional representative, Borah finally consenting to run against both regular and fusionist candidates. Everyone knew that the gold bugs had no chance and anyone who agreed to run for office was greeted as "another lamb for the slaughter."[4]

Bryan's vote in the Northwest was closely linked with fusion. He carried Washington and Idaho where state-wide fusion had been achieved and lost narrowly in Oregon where fusion came less naturally and had the appearance of being improvised for the presidential campaign. Silver was probably the main reason why the Idaho voters in every county of the state returned comfortable majorities for Bryan. In Washington fusionists carried all of the eastern part of the state (except Klickitat) and every county between the Sound and the Cascade Mountains from Olympia to the Canadian border. In several other counties the vote was extremely close: a tie in Clarke

[4] Claudius O. Johnson, *Borah of Idaho*, New York, 1936, Chap. III.

County, a margin of only ten votes in Lewis county, 25 in Island county, and 26 in Kitsap.

The distribution of Bryan and McKinley votes in Oregon followed a different pattern which suggested a more sectional alignment of counties, and at the same time showed very plainly the importance of the urban vote in Portland. The election was marked by a net switch of 12 counties from the Republican to the Democratic column. However, McKinley carried 15 other counties which lay in a broad band along the northern seacoast and the Columbia River, and in the lower valleys of the Willamette, the Deschutes and the John Day rivers. This section, the wealthiest and most productive section of the state, remained safely Republican despite the defections brought about by agrarian reform and free silver. Yet more important was the fact that the Republican organization maintained a wide lead in Multnomah County. McKinley led in the state as a whole by 2,117 votes; but he led in Multnomah county by 5,371. Thus in the Pacific Northwest as in other sections of the country the Republicans owed much to their effective control of the populous centers. In Portland it was machine control exercised crudely enough at election time by ruffians and rascals brought in for the purpose from San Francisco. For a price these men voted as they were told, perhaps not once but several times at different polling places. Jonathan Bourne protested that Bryan actually carried Oregon only to have the victory snatched from him by Republican repeaters. The traffic in ballots helped McKinley at the moment, but it produced a popular resentment which hastened remedial legislation afterward.[5]

Record of Small Achievement

The aftermath of 1896 was as significant as the election itself. So far as national politics were concerned, McKinley was president and enjoyed a good working majority in both houses of Congress. The gold standard was written into law, and beyond the adoption of such minor measures as a postal savings system, the issues of reform were dropped. Returning prosperity and the excitement of the Spanish-American war seemed to quiet the old

[5] Owen, "Oregon Politics," 86-97, citing mainly the *Oregonian* and Bourne correspondence.

complaints and turn popular attention to other matters.

In the states, however, Populism and fusion had more opportunity to show results, or so it seemed at least. In Washington Governor John Rogers and his Populist supporters appeared to have the situation well in hand, controlling as they did both houses of the state legislature. In Oregon the Republicans enjoyed a majority in the legislature, but because of factional dissensions were divided amongst themselves. Pennoyer's election as mayor of Portland showed the strength of reform opinion there, and many Republicans for that matter were ready to admit that political corruption had gone so far that something had best be done about it. Strangely enough, however, the more promising situation proved to be the more disappointing. Rogers urged comprehensive legislation but secured the adoption of only a small part of it. Oregon, on the other hand, realized at first only a few basic reforms, but through them the way was opened to much more.

Washington

The very strength of the Washington Populists led to their undoing. Inexperienced in the responsibilities of government and made heady by their recent victory, they lacked the leadership and self-discipline necessary to agree upon a constructive program and carry it through. Though they had the votes to elect one of their number to the United States Senate, they wasted themselves in needless rivalries and found it impossible even to caucus, too many of them having personal ambitions of their own. After a week of balloting the choice finally fell upon George Turner who, though acceptable on the railroad issue, was more Jeffersonian than Populist and was too much the judge and wealthy mine owner to be a true man of the people. The Ellensburg platform presumably committed the Populists to a number of specific reforms, but they fell to quarreling so with each other over place and patronage that the legislative session (1897) ended with hardly a half-dozen measures approved beyond what the Republicans themselves agreed to.

It was unfortunate that several years of campaigning had not decided the issues of leadership more clearly. John R. Rogers of Puyallup was a man of considerable ability. An intellectual lately become reformer, he had been active in the Union Labor party in

Kansas, and later became a member of the Farmers' Alliance. He had written and published several tracts and pamphlets, even a bit of fiction, setting forth the ideas of the day on agrarian reform. Elected as a Populist to the legislature in 1892, he had a good record to his credit and was recognized especially for his sponsorship of legislation which put the finances of the state more effectively behind the public schools. Yet in 1897 Rogers had not established himself as the acknowledged leader of his party. Before the election of 1896 M. P. Bulger of Tacoma, chairman of the state executive committee, assumed the role of quarterback and attempted to call the plays. After the victory Frank Baker, the new state chairman, claimed the right to dispense the patronage. Rogers was governor not through superior claim but because he was a compromise candidate, acceptable as second best to the supporters of Young and H. N. Belt. Whatever his personal qualities, they were insufficient to give him preëminence either through the arts of conciliation or by the tougher methods of the party boss.

So it was that Rogers lectured the legislature on the dangers of factionalism to no avail. Populist bills suffered various fates. A tax bill that was to have shifted the burden of governmental support from the home owner to the "great properties," when finally adopted, provided only for modest exemptions and some changes in the manner of collection. Proposed legislation establishing maximum freight rates and creating a railroad commission was defeated in the senate by the combined opposition of Republicans and ten of the fifteen Populist members. A bill that looked toward the direct election of United States senators died in committee. An attempt to secure an adequate program of industrial insurance succeeded only in providing publicity of accounts and a meager protection against monopolistic rates. The oft-repeated Populist demand for simplification and economy in government was largely forgotten in measures that created several new state agencies—a bureau of labor, a road commission, and a commissioner of horticulture—which were good in themselves but cost money. Republicans meanwhile made the most of their opportunities to oppose reform while at the same time condemning the Populists for their dissension. The *Post Intelligencer* spoke out with special venom, accusing the Populist legislature of being a "riotous, incoherent tempestuous irresponsible assemblage of men."[6]

A more charitable witness might have found kindly things to say. The Populists recognized at least the importance of practical remedies for specific grievances, and were not much plagued with the romancing of utopians. But with gold discovered in the Klondike, who cared to wrestle longer with the stubborn issues of democracy and public policy? The voters at large frowned alike on the single tax and woman suffrage and defeated both. Republicans won handily in the elections of 1898 and 1900 and Populist voters, chastened by defeat and disillusionment, sought again an affiliation with one or the other of the old line parties. Rogers won reëlection but as a Democrat. Turner found no occasion to remember that the Populists once claimed him for their own. Reform was not dead, but it was clear that Populism as a third party was not to be the means of achieving it. For the next decade those who joined the quest for social justice found it better to work within the organization of established parties rather than to multiply new ones. Still, it was a lesson not yet fully learned which before too long would be repeated.

Oregon

Oregon followed quite another course. Corruption, here more blatant, was not to be ignored even in prosperity. On the other hand, reform was not the prerogative of any particular group or party. The Populists, since they never enjoyed the numerical strength they had in Washington, accepted of necessity the status of a minority and with the eclipse of their organization they sought support for individual measures without laboring the fine points of party and principle. After 1896 many members returned to the Democratic or Republican fold, but demanded basic reforms as the price of their support. As one Republican leader put it, "I have a lot of Pops in my district and I have to do something to keep them happy." Moderates and liberals in both the major parties felt an obligation to prevent the recurrence of scandal. Furthermore the struggle of different factions to control the Republican party machin-

[6] Ridgeway, "Populism in Washington," *PNQ*, XXXIX, 1948, 305-311; also Carroll H. Wooddy, "Populism in Washington," *WHQ*, XXI, 1930, 103-119; Russell Blankenship, "Political Thought of John R. Rogers," *PNQ*, XXXVII, 1946, 3-13.

ery made even the stalwarts more conciliatory than they were ordinarily. All this did not mean that reform came easily. On the contrary, it was achieved through political crisis in the legislature and from a complex contest among individuals and factions to win the prize of public office. Nevertheless, by means often devious the cause of good government was significantly advanced.

In Oregon's "hold-up" legislature of 1897 the Populists' reform strategy led them into an alignment with one Republican faction against another, which offended the men of principle but exploited dissension among the enemy to their own advantage. Jonathan Bourne, recently elected to the house of representatives was candidate for the post of speaker. John Mitchell sought reëlection by the legislature to his seat in the United States Senate. During the early skirmishing there was a compact between the two men and each gave his support to the other. Bourne was a silver man, however, since he owned large holdings in Idaho. Mitchell had spoken for silver too, but was increasingly embarrassed by it and finally came out for the gold standard. Bourne immediately broke with Mitchell, managed a boycott of the Republican caucus, and engineered a coalition of Populists, Democrats, silverites, and even a few Dolph-Simon Republicans which by withholding a quorum effectively prevented the house from organizing to do any business at all. It was a strange and awkward alliance which held together only for purposes of obstruction. In order to hold U'Ren and his Populists in line Bourne promised to give his support to the Populist program which at that time consisted of a registration bill, a measure to regulate the selection and activities of judges and clerks of election, and a constitutional amendment providing for the initiative and referendum. As an effort to secure the speakership for Bourne the coalition failed. It did, however, bring additional support for the measures in question, and they were subsequently enacted.

The problem of maintaining the secrecy of the ballot had been recognized earlier in Oregon and had been dealt with by the legislature. In 1891 a law had been put on the statute books that provided for the Australian ballot and established certain procedures for voting. Yet experience since that time showed plainly the inadequacies of the law regulating elections. In the primary elections in 1896 many a voter had been challenged and pulled out of line, and some imported hireling put in his place to vote for the machine. The remedy for this kind of corruption depended upon ascertaining the qualifications of voters and providing for an accurate counting of the votes cast. The registration law passed by the legislature in 1898 made the qualifications and residence of individual citizens a matter of record. The Holt bill which was put on the statute books soon afterward allowed all full-fledged parties to be represented on local election boards and stipulated procedures that greatly improved the administration of the balloting. These two pieces of legislation materially lessened the evils of political manipulation and made a repetition of the scenes of 1896 improbable. Machine politics by no means disappeared, but there was more acknowledgment of common conscience and a greater reliance upon the judgment and good sense of the rank and file of voters.

22

Politics of the Progressive Era

Oregonians found it quite logical that improved election laws and direct government should be agitated and put into effect together. The one protected the individual in his right to declare himself freely and without duress on political questions. The other charged him with the responsibility for many more decisions than had been required of him previously. In a sense representative government and direct government were not the same thing, and critics soon pointed out that if the citizenry were to be the lawmakers then the legislatures would find but little to do. Direct government enthusiasts saw no contradiction, however. The same principles of democracy that allowed the voter to elect a representative to the legislature should at the same time insure the responsibility of the representative to the people who put him there. Direct government did not short-circuit the processes of republican government but only facilitated the functioning of it. In a day when legislators were likely to be more attentive to special lobbies and pressures than to the general electorate, direct government would restore the ultimate control of public affairs to the people where it properly belonged.

William U'Ren

As a member of the Alliance study group at Lewelling's house William U'Ren had been introduced to J. S. Sullivan's book, *Direct Legislation by Citizenship, through Initiative and Referendum,* which explained the working of these new instruments of government and pointed out their importance. He became enthusiastic about them. By themselves one could hardly call them radical, since they merely implemented the principle of majority rule.

Yet he was bold to believe that once the initiative and referendum were written into the state constitutions they would make possible many reforms that no legislature in the land would adopt. U'Ren was a single taxer, and some years later he remarked that he thought of the initiative and referendum as a means of realizing this specific objective. He was, however, a man of many enthusiasms whose restless activity carried him into crusades for numerous causes. The procedures of direct government had other uses in his mind beyond putting into operation a revolutionary tax system. They opened the way to a broad program of reform which included a review of the whole problem of governmental operation. Incidentally they also made U'Ren himself something of a political czar whose powers, whether because of statesmanship or shrewd management, aroused a certain envy in some who watched him. "Oregon now has two governments," wrote one of his critics, "one in Salem and the other under U'Ren's hat."

U'Ren did not claim the initiative and referendum for any particular party. He identified the Populist party with it and was willing to adopt the direct government amendment as a single-plank Populist platform. But the reform itself was more important to him than the political capital to be made of it. He urged the fusion of Populists with Democrats in order to get a wider support for it, and sought pledges from Republicans too that they would support a proposal for a constitutional convention. In the latter overture he was disappointed since the regulars of the party were skeptical of the idea. He persisted in the effort, however, and turned factional dissension to advantage whenever Republican votes were to be had for a price that he could pay. The maneuvering that took place in the hold-up legislature was not repeated, yet in the end the adoption of the initiative and referendum was successfully accomplished with the aid of a considerable number of Republican votes. Bourne decided for reasons of his own to follow the progressive line, and the rivalry between Simon and Mitchell was so even a contest that neither one dared antagonize the voters by an unfavorable stand on direct government.

To put the initiative and referendum into the Oregon constitution required an affirmative vote by two successive sessions of the legislature and a ratification by the people. This took several years to do. The amendment was proposed and passed by the legislature of 1899. It was again approved in the 1901 session and received an easy majority by popular vote in the election of 1902. U'Ren's success in piloting the measure through these various steps is in part a tribute to his persistence and skill in parliamentary management. He owed as much, however, to a sustained campaign of education and propaganda. By 1895 a Joint Committee, representing Granges, Alliances, and labor unions had circulated 70,000 leaflets describing the initiative and referendum. A new edition of Sullivan's book was published and given a wide distribution. That year U'Ren expressed his belief that "three-fourths of the intelligent voters understand and favor this revolution." From then on the demand for direct government was repeated like a drumbeat until it became in the popular mind the answer to nearly any problem one could mention. By the time the amendment was ratified the initiative and referendum were almost magic words. Their tremendous currency was important not only to their adoption, but to the enthusiastic test of their usefulness which made the next few years a field day for the citizen legislator.[1]

The Oregon System

Following the adoption of the initiative and referendum, Oregon became a laboratory of political democracy that attracted notice throughout the nation. At first the people made but little use of the new "tools" of direct government. In the election of 1904 two initiatives appeared on the ballot: a direct primary law and a local option liquor control measure, both of which passed. Two years later 11 measures were submitted to vote by the people, including woman suffrage, home rule for cities, the extension of initiative and referendum to local and special laws, and gross earnings tax laws on telephone and telegraph companies, sleeping car companies, and

[1] Owen, "Oregon Politics," 80 ff.; Burton J. Hendrick, "Initiative and Referendum and How Oregon Got Them," *McClure's*, XXXVII, 1911, 234-248; Lincoln Steffens, "U'Ren the Law-giver; the Legislative Blacksmith of Oregon and the Tools He Has Fashioned for Democracy," *American Magazine*, XLV, 1908, 527-540; Jonathan Bourne, "Oregon's Struggle for Purity in Politics," *Independent*, LXVIII, 1910, 1374-1378. On the relationship of the Progressive movement to the exposure of fraud, see Stephen Puter, *Looters of the Public Domain*, Portland, 1908, and Lincoln Steffens, "Heney Grapples the Oregon Land Graft," *American Magazine*, LXIV, 1907, 585-602.

refrigerator cars. Of these eight passed and three were rejected, including the suffrage amendment. By 1908 the direct legislation mill was grinding a larger product. In that year 19 measures were presented, 12 of which passed. In 1910 the voters decided on 32 different bills and constitutional amendments; in 1912 on 37; and in 1914 on 29. Within a five-year interval the Oregon electorate declared itself on more than 100 pieces of legislation.

Between 1904 and 1914 no less than 12 amendments to the state constitution were adopted by initiative petitions, including woman suffrage, prohibition, recall by petition and popular vote, home rule for cities, indictment by grand jury, abolition of the death penalty, the reorganization of the judiciary, and changes in the process of amendment itself. An equal number of reforms were embodied in bills that were submitted to the voters and passed. Some of these were measures of hardly less importance than the amendments. A direct primary law, adopted in 1904, was subsequently reënforced by a further stipulation directing the legislature to vote for the people's choice in the nomination of United States senators. Through these initiatives, implemented by "Statement No. 1" (a pledge by members of the legislature to support the candidate with the winning popular vote), Oregon devised a unique and ingenious procedure for the direct election of United States senators some years before the ratification of the Seventeenth (federal) Amendment. In 1910 a presidential primary was added. Measures embodying progressive ideas of social and economic legislation included laws regulating public utilities and freight rates and prohibiting the issuance of free passes by the railroads, gross earnings taxes on sleeping car and refrigerator car companies, employers' liability and workmen's compensation laws, and an eight-hour day for public works projects.[2]

It was remarked at the time that the citizenry of Oregon "got"

---

[2] Allen H. Eaton, *Oregon System, the Story of Direct Legislation*, Chicago, 1912; James D. Barnett, *Operation of the Initiative, Referendum and Recall in Oregon*, New York, 1915; Paul T. Culbertson, "History of the Initiative and Referendum in Oregon," unpublished thesis, University of Oregon, 1941; Burton J. Hendrick, "Lawmaking by the Voters in Oregon," *McClure's*, XXXVII, 1911, 435-450; and "Statement, No. 1," *ibid.*, 505-519; Frederic C. Howe, "Oregon, the Most Complete Democracy in the World," *Hampton*, XXVI, 1911, 459-472; George H. Haynes, "People's Rule in Oregon," *Political Science Quarterly*, XXVI, 1911, 32-62; Charles H. Carey, "New Responsibilities of Citizenship," Oregon Bar Association *Proceedings*, 1908-1910, 18-41.

political decency much as they got religion. Seventy-five percent of the electorate voted on the legislative measures that appeared on the ballot. Grange assemblies and union meetings were devoted to discussions of pending measures. Young women and book salesmen, retired clergy and students working their way through college formed brigades to secure signatures for this petition or that. Receiving five cents per name for their efforts, they invaded office buildings and apartment houses in the cities, and tramped miles from farm to farm in the rural areas. In no other state were the plain people so voluble and argumentative on specific questions of public policy.

Undoubtedly too much was claimed for the "Oregon system." It made news in the popular magazines and aroused much comment in the meetings of political scientists. Lincoln Steffens and B. J. Hendrick, F. C. Howe and G. H. Haynes wrote enthusiastically about it. U'Ren and Bourne insisted that it destroyed the political machine. *Arena Magazine* declared that through these new weapons "the strong arm of corrupt wealth will be shorn of its strength or its power to further rob the millions and debauch the government." Woodrow Wilson, after pronouncing it "bosh" in his Princeton classrooms, was later won to it and termed it a safeguard of politics which weakened the boss and strengthened the voice of the people.

On the other hand, there were those who saw in direct government and progressivism a dangerous trend toward class legislation. The electorate did not actually perform the functions of government under the new system. It was merely a different way of delegating power which undermined the representative form of government and presented democracy with a new dilemma. For all the talk of unseating the professional politicians, it was quite likely that yet more of them would appear as elections and offices were multiplied. In their great zeal to destroy the power of the boss, the "ballot-box legislators" were unwittingly opening the door to the demagogue.

Undoubtedly William U'Ren, working through his People's Power League, was a key figure in the operation of the Oregon system. An interviewer asked him once whether the people voted the way he wanted them to, and he admitted that so far they had. Lincoln Steffens, intrigued by U'Ren's quiet ways, called him "U'Ren the Lawgiver." Though he worked behind the scenes, preferring to be the secretary of an organization rather than its president, he was nevertheless the man to whom many victories of the people might fairly be credited.

But the voting in Oregon gave little support to the demagogue interpretation, or to the idea that any particular group was putting class legislation on the statute books. The striking thing about it was not the alignment of rich against poor, of the country against the city, of labor against capital, but the high degree of agreement and common purpose that existed between these various groups. True, the labor unions of Portland strongly favored the employer's liability initiative which was rejected in the more wealthy districts. Though a universal eight-hour day initiative lost everywhere, the vote for it was four times as strong among the laborers as in the wealthy groups of the population. But in general there was a marked agreement among the several social classes. Considering the vote on 26 progressive measures together, there was 80 percent agreement between the wealthy class and the laboring class, 86 percent between the laboring class and the rural population, and 94 percent between the city and the rural groups. Society in Oregon was not yet highly stratified and no broad differences of opinion set off one class from another. The direct government measures were adopted not because of the pressure of organized minorities but because so many people of varying circumstances and interests approved them.

The dangers and weaknesses of direct government came from too great a zeal in using it. Oregon's enthusiasm for primaries and initiatives went to such length that the system threatened to break down of sheer weight and complexity. In the election of 1910 Oregon voters were asked to choose 34 state and 11 county officers from a list of 131 candidates. In 1912 they were confronted with a ballot measuring 18¼ by 34½ inches which presented 37 direct government measures and six candidates for United States senator in addition to the contests for state and local offices. As a Portland policeman remarked, this was "voting a bed quilt," legislating by the square yard. It presented formidable problems which must be solved if the citizen was to perform his tasks at all intelligently. The people's interest and sense of responsibility continued at a high level. Voters expressed themselves on short bills and long ones, on technical measures and simple ones, on laws and on constitutional amendments with about the same faithfulness. But there was growing talk of the necessity of achieving a shorter ballot. U'Ren himself came forward with proposals that would stagger the terms of various elective officials so that no single election would involve more than a comparatively small number of them. The year 1914 saw the peak in mass appeals to the voters. The number of measures was much smaller in 1916, and in 1918. Yet the decline was not the result of an effort to temper the excesses of reform. Progressivism in Oregon was sensitive to the climate of national politics and world affairs. The zeal for social legislation abated throughout the country during World War I, and in the Far West as elsewhere the domestic issues of politics were less urgent than the vital questions of neutrality and the demands of the war.[3]

Social Legislation in Idaho and Washington

Washington and Idaho shared the mood of progressivism along with Oregon. In both these sister states, however, the initiative and referendum came late (1911 in Idaho and 1912 in Washington) and most of the social and economic legislation of the period was therefore enacted by the legislatures rather than by the electorate directly. In both states the demand for such laws was so great that Republican lawmakers responded to it and put their stamp on a number of measures that would have had little chance of passage a few years earlier.

Idaho writers, looking back on these years, find a difference in matters of reform between the vehemence of the coast states and the "dry and placid" climate of the interior. Idaho did little experimenting in the improvement of government and produced almost no in-

Idaho

[3] George A. Thacher, "Interesting Election in Oregon," *Independent*, LXIX, 1910, 1434-1438; James D. Barnett, "Presidential Primary in Oregon," *Political Science Quarterly*, XXXI, 1916, 81-104; James H. Gilbert, "Single Tax Movement in Oregon," *Political Science Quarterly*, XXXI, 1916, 25-52; Robert E. Cushman, "Recent Experience with the Initiative and Referendum," *American Political Science Review*, X, 1916, 532-539; William S. U'Ren, "State and County Government in Oregon, and Proposed Changes," *Annals of the American Academy of Political and Social Science*, XLVII, 1913, 271-273; G. H. Haynes, "People's Rule on Trial," *Political Science, Quarterly*, XXVIII, 1913, 18-33; Charles Hollingsworth, "So-called Progressive Movement; Its Real Nature, Causes and Significance," *Annals of the American Academy of Political and Social Science*, XLIII, 1912, 32-48; William F. Ogburn, "Political Thought of Social Classes," *Political Science Quarterly*, XXXI, 1916, 300-317; "Social Legislation on the Pacific Coast," *Popular Science Magazine*, LXXXVI, 1915, 274-289.

novations of its own. The state accepted, however, and put into effect a number of ideas that originated elsewhere and were generally popular throughout the West.

Voters approved a woman suffrage amendment in 1905, several years before either Washington or Oregon. In 1907 the legislature passed a law restricting and regulating lobbying, and two years later, after a considerable skirmishing and agitation, adopted the direct primary. In 1911 followed the initiative and referendum amendment, itself a product of the trend of progressivism. A state banking commission, established in 1905, showed a recognition of the need of scrutinizing the activities of banks while the public utilities commission (1913) offered a similar protecton to the consumer in monitoring the rates charged for essential services. A state-wide workmen's compensation program passed the legislature in 1917.

The total product was somewhat meager, and seemed not to bespeak the popular concern that one found in Oregon and Washington. In 1906 six constitutional amendments were placed before the voters; only one of them passed. The general discussion of public affairs failed to catch the imagination in a state which found its excitement in violence at the Coeur d'Alene mines, or the trial of Harry Orchard for killing Governor Frank Steunenberg. Nevertheless the essential features of progressivism found acceptance in Idaho, both in broadening the participation of the people in politics and legislation, and in implementing the principle of state regulation of economic enterprise.[4]

Washington, like Idaho, carried out its progressive legislation through the Republican party but went rather further with it and tested the issues involved in it more thoroughly. Both the railway commission law (1905) and the direct primary (1907) were the result of a mounting popular protest against the intervention of the railroad lobby in political affairs. Previously the railroads had effectively defeated all attempts to establish a regulatory agency despite the fact that the constitutional convention anticipated and authorized the creation of one. Nominating conventions became a hollow mock-

---

[4] *Idaho Encyclopedia,* compiled by the Federal Writers' Project of the W.P.A., Caldwell, Idaho, 1938; Boyd Martin, *Direct Primary in Idaho,* Stanford University, 1947.

ery of democracy when J. D. Farrell put his private car on a siding nearby, and from behind drawn curtains sent out the word as to what should or should not be done. The widespread complaint against such practices eventually produced a reaction against them in the legislature itself. The railway commission bill passed in 1905 with only 11 opposing votes in the House of Representatives and four in the Senate. The direct primary passed the Senate (1907) by a vote of 39 to 1. Here was no party contest, but a general acknowledgement of the desirability of the reform.

Other measures went through with similar top-heavy votes. The 1911 legislature passed such measures as the workmen's compensation law, an eight-hour day for women, and the initiative and referendum amendment by majorities of three to one. A small group of die-hards voted in opposition—an engineer and a manufacturer from Tacoma, a banker from Kelso, a dairyman from Oysterville, a dentist from Vancouver—but there was no signficant pattern in their alignment.

We should not assume from these apparently easy victories that the support for progressive legislation was spontaneous and unplanned. On the contrary, it was the result of skillful agitation and lobbying, and careful organization.

The adoption of woman suffrage in Washington, for example, was realized through the efforts of Mrs. Emma Smith DeVoe and Mrs. May Arkwright Hutton. Mrs. DeVoe devised important points of strategy. There was to be no offensive militancy, no noisy suffragettes arguing shrilly about the place of women, whether at home or in the public forum. This campaign was always in good taste. Its persuasiveness was of frills and ruffles and a man hardly knew when or why it was that he came to think more favorably of ladies at the polls. Mrs. DeVoe was everywhere, traveling, speaking, making friends and influencing people. Hers was the personal note, gracious, winning, and subtle. Mrs. Hutton was of different stuff. A person of means, she directed an energetic campaign from her home in Spokane. Her approach was through the printed as well as the spoken word: books and pamphlets, newspaper stories, and articles in magazines. Briefly it appeared the two might clash and quarrel, but the rivalry was avoided and together they succeeded with an issue more often brought up and more often rejected than any other political proposal of the period.

The initiative and referendum was likewise handled with a deft touch. Having engineered the drive for the amendment in Oregon, U'Ren led a similar campaign in Washington as well. The Direct Legislation League in Washington was the counterpart of the People's Power League in Oregon, an aggressive and efficient propaganda organization that marshaled popular support, steered the desired measures through the legislature, and got out the votes when constitutional amendments required ratification. The League relied upon a number of sympathetic groups, notably the Grange and the labor unions, but welded them together and secured a wider backing from the public generally. Success was the result of hard work and smart politics. Little was left to chance.[5]

Legislation designed to ameliorate the lot of the worker was moderate in its terms, by our present standards, yet at the time it represented important steps forward. Child Labor Laws of 1903 and 1907 protected minors against the more flagrant forms of exploitation. A 1911 law gave women workers an eight-hour day. Two years later the legislature enacted a minimum wage law that benefited both women and children. Under the latter provisions a commission was set up and a study was made of existing conditions. Minimum wage levels were then established for several different groups of occupations: ten dollars per week for office workers and mercantile establishments, nine dollars for telephone operators and industrial workers, and a corresponding scale for other classes of workers. Enforcement left something to be wished for, and when the hotel proprietors protested the nine-dollar minimum, the Commission was reluctant to test the full limits of its legal authority. Despite its limitations, the law still had its benefits in the investigation of conditions and the realization of some improvement in the attitude of employers generally.

More substantial gains were made in the Workman's Compensation Law of 1911. This law not only recognized the principle of collective liability but it set up an industrial insurance department administered by the state. The department operated a state accident fund into which sums were paid by both employees and employers at designated rates varying from $1.50 per 100 dollars of payroll up to

[5] Winston Thorsen, "Washington State Nominating Conventions," *PNQ*, XXXV, 1944, 99-119; "Woman's Victory in Washington," *Collier's*, XLVI, January 7, 1911, Sec. 1, 25; Claudius O. Johnson, "Adoption of the Initiative and Referendum in Washington," *PNQ*, XXXV, 1944, 291-303.

ten dollars per 100 dollars, depending upon the hazards of the industry. Employees covered by the fund received stated payments in case of accident, and provision was made for pensions to dependents: 20 dollars per month to widows and a monthly allowance for children not yet 16 years old.

Though the law was decried as state socialism, its success disarmed the critics and astonished even those who defended it. The coverage was admittedly inadequate; in this respect it was only the first step toward social security. It nevertheless offered a great improvement over other similar laws by eliminating some of the costs of private insurance, by securing prompt and reasonable payment without the necessity of litigation, and by encouraging the prevention of accidents through publicizing safety practices in industrial plants.[6]

Progressives Form Their Own Party

Such, then, was the record of progressive legislation in the Pacific Northwest. Outwardly it might seem that it was accomplished without factionalism or struggle within the political parties. Republican control of the legislatures was never in question. In Washington and Idaho most legislators rode the groundswell of progressive sentiment and supported social and economic measures without feeling that their loyalty to party was called in question. Perhaps Republicanism was gradually changing its spots and the G.O.P. was coming to accept a new political philosophy.

Actually, if one looked more closely, the politics of the progressive era were far from peaceful. The Old Guard learned slowly and gave ground only grudgingly. Progressivism was not always a philosophy; sometimes it was a convenient campaign position assumed because it would win votes when a candidate did not have the regular party organization behind him. Insurgency was at first a personal and individual matter. Later, however, it indicated an alignment within the Republican party and even before 1912 it led to serious defections which resulted in a third-party explosion.

In some respects the experience of Oregon and Washington was much the same. In Oregon Jonathan Bourne exploited the possibilities

[6] Archibald W. Taylor, "Operation of the Minimum Wage Law in the State of Washington," *American Economic Review*, V, 1915, 398-405; Hamilton Higday, "Washington's Unique Compensation Law," *Independent*, LXXIII, 1912, 774-776.

of the progressive movement, especially the direct primary, and won a seat in the United States Senate by doing so. Washington's Miles Poindexter did the same thing. Both men achieved some national prominence for their speeches and writings on progressive themes, though we may wonder how deep were the convictions of either one. Abraham Lafferty of Portland was elected in 1910 as a progressive Republican to the House of Representatives. Borah of Idaho based his politics on a direct appeal to the people and the claim that he was an independent who owed little or nothing to the support of any political machine or to the favor of Big Business.

Democrats appeared more prominently in Oregon. Political observers pointed with some amazement to the spectacle of a Republican legislature (even with the obligations of Statement No. 1) sending to the United States Senate the Democrat Governor George Chamberlain. At a time when Oregon voters were filling the legislature with a solid phalanx of Republicans they elected Chamberlain, then Oswald West, to be governor. These events had no parallel in Washington or Idaho. In both the latter states Republican governors took the initiative in recommending legislation. Washington voters found in Senator Wesley Jones of Yakima a regular Republican politician who without taint of insurgency proved himself a hard-working and conscientious public servant. Since the party organization was being taken more and more out of the hands of the old school politicians and was being made increasingly responsible, there was not the same need for voters to cross party lines.[7]

In all three states the atmosphere of progressivism and reform encouraged a considerable independence on the part of both candidates and voters. To some extent this was reflected in the Socialist vote, which though small, nearly doubled between 1908 and 1912. To a slight degree it could be detected in the strengthening of Democratic forces, especially in Washington where the Bryan vote in 1908 was significant in a number of east-side counties. The most important expression of it came in 1912 when Roosevelt and Taft contested with

[7] Russell G. Hendricks, "Election of Senator Chamberlain, the People's Choice," *OHQ*, LIII, 1952, 63-88; Chester H. Case, Jr., "Oregon System and Oswald West," unpublished thesis, Reed College, 1952; Keith Murray, "Republican Party Politics in Washington During the Progressive Era," unpublished thesis, University of Washington, 1946; Claudius O. Johnson, "William E. Borah, the People's Choice," *PNQ*, XLIV, 1953. 15-22.

one another for control of the Republican party. This was a national rather than a local development, yet it precipitated a clash in the individual states between the progressives in the party and the regulars. The effect of it was to split the Republican party within the region as well as nationally.

In Washington the split reached down to the grass roots. A dozen county conventions, meeting early in 1912, wrangled interminably as Taft and Roosevelt men wrestled for control, and finally sent rival delegations to the state nominating convention at Aberdeen. Here, too, the issue of control was fought bitterly and inconclusively with the result that two state delegations journeyed to Chicago. Since the national committee on credentials was controlled by the Taft forces, the Roosevelt delegation was refused admission, whereupon the Washington progressives joined with other Bull Moose contingents to organize their own party.

In the fall elections Roosevelt carried Washington by a plurality of 26,000 votes. Wilson led in only 12 counties; Roosevelt led in 19, and Taft in 8. Roosevelt led Taft in 31 out of 39 counties. Not only did the Bull Moosers win in the presidential contest; they likewise captured two of the four seats in the lower house of Congress and 38 seats in the state legislature. It was a signal show of strength, yet it demonstrated mainly the size of the independent vote, rather than a significant change of party affiliation as between Republicans and Democrats. Comparing the 1908 election with 1912 only one county (Douglas) shifted from Republican to Democrat.

In Oregon and Idaho the effects of the third-party movement were somewhat different. At first glance the swing to Wilson appeared to be greater since he carried both states and won a plurality in 23 out of 34 counties in Oregon, and in 14 out of 23 in Idaho. Democrat Harry Lane was elected United States Senator from Oregon. What happened, however, was that the defections from the regular Republican organization were serious enough to lose control for Taft without being so large as to win for Roosevelt. The Democratic vote constituted a smaller fraction of the total vote in 1912 than in 1908, in these states as in Washington. But the Progressive vote (1912) ran lower than in Washington: 24 percent in Idaho and 27 percent in Oregon as compared with Washington's 35 percent. In Oregon and

Idaho together Taft won a plurality in 15 counties, and led Roosevelt in 36. On the other hand, the Socialists received a larger proportion of the non-Democratic protest vote, in Idaho as much as 30 percent of it. Since the protest vote as a whole was smaller and was itself divided between Socialists and Progressives, it gave the Democrats control if only by default.[8]

The temporary nature of the protest alignment in 1912 was shown very plainly during the next few years. Republicans bent every effort to healing the party schism and largely succeeded. James Bryan and Jacob Falconer, Washington Bull Moosers, failed to win reëlection to Congress, while the Progressives in the state legislature lost two-thirds of their seats in 1914 and disappeared thereafter. Miles Poindexter won reëlection to the Senate in 1916 but rather in spite of his third-party adventures than because of them. In all three states the third-party protest vote declined to less than 8 percent of the total, and the region, like the nation, returned again to the two-party system.

The healing of Republican wounds did not mean the immediate restoration of the G.O.P. to power, only a realignment within the major parties. C. C. Dill, Democrat from Spokane, served two terms in Congress, and in the 1916 election Wilson carried Washington and Idaho with a margin of some 15,000 votes in each state. Nineteen counties in Washington and nine in Idaho, which had been Republican in 1908 and Progressive in 1912 voted Democratic in 1916, suggesting the extent to which the independent vote of 1912 became the Democratic vote of 1916. Domestic issues were so intertwined, however, with questions of foreign policy that the final eclipse of insurgency is not to be clearly traced or defined. It is significant, by way of comparison, that only nine Oregon counties followed the transition to the Democrats while 14 of the Progressive counties of 1912 reverted to the Republican column. Hughes carried the state in 1916 though by a slender plurality. Thus the Republicans recaptured more of the independent vote in Oregon than they did in either of her sister states. For the moment the issues of progressivism were everywhere put aside. We shall have occasion presently to see how they were revived after World War I.

---

[8] Keith Murray, "Aberdeen Convention of 1912," *PNQ*, XXXVIII, 1947, 99-108; Edgar E. Robinson, "Distribution of the Presidential Vote of 1912," *American Journal of Sociology*, XX, 1914, 18-30.

Development of
Supporting Industries to 1914

INTERPRETIVE KEY

During the early years of the twentieth century the progress of the Pacific Northwest in economic development took a form somewhat different from the earlier boom. While still dependent upon conditions of national prosperity which stimulated emigration and loosened the purse strings of eastern investors, continued growth required the establishment of a variety of types of economic enterprise by which the people could make a living and the investors could profit. Several of these major industries were closely related to the natural resources of the area: agriculture, lumbering, the fisheries, and industrial mining.

Each of these industries expanded tremendously during the years 1890-1914. It was a period of heavy exploitation and the productivity of Northwest resources undergirded the growing regional economy. On the other hand, it was a time when the stern realities of competition in national and international markets became plain, and imposed their requirements upon all producers whether old or new. Success was not easy even when the gifts of the land were bountiful. Only by considerable shrewdness and good management could a bonanza be transformed into substantial and permanent economic gains.

The spirit of the day was thus only half expressed by the booster with his reliance upon advertising and promotion. Equally important were the men who took an industry, with all its headaches as well as its potentialities, and made something of it. A study of such men and of their task and achievements is the subject of the following several chapters.

23

New Developments in Agriculture

Farming in the Regional Economy

The sun shone brightly in the Pacific Northwest and the land was fertile. Though cities and industries were becoming increasingly important in the regional economy, agriculture continued to be a principal means of making a living, as it had been during the pioneer period. Farms represented a larger fraction of the estimated wealth of the area in 1910 than in 1890, and farming supported one of the largest occupational groups. In 1910 nearly one man in four, of those gainfully employed, was engaged in some kind of agricultural or animal industry. There were as many in agriculture as in all lines of trade and transportation put together, and more than twice as many as were employed in the extractive industries of logging, fishing, and mining. If the sawyers and lumber mill workers were counted with the extractive industries, there was a man on the farm for every man in manufacturing of any kind from the bakery to the smelter.

During the first decade of the new century farm values increased nearly 300 percent, three times the rate of growth recorded by the nation as a whole. For the State of Washington alone this meant a gain of 500,000,000 dollars, a figure that put this state in the same class with Kansas, Nebraska, and Illinois. In 1910 the average farm was worth nearly 11,000 dollars compared with a national average of 6,444 dollars. Measuring their position in terms of *per capita* output, Northwest farmers kept pace with the rapidly expanding population. In dollar values they produced in 1910 75 dollars worth of agricultural goods for every man, woman, and child in the region, a figure half again as high as that of 1890. The numbers are somewhat deceptive, for prices advanced considerably during the 20-year interval. Nevertheless the increasingly bountiful harvests of grain, fruit and vegetables gave the Northwest a new importance in eastern markets and abroad as well.[1]

In many places agriculture lost its frontier characteristics. In 1900 it was still possible to buy land in the wheat belt for seven to ten dollars per acre. A decade later the figures stood four times higher. Irrigated lands in Yakima and Chelan counties rose much more, bringing 126 to 146 dollars per acre in 1910. Farm lands in the valleys back of Seattle and Tacoma were priced fully as high, while those around Portland rose to 228 dollars per acre. The day of cheap land was plainly over. For those who established themselves early, the rising values brought substantial gains, but for others who came later farming was an enterprise which required a considerable investment and put them under a heavy indebtedness.

The farmer's financial position was still favorable on the whole in 1910, for the increased property values more than balanced his debt. To be sure, one farmer in three had a mortgage on his place (it had been one in five only a few years earlier) and the average indebtedness had risen in this interval from 1,300 to 2,000 dollars. Nevertheless this figure represented only 22 percent of the value of the farm. The Washington farmer had an equity of 7,000 dollars in his property, which was higher than in any other state except Nebraska.

The highly commercialized nature of agricultural operations brought the farmer more and more into a complex network of marketing and distribution. Ships and railroads offered a means of transport, but many agencies played their part in storing the crops and getting them to the consumer. Sometimes such functions as these were handled by middlemen and the plowman stayed in his field. Increasingly, however, farmers came to study the problems of shipping

[1] The general analysis of agricultural progress offered here is based upon a comparison of the reports of the Census Bureau for 1890, 1900, and 1910. Most of the references cited as supporting the present chapter relate specifically to the years prior to 1920. A few are included, however, which cover the more recent period as well. They are mentioned because they were found helpful, and because they fall into place better here than in later chapters. For example, see Paul A. Eke, "Trends in the Agriculture of the Pacific Northwest," *Proceedings of the Ninth Annual Pacific Coast Economic Conference*, Corvallis, 1930; and Neil W. Johnson and Rex E. Willard, *Trends in Agriculture in Washington, 1900-30*, Washington Agricultural Experiment Station, Bulletin 300, Pullman, Washington, June, 1934.

and merchandising for themselves, developed those products that could be sold most readily, and even began to manage their own storage and selling problems on a coöperative basis.

The pressure to achieve a high productivity put a premium on scientific and technical studies. Chemists analyzed the character of soils, entomologists studied the pests that threatened the crops, and biologists experimented with many varieties of plants to discover those best adapted to western conditions. These were problems which demanded the specially trained expert for their solution. Most of the work was done at the agricultural experiment stations which were established in the important farming areas, and were supported partly by state appropriations and partly by the federal government. One of Enoch Bryan's interests when he became president of the State College of Washington was the reorganization of the experiment station to make the program more effective. C. V. Piper, W. J. Spillman, and Elton Fulmer carried on numerous experiments and published bulletins which put much helpful information at the disposal of the practical farmer. Doubtless their influence at the beginning was not widespread, but as time went on a body of scientific data was built up which was increasingly valuable.[2]

At first glance it would seem that the region was still a single-crop economy. Cereals continued to be the principal products as they had been earlier. In the State of Washington wheat represented 44.5 percent of the value of all crops (1910), indicating a dependence on this one commodity that was greater than in any other state except North Dakota. In the three Northwest states the value of cereals comprised 46.5 percent of the total value of crops raised; for Washington the figure was 54.1 percent. The suggestion in these figures is clear enough that agriculture suffered from a lack of balance and diversification.

Yet a comparison of the grain farms with those of other regions and with other types of farms puts the situation in a somewhat different perspective. Elsewhere the reliance on grain crops was much greater. In eight states of the Middle West, for example, the value of cereals ran above 70 percent of total crop values. If Washington

---

[2] Enoch Bryan, *Historical Sketch of the State College of Washington, 1890-1925*, Spokane, 1928. See also the file of reports and bulletins published by the Agricultural Experiment Stations in the individual states.

farmers put 40 percent of their improved land into grain, so did those in Kansas and Nebraska, Iowa and Wisconsin, even Ohio and Delaware. In the deep South and Texas cotton accounted for two-thirds of the value of everything raised. Apparently the plight of the Northwest was not different from that of other agricultural sections.

Furthermore the growth of the wheat farms was matched by the expansion of animal husbandry and a great increase in the production of forage crops, fruits, and vegetables. Hay and forage were worth in dollars twice as much in 1910 as wheat had been worth ten years earlier, an evidence that cattle raising and dairy herds were considerable enterprises. Oregon's fruit growers contributed 40 cents in farm income (1910) for every dollar that came in from the wheat fields. While the vegetable gardens of the Northwest earned but 8.1 percent of total crop values, the figure for the United States as a whole was only 7.6 percent. In the general ratio of the different kinds of agriculture to each other, the Northwest mirrored the national economy remarkably closely. The region put a slightly smaller proportion of its improved land into grain, a somewhat larger proportion into forage, and almost exactly as much into vegetables. Any conclusion that the local economy was unbalanced should be tempered with the realization that in degree of diversification here was the nation in miniature.

The region possessed an amazing variety of conditions in soil and climate, and the farmers turned it to advantage. The grain belt, the fruit districts, truck gardening areas, dairy industry, and ranching business, each had its own pattern of geographic distribution, and its own organization and methods. Only as we consider these lines individually can we appreciate how they contributed to the economy as a whole.

Wheat and Grains

Of all the different kinds of farmers in the Northwest the ones who carried out their operations on the most princely scale were the wheat farmers. Some of these men could drive their harvesters in a straight line for five miles without crossing the boundaries of their property. In the Palouse hills wheat farms averaged in 1910 384 acres in size; in Adams county they were twice as large (775 acres), representing a capital investment of better than

20,000 dollars. It was reported that the more successful wheat farmers earned the value of their farms in a single year, that they stored one-half to two-thirds of their crop in their own warehouses, and with all their bills paid could laugh at the wheat market. Whitman County wheat men alone produced 10,000,000 dollars worth of wheat in 1909.[3]

North and west of the Palouse were the largest farms, though not necessarily the best ones. In this area the soil was not so rich, and light rainfall forced the operators to learn the methods of dry farming. Failure and disappointment were not uncommon, and a certain amount of consolidation took place.

A considerable amount of experimenting was necessary to develop the varieties of wheat that were best suited to the Inland Empire. The experiment stations put in as many as 20 different kinds of seed, and W. J. Spillman, the agriculturist at Pullman, Washington, began working on special hybrids that would bring a good yield and have the stiff straw necessary for a fairly long harvest season. Both spring wheat and winter wheat were raised successfully, and in some areas of good rainfall a farmer might harvest two crops in a season, one of wheat and one of oats or barley. Of the spring wheats Little Club proved the best all-around variety for humid areas while Bluestem was better for the drier sections. Fortyfold and Turkey Red were the favorites among the winter wheats.

The picture of the wheat grower laughing at the market may have been true of some of them in the best of good times, but it was hardly typical of wheat farmers generally. Most of them depended upon the early sale of their crops, and many of them were not at all happy about the handicaps they suffered in doing so. Thanks to the number of railroads which had been built across Kansas, the farmers there paid only 3.6 cents per bushel to haul their grain to the nearest shipping point. The Washington farmer paid double that amount. Because of the greater distance to Liverpool the ocean voyage cost the Northwest shipper 16.8 cents per bushel, a full ten cents more than his Kansas competitor paid. For a time the Minneapolis millers

[3] Donald W. Meinig, "Environment and Settlement in the Palouse, 1868-1910," unpublished thesis, University of Washington, 1950; Oliver Baker, "Columbia Plateau Wheat Region," *Economic Geography*, IX, 1933, 167-197; William E. Leonard, "Wheat Farmer of Southeastern Washington," *Journal of Land and Public Utility Economics*, II, 1926, 23-39.

thought to reach out to the Far West, but transportation costs were against them and very little wheat from this area reached markets in Eastern United States. Ironically enough, Walla Walla wheat paid five to ten cents per bushel more for transportation to Chicago than to England. The Northwest did compete with Kansas in the Liverpool market even though the net value of wheat at the farm might be eight cents less per bushel. Only the superior productivity of fresh fertile soils made it possible to do so.[4]

In such circumstances as these the grain farmers usually contented themselves with selling their produce to large exporting houses in Portland, accepting prices that were determined by market conditions in England and the Orient. If prices were favorable, say 80 cents or more, wheat usually went to England as grain. If the price fell lower, it was milled in Portland or Tacoma for shipment to the Orient as flour. Of the several port cities Portland was the most favored, yet during several years from 1902 on the export trade from Puget Sound was as large or larger.

Ranching

In the Northwest, as in a number of other areas where agriculture went through a series of stages in its development, the progress of intensive farming was accompanied by a stabilization of livestock and sheep raising and a growth in the dairy industry. Of the various kinds of domestic animals to be found on the farms in the region, horses were by far the most valuable. Useful in many ways as draft animals, they increased with the number of farms until they represented an investment twice as large as the cattle and dairy herds and flocks of sheep added together. Beef cattle totaling 1,000,000 animals were maintained to serve the growing markets within the region, the number rising only slightly during the first decade of the century. Wool production leveled off at about 38,000,000 pounds for the region, Oregon and Idaho each reporting about 2,000,000 sheep of shearing age. Meanwhile dairy herds doubled in size and an industry which in earlier days had been little

[4] Frank Andrews, "Freight Costs and Market Values," U.S. Department of Agriculture, *Yearbook, 1906*, 371-386; A. Berglund, "Wheat Situation in Washington," *Political Science Quarterly*, XXIV, 1909, 489-503; see also U.S.D.A., Bureau of Statistics, Bulletin 89, 1911.

more than a side line now emerged as an important specialty. By 1910 the dairy farmers owned 444,000 milch cows, and delivered 146,000,000 gallons of milk and 37,000,000 pounds of butter fat annually.[5]

The chief change in ranching had to do with the conditions of grazing. Most of the open range was gone and although great acreages of land still remained in the public domain, most of it could be used for grazing only under federal regulations. Between 1890 and 1910 nearly 48,000,000 acres, situated mainly in the Cascade and Blue Mountains, became national forest reserves. After some study and consideration a system of permits was worked out to allow the grazing of cattle and sheep on a lease basis, but the number of animals was closely controlled to protect the vegetation, and the effect was to check the growth of an industry which in previous years had been a rapidly expanding one. Since the sheep cropped the mountain grasses more closely than did cattle, grazing permits were issued more sparingly and this likewise tended to limit the number and size of the flocks.

Despite the vicissitudes of the business, Oregon woolgrowers continued to be a significant and picturesque group. The Basques, an immigrant group who made their homes in Eastern Oregon, were widely known for their skill with sheep, and made of sheep-raising not only an enterprise but a way of life. In the Kittitas Valley, too, and in the Snake River country sheep-raising was an important enterprise. The United States Department of Agriculture did what it could to encourage as careful treatment of fleeces as was given to them by Australian competitors.

Cattle growers found it difficult or impossible to reach markets in the East or Middle West, but they benefited from the growing local demand. Eastward movements by rail declined, but the packing houses in the western cities expanded their trade with the growing urban population, taking a larger number of beef cattle each year.

---

[5] Dexter K. Strong, "Beef Cattle Industry in Oregon, 1890-1938," *OHQ*, XLI, 1940, 251-287; Todd V. Boyce, "History of the Beef Cattle Industry in the Inland Empire," unpublished thesis, State College of Washington, 1937. For references on the sheep industry, see the Minto report, previously cited, and Frederic S. Hultz, *Range Sheep and Wool in the Seventeen Western States*, New York, 1931; also Frederick V. Coville, *Forest Growth and Sheep Grazing in the Cascade Mountains of Oregon*, Washington, D.C., 1898; J. S. Cotton, *Range Management in the State of Washington*, U.S.D.A., Bureau of Plant Industry, Bulletin 75. 1905.

Slaughterhouses in Oregon and Washington did a 21,400,000-dollar business in 1909 as compared with 6,400,000 ten years earlier. Many of these animals came from ranches comparatively close at hand in the Kittitas Valley or the Blue Mountains where they were fattened for market either on native grasses or forage that was grown for the purpose.

Dairy Products

Dairy farming prospered most in the valley lands of Western Washington and Oregon, especially where they were fairly accessible to the urban markets. In Washington the northwestern counties of Snohomish, Skagit, and Whatcom reported (1910) more than 33,000 cows. King County alone had 18,000. The chief dairy counties in Oregon were those in the Willamette Valley: Lane, Linn, Washington, and Clackamas.

Truly impressive production records were made on some of these farms. C. W. Orton of Sumner more than doubled the amount of milk he took from each cow, simply through carefully controlled feeding and good management. Charles Eldridge of Chimacum took a world's record with a cow that gave 3,555 pounds of milk in a single month. One of the most modern establishments in the Far West was Fred Stimson's Hollywood Ranch with its herd of Holstein thoroughbreds which was located across Lake Washington from Seattle. Specialized dairy farms in Western Oregon were of much the same type. A typical one in Tillamook County included 53 acres of bottom land which, together with a house, barn, and machinery represented an investment of 32,790 dollars. The stock consisted of 35 dairy cows, Holsteins, Jerseys, and Guernseys, and a Jersey bull.[6]

Bulletins published by agricultural agencies emphasized the opportunities that awaited those who would reclaim the cut-over timber lands, and described in some detail the manner in which it might be done. One emigrant from the Middle West settled 40 acres of logged-off land, put dairy cows on it, and in a short time built it up from a 1,000-dollar investment to 10,000 dollars. "I make more here in the summer in one month out of cream," he declared, "than I did all

[6] Washington State Bureau of Statistics, *Dairying, Poultry and Stock-raising in Washington*, Olympia, 1912.

year in Kansas. Hurrah for Washington." Perhaps he was too enthusiastic, for many stump ranchers remained close to the subsistence level, and certainly the dairyman did not begin to utilize the great acreages that the logger left behind him. Nevertheless the industry did promise a modest living to a number of families who had but a small operating capital with which to start.

In the central and eastern part of the region, too, dairy herds became more important. In the Kittitas section ranchers used their forage crops for milch cows as well as cattle. In Yakima County and in the grain counties of Whitman and Spokane, the number of dairy cows was only a little lower than in the northwestern counties where the industry was more specialized.

The growing market for fresh milk, cream, and butter in the nearby cities did much to encourage the dairy farmer, but the establishment of condensed milk plants and cheese factories in the Far West gave him other outlets for his produce. Carnation built a plant at Kent in September, 1899, which in a fairly short time was turning out 40,000 pounds of condensed milk per day. In 1906 the canned milk from Washington alone was a half-million-dollar item, more than half of which found its way to Alaska. In Coos County, Oregon, the production of cheese became an increasingly profitable venture. In this area cheese factories turned out 124,586 pounds of cheese in 1909, their output being nearly three times that of the rest of Oregon. One pound of every two pounds produced in the entire region came from these factories in the southwest corner.

In Tillamook County the manufacturing and marketing of cheese was much improved by the organization of dairy and creamery associations, which concerned themselves with standardizing grades and consolidating the merchandizing aspects of the industry. In 1899 the Tillamook Dairy Association was organized as a coöperative. After a few years of financial difficulty the association proved its worth and the coöperative movement spread throughout the area until in 1916 all but two of the cheese factories were operated for the benefit of the dairy farmers who supplied them. In 1909 the Tillamook County Creamery Association began operation. Factories were enlarged and improved. Inspectors from the Association visited them and solicited an interchange of ideas for the perfecting of better processing methods. In 1909 a coöperative selling agency served 16 of the larger factories, handling through its central office 90 percent of the output of the county. While prices in New York and Wisconsin tended to govern those in Oregon, it was possible nevertheless to get a good return for the western producers through storing cheese and selling it on a large scale.[7]

Fruit Growing

If wheat dominated the agricultural scene in Walla Walla, Umatilla, and the Palouse, and cattle and sheep in Eastern Oregon and the mountain grazing lands, fruit-growing was the enterprise of greatest promise in several of the lesser river valleys in Central and Western Oregon and in Central Washington. The Hood River and Rogue River districts, where apples had been grown since the 1850's, became widely known around the turn of the century for their commercial orchards. The Hood River growers developed some of the best Yellow Newtowns and Spitzenburgs in the country, and shipped them by the hundreds of carloads to New York City. In the Wenatchee Valley, Okanogan, and around Yakima, apple "ranchers" achieved a productivity that was unsurpassed even in such old and established fruit-growing states as New York and Massachusetts. In 1890 Oregon and Washington produced only 622,000 barrels of apples. In 1917 the figure was ten times as large. Washington, the number one producer among all the states, was then putting on the market 20 percent of the total commercial crop for the entire nation.[8]

These developments came about partly in response to marketing opportunities that opened up with the railroads. Oregon apples reached the large eastern markets almost entirely by rail. Central Washington growers initially shipped more fruit west to the coast

[7] U.S.D.A., *Yearbook*, 1916, 145-157.

[8] U.S.D.A. *Yearbook*, 1918, 374-375; Portland Chamber of Commerce, *Oregon Apple Industry*, Circular No. 2, 1912; Otis W. Freeman, "Apple Industry of the Wenatchee Area," *Economic Geography*, X, 1934, 160-171; G. H. Miller and S. M. Thompson, *Cost of Producing Apples in Wenatchee*, U.S.D.A. Bulletin 446, 1917, and *Cost of Producing Apples in the Hood River Valley*, U.S.D.A. Bulletin 518, 1917; H. J. Ramsey, *et al.*, *Handling and Storage of Apples in the Pacific Northwest*, U.S.D.A. Bulletin 587, 1917; C. W. Kitchen, *et al.*, *Distribution of Northwestern Boxed Apples*, U.S.D.A. Bulletin 935, 1921; O. B. Jesnes, *Coöperative Purchasing and Marketing Organizations Among Farmers in the United States*, U.S.D.A. Bulletin 547, 1917.

than east. Soon, however, this trend was reversed and by 1910 four to six boxes moved to the East for every one to the coast. Since that time the industry has prospered or languished depending upon the wider market outlets.

Success in reaching large numbers of consumers in other parts of the country spurred the planting of thousands of new trees, and drove land values sharply upward until orchard lands acre for acre were the most expensive agricultural properties one could own. First-class fruit lands cleared and favorably situated around Medford, Oregon, brought 250 dollars to 500 dollars per acre in 1912. In Okanogan a few years later improved apple land was worth two or three times that figure. Bearing orchards in Wenatchee were priced in 1914 on the average at 1,925 dollars per acre, while Oregon orchards brought returns of 10 to 15 percent on investments valued at 4,000 dollars an acre. Some growers reported yearly returns ranging from 800 dollars to as much as 2,000 dollars an acre.

Such figures as these suggest a bonanza to those who were alert to take advantage of them. Certainly the attractions were great. Yet they stimulated speculative land-jobbing around Wenatchee on the part of men from Seattle who had no intention of becoming fruit growers themselves, and they encouraged farmers to plant apple trees in Kittitas County and the Columbia basin areas which soon proved to be quite unsuitable. Fruit growing was a specialty and though the local chambers of commerce might paint a rosy picture of the profits to be made, those who became deeply involved in an orchard enterprise found it was one that not only called for a considerable investment of capital but required their attention to many technical details.

Because of these considerations apple ranches in the Wenatchee area were usually small. The average size in 1914 was 11.4 acres of which 6.5 acres were usually in orchard. Even this operation represented an investment of some 20,000 dollars, and approximately one-third of the farmer's operating costs were interest charges on his capital debt. The size was limited, too, by the amount of work involved in the care and cultivation of the trees which the owner and his family found it best to do themselves. There were a few large orchards but for the most part apple growing was not something to be entrusted to hired help or tenants.

Methods of careful husbandry were the secret of success. Whether one practiced the clean cultivation of the ground or planted a mulch crop of alfalfa, clover, or vetch between the trees, one must have a regard for the soil itself. Most growers conditioned it with plow and harrow; many enriched it with mulch or manure. In irrigated areas furrowing or "creasing" was necessary to carry the water to each individual tree, and a monthly schedule of watering was followed from May to August. Pruning and thinning the trees were tasks that called for skill and good judgment, and spraying involved four different treatments, first with lime sulphur, later with lead arsenate, which extended from the dormant period of early spring until the end of the summer. Harvesting in the fall season required extra help. Pickers, hired at the rate of $2.50 per day, usually picked 50-80 loose boxes in a ten-hour stretch. Following this the fruit was sent to the packing house where they were tightly packed in boxes and stored in specially constructed quarters until they could be shipped to market.

Storage facilities were as important to the fruitgrower as cheap transportation itself and many commercial orchards throughout the country owed their very existence to the developments in artificial refrigeration that were made around the turn of the century. The first big cold storage warehouse was opened in Boston in 1881, and by 1900 there were 6,000 such plants in the United States with a capacity of 50,000,000 cubic feet. These warehouses, together with the refrigerator cars developed by the railroads, enabled the apple grower to move his crop to the large market areas and preserve them there in good condition for sale throughout the year.

The introduction of improved cold storage houses near the western orchards came slowly. Prior to World War I such installations were available for only a small part of the crop. Much of the fruit was moved to eastern storage; the balance was put into local "common storage" houses. These were barnlike structures insulated from the sun, and ventilated in the roof and beneath the floor to conserve and take advantage of the cool night air. Whatever kind of storage was used, it was important to use the greatest care in handling the fruit. This was not always easy, for the packers used laborers who were often poorly trained and careless. It was in improved handling that the packing houses and coöperative association made their greatest contribution to the building up of the business.

The formation of packers' associations and coöperatives began almost as soon as the orchards themselves appeared. The Yakima County Horticultural Union was organized in 1902 as a joint stock corporation which included both fruitgrowers and middlemen. During the next few years it acquired a number of packing houses scattered up and down the valley and built a large cold storage plant at Yakima. In 1913 a group of local packing associations in the same general area established the Yakima Valley Fruitgrowers Association. This was a nonprofit organization which developed cold storage facilities and carried on marketing activities, mainly through fruit brokers, as a service to its members. To the north in the Wenatchee district local associations of growers appeared and organized marketing agencies to serve them. By 1921 the Wenatchee District Coöperative Association numbered 550 members who were grouped around 21 local units. The real development of centralized marketing followed World War I, but the foundations were well laid during the preceding years.

Berries, Vegetables, and Flower Bulbs

Soft fruits and berries, vegetables both for market consumption and for seed, and flower bulbs were specialties that were concentrated for the most part in the most fertile sections of Western Washington and Oregon and in the irrigated districts of Central Washington and Southern Idaho.[9] These farms developed an amazing productivity. Idaho potato growers raised 179 bushels to the acre, the highest output in the entire United States, and so profitable that four-fifths of the irrigated land under cultivation in Idaho was given to this one crop. Hops were still raised in Puyallup and Yakima and sugar beets began to come into their own in a lesser way in Idaho and in the Yakima Valley. Truck gardens sent their crops of perishable vegetables to feed the urban population of the neighboring cities—celery and asparagas, sweet corn and onions, lettuce, peas, and tomatoes. None of the crop records were impressive compared with those of ten years later, yet the pattern

[9] William Stuart *et al.*, *Potato Culture Under Irrigation*, U.S.D.A. Farmers' Bulletin 953, June, 1918; H. J. Ramsey, *Factors Governing Successful Shipment of Red Raspberries from the Puyallup Valley*, U.S.D.A. Bulletin 274, 1915; J. P. Galvin, "Bulb Industry of Western Washington," *Economic Geography*, XX, 1944, 20-24.

was one which has continued to the present time.

Berries became the leading horticultural industry in the Puyallup area where the growers leagued together in a coöperative association of 1,500 members. Here the best varieties of blackberries and raspberries were grown and shipped to an ever-widening market area. The berry wagons were a familiar sight in the streets of the town, some of them coming from five and six miles out in the country. Early shipments reached the nearest markets by express or moved in refrigerator cars to Spokane and Western Montana. Later in the season carlots were shipped as far east as Minneapolis. This kind of long-distance shipping was possible only with the most careful handling, inspection, and grading. Berries of poorer quality went to local canneries.

The beginnings of the vegetable seed industry dated back to the middle eighties when A. G. Tillinghast established his Puget Sound seed gardens near La Conner. By 1904 cabbage seed was shipped east by the carload, and thousands of seed catalogues were being sent out to the four corners of the country. In 1912 Charles Lilly built up his market through national advertising; at the same time he encouraged other farmers to specialize in growing produce for seed. This led a few years later to the organization of the Skagit Valley Seed Growers Corporation which placed a hundred farmers under contract to supply Lilly with a top-quality product. Many a fine mansion on the La Conner flats was paid for out of money from cabbage seed.

George Gibbs of Whatcom did some of the earliest experimental work with flower bulbs, accomplishing more than anyone else perhaps to demonstrate the feasibility of growing them in the Northwest. Out of his efforts there grew another branch of specialized agriculture which in later years became nationally prominent. Climate and soil alike were suitable for it in a few highly localized areas, notably around Bellingham, Lynden, Woodland, and Puyallup, where the earth was a sandy loam well drained, and where the rainfall was adequate and was distributed throughout the year. Farmers in these areas imported their first bulbs from Europe—narcissus, hyacinth, and tulip—and by much study and hard work learned how to propagate them. Three to six years were required to grow native bulbs for sale, and the process involved a great deal of hand labor in planting, weeding, cultivating, digging, and curing. Most of the product was used in the greenhouse forcing trade with shipments of considerable size going to Chicago and New York. The picture of a field of daffodils or tulips, brightly colored against the mountain background, was one long to be remembered.

The general spirit of these years was one of challenge, either to meet the needs of the rapidly increasing population of the region itself or to reach out to some more distant market. While some branches of farming slackened, they were the ones that harked back to the open range, the unsettled countryside. For the most part it seemed that the chief obstacle to the progress of agriculture was the lack of land suitable for farming. Repeatedly the bureaus of immigration pointed to the heavy imports of foodstuffs that had to be brought into the region from other areas. But in 1913 Governor Lister of Washington complained that if he had to find a place for even a thousand new farming families, he would be at a loss to tell them where to find reasonably priced land ready for the plow. This pressure to find land was what spurred the construction of the irrigation canals and we should appreciate what this effort meant to the region. If agriculture was to grow, it would be because men found new ways to carry water to the desert wastes.

24

The Lumber Industry

One might think that economic progress, as it produced cities and industries in the Pacific Northwest, would take the region "out of the woods." The lumber industry was something associated with the pioneer days. Would not the patterns of land use and occupancy change as frontier conditions gave way to those of the modern industrial world? Surely the forests would not dominate the scene. Yet actually the forests continued to be a principal source of support. Conditions of exploitation changed, but forestry and lumbering persisted as one of the largest components in the regional economy. In 1899 the *Pacific Lumber Trade Journal* proclaimed that lumber was king; that all but seven of the towns in Western Washington were dependent upon their big trees. In 1914, nearly 30 years after the railroads had put an end to frontier isolation in the cities of the Far Corner, 55 percent of the payrolls in the region were directly derived from the lumber industry. The output of the lumber camps and mills represented 38 percent of the value of all manufactures, and the capitalized value of the forest lands in the region was estimated to be slightly over one billion dollars. The lumber industry was an enterprise that ranked second only to farming in importance. Whether measured in terms of land values or output, the Pacific Northwest had a stake of three dollars in lumber for every four dollars in agriculture.

The lumber industry thus illustrates very clearly the way the Pacific Northwest economy was expanded and changed under the new conditions of industrialism and finance capitalism, but at the same time remained closely related to the natural products of the soil. Big Business was attracted to the region primarily because of its raw materials. The tremendous expansion of the national economy created a great new market for timber products, and since the virgin forests of the East and Middle West were now largely cut over, the Far West and South assumed an importance as national sources of supply which they did not have before. Speculative buying of timber lands quickly increased their value and the efforts of the large buyers to consolidate their holdings led to complaints of monopoly in the lumber industry just as they had in sugar and petroleum. Meanwhile the financier, the inventor, and the engineer developed a technology in lumbering that put steam power to work at nearly every stage of processing and made the ox team and the simple mill machinery of the earlier years obsolete in a few years time.

The big spurt forward came around 1900 when to a considerable extent the lumber industry of the Upper Mississippi Valley migrated to the west coast. This development had great importance not only because of the expansion of lumbering operations which came about as a result of it, but because of the attendant changes in the pattern of timberland holdings under the pressures of speculative gain.

Timberland Purchases

The era of cheap land was about over and already in 1890 there were signs of a new age in commercial lumbering. Facing a mounting popular protest against cutting on the public domain, and requiring a large and dependable supply of logs for their mills, lumbermen now preferred to own their own timberlands rather than to take their trees from the public domain. As a result immense acreages of timber passed into private ownership. Federal land policy was generous and while it was designed primarily to benefit the individual settler who migrated west and wanted cheap land to live on, the land laws were used by the lumber companies to build up large tracts of timberland without great expense. Dummies and false entrymen who claimed grants under the Homestead law or the Timber and Stone Acts transferred their titles shortly afterward to the company they served. Wagon road and military road grants in Oregon facilitated a concentration of private holdings, and the failure of the state to patent its school lands meant that much valuable timberland which might have been administered by the state was taken up by private claimants instead. Huge federal grants to the Northern Pacific and the Oregon and California railroads were made the basis of some of the largest privately owned timber holdings.

The exhaustion of the forests in the Upper Mississippi Valley and the Great Lakes region greatly increased the demand for timberland in the Pacific Northwest. Middle Western lumbermen, like Ben Healy of Wisconsin, appeared as large stockholders in some of the Puget Sound companies. Contenting themselves at first with the role of absentee owners, they soon took a more active part in the management of the camps and mills. Healy's son-in-law Alfred H. Anderson came west and made himself one of the leaders in the Satsop area around Shelton. Chauncey W. Griggs and his son Everett moved from Minnesota, purchased 80,000 acres from the Northern Pacific, founded the St. Paul and Tacoma Lumber Company, and were soon numbered among the most prominent lumbermen in Washington. California firms like Pope and Talbot were still in the circle of large producers, but increasingly the industry looked toward the East for its leadership as well as its markets. Michigan and Wisconsin men moved west in some number, and the pages of the *West Coast Lumberman*, published in Portland beginning in 1891, contained numerous notices of the visits of Easterners to the Pacific Northwest, and of the purchases of timberlands that followed.

As early as November, 1891, Frederick Weyerhaeuser's name was included among the visitors. The editor denied, to be sure, that this had any great significance, and protested: "It will be a long time before he will plunge very deeply into lands or manufacturing at Puget Sound."

Some few years passed while the St. Paul timber magnate planned his course of action. Then suddenly in 1900 he announced the purchase of 900,000 acres of timberland from the Northern Pacific railroad for a price of six dollars an acre.

This transaction heralded a wave of speculative buying of forest lands in the Far West which had no parallel in the history of the region, or perhaps of the nation. Weyerhaeuser was in a class by himself, so far as land purchasers were considered, his holdings exceeded only by the land-grant railroads which were not in the lumber business as such. Yet what he did on a grand scale, others did to the limit of their resources. In the scramble for stumpage that followed, prices soared to levels previously unheard of, and many speculators, large and small alike, turned a pretty penny trading on the general advance in values.

A few illustrations will serve to show how land prices multiplied sometimes as much as tenfold in a few years. One tract purchased in 1891 for 800 dollars, brought 18,500 dollars when resold in 1909. Another was bought in 1899 for 10,000 dollars and sold again ten years later for 110,000 dollars. A third and larger purchase, this one in Idaho for 240,000 dollars in 1901, brought 2,500,000 dollars in 1909. Great acreages in Oregon and the Sound country, which had been practically without commercial value only a short time before, were eagerly sought out.[1]

This development brought about a change in the pattern of timberland ownership which had far-reaching importance both for the lumber industry and for the progress of forest practice. On the one hand it produced a great concentration of ownership over vast acreages of forest lands. In 1913, according to the Bureau of Corporations, the Weyerhaeuser Timber Company alone owned 26.1 percent of the privately owned standing timber in the state of Washington. Weyerhaeuser and the Northern Pacific Railroad Company together owned 34.7 percent of the privately owned timber in Washington while Weyerhaeuser and the Southern Pacific Company had 22.4 percent of that in Oregon. The Northern Pacific owned 29.8 percent of the private timber in Montana. A full one-half of the private timber in the five states of the Pacific Northwest and California was included in 38 large holdings.

At the same time, speculative profits attracted thousands of small buyers who had neither the means nor the incentives to adopt policies of good forestry. As much as 20 percent of the privately owned timber was held in small acreages (perhaps 1,000 to 2,000 acres) that had less than 60,000,000 board feet of timber each. Thus while three owners controlled 237 billion feet of standing timber in large holdings, some 17,000 owners divided up amongst themselves 205 billion feet more. Because of the small size and isolated location of their holdings, these landowners often found it difficult or impossible to log them

[1] See U.S. Department of Commerce and Labor, Bureau of Corporations, *Lumber Industry*, 4 vols., Washington, D.C., 1913-1914, Vol. I, particularly, 15-26, 65, 100, 109; David M. Ellis, "Recapture of the Oregon and California Land Grant," *PNQ*, XXXIX, 1948, 253-283.

efficiently. Many of them never expected to become lumber operators, but whether they cut their own logs or simply sold their stumpage, the conditions under which they held and exploited their lands usually made for inefficient management. Both the very large private holdings and the very small ones brought dangers and problems that were not to be solved easily.

Experience soon showed that the buying and selling of timberlands and stumpage were enterprises that might or might not be closely identified with the operating of lumber mills and the selling of shingles, boards, and timbers. To some extent the two went together. The rapidly increasing national demand about 1900 and the improved transportation facilities by rail were responsible for both the trading in lands and the expansion of mill facilities. It was true enough, too, as the lumbermen themselves pointed out, that the larger companies which made the big profits were companies which owned both lands and mills. These were the concerns that operated most economically and had the financial resources not only to cut the wood but to get it to market. But increasingly it was realized that the early high margins of profit came from increments in land values rather than from the lumber mills themselves. Once the lumber business was adjusted to the higher values, land ownership ceased to be simply a source of profit and was viewed rather as a capital expense, which under some circumstances might be very burdensome. Meanwhile the operating side of the business was carried on under conditions of sharp fluctuation in volume and in price that seemed to have only a remote connection with land values or land ownership.[2]

The general trend in production was sharply upward during the years 1890 to 1905. Washington's one billion foot output figure of 1888 was doubled by 1895 and trebled in 1902. In 1905 the mills of that state turned out 3.5 billion feet to put Washington in the front rank among the states of the entire nation. Oregon increased its output from 444,000,000 feet (1889) to 1.9 billion in 1909 and Idaho from 27,000,000 feet (1890) to 745,000,000 in 1910. Favorable prices

[2] For realistic analyses of economic conditions existing in the lumber industry, see Cloice R. Howd, *Industrial Relations in the West Coast Lumber Industry*, U.S. Bureau of Labor Statistics, Misc. Pub. No. 349, 1924; and William B. Greeley, *Some Public and Economic Aspects of the Lumber Business*, U.S. Forest Service, Studies of the Lumber Industry, Part I, Washington, D.C., 1917.

prior to 1903 encouraged the building of many new mills (150 in Washington in 1902) and the enlargement of others. The region as a whole attained its peak production for the pre-1917 period in 1913 with a total cut of 7.46 billion feet.

These figures are eloquent testimony to the tremendous capacity of the industry to expand its mechanical facilities both for logging and for milling. Middle Western manufacturers of mill machinery, who were as much interested in developments in the Far West as the lumbermen themselves, placed large advertisements in the trade journals, and kept sales representatives working the new territory. Descriptions of mill layouts, which appeared in the lumbermen's magazines, complete with the specifications of engines, saws, trimmers, and planers, indicate the development of highly mechanized establishments that were a far cry from those that had been the pride of the Far West only a short time previously.

In the logging camps too new machines and tools were devised which handled the heavy timber with speed and precision. Old-timers might smile when Sol Simpson of the Simpson Logging Company sold his bulls and bought first horses and then donkey engines to do his skidding. The newfangled ideas proved their worth and others soon took them up to their advantage. Logging railroads were pushed farther into the inaccessible parts of the mountains, and at Polson's railroad camp, Grays Harbor, the fleet of logging locomotives with their potbellied stacks called attention in picturesque and dramatic fashion to the new importance of steam power. Huge spools of steel wire, delivered at the camps, were spun into rigging that hung like monstrous spider webs against the sky. Until 1911 skidding was done on the ground. After that the spar pole and the high lead rigging found common acceptance. Here indeed was a bold demonstration of power when two men might set the choker on a turn of logs, then stand back to watch them as they were lifted like matchsticks and carried dangling through the air to a loading area 200 yards below them on the mountain slope.

Problems of Production

As early as 1904 lumbermen were plagued by problems of overproduction, for the productive capacity of the mills was expanded more rapidly than the goods could be sold. Despite the fact that output figures increased during several years thereafter, the industry not infrequently ran its mills only five days a week, took several weeks off during the winter for repairs, and closed down a number of establishments altogether. In 1917 William B. Greeley estimated that the output of the mills was only 62 percent of the quantity they were capable of producing.

Stabilization of production was difficult to achieve for several reasons. No single national or world market organization existed which would serve to keep prices uniform and reasonably steady as was the case with wheat, sugar, and other commodities. Lumber prices varied sometimes as much as 50 percent up or down within the space of a year, and it was practically impossible to anticipate such variations or to gauge them closely enough to adjust production to them. Once the mills were operating at a given level, they developed a certain momentum which made them less sensitive to market conditions. Transportation costs, ever a large factor in the operations of the Northwest mills, narrowed their market and often prevented them from shipping to places where they would otherwise have been competitive. Always too there was the possibility that a company would cut to excess because of the necessity of paying taxes on its lands or meeting the interest on its debts.[3]

Because of these various difficulties the leading lumbermen in the region turned their efforts to forming an association of producers through which some degree of common action might be achieved. Victor H. Beckman, one of the Mississippi Valley men who founded in 1895 the *Pacific Lumber Trade Journal*, took the initiative in promoting the organization of trade associations, and pioneered in the gathering of statistical information as the basis for analyzing the market and controlling production. Everett Griggs of the St. Paul and Tacoma Lumber Company was a prominent leader in the movement for more than a decade. Local associations organized during the

[3] F. L. Moravets, *Lumber Production in Oregon and Washington, 1869-1948*, Pacific Northwest Forest and Range Experiment Station, Forest Survey Report No. 100, Portland, 1949; U.S. Bureau of Corporations, Report on the Lumber Industry, Vol. IV, particularly 144. For descriptive details of logging processes, see Stewart Holbrook, *Green Commonwealth . . . Simpson Logging Co. 1895-1945*, Seattle, 1945; and Ralph W Andrews, *This Was Logging*, Seattle, 1954, which contains an excellent selection of pictures by the veteran photographer, Darius Kinsey.

1890's on the Sound and in Portland proved to be short-lived efforts, but soon after 1900 stronger organizations were formed, such as the Pacific Coast Association which had its strength mainly in Washington, and the Oregon Lumber Manufacturers Association (1905). While these groups did not always have the same interests, particularly in matters of railroad rates which favored one or another, both of them grew in membership, and in 1911 they were combined in a single organization, the West Coast Lumbermen's Association. The task of enlisting the support of the Oregon and Washington mills met with varying success, but by the beginning of World War I the Association included in its membership companies which produced 90 percent of the lumber output of the Pacific Northwest, and had established itself as the medium through which common measures within the industry could be agreed upon with considerable effectiveness.

The points on which agreement was sought had to do mainly with prices, with curtailment of production when market conditions were unfavorable, and with the establishment of uniform grades on specified types of lumber. Grades were the assurance of quality, and the acceptance of standards among the mills was of the first importance in selling to markets in other parts of the country. Through the efforts of producers' associations the western mills came to appreciate the importance of recognizing uniform market specifications and observing good grading practices. When it came to agreements on standard prices, there was more than a hint of monopoly practice and restricted competition. They were defended by the manufacturers, however, on the grounds that "cutthroat" competition was wasteful and that price stabilization was something desirable for the industry as a whole. The president of the Oregon association told its members quite frankly that unless prices could be "screwed up a little" there was "little use in getting together our organization." Price lists were adopted by the associations and published with an explicit understanding that they would be enforced upon the members of the association so far as it was practicable to do so. Later (after 1906) when the trust busters sounded the alarm, the published tables became unofficial statements of "prevailing prices." While they were not enforced in the same open manner as before, they had much the same effect, since loyal members were not likely to sell for less.[4]

The lumbermen's trade associations did much to bring order into both the production and marketing of timber products in the Pacific Northwest, but they did not achieve the tight controls that characterized a monopolistic operation. Competition was too complex to be eliminated or "managed" by any group of producers. Wood products faced a growing number of substitutes and rival products, whether of steel, cement, or asbestos, that limited the *per capita* consumption of timber and forced the lumber salesmen to be alert and aggressive to maintain the markets they had so recently won. Interregional competition kept the far western mills watching their costs very closely lest they be shut out of a market by the producers of southern pine. The pattern of milling within the region was such that the large mills, despite their economies and superior efficiency, were never free from the competition of smaller establishments that had less indebtedness and a lower overhead. Thus while the ownership of timberlands was highly concentrated, production of lumber was not. The West Coast Lumbermen's Association lessened competition, but never created a true monopoly.

The Rise of Labor Organizations

The enterprise of the lumber companies which was turned so effectively toward technical improvements and toward the solution of marketing problems did not extend at first into the area of liberal labor policies. The attitude of the employer toward his wage hands was probably no worse than in other industries. Because of their isolation, however, and because of their migratory character, logging operations were marked by long hours, by the lack of a uniform wage scale, and by living conditions that were deplorable. The early twentieth century was a time when private enterprise felt little responsibility for the welfare of the laborer, and the lumber operator, faced by stiff competition, paid no more than he had to in wages and spent only a bare minimum on the temporary living quarters occupied by his men. If challenged as to his practices, he

[4] John Cox, "Trade Associations in the Lumber Industry of the Pacific Northwest," *PNQ*, XLI, 1950, 285-311.

argued that he could afford no more, and that the lumberjack would not know what to do with a clean camp if he had one.

There was a measure of truth in what he said, for the logging camps seemed to attract a group of migratory workers who had lost all connection with a settled life of any kind. Unmarried and without dependents, they were a nomadic lot, reckless to a fault, sometimes happy-go-lucky, sometimes rebellious and complaining, but nearly always lacking in responsibility. This was the group that made a reputation for the logger as a man who accepted loneliness, danger, and privation as a way of living, and escaped from it only occasionally to the doubtful pleasures of the skid road at the nearest city.

As time went on, though, other men were to be found in the logging camps. Some of them were ambitious and able young fellows who worked hard and rose after a short time to higher positions. Others were stump ranchers who were more farmers than timbermen, but worked in the camps until their farms were sufficiently developed to support them. In certain areas, particularly the timbered areas bordering the Willamette Valley and around Centralia (Washington) these men made up as much as 75 percent of the logging crews. Both of these groups were men of purpose and ability, but they did not think of their jobs in the camps as permanent, and therefore took little interest in the improvement of conditions there.

The typical lumberjack was still a different type of individual. Native born or immigrant, of American stock, French Canadian or Scandinavian, it was not improbable that he had followed the lumber industry west from Maine or the Great Lakes just as his employer had. Though he accepted the life of a migratory worker, he looked forward to the time when he could marry and have a home and family. Sometimes, though rarely, he did marry and either brought his wife to the camp or found a place to live in a nearby town. His skill might be those of a pick and shovel man or a whistle punk, a faller, a bucker, a mechanic, or an engineer. In some instances he might have no taste for his work and treat it only as a necessary way of making a living, but more often he took pride in his special abilities, liked his job, and knew that he would do better in it than in something else. Lumbering was his industry and he felt an almost proprietary interest in it, wage earner though he was.

It was this last group that was willing to make sacrifices to improve the level of wages and the conditions of living. These were the men who formed the unions, organized the strikes, and battled with the companies. The drifters might be the radicals but the lumberjacks, together with the shingle weavers in the mills, were the backbone of the organized labor movement among the timber workers.[5]

The Shingle Weavers

In point of time the shingle weavers were the first to organize, the West Coast Shingle Weavers' Union being formed in 1890 with six locals in Ballard, Tacoma, Snohomish, Arlington, Sedro Woolley, and Chehalis. The shingle weavers were a rather small group of mill employees who were well fitted to take the lead in union activity. The dangers of their occupation made them daring. A piecework system of payment put a premium on skill and quickness, while at the same time it put them often under great pressure to earn a living wage. The dependence of an entire crew upon the pace set by the shingle sawyer knit them together as a group.

The shingle weavers carried on a vigorous agitation for higher wages, shorter hours, and better working conditions, and at times enjoyed considerable success. During the early years of the union they advanced the rate of compensation for packing shingles to ten cents per thousand. In 1901, working through a series of strikes in the shingle centers of Western Washington, they were able to secure significant gains, which resulted in a growth of membership and the formation of a number of new local organizations. In 1903 these locals which had been chartered directly by the A.F.L. and loosely associated through a "grand council," formed the International Shingle Weaver's Union of America, composed of some 24 local groups. Within a year the membership reached 1,300 men. The union soon launched a journal, known as the *Shingle Weaver,* which continued publication at Everett for some ten years.

Repeatedly, however, the fruits of victory were snatched away. As panic engulfed the nation in 1893 the shingle weavers lost their ten-

[5] The present sketch of labor problems in the lumber industry is based mainly upon Howd, *Industrial Relations,* and Vernon H. Jensen, *Lumber and Labor,* New York, 1945.

cent rate and packed for as little as three cents per thousand. In 1906 a state-wide strike, fought out to gain recognition of the union, was called off after two weeks, leaving the organization practically destroyed. In 1913 a strike at Ballard took 300 men off the job but failed when the operators brought in strikebreakers. Despite these untoward events, however, the union proved itself an organization to be reckoned with.

Their leadership took more tangible form in 1912 when the Shingle Weavers applied to the A.F.L. to extend the jurisdiction of their union to cover the entire lumber industry. Several attempts had been made by the A.F.L. to organize the sawmill and logging camp workers. In 1905 a charter had been issued to the International Brotherhood of Woodsmen and Sawmill Workers, which organization grew during the first year or so to a membership of 1,250. But the union had no real vitality, members fell away, and in 1911 it was suspended by the Federation for failure to pay the *per capita* tax. The organization was virtually taken over by the Shingle Weavers, the name of the new union being the International Union of Shingle Weavers, Sawmill Workers, and Woodsmen.

The combined organization was wrecked within two years by an unsuccessful struggle to secure an eight-hour day. A strike was called for May, 1914, but the mills at Everett and Raymond anticipated it, and lockouts compelled the men to accept an open-shop employment with the union enjoying no recognition at all. Further strike plans were abandoned in favor of political action. An eight-hour day initiative measure was put forward and local unions were advised to put all their exertions into the support of it. The failure of the initiative spelled disaster for the union. Within a year the number of affiliated locals had dropped from 20 to 5; their membership from 1,768 to 118. A series of lockouts followed, which were lost in nearly every case, and in 1915 the union was reorganized again with jurisdiction only over the shingle weavers. Several timber workers' locals continued in existence, and received their own charter as the new International Union of Timber Workers. The early attempts of A.F.L. to organize the lumber industry as a whole must, however, be considered a failure.

Industrial Workers of the World

In some respects the I.W.W. seemed to have advantages when it came to organizing the logging camps. Their specific demands were much the same as those of the A.F.L. Strikers quit work over disputes involving wages, hours, and working conditions and it was not unusual for them to have the support and even the explicit endorsement of the craft unions. In 1907, for example, the I.W.W. intervened in a sawmill strike in Portland demanding a nine-hour day and a minimum wage of $2.50, objectives which brought a statement of approval from the Central Labor Council in that city. For a time the Shingle Weavers considered affiliating with the I.W.W. rather than the A.F.L., though the final vote of the membership rejected the proposal. At the same time the "Wobblies" had an organizational structure which appealed to the various groups in the lumber industry because it united them on an industry-wide basis rather than dividing them along the lines of their particular craft or specialized skill. Furthermore the I.W.W. soon developed a militant aggressiveness that roused the logger's spirit. Whether or not the men in the camps actually intended to carry out the revolutionary ideas which the union proclaimed, the I.W.W. preamble struck fire in the hearts of the workers as no business unionism could do.

The preamble was assuredly a manifesto for the radicals. Declaring the completely antagonistic interests of employer and employee, it urged the workers to accept the class struggle, and exhorted them to "organize as a class, take possession of the earth and the machinery of production, and abolish the wage system." So long as hunger existed among millions of working people there could be no peace. "It is the historic mission of the working class to do away with capitalism. . . . By organizing industrially we are forming the structure of the new society within the shell of the old."

I.W.W. leaders found the nomadic worker of the western logging camps admirably suited to their purposes. They delighted in his cheerful cynicism, his "frank and outspoken contempt for most of the conventions of bourgeois society." Here was no submissive wage slave. Half vagabond he was, fearful of nothing, always ready to quit his job when the boss got tough or the board was bad. Who could serve better in the advance guard of the labor army? These men would be the guerrillas of the revolution.

Soon after its organization in the summer of 1905 the I.W.W. began work in the lumber industry and quickly formed a number of flourishing local unions. The Seattle group numbered 800 before the organization was a year old. By March, 1907, there were locals at Portland, Vancouver, and Astoria on the Columbia, at Aberdeen and Hoquiam, at Tacoma, Ballard, and North Bend. Membership varied according to the circumstances of the local situation. During the Portland sawmill strike of 1907 the I.W.W. claimed 1,847 members. At Hoquiam in 1912, when strikes were breaking out over wages in the mills there, 250 men joined the I.W.W. in one day. "Overall brigades" made their way to national conventions there to demand representation for the lumber industry, and to play their part in forcing policies of direct action rather than political effort. Yet in 1912 and 1913 the membership seems not to have been large; in 1913 the lumber workers' national union reported only 640 men.

The Wobblies made up in mobility and vigor for whatever they might lack in numbers. Organizers took the initiative and assumed the leadership in many a local dispute, whether or not it was originally their own fight. When a free speech demonstration was called for, the "foot-loose working stiffs" converged on the place by the hundreds to fill the jails and embarrass the police. The Everett "massacre" was precipitated when in 1916 the Seattle I.W.W. chartered a boat (the *Verona*) and took some 250 members to the neighboring city to demonstrate in connection with a strike of the shingle weavers. There they were met at the wharf by the sheriff and a company of armed citizens and volunteers. In the ten-minute shooting battle that followed seven men were killed and 50 others were wounded.

Methods and tactics were of many kinds. The strike was the standard weapon, but since it was not always effective, other measures were devised. Agitators harangued their listeners on the street corners. In 1914 a plan of organization was devised which shifted the focus from the locals which operated in the towns to the job-delegate who worked in the camp and who, if fired, was quickly replaced by another. The wooden shoe and the black snarling cat became the well-known symbols of widespread sabotage.

The efforts of organized labor to improve conditions in lumbering reached a climax in the summer of 1917. Both the A.F.L. and the I.W.W. built up their membership, the one to 2,500 men, the other to about 3,000, representing both the pine sections of the Inland Empire and the fir timber camps and mills along the coast. Conventions held by the I.W.W., the Shingle Weavers, and the Timber Workers all drew up demands calling for an eight-hour, or at most a nine-hour day, higher wages, and improved living conditions in the logging camps. The employers refused to negotiate, insisted upon a ten-hour shift, and formed a Lumbermen's Protective Association to resist union demands, using a strike fund and assessing penalty fines against mills that ran less than a ten-hour shift.

The A.F.L. unions then set July 16 as a strike date. I.W.W. organizers were not at first inclined to extend their strike from the pine country to the fir camps, but the men made it plain that they were going out along with the craft unions. The strike took place as planned, 40,000 to 50,000 men were idle, and by August 1 not more than 15 percent of the mills on the West Coast were running. The eight-hour day became the main issue of the strike with union recognition involved as well. The situation became more serious when the ship carpenters at Grays Harbor refused to handle lumber from the ten-hour mills.

But public pressure mounted against the strikers and while a few mills conceded the eight-hour day, they soon abandoned it. In September the A.F.L. workers returned to their jobs. The I.W.W. transferred their fight to a strike on the job, slowing down their work by intentional inefficiency, and making such trouble as they could through sabotage. The strike found the I.W.W. at the height of its strength. Under wartime conditions the situation changed very quickly. Lumber operators used the issue of patriotism to their own advantage and established the Loyal Legion of Loggers and Lumbermen (the 4L), a "fifty-fifty" employer-employee organization which speedily attained a membership of 100,000, and undermined the position of the genuine labor organizations. On the issue of the eight-hour day, however, the union demands were realized, and in the matter of living conditions at the logging camps great improvement was made. From this point of view the struggle of the previous years was not altogether in vain.

25

Harvests from the Sea

Columbia River Salmon

Fishing like lumbering was still an infant industry in 1880. The salmon streams and the halibut banks were stocked abundantly, but since the local population was small, there was little demand for the fisherman's catch. Of necessity, therefore, he contented himself with supplying a few canneries on the lower Columbia and the Sound and shipping small cargoes to San Francisco.

The salmon fisheries of the Columbia were the most highly developed. Some 30 canneries operating on both banks of the river between Astoria and the Cascades represented a capital investment of 1,000,000 dollars and gave occupation to 2,500 fishermen, half of whom lived in or near Astoria, the rest in smaller canning towns along the river. For the most part these men used boats and gear provided by the cannery companies. One cannery might have 40 to 50 boats, open, flat-bottomed, 26-foot craft, sloop rigged with a centerboard, which were leased to the fishermen together with gill nets 200 to 300 fathoms in length and 40 to 45 feet deep. Two men managed a boat and a net, setting the net on floats across the stream in such a way that the fish encountered it in their upstream migration and were caught in the mesh. The river itself gave them little trouble, but rough water at the mouth of the Columbia was extremely hazardous. More than one boat, lifted up by the great waves on the bar, was tipped end over end; often the men were drowned. Fishermen paid for the use of their boat with their catch, receiving perhaps 65 cents for a fish. The price was several times higher than it had been in 1866 when the first canneries were established.

The canneries operated with Chinese laborers, most of whom received $1.00 to $1.50 a day in wages. It was an unwritten law that a Chinese would be shot on sight if he was found fishing, but he was accepted in the canneries without resentment since the plants had to have cheap labor if they were to operate at all. Chinese workers were faithful and if properly treated were well behaved. Chinese cutters were highly skilled with a knife, some of them cleaning as many as 1,600 fish in a day. They were a migratory group who came to the Columbia in April and left in August, rarely returning for a second year. The canneries paid perhaps a half million dollars in wages to the Chinese and three times that much to the fishermen. In 1880 they produced 530,000 cases of canned salmon valued at 2,600,000 dollars.[1]

Compared with the Columbia River canneries all other fishing enterprises on the river, the Sound, or the coast were very small. At Tacoma two young fishermen from Maine established a fishing station, shipping their catch to Portland and San Francisco. Several companies of Italians and Austrians, Greeks and Portuguese fished out of Seattle, Port Townsend, and Victoria, taking mostly halibut, rock cod, and mackerel. Jackson and Myers ran a cannery for a time at Mukilteo, and later moved to Port Blakeley. At Port Madison a herring fishery owned by one J. P. Hammond gave employment during the winter to a dozen men of various nationalities. Practically all the fishing was done with small boats. With fish selling at Portland and San Francisco at five to eight cents a pound, nobody made much money and the census takers reported a trade worth in 1880 only 181,372 dollars.

As new population and new capital came to the Northwest, the fisheries grew rapidly into one of the region's big businesses. Puget Sound, which had been so undeveloped previously, now became a scene of considerable activity, the fishermen there delivering a product in 1902 worth 5,500,000 dollars. In 1908 Washington ranked fourth in the nation in the value of fish products, surpassed only by Massachusetts, New York, and Virginia. On the eve of World War I Washington alone turned out 20,000,000 dollars worth of fish, a task that occupied 8,500 men in manning the boats, tending the nets, and

---

[1] Oregon State Board of Immigration, *Pacific Northwest; Facts Relating to the History, Topography, Climate, Soil, Agriculture of Oregon and Washington Territory*, New York, 1882; David Starr Jordan, "Fisheries of the Pacific Coast," 47th Congress, 1st Session, Senate Misc. Doc. 124, Part III, 1880, 624-630; David Starr Jordan and Charles H. Gilbert, "Salmon Fishing and Canning Interests of the Pacific Coast," *ibid.*, Part V, 1880, I, 740-753.

harvesting the shellfish. British Columbia caught and sold salmon worth 10,000,000 dollars more. The Alaska fisheries, which were the most productive of all, sent 4,000,000 cases of canned salmon out to the markets of the world. The Pacific coast canneries by themselves could more than encircle the globe with their tins, and provide four pounds of salmon a year for every man, woman, and child in the United States.[2]

From 1890 on the fisheries became increasingly complex in variety and organization. We should therefore look at several of the more important branches of the industry more closely. Salmon, halibut, rockfish and shellfish presented various problems and opportunities, and each attracted a group of fishermen who came to specialize increasingly in their own particular methods and gear. All these branches of the industry went through a period of rapid expansion.[3]

The Columbia River salmon fishery expanded largely through the utilization of more and more efficient gear. In Baker's Bay on the north shore inside the mouth of the river, Washington fishermen built bigger pound nets and more of them until the water was dotted with them. These nets were fixed in position and acted as a kind of fence that guided the salmon into an enclosure or pound where they could be taken more easily. Oregon fishermen continued for the most part to use gill nets put out from small boats. These nets too were larger and more numerous each year and observers declared that when the fish were running the nets overlapped one another and choked the river from one bank to the other, forcing the steamboat captains either to change their schedules or to shut off their engines to avoid fouling the propellers. The gill net men and the pound net operators were bitter enemies. Boat fishermen resented the fixed gear which entangled them and forced them out to dangerous waters on the bar. Washington pound men resented the invasion of their waters by Oregon boats from Astoria. Each group organized its association,

[2] U.S. Census Bureau, *Fisheries of the United States, 1908*, Washington, D.C., 1911; L. H. Darwin, *Fisheries of Washington*, Olympia, 1916; Washington State Fish Commissioner, Biennial Report, 1913; U.S. Bureau of Fisheries, *Canned Salmon Is Cheaper Than Meats*, Washington, D.C., 1914.

[3] Homer E. Gregory and Kathleen Barnes, *North Pacific Fisheries, With Special Reference to Alaska Salmon*, New York, 1939; John B. Cobb, *Pacific Salmon Fisheries*, 4th ed., Washington, D.C., 1930; see also Homer E. Gregory, "Salmon Industry of the Pacific Coast," *Economic Geography*, XVI, 1940, 407-415.

published its own story, and appealed to its legislature or to the federal government for protection. On occasion nets were cut and men were shot as the two groups came in conflict with each other. This kind of altercation and the jealousy which each state felt for the other made the exploitation of the fishery something difficult indeed to control.[4]

On the Oregon side above Astoria floating nets were set from boats but were hauled ashore with horses and emptied on the beach. Higher on the river, between the Cascades and Celilo, rapids and waterfalls presented obstacles which the salmon passed in great numbers at certain favorable spots. At such places the Indians built platforms or stages out over the torrent and fished with spears or dip nets. The white man improved upon these devices, installing instead fish wheels which dipped continuously and practically "pumped" the fish out of the river. Sometimes mounted on a scow and sometimes on permanent foundations, these wheels put in the fisherman's scow some 20,000 to 50,000 pounds of fish per day. They became vested interests that were highly exclusive in character, for there was rarely room for more than one wheel at any single location. Most of them were on the Oregon side of the river, but Washington too had a few of them. Though sharply criticized, they were not outlawed in Oregon until 1927 and in Washington not until 1935.

Salmon Fishing on Puget Sound

On Puget Sound the conditions of fishing were somewhat different. Here too there were "runs" when great numbers of fish moved in through the straits and the San Juan Islands on their way to spawn in the Fraser or Skagit River. Other salmon remained in Puget Sound waters, finding there ample food and a congenial habitat. These fish could be taken at almost any time between May and November. Fishermen were busy during a greater part of the year and they developed gear some of which was adapted to the runs, and some of it to trolling which could be carried on at many varied times and places.

---

[4] U.S. Treasury Department, *Report of the Internal Commerce of the United States for the Year 1890*; Capt. Charles F. Powell and Major W. A. Jones, "Reports of Salmon Fishing on the Columbia River," 50th Congress, 1st Session, Senate Executive Document 123, 1888; Washington Fishermen's Association, *Washington's Salmon Fisheries on the Columbia River*, Ilwaco, 1894.

Fishing methods were suited to the habits and the movements of several varieties of salmon all of which were found in Puget Sound in considerable numbers. King or Chinook salmon averaged over 20 pounds, many of them weighing more than 50 pounds. Sockeye or red salmon, weighing four to ten pounds, were an ideal canning fish. Silvers and pinks were also abundant.

At the approaches to the Fraser, such as Point Roberts, San Juan Island, and Birch Bay, the sockeye followed certain favorite passages. Here the fishermen erected permanent seines or "traps" which functioned in much the same ways as the pounds of Baker's Bay. These traps, which cost several thousand dollars each, delivered a rich catch with a minimum of effort during the seasons of migration. Like the fish wheels, they were criticized for their efficiency, but in 1915 there were some 600 licensed traps in operation in Washington waters.[5]

Sockeyes came in through the border waterways in schools which alert fishermen could detect and capture with purse seines. These seines were floating nets somewhat similar to gill nets except that no attempt was made to entangle the fish in the mesh of the net. A purse seine was set (usually with skiffs from a scow or mother boat) in such a way as to encircle and surround a school of salmon and confine them. A line which ran through the bottom of the seine was then drawn tight so as to close the seine like a purse and prevent the fish from escaping. Having done this the men lifted the net to the surface and "brailed" the fish into the mother boat with a four-foot dip net. A successful seining operation might yield nearly 1,000 fish at a time. It was a very popular method of fishing which led to the development of purse seine boats that were designed and built for that special purpose. Powered at first with gasoline (in recent years with diesel) engines, boats were 60 to 80 feet in length, had a capacity of 15 to 25 tons, and took a crew of five to seven men. In 1912 there were about 100 such boats operating on Swiftsure Bank off the southern shores of Vancouver Island.

[5] Richard Rathbun, *Review of the Fisheries in the Contiguous Waters of the State of Washington and British Columbia*, U.S. Commission of Fish and Fisheries, Document 423, 1899; George A. Rounsefell and George B. Kelez, *Abundance and Seasonal Occurrence of the Salmon in the Puget Sound Region and the Development of the Fishery*, U.S. Bureau of Fisheries, Special Report, 1935; Clark P. Spurlock, "History of the Salmon Industry in the Pacific Northwest," unpublished thesis, University of Oregon, 1940; William A. Carrothers, *British Columbia Fisheries*, Toronto, 1941.

Purse seines and traps accounted for the greater part of the salmon catch on Puget Sound but from 1912 on motor trolling boats began to share in it. They contented themselves with hook and line and caught their fish one at a time. Learning through experience where the best feeding grounds were, they covered a wide area chiefly offshore that was not reached by the other types of gear. Trolling boats were smaller than the purse seiners. They were 30 to 60 feet in length and were identified by the long fishing poles which while traveling stood vertically on both sides of a central mast, and were lowered to carry the lines when fishing. Though the first commercial trollers failed to reach the deeper waters where the large salmon were to be found, and though they hooked (and injured) many fish they did not land, they quickly improved their methods and won a permanent place in the fishing industry. Larger boats were developed. Longer and heavier lines were used, and considerable ingenuity was shown in multiplying the number of hooks and in placing them at various depths. In later years offshore Alaska trollers working beyond the three-mile limit put as many as 12 lines and 30 hooks in the water at once, using a system of in-hauls and power reels. Scandinavian and Finnish fishermen predominated in these boats, and they were the most independent men in the business. Selling entirely to the fresh fish or mild-cured market they secured a premium price for their catch, and operated without any connection with the canneries. Competition was tough and many boats made small profits, if any. Still there was a living in it, and the independent boat owner with his "swivelneck" companion who worked for him for 20 percent of the catch became a familiar sight along the coasts of Oregon and Washington.

Alaska Salmon Fishery

In the varieties of salmon caught, and in the essential techniques of fishing and canning, the Alaska fishery was much like that of the Columbia River and Puget Sound. In Bristol Bay the gill net boats operated much as they did farther south, while in the central and southeastern districts of Alaska the purse seiners and the traps were also like those of the Sound. The types of gear used depended upon local conditions, and were developed through experi-

Flavel House, Astoria. (From West Shore Magazine.)

Portland's First Bridge at Morrison Street. (From Ladd and Tilton, Sixty Milestones of Progress.)

Chamber of Commerce, Tacoma. (From West Shore Magazine.)

A Fine Oregon Mansion of 60 Years Ago. (Courtesy, Oregon Historical Society.)

"They Have Such Lovely Fogs in Seattle." (Drawing by W. Marbury Somervell, From Town Crier.)

Lewis and Clark Exposition Buildings, 1905. (Courtesy, Oregon Historical Society.)

William S. U'Ren, the Lawgiver. (From American Magazine.)

John R. Rogers. (From Rogers, Looking Forward.)

Silver-toned Sextette of the Northwest. (From West Shore Magazine.)

ence. The industry felt the same forces of mechanization, and came under the control of the canneries in the same way. Problems of depletion were the same and essentially the same measures of control were put into effect to conserve the salmon population. The points of difference had to do mainly with the geography of the fishing areas, with the magnitude and complexity of the industry, and with its remoteness from the centers of population.[6]

Salmon canning began in Alaska with some experimental ventures by the Alaska Commercial Company in 1887-1888. The product was shipped to San Francisco where the possibilities of the northern fishery were quickly perceived. During the next years canneries were established in such numbers that the Alaska pack quickly outstripped the Columbia River product. In 1899 Alaska canneries turned out 1,000,000 cases, the Sound produced nearly as much, and the Columbia River dropped to one-third of that figure. From then on to 1914 Alaska accounted for between 2,000,000 and 3,000,000 cases; the Sound 500,000 to 1,500,000, and the Columbia River about 300,000 cases.[7]

The earlier part of this period saw the industry suffering from severe growing pains. The competition to get the fish was intense, far more so than on the Columbia. The natives of Alaska were pushed aside by the cannery men who came in from California and the Sound. As the best trap locations were determined, rivalry led to acts of violence when one group dammed the streams and even destroyed the traps established by another. In the mad rush to get fish, little or no thought was given to problems of depletion. During these hectic years good trap locations might change hands at 20,000 to 90,000 dollars though the trap itself cost but 5,000 dollars to build.[8]

Organization of the Canning Industry

Prior to 1893 most of the canneries were owned and operated by single proprietors or partnerships. Plants were

[6] Gregory and Barnes, *North Pacific Fisheries,* Chaps. 14, 15.

[7] Otis B. Freeman, "Salmon Industry of the Pacific Coast," *Economic Geography,* XI, 1935, 109-129.

[8] See the following documents of the U.S. Bureau of Fisheries: *Reports of Special Agents on the Alaska Fisheries,* 1892-1895; *Fisheries of Alaska,* 1908; and *Report of Alaska Investigations in 1914.*

small, and since little machinery was used, many of them were moved about from place to place in search of more favorable fishing conditions. The next decade was one of rapid change which, while it increased the profits of the larger and more successful canneries, nevertheless forced many smaller ones out of business. The iron chink, developed in 1903, and other machines for making cans and filling and soldering them, tremendously increased the productive capacity of individual plants, which now began to turn out not a few hundred cases a day but several thousand. The cost of canning a case of salmon by such methods was much reduced, but mechanization put a premium upon high capitalization, made a large supply of fish a necessity for survival, and put the problem of marketing in an entirely new light. Despite the improvement of transportation, overproduction quickly glutted the markets and brought ruinously low prices. Out of this situation developed the large packing associations.

The movement toward combination and consolidation advanced rapidly during the early 1890's. Individual cannery owners first entered into coöperative agreements, formed marketing pools, and restricted production as measures to stabilize prices and profits. These steps led to a more thoroughgoing reorganization with the formation in 1892 of the Alaska Packers Association which represented a merger of 90 percent of the canneries operating in Alaska. Individual companies surrendered their plants, received capital stock in the association in return, and accepted a single unified management. A number of the less efficient canneries were closed, cutthroat competition was largely brought to an end, and production was held at profitable levels. The association was a financial success from the beginning, and from 1893 to 1910 it controlled half to three-fourths of the total pack of Alaska salmon. Libby, McNeil and Libby and Pacific American Fisheries, Inc., acquired a number of canneries and established themselves as the other big concerns in the Alaska trade.[9]

The same trend toward consolidation was reflected in the formation of the British Columbia Packers Association and the Columbia River Packers Association, both of which were formed soon after 1900. These organizations functioned in much the same way as the Alaska Packers, though they never produced more than a quarter

[9] David B. De Loach, *Salmon Canning Industry*, Corvallis, Oregon, 1939.

to a third of the total pack. The British Columbia Packers were producing by 1914 280,000 cases a year; the Columbia River Packers Association about half as much. From 1900 to 1920 the Alaska Packers Association produced well over a million cases annually.

Despite the appearance of these large concerns, nothing like a complete monopoly was ever achieved in the salmon fishery, and as the years passed the situation became more competitive rather than less so. Size and financial strength had their advantages, but during the years of rapid expansion new techniques and the necessity of developing new markets kept the industry from being unduly exploited by any monopolistic group.

Big Business methods were important, however, in many ways. Marketing was done through agents and brokers and became increasingly closely related to the food companies through which the outlets were found. Wholesale firms established themselves in San Francisco, Seattle, and Vancouver and storage facilities were built there where the annual pack could be held for distribution throughout the year. The transporting of cannery machinery, materials, and supplies, as well as a large part of the necessary labor force was done in company-owned ships which met the needs of plants scattered over thousands of miles of Alaska coastline far better than any system of public carriers. Fishermen used company boats and gear. Cannery workers included some local laborers, but for the most part they were brought from the centers of population in Washington and California. Some of them were skilled mechanics, many others were Chinese laborers who were rounded up by contractors and were bound to service for the canning season by stiff penalties in case they failed to finish it out. All in all the salmon fishing was hardly to be thought of as an Alaskan enterprise, for with the exception of a few native fishermen, the whole operation was conducted from the outside, from the cities of the Northwest and from San Francisco.[10]

North Pacific Halibut

The halibut fishery, like the salmon canneries, experienced a period of great expansion during the early years

[10] Washington State Bureau of Labor, *Special Report on the Salmon Canning Industry and the Employment of White Labor*, Olympia, 1915.

of the century. During the 1870's and 1880's a few schooners brought fish to Port Townsend and Victoria to be shipped to San Francisco. With the completion of the transcontinental railroads similar shipments were made to the east coast. In fact, fast rail transport and improved refrigeration made it possible for the Pacific fishing boats to sell halibut even in Gloucester itself. By 1915 the industry had grown into an enterprise that handled an annual catch of 66,000,000 pounds.[11]

The invasion of the eastern markets was not something to be achieved easily. Crudely packaged and poorly iced, the first shipments reached their destination in miserably bad condition, and failed even to earn their express charges. Eastern fishermen resented the competition of the western boats while the New England dealers spoke unpleasantly of the "worthless 'California' halibut." High carrying costs, amounting at times to as much as $1.25 per hundred, imposed a heavy burden on the western shipper while the organization of distribution compelled him to ship to New York even though the fish might eventually be sold in the Middle West.

The declining yield of the Atlantic fishing banks offered encouragement, however, to the western fishermen. Halibut prices rose and conditions of competition became more favorable. Larger dealers with better trade connections took an interest, established themselves on Puget Sound, and began operating a fleet of boats. Some of these were eastern firms, like the New England Fish Company (a group of Boston dealers who operated at Vancouver, B.C.) and the International Fisheries Co., which opened a branch at Tacoma. Several other large companies entered the trade in Seattle, the San Juan Fish and Packing Company, the Seattle Fish and Cold Storage Company and the Chlopeck Fish Company being the strongest. In addition to the "company" boats operated by these dealers, local fishermen, including a growing number of Norwegian immigrants, manned a fleet of independent schooners on the nearer banks, selling the catch mainly in the fresh fish market.

Halibut were bottom fish which fed in 40 to 160 fathoms of water

[11] William F. Thompson and Norman L. Freeman, *History of the Pacific Halibut Industry*, International Fisheries Commission, Report No. 5, Vancouver, B.C., 1930; John Q. Adams, "Pacific Coast Halibut Fishery," *Economic Geography*, XI, 1935, 247-257; also *Pacific Fisherman*, February, 1907, January, 1908, and February, 1910.

and the gear used was designed to put as many hooks on the bottom as possible. The common unit of gear was a ten-line skate which consisted of a hemp ground line 500 fathoms long with hooks set on five-foot cotton branch lines or "gangings" spaced nine feet apart. Two men handled these skates from a dory, setting them in strings two to six skates long, anchored and buoyed with an identifying flag at each end of the string. Several strings were set parallel to one another extending either along the edge of the bank or across it.

Life on the halibut boats was no business for landlubbers or weaklings. No little skill was required to set and run the skates without fouling them. Dories put over the schooner's side on a rough day pitched about like eggshells in the stormy sea. The catch varied from 1,000 pounds per skate to as little as 100 pounds, but the crew of the larger boats ran between two and three skates an hour during the course of a good day's fishing which in itself was an arduous exertion. Nor was the day's work done when the fish were pulled into the boat. There still remained the task of transferring them from the dory to the larger boat, cleaning and icing them, and storing them in the hold. Once loaded the boat headed for home port or for the nearest cold storage plant where the cargo was unloaded again to be forwarded to market. Fishermen on the schooners usually fished on shares with the boat taking a third of the catch. On the steamers the men were paid at first by the fish, twenty-five cents apiece large or small. Later the manner of payment was changed, so that on these boats too the fishermen worked on shares, the company taking 25 percent.

While the dories and basic gear remained much the same, important improvements were made in the boats that attended them. Sailing vessels wasted too much time going and coming, especially in the inland waters of British Columbia and Puget Sound. The larger fish companies soon turned to steamers and developed boats especially designed for the trade. Schooners continued to use sail under favorable conditions but installed auxiliary engines which made them increasingly independent of the weather. Both types of vessels were easily recognized by the nests of dories they carried either amidships or on the stern deck. Some fishing was done from shore stations, but for the most part the fishermen preferred to range considerable distances out from their base.

Prior to 1910 nearly all the halibut fishing was done off Cape Flattery and Swiftsure and on the inner banks along the coast of British Columbia and Southeastern Alaska. Summer fishing centered mainly in the southern waters. During the winter months the smaller boats tied up in port while the steamers fished the Alaskan grounds. Beginning in 1910 declining catch records led to a search for new fishing places, driving the boats into deeper water and farther north and west along the coast of Alaska beyond Cape Spencer. Success in these areas staved off for a time the threat of depletion, and for several years prior to World War I the halibut fishermen were chiefly concerned about overproduction and declining prices rather than the exhaustion of the fishing grounds. The disappearance of the fish from Puget Sound and the nearer banks was a danger signal but the full import of it was not appreciated until later.

Shellfish

Shellfish, the Northwest's third fish specialty, did not compare with the salmon and halibut in economic importance, yet they supported an industry of some magnitude which attracted wide attention. Willapa Bay, long famous on the coast for its oysters, had been exporting them to San Francisco for nearly half a century and was still the most favored spot. Other tidal areas at the head of Puget Sound and to the north in Whatcom, Skagit, and Jefferson counties were likewise found to be favorable. In Olympia Captain W. J. Doane made something of a reputation for himself with an oyster pan roast of superior quality. Soon after 1900 Easterners became interested in the industry and put a good bit of capital into it. In 1908 oysters, together with crabs and clams, brought returns of some 460,000 dollars. By 1915 the shell fishery was a million-dollar industry.

Oyster culture required scientific knowledge. Already the beds were threatened with depletion and experiments were undertaken to determine the methods to be used in restoring and maintaining them. In 1907 over 100 carloads of eastern oysters were transplanted as seedlings in the Willapa and Puget Sound districts. The transplanted stock did well, but the problem was to learn how to breed them locally.

By 1915 Professor Trevor Kincaid of the University of Washington was achieving some success in his efforts to overcome these difficulties.[12]

For the most part the oyster beds were managed by commercial corporations on privately owned land, but when the State of Washington surveyed and platted the tidelands, extensive reserves for oyster beds were established, mainly on Hood Canal. This step met with some criticism from the commercial oystermen on the grounds that the reserves should be improved for proper cultivation, which would involve a greater expenditure than the state would be willing to make. As early as 1907 proposals were made for some of the reserves at Willapa Harbor, Shelton, Oyster Bay, Port Orchard, and Hood Canal to be maintained as public lands while the remainder should be offered to the highest bidders in tracts of not more than 50 acres each.

A number of other varieties of fish figured in the Northwest industry, but none of them were of great importance. At certain seasons of the year the smelt filled some of the rivers in Washington and Oregon until their numbers were past believing. Scandinavian immigrants were fond of Puget Sound herring, which they avowed were better than those they had known in Europe. The catch had declined markedly from the time (1870's) when fishermen might take 200 to 300 barrels in a single night, but they were still considered choice and tasty. A few Puget Sound boats went north to Bering Sea in search of codfish though they brought back less than half of what their competitors took to San Francisco. Black bass and perch were abundant, though the latter were hardly of good quality. But the returns from all these varieties together hardly measured a quarter as much as the shellfish. For the most part they were consumed in the local market.[13]

[12] Paul S. Galtsoff, *Oyster Industry of the Pacific Coast of the United States*, U.S. Bureau of Fisheries, Document 1066, 1929; Washington State Fish Commissioner, Biennial Report, 1902; *Pacific Fisherman*, February, 1907.

[13] David Starr Jordan, *Fishes of Puget Sound*, California Academy of Sciences, *Proceedings*, Vol. V, San Francisco, 1896.

26

Metal in the Mountains

Minerals have been like a pot of gold at the end of the rainbow for the far Northwest. They are the source and the material for some of the region's highest expectations and its best stories. At the same time they have proved on many occasions to be the cause of its most disheartening disappointments. Repeatedly men have been driven on to great adventure by the tantalizing thought of untapped resources in the mountains which needed only to be exploited. Some few found fortunes there, and others a living, though a rough and hazardous one. But for the most part, the hills yielded their treasure reluctantly. The story of the mines is no story of easy success. It is a chronicle of titanic struggle, often of dreams ending in disillusionment. Even Montana's mountain of copper and Idaho's rich veins of quartz were opened and placed at man's disposal only by putting the full potential of industrial capitalism to work at the task. Deposits less rich in productivity seemed within the grasp yet never materialized. The rainbow arched over and beyond.

The Northwest vacillated between the optimism of the plunger and promoter and the doubts of the skeptic whose purposes, long cherished, are not even now fulfilled. Each made his contribution to the history of the region, the one through color and excitement, the other through severe and realistic appraisal.

For Montana and Idaho the importance of the mines was beyond contradiction. The copper camps took nearly 4,000,000 dollars worth of ore out of their shafts in a month's time. Coeur d'Alene mined 30,000,000 dollars in gold and silver, zinc and lead, between New Year's and Christmas in 1903. While mining enterprises were of much less importance in Washington and Oregon, these states too felt the fascination of taking wealth out of the ground. Though there was little to glitter in the miner's pan, rich profits were possible in the outfitting and supply trade and substantial reward for those who exploited the work-a-day materials of construction and industry. Coal and iron, even sand and gravel and building stone were important in the appraisal of northwest minerals. The range of interest and activity included not only the placer diggings of the Yukon, but the cement plant at Metalline and the lime kilns of Roche Harbor.

Rush to the Yukon

The turn of the century saw America's last big gold rush, the stampede to the gold fields of the Klondike and the beaches of Cape Nome. It was the greatest excitement since the days of Oro Fino and Virginia City, and contributed even more significantly to the general development of the region. The mines themselves, to be sure, were hundreds of miles away, yet the rush deeply affected the Puget Sound area, inaugurating a vigorous economic advance that quickly lifted the whole Northwest out of the depression doldrums into which it had fallen during the panic of 1893.

Alaska had been mining in a quiet way for some years, but the Yukon burst into the headlines in the summer of 1897. In July of that year the Seattle newspapers carried the news of the arrival of steamers from the north that were freighted with cargoes of nuggets and dust worth a million dollars each. Like wildfire the report of the new Eldorado spread throughout the country, stirring adventurers from every state to go there and seek their fortunes. Within a few weeks the steamers were crowded with strangers bound for Dyea and Skagway, where the rugged mountain trails left the coast, rising abruptly over dangerous passes to the lakes and river waterways that led to the placer grounds of the interior.[1]

What stories were told by the miners who had been on the Yukon during the first days of the rush. "Stranger things than fiction happen here every day," wrote Arthur Perry from Dawson City. Men on Bonanza and Eldorado Creeks vied with each other to see who could produce the richest pan of pay dirt. They measured 280 dollars and said they could just as well have made it a little more. Clarence Berry

[1] Charles M. Gates, "Human Interest Notes on Alaska and the Yukon Gold Rush," *PNQ*, XXXIV, 1943, 205-211.

took out 39 ounces (495 dollars) in one pan, and reports were circulated of a pan that yielded as much as 800 dollars. The first season's digging netted one miner 112,000 dollars, another 94,000 dollars, and Perry offered a list of 22 names of men who made from 12,000 to 50,000 dollars each during one winter.

Such stories of success, and many more, were duly recorded in the newspapers and in promotional pamphlets that were printed and distributed by the thousands. Even the United States Geological Survey put out a *Map of Alaska* with GOLD in brightly colored letters over large areas of the territory, and a description of the routes one might follow to reach them. "Clondyke is almost a household word," declared the Seattle *Post Intelligencer*. "In every city, town and hamlet on the Pacific Coast little else is talked of and people are preparing to go north by the very first means of transportation they can encounter."

To be sure, a great deal happened in Alaska that did not lend itself to such exuberant publicity. Hardships and failure were a common lot. The men who braved the precipitous slopes of Chilkoot pass did not soon forget it. Those who piloted boat or barge through White Horse rapids might well recall this adventure more than the months of drudgery and hard labor they afterwards spent at the diggings. Despite the rich finds, the great majority of prospectors made no more than a bare living and might have made it easier had they stayed at home. Poverty and privation were as much a part of the Yukon rush as a 500-dollar pan.

Nevertheless there was great activity at the placer mines for several years. Asahel Curtis, one of the Seattle photographers who "covered" the mining frontier, found it a busy scene indeed, and one which featured a considerable variety of equipment and machinery. Some miners who had little capital to work with contented themselves with rockers and pans like those used in California 50 years earlier. On the other hand, the valley of Upper Eldorado was laced with elaborate flumes and sluices which zigzagged back and forth on slender trestles. With the building of the Pacific and Arctic Railroad from Skagway to Lake Bennett, heavy equipment could be taken in much more easily, and hydraulic cannon were brought into play that washed tremendous amounts of gravel in a day's time. Here was a powered quest for metal that made the old-fashioned rocker or long tom look like a plaything.

The total output of the placers could only be roughly estimated for there was no adequate system of reporting it. It was said that the U.S. Assay Office at Seattle received 18,000,000 dollars worth of gold by the end of 1900, the number of depositors reaching several thousand each year. Such a figure undoubtedly included a large amount taken from mines situated in Canadian territory. Statistics of production for the Territory of Alaska totalled 17,800,000 dollars for the years 1897-1900. The annual yield did not rise above 10,000,000 dollars until after 1904 when industrial methods were more generally used. Canadian figures for the Klondike districts indicate that perhaps as much as 95,000,000 dollars were mined in British territory by 1900. A few 500-foot claims on Eldorado and Bonanza creeks produced a million dollars each and yields of 250,000 to 500,000 dollars per claim were said to be common occurrences.[2]

The export of gold in such quantities was in itself a stimulus to business activity throughout the Pacific Northwest. As a spur to trade, it was multiplied many times because the prospectors not only found treasure but spent it. They brought a tidy sum with them and paid dearly for transportation and subsistence and for the purchase of supplies and outfits. Those who took the trouble to add up these items came to the conclusion that it might cost nearly a thousand dollars just to get to the Yukon properly equipped to begin digging. This money, together with a great deal of the gold that was mined, passed quickly from hand to hand and produced far more business than one would think if he watched only the output of the gold itself. In those days one made money not only from the mines but from the miners as well.

This fact was not lost upon Erastus Brainerd and his fellow businessmen in Seattle. In less than a month during the summer of 1897 the merchants of the city sold goods worth 325,000 dollars; for several years thereafter Seattle's direct interest in outfitting and supply was very heavy indeed. Goods were piled along the sidewalks higher than a man's head, awaiting shipment to Alaska. Every available

[2] *U.S. Statistical Abstract;* Geological Survey of Canada, Annual Report, new series XII, 1899, 16-38.

steamer was pressed into service. Moran Brothers, shipbuilders, rushed the building of a dozen river boats for use on the Yukon. Sensing the promise of trade with Alaska and the Orient, the Northern Pacific railroad spent a million dollars on the improvement of various waterfront facilities.

Brainerd left no stone unturned to advertise Seattle throughout the length and breadth of the land as the best outfitting center and point of departure for the Klondike. Carefully calculating the circulation of national newspapers and magazines, he distributed information and publicity with a keen eye to the benefits it would bring. There was sharp competition among west coast cities for this trade but Brainerd made sure that the advantages of Puget Sound were widely known. Partly because of their nearer location and partly because of their energetic promotion, the Sound cities exploited the possibilities of the Alaska trade more successfully than did Portland, and Seattle established itself as the most rapidly growing city in the Northwest.[3]

Miners of Coeur d'Alene

Meanwhile in the mountains of Northern Idaho the miners of the Coeur d'Alene district had their first experience with Big Business and heavy industry, and were not at all sure they liked it.

Consolidation of the mines was the trend of the day. For a time local men continued to figure as partners and managers. Captain J. R. De Lama, a local man, shared with Christian and Louis Wahl of Chicago in the ownership of the Wilson mine, one of the largest and richest in Idaho. Simeon G. Reed of Portland was the organizer (1887) of a company which raised a capital of 3,000,000 dollars for the purchase and operation of the Bunker Hill and Sullivan mines. Spokane citizens held sizable mining interests, a fact which expressed itself in the significant number of silver Republicans who joined the Bryan Democrats in a fusion movement in 1896. But eastern men and outside money appeared more and more prominently. New Yorkers sent their experts to carry out a careful reconnaissance on the north fork of the Coeur d'Alene River. The Silver King mine was stocked

[3] Jeannette P. Nichols, "Advertising and the Klondike," *WHQ*, XIII, 1922, 20-26; Jonas A. Jonasson, "Portland and the Alaska Trade," *PNQ*, XXX, 1939, 131-144.

for 2,000,000 dollars in 1893 on the London market, as British investors became increasingly interested in western mining ventures. After a few years Bunker Hill and Sullivan passed into the control of Donald O. Mills of New York City, and other principal properties were reorganized into a few large strong groups. Perhaps the most important development of this kind was the consolidation in 1901 of the Empire State, Standard, and Morning mines under the single control of the Federal Mining and Smelting Company.[4]

Such measures undoubtedly made for more profitable and efficient direction and at first the appearance of strong companies and outside managers were reported with approval as evidence of a stable operation to replace the erratic and unpredictable come-and-go activities of earlier days. But the evils of corporation management soon became apparent as well. Company executives ruled with a heavy hand, heedless often of the safety and welfare of their men. Issues arising between employer and employee produced much ill will and wage earners at the mines reacted to conditions of industrialism in much the same way that American wage earners did elsewhere. Thus Idaho, while it was a frontier in many ways, produced labor organizations which were among the most militant in America, and the Coeur d'Alene mining towns witnessed scenes of violence and proclamations of martial law which put them in a class with Homestead, Pennsylvania, and Pullman, Illinois.

The western miner's heritage of conflict was born of such incidents as those which took place in Idaho in 1892 and 1899. As wages and conditions of employment became increasingly the subject of controversy between miners and mine owners, unions were organized which in the course of a very few years made an important place for themselves in the American labor movement. The mining towns of the Coeur d'Alene were in the forefront in the forming of the Western Federation of Miners in 1893 and Ed Boyce, who served his apprenticeship in the local union at Wardner, rose rapidly to become president of the Western Federation and won national recognition

[4]U.S. Treasury Dept., *Report of the Internal Commerce of the United States in 1890; Jim Wardner of Wardner, Idaho,* by himself, New York, 1900; *Spokane Miner,* Columbia World's Fair Edition, 1893; Frederick L. Ransome and Frank C. Calkins, *Geology and Ore Deposits of the Coeur d'Alene District,* U.S. Geological Survey, Professional Paper 62, 1908.

among the leaders of labor. The battles between union and mine owner were among the most bitter and bloody of the day. Miners staged armed demonstrations and did not shrink from violence or the free use of dynamite. Owners resorted to spotters, imported strike breakers and Pinkerton detectives, and used every trick in the book to destroy unionism root and branch.[5]

The struggle reached a climax during the spring and summer of 1899. On the 29th of April a Northern Pacific train was commandeered to carry miners from a number of Idaho towns to Wardner. There the concentrator of the Bunker Hill mine was blown to bits with 3,500 pounds of dynamite. Governor Frank Steunenberg immediately appealed to President McKinley and 500 federal troops were sent to the Coeur d'Alene area. More than 700 arrests were made, and miners were imprisoned for weeks in a "bull pen" with regular soldiers as guards, under conditions that were atrocious. Repeated protests eventually brought an inquiry into the situation and the withdrawal of troops, but not until they had been there for six months. State officials meanwhile inaugurated a system of permits for employment in the mines which required the applicant to renounce all allegiance to the miners' union. It was years before the union regained its former strength, and the memories of force and deceit lingered on to perpetuate a tradition of class conflict that was inflamed with hatred on both sides.

The problem was not simply a struggle for power between manager and worker, for the issue was deeper than the contest for the control of mining shafts and concentrators. Changing technology inevitably affected conditions of labor. New machinery made miners into mere shovel men, and drove them, if they were not to suffer diminished earning power, to demand that all underground workers be paid at the same rate, whether they were expert miners or not. Market prices of ore likewise had a close relation to wage scales at the mines. Men laboring in the tunnels and shafts of the western mountains found that their pay envelopes depended, in part at least, upon the fluctuating quotations on ore at New York. These things were part of the

[5] *Report of the Industrial Commission on the Relations and Conditions of Capital and Labor Employed in the Mining Industry*, XII, Washington, D. C., 1901, LXXXV-CIX, 389-568. For an account sympathetic to the workers, see May A. Hutton, *Coeur d'Alenes; or a Tale of the Modern Inquisition in Idaho*, Wallace, Idaho, 1900.

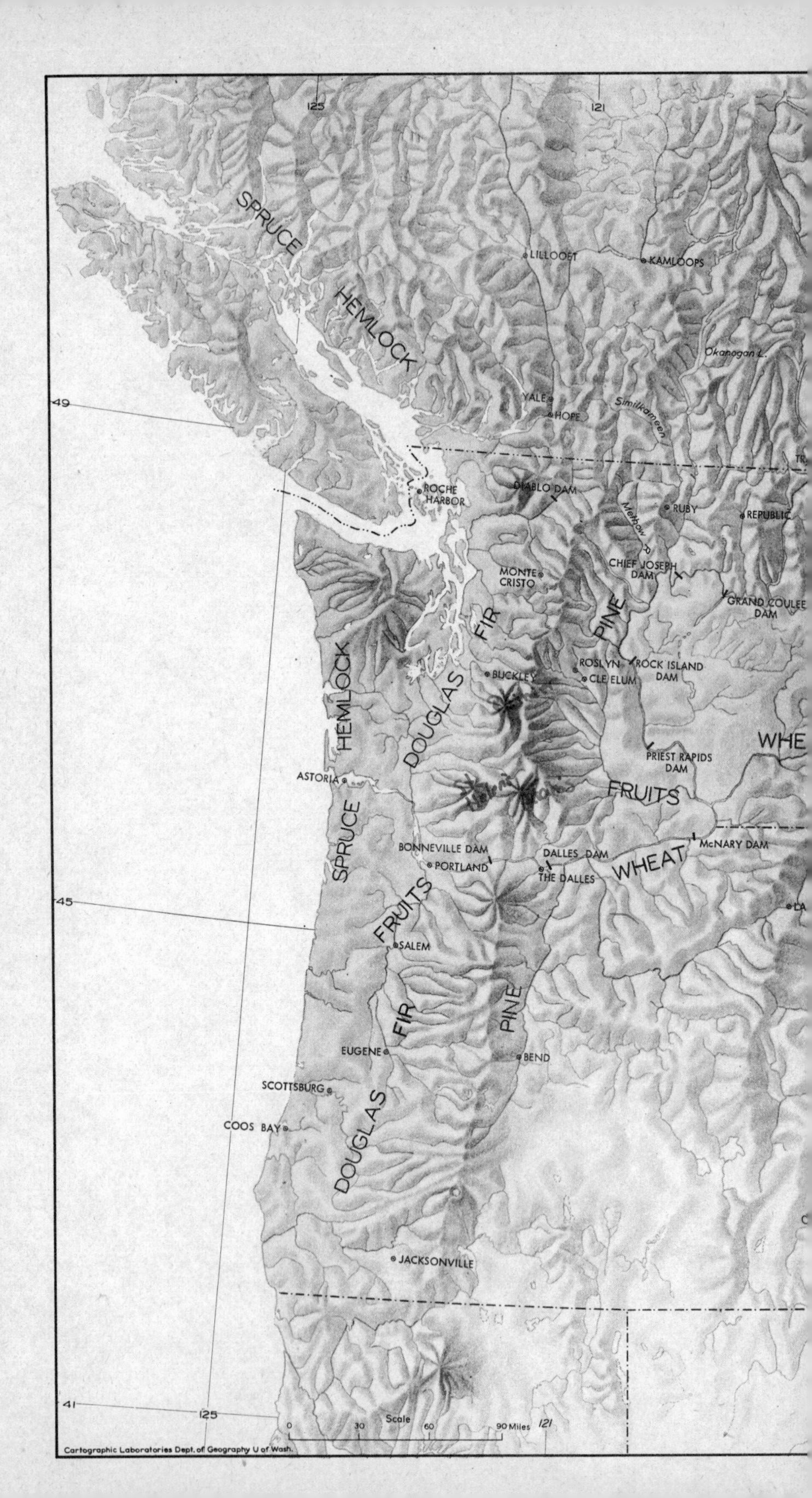
125
121
SPRUCE
HEMLOCK
LILLOOET
KAMLOOPS
Okanogan L.
YALE
HOPE
Similkameen
49
ROCHE HARBOR
DIABLO DAM
RUBY
REPUBLIC
Methow R.
CHIEF JOSEPH DAM
MONTE CRISTO
GRAND COULEE DAM
FIR
PINE
HEMLOCK
ROSLYN
ROCK ISLAND DAM
BUCKLEY
CLE ELUM
DOUGLAS
WHE
PRIEST RAPIDS DAM
ASTORIA
FRUITS
SPRUCE
BONNEVILLE DAM
DALLES DAM
McNARY DAM
PORTLAND
THE DALLES
WHEAT
45
FRUITS
SALEM
FIR
PINE
EUGENE
BEND
SCOTTSBURG
DOUGLAS
COOS BAY
DOUGLAS
JACKSONVILLE
41
125
Scale
0 30 60 90 Miles
121
Cartographic Laboratories Dept. of Geography U of Wash.

113
109
THE PACIFIC NORTHWEST
MINING CENTERS and RESOURCE AREAS
49
HUNGRY HORSE DAM
KALISPELL
LITTLE PORCUPINE DAM
LENE
WALLACE
HELENA
DIAMOND CITY
ELKHORN
PIERCE CITY
ANACONDA
BUTTE
ELK CITY
FLORENCE
ALDER GULCH
VIRGINIA CITY
45
WARREN'S DIGGINGS
BONANZA CITY
Payette R.
VILLE
CENTERVILLE
GALENA
IDAHO CITY
IDAHO FALLS
OISE
POCATELLO
AMERICAN FALLS DAM
South Pass
MINIDOKA DAM
TWIN FALLS
WHEAT
ROCK SPRINGS
41
109
113
John C. Sherman

impact of the industrial revolution, and they were not to be solved by destroying the machines or shooting the guards. On the other hand they were not to be solved by destroying the unions either, or by hiring company detectives, or importing strikebreakers from Missouri. The scenes of violence that took place at Coeur d'Alene, deplorable as they were, illustrated only too well the fact that the bloody battle between labor and management to determine profits and wages and working conditions was being waged not only in the industrial cities of the East, but in the western mining towns as well.

Mining continued to be a principal enterprise in Idaho during the years that followed. By 1917 the mountains had yielded 400,000,000 dollars in minerals, a quarter of which was in silver, and more than half of it in lead. In that year alone the mining companies of Coeur d'Alene realized net profits of 13,000,000 dollars.[6]

Montana Copper

In Butte and Anaconda, even more than in Idaho, mining was an enterprise that harnessed the people and even the state to the chariots of high finance. There was nothing small about Montana, and nothing dull about Butte, "the richest hill on earth." Its honeycomb of shafts became in these years of rapid development a veritable labyrinth of subterranean vaults and passageways. Veins and lodes of copper reached deep into the heart of the mountain, intertwined in an intricate maze of fissures which only the skilled geologist and engineer pretended to understand. Knowledge and luck and dogged persistence carried more than one crew to some new ore bed which they could only guess was there. Forty-five million dollars' worth of metal taken out of the ground in a year was the kind of prize that attracted the biggest money in the country. The contest for the control of it ranged against one another some of the shrewdest and most powerful captains of the time.[7]

[6] James R. Finlay, "Mining Industry of the Coeur d'Alenes," American Institute of Mining Engineers, *Transactions*, XXXIII, 1903, 235-271; Census Bureau, Report of Manufactures, 1900, X, Part 4, 133; C. N. Gerry, "Gold, Silver, Copper, Lead and Zinc in Idaho and Washington," in U.S.G.S., *Mineral Resources*, 1917, Part I, 457-507.

[7] K. Ross Toole, "When Big Money Came to Butte," *PNQ*, XLIV, 1953, 23-29; E. D. Peters, Jr., "Mines and Reduction Works of Butte City, Montana," in U.S.G.S., *Mineral Resources of the United States*, 1883-1884, 336-340, 374-796; *ibid.* (1892), 95-104; U.S.G.S., 19th Annual Report, Part VI, 1897, 137, and 21st Annual Report, Part VI, 1900, 184. See also the reports of the Montana State Inspector of Mines.

In productivity of copper Montana rose to a leading position among the states, far surpassing Hecla and Calumet, the famous Lake Superior mines, and giving ground only occasionally to Arizona. In 1909 the copper camps employed 13,697 wage earners with a payroll of 19,000,000 dollars.

But it was the struggle of the giants that made Montana an exciting battleground. These were the years when the shrewd, inscrutable W. A. Clark found his rival in the rough and genial Irishman, Marcus Daly. Their contest was more than a business matter, a struggle for fortunes in copper. It was personal and political as well. It involved the struggle to control the state capital, the location of which hung for a time in the balance between Helena and Anaconda. It expressed itself in Clark's ambition to win a place in the United States Senate, a post that he finally secured, though in the face of spirited charges of bribery in the state legislature. These were the years, too, when F. Augustus Heinze fought the Rockefeller group to a standstill, matching their every maneuver with a trick of his own so long as he kept the battle close to the mines he knew so well.

It was a war waged at times in Wall Street, where those who mastered the intricacies of stock manipulation bought whole mines without touching a dollar of their own reserves, utilizing for the purpose inflated issues of securities skillfully promoted and sold to an unsuspecting public. Sometimes the battles raged between the mining crews, who tunneled far underground to tap a disputed vein, and attacked each other when they broke through into an enemy shaft, with live steam or any ready weapon that came to hand. On occasion Amalgamated, the Rockefeller-Morgan company, ordered a sudden lockout, hoping thus to direct the wrath of the workers against Heinze, the local favorite. Or again, war shifted to the courtrooms where Heinze's enemies figured his resources in the judges who favored him, and in the costly litigation which for years blocked their efforts to gain control of the hill.[8]

Amalgamated finally took over as one after the other of the local men made their peace and accepted the best settlement they could get. At the instance of Amalgamated, legislation which protected their position was spread upon the statute books of the state. Under

[8] Carl B. Glasscock, *War of the Copper Kings, Builders of Butte and Wolves of Wall Street*, New York. 1935.

similar pressure taxes were adjusted to a level more favorable, even though it meant that the biggest properties paid, percentagewise, the lowest rate. Big Business fared well in Montana but the people who lived there came to have a distinct feeling that the state was not their own. Their resources were too valuable, too compact, and lent themselves too readily to monopoly and absentee control. Montana was a frontier state, "high, wide, and handsome," yet it was not free. The openness of its plains and mountains contrasted sharply with the half hidden chains which shackled its democracy. One finds few examples that illustrate more clearly the way large-scale capitalism extended its dominion into far corners and out-of-the-way places in America, establishing there an economic colonialism more exploitative than any the Revolutionary forefathers had known.

Washington and Oregon Mines

In Washington and Oregon mining never had the epic quality that made the industry important in the Rocky Mountain states. The optimists had their day, and for a time it seemed quite possible that the Cascade Mountains might hold as rich a treasure as the Rockies. But it proved not to be so. Precious metals were elusive and profits came more largely from such industrial materials as coal and sandstone. Even iron was a disappointment.

The mood at the turn of the century was one of hopeful expectancy, for the appraisal of mineral resources was not yet fully realistic. Miners in Oregon turned their attention from the established mining districts of the southwest corner to new developments in Baker County where the placers and quartz districts were soon earning a million dollars a year. Mining journals spoke of numerous deposits in Washington. Claims were established at places where the ore beds seemed most promising: for gold at Republic and Monte Cristo, copper at Index and Chewelah, and iron at Cle Elum and Snoqualmie Pass. Rockefeller bought the mines at Monte Cristo and took out perhaps 3,000,000 dollars' worth of gold and silver. Encouraged by the reports of his scientists, he built concentrators at the mine, and constructed a costly railroad leading to it from Everett where he thought to establish a smelter.[9]

[9] Lawrence K. Hodges, *Mining in the Pacific Northwest*, Seattle, 1897; Washington Geological Survey, Annual Report, 1901; *Mining World*, XXIV, January 27, 1906, 172-173.

A mining output of a million dollars annually was not to be scorned, but compared to Idaho and Montana and even to the anticipated production for Washington itself, the next decade was distinctly disappointing. The geology was deceptive even to the experts. The veins at Monte Cristo narrowed and disappeared, and Rockefeller soon sold out, turning his attention to more rewarding investments. Republic suffered both from stock manipulations and from technical difficulties. The boom of 1899 was followed by collapse, and for several years operations were carried on only spasmodically. In 1914, when Montana ranked eighth from the top among the states in the value of minerals produced, Oregon stood sixth from the bottom.

Washington miners spent much time and printer's ink explaining to themselves and to the indifferent world of investment why it was that the industry failed to grow more rapidly. Wall Street, they said, was diverting capital into other lines, while lesser investors put too much money into wildcat ventures. Many operations were conducted with insufficient means and with inefficient methods of processing. Transportation costs were excessive because of the inaccessibility of the ore beds.

The truth of the matter was that there were few if any bonanza deposits to be found. Most of them were relatively small and of low grade; often they were faulted and hard to follow. The most that could be said was that a number of medium-sized veins would with adequate capital, energy, and good management yield moderately good returns. This at least was the judgment of the geologists, after studying the terrain and the industry for 20 years.[10]

Agencies of scientific study contributed significantly to an appraisal of mineral resources that became increasingly accurate and realistic. Washington's state geologist began publishing his reports in 1891, and though there was but little money to be had, he worked closely with the scientists at the University and other research institutions in planning and executing field studies at places of particular interest. Bulletins appeared which described the formations at Blewett, Index,

---

[10] *Washington Miner*, I, May 1, 1907, 1-2; *Ore Deposits of Northeastern Washington*, U.S.G.S. Bulletin 550, 1914; Arthur H. Fischer, *Summary of Mining and Metalliferous Mineral Resources in the State of Washington*, University of Washington, Engineering Experiment Station, Bulletin 4, 1918; Ernest Patty, *Metal Mines of Washington*, Washington Geological Survey, Bulletin 23, 1921; *Mineral Resources and Mineral Industry of Oregon for 1903*, University of Oregon, 1904; J. S. Diller, *Mineral Resources of Southwestern Oregon*, U.S.G.S., Bulletin 546, 1914.

and Republic. Other more general reports summarized the mineral deposits for the state as a whole. Meanwhile the United States Geological Survey made numerous studies that contributed to the better understanding of the region. Occasionally they were controversial, as when J. E. Spurr described the veins at Monte Cristo not as deep fissures but as superficial joint-planes where the ore was deposited by descending surface waters. Local mining people protested such a view and complained that the publication of the report put the state in an unfavorable light. More often, however, these studies were solid and carefully done, and comprised a highly useful body of detailed information. By 1919 the geologists had pretty well covered the ground; after that mining was no longer a matter of guesswork and speculation.[11]

Coal

Coal mining was the most important branch of the mining industry in Washington. Large deposits of bituminous and subbituminous grades were opened up in the Roslyn area east of the Cascade Mountains, at Newcastle and Black Diamond behind Seattle, and farther south at Carbonado not too far from Tacoma. Seattle had been shipping coal to California for some years, and looked forward to building up the trade with the expansion of population and industry along the whole Pacific coast.

For a decade expansion was fairly steady, production figures rising to 3,000,000 tons in 1903. Thereafter, however, the industry failed to keep pace with the general development of the region. In 1914 coal producers reported no more in output than they had ten years earlier. The increasing use of oil as a competing fuel, and the importation of higher grades of coal from Wyoming narrowed the market for the local product. In 1913 coal mining was a 10,000,000-dollar business, which employed five men for every one in other branches of mining, but there seemed to be scant prospect of any great development in the future.[12]

Wages, working conditions, and industrial relations were touchy

[11] *Mines and Minerals,* XXIII, 1902, 204; *Northwest Mining Journal,* V, 1908, 82.

[12] Bailey Willis, "Report on the Coal Felds of Washington Territory," in the report of the Census Bureau, 1880, XV, 759-771; U.S.G.S., *Mineral Resources of the United States,* 1885, 16, 70, and 1886, 357-369. See also annual reports of the Washington Geological Survey and the biennial reports of the Washington State Coal Mines Inspector.

subjects in Washington as they were in Idaho. The coal miners did not figure in such scenes of violence as occurred at Coeur d'Alene, but they were involved in much the same struggle. In 1888 Negro laborers were imported from the Middle West to work (at lower wages) in the mines at Roslyn. To prevent trouble the United States marshal in Seattle deputized a number of private company guards. The next year rioting broke out at Newcastle and the mine operators demanded the support of troops. Again the marshal deputized guards, which this time brought him into an altercation with Governor Eugene Semple. When Sheriff William Cochrane visited the place he found 30 men from Thiel's Detective Agency in Portland enforcing an uneasy peace with rifles, pistols, and bowie knives.

These incidents were explosive because they found the mining companies and the miners' unions ranged against each other in mutual distrust and hostility. The situation did not altogether change in the ensuing years. Strikes broke out from time to time as a result of tension and complaints. Sometimes there were disputes over safety conditions, the weighing of cars at the mine, or the firing of men. In 1912-1914 the miners' union at one of the Renton mines struck for recognition and had the support of the United Mine Workers in their fight. For two years the men stayed out while the company insisted on an open shop. In this instance the company won, and the miners finally voted to return to work. By 1914, however, most of the companies had contracts with the United Mine Workers, finding such agreements the most satisfactory arrangement.[13]

During these years, too, the state mining inspector reported many improvements in the machinery used at the mines. Since safety and efficiency went together, more attention was given to working conditions and precautions against danger. New power plants and generators made possible a more extensive use of electric lights and ventilating fans. Accidents were investigated in considerable detail, and the inauguration of a state system of workmen's compensation helped to offset the hazards that many a miner faced every day. Safety measures were taken, rescue training was given, and in 1914 a state-wide first aid and mine rescue meet was held on the University of Washington

[13] "Trouble in the Coal Mines, 1889," *PNQ*, XXXVII, 1946, 231-257; Washington Coal Mines Inspector, Report, 1913-1914.

campus. The coal miner led no easy life, but he was not the forgotten man he had been only a few years earlier.

Dreams of a Steel Industry

One of the most persistent dreams, though one which in the end proved vain, was the dream of establishing an iron and steel industry either on the Columbia river or Puget Sound. Simeon G. Reed saw much promise in the furnaces at Oswego, near Portland, and undertook to expand them into a "permanent and handsome paying business." The plan was to use water power from the Tualatin River, bring coal from Puyallup, and take iron ore either from the mountain back of Lake Oswego or perhaps from Baja California and Mexico. Possessed of clear advantages, he thought, the northern mills would "supply the whole Pacific Coast and as far east as Salt Lake." Farther north at Port Townsend, California capitalists built the Irondale furnaces, thinking to use the bog ores of Chimacum mixed with richer ores from Texada Island in the Gulf of Georgia. Seattle likewise aspired to be a center of iron manufacture. The coal fields here were admirably situated close by, while the iron ores of Snoqualmie Pass were of excellent quality. Railroads needed spikes and rails and car wheels. The country was building up. Who could blame the western promoters if they expected steel plants to succeed on the Pacific coast.[14]

Reed interested Henry Villard and Donald Mills in Oswego in 1880. They formed the Oregon Iron and Steel Company, took over the Oswego company and invested nearly 500,000 dollars in it. Elaborate plans were made to build new furnaces, install spike machines, fish plate punches, rail shears, bolt and nut machines, and a machine shop. The venture was, however, a constant trouble and annoyance. Costs of development far exceeded the estimates, while at the same time the price of the finished product dropped in disheartening fashion because of the limited market. Reed withdrew from the

---

[14] C. G. Yale, "Iron on the Pacific Coast," U.S.G.S., *Mineral Resources of the U.S.*, 1884, 286-288; Dorothy O. Johansen, "Organization and Finance of the Oregon Iron and Steel Company, 1880-95," *PNQ*, XXXI, 1940, 123-159; John S. Hittell, *Commerce and Industries of the Pacific Coast of North America*, San Francisco, 1882, 310-314; Joseph Daniels, *Iron and Steel Manufacture in Washington, Oregon, California and Utah*, Seattle, 1929.

business in 1890 and the mill ceased operations four years later. It was revived temporarily in later years, but was dismantled again after World War I. The iron industry was not for novices.

The furnaces at Irondale were never successful either. Twice rebuilt and remodeled during the 1880's, they produced 10,000 tons of iron in 1889 but suspended production soon afterward. From 1900 to 1918 the firm went through repeated reorganizations, each with its pretentious designs which somehow went awry. For several years it was headed by Homer H. Swanly of Pittsburgh until his death in 1904. In 1910 production was resumed again, even more briefly this time, with coke from Pierce County and iron ore from China. A short interval of activity during World War I continued only so long as prices remained at a high level. Sometimes failure followed from policies that were too ambitious. Even so the Irondale plant was basically uneconomic.

The Seattle promoters were even more ambitious for their city than Reed was for Portland. In some ways, perhaps, they had more justification. Certainly the picture was brighter so far as resources were concerned, for the geologists themselves examined the Snoqualmie ore and pronounced it good. Seattle had an advantage, too, in the fact that Peter Kirk, an experienced ironmaster from Cumberland, England, studied the situation carefully and found it encouraging. Doubtless he was too much impressed by the thought that he had supplied steel rails from England to the Seattle, Lake Shore and Eastern railroad when he could have delivered them more cheaply by manufacturing them locally. Probably he was somewhat beguiled by the winning persuasiveness of Thomas Burke whose confidence in A. A. Denny's iron mines in Snoqualmie was born of the boom atmosphere more than sober investigation. But he knew how to make steel and should know, better than most men on the coast, whether he could manufacture it on Puget Sound or not.[15]

He thought he could do it, and after some reconnaissance he picked the eastern shore of Lake Washington as the site for his plant. The Great Western Iron and Steel Company was formed with a paid-up

---

[15] See Lake Washington Belt Line Company's brochure on Kirkland and the Great Western Iron and Steel Company, 1891, for details of the project; also *Eastside Journal*, October 4, 1951.

capital of a million dollars. Shareholders included eastern capitalists as well as such local men as A. A. Denny, Jacob Furth, and Bailey Gatzert. Engineers from Kirk's English company planned the construction of a Bessemer steel plant, a large plate iron works, coke ovens, and brickyards. Buildings went up, the town of Kirkland was born, and in the spring of 1891 the future looked bright indeed.

People say it was the panic of 1893 that shattered the dream, and perhaps it was. The plant never got into production and Kirkland became a ghost town even before the mill brought it fully to life. But when prosperity returned, the mill failed to revive and Kirkland remained a country town for half a century afterward. Was it only hard times, or were there deeper reasons for misfortune?

It was a fact of some importance that not just one iron works failed but that they all did. At one time or another not only Tacoma and Spokane had notions of building such plants, but such lesser places as Sedro-Woolley and Bellingham as well. Not one attempt succeeded. Most of them went no further than leasing the land or drawing the blueprints. The real question seems not to be what made the western men fail, but what made them think they could succeed. Fundamentally the obstacles were in the changing character of the steel industry and the wholly inadequate deposits of ore.

For the nation as a whole the steel industry was coming to be the biggest of Big Business. It subscribed its capital not in millions but billions of dollars, and turned out its products in millions of tons. Business control was tightly centralized and manufacture was carried on on such a tremendous scale that the capacities of the west coast to produce steel, or for that matter to consume it, were infinitesimal in comparison. More and more the needs of the entire country were supplied from the mines and the mills of half a dozen states.

The location of the industry was determined mainly by the raw materials rather than the market. Wherever situated, the mills must practice economies of scale, which meant that they devoured iron ore and coal in mountainous quantities. Hibbing, the fabled center of the Minnesota iron range, sent 6,460,000 tons of high-grade ore to the steel mills of the Midwest in a single year (1917). Eleven mines, all situated east of the Mississippi River, produced a million tons or more annually.

In this kind of game the Northwest had no chance whatever to compete. A few tunnels and cuts were made for exploratory purposes at Snoqualmie, but beyond that there was no development of the ore beds. Even in 1901 the state geologist expressed his doubt that any considerable quantity of metal would be found there. Twenty years later, when the scientists again surveyed the situation, they estimated the total possible deposits of iron in all of Washington at 7,000,000 to 8,000,000 tons, which would be barely enough to keep Hibbing in business for one year. No explanations of the "influence of established industries," no rationalizing of "great, untapped resources" could obscure the fact that the steel industry under twentieth century conditions imposed severe requirements which the Pacific Northwest was quite unable to meet. There was too little ore in the hills.[16]

[16] Washington Geological Survey, 1901, Vol. I, Part 4, 255; Clyde Williams, "Factors in the Production of Iron and Steel on the Pacific Coast," *Mining and Scientific Press*, CXXIII, July 16 and 23, 1921; W. H. Whittier, *Iron Ore Resources of the Northwest*, University of Washington, Bureau of Industrial Research, Bulletin 2, 1917; Solon Shedd, *Iron Ores, Fuels and Fluxes in Washington*, Washington Geological Survey, Bulletin 27, 1922.

The Progress of Urban Civilization

27

Building the Metropolitan Centers

To build in 20 years at Seattle and Portland, Tacoma and Spokane cities of 100,000 to 250,000 population was a considerable undertaking, and one which in itself required much money and man power. During the two decades 1890 to 1910 the skyline was completely altered in each of these places. Palatial hotels, large stores, ten-story office buildings gave the mercantile districts a monumental character, massive and imposing. Seattle's L. C. Smith building towered 42 stories into the air, new and exciting, one of the tallest commercial structures in the United States outside New York City. In each community newly established subdivisions circled the inner nucleus in ever-widening rings of residential neighborhoods, all linked with the center by electric car lines and improved streets. Visitors during World War I hardly recognized the city they had known in earlier years. Old landmarks were gone and the face of things was different. Edward M. Woolley, when he returned to Seattle, felt like Rip Van Winkle awakening after the years to find the familiar haunts had disappeared and everything was new and strange.

We can hardly estimate the energy and resources that went into the creation of this new urban setting. Capital poured into the cities in huge amounts for the construction of buildings and improvements. After the big Seattle fire of 1889, the heart of the city was rebuilt in permanent structures that ranged in cost from 20,000 to 300,000 dollars each. Two million went into hotels, 3,000,000 into dwellings, 8,000,000 into other buildings. In 1890 247 new plats were filed and 13,804 deeds were recorded. After 1900 more pretentious buildings appeared, including a million-dollar railway station, a courthouse equally costly, office buildings and high schools, and churches at 350,000 to 500,000 dollars. Building permits issued from 1903-1906 indicated investments totaling some 33,000,000 dollars. In the two years 1908 and 1909 Spokane put nearly 15,000,000 dollars into buildings. Railways spent in Tacoma alone some 20,000,000 dollars. The building permits issued from 1907 to 1914 in Seattle and Portland together totaled well over 200,000,000 dollars, and for several years averaged 25,000,000 to 30,000,000 dollars a year. City building was a big business that attracted investment capital, spent it generously in the cities themselves, and provided employment for a large number of the region's newly arrived population.[1]

Adventures in Promotion

The cities took the lead in building up business by promotion and advertising and by undertaking the construction of a number of permanent improvements which made growth and expansion possible.

Promotion became increasingly costly and elaborate, more so during the first decade of the century than in any other decade one can point to. Railroads and chambers of commerce turned out a veritable flood of pamphlets and advertising, including everything from purely tourist pieces to informative bulletins that contained solid factual data. Popular magazine articles appeared describing the beauties and advantages of the rising cities of the Far West. Most dramatically of all, the promoters put on their two biggest demonstrations, the Lewis and Clark Exposition in Portland in 1905 and the Alaska-Yukon-Pacific Exposition in Seattle in 1909.

Both of these big trade fairs were done in the grand manner and were spectacles the like of which the Northwest has never seen from that day to this. No extravagance was spared and no opportunity overlooked. Promoters in Portland, encouraged by the Oregon Historical

[1] Edward M. Woolley, "Seattle, Wonder City of the West," *McClure's*, L, January, 1918, 24-25; *Northwestern Real Estate and Building Review*, March, 1890, and February, 1891. See also Joseph Gaston, *Portland Oregon, Its History and Builders*, 3 vols. Portland, 1911; Clarence B. Bagley, *History of Seattle, from the Earliest Settlement to the Present Time*, (Chicago 1916; Nelson W. Durham, *History of the City of Spokane and the Spokane Country*, 3 vols., Chicago, 1912; Robert A. Reid, *Seattle the Queen City*, Seattle, 1914.

Society, planned and pushed the venture for several years before the business community accepted it as their own. Then, as preparations went forward more rapidly, an exposition city went up on the shores of Guilds Lake near Portland with pretentious exhibit halls to house a thousand fine displays contributed from every state in the Union and many foreign countries. Congress appropriated 1,700,000 dollars toward the federal building and its exhibits, and a million more for the coining of Lewis and Clark memorial gold dollars. The United States building, situated on the Peninsula, was the central focus of the entire group. Nearly 2,000,000 people attended the fair, which was enough to pay the expenses of organization and operation and return 21 percent profits to the stockholders. Nor were the benefits confined to the fair itself. Portland was publicized throughout the land, and those who watched the rapid development of the city during the next few years were persuaded that their advertising paid off handsomely.

Seattle's Alaska-Yukon-Pacific Exposition, presented in 1909, was the same kind of big show. Out on the edge of the city the University of Washington campus came alive during the summer months with great crowds of visitors. Several million dollars went into landscaping, roads, and elaborate buildings, a number of which were permanent structures used afterwards by the University for auditorium, library, laboratories, and classrooms. There were towers, obelisks, and arches, flying buttresses and classical colonnades, cascades and fountains, and formal gardens after the manner of Versailles, laid out along a vista to Mt. Rainier. Olmsted Brothers, nationally known landscape architects, drew the preliminary plan for the 250-acre development, but surely the splendor of the finished display must have gone beyond what even they imagined. As for the exhibits housed within, they were indeed varied and impressive, valued (it was said) at 50,000,000 dollars. Those who set them up insisted that nothing was exaggerated. The slogan of the show was simple and straight-forward: "The Truth Is Good Enough." But Truth was a generous word in the Northwest and covered every item of its resources. One could see nuggets from the Yukon, gold ore from Oroville and Republic, silver from Monte Cristo and Coeur d'Alene, copper from Sultan and Chewelah. The Mines Building had amalgamators, sluice boxes, and concentrators. Every log in the pergola which fronted the Forestry Building was a

25-ton monster of the woods with wood enough in it to make a five-room bungalow and woodshed. Spokane farmers built a model dairy barn complete with milking machines. Fisheries experts established a hatchery and oyster bed to illustrate the development of marine species common to Northwest waters. Apart from such local exhibits the spread of products and art pieces from many states and many lands provided a rich fare of information and beauty. Those who craved diversions and recreation found them in abundance at the "Pay Streak" down by Lake Union, complete even to a pioneer show by Ezra Meeker himself.[2]

These extravaganzas were characteristic of their day. In them the high-power booster really came into his own, master as he was of shouting and dazzling display. To a generation that only recently had discovered the power of sensational mass appeals, the expositions seemed a sure way of attracting notice and thus of attracting population and business. In a measure the boosters were right, in that they sensed the crucial importance of people—large numbers of people—to the economic development of the area. Doubtless they put too much confidence in spectacles. The A.-Y.-P. Exposition proved to be worth very little in warding off the effects of economic depression. Yet the optimism and the energy that went into these big trade fairs were important to the cities and to the region as a whole. They were sources of strength which showed itself in other ways as well, most significantly perhaps in the carrying out of a number of substantial improvements. People did not come to the Northwest simply because of advertising. They came, many of them, because the cities were spending on themselves, investing in their own future.

Public Improvements

Generous expenditures went into improved streets, and streetcar lines, sewers, water systems, and electric power plants, the kind of thing every city was faced with as it grew larger. Portland put 6,000,000 dollars into a new municipal water system that delivered its supply to a kitchen sink or fire hydrant from

[2] See Robert A. Reid, *Sights and Scenes at the Lewis and Clark Exposition*, Portland, 1905. Details concerning the Alaska-Yukon-Pacific Exposition are drawn from the official *Information Guide*, catalogues of exhibits, contemporary maps and pictures, and from the report of the A.Y.P. Committee.

the Bull Run reservoir 30 miles away. Seattle and Tacoma both reached even farther up into the Cascade Mountains, exploring problems of sanitation in the watersheds and studying carefully the preservation of the forest cover. Seattle's sewer system involved the excavating of numerous tunnels, and the laying of 428 miles of pipe. Channels and ducts from various parts of the city led to an outlet on the Sound near Ft. Lawton where the discharge was drawn away to deep water no matter what the ebb and flow of the tide.

Portland and Spokane built bridges to bind the different sections of the city together. It was an accomplishment to be achieved only with considerable effort. There is a "ballad" of the period that rehearses the trials and difficulties, each stanza ending with the stubborn but plaintive refrain:

> They're going to build, I feel it yet
> A Bridge Across the Willamette.

Once the first bridge was completed, others followed more easily, even though they were million-dollar projects. Nothing did more to free the community from its confinement within the narrow limits of river and hills. Meanwhile in Spokane people pointed with pride to the new Monroe Street bridge, a tremendous monolithic arch of reinforced concrete, 281 feet long, the construction of which at that time was likewise considered a major accomplishment.

Some of Seattle's most ambitious projects were regrades which involved cutting down its hills and moving tremendous amounts of earth to build up the tide flats. R. H. Thomson, city engineer, took the initiative in planning and carrying out these schemes. He was a man of bold imagination, fertile in expedients and resourceful in his politics. Under his leadership the central part of the city assumed a new and different shape.

Thomson was convinced that Seattle's greatest need was for more level land. The day was gone when a city could prosper clinging to the side of a hill, with nothing flat save a narrow shelf along the waterfront. Railroads required large areas of even ground for their stations and yards and Thompson saw nothing suitable nearer than Auburn, where, before many years, the Northern Pacific located its main switching area. If there was to be any industrial development, this too demanded level land for factory sites, and there was almost none to be had.

To meet this urgent demand for land suited to commercial and industrial purposes Seattle undertook, if necessary, to remove mountains into the midst of the sea. Other cities have filled swamps and built up the land to make it useful, but we may doubt that such operations ever meant so much as they did here. Ten million cubic yards of dirt were shoveled and sluiced down from the hills to make embankments below or to fill large stretches of tideflats which previously had been several feet under water. Some streets were reduced 15 to 25 feet in their grade. At the corner of Fourth Avenue and Blanchard Street the level was lowered 107 feet. The old hotel, perched on top of Denny Hill, was dismantled, the hill cut down, and the New Washington Hotel built in its place. South of King Street on the tide flats, new land was built up to form what is now the principal industrial section of the city. Large hydraulic cannon threw millions of gallons of water daily against the steep slopes while huge specially designed wooden pipes carried water and dirt together to some new location. It was an ingenious feat of engineering, one that was feasible only because comparatively little rock was encountered.[3]

Tacoma faced somewhat similar problems in making its tidelands usable. The Northern Pacific Railroad spent a considerable amount of money on the improvement of the flats at the mouth of the Puyallup River, a project that drew the city still farther east away from the site of Old Tacoma out on the point. The measures adopted were less dramatic than those of Seattle, but here, too, the necessary facilities of the growing metropolis were fitted with no little skill to the contours of a difficult natural setting.

New Port Facilities

The waterfront facilities of the port cities required a large outlay for their development. In Seattle more and larger wharves were needed to accommodate the growing ocean

[3] *That Man Thomson*, ed. Grant H. Redford, Seattle, 1950; Arthur H. Dimock, *Preparing the Groundwork for a City: the Regrading of Seattle, Washington*, New York, 1928; Welford Beaton, *City That Made Itself: a Literary and Pictorial Record of the Building of Seattle*, Seattle, 1914.

commerce, cranes, and other heavy equipment for the handling of cargo, and warehouses for the storage of goods awaiting shipment or distribution. Portland found it a vital necessity to dredge a deeper channel and even to improve the jetty at the mouth of the Columbia River.

A considerable argument arose as to the most desirable way of achieving these purposes. The issue of monopoly was hotly debated and the private wharves were sharply criticized for charging too much in fees while spending too little on expansion. Robert Bridges, a Populist, and for several years member of the Seattle Port Commission, insisted that the waterfront terminals should be impartial public intermediaries between land and water carriers and should not be controlled by either group. Hiram Chittenden, another leader in the development of the port, likewise spoke out vigorously against monopoly along the waterfront, which, he thought, would discourage the growth of the city.

The result of this agitation was the establishment of public port commissions in Portland and Seattle, the improvement of navigation on the Columbia, and the digging of a canal to give ocean-going vessels access to fresh water anchorage on the lakes behind Seattle.[4]

The Port of Portland was created in 1891 as a municipal corporation, vested with the right of eminent domain and with powers to levy taxes and issue bonds for revenue purposes, and charged with considerable authority over the improvement of navigation on the Willamette and the lower Columbia River. During the next 25 years the port commissioners raised and spent nearly 7,000,000 dollars on facilities and services that materially strengthened Portland's competitive position in the handling of ocean commerce. More than half this amount went into river improvement. A drydock was put into operation in 1904 which attracted ships for repairs. In 1912 coaling was provided at competitive costs. For a number of years towing and pilotage services were supplied, even at a loss, in order to overcome the handicaps involved in the long voyage upriver.

The Port of Seattle, established in 1911, was concerned mainly with

[4] Port of Portland Commission, Biennial Report, 1915-1916, Seattle Port Commission, Annual Reports, 1912-1915; Port of Seattle *Yearbook*, 1914; Robert Bridges, *Basic Principles of Port Organization*, Seattle, 1916.

the construction and operation of wharves and warehouses. It was an independent agency largely removed from the frequent changes and pressures of local politics, and directed by men who took a very broad view of the necessities of a growing city. Within five years the commissioners had raised through the sale of bonds 5,750,000 dollars, putting the money into the execution of a comprehensive plan of improved facilities. Along the East Waterway at the mouth of the Duwamish River, four piers were erected with a total berthing space of 5,000 linear feet. The Hanford Street grain elevator had a capacity of 500,000 bushels of grain; not far away were cold storage plants to preserve 2,000,000 pounds of fish and tremendous quantities of apples and other fruits. The Central Waterfront Terminal at the foot of Bell Street, provided 1,200 feet of berthing space and a six-story warehouse of 300,000 cubic feet capacity for canned salmon and miscellaneous storage. Still farther north at Smith Cove a huge double pier which stretched nearly half a mile out into the water, was designed especially for the lumber export trade. Here a big gantry crane picked up loads of as much as 100 tons for delivery to a waiting ship. The Salmon Bay terminal served the fishing fleet with sheltered moorage and 195,000 square feet of open wharf space. The floor space available in all the sheds together totaled nearly 30 square blocks.

The port commission did not succeed without a struggle. Lively contests marked the votes on bond issues, and for a time it seemed that perhaps some private company would secure the public funds and build another Bush Terminal like the one at Brooklyn. But the commissioners weathered the storm and public opinion swung behind them. The Port became a respected public service agency which offered a wide variety of services at attractive rates.

Private Construction

At the same time when these improvements were being made, private construction forged ahead with additional building both in stores, office buildings, and residences. This kind of building was spurred by the highly speculative character of the economic boom. Property values rose rapidly and this in itself attracted investment capital and contributed to still further improvement. Assessed property values in Portland increased from 44,000,000 dollars in 1902 to 144,000,000 dollars three years later and jumped 90,000,000 dollars more in the next two years after that (1907). Real estate transactions in Portland in 1909 comprised a 26,500,000-dollar business. Trade journals in Seattle reported individual transactions that illustrated what was happening there. One tract of land which brought 10,000 dollars in 1887 was sold in 1891 for 600,000 dollars. The townsite of Kensington, priced at 20,000 dollars in November, 1889, brought 100,000 dollars less than a year afterward. Owners of the Central Building advertised for prospects claiming that land values in Seattle's "Inner Business Circle" advanced 25 percent per year from 1900 to 1907. Here, they said, was a "mine of ever-increasing values and ceaseless dividends." Charles Bussell topped such claims as these with other instances where tracts of tidelands were picked up for next to nothing, to be sold again at fantastic profits. One such property, purchased for 400 dollars was sold in pieces for 20,000 dollars and later rose in value to four times that figure. Four and a half acres, for which 444 dollars was paid in 1898, sold in 1902 for 15,000 dollars. "Get the tideland habit" urged Bussell, "it will make money for you while you sleep."

Increments like these attracted many millions of dollars for private building to match the public improvements. Local men in Seattle like Joshua Green, Thomas Burke, and Dexter Horton were responsible for the development of some of the better commercial blocks. Eastern men contributed too, both in money and management, men like J. C. Marmaluke and G. Henry Whitcomb, James J. Hill and the Boston utility firm of Stone and Webster. Residential building was something in which many thousands of persons participated. Bringing a metropolis into being was a task that involved a vast network of capitalist enterprise. The creative power that produced it was national in its scope, and included men of various financial resources who might live almost anywhere.[5]

Architecturally the sections of the cities that offered the greatest interest were the central business districts, where the hotels, stores, and office buildings were located. Building of this kind was not some-

[5] *Raymer's Dictionary of Greater Seattle*, Seattle, 1907; Charles B. Bussell, *Tide Lands, Their Story*, Seattle, n.d.

thing simply local in character. Architecture and engineering were nationally established professions, and many of the men who designed and built the cities of the Northwest were trained in eastern schools which followed the trends and observed the standards that were generally recognized throughout the country. The L. C. Smith Building, Seattle's first real skyscraper, was put up by the typewriter magnate of Syracuse and was designed by Gaggin and Gaggin, a firm of architects in that city. It was a steel frame structure, inspired by the skyscrapers of New York, and might have graced any large city regardless of location. The Metropolitan Tract was developed in similar fashion to become a model "city within a city," its modern medical office buildings being the work of New York architects. The business blocks in downtown Portland were imposing buildings that followed eastern trends and practices in much the same way. The builders of the Northwest reported their activity in their own trade journal and some of their undertakings were noticed in such magazines as *American City* and the *Journal of Engineering*. Except for the local nomenclature, one would have found it hard to identify any of these buildings as peculiarly western or regional in character.[6]

In the process of city growth, the business center encroached upon and eventually replaced the older residential streets, while the newer residential areas pushed out farther and farther into the wild. Churches sold their downtown corner lots at substantial profits and built new buildings perhaps up the hill a few blocks or perhaps in some newer residential district to which their people had already removed. Individual homes which stood in the path of commercial expansion were razed or, if they stood fast, became isolated landmarks of an age gone by, surrounded by overtowering masses of masonry that all but suffocated them. Meanwhile the real estate promoter energetically plied his trade in every quarter. If the proportion of home ownership as compared to tenancy remained unusually high in the Northwest, it was partly at least because the new subdivisions were so laid out as to make it possible.

To be sure, the lots were small. Sometimes they measured only a 40-foot frontage in a city that had many square miles within its limits wholly undeveloped. The better lots were expensive. A man

[6] A. H. Albertson, "City Within a City," *Architect*, XI, January, 1916, 13-55.

might pay 3,000 dollars for his land alone if he wanted a good view of Mt. Hood or Mt. Rainier. But the newcomer could buy according to his taste and his pocketbook, and if he wished to avoid heavy assessments he could do so and still have his own house. The subdivision of realty was an old business in America, one that had moved with the emigrant across the full breadth of the country. Probably it was no better and no worse in the Northwest than in other new communities. If the street and lot lines of a subdivision fell awkwardly across some scenic slope, it was only because Nature here demanded more sensitiveness and imagination than had been yet achieved in the practice of business and simple speculation. Even so the beauty of blue waters or snow-capped mountains brought many a living room to life by the glimpse of it.

Parks and City Planning

The Northwest cities, like those in other parts of the country, felt the influence of the movement for city planning and beautification. Land was acquired for parks, scenic boulevards, and playgrounds, and in 1911-1912 both Portland and Seattle retained planning and landscape specialists to prepare elaborate reports and recommendations that would shape and coördinate the future development of the community.

Park acquistions began with the donation of scattered tracts of land by a few public-minded citizens like Donald Macleay of Portland and Charles Cowen and Ferdinand Schmitz of Seattle. Park commissions were established and as the years passed they were given increasing authority and money necessary to develop a comprehensive system of park areas.

Seattle's city council invited John C. Olmsted, member of a nationally known firm of landscape architects, to study the problem of parks and to recommend a long-range plan. His reports, submitted in 1903 and 1908 became the basis of the present park system, and 1,500,000 dollars in park bonds were approved by the voters toward carrying them out. By 1909 Seattle had five public playgrounds and 14 improved parks appraised even then at twice what had been paid for them. Olmsted's plan called for a varied blending of formal gardens and grassy lawns with larger areas to be preserved unspoiled in their primitive condition. View spots looked out over the city to the mountains. Picnic areas and swimming and boating facilities attracted crowds to the beaches on salt water and fresh. Forest glens and narrow ravines were left as rustic retreats for nature lovers to enjoy perhaps only a few blocks from their homes. A substantial start was made in building a parkway boulevard that would one day circle the city in a scenic belt 50 miles long.

The course of events in Portland was very similar: a survey by Olmsted and a million-dollar bond issue to raise money to carry it out. Under the skillful guidance of the Parks Superintendent, E. T. Mische, a number of new parks were developed, and a boulevard system was laid out to provide a beautiful hillside drive to scenic spots in and around the city.[7]

City planning included much more than parks. In these optimistic years it seemed quite possible that the metropolitan centers might soon become highly congested places of a million, perhaps two million population. Should this take place, it would be well to have definite ideas for the handling of traffic, the grouping of civic buildings, the locating of certain districts in the city to serve particular purposes. Architects and engineers gave their attention to these problems and aroused a good bit of popular interest in them. As a result planning experts visited both Portland and Seattle, studied their needs and worked up comprehensive reports which were given wide circulation.

The Portland plan was done in 1911-1912 by Edward Bennett, a Chicago architect and planner. It called for an ambitious program of construction and embellishment, calculated for a city several times as large as Portland has yet grown to be. A radial spider web of boulevards was to extend from the downtown commercial districts out into the peripheral residential areas. A majestic civic center was to be the focus of interest in the heart of the city while parks situated high on the hills above it would command a panoramic view of the whole development, jewel and setting as well. Rail and shipyards would be concentrated on the flats along the Columbia River.

Virgil G. Bogue, who did the Seattle plan, was an engineer of wide reputation who had worked with F. L. Olmsted in Brooklyn and who more recently had been active in railway construction in the moun-

[7] Seattle Park Commissioners, Report, 1909; George W. James, "Portland, the Gateway of the Columbia." *Twentieth Century Magazine*, II, April 1910, 3-14.

tains of both Americas and in solving engineering problems along the waterfront in Tacoma and Seattle. His plan resembled the Portland plan in some ways and his published report was even more pretentious.

The focal center of the future Seattle, Bogue thought, should be established in the undeveloped area lying south of Lake Union. Here would be located the principal railway depot and an imposing group of civic buildings, designed in the grand manner of the day. The location was central and arterial highways would make it easily accessible from the various sections of the city around it. At several places tunnels would pierce the hills to reach the waterfront or the farther neighborhoods to the east. A funicular railroad along Virginia Street would handle traffic up the steep bluff from the shoreline.

All these ideas were described and diagrammed in considerable detail, and there was logic in what he proposed. He was, however, too much swept away by his enthusiasm and had too little regard for other development projects that were being carried forward at the same time. The more immediate construction then going on tended to center the merchantile district and the civic buildings farther south, where, for the most part, they have remained. The railroad yards did not skirt and encroach upon Lake Union naturally as he thought they would, and the waterfront development on Elliott Bay was not concentrated on Harbor Island as he proposed. Though some of his tunnels have proved feasible and useful, others have not, On the whole Seattle has preferred to take to bridges of one kind or another, rather than tunneling through the hills or under Lake Washington as Bogue suggested. The plan was in many ways prophetic but it asked too much, even of people who were accustomed to dreaming fine dreams and to carrying out a surprising number of them. The Bogue report failed to receive formal approval and is of interest to us now mainly for its might-have-beens. Nevertheless it illustrates for us the way the young Northwest cities, caught up in the currents of urban development just as much older cities were, asked the experts for their recommendations on community planning, but exercised their own discrimination in accepting or rejecting what their visitors said should be done.[8]

---

[8] Edward Bennett, *Greater Portland Plan*, Portland, 1912; Seattle Municipal Plans Commission, Report, 1911.

28

Patterns of Commerce and Manufacturing

The building up of the cities and the expansion of their essential facilities were carried out with the idea that they would earn their way on a larger scale than would be possible for smaller places. Wharves and railroad yards, warehouses, stores, and manufacturing plants were constructed to handle a greater volume of business, and it was only as production and trade were increased that the capital invested in city building would return its profit. Cities, like people, must make a living. The years of rapid growth in the Northwest were important because they witnessed a tremendous increase of economic activity in many varied lines of commerce and manufacturing, in merchandizing, transportation, and banking.

Commerce

Commerce meant buying and selling, transporting goods and storing them. It included moving the crops, handling the fish pack, and forwarding large shipments of lumber. Commission men and jobbers built up the wholesale trade, establishing stocks of commodities in western warehouses to meet the needs of merchants throughout the region, and thus relieving them of the necessity of ordering at long distances from Chicago, St. Louis, or New York. Retailers expanded their stores, offering their local customers a wide variety of merchandise assembled from the four corners of the nation, from Europe, Asia, and Latin America. Commerce might lead a man to far horizons or it might occupy him in the more immediate hinterland close by.

Trade was concentrated to a large extent in the metropolitan centers, yet, since the number of cities was now larger, the exchange of goods became increasingly complex. Portland continued to claim preëminence in the wholesale trade, which in 1908 involved 200,000,000 dollars' worth of business. Businessmen there claimed the city was a distributing center for a territory of 250,000 square miles. Yet Tacoma jobbers established themselves too. Grocery and dry goods firms put up large new buildings with private tracks on Railroad Street. Hardware and furniture companies served not only the city itself but smaller towns nearby. Importing houses handled coffee and tea, spices, herbs, and foreign fruits. The Washington Commission Company shipped its imports as far east as Denver, employing half a dozen traveling salesmen to represent them throughout the entire Northwest area. Most of the wholesalers put men on the road. By 1909 225 traveling men were working out of Tacoma, bringing to that city a wholesale trade of 50,000,000 dollars.[1]

Spokane jobbers treated the whole Inland Empire as their tributary area and aspired to make their city a supply center for the farm lands to the south and the mining districts of Northern Idaho as well. Their location close to the wheat fields and mines favored such a development and did much to make possible the extremely rapid growth of the city as the railroads were extended from the Middle West to the Far West. These natural advantages were in some measure lost, however, because of unfavorable freight rates which were considerably higher to Spokane than to the terminal cities on the coast.

For 20 years the merchants of the Inland Empire contested this discrimination, demanding that rates from Chicago should be no higher to Spokane than to Seattle and Portland. They pointed out repeatedly in hearings before the Interstate Commerce Commission that inequitable freight charges allowed Portland jobbers to sell their goods practically in Spokane's back yard, and in some instances made it impossible for local manufacturing plants to operate at all. On 14 percent of the items enumerated in the Spokane rate case against the Northern Pacific Railroad the rates were high enough to carry the goods from Chicago to Puget Sound and back to Spokane again.

---

[1] *Oregon, Land of Opportunity*, Portland, 1910; *Portland Commercial Review*, Annual Number, July, 1901; *West Coast Trade*, Annual Number, Tacoma, 1892-1913.

On 70 percent of the remaining items there were simliar though smaller differentials. Such rates were defended by the railroads as exceptions to the Interstate Commerce Act on the grounds that there was greater competition at the coast terminals. Only by demonstrating that little real competition did in fact exist were the Spokane traders able finally (1917) to secure the territory around them.[2]

Ocean commerce, whether coastal or foreign, came to be more and more important to the coastal cities. Seattle found the supply trade with Alaska to be highly profitable, even after the Yukon gold rush was ended. During several years prior to World War I this trade amounted to 25 percent of Seattle's domestic commerce. In 1915 the city shipped 17,500,000 dollars' worth of merchandise north to Alaskan ports. Taking both foreign and domestic trade into account, 16 percent (in value) of the city's ocean traffic moved to and from Alaska.

Foreign trade likewise produced a growing volume of business. Portland's wheat ships carried 13,000,000 bushels to foreign ports during the year 1909. Tacoma and Seattle, contending with each other for commercial ascendancy on the Sound, shared in 1895 a foreign trade of 5,000,000 dollars, three-fourths of which went to Tacoma. By 1913 the figure had reached 100,000,000 dollars, divided almost equally between the two ports. Between 1909 and 1914 Seattle's trade with China and Japan averaged some 30,000,000 dollars annually. In the latter year the total foreign trade of the city amounted to 56,000,000 dollars, with 72 percent of Washington's foreign imports coming in at the one city.

Shippers on Elliott Bay pointed with great satisfaction to the low charges which made Seattle the freest port on the Pacific coast. Calculating the costs of wharfage, pilots' fees, towing, and moorage, they asserted that ships entering San Francisco paid an average of 1,153 dollars; at Portland, 490 dollars; at Seattle, only 176 dollars. The further fact that sailing distances were 1,000 miles shorter to the ports of Japan and North China than from California reënforced the conviction that Puget Sound would before long become the principal gateway to the Orient.[3]

---

[2] Douglas Smart, "Spokane's Battle for Freight Rates," *PNQ*, XLV, 1954, 19-27.

[3] Margaret C. Rodman, "Trend of Alaskan Commerce through the Port of Seattle," unpublished thesis, University of Washington, 1930, 14-22; Ole K. Moe, "Analytical

Banking

Banking like merchandising became a big business during the era of urban expansion. Portland had long been the chief banking center with its old local firms like Ladd and Tilton and the branch banks of the Bank of British Columbia and the London and San Francisco Bank. In Washington and Idaho no corporate banking was permitted until late in the territorial period, but private bankers like Dexter Horton in Seattle and Levi P. Ankenny in Walla Walla, had built up a considerable local business in their own communities. With the rapid growth of population, trade, and investment, banking became a central enterprise in the region, for the financing of agriculture, commerce, and manufacturing all depended upon it.

We can get some idea of the rapid development of banking resources by looking at the increasing assets held by the banks of the region. Between 1889 and 1909 these assets for the region as a whole increased more than elevenfold from about 32,000,000 dollars to 355,000,000 dollars, or from 42 dollars *per capita* to about 251 dollars. This was a most important change for it meant that the region improved itself tremendously in the matter of available financial power and was no longer to be considered frontier territory. At the beginning of the century the *per capita* resources of the Pacific Northwest were less than they were in any other section of the country except the South. Ten years later they were surpassed only by New England and the Middle Atlantic states. Idaho was better off than the plains states as a group (178 to 161 dollars); Washington and Oregon banks reported higher figures than those of the Old Northwest, including Illinois and Ohio. The days were over when the Inland Empire and Puget Sound were starved for money and when the banks reported more in loans outstanding than they had in deposits. During the decade of expansion deposits mounted up far beyond the demand for loans. As they did so, the banker's problem

Study of the Foreign Trade through the Port of Seattle," unpublished thesis, University of Washington, 1932; Charles J. Miller, *Pacific Northwest Trade with Far East Pacific Nations,* New York, 1945; Eliot G. Mears, *Maritime Trade of Western United States,* Stanford University, 1935; R. F. Radebaugh, *Pacific Metropolis, Where and Why,* Tacoma, 1913; *Seattle, the Great Shipping and Commercial Center,* Chamber of Commerce, 1913.

was no longer one of finding money to finance improvements and to meet the needs of the enlarging business community. Now it was a matter of finding investment outlets for the surplus savings and reserves that were accumulating. In a word, the region advanced from debtor to creditor financing, as the older sections had done.[4]

Over the region as a whole expansion was brought about through the establishment of many new banking institutions. Between 1900 and 1915 the number of state and national banks together multiplied sixfold until in the latter year some 792 banks were serving the area. This kind of growth was particularly noticeable among the state banks which at the beginning of World War I outnumbered the national banks 575 to 217. Most of the state banks were smaller institutions averaging 300,000 dollars in capital resources while the national banks averaged 1,200,000 dollars.

The rapid increase in the number of banks shows the grass roots development of banking. Even more striking was the growth of large banks in the cities. Here the real financial strength of the region was centered. The big city banks (state and national alike) were five- to 12-million-dollar enterprises. In 1909 four national banks in Seattle possessed more in total resources (38,000,000 dollars) than 64 other national banks in the smaller places (totalling 35,200,000 dollars). Six banks in Spokane and Tacoma added as much again (35,800,000 dollars). Four Portland banks had as much strength as 68 banks in the rest of Oregon (about 32,000,000 dollars).

To some extent the city banks were bigger because the communities in which they were situated were larger and required more in the way of local resources and facilities. Individual deposits at each bank ran into the millions of dollars and while the loans and discounts figures ran perhaps a third less, they too were reported in large numbers in the northwest cities as in others of comparable size.

However, the metropolitan banks fulfilled their more distinctive functions through services they performed for other banks, especially the smaller banks in the area. On the one hand they accepted funds from correspondent institutions which had more in deposits than

[4] The analysis of banking developments offered here is based mainly upon the reports of the U.S. Comptroller of the Currency, the Federal Reserve Board, and the Washington State Bank Examiner.

they could put to work profitably and safely in their own communities. In this way the city banks served as investment outlets for the country bankers who were not in a good position to handle surplus funds. On the other hand, the metropolitan banks made funds available to banks that needed them. Some of this money was carried as a balance with a yet larger bank, situated perhaps in San Francisco, Chicago, or St. Louis. Some of it was sent to smaller banks, either state or national.

The proportion of the two varied in individual cases. In 1909 the national banks in Portland carried just under 3,000,000 dollars in balances with reserve agents while they had 4,130,000 dollars with other national and state banks. The Seattle banks carried a much larger sum with reserve agents (5,700,000 dollars) but considerably less (3,300,000 dollars) with other national and state banks. This would suggest that Portland continued to play the role of a regional financial capital through the intimate relation of city and country banks even after its position of primacy had been challenged by the new cities to the north. Washington's "Big Three" won the same individual treatment that Portland had in the reports of the Comptroller of the Currency, but the responsibilities of their position were new to them, and the demands of their own communities somewhat greater. Nevertheless the metropolitan banks in each city acted as reserve agents for the smaller banks after 1908, and provided a source of capital funds not only for their own locality but in the surrounding area as well.

Manufacturing

As the northwest cities grew larger and the facilities they offered were improved, manufacturing plants increased in number, variety, and productivity. In 1910 Portland claimed 2,000 different establishments which together represented a capital of 30,000,000 dollars and gave occupation to 25,000 employees. For the region as a whole manufactures exceeded farm crops in value. In the cities themselves the Census Bureau found that one man in three of those gainfully occupied was employed in some manufacturing or mechanical occupation. Between 1900 and 1914 the value of manufactures and the number of persons employed more than doubled. By 1914 the manufacturing interest of the Northwest was adding to the value of its raw materials in the amount of some 168,800,000 dollars per year.

Compared with the larger industrial centers of the United States, to be sure, the Pacific Northwest cities made but a small showing. The factories of Detroit and Pittsburgh turned out products at the rate of 400 to 500 dollars *per capita*, while Portland, Seattle, and Tacoma never produced more than 175 dollars *per capita*. Capital went into manufacturing much more cautiously than it did into other kinds of enterprise, and represented only pin money when measured against the sums spent on industrial investments in the East and Middle West. The Northwest as a whole had 4.29 dollars in its farms for every dollar in manufacturing capital.

Nevertheless there were developments which suggested for the Northwest, too, the advances of industrialism. Seattle's big lumber mills with their towering chimneys belching forth smoke and flame gave to parts of the city, at least, very much the atmosphere of a factory community. Moran's shipyard, expanded to undertake the building of the battleship *Nebraska*, possessed all the heavy equipment and machinery that one would find in a similar establishment at Charlestown or Portsmouth. Portland's packing plant, a 3,000,000-dollar installation built and operated by Swift and Company, gave employment to 500 men and had a capacity adequate to handle the slaughtering of 500 cattle and 2,500 hogs and sheep daily. The huge Wheeler-Osgood sash and door factory gave Tacoma (so far as one plant could do it) as good a claim to be called industrial as many a city in New England. Manufacturing output and wage payrolls doubled from 1900 to 1914. Man for man, the industrial workers on the Columbia and Puget Sound produced more goods (in value) in a year than did the factory laborers of Worcester, Lynn, and Bridgeport.

These achievements were on the whole encouraging and lent substance to the confident assumption that growth in manufacturing was a natural part of the general growth of the area. Western boosters took it for granted that manufacturing, like commerce, moved freely into any newly populated section, and could be expected to develop there without difficulty. They did not differentiate between types or conditions of manufacturing, but contented themselves with discovering what products were locally made and what were not. The Seattle Chamber of Commerce published such a list, pointing out the numerous opportunities that existed to produce items currently available only from distant sources.

Yet the turn of the century witnessed far-reaching changes in the geographic distribution of manufacturing throughout the nation. The forces that facilitated the migration of population and the cheap transportation of goods over long distances affected the location of industries very directly. Certain lines of manufacturing were highly concentrated, while others were widely dispersed. Some plants grew to be very large, and by exploiting economies of scale they dominated that particular industry for the entire United States. Old established concerns sometimes gained telling advantages over new ones, a fact of no small importance in cities that were late in developing. Competition became increasingly keen between plants in different places, and success for any city depended more and more upon reaching not only the local market but some part of the farflung national market as well.

Economists have debated among themselves about these matters, and theorists have formulated complex equations to describe the locational distribution of one industry or another. What concerns us here is that manufacturing, contrary to what the boosters believed, did not gravitate to new communities according to any simple law. It is important, therefore, to consider what kind of industrial profile appeared in these far western cities, what lines of manufacturing were principal enterprises, and what others, though of lesser importance individually, nevertheless contributed significantly to the pattern as a whole.[5]

As one might expect, the main lines of manufacturing were those related to the region's natural resources. The secondary ones were for the most part those that were oriented toward the local market. It should be no surprise to discover that products, the manufacture of which was highly concentrated nationally, rarely developed locally. Steel mills did not operate successfully despite a number of attempts to establish them. There was small prospect of making billiard tables

[5] Data on the development of manufacturing appear in the references cited above, but much more fully in the reports of the U.S. Census Bureau.

or cash registers in Seattle when 90 percent of them for the whole country were fabricated in Cincinnati or Dayton. What is not so obvious is that a number of important lines of manufacture, including several with a fairly high degree of national concentration, also flourished on a lesser scale in other parts of the country. Various sections of the trans-Mississippi West had their own plants, situated typically in the main urban centers. These industries developed in the Pacific Northwest cities as elsewhere and became a characteristic part of the regional economy. Meat-packing houses and flour mills, bakeries and breweries, foundries and printing plants were industries that characteristically followed this pattern.

The lumber industry was unquestionably the Number One industry in the cities as well as the states of the Pacific Northwest. In 1910 Seattle's mills contributed a 2,200,000-dollar payroll and employed 3,337 men, while those of Tacoma reached figures only a trifle lower. In Portland the mills did a 10,000,000-dollar business, by far the largest single line of manufacturing in the city. Lumbering, however, was not concentrated in the cities. Mills were scattered about the region in many small places. Communities of less than 10,000 people, which included about half the population in the states of Washington and Oregon, likewise accounted for 45 to 48 percent of the value added in manufacturing in their respective states, largely because of the pattern in the dominant industry. Portland turned out only a third of the total product for the state of Oregon, while Seattle, Tacoma, and Spokane produced together less than 20 percent of the Washington state total. Thus the metropolitan centers were not particularly prominent in the industry that was the major one for the region as a whole.

In manufacturing generally the role of the larger cities was much more important. More than 40 percent of state totals in value added through manufacturing could be traced to the urban centers. In several lines of production the proportion ran much higher. Foundries and printing plants in Portland did three-fourths of the work in their lines for the whole state of Oregon. Washington's Big Three turned out two-thirds of the leather goods manufactured locally and 73 percent of the bakery goods. Seattle and Tacoma produced 46 percent of the milled flour. Seattle alone did half of the state's meatpacking, and brewed 40 percent of its malt liquors.

Urban manufacturing was increasingly a matter of corporate enterprise and large plants. Eighty-five percent or more of the activity of the principal cities was handled by corporations and 75 percent of the output came from plants that produced 100,000 dollars worth of goods or more annually. 40 percent of Seattle's manufactures were the product of large mills that did at least a million dollars' worth of business each year.

But these figures for the large operations do not tell the whole story. The diversity and the balance of industrial activity in the cities stands out rather in the development of a considerable number of lesser lines of manufacture which, though individually small, nevertheless added up as a group to a significant fraction of the total. In Seattle, for example, in 1914, 209 establishments, devoted to the manufacture of various kinds of food products, employed as many workers and supported as large a total payroll as 55 plants devoted to lumber milling. The value of the food products was four times as great as the timber products manufactured. Foundries and printing plants likewise equaled the lumber mills in jobs and wages, and these, too, turned out products of considerably greater value. In none of the larger cities of the region did any one line of manufacturing account for more than 17 percent of the total value of production. Seven different lines in Seattle made up 60 percent of the total. Miscellaneous unspecified small lines made up 28 percent more, while the remaining 12 percent was filled out by a number of industries (including bakeries, dairy and canning plants, and clothing and sheet metal shops) which reported production between 140,000 dollars and 1,500,000 dollars annually. Actually then, so far as dependence on a small number of large payrolls was concerned, the worker in the Far West was not nearly so helpless as the man in Kansas City, Kansas, or Youngstown, Ohio.

The Pace Slackens

Despite the fact that the cities showed considerably more diversification than the region as a whole, their economy too was based on the principal resource industries and was sensitive to any slump that might develop, particularly in the lumber industry. Just *how sensitive* it was it is difficult to determine precisely, for the interrelationships between lumbering and other lines of enterprise were very complicated. The question becomes especially intriguing as we try to understand the reasons for the economic ups and downs that occurred between 1909 and 1914.

These years witnessed a distinct slackening in the pace of economic activity, which was clearly reflected in manufacturing. New population continued to come into Seattle—at least the population figures continued to rise by about 5,000 persons per year—but the rate of growth lessened appreciably. Jobs, payrolls, and manufacturing production had kept pace with population gains during the earlier period; after 1909 these figures faltered. Seattle plants increased their payrolls by only 2,000,000 dollars (1909-1914) and the number of jobs rose by only 1,000. The lumber mills declined in production, and manufacturing related to construction likewise dropped off. A number of lines which might be classified as durable consumers' goods, such things as furniture and mattresses, stoves and furnaces, were operating at a lower level on the eve of World War I than they had been earlier. Food processing lines expanded to take up the slack, as did a number of small shops, but the net effect was to indicate that the boom begun around the turn of the century was now ended.

It is easy to suggest that the lumber industry, plagued by price fluctuations, shipping difficulties, and overproduction offers the main explanation of this situation. It seems plain enough that when a principal source of economic support weakens, the effects are felt at once in many secondary industries. Yet we should not accept such reasoning too quickly, since other factors were undoubtedly involved as well. Probably the building of the cities themselves, as we have described it, was the most important. Many millions of dollars of investment capital had been poured into this undertaking over a period of 20 years, but the major part of the task was approaching completion. Speculative values were high; and the day of reckoning was at hand. To a considerable degree the cities had been living on borrowed money. They must now find ways to pay it back. The problems would be problems of consolidation rather than of expansion. All this in itself involved readjustments that promised to be difficult and at times painful. The connection with the affairs of the lumber industry was important but was not a full explanation. Put them together, however, and the combined result was indeed an economic reorientation that affected every industry and challenged the best business minds in the community.

Nor was the problem confined to the cities alone. The region as a whole was passing into a new stage of economic development. The Pacific Northwest was no longer a frontier that beckoned to people to migrate to it, offering rich resources and profitable opportunities at low values. The years of easy expansion were over. The long pull was beginning, with its promise of more modest growth and its stiff unending competition with other sections and other cities which brought the far Northwest into a kind of equilibrium with them. Under existing conditions of production and distribution it would not be simple to bring about a further development significantly greater than that of other sections, even though the capacity for growth in the Northwest might be clear beyond dispute. Whatever our analysis, the slowing down in production that marked the 1909-1914 years tempered and disciplined the exuberant enthusiasm of the earlier boom period. No one could see then that the necessities of war production would soon bring new opportunities for expansion greater than anything that had yet been realized.

29

Cultural Activities in the Northwest Cities

Life in the cities was much more than trade and construction and city planning. Many of the facts of urban civilization, which evoked exclamations of mingled despair and amazement from those who commented upon them elsewhere, had their counterpart in the communities of the Northwest. Seattle and Portland had their hovels where the "other half" lived, often in conditions of misery and destitution. Poverty and disease were no strangers; crime and organized vice were by no means unknown. Preachers like Mark Matthews thundered from their pulpits against the forces of evil. In matters of city government "practical" politicians consorted with the underworld while the more idealistic sought to cleanse the Augean stables using such novel instruments as the recall and woman suffrage. It was important not only to build a city but to make it habitable. Men must create more than a physical setting. There must be a social environment in which to live together. The raw frontier must develop institutions to serve the people in their human relationships. It must be put in touch with the great heritage of learning and the arts that was the common possession of the Western world.

Social Agencies

The Pacific Northwest shared in many efforts to promote health and established many agencies of social service. Special organizations undertook to minister to the needs of the sick and the underprivileged. Hospitals which, like Providence and Swedish in Seattle and St. Vincent's in Portland, had been established earlier in impoverished or rented quarters, now moved into newly constructed buildings, commodious and well-equipped. Physicians banded themselves together into medical societies to combat the "pestiferous charlatans" who infested the region. Through their support of the University of Oregon Medical School, these men carried the cause of good medical education through the years of crisis that marked the change to modern methods of scientific and technical training.

Seattle's directory of charities included an Orphans' Home, an Industrial School, a Florence Crittendon Home, Seaman's Friend Society, Y.M.C.A., Y.W.C.A., and various benevolent societies, all of which were served by a Bureau of Charities maintained by the Charity Organization Society. Several State Conferences of Charities and Correction were held which considered the more pressing problems of social work, and in 1913 Seattle was host to a national convention of representatives from similar organizations elsewhere. Following the national trend toward the "social gospel," city churches inaugurated various programs of social welfare in the neighborhoods where they were situated. It was an age when government was only beginning to face such problems as these directly, representing the community as a whole. But private institutions and organizations took steps in many ways to alleviate distress and suffering where they were most acute.[1]

Drama, Music, and Art

There was increasing opportunity, too, for cultural enrichment though the conditions of frontier exploitation were not altogether favorable, and outward changes came so rapidly that the progress of mind and spirit inevitably lagged somewhat behind. The energy of promoters, entrepreneurs and artisans undoubtedly found too little expression in things artistic, and the pursuit of material progress left too little time to cultivate the more civilized of human interests and activities. It was not by accident that Bob Considine's eye for dramatic ability was drawn to the vaudeville circuit. The variety show, as he soon demonstrated in sensational fashion, was admirably suited to his audiences. Why should he seek

[1] Clarence Smith, "Seattle Hospitals," *Northwest Medicine*, July 1918, 199; Olaf Larsell, *Doctor in Oregon*, Portland, 1947, 354, 435, 507; *Exponent of Charitable and Philanthropic Work*, I, Seattle, 1901.

to elevate or improve them when they wished only to be entertained? Yet the frontier cities were not wholly content with the cheap and the tawdry. If there were audiences for vaudeville, there were others for Mark Twain and for Mischa Elman. When Schumann-Heinck gave concerts in Seattle, her audience filled the Moore Theatre to the doors. The 1916 concert season included Walter Damrosch with his great orchestra, the Boston National Opera Company, and the Ballet Russe with Nijinsky and Lopokovc. While the Northwest was host to such distinguished visitors only occasionally, they came often enough to show with what pleasure and profit the larger urban communities sought out and supported the musicians and artists, players and lecturers who enjoyed a national reputation.

A better measure of the level of cultural advancement in the region was to be found in the individual artists and men of learning who made their home there, and in the institutions of education and artistic expression which were rooted in the community itself. Portland, for example, had its own symphony orchestra early in the century. Seattle launched one in 1903 under the leadership of Harry West. For several years it was a musician's organization, but in 1907 the Seattle Symphony Society was set up to give the orchestra a more stable sponsorship. Musicians of ability and reputation were brought to the city, and with such men as Michael Kegrize and Henry K. Hadley as conductors, symphony concerts sold out the box office repeatedly. Hadley's successor, John Spargur, enjoyed less popularity, but the orchestra continued on a more modest scale through the war years to 1920. Tacoma and Spokane never had orchestras of their own, but they too arranged special concert programs each year.[2]

Painting and sculpture were more difficult to nourish and sustain. The Northwest produced no artists of great note, and no princely patrons came forward to take the lead in establishing art museums where exhibits could be shown. Nevertheless the initial efforts were made which were to bear fruit in later years. The Portland Art Association, organized in 1892, first established a museum in the city

[2] Eugene C. Elliott, *History of Variety-Vaudeville in Seattle from the Beginning to 1914*, Seattle, 1944; *Town Crier*, Seattle, December 16, 1916, 46; Edward Sheppard and Emily Johnson, "Forty Years of Symphony in Seattle, 1903-43," *PNQ*, XXXV, 1944, 19-28.

library. In 1905, through the leadership and generosity of Henry W. Corbett, W. B. Ayer and Mrs. W. S. Ladd, the Association acquired its own building and began building up a collection of paintings, prints, and pieces of sculpture. Despite severe financial limitations, the early curators, Henrietta H. Failing and after her Anna Belle Crocker, made the museum an important influence in the city. Educational activities were of paramount importance, and led in 1909 to the launching of the Museum Art School where Harry Wentz, artist and teacher extraordinary, gave instruction and inspiration to a growing number of students.

In Seattle the Washington State Art Association, incorporated March 10, 1906, took the lead in assembling and exhibiting art treasures, and promoting the construction of a museum and auditorium building. For a time there was a good prospect of erecting such a structure on the Metropolitan tract, but the project failed of realization. However, a number of exhibits of excellent quality were arranged, first in the public library and later in special quarters rented by the Association. Paintings and pieces of sculpture, some of them executed by such well-known artists as Henry Levy and Léon Bonnat, were presented as part of a growing permanent collection. Others, such as the works of John La Farge and the Dutch painter F. Tadama were presented as special exhibits. Persian rugs, furniture of Chinese ebony, Oriental jade, and Japanese color prints were included in showings that brought many fine pieces of art to the city. These exhibits commanded a wide popular interest. The Art Society numbered 2,000 members in 1912, 800 of whom were life members who had contributed at least 100 dollars each to the program. Perhaps 40,000 people a year went through the galleries.

Meanwhile, though no artists of world renown emerged, a number of local persons did win recognition in the museums of Chicago, New York, and London. Paintings and etchings by such men as E. Frère Champney and Paul Gustin, John Butler and Roi Partridge gave the Northwest some claim to distinction. An old Parisian exclaimed delightedly of Partridge's etchings that they were "just like old lace." Butler's "Mask of Pan" was hailed as a "high water mark in the artistic life of Seattle." Photographs by Imogene Partridge and Edward

Curtis, famous for his portrait studies of Indians, won acclaim far beyond the limits of the region.[3]

Literature and History

The literary folk were not so likely to be found in the cities though some few were there. Frances Victor, journalist and historian, spent her last years in Portland but when she died in 1902 her passing went almost unnoticed. Harvey Scott penned his editorials for the *Oregonian* in English prose of such excellence that they were used as models in the college classroom, yet he failed to rise above fine journalism to achieve real status as a literary essayist. Charles Erskine Scott Wood combined the skill of a corporation lawyer with the sensitivity of the poet and wrote several volumes of verse, some of which were of remarkable beauty and grandeur of speech. He appeared in such conflicting roles, however, as legalist, reformer, single taxer, and anarchist, that his reputation was somewhat marred.

The trend in poetry and fiction emphasized local color and beauty of scenic background. Herbert Bashford, editor of *The Literary West* (San Francisco) took his stand in the August, 1902, issue "for the strenuous intellectual life rather than the strenuousness of financial speculation in the whirlpool of trade," and called upon his fellow writers to breath a new freshness and color into American letters. "Better far a quatrain on a California redwood or a Washington fir than a dozen epics founded on the musty legends of yore." Close by in the same issue Christian Binkley expressed his thoughts of Seattle, "lusty, sordid, wrapped in gray," which he saw only in a moment of poetic vision

grow to
Marble and a thousand masts as one
Pointing aloft.

Sam L. Simpson, writing his best known poem, "The Beautiful Willamette," found his theme in the beauty of rural Oregon. Frederic Homer Balch wrote "The Bridge of the Gods" while a

[3] Adele Ballard, "Seattle Artists and Their Work," *Town Crier*, December 19, 1914, 30, and December 16, 1916, 26; *Museum Auditorium Monthly*, I, Seattle, January 1912.

preacher at Hood River. Ella Higgenson, the most popular and successful of the regional poets of the period, composed her verse at a hillside home in Bellingham. Eva Emery Dye found at Oregon City the people and the atmosphere which brought to life for her and for her readers the characters and events of early Oregon history.

The writing of history was more avocation than profession, yet solid and important work was done. Harvey Scott published his *History of Portland* in 1890. Clarence Bagley's *History of Seattle*, Herbert Hunt's *Tacoma*, and N. W. Durham's *Spokane* presented in some detail the development of the cities in which the authors lived. Frederic G. Young made important scholarly contributions through his editing of the *Oregon Historical Quarterly* and in careful research studies at the University of Oregon. Clinton Snowden's *History of Washington*, John Hailey's *Idaho*, William D. Lyman's *Old Walla Walla Country*, and George Fuller's *History of the Pacific Northwest* were carefully executed and based on much research, though they were more valuable for their factual detail than for their interpretation of events and trends. The most popular works of regional history to come from professional scholars were Edmond S. Meany's *History of Washington* and Joseph Schafer's *History of the Pacific Northwest.* In the broader field of American history and political science the book which raised a great furor locally but won wide recognition was J. Allen Smith's *Spirit of American Government*, a critical analysis of the Constitution of 1787. Smith's work anticipated that of Charles A. Beard and offered a significant new approach to American constitutional interpretation.[4]

Education

The opening years of the century witnessed a rapid enlargement and enrichment of the institutions of education and higher learning. Washington's Barefoot Schoolboy law inaugurated in 1895 the principle of state support for local school districts. While the rural areas and smaller communities were the ones to escape from the one-room school house, the larger cities too

[4] John B. Horner, *Oregon Literature*, Portland, 1902; Alfred Powers, *History of Oregon Literature*, Portland, 1935; Lancaster Pollard, "Sketch of Washington Literature," *PNQ*, XXIX, 1938, 227-254.

found money available both for buildings and operations, perhaps in larger amounts than they would have voted on a purely local basis. School buildings were constructed in considerable number to meet the needs of the growing population. Teaching staffs doubled within a few years, bringing into the city school rooms a number of persons of good education from the older states. Probably the most noteworthy change was the complete differentiation of the high schools which now offered a program of instruction quite separate and distinct from both the elementary schools and the universities. Under the direction of such superintendents as Frank Rigler of Portland and Frank Cooper of Seattle, the city school systems grew to be very sizable operations that called for annual budgets of two million or more. Much remained to be done, but the schools of 1914 were far superior to those of ten or 15 years earlier, and they were turning out graduates who crowded in growing numbers to apply for admission at the institutions of higher learning.[5]

Higher learning might seem at first thought to be something dissociated from the growth of cities. Devoted to the preservation of the wisdom of the ages and the pursuits of science, the tradition of the scholar's study was one of seclusion and contemplation, and the academic campus did not welcome instrusions from the market place. Oregon's colleges were located in many small places in the Willamette Valley.

Nevertheless the colleges and universities grew only as the region grew. Strengthening and improving them depended in the first instance upon economic and financial considerations. To have a faculty, a laboratory, and a library, a school must have a constituency, young people trained for college, and a citizenry sufficiently large and well-to-do to provide an adequate support. Thus the progress of higher education paralleled the progress of urban civilization generally in the Northwest. Significantly, too, the colleges became an increasingly important instrument for the communication and dissemination of urban culture throughout the region. Though most of the colleges were in the small cities rather than in the metropolitan centers, all

[5] Frederick E. Bolton and Thomas W. Bibb, *History of Education in Washington*, Washington, D.C., 1935; Edmund S. Meany, "Educational Advantages of Seattle," *Argus*, December 14, 1912, 41; U.S. Works Progress Administration, *History of Education in Portland, Oregon*, Portland, 1937.

of them were linked more and more closely with urban forces and conditions.

Both the scope and the quality of collegiate instruction, research, and experimentation was tremendously improved in the various institutions of Oregon, Washington, and Idaho. At the State College of Washington President Enoch Bryan built up an institution which included not only the agricultural experiment station and curricula in engineering and the mechanical arts, but a general program in the liberal arts as well. The University of Washington moved in 1895 from its ten-acre campus in the heart of Seattle to a much more commodious one on the outskirts of the city overlooking Lake Washington. Here the school grew rapidly to an enrollment (1914) of 3,300 students, taught by a faculty of nearly 200 persons who represented in their background many of the training centers of the eastern states and Europe. It was a formative period of development. Curriculum changes extended, as they did at the State College, considerably beyond the special functions which the school had served in earlier years. To the study of classical and genteel subjects several of the practical and professional fields were added: Forestry, Engineering, Law, and Teacher Training. The overlapping of subject interests occasioned a sharp rivalry and not a little bitterness between the university and the state college, but each school found a place for itself and each showed great energy and vitality.

In Oregon and Idaho much the same kind of growth occurred, though the populations being smaller, the schools (and the budgets) were smaller too. The University of Idaho opened its doors at Moscow in October, 1892, one unfinished building set down in the middle of a plowed field, with a faculty consisting of the president and one professor. There were then no students, no library, and no laboratory. One could hardly begin with less. Yet in ten years time the infant school grew into a genuine collegiate institution of 140 students. By 1914 the enrollment reached 438, and the organization of four separate colleges had been perfected: Arts and Sciences, Agriculture, Engineering, and Law. Despite the obstacles under which they worked, the regents declared their purpose to offer instruction "equal to the best undergraduate instruction elsewhere." To do this they recognized the need of encouraging original study on the part of students and faculty. "Proper teaching," they declared, "can not be done unless it is intimately associated with that other great fundamental expression of University life—research through which the bounds of knowledge are extended." It was an ideal imperfectly realized, but the goal at least was clear.

In Oregon, the state college at Corvallis was the largest and strongest of the institutions of higher learning. Stressing the value of industrial education and the need of adapting rural education to the needs of the people, this institution more than doubled its enrollment between 1901 and 1908, and again between 1908 and 1912, a growth in students which matched the progress of the University of Washington. The University of Oregon at Eugene remained a much smaller school (662 students in 1913), partly because its location was more remote from the urban centers of population and partly because it suffered somewhat in matters of curriculum. The medical school and law school were of necessity small and expensive. The State Board of Higher Curricula assumed an increasing control of courses and found reason in several instances to change departments and programs from one school to another. As a result of such changes the University lost Electrical and Chemical Engineering to Corvallis. Fine Arts and Music, Economics and Higher Commerce, and the Graduate School were assigned to the University in return, but the net effect of specialization and division between Corvallis and Eugene was to concentrate at the University a number of programs that did not attract a large enrollment. The campus at Eugene harbored a number of able and promising scholars, among them the historian Joseph Schafer who made his mark there before going on to Wisconsin. For one reason or another, however, the school did not develop the strength of numbers, and it was more than once embarrassed by political attacks upon its appropriations.

Meanwhile in Portland a group of trustees took steps to establish the "Reed Institute" in accordance with a bequest of more than a million dollars which dedicated the greater part of the Simeon G. Reed estate as an endowment. They moved slowly and carefully, canvassed the existing educational resources of the city and visited many schools and colleges in other parts of the country. Seeking the advice of the best educational statesmen in the land, they turned to the

General Education Board in New York, which organization included such leaders as President Charles Eliot of Harvard University. These men, after further inquiry of their own, became convinced that Portland's needs and opportunities would be best served by a four-year liberal arts college. They urged that it be founded and maintained on a high level, comparable to the best that any state could offer.

This high goal of academic excellence has been upheld at Reed College since that day. In 1910 the college got its first president, William Trufant Foster, a brilliant young scholar who had trained at Harvard and Columbia. Foster gathered around him a small faculty, carefully chosen men of outstanding ability and high promise. They were young men, most of them not yet forty, who represented, as Foster did, the best graduate schools in the East, or such western institutions as the University of Chicago or the University of California. The college welcomed its first entering class in 1911. The following year it moved to its own 40-acre campus, a tract which had been presented by the W. S. Ladd estate.

From the date of its founding Reed was devoted primarily to the establishment of high academic standards for the leaders of future generations. It did, to be sure, seek out ways to serve the community and enrich its intellectual life. But it "specialized in the humanities" and defended, in season and out, the tangible values in a liberal education. "Education for leadership," as Foster declared in 1913, "is no less practical than the education of plumbers and bookkeepers." The college took as its statement of guiding principles the broad declaration of purposes framed by Thomas Jefferson for the University of Virginia nearly a century before.[6]

---

[6] For the development of the universities and colleges, see the reports of the individual presidents and boards of regents, also the biennial reports of the Idaho State Department of Public Instruction, and Kendrick C. Babcock, *Higher Education in the United States,* U.S. Bureau of Education, Report, 1911; Reed College Record, March, 1911, September, 1911, January, 1914, and Reed College Bulletins, Nos. 1-9, 1911-1912.

Part IV

Frontier No Longer

30

The Problems of Industrial Development

The year 1914 opened somewhat inauspiciously in the Pacific Northwest. The early-century boom had run its course and the people had settled down to plod rather than race ahead in realizing the bright future of their dreams. Urban growth had slowed perceptibly, the resource industries were leveling off in their development, and investment capital found the field less promising than heretofore. As for industrialism, it was something not to be taken for granted. Boosting and youthful energy could not guarantee markets and profits to factories that must compete with larger, better established firms in other sections of the country. If the Northwest was to make further gains in manufacturing it would be because events took place which changed the industrial balance of the nation, and offered new opportunities to the less industrialized areas. What these events might be no one could tell. Before the end of the year, however, the outbreak of war in Europe produced a new situation which in a short time affected every corner of the country. It was the urgency of war that carried the regional economy of the Northwest once more sharply upward to a significantly higher level.

During the years 1914-1919 the number of wage earners and the capital invested in manufacturing doubled while the dollar figures for wages paid and value added by manufacture increased threefold and more. Seattle's labor force jumped from 11,000 to upwards of 40,000, a development which advanced the city in rank among the industrial cities of the United States from 62d to 25th place. Portland made a similar advance from 58th to 40th place. In value of products the three states of the Northwest increased their output from 383,000,000 dollars to over a billion and a quarter.

The war boom featured three components prominently: (1) the recovery and expansion of the lumber trade; (2) the development of food industries related to agriculture and the fisheries; and (3) shipbuilding. The first two of these components were already well rooted in the region and expanded readily in response to the increased demand born of enlarged markets and war needs. The third was strictly a product of military necessity. Though it was the region's second largest industry during the war, it disappeared quickly with the return of peacetime conditions, leaving little more than the memory of bold exploits to be cherished until the yards were built up again in World War II.

Timber and Foodstuffs

The dominance of the lumber industry in the wartime economy was probably only what might have been expected. In Washington lumber manufactures increased almost threefold in value. This single industry employed 40.2 percent of the wage earners in the state and accounted for more than a third of the value added by manufacturing in all lines. Oregon's production of Sitka spruce jumped from 63,000,000 board feet to 215,000,000 in four years. The opening of the Panama Canal made it possible for far western lumber to reach the Atlantic coast markets much more quickly and cheaply than ever before and firms like the Charles McCormick Lumber Company began building their own schooners as carriers. In 1918 Pacific Coast production comprised some 30 percent of the United States total.

These developments did not, however, work any great transformation of the industry. Lumber production, measured in board feet rather than in inflated dollars, increased in Washington and Oregon only 28 percent during 1914-1918. While shipments to the Atlantic Coast held up very well during the war years, the gains were offset by the dislocation of the export trade to the Orient which dropped by as much as 40 percent. In the larger cities the lumber mills expanded their operations only slightly. Seattle mills increased their employment rolls by less than 500 men and Portland by only 1,263. Lumbering was, to be sure, an economic mainstay for the region, but no more than it had been before.

The Northwest likewise made a significant increase in the output

May Flower Mine, Bullion, Idaho. (From Wallace Elliott, History of Idaho Territory, 1884.)

Anaconda Hill, a Copper City in the Making, 1894. (Courtesy, K. Ross Toole.)

The Old Tacoma Smelter. (From West Coast Trade, 1896.)

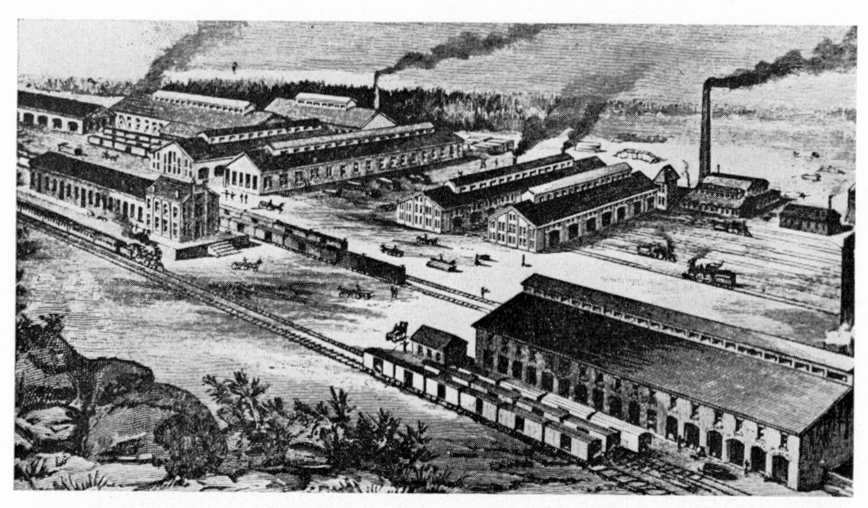

Northern Pacific Railroad Shops, Tacoma. (From West Coast Trade, 1900.)

Lumber Mills Gave Seattle an Industrial Appearance. (From Picturesque Seattle and Puget Sound, 1914.)

Making Pig Iron at Oswego. This Furnace Was Oregon's First Bid for a Steel Industry. (From West Shore Magazine.)

Recent Interior View of Boeing Aircraft Plant, Seattle. (Courtesy, Boeing Airplane Company.)

Recent Exterior View of Boeing Aircraft Plant, Seattle. (Courtesy, Boeing Airplane Company.)

of foodstuffs during the war years, though in these lines too the industrial advances were inconsiderable. The Alaska pack of canned salmon jumped from 4,000,000 cases (1914) to 6,600,000 in 1918. Farmers in the three northwest states increased their wheat acreages by 1,450,000 acres, their harvests by 6,500,000 bushels. Washington apple growers harvested in 1917 a record crop of 4,600,000 barrels to put their state in the top-ranking position in the whole country. In 1918 the dollar value of agricultural crops in Washington and Oregon was almost twice what it had been in 1909.

The greater production of foods brought about a significant growth in several lines of manufacturing as well as in the resource industries themselves. In 1919 Washington ranked seventh among the flour-milling states and eighth in canning and preserving, thanks to the fact that it produced 70 percent of the national output of canned salmon. It also ranked eleventh in the making of butter, cheese, and condensed milk. Oregon ranked tenth in canning and preserving and sixteenth in dairy manufactures. The two states together (1919) turned out food manufactures valued at 326,000,000 dollars, which made them as important as lumber (330,000,000 dollars).

These enterprises did comparatively little, however, to industrialize the larger cities. The canning industry and the dairy manufacturing plants were not concentrated geographically in these places, and the establishments that were to be found in the urban centers did not employ large numbers of men. In Seattle they gave occupation to but 3,000 persons. Only one in seven of the new manufacturing workers who came to Portland during the war found employment in the food industries. To find the manufacturing lines with the big payrolls we must look elsewhere.[1]

Shipyards in War Time

The new and important element in the situation was the mushroom growth of the shipbuilding industry, both for wood and steel vessels. This enterprise was introduced into

[1] The developments of the war years can be seen by comparing the figures in the U.S. Census of Manufactures for 1914 and 1919. See also *Statistical Abstract of the United States,* compiled annually by the Bureau of Statistics of the Department of Commerce and Labor. Some consideration is given to the depression in the lumber industry in the 10th Biennial Report of the Washington Bureau of Labor, Statistics and Factory Inspection, 1915-1916, 89-95; Moravets, *Lumber Production in Oregon and Washington.*

the Northwest on so large a scale that it dwarfed every other save only the lumber industry. It brought millions in capital investment to the region, gave employment to more than 50,000 men, and stimulated the expansion of many secondary bread-and-butter industries to serve the new population that came in to work in the yards.

Shipbuilding began with the construction of wooden sailing vessels at a number of ports in Washington and Oregon. Formerly the schooners and barkentines that made up the lumber fleet had been built elsewhere. Some were foreign "tramp" vessels; of the American ships, nearly all had been constructed in yards on the Atlantic Coast. With the outbreak of war these ships were diverted more and more to other uses, and Westerners began to build for themselves. Late in 1915 Martin Erismann of Seattle drew up plans for a five-masted schooner to be used to carry lumber through the Panama Canal to the Eastern United States. Other men with some experience came forward, men like J. A. McEachern of Astoria, Andrew Peterson and George Mathew of Grays Harbor, and John McAteer of Seattle who had been with the Hall Brothers at Port Blakely and more recently with Todd and Moran. The schooners they built, with characteristic "bald-headed" (no topmast) rigs and auxiliary engines, attracted considerable attention to the Pacific Coast yards. Many of them were hastily constructed and poorly equipped; nevertheless the building of the fleet was one of the significant developments of the war years.

As the European war progressed, Allied powers and neutrals placed orders for American ships, a number of which were constructed in the Northwest. Norwegian shipowners made extensive purchases through the firm of A. O. Anderson of New York. The French government likewise designated a New York company, Cox and Stevens, to arrange for the construction of sailing ships. The Foundation Yards of Tacoma and Portland built 20 five-masted schooners which, bearing the names of French battlefields, carried lumber, flour, and nitrates across the Atlantic to Europe. In 1918 the Swan Shipyard Corporation took over the Olympia Shipbuilding Company and built a number of wooden motorships for the Australian government.

With the entry of the United States into the war the Northwest yards built a considerable number of schooners for the Emergency Fleet Corporation. By the end of the war 28 different yards were active, including not only the establishments in the larger cities, but others at Astoria, Aberdeen and Anacortes, St. Johns and Tillamook, Vancouver and Columbia City. Wooden shipbuilding was a sizable enterprise at some of these places. In Seattle it gave employment to several thousand men, supported in 1919 a 3,000,000-dollar payroll, and turned out 11,000,000 dollars' worth of ships. It was, however, comparatively decentralized geographically, and never featured the huge facilities that were developed at Seattle and Tacoma, Vancouver and Portland to build the steam freighters.

The big steel shipbuilding plants were few in number, so few that the Census Bureau gave no detailed statistics for the industry in Seattle or Portland lest it divulge the operations of individual establishments. In 1918 there were nine yards in all, including Skinner and Eddy, Ames, and J. F. Duthie in Seattle, Todd in Tacoma, and on the Columbia River G. M. Standifer, the Northwest Steel Company, and the Columbia Shipbuilding Company. All of them were of tremendous capacity and together they operated as many as 50 launching ways.

Skinner and Eddy was the giant of the group. In December 1915 this firm began building standardized steel freight steamers, the type that won for the *Niels Nielson* the highest rating the Norwegians could give. Purchasing 27 acres on the Seattle waterfront, the company put 4,600,000 dollars into plant facilities. Later they leased a second yard and doubled their capacity. Skinner and Eddy No. 1 was the teacher and pacemaker of the world, launching ships in 55 days and commissioning them in 20 days more. In the summer of 1918 this plant twice won the blue pennant awarded by the Emergency Fleet Corporation in its speed-up contest.

These and the other steel shipyards boasted the finest plants that money could buy, complete with bending slabs and furnaces, heavy cranes and air hoists, sectional floating dry docks, and well-equipped foundries and machine shops. Quite apart from the private capital invested, the United States government spent 2,000,000 dollars on the Todd yard in Tacoma and almost as much more on housing for the workers there and in Vancouver and on essential transportation facilities in Seattle, Tacoma, and Portland.

The production records as of June, 1919, show how large an operation the shipbuilding industry had grown to be. The U.S. Shipping Board report of that date included 41 yards (wood and steel), 193 launching ways, and totaled 297 vessels delivered by the establishments of the Northern Pacific and Oregon districts and 1,792,000 tons of shipping built at a cost of 458,000,000 dollars. Of these 141 were wooden sailers, 156 were steel freighters of from 3,500 to 8,800 tons capacity. Here was a dramatic demonstration indeed of the industrial potential of the region when conditions favored its full development.[2]

Labor Problems in Seattle

The shipyard workers were responsible not only for records of proud accomplishment but for situations of tension and strife as well. Labor policies and wage levels were the subject of controversy even during the war. After the armistice, when the fervor of patriotism was no longer so much stirred by national peril, these issues came yet more into dispute. In February, 1919, the demands of the shipyard labor unions produced in Seattle a general strike which paralyzed the city for four days and made it appear to the rest of the country that the Northwest was threatened with a proletarian revolution.

War industries in the Northwest were always plagued by a lack of workers. There was, to be sure, a drift of people from the rural areas to the cities, and a migration from places in the interior out to the coast. When W. H. Maloney, mayor of Butte, visited Seattle during the war, he found there a large contingent of former Butte miners holding jobs riveting, bolting-up, holding-on, or working in the machine shops at the shipyards. "Half of Butte seems to have moved to Seattle," he remarked after an hour at a Skinner and Eddy plant. But the demand was so great that the railroads and shipyards faced shortages continually in skilled and unskilled labor. The U.S. Employment Service established offices in the cities, and publicized the opportunities for work as best it could, but failed to find enough men to fill the jobs. By September, 1918, the director was preparing to comb the nonessential industries to find men who could be released for war work.

[2] John Lyman, "Pacific Coast-built Sailers of World War I," *Marine Digest*, May 30, 1942; Portus Baxter, "Growth of Shipbuilding," *Argus*, December 15, 1917; Reports of the U.S. Shipping Board for the year 1918 and for June, 1919.

Faced with this severe necessity of recruiting labor the shipyards attracted men by paying them high wages, in some cases even higher than the national scale allowed. In part the differential was regional, the wage scale in the Far West edging up higher than that in other sections of the country. Beyond that it was a matter of competition between different yards. Some of the smaller establishments had to pay considerable premiums in order to get men at all. Among the big yards Skinner and Eddy paid rates so much above the others that the Portland employers found it difficult to prevent their men from leaving.

All this led to much wage bargaining and negotiation. The Macy Board, a wage adjustment board created by the Emergency Fleet Corporation, tried to establish a uniform national scale, calculated by averaging rates in different cities, but found that such a scale penalized the Pacific Coast yards. When applied in the Far West it brought about wage cuts rather than gains, and led to much discontent on the part of the workers. Special conferences were held at which the representatives of the unions, especially the Metal Trades Council, presented their arguments very ably. Charles Piez, vice-president of EFC, listened sympathetically and promised some kind of adjustment. Nevertheless the year 1918 ended with nothing satisfactory worked out, and the Seattle unions became increasingly restive.

This was the situation that produced the shipyard strike at Seattle early in 1919. Led by the Metal Trades Council the men walked out Tuesday, January 21, demanding a minimum of $6.00 a day as against the current Macy award of $4.16. This time Piez stood firm. "The government is not so badly in need of ships that it will compromise on a question of principle," he declared. "If they [the workers] were successful in securing their demands by this means, the future of the entire shipbuilding industry in your district would be jeopardized." Still convinced of the justice of their demand, the Metal Trades Council then appealed to the Seattle Central Labor Council, asking support in the form of a sympathy strike.

One after another the A.F. of L. unions voted their approval of the proposal. A giant General Strike Committee was organized which finally set the date for the beginning of the strike as February 6. The *Union Record* kept the public informed of developments at the

Central Labor Council and explained the purpose and the nature of the demonstration. Organized labor, it announced, would conduct a peaceful sympathy strike, carrying it out in orderly fashion. Twelve great kitchens would distribute food at low cost. Milk would still go to the babies, and hospitals would carry on all essential services without interruption. Workers were urged not to collect on the streets and to avoid all disturbances with the public authorities or with private citizens.

On Thursday morning, February 6, the city suddenly became strangely quiet. Street cars stopped rolling and taxicabs disappeared from the streets. Restaurants closed their doors, stevedores trooped off the docks, and commercial traffic ceased, save for a few vehicles which carried large placards of exemption. The mails continued to move and the water and power stations were kept going; otherwise business came to a standstill. But the day passed without disorder. Police blotters showed no unusual activity and citizen deputies found little to do. That night troops from Fort Lawton were quartered at the Armory; however, no untoward incidents occurred.

The wholesale walkout continued through Friday. Still there was no violence and the atmosphere of tense apprehension was somewhat relaxed. On the other hand, Mayor Ole Hanson became more resolute, while the striking unions found themselves faced with increasingly difficult decisions. They must either end the strike quickly or accept the responsibility for a situation which in the words of the *Union Record* "will lead NO ONE KNOWS WHERE." Hanson demanded that the strike be called off by 8 A.M. the next morning. From the office of the Seattle *Times* wire dispatches went out announcing to the world that "Attempted Revolution Is Defeated." So far as the press was concerned, the general strike was a subversive movement led by Bolsheviks who had gained temporary control in the labor unions of the city. The *Record* stoutly denied it but it became increasingly plain that the walkout would be continued only in the face of an increasingly hostile public opinion.

The key leaders in the strike organization had favored in the beginning a 48-hour sympathetic demonstration, but the shipyard workers demurred and the terminal date was left undetermined. On Saturday morning the executive body prepared a resolution, to be adopted by the full strike committee, which would have ended the strike that day for all A.F. of L. unions except those in the shipyards. However, the union delegates wrangled over the resolution until far into the night and finally rejected it.

By Monday most of Seattle was heartily sick of the strike, though thankful for the lack of disorder. A number of unions went back to work including the teamsters, the typographical workers, and the sheet metal workers. While other groups awaited directions from their elected delegates, there was less and less disposition to continue the strike and the general committee voted to end it at noon on Tuesday the 11th. Most merchants and business firms took their men back without prejudice, preferring to believe that the responsibility for the affair lay with the leadership in the unions rather than with the members themselves.[3]

Postwar Depression and Recovery

It was one of the ironies of history that the industry which produced such a show of strength and determination on the part of organized labor was the one which collapsed the most quickly with the return of peace. Born of the war and nourished with war contracts, it largely lost its usefulness with the armistice. For a brief moment the U.S. Shipping Board thought it might be otherwise. "A new industry has been created and bids fair to remain an important feature of our commercial structure"—such was the bold prophecy of 1919. Yet even as it was written the actions of the Board belied it. Employment by the Emergency Fleet Corporation, for the country as a whole, which had reached 385,000, dropped by June, 1920, to 75,000 persons. Orders for 146 vessels, nearly a million tons of shipping, were canceled in the North Pacific and Oregon districts. Skinner and Eddy finished their work and terminated their lease for yard No. 2 in November, 1919. In Portland the Columbia River Shipbuilding Corporation put up their facilities for sale, found no buyers, and removed such property as could be salvaged. When the census takers made their canvass of manufacturing in 1921,

[3] Wilfred H. Crook, *General Strike*, Chapel Hill, 1931, 528-543; General Strike Committee, *Seattle General Strike*, Seattle, 1919. The authors are indebted also to Robert B. Gibson, author of an unpublished manuscript, "The Radical Experiment," University of Washington, 1951.

they found the shipbuilding industry doing less than one-tenth of the business they had done two years before. Seattle and Portland yards together had only a thousand men at work. The total tonnage of ships launched in the region did not exceed 50,000. For 20 years thereafter shipbuilding had comparatively little importance in the economy of the Northwest.

What happened in this extreme way in shipbuilding occurred to a lesser extent in other industries as well, and the whole level of manufacturing dropped abruptly in the years immediately following World War I. Industrial payrolls in Washington declined by 100,000,000 dollars while the output of manufacturing plants fell to one-half what it had been during the war. Employment in Oregon dropped 31 percent between 1919 and 1921 and the figure for value added through manufacturing in Idaho dropped 41 percent.

Flour mills, slaughter houses and canneries cut back their activities, and condensed milk plants refused to take the farmers' supply, forcing them to go into processing and marketing for themselves. Foundries, car shops, and printing establishments experienced a period of retrenchment. The lumber industry laid off 15,000 men in Washington alone and reduced its cut by more than a billion board feet. Seven thousand men were laid off in Oregon. Dislocations were painful and readjustments took time to work out.

But despite the setbacks that accompanied the return to "normalcy," manufacturing in the Northwest stabilized at figures well above the prewar years. By 1923 employment and production figures were moving back up again. The rest of the decade had its ups and downs, but the Northwest shared reasonably well in the national prosperity and by 1929 industrial productivity in the region (as measured by the value added through manufacture) was back up where it had been during the war boom.

Economic recovery and advancement were based at first upon the development of the lumber industry, even more than it had been before the war. In two years (1921-1923) the productivity of this single enterprise increased by 90,000,000 dollars in Washington alone, climbing from 37.3 percent of total value added up to 52.1 percent. In Oregon the industry was a central factor in the same way, advancing from 35 per cent to 45 percent of total value added by manufacture in that state. The timber trade with the Orient was built up with much energy, and larger shipments reached Chicago and the Atlantic Coast as the southern pine belt was cut over and as marketing methods were made more effective. An annual cut of 11.7 billion board feet was achieved for the region as a whole, which meant jobs for more than 100,000 men.

Those who measured the progress of the region in the diversification of its manufacturing found more grounds for satisfaction after 1923. Lines allied to lumbering, such as furniture and more especially the making of pulp and paper, achieved significant growth. Food processing plants, which suffered badly after the armistice, expanded to turn out more in peacetime than they had produced in war. Shipyards and foundries maintained a sizeable operation though it was far below the level of 1919. On the other hand, printing and publishing establishments increased in number and size well above the wartime level, and the manufacture of clothing grew to be twice the industry in 1929 that it had been ten years before. Construction was resumed in a new building boom that gave employment to several thousand workers in the cities. Portland reached its peak in 1925 when building permits to the amount of 38,500,000 dollars were issued. The Seattle boom did not go quite so high (34,800,000 dollars in 1928), but it was sustained for several years at about 30,000,000 dollars a year. Tacoma and Spokane enjoyed much less activity but here too the building trades had a significant part in economic diversification and growth.

The distribution of manufacturing among these various lines was not greatly changed from the pattern of earlier years. As before, many small enterprises together accounted for some 30 percent of the total output. These plants served the local markets and did little to add to the industrial stature of the region. Nevertheless they tended to grow with the population and helped almost as much as the secondary lines mentioned above to make up for the cutting back of war industry after 1919. The geographic distribution likewise remained much the same. In Washington the three large cities accounted for some 40 percent of total value added by manufacture. Portland, however, declined percentagewise, as manufacturing in the lesser cities expanded and gained for them a larger share of the total.[4]

[4] See U.S. Shipping Board, 4th Report, 1919-1920. The U.S. Census of Manufactures permits a close analysis of trends, since reports were issued every two years.

At the time, these evidences of expansion were taken to be signs of continuing growth in the region. As we look back from the vantage point of the present, however, the perspective changes. To be sure, the indexes that have been constructed of economic activity show steady advances during the 1920's in postal receipts, department store sales, and the purchases of gasoline and life insurance. Freight car loadings likewise moved upward though not as strongly. But the gains suggest a much lower rate of growth than the region had enjoyed earlier. It appears, too, that the regional share in the national economy was becoming smaller rather than larger. More and more the situation was coming to be like Alice in Wonderland. One must run as hard as one could to stay in the same place. To advance one must run much faster.

These are the conclusions of economists who have reflected upon the matter in recent years. They follow from statistics of migration and population growth and from calculations of income payments to individuals in the Pacific Northwest as compared with the United States as a whole. For several decades preceding 1910 the population of the region had doubled every ten years. From 1910-1920 and 1920-1930 the increase was less than 20 per cent. The slower rate of growth was the result of a slackening in westward migration and a low birth rate, which in Oregon fell to 14.1 per thousand, the lowest figure in any state of the Union (1930). The gain in population was lessened also by a considerable outward migration, for 50,000 native Oregonians left their home state during the decade following the war. As for income payments to individuals, there are indications that the Pacific Northwest, like the agricultural West and most of the South, was declining during the years 1919-1932 in the proportion which regional figures bore to those of the nation at large. The development of the area was slowing perceptibly and whether people saw the reasons clearly or not, economic opportunities were less attractive, based as they were on natural resources that were no longer as cheap and abundant as they had been 20 years earlier.[5]

[5] See indexes of economic activity in the region published in *Pacific Northwest Industry* by the Bureau of Business Research, University of Washington; Paul B. Simpson, *Regional Aspects of Business Cycles and Special Studies of the Pacific Northwest*, Eugene, Oregon, June 1953.

Era of the New Deal

The depression years that followed 1929 made plain the vulnerable character of the regional economy. Lumber exports dropped to less than half, and rail shipments of forest products to one-third of their former value. Agricultural markets dried up, producing widespread distress. Wheat farmers were hard hit by the decline of the export trade and many gave up their tractors and went back to horses. Apple growers, no longer able to send large shipments to Europe, pulled up and burned their trees to avoid the expense of maintaining them. The 1932 salmon pack was 120,000,000 pounds under 1929. Mining output in Idaho dropped (1929-1932) from 32,100,000 to 9,500,000 dollars.

General conditions reflected these reverses in the major resource industries. The wholesale trade in Washington fell 47 percent by 1933. Factory employment declined even more sharply, individual incomes dropped to about 55 percent of the 1929 level, and bank debits in the cities of Western Washington were 2.2 billion dollars less in 1934 than in 1929. Tax delinquencies in Oregon amounted to some 40,000,000 dollars by 1936, bringing losses in private ownership of land affecting an area as large as the state of Delaware. Migration into the region, which formerly had been something to be encouraged, now menaced the welfare of the people already living there, since it intensified the competition for limited opportunities and put added pressure on the relief agencies. Years of drought brought about the migration of thousands of Dust Bowl refugees to the Far West; on the other hand, many natives sought their fortunes elsewhere. Two persons left Oregon for every three who came.

While the depression hit the region with particular severity, the recovery program undertaken by the national government brought benefits to the Pacific Northwest rather more than to other sections. Public works construction brought about the expenditure of large sums of federal money in this region. More than half of the 61,000,000 dollars put into the building of Grand Coulee Dam by January 1, 1940, was spent in Oregon and Washington. Pay night at Grand Coulee itself was marked by all the free spending exuberance of a boom town at the height of its prosperity. Since such large projects generated a great deal of secondary activity, it has been estimated that perhaps two-fifths of the increase in incomes occurring in the region between 1933 and 1939 can be attributed, directly or indirectly, to public construction.

Whatever the fraction there can be no question that the federal program stimulated a significant recovery after 1933. In 1937 income figures stood fairly close to the level of 1929 and industrial productivity was greater than it had been in 1925. During the two years 1936-1937 Washington manufacturers increased their payrolls by nearly 45,000,000 dollars and their output by 200,000,000 dollars. Thanks to the monetary policies of the federal government, Idaho silver mines expanded their annual production (1932-1937) from 1,800,000 to 15,100,000 dollars.

The development of the airplane industry had to do less with measures of economic recovery than with military preparedness. In Seattle the Boeing Airplane Company struggled through years of slow growth, but established itself as one of the leading producers in the country. In 1934 engineers developed the design of Project 299, grandfather of the flying fortress. Two years later the Army Air Corps placed its initial order for 13 heavy bombers, which were delivered in August, 1937. Boeing planes pioneered a number of new features for military and commercial aircraft, demonstrating durability and ease of handling that had been thought impossible in planes so large. With the development of the turbosupercharger they established impressive performance records not only for long-range flying but for high altitude flight as well. The Boeing plant has been called a "foot-loose" industry, located in the Northwest only because the founder of the company happened to live there. Aircraft could be delivered, however, under their own power to any part of the world, and geographic considerations were less important in the location of factories than was usually the case in manufacturing. At the same time the building up of a team of engineers, technical experts, and executives served to root the enterprise on Puget Sound and thus gave the Northwest an industry which in a few years would become a main reliance for the regional economy.[6]

---

[6] *Oregon Looks Ahead*, Oregon State Planning Board, November, 1938; *Economic Survey of the State of Idaho*; Part I. *The Economy of Southwestern Idaho with Refer-*

Developments in Labor Organization

During the years of economic recovery the Pacific Coast became a proving ground for the trial and testing of labor organizations and labor policies. Along the waterfront some progress had been made in the Northwest after World War I in "decasualizing" the longshoremen. The working force had been somewhat stabilized, wages had been established at good rates, and labor representatives had been allowed to participate in the management of hiring halls. Nevertheless from 1934 to 1941 the port cities were the scene of a series of strikes which tied up shipping for months at a time and which ranged labor and management against each other in bitter warfare.

In 1934, after a three-month strike, the International Longshoremen's Association successfully challenged the position of the "blue book" (company) unions and secured an acceptance of its demand for a six-hour day, a 30-hour week, and a basic wage rate of $.95 per hour. Three years later the Pacific Coast unions withdrew from the I.L.A., which was affiliated with the American Federation of Labor, and formed the International Longshoremen's and Warehousemen's Union affiliated with the C.I.O. From then on the waterfront was a C.I.O. stronghold defended by the longshoremen, the fishermen, the salmon cannery workers, and the inland boatmen. They were a militant left-wing group. Harry Bridges, their leader, soon came under attack and his enemies long demanded (though in vain) that he be deported to his native Australia. The charges of his Communist affiliation were never proved, but some members of the union followed the party line and gave the organization a distinctly reddish appearance. There was much strife and controversy in the harbors despite favorable contracts and awards. Picket lines gave trouble repeatedly, and loading operations were often interrupted by the refusal of the

---

ence to Irrigation Development, Idaho State Planning Board and University of Idaho, December, 1940; *Development of Resources and of Economic Opportunity in the Pacific Northwest*, Pacific Northwest Regional Planning Commission, Report to the National Resources Planning Board, 1942; Davis McEntire and Marion Clawson, "Migration and Resettlement in the Pacific Northwest 1930-40," *Social Science*, XVI, April, 1941, 102-115; James C. Rettie, "Economy of the Pacific Northwest; Present Status and Outlook," *Ibid.*, 116-123; Thomas Collison, *Flying Fortress*, New York, 1943; Harold Mansfield, *Vision; a Saga of the Sky*, New York, 1956.

men to handle "hot" (nonunion) cargo. Organized slowdowns and disputes over lift boards and labor-saving machinery doubled the costs of moving cargo. Not until December, 1940, was there a material improvement in efficiency and a more satisfactory adjustment of the conflicting interests of labor and management.[7]

The C.I.O. was less successful in the logging camps and lumber mills. Labor unions had almost disappeared in the lumber industry after 1923, and when they were reëstablished with the National Recovery Administration ten years later, they fell under the general jurisdiction of the A.F. of L. carpenters. Building up its membership very rapidly, the A.F. of L. union functioned as the timber workers' bargaining agency for several years. The big strike carried out under its leadership in 1935 took half the men in the Douglas fir belt off their jobs in a successful drive to win the principle of union recognition.

But the carpenters met with opposition and insurgency within the timber workers' unions from the beginning. Many of the members found them too conservative, and too narrowly specialized in their outlook when lumbering called for a broader industrial type of labor organization. No single leader succeeded in dominating and controlling the timber workers as Bridges did the longshoremen or Dave Beck the teamsters. Depression dogged the industry, held wages down, and kept laboring conditions highly competitive. Millowners found it possible, even necessary, to negotiate locally rather than on an industry-wide basis. The result was that the pattern of union organization continued to be complicated and uncertain until the outbreak of World War II.

In 1937 insurgency expressed itself in the formation of the International Woodworkers Association (I.W.A.) which secured a charter from the C.I.O. There followed several years of rivalry and violence as the C.I.O. and the A.F. of L. struggled for preëminence. Portland became a battleground where goon squads roamed at large and the police were powerless to put a stop to terrorism. At Grays Harbor, Everett, and Tacoma mills were shut down repeatedly while the

[7] "Decasualization of Dock Labor in Seattle," *Monthly Labor Review*, XIX, October 1924, 868-870; F. P. Foisie, "Stabilizing Seattle's Longshore Labor," *National Conference of Social Work*, 1925, 302-307; John Blanchard and Dorothy Terrill, *Strikes in the Pacific Northwest 1927-40; a Statistical Analysis*, Portland, 1943; James Clinton Harris, *Study of the Pacific Coast Longshore Industry*, Eugene, 1942; Paul Eliel, "Labor Peace in Pacific Ports," *Harvard Business Review* XIX, Summer 1941, 429-437.

local unions wrangled over their status. Elections were held only to be challenged and disputed. Conferences were summoned in Washington, D.C., only to adjourn without reaching decisions. Wage agreements, hours, and specific contract provisions were worked out on a short-term basis with any union that seemed to be top dog at the moment. The general issue of jurisdiction continued for some time in a stalemate and no one could say how it would finally be resolved. Later there developed a rough division of control, the A.F. of L. being the stronger in the mills, the C.I.O. in the forests.

The big A.F. of L. empire was built up shrewdly if without scruple by Dave Beck and his teamsters' union. The first conquests were made in Seattle where the truck drivers, using wrenches and jack handles, if necessary, to "perfect their organization" achieved a position well nigh invulnerable. Having thus established themselves, they then extended their power by bringing within their control a number of subsidiary groups—warehousemen, milkmen, brewery workers, even the department store clerks. The teamsters followed the maxim that anything with wheels (even perhaps anything that could be moved) should properly be brought within their jurisdiction and control. It was a goal not fully realized, for they encountered obstacles when they tried to establish their sway over the loghaulers and the Boeing machinists. Nevertheless Beck made himself one of the strongest labor leaders in the country and achieved a national prominence which in later years (1952) carried him to the presidency of the International Brotherhood of Teamsters.

Ingenious and resourceful in his methods, Beck was quick to adapt his tactics to changing circumstances. Strong-arm practices gave way to more respectable negotiations which emphasized the common interests of unions and employers. Laundrymen and dry cleaners, bakers and garage owners came to see the advantages of paying higher wages to their union employees when the costs could be offset by charging higher prices, and when they had some assurance that unprofitable competition would be discouraged. Beck fell into step with the chamber of commerce, and Seattle became a "peaceful" closed shop town.[8]

---

[8] Vernon H. Jensen, *Lumber and Labor*, New York, 1945, Chaps. 8-14; "After the Battle; Present Relations Between Labor and Management," *Fortune*, XXXI, February 1945, 176-179; "Dave Beck," *ibid.*, XXXVIII, December 1948, 191-197.

World War II and After

The outbreak of World War II produced a transformation as important to the region as that of 1917 and even more spectacular. The "battle of production" stimulated business even before the attack on Pearl Harbor. With the entry of the United States into the war government contracts, especially for ships and aircraft, produced a tremendous expansion in manufacturing. Shipbuilding became the Number One industry in the region. Boeing employees numbered more than 40,000 persons, distributed among the main plants in Seattle and Renton and in lesser shops in Bellingham and Chehalis, Everett and Aberdeen. Employment in the various aircraft, shipbuilding, and metals plants of the Northwest increased twentyfold to reach a total of a quarter of a billion dollars.

Military contracts and the demand for foodstuffs meant much more to the Pacific Northwest than they did to the country as a whole, if we may judge by comparing them to prewar levels of production. Seattle ranked among the top three cities in *per capita* war orders, and Washington near the top among the states. In four years time 1941-1944 these contracts amounted to 5.59 billion dollars in Washington alone. During this period the regional index of business activity climbed 63 points. In 1946 the farmers' cash receipts were 244 percent above the 1935-1939 figures.

Manufacturing plants large and small were caught up in the complex web of war production, no matter where they were or whether they had previous experience. Naval repair yards at Bremerton sent most of the Pearl Harbor fleet to sea again stronger than it was before. Half a hundred flattops were launched at the Kaiser shipyards by July, 1944. Walla Walla took time from agricultural occupations to make castings for the Portland yards, and agricultural implement manufacturers in Yakima turned to the production of destroyer parts. Liberty and Victory ships, built by amazingly rapid methods of welding and assembly, took their propellers from brass foundries in Seattle, their galley stoves, windlasses, and steering engines from iron works in Everett. Pacific Car and Foundry Company contributed General Sherman tanks and tank retrievers for the battlefields of Europe, while in nearby Kent a small garbage can factory became an important supplier of rifle clips.

Northwest resources were exploited on a larger scale than ever. Mines, forests, and fisheries produced generously of their bounty. Food plants in the Yakima Valley processed 4,700,000 cases of canned fruits and vegetables and 39,000,000 pounds of beet sugar. Meanwhile new hydroelectric installations at Bonneville and Grand Coulee made possible a great expansion of cheap electrical power. Between 1939 and 1944 the energy sold increased from 129,000,000 to nine billion kilowatt hours. This development ushered in a new age for the electro-process industries and for manufacturing generally, which promised much both for the war and afterward. Twelve large plants were built at a cost of 160,000,000 dollars, including establishments at Spokane and Vancouver for processing aluminum and others for making calcium carbide and ferroalloys.

Wartime observers prophesied that the Northwest was entering upon an era of great industrial growth, yet their pride of achievement was tempered with lingering doubts as to the permanence of the changes that were being brought about. With the return of peace the shipyards would undoubtedly disappear as they had in 1920, and the aircraft plants would suffer cancelled contracts as well. What would be the prospects of employment and industrial "reconversion" then? No one could say, though the research analysts made inquiries as best they could to determine what measures of postwar adjustment were possible and likely.[9]

Happily those who felt apprehension for the future were spared the realization of their fears during the first postwar decade. Though many war workers left the region, other newcomers took their places with the result that the gain in population was maintained and even increased. Business activity hardly faltered with the end of the war; thereafter the general index continued its strong steady rise until in 1952 it stood at 261. After watching it for several years the statisticians shifted their base year from the 1935-1939 average to 1947. Henceforth the new postwar level would be taken as the normal state

[9] *War Production in Washington*, compiled by the Secretary of State, Olympia, 1943; *Counties of Washington, Supplement*, compiled by the Secretary of State, Olympia, 1944; *Pacific Northwest Goes to War; State of Washington*, ed. and pub. by Art Ritchie and William L. Davis, Seattle, 1944; Puget Sound Regional Planning Commission, *Puget Sound Region; War and Post War Development*, Washington, D. C., 1943; Washington State Planning Council, *Employment and Payrolls; Basic Industries of Washington, 1920-44*, Olympia, 1945; Maurice W. Lee, "Appraisal of the Pacific Northwest," *Harvard Business Review*, XXVI, 1948, 282-304.

of affairs to which subsequent changes would be compared.

The situation in 1947 was in some ways so different from 1939 that it did seem the region was entering upon a new stage of economic development. Even though factory employment dropped nearly one hundred points on the index with the ending of World War II, it stabilized at a level 50 points above the prewar figure. Aircraft plants employed twice as many men as in 1939, and shipyards three times as many. In nine of 16 major industrial groups Northwest manufacturers registered important gains and conserved them. The total value added by manufacturing for the region as a whole increased 265 percent. Building and private construction, long neglected during the years of depression and war, rose to a level five times as high as during the middle 1930's. Business activity in banks and department stores was two and three times as great.

Several factors accounted for the industrial growth that was taking place. Part of it resulted from large government expenditures which continued after World War II due to the disturbed state of world affairs. Manufacturing plants constructed during the war were available to be used by private industry afterward. The pent-up demand for consumers' goods expanded the market for goods in the Northwest itself, now proportionally larger because of the heavy increase in population.

Yet those who made careful appraisals of the postwar economy were not persuaded that the new conditions were basically different from the old. The development of the region was still dependent upon resources, and was directly related to the extractive industries. Eighty percent of its manufacturing continued to be concentrated in five major groups: lumber, food processing, paper, transportation, and primary metals. Industrial diversification increased somewhat within these groups, but the general balance as between groups (save for the aluminum and aircraft industries) was not greatly changed from what it had been earlier.

Manufacturing, despite its gains, occupied a comparatively smaller proportion of the population. Of the total population increase in the United States 1939-1947, 8.9 percent represented the share of the Pacific Northwest states. Yet the region realized only 2 percent of the national increase in manufacturing workers. Save for a few exceptions, important ones to be sure, the region continued to be a place of small shops and branch plants, which did not feel industrialized as eastern cities did. It was still an area set apart by great spaces and long distances from the more populous sections of the country. The pattern of freight rates still presented serious obstacles to the establishment of industries which were at all sensitive to transportation costs. Furthermore, the people themselves were not especially industry-minded. The business community suffered a lack of entrepreneurship, put comparatively little of its investment capital into the development of new industrial enterprises and contributed only half-heartedly to the research and experiment that would lead to the introduction of new products.[10]

Resources were still the focus of economic development, and it was well that steps were taken to maintain the resource base of the economy. Measures of conservation assumed increasing importance for the forest industries and fisheries, while reclamation was vital to the further expansion of agriculture. The utilization of water power for electric energy promised for a time at least to give the region an advantage in attracting new manufacturing. Differences of opinion were expressed as to how far such programs as these would support the continued growth of the area but there was general agreement that resource development was imperative. The emphasis on resource management gave a new importance to the endeavors in this field that had been going on, not too successfully, for several decades. Often the temper of the times had not been favorable. Now perhaps the necessity for action was more compelling.

---

[10] V. B. Stanbery, *Growth and Trends of Manufacturing in the Pacific Northwest, 1939-47*, U.S. Department of Commerce, Office of Field Service, 1950; *Annual Survey of Manufactures*, 1953, U.S. Dept. of Commerce, March 30, 1955; Edwin J. Cohn, Jr., *Industry in the Pacific Northwest and the Location Theory*, New York, 1954.

31

Water for a Thirsty Land

Farmers and irrigators, who made it their business to be acquainted with Nature's moods and eccentricities, found her perverse and exacting in many parts of the Inland Empire. The first white men to pass that way had remarked upon the cheerless desert wastes, the hills seamed and cut by dry ravines, the plains smoking with dust, the soil baked and brittle, "to all appearances never visited by the dews of heaven." For a people who searched out the grassy valleys and well-watered plains for their settlements, the plateau was a god-forsaken country and few of the early emigrants thought twice of remaining there to live. For many years it continued barren and unyielding, save to the cattlemen whose animals found subsistence on the bunch grass.

The generation of 1900, however, found more promise in the place. Climate and rainfall were not to be changed by prayer and good living. But the possibilities of leading water from a mountain stream, perhaps for many miles to an orchard or garden, encouraged the farmer to dream of man-made oases where vegetation would grow as lush as in Iowa or Virginia. The soil itself was fertile and the snows of the overtowering ranges held all the moisture one could desire. The problems of irrigation had to do not so much with the source of supply as with the mechanics of storage and distribution. The devising of reservoirs and the construction of canals presented difficulties in expense and engineering, but the basic elements of soil and water were present in abundance. It was mainly a matter of bringing them together.[1]

[1] The most useful references for a general coverage of the progress of irrigation in the Pacific Northwest are the reports on the subject by the U.S. Census Bureau and the U.S. Reclamation Service. See also John H. Lewis, *Irrigation in the State of Oregon*, U.S. Dept. of Agriculture, Office of Experiment Stations, Bulletin 209, 1909; Osmar L. Waller, *Irrigation in the State of Washington*, U.S.D.A., Office of Experiment Stations, Bulletin 214, 1909; and Mary G. Lewis, "History of Irrigation Development in Idaho," unpublished thesis, University of Idaho, 1924.

The great lava plateau of Southern Idaho and Eastern Oregon, which stretched from the foothills of the Rockies westward to the Cascade mountains, was as parched a land as any in the West. Yet the ground was good and the watershed was so intricately figured that one might find land not too far from some tributary stream in any one of a score of valleys lying at the base of the mountains, from Henry's Fork and Bear Lake to Boise and Payette, Malheur and Owyhee. In Southern Oregon ancient lake beds, marshes, and "lost" rivers challenged the engineer to make them useful. Farther north, in the middle valley of the Columbia and its tributaries, the farm lands were screened from the rain clouds and the river channels were deeply carved below the valley floor, but here, too, there was water to be had, if practicable ways could be found to distribute it.

Irrigators were fortunate in that the varied topography presented many levels of difficulty, so that they might begin with the easy ones and progress to those more technical and costly. Individual farmers started with short, improvised ditches such as those first constructed at Bloomington and Canyon Creek in Bear Lake County, Idaho, in the Methow and Okanogan valleys in central Washington, or in Jackson and Josephine counties in Southern Oregon. Somewhat later private companies raised money in larger amounts for an operating capital and undertook more ambitious projects, including canal systems to serve as much as 200,000 acres (near Boise) and reservoirs that would gather and contain the spring runoff for use during the summer months. By 1914 planning and construction had progressed to the point of reclaiming whole valleys by putting agencies of the United States government directly behind the work.

Irrigation might begin with the expansion of an enterprise which had been carried on in a more limited way without it. Cattlemen in the Harney Basin turned to it in an effort to enlarge the area from which they harvested forage crops. In this section the spring flood waters flowed early and then subsided, leaving the soil moist and productive. Irrigation spread the water over wider acreages. Apple growers in the Hood River district increased the output of existing orchards and developed larger ones. Many a farm in the Willamette Valley was made the richer through the use of supplemental water, though the climate was not considered arid. Here

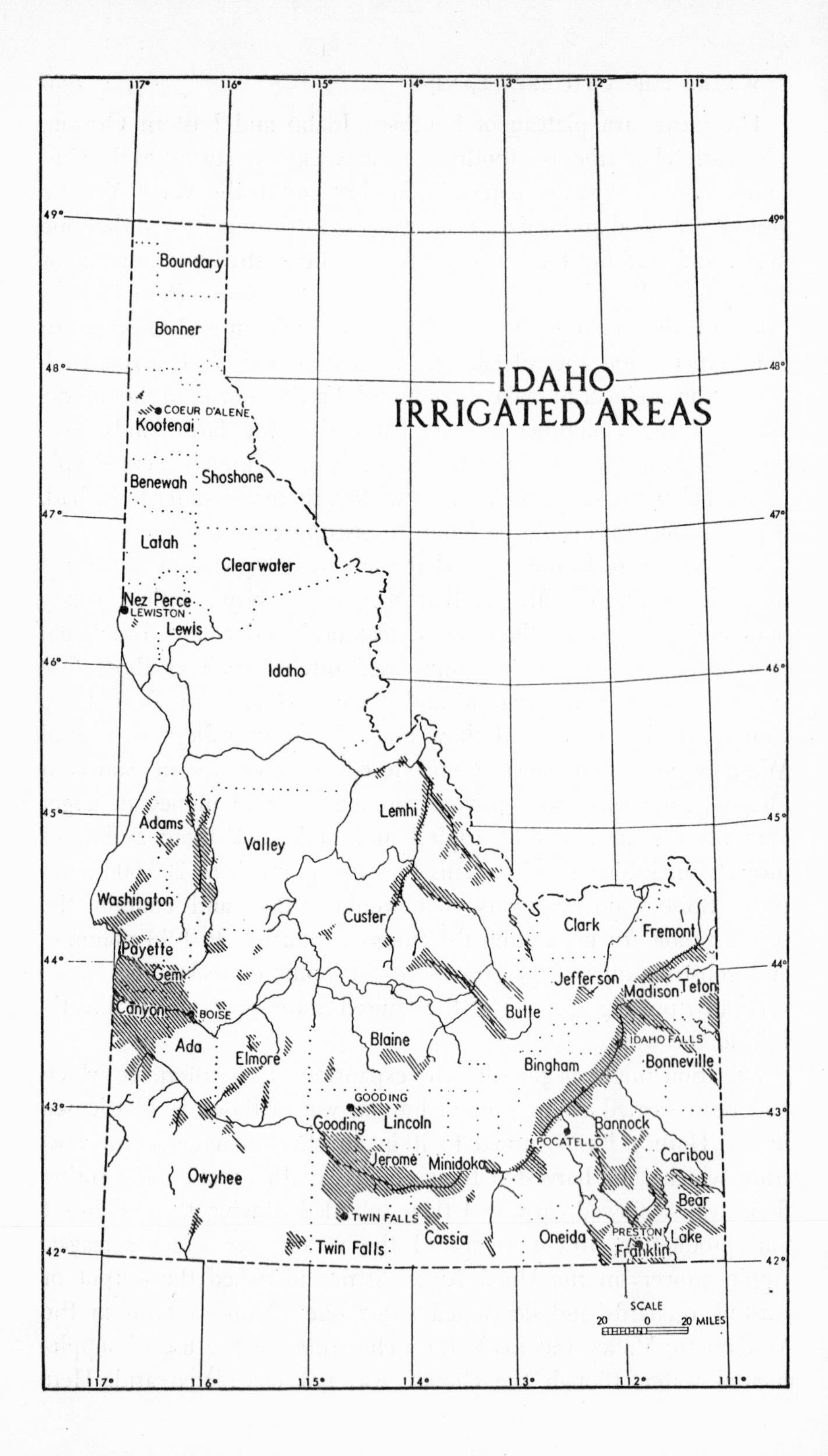
IDAHO
IRRIGATED AREAS
117°
116°
115°
114°
113°
112°
111°
49°
48°
47°
46°
45°
44°
43°
42°
Boundary
Bonner
COEUR D'ALENE
Kootenai
Benewah
Shoshone
Latah
Clearwater
Nez Perce
LEWISTON
Lewis
Idaho
Adams
Valley
Lemhi
Washington
Custer
Clark
Fremont
Payette
Gem
Jefferson
Madison
Teton
Canyon
BOISE
Butte
Ada
Elmore
Blaine
IDAHO FALLS
Bingham
Bonneville
GOODING
Gooding
Lincoln
Bannock
POCATELLO
Jerome
Minidoka
Caribou
Owyhee
Bear
TWIN FALLS
Twin Falls
Cassia
Oneida
PRESTON
Lake
Franklin
SCALE
20
0
20 MILES

the benefits were great because of the light rainfall during the growing season.

For the most part, however, irrigation was the magic by which wholly new garden areas were created in places that previously were desolate and uninhabited. It was like Aladdin's lamp in its power to create wealth and productivity where none had existed before. It was a dramatic and spectacular demonstration of man's power to alter the environment in which he lived, which touched his agricultural environs no less than the urban setting in which he placed his cities.

Success was intermingled with failure. If there was sudden wealth, there was also conflict and distress and precarious living. One might make a fortune, or one might lose one. The Walla Walla wheat farmers and others who tilled their fields trusting to the summer rains were skeptical of the complicated management and the elaborate routine that irrigators found essential. Water rights were the subject of stormy dispute and protracted litigation, and the law itself was often defective in upholding one's claims to a share of the mountain torrent. But while the problems were many and perplexing, irrigation held such promise of return that agriculturists were wedded to it more and more. Rich harvests in the end overcame all doubts.

The paradox of irrigation was that while it stimulated individualism and fed upon private speculation, it was actually ill suited to either one. The possibilities of achievement that a single farmer or a single company might realize in constructing and operating an irrigation system were limited indeed. Repeatedly they made the attempt only to meet with failure and disappointment. Circumstances were against them, and the trend of a half-century evidenced a steady decline in the role they were to play. Reclamation demanded for its success a collective, institutional approach. Individualism and capitalism might flourish and prosper once the land was watered, but the task of watering it was one that called for social action. Sometimes it was by water users joined together and organized in a mutual effort, and sometimes through governmental measures which provided a more sure and equitable protection of individual claims and interests, and made larger funds available.

Irrigation by Private Enterprise

The first considerable advances in irrigation were part of the general progress in agriculture that came during the years of boom and prosperity at the turn of the century. Some 385,000 acres were reclaimed during the 1890's in Idaho alone, an expansion that trebled the irrigated land in extent and brought the total area served to 600,000 acres. By 1902 Oregon farmers were irrigating 440,000 acres. Development in Washington was more limited, but here, too, three farms were irrigated in 1900 for every one counted in 1890. By 1909 30,000 farms, totaling nearly 3,500,000 acres, were served by canals and ditches in the region as a whole, at a total cost in irrigation enterprises of 70,000,000 dollars.

The major part of this expansion was accomplished by private enterprise. Not only were farmers impressed by the crop returns, but investors and speculators were attracted by the prospect of increased land values, as desert lands worth five dollars an acre or less brought many times that amount when irrigated. Sizable sums of capital could be had for the construction of improvements, through individuals and partnerships, through coöperatives formed by groups of water users, or through commercial companies. In 1909 90 percent of the irrigated acreage in Oregon and 75 percent in Idaho were classified under these agencies of private operation. Individuals and partnerships were responsible for 59.8 percent (in acreage) of Oregon's irrigation. Idaho's coöperatives accounted for 43.9 percent of the acreage irrigated in that state.

This was possible because so large a proportion of the improvement was done at a comparatively low cost per acre. In 1905 one-half of Oregon's irrigation was achieved by temporary dikes and dams which simply forced the spring flood waters over a wider area. The average cost of irrigation works in Oregon and Idaho was $16.25 per acre, the average annual charge for maintenance and operation was $0.69 per acre. This meant that only the easiest undertakings were attempted. The farms that were served were situated on valley lands bordering the secondary streams. The higher bench lands and extensive tracts lying along the major rivers could only be reached with more elaborate canal systems or expensive pumping operations. These larger irrigation works required more capital and stronger organizations to manage them.

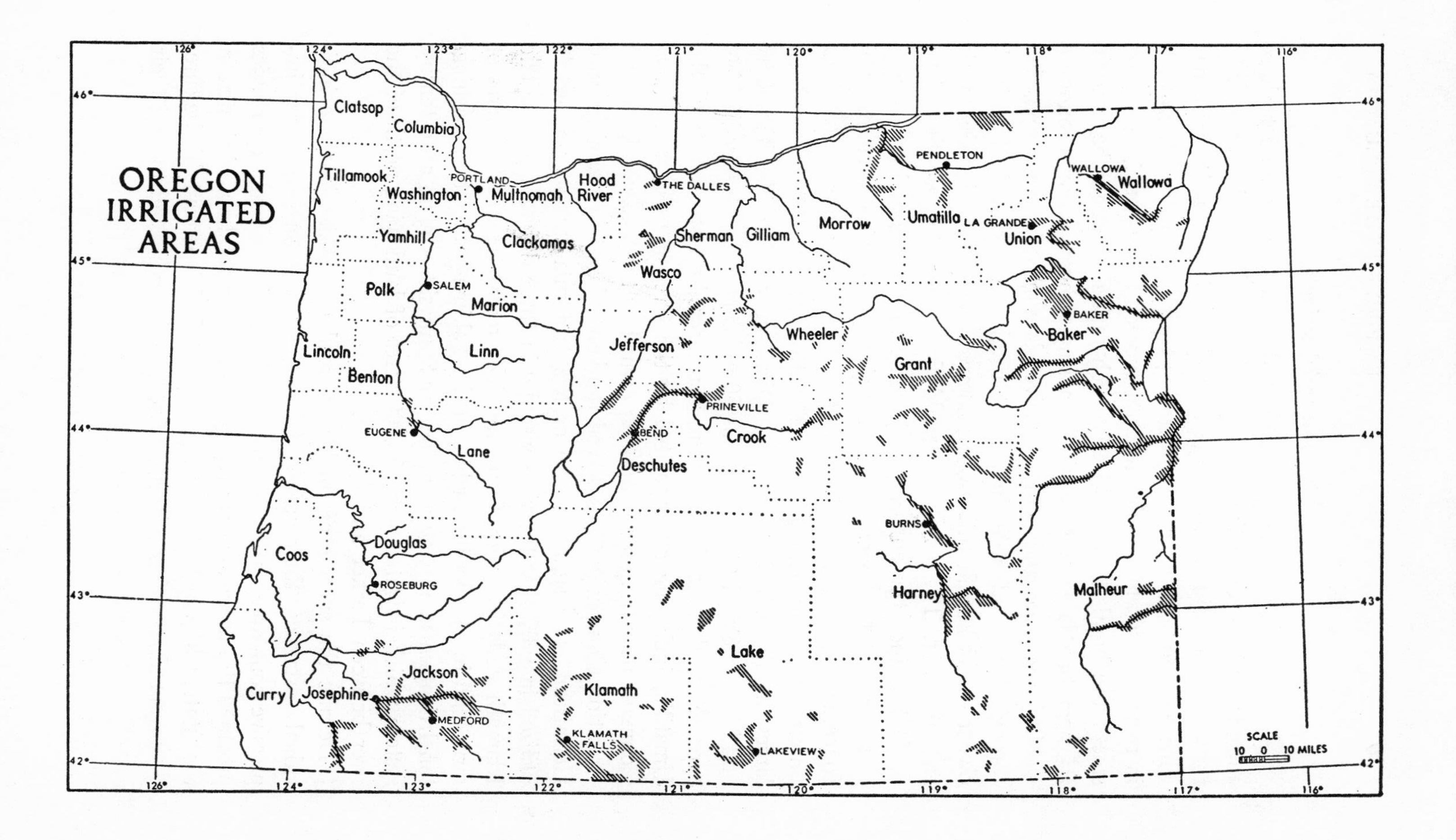
OREGON
IRRIGATED
AREAS
Clatsop
Columbia
Tillamook
Washington
PORTLAND
Multnomah
Hood
River
THE DALLES
Sherman
Gilliam
Morrow
PENDLETON
Umatilla
LA GRANDE
Union
WALLOWA
Wallowa
Yamhill
Clackamas
Wasco
Polk
SALEM
Marion
Linn
Jefferson
Wheeler
Grant
BAKER
Baker
Lincoln
Benton
PRINEVILLE
BEND
Crook
EUGENE
Lane
Deschutes
BURNS
Harney
Malheur
Coos
Douglas
ROSEBURG
Lake
Klamath
KLAMATH
FALLS
LAKEVIEW
Jackson
Curry
Josephine
MEDFORD
SCALE
10 0 10 MILES
126°
124°
123°
122°
121°
120°
119°
118°
117°
116°
46°
45°
44°
43°
42°

Commercial Irrigation

Commercial companies seemed to have advantages in meeting the problems of the costly developments, and for a while considerable reliance was placed in them. It was a day when corporations were demonstrating their strength and usefulness in many fields; why should they not succeed in this one? By issuing stocks and bonds they could raise such capital as might be needed. By operating large systems under a single management economies would be realized and comprehensive planning that was impossible through local and individual effort would be achieved. The landowner would benefit because the company would provide the magic gift of water. The company would find the enterprise financially profitable since the land would become productive and valuable.

The expectations were logical enough and a number of commercial concerns were formed. The Payette Valley Irrigation and Water Power Company operated a system that was in 1890 one of the largest in Idaho. The Ridenbaugh Ditch, operated by the Boise City and Nampa Canal Company, was 50 miles long and watered 25,000 acres. Several large ditches were constructed in the valley of the Umatilla, including one operated by the Oregon Land and Water Company near Irrigon and another owned by the Maxwell Land and Irrigation Company which served the bench lands in the vicinity of Hermiston. The summer flow of the Umatilla was so completely utilized in 1909 that the river was dry in three different places. The Klamath Falls Irrigation Company delivered water to 2,000 acres of farm land in that locality, while in the Yakima Valley the Washington Irrigation Company operated the Sunnyside Canal, an extensive system which irrigated some 36,000 acres of land lying north of the river between Parker and Prosser.

Despite the success of the commercial companies in these individual instances, their accomplishments as a group were not impressive compared with other forms of operation. Oregon companies provided the water for only 11.3 percent of the total land irrigated in that state, while in Idaho the figure was only 3.1 percent. To be sure, they were able to finance somewhat larger systems and to lead their canals to some of the less accessible locations which lay beyond the reach of other private ditches. Nevertheless they encountered many difficulties, and their experience soon demonstrated the weaknesses of the commercial type of enterprise for the purposes of irrigation.

The corporations formed were of two types, both of which had their shortcomings. Some were land and water companies that combined irrigation with land speculation. The profits that attracted these concerns were derived from the increased land values that resulted when arid tracts of "desert" were transformed into orchards or vegetable gardens worth fancy prices. Water was a necessity and they did what they had to in order to provide it, but their interest in irrigation usually did not extend beyond the acreage they owned and ended when the land was sold. Sometimes the service was good, as in the case of the Washington Irrigation Company. Sometimes it was poor, the construction flimsy, and the maintenance woefully inadequate. Whatever their policies were, the companies had a limited, short-term view whereas the needs of the water users called for a comprehensive, long-range program.

Other corporations thought to provide the water without buying and selling the land itself. Since the value, as they saw it, attached to the water and not the land, they trafficked in water rights, selling a perpetual right for perhaps 10 dollars per acre, and adding an annual maintenance charge to it. Presumably these companies had a more enduring interest in the water service, and were not obliged to shoulder the burden of heavy investments in land purchases. They were, however, trading in claims for which the title and value were not beyond question, and the satisfaction of which in the indefinite future was not theirs to guarantee. They were dealing, moreover, with landowners whose position was often stronger than their own. The land had many owners, the canal but one. Investments in dry lands could be bought at low prices and the speculator could afford to wait some years for water if there was a prospect of getting it in the end more cheaply. Saddled with heavy construction costs, the canal company had to realize its returns quickly or face bankruptcy. A number of companies failed and saw their water systems transferred to the men who owned the land.

Carey Act

The Carey Act, placed on the statute books by Congress in 1894, was so drafted as to improve the opportunities of the commercial companies by giving them more security and protection. The federal government did not deal with the corporations directly. But provision was made that tracts of public land would be transferred from the national domain to the jurisdiction of the states in which they were situated, if the states would see that they were reclaimed. The states then signed contracts with individuals or commercial companies to construct and operate the necessary canal systems.[2]

This was a second attempt on the part of the United States government to encourage the reclaiming of arid areas in the West by granting lands from the public domain to those who would undertake to make them productive. An earlier law, the Desert Land Act of 1877, provided that grants could be made directly to individuals at $1.25 per acre, if they could show that irrigation of at least 80 acres had been accomplished on a 640-acre tract. The terms had some importance in Idaho and Oregon, where 800,000 acres were taken up by 1910. But no supervision was attempted and no machinery was set up that would allow the reclaiming of larger tracts under private enterprise utilizing the means of corporate management and the issue of bonds. The Carey Act was an extension of the earlier policy, and the philosophy behind it was much the same. The differences had to do mainly with the adaptation of federal land grants to the requirements of large-scale private financing and construction.

In matters of administration the Carey Act left most of the responsibility with the states. A state included in the act must accept its provisions, make application to the United States for grants of lands, submitting a map and plan of development in support of each application, and set up an administering agency under whose direction the improvements would be carried to completion. The states undertook to examine each proposed plan for feasibility and adequacy of

---

[2] Guy Ervin, *Irrigation Under the Provisions of the Carey Act*, U.S.D.A., Office of the Secretary, Circular 124, February, 1919; Wells A. Hutchins, *Commercial Irrigation Companies*, U.S.D.A., Technical Bulletin 177, March, 1930.

water supply, and to manage the sale of lands to settlers. No lands were to be leased or disposed of except to secure reclamation and settlement, and not more than 160 acres could be sold to one person. Idaho and Washington accepted the provisions of the act in 1895, and Oregon in 1901. Idaho and Oregon both assigned the task of supervision to the State Engineer since he was the officer who had charge of the listing and certification of water rights.

When the states applied for specific grants, the plans and proposals contained in the applications were drawn up by the companies, and the contracts which the companies subsequently concluded with the states stipulated the terms under which they would provide water and sell water rights. The price of the water rights was governed by the cost of constructing the system, estimated as accurately as possible though it often proved to be too low. The companies were given a measure of protection in that the state sold the land only to those who bought water rights with it, and after 1896 made the cost of constructing the canals a lien upon the lands that were benefited. Thus assured of a return on their investment, the irrigation companies went to banks and financing agencies and sold bonds to pay for the construction.

Idaho made of the Carey Act a very good thing; in fact, three-fourths of the land irrigated under the law was situated within the borders of this one state. The Twin Falls South Side project, which was set up to encompass 240,000 acres, was highly successful and served as a model for a number of others. Between 1904 and 1911 35 requests were processed, which together contemplated the irrigation of 2,000,000 acres of land in the Snake River Valley at an estimated cost of $66 millions. By 1912 a full third of that amount had been actually expended. The Twin Falls North Side Land and Water Company submitted proposals covering 200,000 acres and 16 other companies signed contracts for canals serving from 12,000 to to 112,000 acres each. Financial reverses put a stop to further development in 1913 and for several years little was done. The achievements of the companies fell far short of their goals, and many companies failed even to get their applications approved. Nevertheless Idaho's Carey Act projects covered in 1917 no less than 868,000 acres of which 456,000 acres were in productive use.

Save for Idaho the Carey Act was generally taken to be a failure. The State of Oregon selected 432,203 acres and signed several contracts with private companies operating in the Deschutes Valley, but none of the projects was successful or important. In Washington no projects were approved, though the Washington Irrigation Company pressed for one in the Yakima Valley. The reasons for failure were partly technical and partly administrative. The engineering done by the companies was very imperfect, and their surveys were often inadequate. Construction costs were poorly estimated, yet once the water rates were established, they could not be increased later. The states gave the projects little real supervision and paid too little attention to determining the adequacy of the water supply. As for the settlers, some got too little water and others too much. The experience of many was one of misfortune, which gave the projects a bad name and discouraged the sale of Carey Act lands. Even when the act was amended (1901) to extend the period of repayment, the burden of financing was a heavy one both for the settlers and the companies, and it became increasingly clear that some further government aid would be necessary. Beyond this there was a pressing need to clarify the legal status of conflicting water rights and to establish in each state some procedures by which outstanding claims could be reconciled and recorded.

Water Rights

Issues of law were thorny where they touched the establishment of water rights. There was no uniformity among the states as to the valid basis of such rights and for some years there was no way of determining from the public records how much water was subject to valid claims and how much remained unappropriated. Oregon and Washington followed at first the common law of riparian rights which favored the landowners along the banks of the streams and made no provision for the diversion of water that would be consumed in the process of irrigation. Later this principle was modified, partly by court decisions and partly by state legislation, to recognize the doctrine of appropriation for beneficial use. According to this interpretation, priority of application for actual use established a claim as against another claimant who could not prove that he used what he claimed for beneficial purposes. Claims by appropriation could be made for the utilization of lands situated back from the stream as well as along the banks, provided it was practicable to water them by an irrigation canal. The conflict of overlapping claims based on the two principles inevitably led to much confusion and litigation.

Washington and Idaho both incorporated provisions in their state constitutions which declared that the use of waters for purposes of irrigation should be deemed a public use, a principle which Oregon recognized by statute in 1891. Washington included also a clause which permitted the condemnation of such land as might be needed to secure right of way for an irrigation canal. Idaho asserted the power of the state to regulate and control the distribution of water, protected the right of individuals to divert unappropriated water, and outlined certain principles that should govern distribution when the water supply was inadequate to supply the full needs of all claimants. In all three states, however, there remained the further problem of maintaining an administrative jurisdiction over the filing and certifying of claims based on appropriation.[3]

The practical importance of this became evident as the engineers began to study and measure the water flow in the various rivers that were being put to use for irrigation. The success of an irrigation system depended upon its having a capacity adequate to satisfy the legal claims of the water users who were dependent upon it. But how much water would be necessary? State laws in Washington and Oregon required at first nothing more than a posting or filing of claims which gave notice of the intended diversion, indicating the amount of water to be appropriated. No proof of actual use was called for, and no state agency was empowered to limit the claims to the amount of water actually available in the river. In 1905 a little figuring disclosed the fact that the existing known water claims in the Yakima Valley considerably exceeded the total flow of the river. Obviously not everyone was getting his water, but any irrigation system ran the danger of

[3] U.S. Census Bureau, "Report on Irrigation," 1910, V, 842-843; Ray P. Teele, "Recent Irrigation Legislation," U.S.D.A., Office of Experiment Stations, Report, 1909, 399-401; Ray P. Teele, "State Engineer and His Relation to Irrigation," U.S.D.A., Department Bulletin 168, 1906; Marvin Chase, *Water Code and Its Administration*, Office of the Washington State Hydraulic Engineer, Bulletin No. 1, Olympia, 1918.

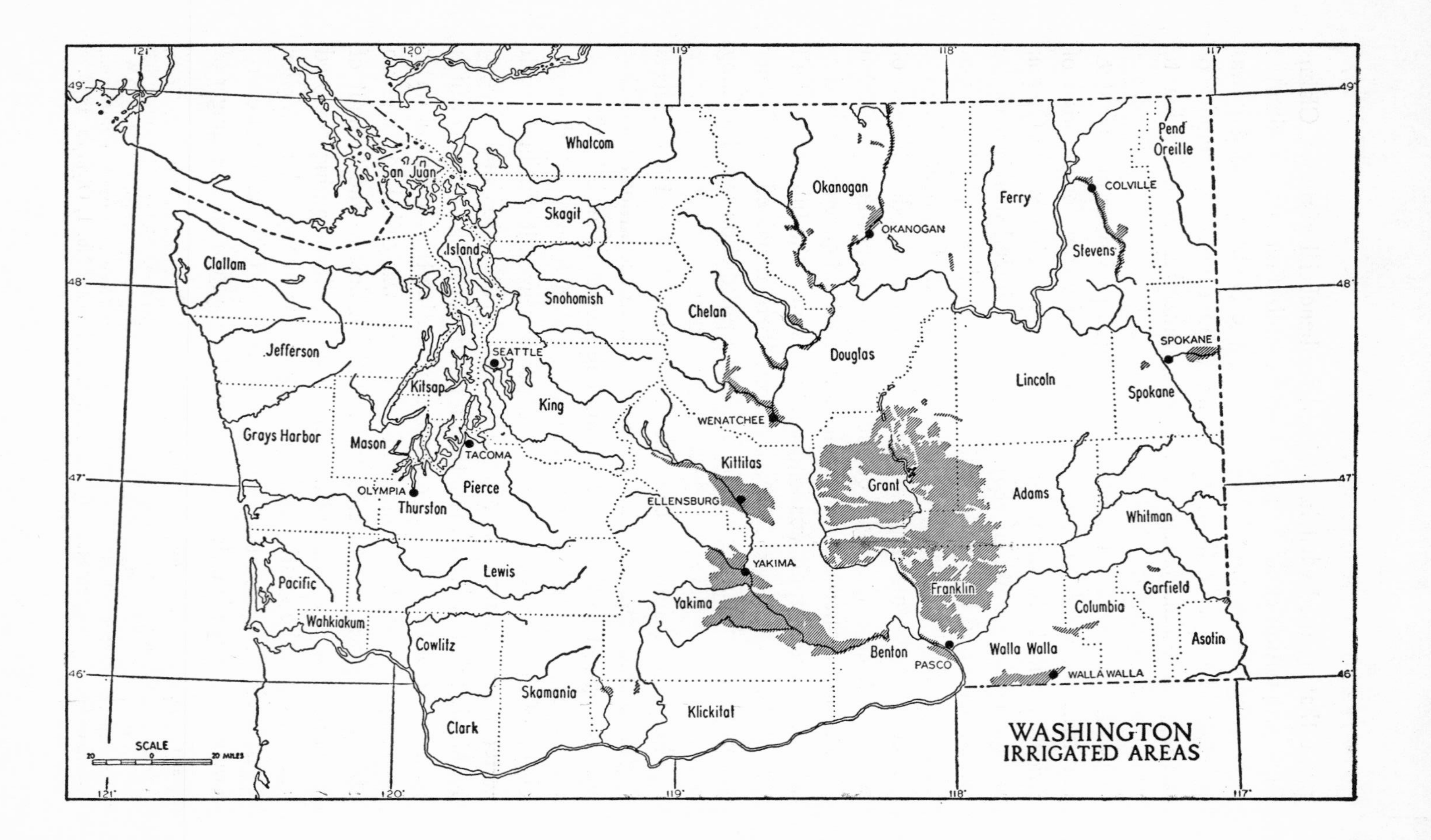
WASHINGTON
IRRIGATED AREAS
Whatcom
San Juan
Skagit
Island
Clallam
Snohomish
Jefferson
Kitsap
SEATTLE
King
Grays Harbor
Mason
TACOMA
OLYMPIA
Thurston
Pierce
Lewis
Pacific
Wahkiakum
Cowlitz
Clark
Skamania
Okanogan
OKANOGAN
Chelan
WENATCHEE
Kittitas
ELLENSBURG
YAKIMA
Yakima
Klickitat
Douglas
Grant
Franklin
Benton
PASCO
Ferry
Stevens
COLVILLE
Pend Oreille
Lincoln
Spokane
SPOKANE
Adams
Whitman
Walla Walla
WALLA WALLA
Columbia
Garfield
Asotin
SCALE
20 0 20 MILES
49°
48°
47°
46°
121°
120°
119°
118°
117°

embarrassment if all the claims had to be supplied at once. Similarly the filings in five Eastern Oregon counties totaled 810,025 second feet, or enough water to cover the entire area each year to a depth of 23 feet, which was patently absurd. Total recorded claims for power in Oregon amounted to 50 times the low-water flow of the Columbia River.

Plainly some action was necessary to regulate and police the filing of claims to water rights. The states took steps as best they could. Idaho followed the Wyoming system, declaring the principle that the rivers belonged to the state and that water rights must be acquired by application to the state. The state law required that the construction of improvements be completed within a stated period of time and that applicants must submit proof of actual use of the water claimed. The state engineer then issued a certificate defining the amount of the appropriation. The engineer also assisted the courts by making surveys in cases where preëxisting claims were being adjudicated. Here, however, his powers were limited since he could act only when individuals disputed each other's claims and sought a settlement by judicial procedures. Because many claims could only be resolved judicially, much confusion persisted. Nevertheless Idaho made real progress, so much so that by 1909 55.5 percent of the area being irrigated was covered either by a court adjudication or by a state permit.

Oregon moved more slowly, but enacted in 1909 a regulatory law which put the control of water rights on much the same basis. The state engineer, who previously had possessed no real authority, now became a key figure. Persons seeking water rights must make application to him, must begin work within the year and complete the improvement within five years, and demonstrate beneficial use of the water appropriated. Water rights acquired by purchase from canal companies were limited by the main source of supply. Provision was also made for the definition of rights acquired prior to 1909 by a Board of Control consisting of the state engineer and several division superintendents upon petition by the water users in the area. The decisions and awards of the engineer and the Board were made matters of permanent public record.

Washington enacted its water code in 1917, establishing a comprehensive system of adjudication and state control administered through the newly created office of the hydraulic engineer. The purpose of the code was to provide for the recording of water rights, both those already existing and those that might subsequently be established, and to provide the means of adjusting conflicting rights and supervising the operation of irrigation works. Both the engineer and the courts had a part in this procedure which culminated in the issuance of certificates of rights and included a thorough investigation of all diversion dams, canals, and measuring devices.

Federal Regulation

These improvements in the state procedures governing water rights did much to give water users a new legal security, which was necessary if irrigation agriculture was to expand. It was imperative, however, to give them economic security as well. Provisions of law and administrative regulations were of little use if the water supply for irrigation was limited to the fluctuating stream flow of rivers that ran full in the spring but went dry in summer. Any program of real expansion must look toward the impounding of water in large reservoirs, the construction of diversion dams higher up on the rivers, and the building of long canals leading from them to plateau and bench lands which otherwise lay well above the stream beds. Such a program exceeded the capacities of individualism and private enterprise. It was doubtful that it could be realized by state sponsorship or intervention. Because of the close connection of reclamation with the administration of the remaining public domain, and because of the great concern aroused by John Wesley Powell and his followers in the United States Geological Survey, there were good reasons why Congress should commit the federal government still more deeply to the furtherance of irrigation. With the passage of the Newlands Act in 1902, a new era began. This time Uncle Sam did not content himself with granting land while others did the planning and the work. The new program put him into the reclamation business directly.[4]

---

[4] John T. Ganoe, "Origin of a National Reclamation Policy," *Mississippi Valley Historical Review*, XVIII, 1931, 34-52; see also the first and second reports of the U.S. Reclamation Service, 1902-1903.

Three main purposes governed the reclamation program as carried on under the Newlands Act: (1) to plan and construct the major improvements by means of a federal agency, rather than leaving this task to states and commercial companies; (2) to design and carry out each project in such a way as to provide the maximum benefits for the entire area in which it was located; and (3) to make the federal projects self-liquidating, by charging the costs against the lands that were served by them, and eventually by transferring the ownership and management of the canals (though not the dams and reservoirs) to associations of water users. No one knew by what specific ways and means these ends could be accomplished, but throughout the years that followed all three objectives were consistently pursued.

The new agency to which the program was entrusted was the United States Reclamation Service. This office, which became the Reclamation Bureau in 1923, was charged with the development of all federal projects except a few on Indian reservations. Reclamation Service engineers made detailed investigations and plans before any projects were approved, to determine the costs that would be involved and the conditions that must be met to satisfy federal requirements. The Reclamation Service also had control of all expenditures made from the Reclamation Fund, and managed the construction and operation of dams, canals, and other improvements.

The Reclamation Fund, as established by the Newlands Act, was fed and replenished from the revenues received by the United States by the sale of federal lands in 13 western states and three territories where the projects were to be built. It was stipulated that the "major part" (i.e., 51 percent) of the sums "covered into the fund" from a particular state should be expended in that state, while the remainder might be expended on projects situated in any one of the states. In this way each state was assured of a proportionate share of the benefits, while at the same time there was sufficient latitude in the distribution of the money to allow planning on a national scale and to permit the construction of improvements that were too expensive to be built from the funds received from one state alone. The Reclamation Fund was to be a revolving fund, since expenditures for the construction of projects were to be repaid into it by the water users over a period of ten years as the land became productive. By the end of the year 1903 revenues to the amount of 5,800,000 dollars were available in the fund from land sales in the three states of the Pacific Northwest.

Investigations were initiated at once in these states looking toward the approval of projects in each one. The situation proved to be a complicated one. The largest revenues had come in from Oregon, yet serious difficulties stood in the way of launching large undertakings there. The pattern of land ownership was unfavorable because the federal domain in the extensive arid areas was cut up by wagon road grants and swamp land selections. The water supply was generally limited, since the streams flowed out of the lower rather than the higher mountain areas. Basins that might have served for storage purposes were already being used for cattle ranches. The Deschutes River was perhaps the best river for irrigation, yet its flow had been largely appropriated by various Carey Act corporations. In Washington, too, there were not too many opportunities. In the valley of the Palouse River and the Big Bend of the Columbia River large areas were suitable for irrigation, but the costs were prohibitive and probably would continue to be so for some years. In the Yakima Valley problems of land ownership, water rights, and previous development seemed to make federal action impracticable. Numerous small reservoirs could be built in the Okanogan country, but no system of any size. Idaho offered some of the best opportunities but here again the work that had already been undertaken made it difficult to know how the federal government should proceed.

The Federal Projects

Despite the obstacles and complexities, the next few years witnessed substantial achievements. Six projects were approved. The Umatilla and Klamath projects in Oregon were authorized as well as the Okanogan and Yakima projects in Washington. In Idaho plans were carried out to enlarge and consolidate the development of the Boise-Payette district, and a beginning was made on the Minidoka project in the central Snake River Valley. Solutions were found to technical and administrative problems, and several of the big dams and reservoirs became a reality. In 1909, 125,000 acres of arid land were being watered by the facilities of the United States Reclamation Service.[5]

The underlying secret of success was the early recognition that the program would assuredly fail if the federal projects were to be located only in places that were unoccupied and undeveloped. In some of the most promising areas irrigation was already being carried on in a limited way under private enterprise, or in some cases under the Carey Act. Such efforts deserved support, and the Reclamation Service devoted itself to measures of mutual effort as well as to the projects that were wholly new.

Both the Oregon projects were developed in areas where irrigation was already practiced. The Umatilla project was undertaken in the vicinity of Stanfield and Hermiston where several private companies were operating and three-fourths of the land was privately owned. The first federal investigations contemplated the possibility of irrigating lands on the lower Umatilla River by gravity from the Columbia and Snake rivers. It was decided, however, to use the Umatilla River instead, enlarging the capacity of the system by providing storage reservoirs. Cold Springs Reservoir, completed in 1908, was filled from the Umatilla by means of a diversion dam and feed canal leading from a point south of Echo. Structures were of permanent construction, concrete dams and cement-lined canals. Costs of 60 dollars per acre were assessed against the lands which, with water, were valued at three or four times that amount.

The Klamath project, too, was located in an area which had long been served by private canals. Here an elaborate plan was worked out which called for storage reservoirs at Clear Lake and Miller Creek (Gerber Reservoir), several diversion dams on Lost River, and a network of canals that would irrigate the land south of Klamath Falls and control the flow into Tule Lake in Northern California. The system was designed to serve 187,000 acres, the requirement being that the large private holdings must be subdivided and sold in tracts of not more than 160 acres before government water would be made

[5] For details on the progress made in constructing the federal projects by 1910, see the Report of the U.S. Reclamation Service for 1909-1910; a more complete description covering later years as well is given in U.S. Bureau of Reclamation, *Reclamation Project Data*, Washington, D.C., 1948.

available to them. By 1912 the Main Canal, Clear Lake dam, Lost River diversion dam, and many of the distribution structures had been completed.

The approval of the Okanogan project resulted from the petitions of residents in the area. It was a modest development, consisting of two storage reservoirs on Salmon Lake and Salmon Creek near Conconully, a diversion dam on the lower waters of Salmon Creek, and

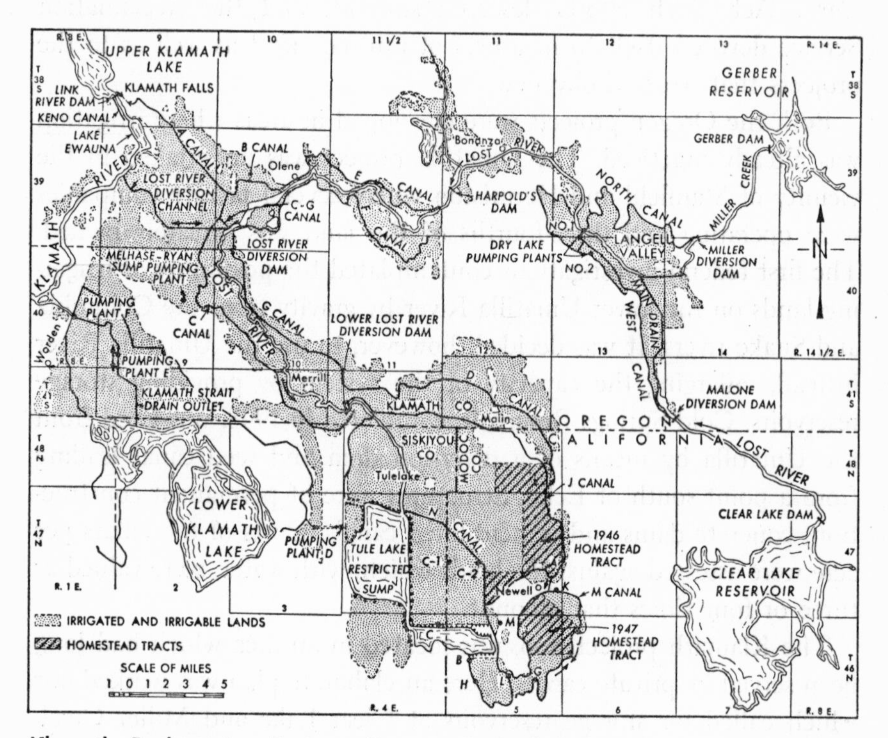

Klamath Reclamation Project. (From U.S. Reclamation Bureau, Reclamation Project Data, 1948.)

distribution canals to serve some 7,700 acres lying west of the Okanogan River in the vicinity of Omak. The land was devoted principally to fruitgrowing.

In the Yakima Valley private and commercial development of irrigation had gone so far that the Reclamation Service at first saw no prospect of carrying out any construction there. The Washington Irrigation Company not only had extensive landholdings in the central section of the valley, but had a bill before the Washington state legislature which would allow it the right to use Lake Cle Elum for storage purposes as part of its private irrigation system. Should Cle Elum and the other mountain lakes come under private control, it would seriously jeopardize plans for the comprehensive development of the whole valley under federal auspices. Federal engineers were likewise dubious of success so long as the appropriations for water rights were known to be excessive. They were willing to recommend a federal project only on condition that the outstanding water rights be reduced to a realistic figure, and that the Washington Irrigation Company sell its water system though not its lands to the United States.[6]

The federal demands precipitated a lively political flurry in the Yakima Valley during the course of which Wesley Jones of Yakima and A. J. Splawn of Cowiche led the drive for a program of national irrigation. As a result of strenuous efforts the private reservoir bill was defeated, and the private company was finally brought to accept the federal terms. Colonel William W. Robertson, editor of the Yakima *Republic*, aided the cause materially with his vigorous editorials. The reduction of water rights was accomplished by an energetic campaign up and down the valley to prevail upon those who had filed appropriations to scale them down.

Early in 1906 work was begun on the Sunnyside and Tieton units of the Yakima project. So far as the Sunnyside was concerned, it meant improving and enlarging the existing canal and reconstructing the diversion dam. The Tieton development involved the building of a diversion dam on the Tieton River and a canal system to water 27,500 acres lying between the river and Ahtanum Creek west of North Yakima. In addition to these local improvements, several mountain reservoirs were established at Lake Cle Elum, Bumping Lake, Lake Kachess, and Lake Keechelus. These facilities guaranteed an adequate stream flow throughout the year and permitted the construction of canals leading to the higher benches and lands in the upper valley later. The Yakima project as a whole was intended ultimately to serve 450,000 acres in South-central Washington. Ex-

[6] Calvin B. Coulter, "Victory of National Irrigation in the Yakima Valley, 1902-06," *PNQ*, XLII, 1951, 99-122.

penditures through 1910 amounted to 3,500,000 dollars.

The Reclamation Service projects in Idaho required equally complex negotiations and even more ambitious planning. The development of the bench lands between the Boise and Snake rivers was undertaken in response to petitions signed by local irrigators who found the improvement of the higher elevations too much for them. It involved the incorporation of a number of existing canals into the project system. Agreements were concluded with landowners and with canal companies which gave the Reclamation Service adequate control while at the same time recognizing individual property rights and giving a firm commitment to supply water in the future. In some instances where there were no water companies with which the Reclamation Service could negotiate, associations of water users were formed, and contracts were negotiated with them under which they undertook to repay the project costs. Similar contracts were signed with several local irrigation districts, such as the Pioneer Irrigation District, the Riverside Irrigation District, and the Nampa-Meridian District. Only as these contractual arrangements were perfected could the Reclamation Service proceed with the work of construction.[7]

The Boise project featured particularly the Boise River diversion dam southeast of the city of Boise and the Deer Flat reservoir southwest of Nampa, together with low line and high line canals. These facilities were well advanced toward completion by 1910. Additional storage was secured with the construction of the Arrowrock dam, a tremendous concrete, arch-gravity type of structure 354 feet high from river bed to crest and 1,150 feet long, which created a reservoir with a capacity of 286,600 acre-feet. This dam, finished in 1915, brought into existence the first of a series of huge storage basins that gave reclamation in Southern Idaho a greatly increased potential.

The Minidoka project differed from the rest in that irrigation in this locality was a new venture. The United States Geological Survey had made studies and private parties had been somewhat interested, but beyond a few surveys little or nothing had been done. The plan adopted by the Reclamation Service included a storage dam on the

[7] Wells A. Hutchins, "Irrigation District Operation and Finance," U.S.D.A., Department Bulletin 1177, 1923.

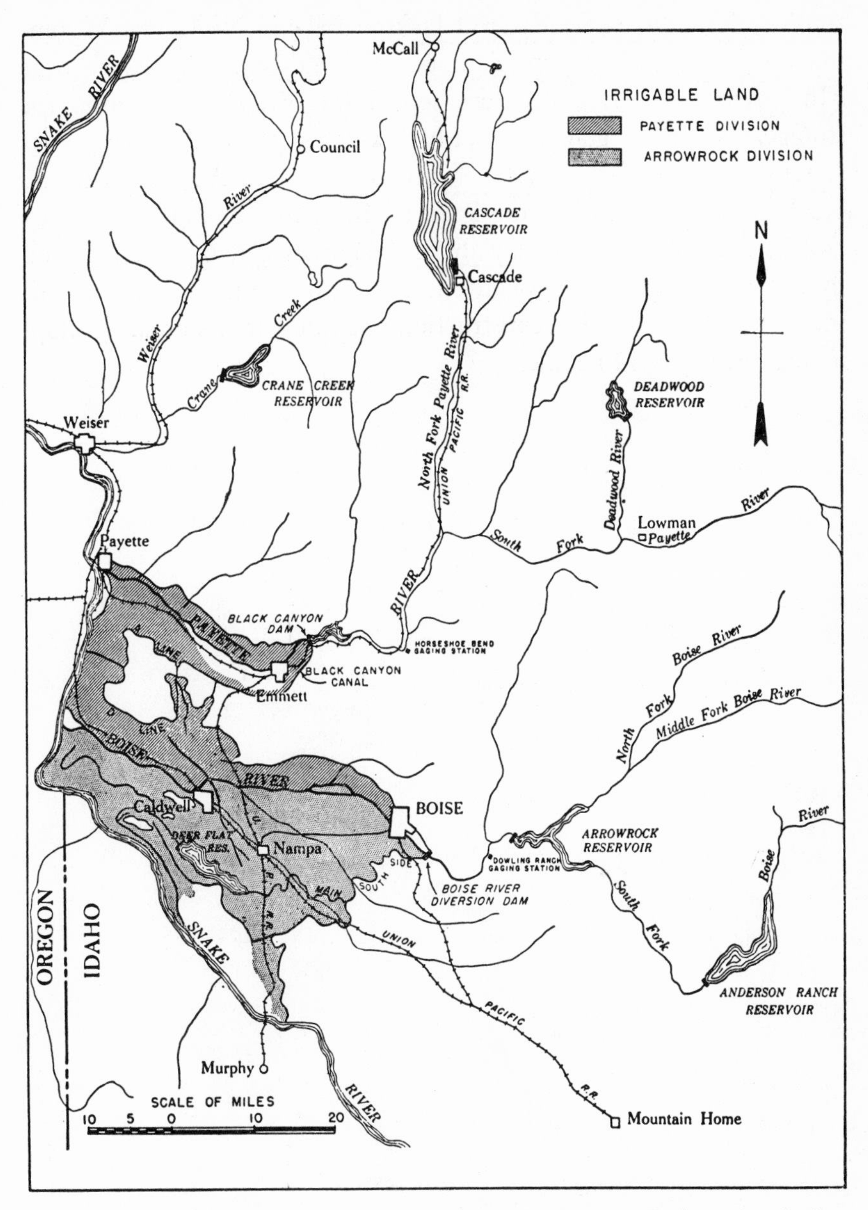

Boise Reclamation Project. (From U.S. Reclamation Bureau, Reclamation Project Data, 1948.)

south fork of the Snake River at Jackson Lake in Northwest Wyoming and a general-purpose dam on the middle Snake River near Minidoka. The latter structure served for diversion purposes, for storage, and for the generation of hydroelectric power. A gravity canal system led from this dam to an area adjacent to Acequia, Rupert, Heyburn, and Paul, while the lands south of the river around Burley and Declo, some of which lay above the gravity canals, were irrigated by a pumping system. Though one could not see it then, the multipurpose dam forecast the construction of a number of similar developments in the years to come.

32

Progress of Reclamation

From 1914 on irrigation became an increasingly expensive undertaking, and one that was justified only in areas where the crop returns were high. The average first cost of putting water on irrigated lands for all enterprises in Oregon increased between 1910 and 1940 from $15.36 to $40.41 per acre, while the Reclamation Bureau contracts for repayment schedules on its major facilities amounted in some cases to more than a hundred dollars per acre. Annual operating and maintenance costs advanced likewise from $.75 to $1.25 per acre in Oregon and as high as $4.14 per acre in Washington (1930). These trends raised serious problems of finance and administration since most of the burden had to be borne by the water users.

Financing became difficult during the decade following World War I when agricultural prices slumped from their former high levels. In many places where small water systems had been built during the first flush of enthusiasm for reclamation, especially by individuals or private companies, the decade of the 1920's was a time of retrenchment and readjustment. Some of these enterprises failed; others had to be reorganized. The acreage served by them shrunk by 33 percent. In Idaho commercial irrigation companies went out of business almost entirely, and in Oregon and Washington their operations dropped to less than half of what they had been. Many irrigation districts, too, found it impossible to finance further improvements, or even to pay the interest on their outstanding bonds. On the basis of incomplete reports by the Census Bureau, the total land irrigated in the Pacific Northwest was significantly less in 1930 than in 1920, perhaps by as much as 200,000 acres.

Idaho suffered particularly since many of the earlier canals and ditches had been laid out through the zeal of local promoters without taking account of the danger of limited water supply. Water shortages developed in the Boise Valley as early as 1924 and subsequently in the Payette and Weiser areas where crop losses ran into the millions of dollars. In any one of several districts—Bear River, Henry's Fork, Weiser basin, even in the Snake River section itself—the decline in acreage irrigated that took place during the decade was greater than the expansion which the Reclamation Bureau claimed for itself in the entire region. It took 20 years to consolidate Idaho's earlier expansion and to provide adequate water for an agricultural empire that had been built up originally in piecemeal fashion without adequate planning or engineering.[1]

The record of the state governments was disappointing whether they established irrigation enterprises directly or supported those of the local districts. In Washington the state attempted to colonize settlers on irrigated lands in the Hanford-White Bluffs area of the Columbia basin but failed dismally. Some 60 families were assigned to 20-acre plots of land which were to be watered from wells using electric pumps. The general idea was perhaps a reasonable one, for the record of irrigated farms in previous years was for the most part a very good one. Unfortunately, however, the soil conditions were unfavorable and there was too little appreciation of the difficulties of administration. In the face of agricultural depression the farmers and the state alike lost their enthusiasm for the venture and White Bluffs soon became a ghost project inhabited by only a few of the more stubborn or hardy colonists.

As for the financing of the local districts, the efforts of state agencies to support the prices of irrigation bonds were unavailing. Authorities in Oregon were embarrassed, for they had only recently inaugurated a procedure for the certification of such bonds as legal investments for trusts. In Washington the state government established a revolving fund to be used to buy irrigation bonds and thus reëstablish their market value. Presumably they would soon be sold again and the

[1] See reports on irrigation by the Bureau of the Census, 1920, 1930 and 1940, also Bureau of Reclamation, *Reports on the Engineering, Agricultural and Economic Feasibility of the Kittitas Division, Yakima Project, Washington, Baker Project, Oregon, Vale Project, Oregon, Owyhee Project, Oregon-Idaho,* Washington, D.C., 1925. Irrigation problems in Idaho are treated in the biennial reports of the Department of Reclamation, State of Idaho. For a general analysis, buttressed with specific figures, see Ray P. Teele, *Economics of Land Reclamation in the United States,* New York, 1927.

money would then be used to aid some other district. This plan, too, was unsuccessful since no real attempt was made to distinguish between good bonds and bad, and no supervision was exercised over the operations of the districts in question. After spending some 1,400,000 dollars fruitlessly Washington gave up the scheme and allowed the bond buyers to judge irrigation values for themselves.[2]

Federal Projects

While the state and local agencies of government found the problems of irrigation too big for them to manage, the federal government moved ahead, and the federal program became more vitally important to the economic development of the region. With the larger funds that were available and the technical knowledge and skill of the federal engineers, the Reclamation Bureau carried more and more of the burden of planning and building necessary improvements in the region. Congress supplemented the Reclamation Fund by adding other special appropriations to it, and extended the period of repayment from 20 to 40 years. These steps made it possible to undertake a number of major facilities in the Snake River Valley, the Yakima Valley, and in the Umatilla and Klamath projects in Oregon. Any real enlargement of the area of farm lands to be irrigated involved big dams and reservoirs, siphons, flumes, and tunnels that only Uncle Sam had the means to build.

In Washington the Reclamation Bureau set up the Kittitas Division of the Yakima project after several attempts to finance the system privately had failed. This plan called for a diversion dam on the Yakima River near Easton, and 76 miles of main canals which fanned out north and south to serve extensive agriculture areas lying on both sides of the river. Farther down the valley the Tieton division opened to cultivation some 27,500 acres situated west of Yakima, storing the necessary water behind a newly constructed dam (1925) on the Tieton River.

---

[2] Washington State Department of Conservation and Development, *Special Statistical Report on the Reclamation Revolving Fund, Land Settlement, Whitestone Reclamation District, Kittitas Project and Columbia Basin Project,* Olympia, 1925; Ross K. Tiffany, "State Reclamation in Washington," American Society of Civil Engineers, *Proceedings,* LIII, 1927, 913-923; Wells A. Hutchins, *Irrigation Districts, Their Organization, Operation and Financing,* U.S.D.A., Technical Bulletin 254, 1931.

The Umatilla and Klamath projects in Oregon were enlarged and improved with the building of three large structures. The Malone and Gerber dams served the Langell Valley district of Lost River southeast of Klamath Falls, and controlled the flow into Tule Lake. The McKay dam and reservoir was situated on McKay Creek south of Pendleton. The greater part of the storage there benefited local irrigation districts operating systems around Stanfield and Westland, which took the water on contract.

The Vale and Owyhee projects were likewise the scene of important construction though the fruits of it were not realized until the 1930's. In 1926 the Bureau of Reclamation purchased a one-half interest in the Warm Springs Reservoir, which had been established (1919) by a local irrigation district, and contracted to build a diversion dam, canals, and drainage works along the Malheur River. The Harper diversion dam was built soon afterward and by 1930 the first project units at Harper and Little Valley were receiving water. The Owyhee project, situated somewhat farther south, was organized at the same time and in much the same way, through contracts signed with several irrigation districts. Work started on the storage dam and canal system in 1928, first water being delivered to project lands in 1935. This was one of the most ambitious undertakings of the period, the plan calling for the irrigation of more than 100,000 acres of land lying west of the Snake River in Oregon and Idaho. Owyhee dam, 417 feet high and 833 feet long at the crest, was capable of storing behind it more than one million acre-feet of water. A tunnel 15 feet in diameter and 3.5 miles long led from the dam to Tunnel Canyon where North and South canals originated. These big ditches, which had a combined length of 107 miles and a diversion capacity of 1,840 second feet, distributed the water supply to the Mitchell Butte, Succor Creek, and Dead Ox Flat divisions which served the area around Homedale, Idaho, and from Adrian, Oregon, northward to the Malheur River and beyond.

Irrigation activity in Idaho centered in the construction of additional dams, storage facilities, and canals in the Boise and Minidoka projects. The lower Payette River valley was given adequate irrigation through the construction of the Black Canyon diversion dam (1924) and the Deadwood dam and reservoir (1931). The gravity distribution system for the Payette division was finished in 1935. The Minidoka project was greatly strengthened with the construction of American Falls dam (1925-1927) to store 1,700,000 acre-feet of water. This dam brought benefits to a number of irrigation districts and companies lying below it and to the Lake Walcott power plant as well. Not only were existing areas served more adequately, but new farm lands were brought under cultivation with the building of a main canal from Milner dam northward through Jerome county to Gooding and the Big Wood River.[3]

Thanks to these improvements, the cause of irrigation was materially advanced and the transition from quick speculation and rule-of-thumb construction to long-range planning and careful engineering was to a considerable extent achieved. More than 7,500 new farms began operations on irrigated land during the decade following World War I while the dollar investment in reclamation projects by the federal government and local irrigation districts together increased by some 38 million dollars. In Idaho irrigation became more indispensable than ever to agriculture. Crop yields per acre ran two to three times higher with irrigation than without; in 1930 two farms out of three were dependent upon canals and ditches. In Washington the returns from irrigated lands averaged $150.97 per acre in the value of crops raised as compared with a general average of $39.56.

Columbia Basin

Washington's big problem was not to build dams and reservoirs to supply water for existing farms but to open up new agricultural areas and thus provide a means of support for a larger farming population. The area that offered the greatest promise was the Columbia basin.

The Reclamation Bureau hesitated to go into this section mainly because the cost of bringing water to the parched soil was so great as to be prohibitive. Several times prior to World War I engineers and irrigators had considered the feasibility of projects in the vicinity of Priest Rapids and Quincy, only to abandon the idea. The Great Northern Railroad and the Northern Pacific both had been interested.

---

[3] For details on the various federal projects, see Bureau of Reclamation, *Reclamation Project Data*, Washington, D.C., 1948.

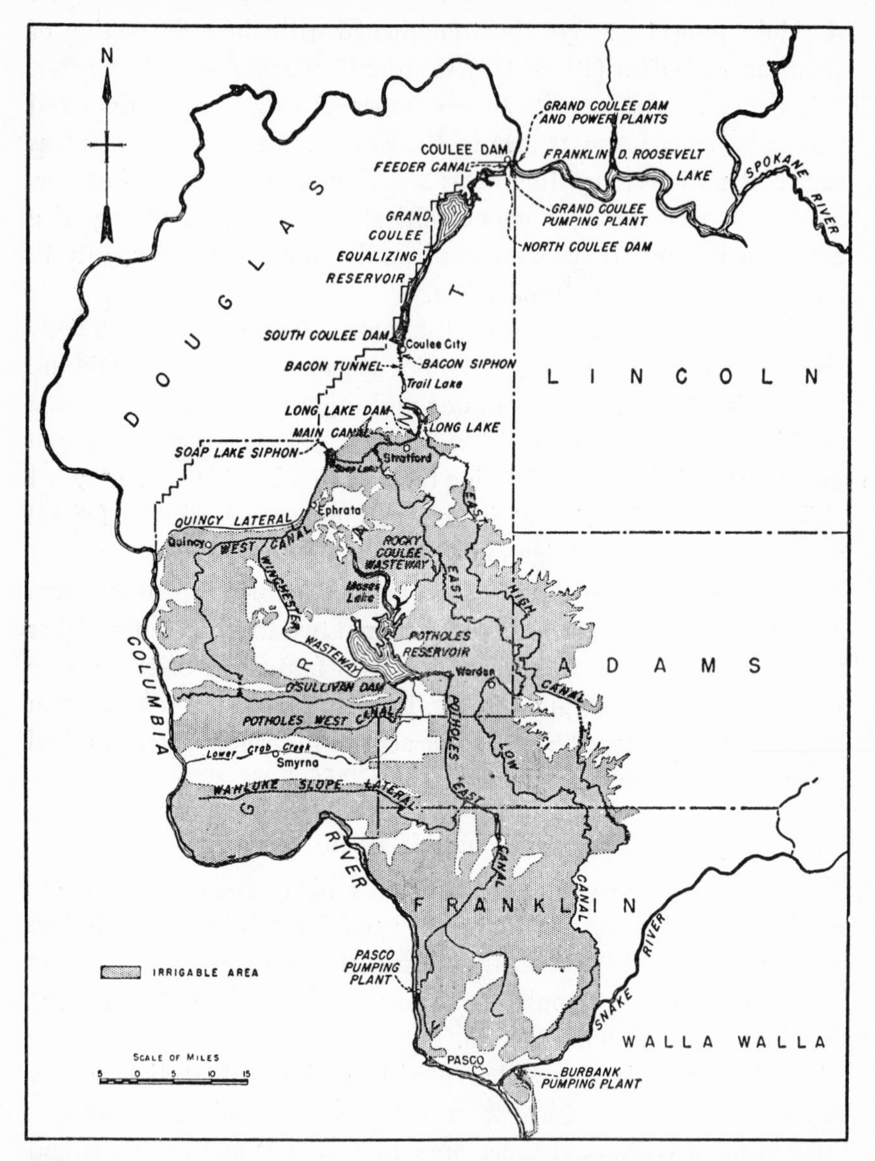

Columbia Basin Reclamation Project. (From U.S. Reclamation Bureau, Reclamation Project Data, 1948.)

The state authorized surveys and the Reclamation Service made investigations and wrote reports, but always came to the same conclusion. Pumping on so large a scale seemed a doubtful expedient while a canal system which drew its water from the Cascade Mountains, perhaps, from a reservoir at Lake Wenatchee, presented major difficulties. All the early proposals were rejected and it was not until 1918 that new ones were devised. They too were so staggering in their requirements that they seemed beyond the realm of possibility.

Two plans were put forward. One called for a gravity system that would have its source of supply not in Lake Wenatchee but in Lake Pend Oreille a hundred miles to the northeast. This would be exclusively an irrigation project, though at certain times of the year, when the water was not required for agricultural purposes, it could be turned into the Spokane River and would be of some benefit to hydroelectric power plants there. Its costliness resulted from the long canals, tunnels, and siphons which would be necessary to carry the water at the proper grade through intervening ridges and across or under the Spokane River. The entire expense would have to be borne by the land, a total estimated at 300,000,000 dollars. This plan originated with E. F. Blaine, horticulturist for the Sunnyside division of the Yakima project. He urged it in a speech to the Spokane chamber of commerce and it had its principal support in Spokane. Governor Ernest Lister thought favorably of it and it was with his encouragement that the state legislature set up the Columbia Basin Commission to investigate and promote it. The private power interests liked it since it would benefit them without raising the troublesome issues of competition with public power installations.

Almost at the same time James O'Sullivan and William Clapp of Ephrata, and Rufus Woods, editor and publisher of the *Wenatchee World*, proposed an alternative plan, the main feature of which was a dam at Grand Coulee. Many centuries ago, perhaps as early as 20,000 B.C. when glaciers covered a great part of the region, ice had blocked the course of the Columbia River which then carved out a new channel and valley floor extending south toward Soap Lake. Later the glaciers withdrew, the ice dam melted and the river resumed its old channel again, eroding it slowly but relentlessly until the river flowed some 600 feet below the rim of basalt which confined it.

O'Sullivan's plan was to raise the level of the river with a dam and pump water over the rim into the upper end of the coulee. It could then be stored and distributed by canal to irrigate more than a million acres of fertile but arid soil.

It was a bold and imaginative scheme. The dam itself must of necessity be a colossal structure, perhaps 400 feet high, and more than 4,000 feet long, "the biggest thing in one piece that man had ever made." O'Sullivan was convinced, however, that the difficulties were primarily those of magnitude, that no problems of engineering were involved which had not already been solved on a smaller scale in the construction of existing dams elsewhere. Colonel Hugh L. Cooper, an engineer of national reputation, expressed a similar opinion when he visited the site. "Gentlemen," he declared, "when you irrigate the Columbia basin, you will do it with water from the Columbia river, by a dam at the head of the Grand Coulee."

The story of Pend Oreille and Grand Coulee during the ensuing decade is a story of controversy and contrary promotion in which the rival groups contended with each other to establish their own propositions and discredit their opponents, played politics for their own purposes, and sought to prevail upon Congress and the federal government to adopt the plan of their choosing. Each side cherished a deep distrust of the other; even now feelings run high in the Quincy basin at the memory of the struggle. The gravity plant won a general approval at the start and more than once the advocates of Grand Coulee all but gave up the contest. It was a strange mixture of good luck and good judgment, of "practical" lobbying and long-range statesmanship, of complexities in financing and technicalities of interstate relations, which in the end brought a decision in favor of the multipurpose plan and the high dam.

One could hardly say that Ephrata and Wenatchee spoke more persuasively than Spokane. Rather it was a matter of federal engineers coming to their own conclusions about the practicability of the dam, and economists demonstrating the advantages of repaying the cost of it with revenues drawn from hydroelectric power as well as from irrigation. It was hard to defend the Pend Oreille plan in the face of Army estimates that the farmer's repayment charges would be 400 dollars per acre as compared with 85 dollars per acre, the figure that would be possible with marketable power available at the Grand Coulee generators. There were the pessimists, of course, who doubted that anyone would buy the power, but since the private power companies were themselves planning for expansion, the general prospects could not be wholly dark. Furthermore the Pend Oreille project required legal clarification of water rights in Idaho to permit the diversion of so large a supply into Washington. Legislation was introduced several times but failed to pass. Without it there could be no real progress in carrying out the gravity plant, and it was finally given up. In 1931 the Army Engineers and the Reclamation Bureau came to agreement on the Grand Coulee project. When the Roosevelt administration set up its recovery program, Grand Coulee dam was included as one of the projects of the P.W.A. Construction began in 1933 and continued for eight years; in 1941 the first generators began to turn. Within three years they were supplying current to several large aluminum plants and to the plutonium plant at Hanford.[4]

The construction of Grand Coulee dam was so large an undertaking that little was done in building the distribution system for irrigation until after the dam itself was finished. Considerable attention was given, however, to studies of the economic aspects of agriculture in that area, to crops and markets, and to the administrative regulations that would promote the settlement of the Columbia basin. Individual farms in the new project were restricted in size to operating units of 40-160 acres, and landowners holding more than the latter amount agreed (as a condition to receiving their water) to sell the excess at prices based on pre-irrigation valuations. Land speculation was thus tightly controlled, and farmers thinking to go into the basin had the assurance that they would be free of the burden of high-cost land which had weighed so heavily upon the settlements developed earlier by private promoters.

World War II delayed for several years more the construction of canals, but soon afterward work on the irrigation system was begun. Two earth-and-rock impounding dams were built in the Grand Coulee to create there an equalizing reservoir 27 miles long supplied with

[4] See George Sundborg, *Hail Columbia: the Thirty-Year Struggle for Grand Coulee Dam,* New York, 1954; Bruce C. Harding, "Water from Pend Oreille: the Gravity Plan for Irrigating the Columbia Basin," *PNQ,* XLV, 1954, 52-60; Richard Neuberger, *Our Promised Land,* New York, 1938, Chaps. 3-4.

water from the pumps at the main dam. From the reservoir a main canal system led southward toward Adrian, dividing just north of the town to form the West Canal 80 miles in length, and the 130-mile low East Canal. The land first to be watered lay in three sections including Adrian, Soap Lake, and Ephrata, and areas to the south and southwest. The plan called for the irrigation of approximately 160,000 acres during the decade of the 1950's. The system would eventually include other canals and a reservoir in the potholes district, and an East High Canal which together would serve 1,029,000 acres lying in the central plain.[5]

Idaho and Oregon

While the Columbia basin project was perhaps the most spectacular reclamation venture to be carried forward during the 20 years 1935-1955, it was but a part of a far larger program of land improvement which included many other undertakings large and small. In Idaho the main emphasis was upon additional storage dams and reservoirs, strategically placed on the upper waters of streams that served existing projects. More than a million acre-feet of reservoir capacity was provided during the 1940's through the construction of the Anderson Ranch dam and reservoir on the south fork of the Boise River, and the Cascade dam on the north fork of the Payette River. In 1939 the Upper Snake storage project was launched which included dams and reservoirs at Jackson Lake and Grassy Lake in Northwestern Wyoming, and Island Park north of Ashton, Idaho. The Island Park dam was an immense rock-faced earth fill 91 feet high and 9,448 feet long at the crest. These various improvements stored nearly another million acre-feet. They were situated above the main reservoirs and dams serving the Snake Valley and did much to answer the complaints of water shortage by the farmers in that area.

The Wickiup dam and reservoir on the Deschutes River south of Bend, Oregon, was a somewhat similar development, though its benefits were not so general. The dam itself was even larger than the

[5] U.S. Reclamation Bureau, *Columbia Basin Project; Soil and Economic Conditions*, 1928; also published by the same agency, *Grand Coulee Dam and the Columbia Basin Project*, 1938, *Columbia Basin Land Use Problems and Policies*, 1940, and *Comprehensive Plan for the Development of the Columbia Basin*, 1948.

Island Park dam; the distribution system served 50,000 acres in the vicinity of Madras and Culver.

In Oregon, however, the emphasis was not so much on the large projects as the small ones. In the southwestern part of the state, and even in the Willamette Valley, there were many farming districts where the annual rainfall was too high for the climate to be called arid, but where it was nevertheless excessively dry during the growing season. In such places supplementary irrigation spelled the difference between low crop yields and abundant ones. The studies of planning and land development therefore made much of proposals to build numerous small dams. Five such dams, for example, costing $200,000 to build, might store 15,750 acre-feet of water. The farms that were served could be expected to produce 15,700 tons of alfalfa at eight to ten dollars per ton. The value of crops would more than exceed the cost of the dams in two years time.

Considerations of this nature gave Oregon a particular interest in the legislation passed by Congress in 1937 which authorized the expenditure of federal money for small reservoirs, the costs to be repaid by the local water users without interest over a 40-year period. Another law, the Water Facilities Act, permitted the construction of federal-financed small dams and pumping installations on a somewhat similar basis. Such a program was tailored to the needs of the Pacific Northwest. It supplemented the larger projects and helped the main agricultural sections as well as the newly developed arid areas. By 1951 the Willamette Valley plain, which had only 12,000 acres irrigated in 1930, reported 100,000 acres served with supplemental water.[6]

[6] Richard M. Highsmith, "Irrigation in the Willamette Valley," GR, XLVI, 1956, 98-110; Oregon State Planning Board, *Land Development in Oregon Through Flood Control, Drainage and Irrigation*, Works Progress Administration, July, 1938. See also Idaho State Planning Board, *Water Resources of Idaho*, 1937; and Washington State Planning Council, *Reclamation, a Sound National Policy*, 1936.

33

The Early Conservation Movement

While loggers, lumbermen, and speculators were concerning themselves with the exploitative aspects of forest resources, the conservationists felt a growing apprehension. The rate of cutting was prodigious and could be expected to increase yet more. To keep the mills going in Portland alone 80 acres of forest had to be cut every 24 hours. Estimates of remaining standing timber for the country as a whole did not exceed 2,500 billion board feet, of which 100 billions were cut or destroyed annually. Since the current rate of growth of new trees did not exceed 40 billion feet, it seemed more than likely that the supply would be exhausted to meet the needs of a single generation. Practically no reforestation was being attempted on private lands, yet these areas contained two-thirds of the trees. The national forests, extensive though they were, could not meet this kind of demand for more than four or five years. Such calculations led Gifford Pinchot to predictions of timber famine as something very real and ominous. Within a few decades, if the forests were exhausted the lumber industry, fourth greatest in the country, would disappear. The building trades would be prostrated. Agriculture and commerce would soon be blighted. Waterpower would dry up. "In short, when the forests fail, every man, woman and child in the United States will feel the pinch." As for the Far Northwest, who could doubt but that the cycle would follow the experience of Maine, Michigan, and Minnesota where exhaustion of resources had been a matter of a few decades at most.[1]

---

[1] Roland Phillips, "Vanishing Forests of America," *Harper's Weekly*, LII, March 28, 1908, 10-12; Royal S. Kellogg, *Drain Upon the Forests*, U.S.D.A., Forest Circular 129, 1907; Gifford Pinchot, *Fight for Conservation*, New York, 1910, and "Uncle Sam's Woodlot," *Independent*, LXIV, June 18, 1908, 1374.

Western Views on Conservation

These gloomy prophecies were called in question, however, in the region itself. There the arithmetic looked different, for the timber stands reached a figure of 1,500 billion board feet and the annual cut was little more than five billion. The difficulties seemed to lie in stimulating enterprise and expanding the lumber trade, and local sentiment opposed the forest reserves as measures that had the effect of "locking up" the resources of the region and putting economic enterprise in a strait jacket.

The governor of Washington declared that Pinchot had done more to retard the growth and development of the Northwest than any other man. The editor of the Seattle *Post-Intelligencer* voiced his protest with equal vehemence:

> The recent abuses of power have grown to the point that there will be bitter revolt against the entire policy of forest reserves and an appeal to Congress to repeal all of the laws on the subject. The growth of such a great state as Washington can no longer be hampered, and its development hampered, to please a few dilettante experimentalists, however well intentioned and patriotic in purpose they may be. Their idea that the greater part of this state must be kept in primeval wilderness for the benefit of wealthy lumbermen and city sportsmen does not appeal to the people of Washington, who are inviting immigrants to build up the country.

To be sure, the movement to recapture the land grant made to the Oregon and California Railroad had strong support in the Far West, but not entirely from motives of restraint. These lands were already locked up in the sense that they were held by a giant monopoly, the Southern Pacific Company, which had few friends in the West. Recapture was called for not to build larger reserves but to return the lands to the General Land Office where they could be disposed of cheaply through the Homestead Act and other land laws to a host of small local speculators. If, when the recapture law was passed in 1912, the Land Office reclassified the lands, released only the tracts suitable for genuine homesteading and held those valuable for their timber, it was a policy quite at variance with the wishes of the entrepreneur whether he spoke for a middle western lumber company or was himself a western speculator.

Yet there were conservationists in the West as well as in the East, and the prevailing opinion for or against the forest reserves was determined by a balance of the interests of local groups that was often quite complex. Townspeople felt a vital concern for the protection of their watersheds and supported the forest reserves that would give them such benefits. Irrigators and farmers in the Blue Mountain section challenged the views of the lumbermen for the same reason. Naturalists and recreation groups had their representatives who often spoke out very persuasively. A few newspaper editors like Harvey Scott of the Portland *Oregonian* were known for their independence and public spirit, or spoke for conservation, as W. H. Cowles did in the Spokane *Spokesman-Review*, out of a personal regard for Gifford Pinchot. Cattle and sheep men at times had their reasons for urging the creation of reserves. Educators in western colleges were friendly to them. A number of the field men in the United States Forest Service did much to win public opinion to measures of conservation. Conservation then was not something imposed upon the Northwest from the outside; it was a program which, though it encountered the opposition of special interests, had a broad popular support not only in the East but in the West itself.[2]

The Role of State Government

Some of the safeguards against too rapid an exploitation of forest lands were measures adopted by the states of the region. True, they were likely to reflect the mistakes and the poor statesmanship of earlier years. Oregon lost the greater part of its public domain through circumstances that bordered on the scandalous before the legislature passed a protective law in 1890. Even then the experience of the state was so unhappy that those who would save the remaining timberlands relied mainly on the federal rather than the state authority. In Washington timber thievery had been so extensive that one of President Grant's federal investigators estimated it to be in the neighborhood of 40,000,000 dollars. It was at federal instance, therefore, that the state constitution of 1889 contained a

---

[2] Seattle *Post Intelligencer*, March 7, 1907; David M. Ellis, "Oregon and California Land Grant, 1866-1945," *PNQ*, XXXIX, 1948, 253-283; Roy Robbins, *Our Landed Heritage*, Princeton, 1942, 343-363; Lawrence Rakestraw, "Uncle Sam's Forest Reserves," *PNQ*, XLIV, 1953, 145-151; E. O. Siecke, "Development of Oregon's Forest Policy," *Commonwealth Review*, I, 1916, 189-199.

clause that prohibited the sale of state lands for less than ten dollars per acre, a provision that gave at least a meager protection.

When it came to setting up administrative agencies to manage the state lands and sales therefrom, differences of opinion developed. There was something to be said for the proposal that a single agency, probably the state land commissioner, should be given full authority and should also be held responsible for these lands. Usually, however, other agencies and institutions likewise had an interest in them, and shared the responsibility for their administration and sale. State universities considered the land grants made for their support to be subject to their own control. The administration of the school lands involved superintendents of public instruction in questions of sale and price. Often these educational officers, who wished to realize the full returns from their endowment, were more public-spirited and more exacting in their negotiations with purchasers than the land commissioner himself.

They were not, however, concerned primarily with timber as such. For some years none of the states in the Northwest had a state forester, nor did any of them have a code of law which spelled out even the outline of a long-range forest policy. Such legislation as was passed had to do rather with the taxation of private timber lands and with certain requirements and immunities directed toward the lumber companies. Only through the institutions of higher learning did the states make any systematic study of the problems of lumbering and forestry. Washington launched its School of Forestry in 1907 at the University; Oregon set up a similar one at the State College at Corvallis. These schools were purely educational and research agencies which had no powers of regulation. They devoted themselves primarily to the training of professional foresters who were qualified either for private or public positions. Nevertheless they did concern themselves with problems of conservation as well, and members of their faculties, such as B. P. Kirkland at the University of Washington, contributed not a little to the analysis of administrative and economic problems.

Progress of Fire Protection Programs

Perhaps the point at which the states participated most directly in conservation was in the development of fire protection. Fire was a terrible thing in the pine and fir country. It scorched and ravaged the land from the days of the earliest settlements, yet no measures of prevention were devised for many years. Charles E. Laughton, one of Washington's first lieutenant governors, termed fire "the most insidious enemy we have to contend with," a weapon of desolation that mowed down mighty trees like grass before the scythe and left utter destruction in its trail. During the dry summer months the forest jungle became (in Stewart Holbrook's phrase) the biggest box of tinder on earth. Whatever the source of the spark, whether from lightning, a careless logger's match, or a locomotive's smokestack, the result was a holocaust that produced scenes of tragedy and often death.

The year 1902 was one long to be remembered in the Lewis County country south of Puget Sound. It was the year of the Yacolt Burn, a tremendous series of fires which wiped out a score of villages, rendered farmers and stump ranchers destitute, and left sawmills and shingle mills little more than blackened ashes. Seven hundred thousand acres of blazing timber formed a mighty torch that was visible from Eugene to Bellingham. That year fire losses in Oregon and Washington were estimated at 12,767,100 dollars.

Such catastrophe demanded action and within a few years the states established a system of fire wardens and the private lumber companies organized their own fire-fighting crews as well. In 1908 a number of the larger timber owners formed the Washington Forest Fire Association, assessed themselves a penny an acre and put some 80 men in the field through the dry season. As the result of negotiations the Association came to a voluntary agreement with the state fire warden which brought its benefits to both by insuring the best possible use of the men who were available.

The beginnings of a partnership came naturally, for the advantages of common action were clear to all, and the fire-fighting program was free from much of the controversy that marked the discussion of other aspects of conservation. Furthermore the pattern of land ownership, which resembled a great checkerboard with state lands interlaced in alternate sections with others that were privately held, made it obvious that only a coöperative effort could be efficient.

During the next several years the fire-fighting organizations were built up into much stronger forces. Washington's state expenditure was increased nearly fourfold between 1907 and 1911; in the latter year the fire warden had a biennial appropriation of 75,000 dollars at his disposal. Intensive educational work was done through the press and women's clubs and directly with loggers, lumbermen, and railroads. Working relationships between the state and the Washington Forest Fire Association were further improved. Federal funds too were allocated to the states under the Weeks Act of 1911. The sums were small at first, 10,000 dollars each to Washington and Oregon, and 10,500 dollars to Idaho and Montana. They were made available on a matching basis in the belief that for every federal dollar allocated, three to five dollars would be spent from state or private funds, an estimate which in the Far West was probably very conservative. In 1917 the United States Forest Service experts estimated that the costs of fire protection ranged from 1/10 of a cent to 1/3 of a cent per thousand board feet.

At the same time a beginning was made, though a small one, in state reforestation by sowing seed and planting areas that had been cut over. Idaho made the best showing, with more than 10,000 acres reforested in 1913. Oregon rehabilitated better than 8,000 acres; Washington only a third of that. The record was modest enough, but it was at least a token recognition of the task to be done.[3]

The Role of the Federal Government

The big struggle to save the Northwest forests was waged over the conservation program of the federal government. State forest lands were never more than a small fraction of the regional total (15.6 billion feet out of a total of 1,131.5 billion feet in the region). State forestry agencies were never more than a frail reed to lean upon. In the contest to determine what timberlands should be set aside, and to establish the standards of good forest practice and sustained yield, Uncle Sam himself took the chief initiative for a number of years. The national forests and the national parks were the reserves set up on such a scale that they could be a

[3] Stewart Holbrook, *Burning an Empire*, New York, 1943, Chap. 10; see also the reports of the Washington State Forester and Fire Warden, 1907-1914; the reports of the Chief Forester, U.S. Forest Service, 1903-1913, and the reports of the Washington Forest Fire Association.

really important element in protecting the timber supply and perpetuating the forest industries. The United States Forest Service, of all the agencies in the field, public and private, was the only one strong enough to be a formative element in the development of an enlightened forest policy.

This is not to say that the public lands were enough in themselves to insure a supply of lumber or that the private companies did not participate from the beginning, one way or another, in the establishment of practices adapted to long-term use. The larger companies, possessed of lands far beyond the needs of current operations, shared significantly in the task of managing the nation's timber resources. Confronted by problems of overproduction, they often cut more sparingly than did their weaker competitors. Bearing a heavy burden of taxation and financial indebtedness, their experience (if not their proposals of tax exemption) contributed much to the economist's thinking about tax reform and his analysis of the proper division of costs as between the private industry and the public. If effective measures were to be adopted, the industry as well as the public forester must accept them.

It remained true, however, that the conservation movement channeled mainly through the government agencies for some time. The effort to preserve the source of supply found expression in the establishment of forest reserves by the federal government from its own public domain. The formulation of a forest policy, which could be practiced on both public and private lands, was a task carried out by a special federal agency, the United States Forest Service.

Establishing the Forest Reserves

The Forest Service did not at first have control of the federal reserves. Originally established in the Department of Agriculture, it was a technical and educational rather than an administrative agency. The reserves themselves were handled by the Department of the Interior. Some of them were Indian reservations. A few, like Yellowstone and Mount Rainier, were National Parks. Still others were designated specifically as forest reserves, but they were administered by the General Land Office which, in 1901, had its own newly established Forestry Division. Not until 1907 were the forest reserves placed under the direct administration of the Forest Service, to be handled as National Forests.

Because of its very limited powers and its concern with a problem that required the coöperation of the private timberland owner for its solution, the Forest Service was not much given to cracking the whip. President Theodore Roosevelt delivered a characteristic tirade against the men who "skin the country and go somewhere else . . . whose idea of developing the country is to cut every stick of timber off of it, and then leave a barren desert for the home maker who comes in after him. That man is a curse and not a blessing to the country." But Gifford Pinchot, chief forester, appealed to the better judgment of the lumberman without indicting him. The great bulk of the forests were and would remain in private hands. Forestry would succeed only as the private landowners, large and small, were persuaded of its advantages. "The forests of the private owners," he insisted, "will have to be set in order if the overwhelming calamity of timber famine is to be kept from this nation." Later Pinchot would do some fulminating of his own. This earlier mood was that of the crusader whose tremendous energy and enthusiasm were rooted in a conviction that the lumberman and the forester had much in common. Only preach, practice, and demonstrate the practical values of good forestry and the lumber industry would surely be won over to it.

Much of the western opposition to Pinchot and the Forest Service was opposition to the reserves. When Congress placed the reserves under the Forest Service and when President Roosevelt greatly enlarged them in a series of sweeping proclamations just before his powers to do so expired in 1907, they created a landed empire of 150,000,000 acres over which Gifford Pinchot was to rule. The larger part of it lay in the states of the Far West: 65,000,000 acres in Oregon and Washington, Idaho and Montana. Seventy-one billion feet of timber were included in the national reserves in Idaho, while only 50.1 billion feet remained in private hands. Of Oregon's 545.8 billion feet of standing timber, nearly one-fourth was in National Forests; of Washington's 391 billion feet, slightly over one-fifth. Such facts as these put the Forest Service in a different perspective in the Pacific Northwest than elsewhere, and they help to account for the vitriolic protests that came from that part of the country. Uncle Sam was viewed as a powerful absentee landlord, whose benevolence was by no means proved and might well be doubted. Just as the lumber industry was becoming interested in the western forests, they were to be made inaccessible by federal mandate. The threat was real enough whatever Pinchot might say. The legislature in the State of Washington expressed itself in outspoken opposition in a memorial to Congress. Now Senator Charles Fulton of Oregon introduced a rider on the appropriation bill (1907) which provided that "Hereafter no forest reserve shall be created, nor shall any addition be made to one heretofore created, within the limits of the States of Oregon, Washington, Idaho, Montana, Colorado or Wyoming except by act of Congress."[4]

Forest Service Policies and Practice

The Forest Service record during the ensuing years was not one to substantiate such alarm. In the policies that were formulated and the regulations that were put into force high purpose was tempered with a frank recognition of the realities of the local as well as the national situation. Timber resources were not to be locked up. They were to be used according to need and cut according to plan. No compromise was made with the speculator, but whenever there was a real demand for lumber, stumpage was offered for sale at fair minimum prices. The quantity and variety sold depended upon the market and the situation in the private forests. Little Douglas fir was sold, since plenty of private stumpage was available. On the other hand, Idaho white pine was in considerable demand, and to a lesser extent western red cedar and yellow pine from Eastern Oregon and Washington. In 1910 574,000,000 feet of stumpage was sold from the National Forests of the Pacific Northwest. Of this amount 379,000,000 feet were cut, which represented perhaps 7 percent of the total for that year. The figure was subsequently increased somewhat and in 1913 several large contracts were signed with private purchasers which allowed them to do the

[4] John Ise, *United States Forest Policy*, New Haven, 1920; Herbert A. Smith, "Early Forestry Movement in the United States," *Agricultural History*, XII, 1938, 326-346; Andrew D. Rodgers III, *Bernhard Eduard Fernow: A Story of North American Forestry*, Princeton, 1951; *Forest Preservation and National Prosperity*, U.S. Forest Service, Circular 35, 1905; Darrell Smith, *Forest Service, Its History, Organization and Activities*, Brookings Institute, 1930; Jenks Cameron, *Development of Governmental Forest Control in the United States*, Baltimore, 1928.

cutting over a period of 22 years and to pay prices that were adjusted every five years to meet market conditions.

In determining the conditions under which the trees were to be cut on the national reserves the Forest Service followed a practical and flexible approach to reforestation, which was demonstrated on its own lands and which was recommended for adoption by the private operators as well. The chief point of it was that strip cutting might under some circumstances be advantageous. Douglas fir usually grew in stands of uniform size, and seedlings prospered best in the open rather than in the shade of other trees. These facts argued for a complete rather than a partial cut, provided a method of natural reseeding could be discovered. This problem was met by leaving seed trees in each cutover tract, and by cutting tracts of limited size so placed that additional reseeding would be accomplished through windfalls from trees left standing around them. Meanwhile nurseries were established in National Forests at Pocatello and Helena, the Bitterroots and Snoqualmie. Stocks of seedlings were built up until, as early as 1910, the annual capacity of the nurseries reached 10,000,000 plants.

The program of the Forest Service was publicized and carried to the people in many pamphlets and circulars and in many articles in the popular magazines. As research and experimentation went on, the results and recommendations were made generally available, and the foresters and rangers became a corps of educators who did much to influence public opinion in the areas to which they were assigned. These men identified themselves with the region in which they lived, and the Forest Service policy of decentralizing the administration of the reserves served to relieve in some measure the local resentment against the absentee.

Partnership Between Government and Business

By 1917, then, the ramifications of the lumber industry and of the problem of reforestation had been well explored. A full meeting of minds as between the foresters and the lumbermen had by no means been reached. Only a few private operators did more than pay lip service to the principles of conservation. Most of them approved of it to the extent that it meant fire protection and such curtailment of logging as might serve to support good prices. Some were reassured when they discovered that national forests relieved them of the necessity of carrying the burden of a future timber supply while at the same time providing them with stumpage to meet current needs. Still others were die-hards of the old school that Roosevelt had condemned, who cut their stumpage when and where they liked, complained bitterly about their taxes, and got rid of their lands for what they could get when the logging crews had finished with them.

And yet the basis of a better understanding was becoming clear. Much of what the lumbermen had said in protest against conservation at their expense was being acknowledged. Professor Fred R. Fairchild's proposals that timberland taxes be changed from regular annual levies to a yield basis were being given currency. Many points in the economic position of the industry were emphasized in William B. Greeley's study of it, prepared and published by the Forest Service in 1917. Professor Burt Kirkland's recommendations for a sustained yield program were stated in terms basically sympathetic to the industry. Edward T. Allen's manual, which urged the adoption of long-range logging practices, was published in 1911 under the title *Practical Forestry in the Pacific Northwest.* Within the industry business was business, but the long view might be good business too. Greeley was hopeful, on the whole, as he proposed that government and business coöperate in planning for the future. The national forests were essential to his program. They should serve, he said, "as a governor of the industrial machine which manufactures and distributes forest products by maintaining not only competitive but stable conditions in the lumber trade." Public interest demanded that both monopoly and wasteful overproduction be avoided. Conservation would not stifle enterprise but sustain it. The partnership of government and business was by no means cemented, but it was a practical goal toward which both should progress.[5]

[5] Fred R. Fairchild, "Present State of Forest Tax Legislation," *American Forests,* XVIII, 1912, 653-655; Frank Lamb, "Problems of Conserving Forest Resources of the Pacific Coast States," *Pacific Lumber Trade Journal,* XIV, June, 1908, 20, 22, 25-26; Burt P. Kirkland, "Continuous Forest Production of Privately Owned Timberlands as the Solution of the Economic Difficulties of the Lumber Industry," *Journal of Forestry,* XV, 1917, 15-64; William B. Greeley, *Some Public and Economic Aspects of the Lumber Business,* Washington, D.C., 1917, and *Forests and Men,* New York, 1951.

The Wheat Fleet in Portland Harbor. (Courtesy, Oregon Historical Society.)

River Steamers Entering Cascade Locks, Columbia River.

The Canyon City Stage, Precursor of the Freeway. (Courtesy, Oregon Historical Society.)

Fleet of Logging Locomotives, Grays Harbor. (Courtesy, University of Washington Library.)

Boeing B-52 in Flight Near Mt. Adams. (Courtesy, Boeing Airplane Company.)

Columbia River Steamers Tied Up to the Bank. (Courtesy, Oregon Historical Society.)

Skiing Comes Next to Flying: a Snow-Covered Slope in the Cascade Mountains. (Courtesy, University of Washington Tyee.)

34

Advances in Forestry

The conservation movement made comparatively little headway in the field of timber resources during the years of rapid expansion that followed World War I. This was the time, to be sure, when Gifford Pinchot urged the dangers of timber famine even more vehemently than before. Federal reports documented the fact of depletion with impressive statistics, and numerous magazine articles kept the issue before the public. The nation as a whole, it appeared, was using up its trees four times as fast as they were growing. In the Pacific Northwest the privately owned forests were being devastated at an alarming rate while almost nothing in the way of systematic reforestation was being attempted.

Yet the lumber industry had little incentive to curtail production so long as every effort was devoted to enlarging markets and increasing shipments by land and sea. Furthermore, the margin of profit was a narrow and uncertain one. High transportation costs, burdensome taxes and interest charges, and the risk of large losses by fire deterred all but a few companies from spending anything to provide forests for the future. Fred Ames of the Forest Service admitted that conservation would appeal to the lumbermen only when it would pay. For several years the pressure to cut heavily was so great that even the national foresters with their slogan, "Use wood and conserve the forests," were misquoted. William B. Greeley, chief forester, was forced to take to the columns of the *West Coast Lumberman* to explain that he did not mean there was "plenty of wood for all future needs." Despite his sympathy for the private companies, the danger of depletion was very real, and he urged the industry to support the Forest Service program and to take a greater responsibility for the reforesting of their own lands.

While the progress in private forestry was very slow, these years of the 1920's were nevertheless important, for the program of coöperation between government agencies and the lumber industry was more fully outlined in federal and state legislation, and the idea of mutual interest and common responsibility was increasingly recognized as a guiding point of policy.

The decision to adopt measures of joint endeavor instead of relying upon governmental control was argued at some length in Congress. Conservationists of the Pinchot school urged that strict regulations be imposed by federal law to limit the cutting of timber on private lands as well as in national forests. There was likewise a disposition to undertake the rehabilitation of cutover lands by purchasing them and making them into government reserves. These proposals showed a highly critical attitude toward the lumber industry, and a general conviction that the answer to the problem of depletion must be found in the direct exercise of federal authority.

These views did not prevail, however, partly because the postwar period of political conservatism was unfavorable, and partly because prominent leaders, including lumbermen like George Long, and foresters like Greeley and Ames recommended a different course. If the lumber industry was to have a larger part in the conservation movement, federal policy should give encouragement to such activity. Certain very practical inducements were necessary. Long made the plea for the industry. "Help the lumbermen with forest fires and forest taxes," he counseled, "and they will find a way to regrow the timber."[1]

Program of Coöperation

In the Clarke-McNary Act, adopted in 1924, Congress said nothing about federal regulation, but wrote the principle of coöperation into every paragraph. The Secretary of Agriculture was authorized to coöperate with state officials or other suitable agencies to recommend systems of fire protection for "the continuous production of timber" on lands that were suitable for it.

[1] *Timber Depletion, Lumber Prices and . . . Concentration of Ownership,* U.S. Forest Service, 1920; Gifford Pinchot, "Economic Significance of Forestry," *North American Review,* CCXIII, February, 1921, 157-167; Jenks Cameron, *Governmental Forest Control,* 388-426; William B. Greeley, *Forests and Men,* 76-114; *West Coast Lumberman,* LIII, January 1, 1928, 32; George P. Ahern, *Deforested America,* Washington, D.C., 1928. An early investigation of the possibilities of reforestation by the larger companies operating in the Grays Harbor area is reported in *West Coast Lumberman,* XLVIII, September 1, 1925, 25.

He was to coöperate likewise with the states to provide tree seeds and plants and to give aid in the better management of woodlots. Other provisions looked toward the purchase of cutover lands and the acquisition of other forest lands by mutual agreement with the owner "to insure future timber supplies."

The next few years witnessed a noteworthy improvement in fire protection and taxation, and in experimental work in forestry. Federal appropriations for fire fighting were considerably increased, and were matched by larger sums provided by the states and by the industry as well. Forest experiment stations were set up and research programs were launched, an approach to the problem which was authorized and supported under the terms of the McSweeney-McNary Act of 1928, again in coöperation with public agencies and institutions and with private organizations. Forest tax laws were made the subject of a more thorough study by Professor Fred R. Fairchild of Yale University, who visited a number of western and southern states and based his recommendations on a close knowledge of the economic problems of the industry. Soon afterward the question of tax revision was brought before the state legislatures both in Washington and Oregon, and new laws were adopted that incorporated the essential features of Fairchild's report. By the provisions of these acts forest lands were made subject to a low annual assessment combined with a yield tax amounting to 12½ percent of the value of such timber as was cut from them. By levying the yield tax only as the lands brought returns, landowners were encouraged to undertake long-term plans of conservation and reforestation. Washington and Oregon also passed forest codes which, without limiting the cut, did require slashing to be burned and the cutover lands to be left in better condition for reseeding. The Knutson-Vandenberg Act adopted by Congress in 1930, expanded the tree-planting program in the national forests and provided that purchasers of timber from these reserves might be required to pay part of the cost of clearing and planting.[2]

[2] For the Clarke-McNary Act, see 43 Statutes at Large, 653; McSweeney-McNary Act, 45 Statutes at Large, 699; Knutson-Vandenberg Act, 46 Statutes at Large, 527. See also J. V. Hofman, *Natural Regeneration of Douglas Fir*, U.S.D.A., Department Bulletin 1200, April, 1924; Fred R. Fairchild, *Forest Taxation in the United States*, U.S.D.A., Misc. Pub. 218, 1935; General Laws of Oregon, 1929, Chap. 138; Laws of Washington, 1931, Chap. 40. Washington's Governor Roland Hartley took a personal interest in the problem of state reforestation.

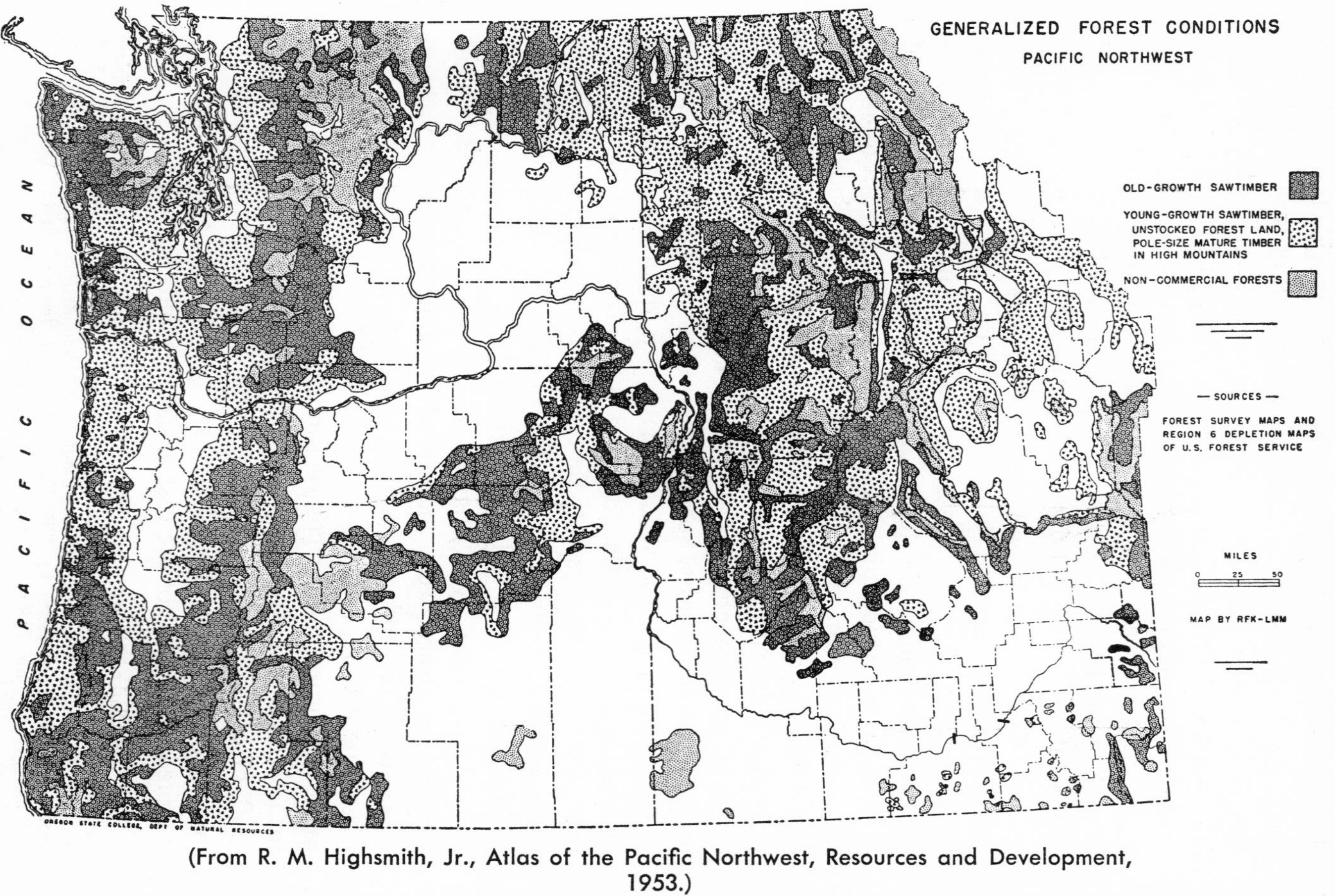

(From R. M. Highsmith, Jr., Atlas of the Pacific Northwest, Resources and Development, 1953.)

All these measures had to do mainly with protection and replacement of the forests and avoided the more controversial problem of determining a long-range balance between lumber production and the rate of forest growth. When it came to putting limits on the amount of lumber to be put on the market, it was, oddly enough, the industry that took the initiative rather than the government.

Sustained Yield

The years of expansion (1923-1927) passed all too quickly and the lumbermen were soon beset again with falling prices and overproduction. The mill men, as before, turned to measures of control which would alleviate the evils of excessive competition. At this point they became distrustful of the Forest Service not because timber was being locked up but because too much of it was available to be sold. When David Mason, a consulting forester in Portland, came forward in 1927 with proposals for a sustained yield program, the purpose of it was to take off the market a considerable quantity of timber in the national forests and on other federal lands which, if sold at auction according to the prevailing practice, threatened to depress prices even more.

Mason's plan called for the establishment of sustained yield units that would include large tracts of timberland some of which would be privately owned while the remainder would be in forest reserves. For such units schedules would be established on a sustained yield basis, which would be calculated over a period of 40 years or more, the time that it was anticipated the existing timber would last at current rates of production. Such a plan, he argued, would not require any curtailment of cutting below the current level, but it would commit the reserves, especially the public reserves, to be held off the market until some time safely in the future when they could be drawn upon without upsetting timber values.

Mason preached the doctrine of sustained yield early and late and for a time filled his diaries with references to many conferences with lumbermen and with government officials during which he urged the advantages of "sustained yield." As he outlined it, the program would not only obligate the National Forest Service to keep timber off the market during the current slump in the lumber trade, but it would include commitments to make the timber available later on long-term contracts with individual lumber companies. Thus the supply would be stabilized according to the needs of the industry, and there would be very real incentives in terms of self-interest that would lead the stronger companies to endorse the plan.[3]

Such a program was a two-way street. Greeley later recalled his own response on one occasion when a lumberman applied for a long-term contract to cut trees from the national forests. The concession was worth a price and Greeley exacted it. When the contract was approved it was on the condition that the applicant adopt the same forest practices for his own private timberlands that were enforced in the national forests. Generally speaking the Forest Service looked somewhat skeptically on contracts and sustained yield arrangements that gave preferential treatment to individual large companies to the exclusion of other operators in the area. On the other hand, any plan that promised to effect better conditions on large acreages of private timberlands deserved careful study. The balance of advantages to government and industry determined the character of the negotiations between them during the next two decades.

The national lumber code, drawn up in 1934 during the short life of the N.R.A. embodied much the same kind of bargain. The industry wanted price increases and was willing to accept wage and hour commitments along with them. To secure government approval of the terms they considered desirable, industry representatives agreed to the inclusion of Article X which pledged the operating companies to put into effect "practicable measures" of good forestry to give protection against fire, prevent damage to young trees, and provide for restocking cutover areas. Coöperation was declared to be reciprocal, and carried its obligations for governmental agencies as well as for the industry itself. When the N.R.A. was held to be unconstitutional and the code lost its legal authority, the industry continued the main provisions in force voluntarily as an undertaking in industrial self-government which promised both immediate and long-range benefits.

The revested land grant of the Oregon and California Railroad presented special problems of administration in which the lumber

[3] David T. Mason, "Sustained Yield as a Remedy for Overproduction," *West Coast Lumberman,* LIII, October 1, 1927, 35; also *Forests for the Future: the Story of Sustained Yield as Told in the Diaries and Papers of David T. Mason, 1907-1950,* ed. Rodney C. Loehr, Minnesota Historical Society, 1952.

industry took a direct interest. When the federal government recaptured this grant from the Southern Pacific Company in 1917, Congress provided for the management of it by the Department of the Interior under conditions stipulated in a special law passed for that purpose. It was a large tract of more than 3,000,000 acres which included some of the best timberlands in Oregon. The program adopted by the National Forest Service did not apply to it, and the governing legislation required the Department of the Interior to sell such timber from it as might be applied for at current market prices. Mason saw even more of a threat to prices from this quarter than from the national forests. He therefore took an active part in promoting legislation (1937) which modified the administration of the grant and applied to the Oregon and California grant the principles of sustained yield "for the purpose of providing a permanent source of timber supply, protecting watersheds, regulating stream flow, and contributing to the economic stability of local communities and industries, and providing recreational facilities."

Under the terms of this legislation the annual timber cut from the Oregon and California tract was limited to 500,000,000 board feet or so much of that amount as could be sold at reasonable prices on a normal market. The Secretary of the Interior was authorized to establish sustained yield units, recognizing the need to provide a permanent source of raw materials for the support of dependent communities, and giving "due consideration" to lumbering operations that were already established. Timber sales from a forest unit were to be limited to its productive capacity, and the same principle was to be applied to the grant as a whole as soon as the annual rate of growth could be determined. Coöperative agreements could be negotiated with federal or state agencies and with private forest owners and operating companies to put the program into effect on lands which were not administered directly by the Department of the Interior. Thus the main features of Mason's plan were written into law in comprehensive fashion for the Oregon area.

In connection with some of the sustained yield hearings held in Oregon, certain facts appeared which threw still further light on the interest that particular towns and localities might have in the program. At Bend, for example, it was pointed out that if the lumber companies operating there were left wholly to their own devices they might very well cut and get out, leaving the town in a few years time deserted and without means of support. If, on the other hand, a strong company was assured of a source of supply from public land forests through a long-term sustained yield contract, it could stabilize its operations, add to its investment in mill facilities, and adopt a reforestation program that would be a support for the town perhaps indefinitely.

Here the plan presented something of a dilemma. Was the company the servant of the town or master and patron of it? Instances of desertion and blight could certainly be cited. Other instances could be mentioned too, where a lumber company had shown a sense of responsibility for the welfare of the community in which it was located. Probably it was not healthy for a town to be dependent upon a single enterprise for its livelihood. If, however, such a situation was inescapable, was it advisable perhaps to recognize and make the best of it? The questions were not easy and were not to be answered in terms of any simple formula. Government and business had certain interests in common, but they had points of difference too. The partnership between them was partly a matter of statesmanship on both sides; partly it was a matter of handling each local situation on its own merits.

In 1944 Congress extended the sustained yield plan from Oregon to other states by enacting further general legislation. Under individual agreements with private owners, sustained yield units could be set up which would include both public and private lands, to provide a coördinated management and a single schedule for harvesting and reforesting all the lands in the tract. In other situations where particular communities were dependent upon their wood-processing industries, sustained yield units could be established wholly from federal timberlands which would be harvested without competitive bidding for the benefit of communities specified in the plan. Here the cut was not necessarily to be pledged to a single company, though the operators who supplied the local industries would be preferred. Timber properties administered by state or local agencies could be included in either type of unit through special agreement.[4]

---

[4] N.R.A. *Code of Fair Competition for the Lumber and Timber Products Industries,* August 19, 1933, Washington, D.C., 1935. For the Oregon and California Land Grant,

Despite the broad terms of the 1944 law, very few new units were actually set up. Forest Service policy stipulated that at least 20 percent of the merchantable timber assigned to a unit should be owned by the private coöperators. So long as prices continued to be high, the pressure to realize returns from their timber holdings made private landowners reluctant to accept the restrictions which a long-range commitment entailed, with the result that few applications for agreements were submitted. In 1946 a 100-year plan was agreed to by the Forest Service and the Simpson Logging Company of Shelton, Washington, covering approximately 270,000 acres on the Olympic peninsula. The terms committed the company to fire and insect control measures, and to approved silviculture practices, and in return pledged to the company's use the timber from the national forest lands which comprised 80 percent of the total stand in the unit. The agreement was designed to be a model for future plans, but since the restraints applied at once, while the benefits were deferred some years into the future, the arrangement was one that had only a limited appeal. In the establishment of federal units for dependent communities the Forest Service again moved slowly. After prolonged negotiation, a plan was put into effect for the benefit of the Grays Harbor communities, but the difficulties of administration and of determining the proper requirements of dependency were so great that the federal unit approach had little if any usefulness elsewhere.

The sustained yield unit law was born of a period of depression and was hardly suited to the boom of World War II and the years of heavy construction that followed it. Mason's "s. y." agreements no longer served the purposes either of the lumber industry or the Forest Service. From the industry's point of view the chief reason for having them was gone. The demand now was for more timber from the national forests, and there was no serious reason to complain about the competitive bidding by which such timber could be bought. On the other hand, the conservationists might well feel little enthusiasm

see 50 Statutes at Large 874, and David M. Ellis, "Oregon and California Land Grant, 1866-1945," *PNQ*, XXXIX, 1948, 253-283. For the Sustained Yield Act of 1944, see 58 Statutes at Large 132. The thinking at the state level is suggested in Oregon State Planning Board, *Oregon's Forest Problem*, Salem, 1936; Washington Forest Advisory Committee, *Long Range Forest Program for the State of Washington*, Olympia, 1942; and Pacific Northwest Regional Planning Commission, *Pacific Northwest Forest Resources: Problems of and Program for Conservation and Utilization*, Portland, 1937.

for a partnership venture which pledged four trees in the national forest to one on private lands. There was, moreover, strong political opposition to committing large tracts of national forest to the use of any single timber company.

Timber Is a Crop

Though Mason's proposal to achieve a sustained yield by formal contracts was but little used in the Pacific Northwest, conditions of prosperity did promote a wider acceptance of the idea of growing timber and harvesting it as a crop. Years earlier foresters had come to the realization that the important thing about the Pacific Northwest in the long view was not so much its great stands of virgin timber as the unusual geographic and climatic conditions which made it possible to reproduce a forest stock comparatively quickly and in great profusion. Repeatedly men expressed their astonishment at the way a clear cut slope, "devastated" and abandoned by the logging crews, produced in little more than 20 years a thick and flourishing "junior forest." Timber was a crop and the land should be dedicated to it. The lumber industry should become as stable and permanent an enterprise as agriculture.

So the conservation program laid less emphasis upon limitations in cutting and made more of measures that would raise the rate of growth of younger trees. More and more private companies put foresters on their payroll or secured the services of consultants. Logging was done more systematically and cleanly, leaving the ground in good condition for reseeding. A nursery was established at Nisqually which, after a few years, distributed millions of seedlings to tracts which could not be reforested naturally.

Lumbermen took pride in these accomplishments. In 1941 the Clemons Tree Farm had been established near Elma and Montesano, initiating a movement that quickly spread to 36 states. By 1954 Washington alone had more than two hundred tree farms, 129 in the Douglas fir country and 80 more in the eastern pine section for a total of 3,000,000 acres. Weyerhaeuser found it to be good business and good public relations as well. Many a small company drew just as much satisfaction from the fact that their farms too were registered, and their standards of management were high.

Undoubtedly there was a measure of shrewdness as well as good will in all this. Greeley's remarks were very much to the point when he argued that the industry by regulating itself would stave off the threat of federal intervention. Furthermore the times encouraged such self-improvement, for business generally found it advantageous to invest in the future. Lumbermen spent more generously both on forests and on mill machinery because they felt that their investments would pay off. Meanwhile technology promised much in the full utilization of every log, and developed new processes which made a small tree as good as a big one for many purposes.

The stress on full utilization and a high rate of replacement led naturally to a modification of some of the earlier notions about the timber budget. The old idea of establishing a balance between total cut and total growth was supplanted by more complex plans which determined the cut in a particular locality according to local conditions. Professor Kirkland's timber budget as worked out in 1944 was a very different thing from the earlier general formulae. He urged the establishment of control tracts which could be studied carefully for their characteristics and for the best type of logging and reforestation. The cutting schedules would sometimes emphasize selective cutting, sometimes clear cutting. Once determined, they could be applied to larger areas. At the same time, there was more planning on a national scale, which provided for a higher allowable cut in the Pacific Northwest during the years just ahead while other sections were bringing their junior forests to maturity. The arguments fitted nicely together to harmonize the idea of heavy cutting with long-range resource management.[5]

The industry viewpoint by mid-century had come to accept public ownership and administration of timberlands, as practiced by the National Forest Service and on some of the municipal watersheds. The point was vigorously urged, however, that timber lands should

[5] Stanley F. Horn, *This Fascinating Lumber Business*, Indianapolis, 1951, Chaps. 3, 5; Burt P. Kirkland, *Forest Resources of the Douglas Fir Region*, Portland, 1946; Joint Committee . . . of the National Research Council and the Society of American Foresters, *Problems and Progress of Forestry in the United States*, Washington, D.C., 1947; *Washington Forest Facts*, 1954 ed., compiled by the American Forest Products Industries, Inc., Washington, D.C., 1954; Luther H. Gulick, *American Forest Policy*, New York, 1951; West Coast Lumbermen's Association, Joint Committee on Forest Conservation, *West Coast Tree Farms*, Seattle, 1943.

be in private hands so far as possible. Public ownership was the subject of complaint because it took land off the tax rolls, and although the Forest Service adopted the practice of making lieu payments to counties in which the national forests were located, the objection was never altogether stilled. It was voiced most loudly and persistently when large tracts of timber were placed in national parks where the policies against logging were more strict. The boundaries of the Olympic National Park were especially the subject of controversy, the lumber companies and the local chambers of commerce lining up against the conservation organizations in lively contests of lobbying and public debate. Congressman Mon Wallgren's bill of 1938, establishing a park nearly a million acres in extent, was strenuously opposed not only by the industry but by the Washington State Planning Council as well. Governor Clarence Martin, however, viewed the matter as an interagency fight between the Forest Service and the National Park Service, in which the State of Washington should have no part. The broad popular support for the park could not be denied. The industry had not yet proved its purpose so far as conservation was concerned. Exploitation still threatened the forests, and the nation at large saw the federal conservation agencies as the more sure protection of the region's vital resources.[6]

[6] Washington State Planning Council, *Study of Parks, Parkways and Recreation Areas*, Olympia, 1941; Fred Cleator, "Olympic National Park; a Review of the Past," unpublished digest of actions and opinion, University of Washington School of Forestry, n.d. See also the file of pamphlets and clippings in the Forestry Branch, University of Washington Library.

35

The Conservation of North Pacific Fisheries

Programs of research and regulation were a matter of grim necessity in the Pacific Northwest fisheries. Now and again conditions of overproduction occurred, to strengthen the arguments of conservation with considerations of price stabilization. For the most part, however, the problems of resource management were intensified by the bitter facts of depletion, brought home inescapably as industries which once had prospered met with adversity, and fishing fleets faced ruin because there were no fish. Both the halibut and salmon fisheries offer examples of enterprises that were saved from exhaustion to be rehabilitated through a scientific analysis of the causes of depletion, and the adoption of suitable measures of control. Both of them illustrate also the complexities which made solutions difficult when conflicts of interstate or international jurisdictions were involved.

Halibut

The declining productivity of the halibut banks had been appreciated by such scientists as William F. Thompson even before World War I. He had presented data to show that while the total catch increased from 1907 to reach a peak in 1913, the returns per skate were dropping so that more intensive fishing was necessary and the boats were forced to range farther and farther north into Alaskan waters. The American-Canadian Fisheries Conference of 1918 considered the problems of the halibut fisheries along with others, and gathered testimony through hearings which confirmed Thompson's views. There was a general agreement that a closed season was desirable, and that a thorough study of the life history and habits of the halibut species was needed. Since the fishing was done outside the limits of territorial jurisdiction, any effective controls would have to be exercised jointly by the United States and Canada through a treaty agreement.

The first attempt to negotiate a treaty failed, owing to the fact that tariff provisions were included which Congress found objectionable. Reciprocal privileges were also allowed to the fishermen of each nationality in the ports of the other, a point that was found to be unacceptable in view of the disputes which had arisen previously out of similar arrangements in the North Atlantic fishing ports. In 1922, however, the treaty was rewritten and approved, with the controversial clauses eliminated. Two years later it was ratified and went into effect. A closed season was inaugurated, lasting from November to February, and a special international commission went to work on a thorough scientific study. The commission had at first no regulatory powers, but was authorized to gather data from the fishermen as a means of analyzing the trends in the halibut population on the various banks, and to make recommendations for the preservation and development of the fishery.

As a result of this study a number of important facts became clear. Statistical tables documented the degree of depletion. South of Cape Spencer, for example, the catch dropped from 56,900,000 pounds in 1911 to 22,600,000 pounds in 1930. For the fishery as a whole, the total catch declined substantially between 1915 and 1930 although the number of skates more than doubled. West of Cape Spencer the catch per skate fell during the same period from 266.1 pounds to 64.7 pounds. There could be no doubt that depletion was caused by the increasingly intensive fishing. The commission therefore recommended in its report that fishing boats be licensed, and that the total annual catch be reduced to a point where the yield could be stabilized. The use of unduly destructive fishing gear should be prohibited; the existing closed seasons should be extended to February 15, and areas populated by immature fish should be closed altogether. These recommendations were incorporated into the provisions of a new treaty in 1930, and the International Fisheries Commission was transformed from a research body into a full-fledged regulatory agency. The initial catch limit was set at 46,000,000 pounds.

The catch per skate increased 89 percent in Area 3 west of Cape Spencer and 77 percent in Area 2 lying to the south. The program was so successful that the commission raised the quota by 2,000,000 pounds in 1938 and 6,000,000 pounds more in 1940.

Although the main framework of regulation was established and administered by the International Fisheries Commission, the fishing industry was consulted as each step was taken. With the approval of the Commission an organization of the boat owners and fishermen's unions was formed to put into effect additional regulations governing the operations of the individual boats within the total catch limits. This agency, known as the Halibut Production Control Board, was established in Seattle in 1932 for the purpose of stabilizing halibut prices during the year through a system of "orderly marketing." Under the auspices of this Control Board representatives of the fishermen and boat owners negotiated an annual plan known as the "Halibut Curtailment Program," and worked out regulations designed to prevent excessive price fluctuations by "splitting the fleet" into halves, scheduling landings more regularly, and enforcing periodical lay-ups that spread and reduced production. Basic per-man-per-trip quotas were also established which ran 2,500-3,000 pounds in Area 2 and 3,500-4,000 pounds in Area 3. Canadians coöperated in the program of curtailment, and Americans and Canadians together discouraged the invasion of the North Pacific by competing boats from the countries of Europe.[1]

Fraser River Salmon

The rehabilitation of salmon runs in the Columbia and Fraser rivers presented problems no less pressing than the building up of the halibut fishery. Questions of jurisdiction were even more complicated, since they involved not only international relations but the relations of states to each other and to the federal government. Programs of research and experimentation were just as demanding, particularly the tracing of the long migrations which carried the salmon from their spawning grounds on the river tribu-

[1] William F. Thompson and Norman L. Freeman, *History of the Pacific Halibut Industry*, Vancouver, B.C., 1930; John Cobb, *Scientific Problems of the Fisheries of the North Pacific*, San Diego, 1919; Jozo Tomasevich, *International Agreements on Conservation of Marine Resources*, Stanford University, 1943, Chaps. 9-14.

taries far out to sea and back again. Most perplexing of all, practical solutions were difficult to plan and execute because of the conflicting interests of rival industries, especially between the fishermen who would keep the rivers open and those who would build dams across them for purposes of irrigation, flood control or power development.

The restocking of the Fraser river system with sockeye salmon offered a particular challenge, since its numerous tributary streams and chains of lakes made this stream "potentially the best sockeye river in the world." For many years the dangers of intensive fishing were pointed out, and conferences of experts repeatedly urged the adoption of common safeguards by the United States and Canada. Always there was some reason why the United States refused to approve a treaty. American fishermen and canneries felt they would be adversely affected, and Governor Roland Hartley protested that the treaty would deprive the State of Washington of its rightful authority to handle the fisheries problem for itself. In 1930 a treaty was signed but it failed of ratification in the United States, mainly because it provided for an equal division of the catch between the two countries and the Americans were then taking more than that. During the next few years, however, the American boats lost their competitive advantage and therefore came to view the treaty more favorably. Supplementary articles were drawn and accepted which protected the rights of the State of Washington. Soon afterward the Senate voted to ratify the treaty, opening the way at last to real progress in the repair of the Fraser River salmon streams.

As in the case of the halibut treaty, the sockeye agreement provided for some years of scientific study before the program of reconstruction was begun. Under the direction of a joint Canadian-American commission, biological and engineering studies were made to determine the kind of regulations that would be needed and the channel improvements that would have to be built.

The most urgent engineering problems were those encountered at Hell's Gate Gorge where in 1913 a railroad construction crew had blasted a great mass of rock from the canyon wall into the river bed. No serious attempt had been made to clear away the rubble and it presented a formidable barrier to the migrating sockeye. Despite Professor Thompson's efforts, officials were slow to realize how serious it was. Until the Hell's Gate fish channels were reopened other measures of rehabilitation would be of little value. So in 1945 the work in the canyon was begun, to be completed three years later. At some points rock was removed from the river bed to permit a normal use of the main stream once more. At other places tunnels and ladders were built which allowed the fish to go around an obstacle or even through it. All in all 1,500,000 dollars was spent on improvements that made the Fraser fit for a fish to swim in.

There have been few conservation programs more immediately and strikingly successful than this one. Within three years the cost of the improvements had been repaid tenfold in the value of fish. In 1953 the Fraser yielded 4,000,000 sockeye worth 10,000,000 dollars, the largest catch since 1917. On the strength of such a record the State of Washington embarked upon an elaborate program of fishways and stream improvement designed to rehabilitate other salmon streams in the same way.[2]

The Columbia River, like the Fraser, was one of the great salmon streams of North America. Yet its productivity was seriously threatened by intensive fishing, by the construction of hydroelectric and irrigation dams, and by neglect of the smaller tributaries which in too many instances were so much clogged with brush and other obstructions that salmon could no longer spawn in them. Rehabilitation of this watershed was a many-sided problem.

Measures designed to insure an adequate escapement of fish were more than ordinarily complicated, since the lower Columbia was a boundary between Oregon and Washington and the two states did not agree in their laws and regulations. In 1910 the legislatures established a joint committee on fisheries in order to achieve more uniformity in their policies, and a few years later they drew up an interstate compact which established a concurrent jurisdiction over the lower river. The compact received the approval of Congress in 1918 but did not result in identical regulations as had been hoped. In test cases the courts ruled that in spite of the common jurisdiction the two states could still act independently in regulating their own

[2] William A. Carrothers, *British Columbia Fisheries,* Toronto, 1941; Roderick Haig-Brown, "Canada's Pacific Salmon," *Canadian Geographical Journal,* XLIV, 1952, 109-127; Tomasevich, *Conservation of Marine Resources,* Chaps. 15-18; Washington State Fisheries Department, Annual Report, 1953, 49.

citizens. Thus fish wheels were outlawed by Oregon in 1927 but continued to be legal so far as Washington was concerned until 1935. Similarly fish pounds and fixed gear were prohibited on the Washington side of the river in 1935, but were continued in use on the Oregon side below the Cascade rapids. When the Oregon State Planning Board studied the problem of preserving the Columbia River salmon in 1938, they urged once again the importance of uniform measures, and proposed the creation of a Joint Columbia River Fisheries Commission.[3]

The building up of the lower tributaries of the Columbia River was the more imperative because of the necessity of shifting the salmon runs to streams that were not closed by hydroelectric dams. It was not always a matter of choosing between power and fish. At Bonneville dam, McNary, and Rock Island, fish ladders and elevators were constructed which made it possible for salmon to pass by. Grand Coulee dam, however, could neither be scaled nor skirted and more than a thousand miles of salmon streams above it had to be abandoned.

This situation called for unusual methods of fishing and artificial propagation. Adult fish were intercepted in their upstream journey at Rock Island, their eggs were stripped and fertilized, and the fingerlings were reared in pools at a large hatchery established nearby at Leavenworth on the Wenatchee River. Tank trucks then took them to "planting areas" in tributaries that entered the Columbia below Grand Coulee dam. These fish transferred their affections to the streams in which they were placed and returned to them when it came time to spawn. In this way the productivity of the upper river was saved from loss and the stock of fish in the lesser streams below was greatly multiplied.

The growing importance of the lower tributaries led to still other measures of conservation, some of which were undertaken by individual states while other were coöperative. In 1949 the Washington state legislature declared the lower Columbia watershed to be a sanctuary which was to be administered with a special purpose to build

[3] Oregon State Planning Board, *Commercial Fishing Operations on the Columbia River*, Salem, 1938; James Carty, "Washington-Oregon Fisheries Compact, with Special Reference to Legislative and Judicial Problems," unpublished thesis, State College of Washington, 1949; Washington State Fisheries Department, Report, 1953.

up the native stocks of fish. The provisions of this law were soon contested by the city of Tacoma which applied to the Federal Power Commission for permission to build a hydroelectric power dam on the Cowlitz River. The alternatives of fish or kilowatts were particularly difficult here, since the Cowlitz lay within the sanctuary and the building of the dam would mean the loss of the last large spawning stream in the watershed. The final decision was long delayed in court litigation and at the time of this writing (March, 1956) was not yet determined. State and federal authority on this point were sharply opposed.

The working relations of the state fishery departments in Washington and Oregon and the United States Fish and Wildlife Survey were much happier. In 1948 the three agencies entered into a cooperative agreement to carry out a 20-year plan of research and development. A number of new hatcheries were built in the lower Columbia watershed, fishways were constructed at points that were obstructed, and a comprehensive plan of stream clearance was undertaken. At the same time the problem of escapement was carefully studied and common measures were put into effect to insure adequate runs of fish. Experts estimated that with a sustained program of river improvement the Columbia River system could be made to yield annually nearly double the 28,000,000 pounds of fish that were currently produced.[4]

[4] Washington State Legislature, Interim Committee on Fisheries, *Report on Problems Affecting Food Fisheries of the State of Washington*, 1949; Tim Kelley, "Fishery Conservation in Washington," *PNQ*, XXXVIII, 1947, 19-34; Washington State Fisheries Department, *Salmon Rehabilitation and Hatcheries* (1952).

36

Forty Years of Politics, 1916-1956

In Northwest politics, as in national politics generally, World War I was a turning point which marked an end of the era of progressivism and witnessed a decline of popular interest in economic and social reform. The issues of neutrality and the challenge of war drew the attention of the people from domestic questions to the external problems of world affairs. Politics was never adjourned altogether, but both the major parties supported the war while political dissent was discouraged since it was likely to be viewed as subversive. At the same time, wages were raised, working conditions were improved, and governmental controls were extended partly because the war boom brought a prosperity that permitted it, and partly because the crucial demands for record-breaking production and transportation made it necessary to get the jobs done. The sense of moral urgency was diverted from the exposure of monopoly and political manipulation to the great crusade to "save the world for democracy."

Preference for Republicans

The decade of reaction following the Peace of Versailles was a period of political conservatism which restored the Republicans to power in every state of the Northwest. Presidential elections in 1920, 1924, and 1928 resulted in Republican majorities, and Congressional delegations were Republican almost to a man. The only significant upsets were the election in 1922 of Clarence Dill, a Spokane Democrat, to replace Miles Poindexter in the United States Senate, and of Sam B. Hill who held a seat in the

House of Representatives for the next six terms. In the state capitols Republican governors (save for Walter Pierce of Oregon) maintained an unbroken rule, challenged only feebly by a handful of Democrats in the legislatures.

Republican habits of voting were so confirmed that incumbents holding seats in Congress were returned to office with an almost monotonous regularity. Burton French of Moscow, Idaho, who had been in the House of Representatives from 1903 to 1915, was reëlected in 1916 and thereafter served continuously until 1933. Addison Smith of Twin Falls kept his seat in the House for ten terms (1912-1932), and Borah was a fixture in the Senate from 1907 until his death in 1940. Oregonians treated their Congressmen in much the same way. Counting his years of service before as well as after World War I, Willis Hawley of Salem held his seat in the House of Representatives for 13 consecutive terms (1907-1933). Nicholas J. Sinnott from the Dalles, who was first elected in 1912, remained at his desk through eight terms. In the United States Senate Republicans took the places of the Democrats George Chamberlain and Harry Lane, and Charles McNary lived out a long career there. Robert Stanfield was something of an exception. He failed of reëlection to the Senate in 1926, after a single term, but Oregon editors took pains to explain that it meant no breach of party regularity, no wavering in Republican control. Fred Steiwer, they said, took his place because Stanfield on occasion showed a personal indifference to the observance of prohibition.[1]

From 1918 to 1932 Washington voters changed only three names in their entire Congressional delegation. In the lower house Republicans Miller and Summers, Johnson and Hadley worked together as a team for 12 years without a single substitution. Hadley served nine consecutive terms and Johnson ten. Wesley Jones was a member of the Senate for 22 years. The citizenry of this state, as of the others, showed an unusual confidence in the men of their choice who spoke for them in national affairs, and the wheels of party machinery turned with remarkably little squealing.

[1] See "Old Guard Defeated in Oregon," *Literary Digest*, LXXXIX, June 5, 1926, 12-14. The roll of Representatives and Senators from the northwestern states can be constructed from the *Biographical Directory of the American Congress, 1774-1949*, Washington, D.C., 1950.

New Approach to Administration

The new mood in government and politics expressed itself in the direct government measures that were put before the voters and in the efforts that were made to reorganize the structure and operations of state government. There was less enthusiasm for legislation that would increase the regulatory powers of government over business enterprise or make political democracy more effective. Instead the emphasis was upon the mechanics of government, the practical problems of taxation and governmental finance, and the problems of roadbuilding, irrigation, and veterans' benefits.

In Washington the most important piece of legislation dealing with government reorganization was the Administrative Code of 1921. This measure was inspired by the efforts on the part of Governor Lowden of Illinois to make the administration of government in his state more orderly and efficient. Governor Louis F. Hart became interested in the venture and took the initiative in securing somewhat similar legislation for Washington. The Code provided for the establishment of ten administrative departments which ranged in their jurisdiction from Agriculture to Highways and Health, Labor and Industries and Public Works. More than 75 regulatory commissions and boards were abolished, their powers transferred to one or another of the new departments. The main purposes were to reduce the multiplicity of governing agencies and to eliminate a wasteful duplication of functions and overlapping of responsibility. Economy and efficiency were popular watchwords among the supporters of the code. It had its appeal for politicians and administrators as well, since it created a number of well-paying positions and increased the governor's patronage through his powers of appointment and control. As the lines of authority were gathered into the governor's hands, party organization was also somewhat changed. The chief executive did not immediately become the titular head of the Republican organization. On the contrary, the period was marked by bitter wrangling between the governor and other leaders in his own party. Several of Roland Hartley's messages to the legislature were full of invective, directed against the elective officials that he could not control and the lumber and education lobbies for which he cherished a deep distrust. On the whole, however, the trend of the period was in the direction of consolidating administrative and political power in the office of the governor.

The process of overhauling governmental machinery did not go so far in the other states. The weaknesses in Oregon were recognized to be much the same and preliminary steps were taken to remedy them. The legislature set up committees to study the matter and in 1919 D. J. M. Mathews of the University of Illinois made a study and submitted a report which proposed a comprehensive consolidation into ten executive departments responsible to the governor. When it came to enacting the plan into legislation, however, Oregon politicians faltered and found reasons to object. Bills were before the legislature during every session, yet few of them reached the floor and none of them passed. Largely ignoring Mathews' proposals, legislators attacked the problem piecemeal, disagreed as to the establishment of individual departments, and made scant progress with any of them. Some measure of scrutiny and control of administration was achieved through centralized financial procedures, and a few departments were established (1929, 1931), for Higher Education, Agriculture, and State Police. But many areas of state government continued to be served by agencies and commissions which overlapped and duplicated in their functions, yet stubbornly resisted change.[2]

Signs of Discontent

Republican ascendancy and the political longevity of the people's representatives were outward evidences of tranquillity in public affairs, yet, if one looked more closely, there were signs of stress that pointed to organized dissatisfaction and dissent. The Nonpartisan League, though it never developed the political power as a militant farm organization that it had in Minnesota and North Dakota, was nevertheless something of an agrarian storm center in Idaho and Washington as well. In Idaho the League had a short life, but it prepared the ground for a strong minority vote by the Farmer-Labor party in 1922 and the Progressives in 1924. In Wash-

[2] Walter S. Davis, "New Civil Administration Code in Washington," *American Political Science Review*, XV, 1921, 568-576; James D. Barnett, "Reorganization of State Government in Oregon," *ibid.*, IX, 1915, 287-293; Charles McKinley, "Oregon State Government Reorganization," *National Municipal Review*, XX, 1931, 646-650, and "Oregon Administrative Reorganization Report," *ibid.*, XL, 1951, 262.

ington, League petitions forced referendum votes successfully on measures that would have put restraints upon the independent voter, and League votes helped to send Clarence Dill to the United States Senate. Incidents of violence in Washington indicated a considerable fear of agrarian radicalism. Oregon too showed signs of unrest. Here the Ku Klux Klan made a brief but spectacular bid for power, claiming a victory over the Republicans in the 1922 gubernatorial election. Their votes carried the day for Walter Pierce, Democrat, a dirt farmer from La Grande, though he was embarrassed by their support and was unsympathetic to their purposes. Klan votes were behind a measure that struck at the Catholics by requiring all children of school age to attend the public schools. Since Catholicism was in no sense a serious threat, however, political observers interpreted the movement as an expression of agrarian discontent, a protest against the Republican management of things, and a demand for economy in government and measures of relief that would assure the farmer a living wage.[3]

Election of 1924

The presidential election of 1924 was marked by a vigorous protest vote throughout the Northwest, one that was registered not so much through the Democratic party as through the Independents and third-party candidates. The pattern was a familiar one which repeated the precedents of the Populist and Progressive elections of earlier years. Pacific Northwest voters had little use for an opposition party that failed to speak out, or played the political game like Tweedle Dee and Tweedle Dum. Their own Democrats, Dill and Hill and Pierce, were worthy of support and got it, but John W. Davis, the national Democratic nominee for President, had no great backing. Old Bob LaFollette was more popular and his vote cut deeply into Republican and Democratic totals. In Washington and Idaho the Democratic vote was reduced to half of what it had been in 1920 and in Oregon it was substantially diminished. The result was a three-way contest which, though it left the

[3] Anne Greenwood, "Bill Borah and Other Home Folks," *Nation*, CXVI, February 28, 1923, 235; M. R. Stone, "Idaho, Remnant of the Old Frontier," *ibid.*, CXVI, June 13, 1923, 692-695; W. Roberts, "Ku Kluxing of Oregon," *Outlook*, CXXX, March 14, 1923, 490-491.

Republicans still in the saddle, nevertheless shook them up considerably. In many counties they won only because the opposing vote was split. In some the LaFollette forces fought them to a standstill, or yielded only by the slenderest of margins.

Idaho Progressives trailed the Republicans by some 15,000 votes in a total of 148,295. In 19 counties out of 44 they offered a very real threat; in all but five they surpassed the Democrats. Oregon Republicans won no more than a plurality in 11 counties which included the Portland area and the northeast corner of the state. Though the defections from the Democratic vote were less significant, Republican strength was materially reduced.

In Washington the greatest challenge to Republicanism percentagewise appeared in the rural counties: Douglas, Grant, Benton, and Kittitas in the central part of the state, and on the Sound, Skagit, Island, Kitsap, and Snohomish. But all three urban counties were invaded too. In King and Spokane the Republicans eked out no more than a four to three victory over the Progressives while in Pierce they won by 2,000 votes in 44,818 total. The outcome left the Republicans in control, but the protest vote was strong and widespread throughout the state.[4]

In the years that followed, the farm relief problem continued to be troublesome and developed political undertones of McNary-Haugenism. In the Palouse country men like F. J. Wilmer kept in touch with the national movement and helped to organize the local support for it. Distress in the grain belt was something that no Congressman could ignore, no matter what party he represented. When the roll-call votes were taken on the McNary bill in April and May, 1928, every northwestern Senator except Borah was recorded in favor of it, and in the House of Representatives only Albert Johnson of Grays Harbor and Franklin F. Korell of Portland's third district voted with the nays.

Battle of the Kilowatts

The issue that revived the popular resentment of monopoly and corporation lobbying was the issue of public

[4] See figures given in Edgar E. Robinson, *Presidential Vote, 1896-1932*, Stanford University, 1934.

power. For 20 years and more a vigorous battle had been waged between the big private utilities and the municipal power systems in Seattle, Tacoma, and Portland. Stone and Webster, a Boston firm, was strong in the Puget Sound area while Washington Water Power served a large part of the Inland Empire. In Portland and vicinity, Portland Electric Power Company and Northwestern Electric Company were dominant private utility companies. These companies managed their operations on generous margins of profit and showed but little interest in spreading the benefits of cheap electric power to large mass markets or to widely scattered rural areas. On occasion they secured water rights with only a small investment, then capitalized them at a much higher value and charged proportionally high rates. The chief threat to such practices came from the publicly owned systems in Seattle and Tacoma. Within a few years time Seattle's City Light forced repeated rate reductions until power which had been purchased previously for 20 cents could be had for six cents or less. The private companies resisted this kind of competition with every resource at their command. They attacked the public city systems with many arguments and complaints, issued propaganda to undermine popular confidence in them, and spent considerable sums of money in political activity to prevent the enactment of legislation that would make possible the extension of existing public power installations or the establishment of new ones. The drive to develop more fully the hydroelectric resources, which the region possessed in great abundance, involved a great deal of popular education and some of the most strenuous politics of the decade.

The agitation in Oregon centered in the city of Portland where inquiries brought to light the fact that rates were much higher than they needed to be. Rate experts pointed out that Portland Electric Power Company charged its customers on the basis of 8 percent profits on an operation valued at 8,000,000 dollars, though in actual output the figure should have been 1,440,000 dollars. Another company in the area capitalized its water rights at 10,000,000 dollars though the development actually cost only 1,230,000 dollars. Popular protests against this situation became increasingly widespread not only because the companies' charges were out of proportion to their investments but because the resulting high rates prevented the same encouragement of manufacturing that was possible in the Puget Sound cities where there were strong municipal power plants.

Throughout the 1920's George Joseph of Portland was the apostle of public power. During several terms in the state legislature he had fought the private utilities at every turn. His efforts were largely responsible for the defeat of a proposal that would have merged Portland Electric Power Company and the Northwestern Electric Company in a single private monopoly. Repeatedly he sponsored constitutional amendments that would have allowed the development of public power, but always in vain. The climax of a long career was his successful candidacy in 1930 to win the Republican nomination for governor, a contest that found him running in the party primary against Henry Corbett and Walter Norblad. The votes he won were cast in protest against the control of the Republican party by the conservative politicians, but they expressed also a growing popular concern with the issues of hydroelectric power.

The campaign was hard fought and the victory was bought with a price. Only a few weeks after the election Joseph was stricken with a heart attack and died, leaving the public power forces without a leader. By this time, however, the movement was so strong that it drew new leadership to it. Julius Meier, a prominent Portland merchant and one of Joseph's close friends, agreed to run in his place, pressed the cause of public power vigorously and effectively, and won the gubernatorial election. That same year the Oregon voters put their stamp of approval on legislation which authorized the formation of public utility districts, and thus opened the way to the spread of public power into the rural areas.[5]

In Washington the State Grange was the leading organization to urge liberal power legislation for the benefit of sparsely populated counties. Grangers backed a number of bills in the state legislature and took the lead in soliciting signatures for initiatives that would

[5] Stiles Jones, "What Certain Cities Have Accomplished Without State Regulation," *Annals of the American Academy of Political and Social Science*, LVII, 1915, 72-82; Emerson P. Schmidt, "Movement for Public Ownership of Power in Oregon," *Journal of Land and Public Utility Economics*, VII, 1931, 52-60; V. MacMickle, "Jolt for High Light Bills," *Nation*, CXXXII, January 28, 1931, 96-98; Charles B. Frisbie, "Exciting News from Oregon," *ibid.*, CXXXI, December 24, 1930, 707; George N. Joseph, "George W. Joseph and the Oregon Progressive Tradition," unpublished thesis, Reed College, 1952.

allow the municipal systems to serve the surrounding rural districts. Yet they were unable to secure the passage of any of them. Initiative No. 52 won a favorable vote in 1924 which placed the measure before the legislature, but both houses voted adversely on it. Subsequent efforts were no more successful. Only as the Grange was joined in its efforts by other groups did the public power measures win approval at the polls.

The political figure who identified himself most actively with the power issue was Homer T. Bone of Tacoma. Bone had been legal counselor for the city of Tacoma as early as 1911, and from then on had been doing what he could to forward the cause of cheap electricity. He moved from party to party during these years, running with the Socialists in 1912, the Progressives in 1924, the Republicans for a while thereafter, and finally with the Democrats in 1932. Yet his advocacy of public power was more constant. He gave his name to the bill introduced in 1924, and campaigned aggressively for the adoption of this and similar measures until public power was taken up by the federal government during the New Deal. His authorship and energetic support of the Public Utility District law in 1930 had much to do with securing a successful vote on it.

Political observers pointed out at the time that the popular vote which legalized the establishment of public utility districts was a protest against the private companies more than an affirmative vote for an elaborate program of public power. The developments of the next few years gave reason for thinking so. Spokane County formed a P.U.D. in 1932, but it remained inoperative. Of the three counties that took action in 1934 only Mason County was able to provide actual service. In 1939 no more than four P.U.D.'s had solved the problems involved in finding sources of power and acquiring or building transmission systems. It was not that politics were unfavorable, or that the people had lost heart. But the technical difficulties were formidable and they required federal policies and federal appropriations for their solution. The construction of Bonneville dam, and later of Grand Coulee dam, and the establishment of the Bonneville Power Administration gave the P.U.D. legislation of 1930 an importance that it could not have had otherwise. By the end of 1942 thirteen P.U.D.'s were in operation, most of them served with power from Bonneville at low wholesale rates. Thus the issues of public power helped to swing the Pacific Northwest behind the New Deal. In the meantime the P.U.D. legislation showed the strength of the political demand that something be done to contest the monopolistic practices of the private utilities.[6]

What of the Democrats?

The elections of 1928 and 1930 were significant as marking a return to the two-party system. Third-party voting dropped to the lowest level in nearly 30 years leaving the Republicans entrenched in power, apparently more securely than ever. Percentagewise the vote for Hoover in 1928 was considerably stronger than the vote for Harding in 1920. Washington's Roland Hartley defeated Scott Bullitt of Seattle for governor by 67,000 votes. The losses of 1924 were repaired and the party seemed stronger than it had been since the days of Roosevelt and Taft.

Where there was a protest vote it was registered through the major parties. Sometimes this meant a contest in the primaries, a victory for George Joseph, a race between Scott Bullitt and the conservative Stephen Chadwick, or a spirited challenge of Albert Johnson by Homer T. Bone which all but succeeded. On occasion it meant a test of strength between the parties, such as the one which reëlected Clarence Dill to the United States Senate. Both parties had their liberals and their conservatives and both trimmed their sails somewhat to meet the winds of discontent.

But there was little evidence to suggest a trend toward Democratic rule. Democrats profited by the disappearance of Farmer-Labor and Progressive minorities, yet not so much as the Republicans. Al Smith won a larger relative vote than James Cox had in 1920 and proved himself much stronger than John Davis had been in 1924. There were Democrats in the state legislatures and party conventions whose names would soon be more widely known, men like General Charles Martin, and Walter Pierce and Peter Zimmerman of Oregon, C. Ben

[6] Elliott Marple, "Movement for Public Ownership of Power in Washington," *Journal of Land and Public Utility Economics*, VII, 1931, 61-66; James K. Hall, "Washington's Public Ownership District Power Law," *National Municipal Review*, XX, 1931, 342-348; William A. Smith, "Development of Public Utility Districts in Washington," unpublished thesis, University of Washington, 1950.

Ross of Idaho, and Lewis Schwellenbach and Clarence Martin of Washington. But the Democratic party lacked a constructive program, captured only one vote in three, and gave no promise of winning a majority anywhere. The Pacific Northwest followed the national trend rather than anticipating it, and there was as yet no sign that economic depression would bring about political revolution and carry the Democrats into office.

Whatever the signs and portents, the elections of 1932 saw the voters of the Pacific Northwest turning to the Democratic party as they had not done in many years. Franklin Roosevelt won sweeping majorities which made Wilson's victories of 1912 and 1916 seem precarious by comparison. Never had there been such a complete reversal, so unanimous a disposition to turn somersaults. In 1928 Fremont County, Idaho, had the unique distinction of being the only county in the three states of the Pacific Northwest to vote for Al Smith. In 1932 Bear Lake County, Idaho, and Benton County, Oregon, were the only counties to claim the contrary honor of remaining loyal to Hoover in the hour of his defeat. It seemed not to matter what their previous record had been. Some counties had been centers where protest voting was habitual and every third-party candidate had found support. Others had not declared for a Democratic president in two generations. All voted now for Roosevelt regardless of their prior political coloring. Not only that, but they voted for Democratic governors also, and sent Democrats to the state legislatures in such numbers as to give the party full control at the state as well as the national level.

Washington: Radicals Under Rein

One could hardly say that the Democrats in the Northwest were prepared for the responsibilities of office, or that they were always qualified. Developments in the State of Washington took on the appearance of "circus politics" and because of instances of eccentricity and opportunism they attracted the attention of the nation for reasons that were not at all laudable. The voice of the people was indeed unpredictable and undisciplined. As one commentator explained, the Washington voter had never been roped or branded by any political party. Certainly he was under no restraints now, and felt no compulsion to follow the dictates of the existing party organization. So it came about that the man elected to be attorney general was a lawyer who, it was said, had not practiced in 15 years. One of the newly chosen members of the legislature did not have the price of a ticket to Olympia; another was unable at first to serve since he was detained at the moment in a county jail. Vic Meyers of Seattle, the new lieutenant governor, was known chiefly as a popular band leader who on one happy occasion had campaigned for the office of mayor promising "a hostess in every streetcar." There was in these elections a carefree exuberance that left one amazed and breathless. Andrew Jackson had once expressed the view that there was nothing mysterious about government that ordinary people could not understand and manage. Now it looked as if perhaps Washington was going back again to the days of Old Hickory.[7]

Radicalism became something more urban than rural. The New Deal program was welcomed in the agricultural counties of the Inland Empire and on the Sound, the more so in some cases because in earlier days they had been centers of Democratic strength. But the significantly new element in the situation was the Washington Commonwealth Federation which drew its strength chiefly from the labor unions and the Unemployed Citizens League in Seattle. The Sound cities had not previously developed anything resembling a Democratic machine. The Republican party had much the better organization and Tammany had no branch offices from which to direct the political affairs of these communities. Radicalism had been discredited since the days of the Wobblies and the General Strike, and there were no groupings within the lower classes that could be used to challenge Republican control. Now, however, the Democrats had something new with which to work.

Leaders in the party, and for that matter the members of it, were divided in their attitude toward the new organization. Conservatives like Stephen Chadwick would have nothing to do with it. Composed

[7] Earl W. Shimmons, "Revolt in the Far Northwest," *Nation*, CXXXV, November 9, 1932, 452-453; "Seattle's Unemployed Citizens League," *New Republic*, LXXIII, November 30, 1932, 56-57; Mary McCarthy, "Circus Politics in Washington State," *Nation*, CXLIII, October 17, 1936, 442-444; "Progressives in Seattle," *New Republic*, XCII, October 20, 1937, 285; "Politics on the West Coast," *Fortune*, XXI, 1940, 40-53.

as it was of old age pensioners and unruly elements of labor, socialists, technocrats, and liberals of diverse colors, its program emphasized "production for use" while its leadership often featured the arts of the demagogue. The rank and file of the middle class were suspicious and uneasy about it and the farmers, even some of the laborers, rejected the radical ideas that were advocated and proclaimed by it.

On the other hand, the Federation unquestionably delivered votes in some number, a fact to which none of the hustling young politicians could be indifferent. Claiming a membership of some 30,000, the Washington Commonwealth Federation elected as many as 27 representatives and several senators to Washington's state legislature. In 1936 it threatened to take over the direction of the Democratic party, forcing the Old Guard into the back seat during the fall convention while Howard Costigan directed the strategy. However one might view its principles, there could be no doubt that organized labor was becoming politically articulate and powerful as it had not been before, and that the issues of relief, social security, and old age were matters from which one must make political capital as best one could.

It is not surprising, therefore, to find that the company of those who solicited the support of the Federation included not only the radicals but some of the more moderate liberals as well. The roster included such names as Marion Zioncheck, the Seattle congressman, and John C. Stevenson, unsuccessful W.C.F. candidate for governor, but it included also Homer T. Bone, John Coffee, and Warren Magnuson, all of whom turned in creditable records in the United States Senate or House of Representatives, or both. Clarence Dill accepted W.C.F. candidates and received its support himself although, ironically, he suffered a series of defeats thereafter, and finally withdrew from public life. In this case the affiliation with W.C.F. proved to be an encumbrance, for Dill was beaten by men who were more conservative: Lewis Schwellenbach in his own party, and Republicans Arthur Langlie and Walter Horan.

The Washington Commonwealth Federation was never in the saddle, for a combination of moderate and conservative elements proved strong enough to keep the radicals under restraint. Clarence Martin, a well-to-do Democrat who traveled the middle of the road, early established his leadership in the party organization and twice won election as governor. Probably he represented fairly accurately the general mood of the people. Accepting and carrying out the New Deal program in its essentials, he resisted the extreme demands of the W.C.F. In the elections of 1936 a number of candidates who enjoyed Federation support were victorious, yet the radical measures on the ballot were all defeated. Martin himself defeated Stevenson in the primaries through the assistance of several thousand Republicans who, taking advantage of the open or "blanket" primary provisions adopted by initiative in 1935, voted for Martin rather than for Hartley. A somewhat similar situation arose in 1940. This time Dill defeated Martin in the primary, whereupon the conservative Democrats voted with the Republicans to elect Arthur Langlie. Confronted with Democratic majorities in the legislature and Democrats in the other elective offices, Langlie's administration was torn by much bickering. Nevertheless it illustrated the temper of the times in Washington where political extremes were avoided through the combined efforts of the moderates in both parties.

From 1940 on the political pendulum swung farther to the right as the New Deal lost favor in the rural counties and Republicans captured several seats in Congress. Ten counties in the central and eastern part of the state changed from Democrat to Republican in the presidential elections of 1940 and 1944. Walter Horan established himself in the fifth Congressional district after defeating Dill in 1942, and Hal Holmes was equally successful in the fourth district, Knute Hill's bailiwick. Fred Norman and Russell Mack brought the third district into the Republican fold though not so solidly, and by 1948 Thor Tollefson represented the sixth district. In the Senate Harry Cain of Tacoma upset for one term a succession of Democratic victories unbroken since 1932.

Despite these developments, the middle decades of the century found the Democrats still vigorous and powerful. Though Bone left the Senate to become a federal judge, and Schwellenbach to become Secretary of Labor, the roll of Washington senators continued to be weighted in favor of the Democrats, including as it did such names as Monrad Wallgren, Warren Magnuson, and Henry Jackson all of whom had served previously in the House of Representatives. A further demonstration of Democratic strength was the election in

1952 of Don Magnuson of Seattle to be Congressman-at-large. The first Congressional district, which included Seattle and Kitsap County, was something of a political barometer owing to the heavy concentration of urban population and the strength of organized labor. This was Warren Magnuson's constituency during the years of New Deal ascendancy. Thereafter it was not held securely by either party. Even here in the Washington Commonwealth Federation stronghold, extreme political views met with resistance. Hugh DeLacy was defeated after a single term in Congress, and thereafter the Democrats presented candidates who were more discreet in their liberalism.[8]

Idaho: Struggle of Factions

Idaho Democrats likewise showed unprecedented strength during the New Deal era. The northern Congressional district which for 30 years had been Republican now entered upon 20 years of Democratic rule. Compton White was returned to the House of Representatives as faithfully as Burton French had been before him. D. Worth Clark of Pocatello served two terms with White in the lower house, while another Democrat, James P. Pope of Boise, sat with Borah in the Senate. In 1938 Clark succeeded Pope, to be followed in turn (1944) by Glen Taylor.

Meanwhile the popular favorite "Cowboy" C. Ben Ross won election as governor three times in succession, though the unwritten law of the state forbade a man to run more than twice. Ross was a veteran politician who sensed the mood of the people with uncanny accuracy. Sometimes he would talk of ranching, sometimes of the way he had reduced the state's indebtedness. On occasion, he would throw away a prepared speech and preach a sermon, evoking from his audience approving Amens and Hallelujahs. There was a hint of Huey Long and Theodore G. Bilbo in him, something of the same art of demagoguery and the same consuming political ambition. In

---

[8] Claudius O. Johnson, "Washington Blanket Primary," *PNQ*, XXXIII, 1942, 27-40; Daniel M. Ogden, Jr., "Blanket Primary and Party Regularity," *ibid.*, XXXIX, 1948, 33-38; George Gallup, *Political Almanac*, Princeton, N. J., 1952; Paul T. David, *Presidential Nominating Politics, 1952*, Baltimore, 1954, V, 161-184. See also Edgar E. Robinson, *They Voted for Roosevelt; the Presidential Vote 1932-44*, Stanford University, 1947.

1936 even Borah had reason to feel the strength of his attack, for Ross wanted Borah's seat in the Senate.[9]

This was the challenge of one popular favorite by another and in such a contest Borah held his own. More significantly, when Borah died in 1940, it was not Ross but Republican John Thomas who took his place. Republicans also captured one of the two seats in the House of Representatives, claiming it repeatedly for Henry Dworshak of Burley. For several years the struggle between the parties was unresolved and one could not say that Idaho was either Democratic or Republican.

Party politics became a matter of geographic sectionalism. Democrats were strong in Lewiston, Kellogg, and the Coeur d'Alene country while Republicans controlled Canyon and Payette counties. In the Snake River basin the Boise area went Republican while Pocatello continued Democratic. Idaho had no concentration of urban population and organized labor was not a significant factor for some years. The political pattern differed in this respect from the situation in Washington and Oregon where the metropolitan centers took on a new importance.

Both the major parties knew the meaning of internal division, and experienced factional controversies born of the struggle of liberals and conservatives to gain control. For a time Ben Ross made himself boss of a Democratic machine that delivered votes when and where they were needed. In the late 1930's, however, this organization split and Democrats of differing persuasions came forward, each with his own constituency and his own political views. D. Worth Clark, isolationist and conservative, spoke for a wing of the party which, though Democratic, became increasingly critical of the New Deal. Party liberals found their leadership in Francis Ristline and Glen Taylor.

Republicans, too, had their difficulties with the independent voter. The organization wing bent its efforts to overcoming Borah's "liberals" and by 1940 was largely in control of the party. As a result Idaho Republicans remained faithful to Dewey even during the national

[9] W. D. Gillis, "Governor Guided by Divinations," *American Mercury*, XXXIII, 1934, 113-117; Walter Davenport, "Storm Warnings in Idaho," *Collier's*, XCVII, April 4, 1936, 10-11; "Cowboy Ben Ross Aims at Borah's Job," *Newsweek*, VIII, August 22, 1936, 8.

stampede to Wendell Willkie. In the next decade the Young Republicans dropped out of the precinct organizations, leaving the conservatives even more in command.

By mid-century Idaho was once more in the Republican column. Glen Taylor lost a good many supporters because of his desertion of the Democratic party in 1948 to run as Progressive candidate for Vice President. He suffered also from the workings of the open primary, for in 1950 Clark defeated him for nomination on the strength of several thousand Republican votes. The conservative trend favored the Republicans, particularly since they were able to present a more united front. In the national Republican conventions Idaho followed Dewey and later Taft. In 1952 the delegation switched to Eisenhower only when he had already won a majority support.[10]

Oregon: The Power of Tradition

Those who witnessed the change of party fortunes in Oregon disagreed somewhat as to the interpretation of it. Palmer Hoyt, editor of the *Oregonian*, spoke of the almost magical personal influence of Franklin Roosevelt, but insisted that Oregon was opposed to the New Deal. He cited as proof the rejection by the voters of a number of tax proposals and free-spending measures put up for adoption by the state. Others said that Oregon voters accepted the main purposes and features of the New Deal program, but were only halfhearted in their support of the Democratic party. There was a case to be made for both opinions. Certainly local self-sufficiency and economy were considerably changed as Oregon took advantage of federal matching funds for old age assistance, social security, and grazing loans. Farmers in the grain belt were won to crop controls through their wheat checks, while those in the Willamette Valley who complained did so because the recovery program made it more expensive to employ farm labor. There were still vestiges of Populist thinking in Oregon, and electors felt the appeal of politics which reoriented the government to put it at the service of the people.

For a time this produced a striking change in the balance of political parties and put the Democrats in positions of responsibility which they had not held in many years. General Charles Martin was

[10] David, *Presidential Nominating Politics*, V, 26-38.

first elected congressman, then governor. Walter Pierce served five terms in Congress, and was joined for one term (1937-1939) by Nancy Honeyman of Portland, so that two of Oregon's three seats in the House of Representatives were held by Democrats. In the state legislature, too, the Democrats once more had their day. In 1935-1936 they controlled the lower house by a comfortable majority and had only four seats less than the Republicans in the Senate. In Multnomah County the gains were as impressive as in King County, Washington. Between 1930 and 1934 Democrats captured 11 out of 12 Republican seats from these districts and put themselves in complete command. Monroe Sweetland made the Commonwealth Federation a force in Oregon as it was in Washington, the more significantly perhaps since he evaded the blandishments of the Popular Front.

But such successes were short-lived. Factional differences within the Democratic party became unmanageable and made possible an early return of the Republicans to power. In 1938 the Commonwealth Federation opposed the renomination of Charles Martin. Republicans then elected Charles Sprague as governor, replaced Nancy Honeyman with Homer D. Angell in Congress, and regained control of the state legislature. Soon afterward they captured a majority once more in Multnomah County.

The issues of the day cut across party lines not only locally but in national affairs. Multnomah County legislators of both parties were outnumbered by rural members of the legislature and tended to draw together on many matters. The benefits of the New Deal were no longer identified simply with Democratic votes. McNary supported not only the farm relief program but public power as well, and Guy Cordon, who took McNary's place in the Senate, labored no less energetically to secure federal appropriations for additional transmission lines that would round out the Bonneville power system. Not all Republicans were so minded, but it was characteristic of Oregon to accommodate the Republican party to the changing needs of the people, and it was a common thing to find both liberals and conservatives within the party.

Thus the Republicans gained in strength while the Democrats were progressively weakened until during the 1940's Oregon seemed to be almost a one-party state. By 1952 Richard Neuberger, one of the few Democrats in the legislature, referred to himself and his wife as the "poor relations" of Oregon politics, who were pointed out by the doorkeepers as curiosities for visitors in the galleries to notice. Probably it was true, as he said, that some Oregon counties had not sent a Democrat to the state capitol "since the railroads crossed the Great Divide." But it was even more noteworthy that in four years time (1938-1942) the number of Democrats in the state Senate dropped from 12 to three; in the House of Representatives, from 38 to nine. It was not that Oregonians had never known the rule of Democrats. They had tried it, but the circumstances were exceptional and Democratic control, as they knew it, savored of labor unions, pensioners, and the heavy hand of federal bureaucracy. The Republican tradition was strong and Oregon found it easy to return to it again.

Still, it was hardly accurate to call the Oregon system a one-party system. Politics there had long been marked by a considerable independence exercised both by the voters and by their representatives. Wayne Morse, elected to the Senate as a Republican in 1944, was a law unto himself and finally bolted the party eight years later. On the other hand the Democratic party had the strength of votes, though its organization left much to be desired. The great increase in industrial workers which took place during World War II had its importance for politics as well as for economic development. In 1950 the number of registered Democrats exceeded the Republicans by some 6,000 names. Two years later, despite the Eisenhower victory, Democratic registrations dropped below the Republican by only a few thousands. Neuberger was hardly to be called a poor relation when his Democratic supporters were strong enough to send him to the United States Senate. Thus the balance of political forces was more even than might at first appear. Oregon's tradition was Republican, but the people had a reputation for finding ways to cope with both radicalism and reaction.[11]

[11] Waldo Schumacher, "Ballot's Burden, an Analysis of the 1932 Election in Oregon," *Commonwealth Review*, XV, 1933, 96-107; for the Oregon election of 1934 see *ibid.*, XVI, 1934, 193; Palmer Hoyt, "In Conservative Oregon," *Review of Reviews*, XCIII, March, 1936, 43; "Lively Feud," *Nation*, CLXV, August 23, 1947, 176; Richard Neuberger, "Two-Party Blues in a One-Party State," *New York Times*, Magazine Section, February 1, 1953, 16. For election returns and recent analysis, see *Oregon Blue Book*; Gallup, *Political Almanac*, and David, *Presidential Nominating Politics*, V, 186-215.

37

Mid-Century Appraisal: A Survey of Cultural Progress

The attainment of maturity in cultural and intellectual pursuits in the Pacific Northwest was above all the achievement of individual persons whose training and ability made it possible. In a way, perhaps, it was a matter of chance that these individuals happened to live on Puget Sound or the Columbia River rather than somewhere else. Scholars and artists are citizens of the world, not simply of a particular locality, and the accident of residence here or there may have little to do with their accomplishments. Nevertheless, the search for knowledge and the expression of creative energies in art and literature required nutrition and encouragement in the local setting. Only as the isolation and provincialism of frontier society were overcome and a truly cosmopolitan community was built up could there be a fulfillment of the cultural aspirations of the people. In this sense there was a very real connection between regional development generally and the progress of learning and the arts. The advance of the region as a whole made possible the achievements of its leaders. On the other hand, each citizen of the world who made his home in the Northwest contributed his share to the further elevation of the general level of popular interest and support.

Architecture

The relation of the artist to the community was of course different in the several fields of artistic endeavor. Architects, for example, were in close touch with construction, and found their opportunities in the building boom that took place during the 1920's and again during and after World War II. Stately churches lifted their spires high above the street and Gothic classroom buildings appeared on the college campuses. Residential architecture exhibited a variety of styles and designs, the two-story cottages and Puget Sound "ramblers" being especially popular. Courthouses, libraries, museums, schools, and other public buildings all presented their challenge to the architect's skill and artistry. So far as trends in style were concerned, the earlier years were not marked particularly by originality. For the most part they witnessed a conformity to accepted designs or national tastes that were reminiscent of Europe or New York.

Beginning in the 1930's the region fared better. Architects everywhere were breaking away from the traditional and in the Northwest, where old ties were not so strong and the setting was more provocative, they were able to design with a maximum of freedom. An intermingling took place of influences from East and West. Pietro Belluschi, trained at Rome and Cornell, developed in Oregon a fresh interpretation of architectural design and became one of the region's most prominent spokesmen. Students of Walter Gropius went out from his classes at Harvard to practice their profession in the Far West, feeling that they could do more with it there. On the other hand, the western training schools produced a generation of designers who were quite capable of holding their own in any community. Some few, like Welton Beckett and Minoru Yamasaki, achieved distinction outside the Northwest. Others contributed richly to the architecture of the region itself, and freed it to a considerable extent from its dependence upon eastern firms.

There was no simple transition from dependency to self-reliance. When in 1936 Oregon invited the architects of the nation to submit plans in competition for the new state capitol in Salem, the local men played a minor role. The winning design was executed by Trowbridge and Livingston, and Francis Keally of New York, and the acrimonious debate over the merits and faults of the plan raged among the architects of New York, Philadelphia, and Los Angeles, as well as in Oregon itself. Perhaps this was a special case, for public buildings in the Northwest were even then being designed by western architects. Carl Gould's plan for the Seattle Art Museum (1933), dignified and beautiful in its external simplicity, was a functional design, admirably suited to its highly specialized purposes. Belluschi's plan for the Portland Art Museum (1936) was marked by the same qualities.

Still there could be no doubt that the region gained greatly in stature and competence during the ensuing years. Regional firms made a very real impact on the architecture of home and church, hotel and office building. Belluschi and John Yeon won increasing recognition not only in Oregon but nationally, for churches that contributed significantly to the new trend in religious architecture, and for residences that adapted local materials to the special regional opportunities afforded by climate and landscape. Belluschi's design for the Equitable Savings and Loan Association Building in Portland (1948) was much talked about among those interested in skyscrapers. It seemed to be the last word in its application of modern principles, a reënforced concrete frame encased almost completely in glass. In 1951 Belluschi returned to the East, to become dean of the School of Architecture and Planning at Massachusetts Institute of Technology. A firm of associates continued his practice in Portland.

Seattle developed its large firms and its small ones. Naramore, Bain, Brady, and Johanson built up an extensive practice and handled such major structures as the Public Safety Building, the Veterans' Administration Hospital, and the University of Washington Health Sciences Building. Young, Richardson, Carleton, and Detlie did the Children's Orthopedic Hospital, and John Graham planned the Northgate Shopping Center, a model group of retail stores that attracted wide attention. Paul Thiry and John Durham were known for their churches and George Wellington Stoddard for his dramatic football stadiums. By the time the American Institute of Architects held its national meeting in Seattle (1953), the visitors found the local chapter vigorous and capable, with substantial achievements to show.[1]

Painting

Painters and sculptors were more removed from the busy rush of building and were less influenced by the trends of regional development. Yet they too were sensitive both to the local

[1] Articles on northwestern architecture appear in *Architectural Record,* CVIII, December, 1950, 9; CXIII, April, 1953, 139-142; The Portland Art Museum is treated in *Mouseion,* Nos. 33-34, 1936, 53-80; the Oregon State Capitol in *Architectural Record,* LXXX, August, 1936, 76-80, and *Pencil Points,* XVII, July 1936, 352-374. See also *Guide to Seattle Architecture,* Seattle, 1953.

environment and to wider movements in the field of art which impelled them to experiment with new forms and techniques.

The decade of the 1920's was not a time of significant achievement. Americans generally were trying to find themselves, the artists perhaps even more than the rest. Mark Tobey, who came west in 1920 and joined the faculty of the Cornish School, later remarked that the mood of the day would turn any creative heart into an organ without blood. It was hard to find nourishment and stimulation in the Northwest, and Tobey left after a short while, to spend several years in Europe and the Near East.

Portland lost C. S. Price for 14 years (1915-1929) in much the same way. Price was a successful illustrator, a cow hand turned artist, largely self-taught, who won many a reader to *Pacific Monthly* and to *Sunset Magazine* with his cattle and horses and stagecoaches drawn in the popular style of Charles Russell. It was a good living, but there was no growth or depth in it. Restless and dissatisfied, Price left Portland for California, San Francisco first and later Monterey, where he joined a small group of artists and lived out the "lonely struggles of the years of search." It was important, though, that the artists of the region recognized the dangers of isolation and provincialism, and sought out the art of other times and other cultures.

During these years the trend toward formal training brought other newcomers of ability to the Far West, who were to exercise a formative influence upon a whole generation of younger men. Ambrose Patterson came to Seattle (1919) with the full equipment of a professional, having been trained in Paris and Australia. Walter Isaacs, who likewise had his instruction from the French masters, had learned from Othon Friez the simplification of form and color, and from Charles Guerion a rigorous exactitude. These men and Raymond Hill, the water colorist, gave the University of Washington a new importance as a center of artistic endeavor. By their knowledge of the history of art and their solid respect for traditional methods, they encouraged in their students a high level of competence, and promoted an appreciation of the enduring qualities by which great art is recognized.

In the community at large a group of painters who lived by their art formed in 1925 an association known as the Puget Sound Group with club rooms first in the Boge Building Annex and afterward for some years at Eustace P. Ziegler's studio. This company of congenial spirits found pleasure and profit in mutual stimulation and companionship, and did what they could to advance the cause of the fine arts in their city.

The depression years of the 1930's were years of trial and testing, but they were fruitful years, thanks to the substantial encouragement that was given the artist by government agencies and by individual patrons. In these lean times the W.P.A. Federal Art Project was of material assistance to many a person who was not well established. C. S. Price and Kenneth Callahan, Guy Anderson and Morris Graves, all of them significant names among Northwest painters, grew in maturity and kept their creative talents alive through the commissions to which they were assigned. Numerous post offices, hospitals, and federal buildings became the setting for mural canvases executed by these and other local artists.

At the same time the cause of the fine arts was greatly strengthened by the establishment of improved museum facilities, and the enrichment of art collections both in Oregon and Washington. The University of Oregon acquired an outstanding collection of Oriental art assembled by Murray Warner. In 1933 Seattle built its Art Museum through the generosity and civic spirit of Mrs. Eugene Fuller and her son Richard E. Fuller. It was a beautiful building placed amid the spacious lawns and gardens of Volunteer Park which became the permanent home of the paintings and art pieces assembled through the years by the Seattle Fine Arts Society. The Fullers not only presented the building to the city but gave with it a valuable collection of Oriental jades, Chinese snuff bottles and Japanese art treasures. Theirs was a continuing interest, and through the years that followed they broadened the scope of the collection to cover the entire field of Asiatic art, and encouraged the building up of a representative group of art pieces representative of European and modern art as well. Other patrons and donors joined in the effort, especially Mrs. Donald E. Frederick and Mrs. Thomas D. Stimson, both of whom contributed outstanding items. The Museum gave tangible support to the efforts of Northwest artists, and acquired a considerable number of their paintings. The continued expansion made the institution an important civic enterprise.

Expression through painting was a varied and individual matter.

Some artists painted what they saw in the outer world around them. Walter Isaacs did portraits of University faculty—Savery, Cory, and Lee Paul Sieg—though he was known also for his scenic studies and still life. Raymond Hill established a small "Art Vacation" program at Chelan, a choice spot for landscapes. Ambrose Patterson journeyed to La Push and after careful observation and delineation, painted his interpretation of an Indian Shaker Meeting. Kenneth Callahan found inspiration both in logging camps and in the Seattle skyline, executing the one in bold "folk" terms, the other in drawing meticulous and finely executed.

Even the more imaginative and experimental artists were not wholly indifferent to the world of material reality. Morris Graves painted his "Joyous Young Pines" as he had actually seen them. For all his sense of cultural starvation, the Puget Sound weather pulled him back repeatedly from his wanderings. "You get into it like an old coat," he explained. When he went later to paint in Ireland, he remarked that he had memorized the Northwest and took it with him to use as he might need it. Tobey likewise took nourishment from the regional environment, put down on canvas his impressions of Seattle, the crowded wartime city, and enjoyed his studio in the University district until a supermarket came in across the street and drove him from his familiar haunts.

But for these men the relation of the painter to the setting in which he did his work became increasingly complex. Price developed a mysticism in which his animals became potent symbols and his themes, no longer simply narrative, took on "ineffable meanings . . . close to the core of life." Perhaps the mystic in him established some communion with the forests, the fogs, the cold waterways of his native land. From his seclusion in Oregon he searched them more and more for the abstract elements with which he might convey the deeper meanings of his art, and express the felt nature of things, "the truth [that] lies behind the appearance."

Mark Tobey was always unpredictable, springing surprises, experimenting with new techniques and leaving them as others took them up. Prolific in his devices, he ranged from violent caricature to the most involved abstraction, from enchanted scenes in brilliant color to designs of tortured fantasy. Outward appearance was to him but superficiality. His paintings spoke of the inner essence of life, of the turmoil and excitement of the cities, of man's hopeless entanglement in a world of confused and changing values. His pictures were the product of no region or locality, for they were concerned with universals. They had to be read slowly and interpreted, and they revealed their tenor only to a responsive heart.

Morris Graves was even more the spiritual mystic. His subject matter, intricately symbolic, was elaborated in sequences and series, in birds and fish and pine trees, each of which represented something elemental in life. His art was not intellectual but intuitive, as if by the processes of Oriental contemplation he could fathom the deepest meanings in men's existence, "stilling the surface of the mind and letting the inner surface bloom." Some critics spoke of his compelling honesty, his abiding feeling for taste, his attempt to combine, not altogether successfully, the decorative qualities of Asiatic art with western abstraction. Others confessed that his paintings left them with a sense of riddles that had no answers, of symbols with lost meanings that gleamed fitfully, veiled and intangible, like artifacts from a vanished age. Drawn from some remote spiritual level, they seemed to dissolve beneath one's gaze yet continued somehow to haunt and captivate the imagination.

That the Pacific Northwest could produce, or at least give asylum to such a group as this entitled it to more than casual notice. However one might interpret the artists and their work and however one explained their seclusiveness and eccentricity, these men developed a new language in painting that challenged both critics and fellow artists. Tobey and Graves were spoken of in Paris as leading "*une école du Pacifique,*" a Pacific Coast school of painting. Their originality and their importance were proved in the number of canvases that were acquired and exhibited by the great metropolitan museums.[2]

Literature

Literature no less than the graphic arts required favorable cultural environment and found it partly in the

[2] Walter Isaacs, *Painter Looks at Nature*, University of Washington Chapbooks, No. 2, 1928; *Catalogue of an Exhibition by Mark Tobey*, Portland Art Museum, 1945-1946; Fred S. Wight, *Morris Graves*, Berkeley, 1956; *Retrospective Exhibition of the Paintings of C. S. Price, 1920-42*, Portland Art Museum, 1942; "Mystic Painters of the Northwest," *Life*, XXXV, September 28, 1953, 84-85. A helpful collection of pamphlets and clippings is available in the Art Library of the University of Washington.

region itself and partly in conditions which made the poet, novelist, and essayist feel themselves included in the wider tradition of good writing.

The emphasis was still upon cultural autonomy as it had been earlier. Undoubtedly there was too much provincialism in this, too much straining to point out to the world the unique possessions of the Northwest without establishing rigorous standards either for significance of subject matter or excellence in style. In 1939 Russell Blankenship commented wryly on the preoccupation with frontier hardship and scenic grandeur which gave much of the regional writing a distressing sameness and marked it for mediocrity. Ten years later a conference of writers and critics, assembled at Reed College to consider the strengths and weaknesses of regionalism in literature, heard Joseph Harrison, Blankenship's colleague at the University of Washington, enter a plea for the elements of universality rather than local uniqueness as being the key to greatness in literary expression.

The most significant achievements of the 1920's stemmed from the critics and interpreters rather than the poets and novelists. Tracing the progress of American writers in producing an indigenous literature, Vernon Louis Parrington explored the theme in the larger area of colonial and early national experience and found a new importance in it. His *Main Currents of American Thought* (1928), which won recognition throughout the nation as a pivotal study, had a particular relevance for the writers of his own region, for he interpreted literature as the expression of ideas and the crystallization of experience which linked the American scene with the broader background of English and European thought. Regional literature must likewise express the larger themes of the age if it was to have more than a local and passing importance.

The Pacific Northwest produced no Mark Twain or Rölvaag to lift its stories and its characters wholly above the level of local color writing. It did breed a number of gifted authors who put a new vigor into its literature and developed a very creditable degree of fine craftsmanship.

While Parrington was working over his appraisal of the larger figures of American literature, Honoré Willsie Morrow published her popular Oregon novel, *We Must March,* and James Stevens offered a collection of *Paul Bunyan Stories* that did much to endear to the hearts of Americans everywhere this folk hero of the western logging camps. Some few years later Harold L. Davis completed his prize-winning book, *Honey in the Horn* (1935), a novel of herders and horse traders, sawmill workers and hop pickers projected against an early twentieth-century Oregon background. It was a man's book, racy, pungent, and unconventional, "a literary long drink and a heady one," that stood out especially for its irrepressible chest-thumping robustness. Unrestrained and lacking in balance, it was redeemed by its anecdotes and shrewd humor and had vitality enough to burst its bindings.

Nard Jones declared the purpose of the rising group of younger writers to become more than regionalists. His *Wheat Women* (1933), a novel of life in the Walla Walla country, attracted favorable notice for its theme and its setting, though the story was of uneven merit. Similarly Archie Binns's *Lightship* (1934) won plaudits from the reviewers for its faultlessly simple prose and its human qualities of insight and understanding. Robert Cantwell's *Land of Plenty* (1934) was a different species, a proletarian novel of the mill town which contrasted almost savagely with Binns, pointing out the rough and brutal side of life when industrialism made its impact on the Northwest.

During the next 20 years a considerable number of regional novels and nonfiction volumes found their way into print. Archie Binns wrote sympathetically of the Puget Sound frontier in such books as *The Land Is Bright* and *Mighty Mountain, The Roaring Land* and *Northwest Gateway*. Nard Jones not only wrote several novels but added a work of general regional characterization in *Evergreen Land*. By mid-century Murray Morgan was becoming known through his *Skid Road,* an informal history of Seattle, *The Dam,* a popular account of Grand Coulee, and *Last Wilderness,* a delineation of past and present on the Olympic Peninsula. Stewart Holbrook ranged widely over many topics in the development of the American West, always engagingly and with characteristic spirit. Forestry and lumbering had a special place in his affections, and the railroad builders won his admiration. In *Far Corner* he offered thumbnail sketches of a number of lesser characters and places in the Northwest, done with a deft touch and sure sense of human interest.

The latter years, which were somewhat dominated by the free lancers, were distinguished by technical skill and by an amazing productivity rather than by the more lasting qualities of thoughtfulness and philosophic penetration. The successful writers went on tirelessly from one book to the next. Richard Neuberger wrote numberless articles for the popular magazines and Betty McDonald established a new sales record for a Northwest author when *The Egg and I* sold more than a million copies. Persons of more modest attainments failed through no lack of zeal. Each year saw its yield of novels which, though of no great import in plot or message, had interesting sidelights on the region and witnessed its great desire to be heard and understood.

Assuredly, the writers' accomplishments were not to be measured wholly in their royalties. When Stewart Holbrook surveyed the regional field in 1945 and published his *Promised Land,* a book of representative selections from Northwest novels and essays, it proved to be something of a landmark in the literary history of the area. In the variety of their interests, in their professional competence and in their appreciation of literary values, these authors were entitled to be considered able spokesmen for their generation. They had come a long way in 30 years, even though the truly *big* book in the field of fiction or regional interpretation was still to be written.[3]

Meanwhile scholarship and research were pursued assiduously in every branch of learning. Anthropologists distilled the results of their field work into closely packed monographs, while economists and sociologists studied the communities of their own day and incorporated their findings in descriptive and technical studies. Works of formal history and biography appeared, some treating of regional subjects while others evidenced the writer's interest in broad areas of knowledge which had no advantage in local perspective. J. Allen Smith finished a second book, *The Growth and Decadence of Constitutional Government* (1930), in which he raised searching questions as to the impact of political and administrative centralization on

[3] Russell Blankenship, "Half Century of Cultural Progress: Literature," *Building a State; Washington 1889-1939*, Washington State Historical Society, 1940, 178-183; Joseph B. Harrison, "Regionalism Is Not Enough," *Northwest Harvest, a Regional Stocktaking*, Portland, 1948, 146-155.

American democracy. Scientists gauged the resources and products of the region and offered their proposals for the further development of them.

Universities and Colleges

Such activities were centered for the most part in the colleges and universities, and prospered or not depending upon the conditions existing there. These schools experienced a rapid expansion during the two periods of postwar development when population increases and high enrollments greatly spurred their growth. New laboratories and dormitories went up on the college campuses, faculties were enlarged and a number of new programs of research and publication were undertaken which contributed significantly to the advance of knowledge in the Northwest.

The University of Washington grew from a school of 4,000 to one of 10,000 students between 1914 and 1926. The campus quadrangle took shape with the construction of several classroom buildings and the first wing of the main library, a cathedral type of structure that was designed to be the architectural focus of the entire development. These years witnessed also a number of administrative reorganizations which gave a new importance to law and journalism, marine biology and business administration. The State College of Washington doubled its enrollment and strengthened its program not only in fields of study related to agriculture, but in the arts and sciences, engineering, mining, and home economics as well. A legislative survey (1915) gave attention to the problem of defining the areas of special interest of each school, but for a number of subjects it was not felt to be necessary to assign the responsibility exclusively to either institution.

Jurisdictional problems plagued Oregon much more. The rivalry of Eugene and Corvallis became increasingly intense and produced finally (1931) a full-scale inquiry and reorganization. The two schools were put under a single governing board and policies were formulated that envisaged a considerably sharper division of functions than was attempted in Washington. Specialization was logical enough, but institutional loyalties were strong and the concept of a university was never wholly fulfilled so long as the program of studies was split between two places situated 40 miles apart. The later trend was less severe in its separation of the sciences and the arts, and allowed the development of a comprehensive program at both schools though still preserving the special emphases of each one.

Private colleges continued to occupy a prominent place in higher education. The church-sponsored schools felt the same general impulse that produced the growth of the public institutions, and joined in the movement to improve and enlarge their facilities. The College of Puget Sound moved to a spacious new campus in Tacoma (1924) while Willamette University carried out a "forward movement" that brought money for several new buildings, higher faculty salaries, and a larger endowment. Lutherans reorganized and combined their schools at Parkland, Washington, and the Seventh Day Adventists improved their college at Walla Walla. Catholic institutions of higher education were strengthened especially at Gonzaga (Spokane) and Seattle. Though the funds came slowly, and the presidents had to devote much of their time and attention to financial and promotional efforts, the private colleges nourished the academic traditions of scholarship and claimed many devoted supporters.[4]

Depression years were lean years on the campuses. Salaries were cut sharply and minimum budgets discouraged all but the essential activities of the colleges and universities. Following World War II, however, a further transformation took place the importance of which would be hard to exaggerate. Millions of dollars went into the expansion of the physical plant, until returning alumni hardly recognized the old familiar places. With more generous funds the schools of the Far West were able to attract able scholars from other sections to be teachers or to hold key executive positions. New medical schools were established and old ones were strengthened. Cyclotrons and cosmic ray laboratories gave evidence of the new era in the study of physics in which the western schools took an active part. Research funds became available in substantial amounts, either from the insti-

---

[4] Bolton and Bibb, *History of Education in the State of Washington*, Washington, D.C., 1935; Enoch Bryan, *Historical Sketch of the State College of Washington, 1890-1925*, Spokane, 1928; *Survey of Public Higher Education in Oregon*, U.S. Office of Education, Bulletin No. 8, 1931; Joseph Schafer, "University of Oregon: the Formative Period," *Commonwealth Review*, VIII-IX, 1926, 91-105; Robert M. Gatke, *Chronicles of Willamette*, Portland, 1943.

tutions themselves, or from contracts through which nonacademic government agencies supported special investigations. Contract research required good judgment and firm policies on the part of the colleges to keep it focused on lines of inquiry that promised to result in significant contributions to higher learning. When effectively administered it greatly increased the productive potential of the institutions to which the work was entrusted, and added to their usefulness. At the same time the universities and colleges came to serve their own communities and the citizenry of their states through a wide variety of extension courses and adult education programs.

Trends in Public School Education

The educational program of the public schools was as vital to the public welfare as the growth of the colleges, and offered fully as great a challenge. In terms of finance and administration, curriculum development and teacher training, the problems involved in expanding the elementary and secondary school systems throughout the region were formidable indeed. From World War I to mid-century there was little letup in the attempt to provide facilities. In 1955 the region faced the future fully aware that the next 15 years would require even greater efforts.

Methods of financing varied from state to state but in all cases were marked by an increasing reliance upon state funds since revenues from local real estate taxes were uneven and often quite inadequate. Washington shifted the sources of school support more completely than Oregon and Idaho, the change coming about naturally as a result of the increasingly large state appropriations. By 1948 more than 70 percent of the sums spent for the common schools came from state taxes. It was a trend that was not easily reversed, though Republicans offered arguments and passed bills that aimed at raising more of the money from local sources. Voters in the rapidly growing areas approved special levies for buildings and even for operating budgets, but there was a strong opinion in favor of limited general millages. At the same time the policy of drawing upon other types of taxes was defended on the grounds that it was more equitable in the amounts drawn from different localities. While both Oregon and Idaho recognized the principle of state support, and raised increasing sums from general taxes, neither state contributed more than 31 percent of the total amounts required. The school districts and counties continued to shoulder the major part of the burden.

The general trends in school administration lay in the direction of more comprehensive coördination and supervision at the state level. For a time the superintendents of public instruction and the state boards of education maintained only small offices and occupied themselves mainly with fact-finding and advisory functions. After 1930, however, they became concerned increasingly with specific questions of state-wide administration. During the depression years there was an urgent need to effect economies by consolidation and uniformity in business matters so that every dollar spent on education would bring the greatest possible return. Later, when huge sums were being spent on the construction of new school buildings, buses, and equipment, the states exercised even greater vigilance in supervision wherever state dollars were used. Through their control of credentials, their vigorous sponsorship of the educational programs before the legislatures, and through professional educational associations the state educational agencies came to exercise a powerful influence over local administrators and classroom teachers as well. School boards still played an important role in the individual districts, but the management of the schools lost much of the grass-roots democracy of the earlier years. More and more policies and practices were developed by the experts in the state offices.[5]

As for the classroom itself, the region followed the national trend in its concern for the nonacademic student. Teacher training programs placed an increasing emphasis on methodology and "professional" courses, and administrators considered subject matter specialization to be less valuable in teaching than personality and a passing acquaintance with several different disciplines. For some years col-

[5] Washington State Planning Council, *Survey of the Common School System* (1938); George D. Strayer, *Public Education in Washington*, Olympia, 1946; Zeno B. Katterlee, "History and Development of School Finance in Washington," Washington State College, *Research Studies*, XV, September, 1947, 192-200; *Report of the (Oregon) Educational Commission to Governor Julius L. Meier*, January 1, 1935; Oregon Board of Education, Legislative Advisory Committee, *Study of Public Elementary and Secondary Education in Oregon*, Salem, 1950; Idaho Education Survey Commission, *Public Education in Idaho*, Nashville, 1946; William Gartin, "Financial Aspects of Public School Education in Idaho," unpublished thesis, University of Washington, 1930.

lege preparatory work went out of fashion while the curriculum was shaped and adjusted to the needs of those whose education would go no further than the high school. Not until mid-century, when entrance into college once more became competitive, did the high schools turn again to the more intensive schooling of those who must meet the rigors of examinations and high scholarship.

A Time and Place for Recreation

The Northwest gave thought increasingly to recreation, finding it necessary to plan and develop facilities more systematically as the population grew larger. In earlier times hunting and fishing and mountain climbing were enjoyed by a comparatively small number of people who asked no conveniences as part of their pleasure. As the years passed, however, the spokesmen for recreation urged that more of the region's beauty spots be made generally accessible. Asahel Curtis led a drive to build good auto roads in Mount Rainier National Park, and Oregon nature lovers promoted similar improvements for Mount Hood and Crater Lake, the Columbia River gorge, and the beaches south of Tillamook. One of the latest of these projects was a road to Hurricane Ridge on the mountain slopes of the Olympics south of Port Angeles. Opening Mount Hood and Mount Rainier to the public greatly increased the need of shelter in these parks. Lodges and hotels were constructed and comfortable camping facilities were provided. Timberline Lodge on Mount Hood, a massive log structure, was put up during the New Deal as one of a number of federal projects. Paradise Valley had its lodge and inn which attracted thousands of people during the summer months, though the terms of the concession were the subject of some controversy, and further developments were urged.

Skiing and mountaineering were enjoyed at these centers in the national parks, but at many other places too. The Mazama Club and the Mountaineers maintained lodges, gave instruction in snow and rock climbing, and managed a variety of hiking trips each summer. The National Forest Service adopted flexible policies of administration during the 1930's which encouraged an extensive and varied recreational program, supported and served by concessions at places where small commercial establishments were practicable. Mount

Baker and Stevens Pass attracted skiing enthusiasts on the weekends, and Snoqualmie and Naches Pass were favored by many city dwellers who could reach them in little more than an hour's drive. Skiing became in the years following World War II not only sport but good business, and the equipment shops found a ready market for the finest imported skis, boots, and bindings. The snowfields in these mountain playgrounds were among the finest in the world, and growing crowds showed their appreciation of them.

Hunting and fishing likewise took thousands of sportsmen to vacation haunts during the open seasons of the year. The shooting of elk and deer, duck and pheasant were carefully administered under state regulations which conserved the species but permitted a sizable take each year. Hunters were a select group, easily identified by the bucks fastened like a victor's emblem to the fenders of the cars returning home from Bend or Ellensburg. Salmon fishing was more universal and more democratic. There were those, to be sure, who made it a rather expensive hobby, purchasing boats, outboard motors, and fishing gear until the resort owners figured the total outlay in equipment (1951) at not far from 10,000,000 dollars. One enthusiast who was willing to discover and face the truth, counted his costs and figured that his catch of Chinook in one good year cost him 27 dollars per pound. But there were thousands who fished more modestly, buying only the essential gear and renting boats and motors as they needed them. Estimates of the number of man-trips made by the salmon fishermen in 1951 exceeded 600,000 in number. These covered a wide range of voyages, from a couple of hours at Holmes Harbor (Whidbey Island) to the all-day excursions that went out from Cape Flattery and Westport.

The sheltered waters of Puget Sound and the inland lakes and rivers gave the Northwester many opportunities for pleasure boating. Yachtsmen arranged their cruises offshore or spent vacation periods in the San Juan Islands and the Strait of Georgia. Small sailboats of half a dozen racing classes dotted Lake Washington on a breezy day. Chris-Crafts, Century runabouts, and speedy outboards skipped lightly over the waves, their water skiers swinging in wide arcs across the foaming wake. Thanks to Stan Sayres' racing hydroplanes, Slo-mo IV and Slo-mo V, Seattle made its August Sea Fair the principal festival of the year for civic promotion. Water sports likewise became a favorite recreation on the slack waters of Lake Roosevelt above Grand Coulee dam, breaking the stillness of the desert with the whine of motors.

Parks and recreation areas were acquired by the states and administered for the people at well-chosen sites throughout the region. This program developed comparatively late, for natural beauty was so common that it hardly seemed necessary to buy acreage to preserve it. After World War II, however, park and recreation commissions became more active, and funds were made available which permitted a significant expansion of their efforts. State parks were crowded with tourists and campers who assembled there to pitch their tents and build their fires. Historical museums offered entertainment and instruction to those who were curious to learn what personages had been there before them, and what events had taken place there. Washington took the lead in this movement, and it was more important there, since federal and local agencies largely met the need in Oregon and Idaho.[6]

The last areas to be served were the suburbs, which circled the cities in ever-widening rings. These communities were the scene of large real estate developments where speculative builders and promoters were quite capable of putting up homes for several thousand new inhabitants within the space of a few months. Such settlements were virtually towns, yet scant provision was made for meeting the civic and social needs of those who lived there. School boards found it difficult to buy land except at a speculator's price, and developers felt no responsibility to include playgrounds in their plats. At the same time county park agencies rarely had the money or the vision to purchase and develop sites according to any comprehensive plan. Metropolitan park commissions were slow to develop, with the result that suburban needs were largely lost to view. Only when there was some kind of local incorporation did civic needs receive adequate study leading to action. Even where planning commissions pointed

[6] Joseph Hazard, "Winter Sports in the Western Mountains," *PNQ*, XLIV, 1953, 7-14; Eldon Hauck, "Sportsmen Fish for Chinook," *ibid.*, XLIV, 1953, 135-139; Washington State Parks and Recreation Commission, *Official Guide to Washington State Parks*, 1953. See also Washington State Fisheries Department, Report, 1949.

the way, the establishment of civic and recreational facilities came slowly.

Programs of Social Betterment

As recreation came to require more and more planning and conscious civic effort, so too did various other programs of social betterment. The establishment of churches to serve the growing population was something that could not be left to take place spontaneously. Sometimes individual city churches sponsored new churches in rapidly growing areas nearby. More often interdenominational councils of churches made comity assignments to one denomination or another, and the machinery of denominational planning and expansion gave guidance and support to the efforts conducted in the local communities. In these activities the Northwest took its place in a national movement. It received much new strength in the churches that were founded there. At the same time the region contributed leadership to national organizations. The election of Dr. Paul Wright, pastor of Portland's First Presbyterian Church, to be the national moderator (1955), was but one illustration of the growing participation of the region in the religious affairs of the nation at large.

In most fields of social welfare and community effort, the Far Northwest followed the general trend in organization and program. The cities had their Good Neighbor funds, their Councils of Social Agencies. State institutions and juvenile programs felt the influence of improved professional leadership, though politics and costiveness presented their obstacles to rapid improvement in administration. Hospitals in far western communities received their share of grants from the national foundations for the enlargement of their facilities and services.

In some few instances one could say the region led the trend. The Group Health Coöperative of Puget Sound was one of the pioneer ventures in the country in the field of prepaid medical coverage, and one which met with a strong popular response. The program of orientation and guidance for foreign students, set up at the University of Washington under the direction of James Davis, won recognition and commendation throughout the nation. John Richards won election as national president of the American Library Association for his record of energetic and resourceful leadership in library administration, not only for his own institution, the Seattle Public Library, but in the wider field as well. These evidences of progressivism and imaginative leadership in humanitarian endeavor, no less than the Pulitzer awards won by Northwest poets and scientists and the Rhodes scholarships captured regularly by the students of Reed College and the University of Washington, indicated that the region was coming of age in its realization of social and intellectual achievement.

A Nation Knit Together

In some ways the Pacific Northwest was still, at mid-century, the "far corner" of the United States. In general viewpoint, as in economic enterprise, it made a difference that the broad belt of mountains and plains separated this section of the country from the more populous eastern states. Professional and business people lived and worked in an atmosphere far removed from the hustle of Chicago and New York. Their thinking was likely to be that of the provinces, not of the brain centers where the major decisions of the nation were formulated and determined. Geography still presented barriers to travel and limited the outlook of the people. Many who grew up by Pacific shores had never seen New England or the deep South, had never crowded the galleries of the national capitol in Washington, D. C., or enjoyed the eastern concert stage or theater.

Notwithstanding the great open spaces, however, distance was not the dimension of living that it had been earlier. By ordinary air transport New York and Washington were only ten hours away. In 1955 a Boeing jet plane crossed the continent not once but twice between dawn and dinnertime. Scholars and salesmen, clerics and politicians attended the national meetings of their guild, whether in Boston, St. Louis, or Los Angeles. Corporations and colleges recruited from the entire nation, and did much to bring about an intermingling of people from every section. Foundation grants and fellowships opened new opportunities for travel and study, and made possible extended visits to the countries of Europe and Asia. Radio and television largely destroyed cultural provincialism, bringing to Northwest homes a varied fare of entertainment and instruction, ranging from prize fighting to grand opera.

By mid-century isolation was more a local and individual than a regional problem. The country as a whole was knit together and the Pacific Northwest was one with the nation as never before. In cultural opportunities this region had possibilities comparable to any other. It was up to the people now, each man in his own way, to take advantage of them.

Index

INDEX

Abalone shells, 18
Aberdeen, Lord, 266
Abernethy, George, 245, 270
Abolitionism, Oregon, 317
Absenteeism, territorial, 329, 401
Adair, John, 335
Adams, John Quincy, 189, 192, 194-198
Administrative code, Washington, 630
Admission, of states, 319, 400-413
Adventure Cove, 68
Agrarian reform, 414-429
Agricultural Experiment Stations, 447, 449
Agricultural Society, Oregon, 349
Agriculture, 149, 155, 161-163, 216, 223, 333, 348-350, 384-388, 445-459; markets, 281
Aguilar, Martin, 25
Ainsworth, J. C., 339, 342
Airplane industry, 556
Alaska, commerce, 520; fisheries, 477, 480, 486; fur trade, 28, 193
Alaska Commercial Company, 481
Alaska Packers Association, 482
Alaska-Yukon-Pacific Exposition, 507
Alder Gulch, 323
Aleutian Islands, 29, 34
Alexander, John B., 388
Allen, Edward T., 608
Alphabet, Nez Perce, 215
American Board of Commissioners for Foreign Missions, 213-217
American-Canadian Fisheries Conference, 621
American Falls Dam, 591
American Federation of Labor, 471, 549
American Fur Company, 122, 138, 166, 172
American Home Missionary Society, 353
American party, 243
American Philosophical Society, 91-92
Ames, Fred, 609
Anaconda Copper Company, 393
Anaconda, Montana, 495
Anderson, A. O., 546
Anderson, Alfred H., 462
Anderson, Guy, 651
Anderson Ranch dam, 596
Angell, Homer D., 645
Anian Strait, 23, 28
Ankenny, Levi P., 521
Annuities, Indian, 308
Anti-monopoly Sentiments, 280
Applegate, Jesse, 244, 259, 297
Apples, 454
Appointments, territorial, 401
Appropriation, water rights, 574
Architecture, 351, 513, 647-649
Armstrong, Major A. N., 231
Army, U.S., 311
Arrowheads, obsidian, 7
Arrowrock Dam, 584
Art, Indian, 6; Northwest cities, 351, 532, 647
Arteaga, Ignacio, 40
Ashley, William H., 164
Assumption Bay, 30
Astor, John Jacob, 121-131
Astoria, fisheries, 475
Athabaska Pass, 133
Atkinson, George H., 353, 356
Auburn, Washington, 509
Aurora, Oregon, 357
Australia, 31
Ayer, W. B., 533

Bagley, Clarence, 535
Bainbridge Island, 54
Baker, Frank, 426
Baker, James, 74
Baker County, Oregon, 497
Baker's Bay, 335, 477
Ball, John, 176
Ballard, David W., 330
Banking, 521-523
Banking commission, Idaho, 437
Banks, Sir Joseph, 61
Barkley, Charles, 42-44
Barlow, Samuel K., road, 261

Barry railroad survey, 373
Barton, Dr. Benjamin, 97
Bashford, Herbert, 534
Baskets, Indian, 11
Basques, Oregon, 451
Battleship *Nebraska*, 524
Bear Lake, 166, 168, 565
Beaver, Herbert, 207
Beaverhead river, 100
Beck, Dave, 559
Beckett, Welton, 648
Beckman, Victor H., 466
Belcher, Edward, 154, 232
Bella Coola Indians, 8; River, 85
Belluschi, Pietro, 648
Belt, H. N., 426
Bend, Oregon, 615
Benedict, Ruth, 8
Bennett, Edward, 516
Bennett, Thomas W., 331
Bentinck's Arm, 55, 85
Benton, Thomas, 253
Bentzon, Count, 194
Bering, Vitus, 28
Bering Strait, 32, 34
Berries, Washington, 458
Berry, Clarence, 489
Billings, Joseph, 35, 39, 62
Binkley, Christian, 534
Binns, Archie, 655
Bishop, Charles, 75
Bishop of Quebec, 218
Bitterroot Valley, 105
Black, Arthur, 169
Black Diamond, Washington, 499
Blackfeet Indians, 108, 119, 172
Blaine, E. F., 593
Blalock, H. G., 409
Blanchet, A. M. A., 219
Blanchet, François Norbert, 219-221, 234
Blankenship, Russell, 654
Blankets, Indian, 10
Blewett, Washington, 498
Blind Pool, 377
Blue Mountains, 131, 387
Boating sports, 662
Boats, Columbia river, 261; fishing, 475, 479, 485
Bodega Bay, 194
Boeing Airplane Company, 556, 560, 665
Bogue, Virgil, 516
Boise, Idaho, 387, 565
Boise Basin, 324
Boise project, reclamation, 584
Boit, John, 68-69
Bonds, irrigation, 573, 588; railroad, 370, 374, 380
Bone, Homer T., 636, 640
Bonnat, Léon, 533
Bonneville, Benjamin, 172-173
Bonneville Power Administration, 637, 645
Boosters, 364
Borah, William E., 423, 441, 629
Borst, Joseph, 301
Boston men, 74
Botany, 153-154
Boundaries, territorial, 327, 403
Boundary, Canada, 188-200; treaty, 267
Bourne, Jonathan, 424, 428, 440
Boxes, Indian, 11
Boyce, Ed, 493
Boys and Girls Aid Society, 354
Brainerd, Erastus, 490
Brayman, Mason, 331
Bremerton, Washington, 560
Bridges, construction, 509
Bridges, Harry, 557
Bridges, Robert, 422, 511
Brigade, fur trade, 155
British Columbia, Indians, 14; posts, 155 156
British Columbia Packers Association, 482
Broughton, William, 55-56
Brown, Tabitha, 355
Browne, J. J., 409
Bryan, Enoch, 447
Bryan, James, 443
Bryan, William Jennings, 423
Bryant, William P., 295
Building permits, 506, 553
Bulger, M. P., 426
Bullitt, Scott, 637
Bumping Lake, reservoir, 583
Bunker Hill mine, 394, 492, 494
Bureau of Charities, Seattle, 531
Bureau of Corporations, 463
Burke, Thomas, 379-381, 502, 513
Burnett, Peter, 256, 272, 275, 285, 296
Bush, Asahel, 294, 316
Business conditions, Oregon, 274-275
Butler, John, 533
Butte, Montana, 393, 495
Byrd, William, *History of the Dividing Line*, 249

Caamano, Jacinto, 49
Cabrillo, Juan Roderiguez, 22
Cain, Harry, 641
Calhoun, John C., 264
California, Jedediah, Smith in, 168
California Stage Company, 348
Callahan, Kenneth, 651
Calapooya, Oregon, 353
Camas roots, 15

Camping, 663
Canada, halibut conservation, 623
Canneries, salmon, 475, 481
Canning industry, 545
Canoe River, 132
Canoes, Indian, 11, 17
Canton market, 40
Cantwell, Robert, 655
Canyon Road, 338
Cape Arago, 33
Cape Disappointment, 45
Cape Flattery, 662; fisheries, 486
Cape Foulweather, 33
Cape Frondoso, 30
Cape Nome, 489
Cape of Good Hope, 32, 74
Cape Perpetua, 33
Cape San Roque, 30
Cape Spencer, Alaska, 486
Capital, investment of, 281
Capitol, Oregon Territory, 295
Capitol locations, Idaho Territory, 332
Carbonado, Washington, 499
Carey Act, 572
Carmichael, Lawrence, 226
Carver, Jonathan, 82
Cascades, Columbia, 17, 339
Catherine II, 39
Catholic colleges, 658; ladder, 221; missions, 218-221, 231
Cattle, 149; drives, 226, 279; raising, 386-388
Cave dwellers, 6
Cayuse War, 284
Cedar bark skirts, 10
Celilo, Oregon, 377
Central Labor Council, Seattle, 549
Central Pacific railroad, 370
Centralia, Washington, 399
Chadwick, Stephen, 637, 639
Chamberlain, George, 441, 629
Champney, E. Frère, 533
Champoeg, meeting, 242
Charbonneau, Toussaint, 100, 109
Cheatham, Neal, 422
Cheese, manufacture, 453
Chehalis River, 13
Chelan, Washington, 652
Chief factor, 151
Child labor laws, Washington, 439
Chilkoot Pass, 490
Chimacum, Washington, 501
China, American commerce, 60, 63
China market, 73
Chinese labor, 352, 475, 483
Chinook Indians, 11, 12, 75
Chinook Pass, 18
Chinookan languages, 8
Chirikov, Alexei, 28
Chittenden, Hiram, 511
Church of England, 207
Churches, 664; Oregon, 219, 352-354; urban, 531
"Circus politics," 639
Cities, 395-399; building, 505-517; Oregon, 334-338; social welfare, 664
City planning 516; Portland, 351
Civil rights, 311
Civil War, politics, 320
Clackamas Indians, 212
Claims associations, mining, 326
Clapp, William, 593
Clark, D. Worth, 642
Clark, N. S., 312
Clark, W. A., 496
Clark, William, 11-12, 99
Clarke, John, 134
Clarke-McNary Act, 610
Clark's Fork River, 105, 115, 378
Class legislation, Oregon, 435
Clatsop Plains, 256, 282
Clayoquot Sound, 43
Cle Elum Lake reservoir, 583
Clearwater River, 105
Climate, Oregon, 255
Clothing, Indian, 10
Coal mining, Washington, 499-501
Coastal Indians, 7-13
Cochrane, William, 500
Code, provisional government, 242
Coeur d'Alene, Idaho, 393, 488, 492-495
Coffee, John, 640
Cold Springs reservoir, 581
Colleges, Oregon, 355
Colleges and universities, 536-539, 657-659; church sponsored, 658
Colnett, James, 35, 42, 45-47
Colonialism, Oregon, 297; territorial, 401
Colonization, 42, 173, 196, 203, 223
Colter, John, 102, 108, 109, 116
Columbia Basin, irrigation, 591
Columbia Department, 145
Columbia River, 30, 52, 56, 70, 86, 114; diplomacy, 189-200; fisheries, 475, 625-627; fur trade, 75-78; steamboats, 338
Columbia River Company, 178
Columbia River Gorge, 661
Columbia River Packers Association, 482
Columbia River Shipbuilding Company, 547, 551
Colville, 388; Indians, 14
Commerce, 390-392, 491, 518-520; Indian, 18; Oregon, 274-280, 347; supply trade, 322; with Orient, 59, 204

Commercial facilities, 398, 512
Commonwealth Federation, 639, 645
Communications, fur trade, 152
Communist societies, Oregon, 357
Competition, fur trade, 152, 156, 159
Concerts, musical, 532
Congress, and territories, 402; U.S., land laws, 290-292
Conservation, fisheries, 621-627; lumber, 598-608, 609-620
Conservatism, Oregon, 359
Considine, Bob, 531
Constitutional amendments, Oregon, 433; conventions: 1878, 404; 1889, 407-411; Oregon, 316, 318-320
Construction, railroad, 378; urban, 505, 514, 553
Continental Divide, 103
Continentalism, American, 187-188
Contract research, 658
Conventions, political, 418, 422, 437
Cook, James, 31
Cooke, Jay, 342, 369, 371
Cooper, Frank, 536
Cooper, Hugh L., 594
Coöperatives, dairy, 453; fruit, 457; irrigation, 568
Coöperation, timber conservation, 610
Coos County, Oregon, 453
Copper mining, Montana, 393, 495-497
Corbett, Helen Ladd, 358
Corbett, Henry W., 348, 533, 635
Cordon, Guy, 645
Corn Laws, British, 266
Cornish School, 650
Corporations, constitutional provisions, 410; irrigation, 571
Correll, Mrs. Charles, 358
Corruption, political, 295-296, 405, 410, 414, 417; Idaho, 331
Corvallis and Yaquina railroad, 346, 382
Costigan, Howard, 640
Couch, John H., 274
Counties, provisional government, 298
Cowen, Charles, 515
Cowles, W. H., 600
Cowlitz Convention, 302
Cowlitz Plains, 300
Cowlitz River, dam, 627
Cowlitz Valley Farms, 162-163
Cox, Ross, 137
Cox and Stevens, 546
Crater Lake, 661
Credit, Oregon, 275
Crevecoeur, *Letters of an American Farmer*, 249
Crocker, Anna Belle, 533
Crockett, Davy, 250
Crook, A. J., 421
Crooks, Ramsay, 125, 130, 134
Crops, 149
Cultural activities, urban, 530-539, 647-666
Curry, George L., 285, 295
Curtis, Asahel, 490
Curtis, Edward, 534
Customs, Indian, 8

Dairy farms, 451-454
Da Lama, J. R., 492
Dalles, Columbia, 17, 152, 339, 388; mission, 211
Dalles Military Road, 415
Daly, Marcus, 496
Damrosch, Walter, 532
Davis, Harold, L., 655
Davis, James, 664
Davis, John W., 295, 632
Davis, Napoleon, 416
Day, John, 130
Day with the Cow Column, 259-260
Deady, Matthew P., 320
Dean Channel, 85
Deception Bay, 45, 52
Deer Flat reservoir, 584
De Lacy, Hugh, 642
Delegate, territorial, 293
Delegation, to St. Louis, 219
Demers, Modeste, 219-221
Democrats, Oregon, 229
Denny, Arthur A., 379, 503
Departments, state administrative, 630
De Smet, Peter John, 220
De Voe, Emma Smith, 438
Desert Land Act, 572
Dexter Horton bank, 409
Dialects, plateau, 14
Dill, Clarence, 443, 628, 632, 637, 641
Diplomacy, Louisiana, 92-98; Nootka Sound crisis, 47-48; North Pacific, 184-200
Direct government, Oregon, 430-432
Direct Legislation League, 439
Direct primary, 432, 437, 641
Districts, provisional government, 298
Diversification, industrial, 553
Dixon, George, 34, 41, 44
Dodge, Grenville, 370
Dolph, Joseph N., 415
Dominis, John, 157
Donation Land Act, 290-292, 306
Douglas, David, 153

Douglas, James, 154, 207, 229, 230, 300
Douglas, William, 45
Drake, Francis, 24
Drouillard, George, 101, 102, 106
Drury, Clifford, 215
Dryer, Thomas, 318
Duncan, Charles, 42
Duniway, Abigail Scott, 420
Durham, John, 649
Durham, N. W., 535
Dust Bowl, refugees, 555
Duthie, J. F., 547
Dworshak, Henry, 643
Dye, Eva Emery, 535

East Indian voyages, 64
Ebberts, George W., 183
Economic conditions, Oregon, 276-277; Washington Territory, 313; 1919-1955, 551-563
Education, 154, 219, 355, 535-539, 657-661
Eells, Cushing, 215, 356
Eight-hour day, Oregon, 433, 435; Washington, 439
Eldridge, Charles, 452
Elections, political, 319, 420-424, 435, 628; 1896, 423; 1912, 442; 1916, 443; 1924, 632; 1928, 637; provisional, 234, 243
Electric power, rates, 634
Eliot, Thomas Lamb, 354
Eliza, Francisco, 48, 49
Elk City, Idaho, 323, 392
Ellensburg, Washington, 387, 399
Ellicott, Andrew, 97
Elliott railroad survey, 373
Elman, Mischa, 532
Emergency Fleet Corporation, 546-548
Employer's liability, Oregon, 433, 435
Employment Service, U.S., 548
Enabling acts, Oregon, 318
England, maritime fur trade, 40
Erismann, Martin, 546
Ermatinger, Francis, 177
Escurial convention, 48
Etches, Richard Cadman, 41, 42
European and Oregon Land Company, 374
European tours, 351
Everett "massacre," 473
Expansion, American, 187-188, 203, 246-253
Expeditions, Snake, 145
Exploration, 20, 24, 26, 37, 39
Export trade, Orient, 544; wheat, 450
Expositions, trade, 506
Express, overland, 149, 153

Failing, Henrietta F., 533
Fairchild, Fred R., 608, 611
Fairhaven, Washington, 382
Falconer, Jacob, 443
Falkland Islands, 74
Farm machinery, 386
Farm mortgages, 446
Farm relief, 633
Farmers' Alliances, 417, 419
Farms, Northwest, 343
Farnham, Russell, 137
Farrell, J. D., 438
Federal Mining and Smelting Company, 493
Ferrelo, Bartolome, 23
Ferry, Elisha P., 413
Fidalgo, Salvador, 48, 49
"Fifty-four forty or fight," 264
Finck, Heinrich Carl, 357
Finlay, Jacques, 115
Finlayson, Duncan, 158
Fire protection, 601, 610
Fish wheels, 478
Fisheries, conservation, 621-627
Fishing, Indian, 12; industry, 475-487; sport, 662
Flathead House, 147
Flathead Indians, 15, 115
Florence, Idaho, 392
Flower bulbs, 458
Floyd, John, 198
Food, Indian, 6, 12, 16
Food manufactures, 526, 545
Forage crops, 498, 565
Ford, Sidney, 301
Foreign trade, Washington, 520
Forest reserves, 416, 451, 604-609
Forest Service, U.S., 661
Forestry, 1890-1917, 598-608; 1920-1955, 609-620; schools, 601
Forrest, Charles, 300
Forts: Alexandria, 155; Astoria, 127, 135 139, 142, 188-190; Benton, 387; Boise, 180, 213; Bonneville, 173; Cass, 172; Chipewyan, 84, 85; Clatsop, 105-107; Colvile, 148, 310, 321; Fraser, 112, 155; George, 139-140, 148; Hall, 178; Langley, 156; Laramie, 213; McKenzie, 172; McLeod, 112, 155; Missouri River, 172; Nez Perce, 141, 148; Nisqually, 162; Nisqually mission, 211; Okanogan, 132; St. James, 112, 154; Union, 172; Vancouver, 148-149, 152-154, 213, 214; Victoria, 265
Foster, Philip, 271, 273
Foster, William Trufant, 539
Foundation shipyards, 546

Four Lakes, battle, 312
France, exploration, 37; fur trade, 80-81; Mississippi river, 91-98
Fraser, Simon, 111
Fraser River, 7, 84, 321; salmon, 623
Frazier, Robert, 102
Frederick, Mrs. Donald E., 651
Free Negroes, Oregon, 316
Free trappers, 165-166
Freight rates, 391; Spokane, 519
Fremont, John C., 200
French, Burton, 629
French Canadians, 218, 225, 231, 240
French Prairie, 163, 219
Frontier, interpretation, 249-254
Frost, J. H., 211
Fruit growing, 349, 448, 454-457
Fuca, Juan de, 24, 30; Strait, 33, 43, 51
Fuller, George, 535
Fuller, Mrs. Eugene, 651
Fuller, Richard E., 651
Fulmer, Elton, 447
Fulton, Charles, 608
Fur trade, business details, 116, 152; French, 38, 80; maritime, 35, 39, 58-78; posts, 146-149; Rocky Mountain, 164; Russian, 28
Furth, Jacob, 503
Fusion, political, 420

Gaines, John P., 294
Gairdner, Meredith, 154
Galiano, Dianisio, 49
Gallatin, Albert, 190
Gallatin Valley, 108
Garden of the World, 251
Garnett, Robert, 312
Gateway to the Pacific, 204
Gatzert, Bailey, 503
Genet, Citizen, 91
General strike, Seattle, 548-551
Geology, mining, 498
Gerber reservoir, 581
German communities, Oregon, 357, 358
Ghent, Treaty of, 188-190
Gibbon's Pass, 108
Gibbs, George, 301
Gibson, Robert, 46
Gill nets, salmon, 475, 477
Gilman, Daniel H., 380
Ginseng, 64
Gold rush, Alaska, 489
Gold rushes, Northwest, 310, 321-326
Gold spike, 370, 378
Gonzaga University, 658
Goose Lake, 375
Goulburn, Henry, 190
Gould, Carl, 648
Government, American ideas, 263, 319; Idaho territory, 327-333; Indian, 8; provisional, 225-245; territorial, 254, 289-290, 292-297, 400-413
Grain farms, 149, 385, 447-450
Grand Coulee Dam, 555, 593, 663
Grand Teton range, 128
Granger movement, 346, 416, 635
Grant, John, 649
Grant, Ulysses S., 358
Graves, Morris, 651-653
Gray, Robert, 53, 65-71
Gray, William H., 213-217, 239
Grays Harbor, 69; sustained yield, 617
Grazing, permits, 451
Great American Desert, 258
Great Britain, relations with Spain and U.S., 90-95
Great Falls of Missouri River, 107
Great Northern railroad, 381
"Great Plains of the Columbia," 306
Great Reinforcement, 210
Great Western Iron and Steel Company, 503
Greeley, William B., 608, 614, 619
Green, Joshua, 513
Green River, 128, 166, 173
Griffin, John S., 355
Griggs, Chauncey W., 462
Griggs, Everett, 466
Grist mills, 216, 223
Group Health Cooperative, 664
Guidebooks, 258
Gulf of Georgia, 49
Gunn, James, 421
Gustin, Paul, 533

Habeas corpus, 311
Hadley, Henry, 532
Haida Indians, 8
Hailey, John, 535
Halibut, closed season, 622; conservation, 621-623; depletion, 486, 621; fisheries, 483-486
Halibut Production Control Board, 623
Hanford, plutonium plant, 595
Hanford-White Bluffs, irrigation, 588
Hanna, James, 41
Hanson, Ole, 550
Harbor Improvement, Seattle, 512
Harney Basin, 565
Harney Valley, 387
Haro, Lopez de, 40
Haro Channel, 49, 268
Harrison, Benjamin, 407, 420
Harrison, Joseph, 654

Hart, Louis E., 630
Hartley, Roland, 624, 630, 637
Haswell, Robert, 68
Hatcheries, fish, 626
Hawaiian Islands, 35, 74, 279
Hawley, Willis, 629
Haynes, G. H., 434
Head flattening, Indian, 19
Healy, Ben, 462
Heceta, Bruno, 29
Heinze, F. Augustus, 496
Helena, Montana, supply trade, 340
Hell's Gate Gorge, 624
Hendrick, B. J., 434
Henry, Andrew, 119, 164
Henry's Fork, 565
Henry's Fort, 119, 128
Herd laws, 386
Heron, Francis, 153, 171
Hibbing, Minnesota, 503
Higgenson, Ella, 535
Hill, James J., 381, 513
Hill, Knute, 641
Hill, Raymond, 650, 652
Hill, Sam B., 628
Hines, Gustavus, 211
Historical museums, 663
History, writing, 535
Hogg, T. Egenton, 346, 382
Hogs, 149
Hoh River, 30, 44
Holbrook, Stewart, 655
"Hold-up legislature," Oregon, 428
Holladay, Ben, 341, 374
Holman, Joseph D., 335
Holmes, Hal, 641
Holmes Harbor, 662
Holy Alliance, 195
Home rule, Oregon cities, 433
Homestead Act, 343
Honey in the Horn, 655
Honeyman, Nan, 645
Hood River, 565; orchards, 454
Hood's Canal, 54
Hopkins, Mark, 370
Hops, 384; Washington, 457
Horan, Walter, 640
Horses, breeding, 387; fur trade, 152, 155; Indians, 15-16
Horton, Dexter, 513
Hospitals, 530, 664
Houses, Indian, 10, 15
Howard, Tilghman A., 236, 255
Howe, F. C., 434
Howse, Joseph, 120
Howse Pass, 115
Hoyt, J. B., 409
Hoyt, Palmer, 644
Hudson, Thomas, 45-46
Hudson's Bay Company, 82, 143-165, 198, 206, 235, 265, 267, 268, 279, 280
Humboldt Valley, 375
Hunt, H. H., 279
Hunt, Herbert, 535
Hunt, Wilson Price, 125, 128
Hunting, Indian, 7, 12; sport, 662
Huntington, Collis P., 370, 375
Hutton, May Arkwright, 438
Hydroelectric power, 398, 561

Idaho, livestock, 387; mining, 323-327; Panhandle, annexation, 403, 406; Territory, 327-333; water rights, 577
Ildefonso, Treaty, 92
Immigrants, 217
Imperialism, British, 185
Implements, Indian, 6, 12
Improvements, urban, 508
Inauguration ceremonies, statehood, 412
Independence Creek, 378
Independence party, 243
Index, Washington, 498
Indian agents, 238, 242; treaties, 307; wars, 267-268, 283, 309-314, 332
Indians, Northwest, 6-19, 33, 69, 261
Industrial location, 525
Industrial Workers of the World, 472-474
Influenza, 157
Initiative and referendum, Idaho, 437; Oregon, 428, 430-432
Inland Empire, farming, 385
International Fisheries Commission, 622
International Longshoremen's Association, 557
Interstate Commerec Act, 520
Interstate Compact, fisheries, 625
Investment capital, 505; Oregon, 340, 348
Irondale, Washington, 501
Iroquois Indians, 220
Irrigation, 1890-1914, 564-586; 1914-1955, 587-597; bonds, 588; constitutional provisions, 412; districts, 587; districts, Oregon, 590
Isaacs, Walter, 650, 652
Isle of Sorrows, 30

Jackson, Henry, 641
Jackson, John R., 300
Jackson's Hole, 166
Jacobs, Orange, 401
Jefferson, Thomas, 38, 88-98
Jefferson River, 103
Jervis Inlet, 54

Jesuit missions, 219-221
Jews, Oregon, 354
John Day Valley, 415
Johnson, Albert, 633, 637
Johnson, Overton, 273
Joint occupation, 191, 197, 266
Jones, John Paul, 38, 60
Jones, Nard, 655
Jones, W. C., 423
Jones, Wesley, 441, 583, 629
Joseph, George, 635
Judges, Oregon Territory, 295

Kachess, Lake, reservoir, 583
Kaiser shipyards, 560
Kalama, 371
Kamchatka, 28, 38
Kamiah, 215
Keechelus, Lake, reservoir, 583
Kegrize, Michael, 532
Keil, William, 357
Keith, James, 190
Kelley, Hall Jackson, 173-174, 181
Kendrick, John, 65-67
Kenekomitt, 69
Kennedy, John, 154
Kettle Falls, 147-148
Kidder, Jefferson P., 401
Kincaid, Trevor, 487
King George's Sound Company, 41
Kinnear, J. R., 410
Kipling, Rudyard, 396
Kirk, Peter, 502
Kirkland, Burt P., 601, 608, 619
Kirkland, Washington, 503
Klamath Lake, 373
Klamath project, reclamation, 581, 590
Klondike, Alaska, 489
Knights of Labor, 418
Know Nothing party, 315
Knutson-Vandenberg Act, 611
Kone, W. W., 212
Kootenai House, 114
Kootenai Indians, 14
Korell, Franklin F., 633
Ku Klux Klan, 632
Kullyspel House, 115
Kurile Islands, 28
Kwakiutl Indians, 8
Kygarney, 74

Labor, Chinese, 475, 483; constitutional provisions, 412; disputes, 557-559, in Idaho, 494, in Washington, 500, 548-551; force, 314, 352, in Seattle, 543; legislation, 433, 438, 439
Labor unions, 557-559; lumber, 468-474, 558; Oregon, 435; politics, 639; shipbuilding, 548
Ladd, William S., 339, 348, 360, 539
Ladd, Mrs. William S., 533
La Conner, Washington, 384, 458
La Farge, John, 533
La Follette, Robert, 632
La Verendrye, Sieur de, 81
Lafferty, Abraham, 441
Lake Bennett, 490
Lake Roosevelt, 663
Lake Washington, 662
Land cessions, Indian, 307
Land claims, 242, 271
Land grants, railroad, 370, 372, 414
Land holdings, timber, 461-464
Land policy, 257, 343
Land speculation, Columbia Basin controls, 595
Land titles, 236, 290-292
Land values, irrigation, 571; orchards, 455; Oregon, 375; Seattle, 513
Lander, Edward, 305, 311
Lane, Harry, 442, 629
Lane, Joseph, 293, 294, 302
Langlie, Arthur, 640
Languages, Indian, 8, 14
Lapérouse, Count, 37
Lapwai, 214
Laughton, Charles E., 602
Laurel Hill, 262
Law codes, Idaho Territory, 331
Lawlessness, mining, 327
Lease, Mary Ellen, 420
Le Breton, George, 241
Ledyard, John, 35, 59-63
Lee, Daniel, 211
Lee, Jason, 208-211, 227
Legal tender, wheat, 277
Legislation, territorial, 402
Legislature, Washington, 410
Lemhi Pass, 105
Leschi, 309
Leslie, David, 211, 232
Lesseps, Ferdinand de, 63
Levy, Henry, 533
Lewelling, Seth, 418
Lewis, James Hamilton, 422
Lewis, Meriwether, 92, 99
Lewis and Clark Expedition, 95-110
Lewis and Clark Exposition, 506
Lewis and Clark Pass, 107
Libby, McNeil and Libby, 482
Libraries, 153, 357, 665
Lieu land, 416
Lilly, Charles, 458
Lindsley, A. L., 353

Linn, Lewis F., 232, 236, 257
Linnton, Oregon, 272
Liquor control, Oregon, 432
Lisa, Manuel, 116
Lister, Ernest, 459, 593
Literary West, 534
Literature, 357, 534, 653-656
Lituya Bay, 38
Liverpool, wheat trade, 449
Livestock, 226, 239, 322; industry, 349, 386-388, 450-452
Loggers, characterized, 469
Lok, Michael, 23
Lolo Pass, 105, 107
Long, George, 610
Longshoremen, 557
Louisiana Purchase, 87, 92-98
Lovejoy, Asa L., 336
Lumber industry, 279, 346, 389-392, 460-474, 544, 552; conservation, 598-620; distribution, 526; labor unions, 468-474, 558; trade, 160, 390, 466, 544, 552
Lumbermen's Protective Association, 474
Lutherans, college, 658
Lyman, Horace, 353
Lyman, William D., 535
Lyon, Caleb, 330

McAteer, John, 546
McCarver, Morton M., 272
McClellan, George, B., 306
McClellan, Robert, 125, 130, 134
McCormack, E. P., 416
McCormick, Charles, Lumber Company, 544
McDonald, Betty, 656
McDonald, Finan, 115
McDougall, Duncan, 125, 126, 137
McEachern, J. A., 546
McGillivray, Simon, 123
McGinn, Henry, 415
McKay, Alexander, 84, 125, 126
McKay, Thomas, 177
McKay Dam, 590
McKenzie, Donald, 125, 128, 134, 141
McKinley, William, 424
McLoughlin, Dr. John, 150-152, 169, 218, 231
McNary, Charles, 629
McNary-Haugen bill, 633
McSweeney-McNary Act, 611
Mack, Russell, 641
Mackay, John, 41, 43
Mackenzie, Alexander, 83-86
Macao, 38, 42, 44
Macleay, Donald, 515
Magnuson, Don, 642
Magnuson, Warren, 640
Main Currents of American Thought, 654
Makah Indians, 11
Malheur River, 262; irrigation, 565, 590
Maloney, W. H., 548
Mandan villages, 102, 108
Manifest Destiny, 248-249
Manufacturing, 397; 1890-1914, 523-529; 1914-1955, 543-563
Marias River, 107
Marine department, 156-158
Mark Twain, 532
Marketing, dairy products, 453, 552; fisheries, 483; fruit, 454
Markets, Oregon, 276
Marmaluke, J. C., 513
Marsh, Sidney H., 355
Martial law, 310-311, 494
Martin, Charles, 637, 645
Martin, Clarence, 620, 638
Martinez, Don Esteban Jose, 40, 46
Mason, David, 613
Massacre, Whitman, 217
Mathew, George, 546
Mathews, D. J. M., 631
Mats, Indian, 10
Mazama Club, 661
Meany, Edmond S., 535
Meares, Cape, 45
Meares, John, 42, 44, 46
Meat packing, 387, 452, 524
Medical education, 154
Medical schools, 531
Meek, Joseph L., 183, 241, 287
Meeker, Ezra, 508
Meier, Julius, 635
Mercer, Asa, 356
Merchants, 186, 348; Oregon, 276, 354
Merk, Frederick, 198
Metal Trades Council, Seattle, 549
Metalline, 489
Metallurgical industry, 398
Methodist Mission Society, 208-212
Methodist missions, 222-223
Methow Valley, 565
Metropolitan centers, 336, 505-517; banking, 522; histories, 535; manufacturing, 526; politics, 639, 645; schools, 536
Metropolitan Tract, Seattle, 514
Meyers, Vic, 639
Michaux, André, 92
Middleton, Henry, 196
Migration, to Oregon, 255-262
Migratory workers, lumber, 469
Miles City, 387
Militia, 284, 311

Miller, Joseph, 125, 128
Mills, Donald O., 493, 501
Milton City, Oregon, 334
Milwaukee, Oregon, 273, 336
Minidoka project, reclamation, 584
Minimum wage laws, Washington, 439
Mining, 312, 321-327; industry, 392-394, 488-504
Mische, E. T., 516
Mission party, 228
Missionaries, 49, 203, 206-224, 225, 230
Missouri Fur Company, 116
Missouri River, 80, 164, 172
Mitchell, John H., 385, 415, 428
Money supply, Oregon, 277, 418
Monopoly, 418; constitutional provisions, 410; steamboat, 345
Monroe Doctrine, 197
Montana, livestock, 386; mining, 323-327, 495-497
Montana Central railroad, 381
Monte Cristo, Washington, 497
Monticello memorial, 302
Montville Institute, 353
Moore, Miles, 413
Moran Brothers, 492
Morgan, Murray, 655
Mormons, Idaho, 332, 406, 412
Morris, B. Wistar, 355
Morris, Robert, 60
Morrison, Robert W., 255
Morrow, Honoré Willsie, 654
Morse, Wayne, 646
Mountaineering, 661
Mt. Adams, 105
Mt. Baker, 54, 662
Mt. Hood, 105, 661
Mt. Olympus, 45, 54
Mt. Rainier, 54
Mt. Rainier National Park, 661
Mt. St. Helens, 212
Mountain men, 165-170, 229
Muir, John, 396
Mullan road, 324, 387
Multnomah River, 107
Municipal power, 634
Museums, art, 533, 651; historical, 109, 663
Music, 357, 532

N. R. A. lumber code, 614
Naches Pass, 662
Naramore, Bain, Brady, and Johanson, 649
Naval repair yards, 560
Navigation, free, 199
Neah Bay, 49
Neahkahnie Mountain, 26
Nelson, Thomas, 296
Neuberger, Richard, 646, 656
New Albion, 25
New Caledonia, 112, 145-147, 154-155
New Deal, 555, 644
New Dungeness, 53
New England, emigration, 350; influences, 352, 359
New England Fish Company, 484
New Georgia, 55
New Zealand, 31
Newcastle, Washington, 499
Newell, Robert, 183, 244
Newettee, 74
Newlands Act, 1902, 579
Nez Perce Indians, 14, 105, 215
Noncolonization principle, 197
Nonpartisan League, 631
Nootka Sound, 7, 33, 40, 45, 66; dispute, 45-48, 50
Norblad, Walter, 635
Norman, Fred, 641
North West Company, 83, 111, 120
Northern Oregon, 298-302
Northern Pacific Railroad, 342, 370, 378, 387, 463
Northwest Passage, 22
Northwest Steel Company, 547
Notre Dame de Namur, Convent, 219
Nunez Gaona, 49
Nuttall, Thomas, 154, 180

Obsidian, 7
Occupation, basis of sovereignty, 48, 186
Officials, territorial, 401
Ogden, Peter Skene, 145, 154, 167, 283
Okanogan, 14, 155, 565; orchards, 455; project, reclamation, 582
Okhotsk, 28
Old Dominion mine, 394
Olmsted, John C., 515
Olmsted Brothers, 507
Olympia clique, 303
Olympic mountains, 661
Olympic National Park, 620
Omnibus Bill, 407, 412
O'Neill, James, 233
Orchard, Harry, 437
Oregon, boundary treaty, 267; code, 242, described, 174; migration to, 255-262; River of the West, 82; statehood, 315-320
Oregon and California Railroad, 341, 346, 372-376; land grant, 599, 615
Oregon and Montana Transportation Company, 340
Oregon and Southeastern Railroad, 382

Oregon and Transcontinental Company, 378
Oregon Central Railroad, 373
Oregon fever, 257
Oregon Improvement Company, 378
Oregon Institute, 355
Oregon Iron and Steel Company, 501
Oregon Producers' Exporting and Importing Company, 282
Oregon Shipbuilding Company, 348
Oregon Short Line Railroad, 381
Oregon State College, 538
Oregon Steam Navigation Company, 338-341, 345, 371, 377
Oregon system, 432-436
Oregon Territory, created, 287
Orford, Cape, 52
Organic code, territorial, 303
Orient, American commerce, 59
Oriental art, 651
Oro Fino, Idaho, 323, 392
Orphanages, Oregon, 355
Orton, C. W., 452
O'Sullivan, James, 593
Oswego, Oregon, 501
Outfits, fur trade, 165
Outfitting business, 491
Outhouse, John, 354
Overland mail, 341
Overton, William, 336
Owens, Henry C., 415
Owings, Nicholas, 364
Owyhee district, 324, 565
Owyhee project, reclamation, 590
Oyster industry, 486

Pacific American Fisheries, Inc., 482
Pacific Car and Foundry Company, 560
Pacific City, 335
Pacific Fur Company, 122, 124-125
Pacific Mail Steamship Company, 341
Pacific Railroad Surveys, 305
Pacific University, 353
Pack trains, 340
Packing associations, fish, 482
Packing houses, fruit, 457
Painting, 533, 649-653
Palmer, Joel, 309
Palouse country, 385
Panama Canal, 544
Paradise Valley, 661
Parker, Samuel, 213
Parkland, Washington, 658
Parks, city, 515; state, 663
Parrington, Vernon Louis, 654
Parsnip River, 84
Parties, political, 441
Partition, territorial, 197-200, 403
Partridge, Imogene, 533
Partridge, Roi, 533
Patterson, Ambrose, 650
Patterson, Robert, 97
Patrons of Husbandry, 416
Payette, Idaho, 565
Payette River, irrigation, 590
Peace River, 84
Peale's American Museum, 109
Pend Oreille, Lake, 115, 340; irrigation plan, 593
Pendleton, Oregon, 387
Pengra, B. J., 375
Pennoyer, Sylvester, 419, 421, 425
People's Party, 418
People's Power League, 439
People's Transportation Company, 340, 346
Perez, Juan, 29
Perry, Arthur, 489
Perry, William, 275
Peter the Great, 26
Peterson, Andrew, 546
Petition, for government, 227, 232
Pettygrove, Francis W., 274, 336
Peu Peu Mox Mox, 308, 309
Philippine trade, 23
Piegans, Indians, 108
Pierce, Walter, 629, 632
Piez, Charles, 549
Pig War, 268
Pinch, Jeremy, 117, 118
Pinchot, Gifford, 598
Pioneer letters, Oregon, 256
Pioneer Lyceum and Literary Club, 238
Piper, C. V., 447
Place names, Puget Sound, 54
Placer mining, 325, 392; Alaska, 489
Plains, travel, 258
Planning commissions, 663
Plateau Indians, 13-19
Platforms, political reform, 418
Platte River, 170, 370
Pocatello, Idaho, 399
Poetry, 534
Poindexter, Miles, 441, 443, 628
Point Grenville, 29
Political parties, 243, 293, 419-422, 639-644; Oregon, 315-318, 360
Politics, 1896-1916, 430-443; 1916-1956, 628-647; agrarian, 414-429; frontier, 254, Idaho Territory, 328, Oregon, 228, 286, 315-318, 360; statehood, 407; Washington Territory, 303
Polk, James K., 265
Poltito Palton Lake, 117, 118

Pompey, 101
Pope, James P., 642
Pope and Talbot, 389
Population, growth, 554; Idaho, 333; Oregon,248, 252; statistics, 343; urban, 395; Washington, 324, 383
Population centers, Indian, 13
Populist party, 420-429, 431
Port Blakeley, 389
Port charges, 520
Port commissions, 511
Port des Français, 38
Port Gamble, 389
Port Ludlow, 389
Port of Seattle, 511
Port San Juan, 45
Port Townsend, 301, 390, 399
Portages, Columbia River, 339
Portland Academy and Female Seminary, 354
Portland Art Association, 532
Portland Electric Power Company, 634
Portland, Oregon, 336, 347, 351, 395, 511
Portlock, Nathaniel, 34, 41, 44
Post system, fur trade, 146-147
Posts, fur trade, British Columbia, 155
Potatoes, Idaho, 457
Potlatch, 8
Pound nets, salmon, 477
Powell, John Wesley, 578
Pratt, Orville C., 296
Price, C. S., 650, 652
Prices, fur trade, 146, 152, 165; lumber, 466, 613; Oregon, 278; real estate, 350
Prince William Sound, 44
Printing, missionary, 215
Private utilities, 634
Probate judge, 233
Profits, fur trade, 166
Progressive Party, 440, 632
Progressivism, political, 430, 443
Prohibitionists, platform, 418
Promishlennik, 29
Promontory Point, 370
Promotion, urban, 492, 506-508
"Proper Oregonians," 360
Protestant Crusade, 224
Provincialism, cultural, 647, 665
Provisional government, 225-245, 284, 286
Public indebtedness, 405
Public lands, Oregon, 415; timber, 599-601; trespass, 414
Public power issue, 633
Public schools, 659-661
Public utilities, Idaho, 437; Oregon, 433; districts, 636
Public works, construction, 555
Puget, Peter, 54
Puget Sound, early settlement, 301; explored, 53-55; fisheries, 476, 478
Puget Sound Agricultural Company, 161-163, 267
Pulitzer awards, 665
Purse seines, 479
Puyallup, Washington, 384

Quadra, Bodega y, 29, 40, 48
Qualchian, 313
Quartz mining, 325
Queen Charlotte Island, 29
Queets River, 44
Quesnell, Jules, 112
Quimper, Manuel, 48
Quinault Indians, 11
Quivira, 20

Radicalism, Washington, 639
Raids, Indian, 9
Railroads, 368-382; Oregon, 341; rates, 519; regulation, 410, 415, 418, 433, 437; surveys, 305
Ranges, cattle, 386
Rate wars, steamboat, 340
Ray, Verne, 14
Real estate, prices, 350
Recall, Oregon, 433
Reclamation projects, federal, 584, 588-597
Reclamation Service, U.S., 579
Recreation, 661-663
Red River, migration from, 235
Reed, Simeon G., 339, 348, 360, 492
Reed College, 538, 665
Reforestation, 609
Reforms, political, 414-429, 430-443
Refrigeration, fruit, 456
Registration bill, Oregon, 428
Regrades, Seattle, 509
Religion, 410; Indian, 212
Rendezvous, fur trade, 165
Republic, Washington, 497
Reservations, Indian, 308
Reserve agents, banking, 523
Reservoirs, irrigation, 583, 596
Resources, mineral, Washington, 498, 504
Rezanov, Baron, 192-193
Rhodes scholarships, 665
Rice, L. A., 285
Richards, John, 665
Richmond, John P., 211
Rigler, Frank, 536
Riparian water rights, 574
Road, Barlow, 261
Road to Oregon, 257-262

Roads, auto, 661; Idaho, 324; military, 415; Oregon, 338; wagon, 344
Robertson, William W., 583
Robinson, Frederick, 190
Roche Harbor, Washington, 489
Rockefeller, J. D., 497
Rocky Mountain Fort, 112; fur trade, 164
Rogers, John R., 422, 425
Rogers, Robert, 81
Rogue River, 373; Indians, 309; orchards, 454
Roosevelt, Franklin, 638, 644
Roosevelt, Theodore, 442, 605
Rosario Strait, 49, 268
Roseburg, Oregon, 374
Roslyn, Washington, 500
Ross, Alexander, 134, 137, 167
Ross, C. Ben, 637, 642
Ross, Charles, 154
Routes, Astorians overland, 127, 131
Routes, Northwest mining, 324
Row River, Oregon, 382
Rush, Dr. Benjamin, 97
Rush, Richard, 190, 198
Russell, Lord John, 266
Russia, exploration, 26, 39; and Oregon boundary, 192-198
Russian Alaska, 161

Sabotage, I. W. W., 473
Sacajawea, 100, 106
Sacred Heart, mission, 220
"Sage of Yoncalla," 297
Sahaptin language, 14
St. Francis Xavier, mission, 220
St. Ignatius, mission, 220
St. Joseph's school, 219
St. Louis, Jesuits, 219
St. Louis, merchants, 88
St. Mary, mission, 220
St. Paul's mission, 219
Saint Roc, 215
Saleesh House, 115
Salem, Oregon, 375
Salem clique, 315, 319
Salem Convention, 419
Salish language, 14
Salmon, conservation, 623-627; fisheries, 12, 17, 180, 475-481; sport fishing, 662, varieties, 479
Salmon River, 13, 323
San Juan Islands, 662
San Juan water boundary, 268
San Poil Indians, 14
Sandwich Islands, 32
Saskatchewan River, 81
Satsop district, 389
Sauvies' Island, 7, 179
Sawmills, 160, 346, 389, 524
Sayres, Stan, 662
Scandinavians, 480, 487
Schafer, Joseph, 535, 538
Schmitz, Ferdinand, 515
School lands, Oregon, 416
Schools, Oregon, 219, 354; state support, 659; Washington, 356
Schumann-Heinck, Madame, 532
Schwellenbach, Lewis, 638
Scott, Harvey, 534, 600
Scott, Thomas Fielding, 353
Sea otter, 35, 39, 71-73
Seattle, Washington, 395; developments, 505-517; general strike, 548-551; manufacturing, 524-528; outfitting, 491
Seattle and Montana Railroad, 382
Seattle and Walla Walla Railroad, 379
Seattle Fine Arts Society, 651
Seattle, Lake Shore and Eastern Railroad, 379-381
Seattle Sea Fair, 662
Seattle Symphony Society, 532
Secret ballot, 428
Secret societies, Indian, 8
Sectionalism, Idaho, 332, 643
Self-government, Oregon, 297
"Self supporters," missionaries, 217
Semple, Eugene, 500
Senate, U. S., elections, 425, 433
Seton, Alfred, 178
Settlement, 42, 49, 173, 217, 223, 235, 300
Seventh Day Adventists, 658
Sewer systems, urban, 509
Shannon, George, 101
Shaw, Samuel, 64
Sheep raising, 386-388
Shellfish, 486
Shingle weavers, 470
Ship building, 282, 339, 345, 348, 492, 524, 545-548, 560
Shipping, labor unions, 557
Ships, Hudson's Bay Company, 156-157, 159
Shively, J. M., 258
Shoshonean language, 14
Shoup, George, 421
Silver, coinage, 418, 422
Silver King mine, 492
Silver Republicans, 422
Simmons, Michael T., 300
Simpson, George, 144, 169
Simpson, Sam L., 534
Simpson, Sol, 465
Simpson Logging Company, 617

Sinclair, John, 176
Single tax, 431
Sinnott, Nicholas J., 629
Skagit Valley Seed Growers' Corporation, 458
Skate, halibut gear, 485, 622
Skiing, 661
Skinner, Alonzo, 335
Skinner and Eddy, 547, 551
Slacum, William A., 200, 227
Slavery issue, 316-319
Smith, Addison, 629
Smith, Al, 637
Smith Asa Bowen, 215
Smith, Delazon, 318
Smith, Elijah, 379
Smith, J. Allen, 535, 656
Smith, Jedediah, 167-170
Smith, L. C., building, 505, 514
Smith, Levi, 301
Smith, Solomon H., 177
Snake River, 128, 145; irrigation, 573
Snoqualmie Pass, 501, 662
Snowden, Clinton, 535
Social agencies, 531
Social conditions, Oregon, 359
Social legislation, Idaho, 436; Oregon, 433; Washington, 437
Socialist Party, 441, 443
Society Islands, 32
South Pass, 166, 171, 258
South West Company, 122
Southern Pacific Company, 463
Sovereignty, interpreted, 186
Spalding, Eliza, 213-217
Spalding, Henry Harmon, 213-217, 356
Spanberg, Martin, 28
Spargar, John, 532
Speculation, land, 271, 292, 334, 415, 513; irrigation lands, 571; timber lands, 461
Spillman, W. J., 447, 449
Splawn, A. J., 583
Spokane, Washington, 398; freight rates, 519
Spokane House, 115, 147
Spokane Indians, 14
Spokane Plains, battle, 312
Sporting goods, 662
Sprague, Charles, 645
Sprague, Washington, 388
Sprague River, 375
Spurr, W. E., 499
Stage lines, 340, 348
St. Paul and Tacoma Land Company, 371
St. Paul and Tacoma Lumber Company, 462
Standifer, G. M., 547
Stanfield, Robert, 629
State College of Washington, 447, 537, 657
State Engineer, Idaho, Oregon, 577
State regulations, fisheries, 626; irrigation, 573
Statehood movements, Oregon, 315-320; Idaho, Washington, 400-413
Statement No. 1, 433
Statistics, agriculture, 445-448; banking, 521; census, 383; coal mining, 499; commerce, 520; economic, 1929-1939, 555; fisheries, 476; irrigation, 568; lumber, 464; manufacturing, 524, 543, 552, 560; mining, 491, 495, 496; shipbuilding, 547; urban, 395, 506
Steamboats, Oregon, 157, 338, 374
Steel industry, 501-504
Steffens, Lincoln, 434
Steiwer, Fred, 629
Steptoe, Edward J., 312
Stetson and Post, 391
Steunenberg, Frank, 423, 437, 494
Stevens, Isaac I., 305, 369
Stevens, James, 655
Stevens Pass, 662
Stevenson, John C., 640
Stevenson, R. A., 411
Stimson, Fred, 452
Stimson, Mrs. Thomas D., 651
Stoddard, George Wellington, 649
Stone and Webster, 513
Stone carvings, Indian, 7
Stores, Oregon, 276
Strait of Georgia, 662
Strange, James, 41
Strikes, lumber, 470-474
Stuart, David, 125, 132
Stuart, John, 112
Stuart, Robert, 125, 134
Stuart's Lake, 154
Sublette, Milton, 178
Sublette, William, 178
Subsidies, to railroads, 370
Suburbs, development, 663
Sugar beets, 457
Sullivan, J. S., 430
Sunnyside canal, 583
Superintendents of public instruction, 660
Supply trade, miners', 322
Sustained yield, timber, 613-618
Sutton, G. D., 419
Swan Island, 107
Swan Shipyard Corporation, 546
Swanly, Homer H., 502
Sweetland, Monroe, 645
Swiftsure Bank, 479

Sylvester, Avery, 275, 279
Sylvester, Edmund, 301

Table Rock Treaty, 309
Tacoma, Washington, 396; as terminal, 371
Tacoutche Tesse, 84
Tadama, F., 533
Taku River, 156
Tax laws, Oregon, 432
Taxes, 242, 244; timber land, 608, 611
Taylor, Glen, 642, 644
Teakwhit Head, 72
Teamsters' Union, 559
Tenino Indians, 14
Terminals, railroad, 371
Territorial government, 289-290, 292-297, 372; Idaho, 327-333
Territory of Columbia, proposed, 302
Test oaths, Idaho Territory, 331
Texada Island, 501
Thayer, William, 415
Theatre, Oregon, 357
Thiel's Detective Agency, 500
Thiry, Paul, 649
Thomas, John, 643
Thompson, D. W., 157, 331
Thompson, David, 112-115, 131-133
Thompson, Robert R., 339, 348, 360
Thompson, William F., 621, 624
Thomson, R. H., 509
Thorn, Jonathan, 126-127
Three Arch Rocks, 45
Three Forks, 103, 108
Thurston, Samuel, 287, 293, 334
Tibbitts, Calvin E., 177
Tidelands, 402; reserves, 487; Seattle, 510, 513
Tieton River, reclamation, 583, 589
Tillamook Bay, 45
Tillamook County, 452
Tillinghast, A. G., 458
Timber famine, 598
Timberlands, 461-464; management, 619; U.S., 600
Timberline Lodge, 661
Tipis, Indian, 15
Tipping, William, 42
Tlingit Indians, 7
Tobey, Mark, 650, 652
Todd Shipbuilding Company, 547
Tollefson, Thor, 641
Tolmie, William F., 153
Tomales Bay, 25
Tonquin, 126
Tourists, Oregon, 351
Town builders, 252-253
Towns, Oregon, 270, 272
Townsend, John K., 180
Townsite speculations, 334
Trade, Indian, 18; missionaries, 230
Trade associations, lumber, 467
Trade winds, Pacific, 22
Traders' goods, 76
Trails, Indian, 13
Transcontinental canoe routes, 80
Transcontinental rail connections, 342, 372, 375
Transportation, air, 665; costs, farm, 449; river, 324, 338, 345, 346
Trappers, American, 169, 171
Travel, Indian, 13; wagon, 257-262, 272
Treaties, boundary, 267; halibut, 622; Indian, 307; salmon, 624
Tree planting programs, 611, 618
Tribal structure, Indian, 15
Trolling boats, salmon, 480
Trowbridge and Livingston, 648
Trusts, constitutional provisions, 410
Tshimakain, 215
Tsimshian Indians, 7
Tualatin Plains, 163, 235
Tumwater, 300
Turner, George, 409, 425
T'Vault, William G., 260
Twin Falls, Idaho, irrigation, 573

Umatilla, 385; Indians, 15; reclamation project, 581, 590
Umatilla River, 131, 340
Umpqua River, 373, 375; Indians, 169
Underhill, Ruth, 9
Unemployed Citizens League, 639
Union Pacific Railroad, 370, 391
Union Pass, 128
Unions, recognition, 471; Seattle, 549
United Mine Workers, 500
United States, fur traders, 158; Forest Service, 603-609; Reclamation Service, 579
University of Idaho, 537
University of Oregon, 538
University of Washington, 537, 657, 664
Unknown Continent, 31
Urban development, 394-399, 505-517
Urdaneta, Andres de, 22
U'Ren, William, 418, 422, 428, 430, 434, 439

Valdes, Cayetano, 49
Vale project, reclamation, 590
Vancouver, George, 34, 48, 50-55
Vancouver Island, 29, 33, 49

Variety vaudeville, 358, 531
Vegetable seed, 384, 458
Venison, 156
Vest, George G., 413
Victor, Frances F., 534
Victoria, B. C., 322
Vigilante committees, 332
Villages, Indian, 8
Villard, Henry, 376-378, 501
Viscaino, Sebastian, 25
Volunteers, territorial, 311, 332
Voorhees, Charles, 372
Voyage of a Summer Moon, 114, 131-133

W. P. A. Federal Art Project, 651
Wages, cannery, 475; farm, 314; fur trade, 166; Oregon, 274; shipbuilding, 549
Wagon travel, 170, 257-262, 324, 340, 344
Waiilatpu, mission, 214, 238
Walker, Elkanah, 215, 356
Walker, Joseph, 178
Walla Walla, 308, 356, 377; college, 658; separation, 403, 406
Wallace, Leander, 301
Wallace, William H, 329
Waller, Alvin F., 211, 231
Wallgren, Monrad, 620, 641
Wallula, Washington, 340, 377
War of 1812, 188
War production, 544-548
Wardner, Idaho, 394, 494
Warner, C. H., 409
Warner, Murray, 651
Warner's Diggings, 392
Wars, Indian, 9, 76, 310-314
Washington Commonwealth Federation, 639
Washington Forest Fire Association, 603
Washington State Art Association, 533
Washington Transportation Company, 344
Washington Territory, 302, 303-314
Water code, Washington, 577
Water companies, 571, 573
Water Facilities Act, 597
Water rights, 412, 571, 574
Water systems, urban, 509
Waterfront, Seattle, 511
Waterpower, Williamette, 231
Weapons, Indian, 6
Weaver, James B., 420
Weaving, Indian, 6
Webster, Daniel, 264
Weeks Act, 1911, 603
Wells Fargo Express, 341
Wenatchee, Indians, 14; orchards, 455
Wentz, Harry, 533
West, Oswald, 441
West Coast Lumbermen's Association, 467
Western Federation of Miners, 493
Westport, Washington, 662
Weyerhaeuser, Frederick, 462
Weyerhaeuser Timber Company, 463
Wheat, transportation, 277, 338, 347; varieties, 449
Wheeler-Osgood factory, 524
Whigs, Oregon, 229
Whitcomb, G. Henry, 513
Whitcomb, Lot, 273
White, Compton, 642
White, Elijah, 210, 225, 230, 235, 237, 258, 335
Whiteaker, John, 318
Whitman, Marcus, 213-217, 283
Whitman, Narcissa, 213-217, 283
Wholesale trade, 519
Wickiup Dam, 596
Wilbur, James H., 353
Wilkes, Charles, 200, 234
Wilkes, George, 253, 368
Williamette Falls, 272, 273
Williamette Mission, 209-211
Williamette University, 355, 658
Williamette Valley, 231, 251; irrigation, 597; railroads, 374
Willapa Bay, 486
Williams, E. B., 419
Williams, Joseph, 218, 233
Willson, W. H., 211
Wilmer, F. J., 633
Wilson, Edgar, 421
Wilson, Woodrow, 434, 442
Wind River, 128, 170
Windemere, Lake, 114
Winnemucca, Nevada, 373
Winnipeg, Lake, 81
Winship, Nathan, 77
"Wolf meeting," 239-240
Woman Suffrage, Idaho, 437; Oregon, 432; Washington, 438
Wood, Charles Erskine Scott, 534
Wood, Tallmadge B., 256
Woods, George L., 415
Woods, Rufus, 593
Wool, John E., 311
Wool growing, 387, 450
Woolley, Edward M., 505
Work, John, 152
Workmen's Compensation, Idaho, 437; Oregon, 433; Washington, 438, 439
World War I, manufacturing, 543-551
World War II, manufacturing, 560
Wright, George, 312
Wright, Paul, 664

Wyeth, Nathaniel J., 173-181
Wygant, Theodore, 261, 262

Yacolt Burn, 602
Yakima Indians, 14, 308
Yakima project, reclamation, 583, 589
Yakima Valley, 387; water rights, 575
Yakima Valley Fruitgrowers Association, 457
Yakutsk, 62
Yamasaki, Minoru, 648
Yankee ships, 156, 157
Yantis, J. L., 353
Yaquina River, 13, 32, 346
Yellowstone River, 88, 108, 164
Yeon, John, 649
York, 101
Young, C. W., 422
Young, Ewing, 182, 226, 233
Young, Francis, 535
Young, Richardson, Carleton, and Detlie, 649
Yrujo, Spanish minister, 95-96
Yukon, Alaska, 489

Ziegler, Eustace P., 651
Zimmerman, Peter, 637
Zioncheck, Marion, 640

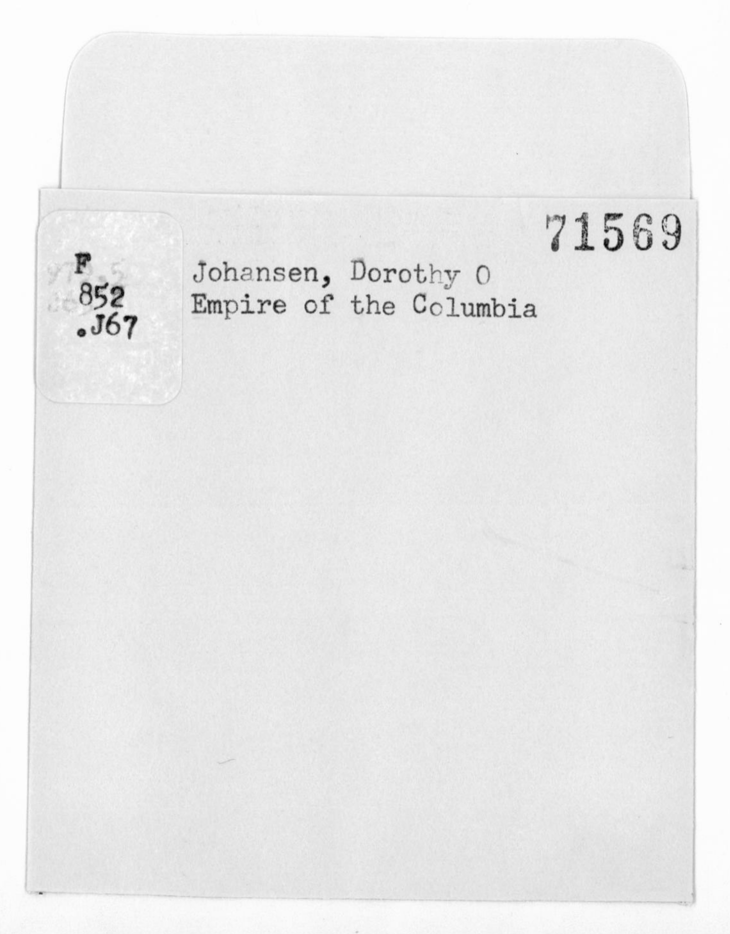
71569
F
852
.J67
Johansen, Dorothy O
Empire of the Columbia

Calvert Island
125
121
Canim L
B R I T I
Chilko L
Queen Charlotte Strait
Columbia
North Thompson R
Adams L
Shuswap L
Thompson R
Kamloops L.
KAMLOOPS
VANCOUVER ISLAND
Lillooet R
C O L U M B
Fraser R
Nootka Sound
Strait of Georgia
Okanogan L
49
Similkameen R
PENTICTON
NANAIMO
VANCOUVER
NEW WESTMINSTER
Barkley Sound
BLAINE
BELLINGHAM
Mt. Baker
OROVILLE
Strait of Juan de Fuca
NEAH BAY
ANACORTES
VICTORIA
MT. VERNON
Okanogan
REPUBLIC
OMAK
FORKS
PORT ANGELES
PORT TOWNSEND
Lake Chelan
Columbia R
OLYMPIC NATIONAL PARK
EVERETT
W A S H I N G T O N
BREMERTON
SEATTLE
WENATCHEE
TACOMA
HOQUIAM
ABERDEEN
OLYMPIA
EPHRATA
ODESSA
RITZVIL
MOSES LAKE
Mt. Rainier
ELLENSBURG
CHEHALIS
YAKIMA
Yakima R
Snake R
Mt. St. Helens
ASTORIA
LONGVIEW
Mt. Adams
RICHLAND
PASCO
KENNEWICK
PROSSER
WALLA
Columbia R
HERMISTON
TILLAMOOK
PORTLAND
VANCOUVER
WHITE SALMON
Umatilla R
PENDLETON
THE DALLES
45
OREGON CITY
Mt. Hood
John Day R
BLUE MTS
Grande R
Willamette R
SALEM
Deschutes R
NEWPORT
MADRAS
ALBANY
CORVALLIS
O R E G O N
EUGENE
SPRINGFIELD
BEND
REEDSPORT
Umpqua R
Malheur R
COOS BAY
BURNS
Malheur L
ROSEBURG
Harney L
Crater Lake
Rogue R
GRANTS PASS
MEDFORD
JACKSONVILLE
Klamath L
KLAMATH FALLS
LAKEVIEW
CRESCENT CITY
Klamath R
Mt. Shasta
CALIFORNIA
N E
41
125
Scale
0 30 60 90 Miles
121
WINNEMUCCA
Cartographic Laboratories Dept. of Geography U of Wash.